# Praise for *Myself Among Others*

"Anyone can write about the music played at a jazz festival. Very few people can write authoritatively about what it takes to run one. George Wein can do both, and in *Myself Among Others* he does both very well."

—*New York Times*

"George Wein is one of the two most influential jazz producers and promoters of the postwar era . . . he must be judged one of the most beneficial presences the music has known."

—Jonathan Yardley, *Washington Post Book World*

"[Wein is] a jazz world miracle worker . . . Offers an exhaustive look at a life lived upon the most exciting jazz stages of the 20th century."

—*Los Angeles Times Book Review*

"This will be a primary source of musical and personal information for decades, generations, perhaps even centuries, to come."

—*Buffalo News*

"Wein's anecdotes about a half-century behind the scenes provide a rare glimpse into jazz history."

—*Boston Globe*

"The book is irresistible."

—*Boston Phoenix*

"A sprawling mix of biography, anecdote, philosophy, hard-won lessons and musical history."

—*Providence Journal*

"Fearless, inventive and funny, Wein is a man whose love of music and fierce devotion to what is right have changed the landscape of American music."

—*New Orleans Times Picayune*

"Wein here recounts his numerous encounters with some of the most significant jazz musicians of the 20th century . . . Wein also provides a keen and sobering insight into the business end of jazz music . . . This important and fascinating memoir is well written and easily worth the price. Highly recommended."

—*Library Journal*

"Wein has crammed his book with recollections that provide insight into the personalities of Duke Ellington, Thelonious Monk and many other music legends he's presented . . . Wein rates as one of the best friends jazz and folk music ever had."

—*Boston Herald*

"The book is entertaining, informative, funny, sad and sometimes deeply serious. An invaluable slice of American cultural history."

—*Hartford Courant*

"An engaging and often insightful account."

—*Time Out New York*

"A terrific new, can't-put-it-down autobiography."

—*New York Observer*

"George Wein is one of the most successful of all music producers . . . [his] story is inspiring."

—*Austin Chronicle*

"Presents the story of a 50-year career with smooth transitions, mellow flow and continuity . . . an important, valuable addition to the jazz history shelf. It's a fact-filled, melodic memoir, swinging with emotion and energy."

—*Publishers Weekly*

# Myself
# Among Others

## GEORGE WEIN
### WITH NATE CHINEN

**DA CAPO PRESS**
A Member of the Perseus Books Group

Designed by Reginald R. Thompson
Set in 11-point Garamond by the Perseus Books Group

Cataloging-in-Publication data for this book is available from the Library of Congress.

First Da Capo Press paperback edition 2004
ISBN 0-306-81352-1

Published by Da Capo Press
A Member of the Perseus Books Group
http://www.dacapopress.com

Da Capo Press books are available at special discounts for bulk purchases in the U.S. by corporations, institutions, and other organizations. For more information, please contact the Special Markets Department at the Perseus Books Group, 11 Cambridge Center, Cambridge, MA 02142, or call (800) 255–1514 or (617) 252–5298, or e-mail special.markets@perseusbooks.com.

1 2 3 4 5 6 7 8 9—07 06 05 04

# DEDICATIONS

## TO MY WIFE JOYCE
## WHO IS EVERYTHING TO ME.

&

## TO PETE AND TOSHI SEEGER

*I wish I had
as much courage and belief in myself
as they have in themselves to face life
with a never-ending message of hope
that the world can be a better place.*

# Contents

# PART THREE

# Acknowledgments

MY FIRST ACKNOWLEDGMENT has to be to all the musicians who have worked with me for so many years. I have only mentioned a few of their names in this book, and I beg them as a group to forgive me if they feel I have forgotten them. Believe me, I haven't.

During my career since 1948, I have spoken at too many funerals, given a multitude of interviews, and told a wealth of stories, either sitting with journalist friends or in public forums. Some of these stories as told by other authors have appeared in biographies of musicians in ways that might resemble anecdotes in this book. They usually represent only a fragment of the whole picture.

With the exception of the recollections of Elliot Hoffman when he and his wife, Nancy, served as road managers for a John Coltrane tour in Japan, all recounting of experiences here are personal. None of the stories are legendary, hearsay, or apocryphal.

This book has been a work in progress for many years. Michael Zwerin, Ken Franckling, Nalini Jones, and the brilliant novelist AJ Verdelle all gave their talent and knowledge, but the book did not really get started until Lolis Elie, Jr., got me to put many thousands of words on tape; those words were transcribed with undying effort by Susan Whitred. Because I'm computer illiterate and wasn't about to write the book in longhand, I sent the pages and notes to Bill Zavatsky, an English teacher at Trinity School in New York City and an avid jazz fan. He expressed interest in my story, but explained that he had a job and that I would need someone full-time to work with me. He recommended a man that he had just met who was twenty-two years old and a recent graduate of the University of Pennsylvania. By coincidence, this young man had sent me a résumé, which my assistant at that time, Regina Barrier, had brought to my attention. Thus, I met Nate Chinen, who devoted the next few years of his life to this memoir. In addition, Jennifer Huang, who is now a third-year student at St. John's University School of Law, gave me all her spare time for the past four years, utilizing her skills in understanding and transferring my thoughts to a computer.

The photos have been edited and chosen with the help of Lee Weissman. A special thanks goes to all the photographers, including David Redfern, Bill Cunningham of the *New York Times*, Ira Kaye, Walter Karling, Michael Smith, Pierre Lapijover, John Abbot, Lee Friedlander, and Steve Sherman. Also thanks to Dale Parent, grandson of Bobby Parent and curator of the archives of his grandfather's invaluable collection of jazz photos; Milt and Mona Hinton, and Hinton Archives curator David G. Berger; and the late Jules Cahn, and Sally Stassi and John Magill of the Historic New Orleans Collection.

Dan Morgenstern and his staff at the Rutgers Institute for Jazz Studies provided Nate with total access to their archives, for which we are especially grateful.

In New Orleans, Quint Davis has been with me from the beginning in 1970, and has become one of the world's greatest producers of festivals. He and I are supported by EJ Encalarde, Karlton Kirksey, Louis Edwards (the prizewinning author), Nancy Ochsenschlager, Tague Richardson, Laura Cottingim, Reginald Toussaint, and Badi Murphy. Deepest gratitude to Arthur Davis, Sr., whose support of his son, Quint, and me has made it possible for the New Orleans Jazz and Heritage Festival to exist.

I am indebted to many people for whom I would like to give thanks:

For the Ohio Valley Jazz Festival, the late Dino Santangelo and his brother Joe Santangelo; to Brown & Williamson, sponsor of the KOOL Festival, namely Brad Broecker, Frank McKuehn, and others; to Hampton University's school president, Dr. William Harvey, Lucius Wyatt, John Scott, Bill Cope, Joe Tsao, and George Wallace; to the Playboy Jazz Festival, Dick Rosenzweig, and, of course, Hugh Hefner.

The Grande Parade du Jazz and my European operations would never have existed without Simone Ginibre and her son, Jean-Noel Ginibre, and Jean-Pierre Vignola.

Laura Loughlin, president of Festival Marketing Inc., a subsidiary of Festival Productions, Inc., made my life easier.

To JVC, Harry Elias, Karl Bearnarth, Shimizu-san, Adachi-san, Hattori-san, Bojo-san, and so many others. To Mellon Bank, Sandy McLaughlin, Dick Torbert, Marty McGinn, and Jim McDonald; to American Express and Ken and Kathy Chenault, who have become close friends; to Ernest Fleischmann, Robert Harth, Ann Parsons, and Deborah Borda of the Los Angeles Philharmonic at the

Hollywood Bowl; to the Saratoga Performing Arts Center and Herb Chesbrough; to the Verizon Music Festival, Bruce Gordon, Pat Hennebry, and Dana Moscato; to the late Ben Barkin who was truly an important figure in my life; to the Essence Music Festival, Ed Lewis, Susan Taylor, and Harry Dedyo.

My life in New York City, aside from business, has become dedicated to major cultural institutions. I serve on the boards of Carnegie Hall, of which Sandy Weill is chair; Jazz at Lincoln Center; and the Apollo Foundation, where Dick Parsons, CEO of AOL Time Warner, has asked me to serve. The Museum of Modern Art, where I've had the opportunity to meet and work with the generous Agnes Gund, David Rockefeller, Jr., and the Friends of Education Committee; and all the people from the Studio Museum in Harlem, where Joyce is on the board.

No one has been more important to the growth of FPI than Darlene Chan (who has been with me for more than thirty years) and her staff in California—Ellen Shimomura, Jeff Wallace, Zarina Rico, Friday Van der Most, and Caren Culver.

In New York, Charlie Bourgeois has been with me since 1950, and is still the first one in the office and the last to leave. John Phillips, president of FPI, with the help of Cara MacGilvray, is most responsible for the loyalty JVC has shown to us. Dan Melnick has filled the void created by the loss of Marie St. Louis. Rick White, Art Edelstein, and Scott Foster are invaluable, as are Andrianna Riley-Roach and Carol Ogle. Lois Kuhlmann and Freda Matthews have both been with FPI for more than twenty years. A special thanks to the people who make life livable: Bearle Bowen, Beverly Speede, Andrew Gluchowski, and Cliff Vinson. And a welcome to Melanie Nañez, my assistant, who devoted a lot of her time to the finishing of this book.

The Newport Festivals could not function without the contributions of Jill Davidson, Tim Tobin, and, of course, Gordon Sweeney, who has been with us since 1954.

The Jones family, with Robert and Marguerite, their two beautiful daughters, Nalini and Radhika, and their son, Christopher, have been part of the FPI family since Bob walked into the office of Air India in Paris while managing a tour with Duke Ellington and walked out with a gorgeous wife. Tracy Reid has become the right arm of Bob Jones in his work on the Newport Apple and Eve Folk Festival.

A special nod to Deborah Ross, who, in addition to her work at FPI, works closely with Joyce and me on our personal affairs.

FPI has kept out of legal trouble since the beginning of the organization, thanks to our close friend Elliot Hoffman who came to the Newport Jazz Festival forty years ago and realized that we needed legal help that we couldn't afford. He volunteered his services, which we accepted, and he has been my lawyer and friend every since.

Thank-you also goes to our accountant, Lester Dembitzer, and his assistant, Raquel Lieberman.

My gratitude as well goes out to those at Da Capo Press and the Perseus Books Group who helped bring this book to fruition—John Radziewicz, Kevin Hanover, Chris Coffin, Fred Francis, Alex Camlin, Steve Cooley, Frank Pearl, Jack McKeown, Matty Goldberg, Andrea Schulz, and Dan O'Neil.

I wish it were possible to acknowledge everyone who has been helpful to me in my life, but the list would involve hundreds. Quite a few have been mentioned in this narrative. There are a few close friends that I would like to cite: Ed Bradley of *60 Minutes*; Hugh Fierce, president of Jazz at Lincoln Center; the late Nesuhi Ertegun, with whom I bonded in spite of his having to produce *Wein, Women and Song* as his first project at Atlantic Records; his brother Ahmet Ertegun, a force unto himself; Kym Bonython, Australia's soldier of fortune and most ardent jazz fan and producer; and Roger Luccioni, the bass-playing doctor from Marseilles.

Thanks to Sue Auclair whose work in Boston has kept our reputation alive and well.

A very special thanks to the brilliant Leroy Nieman for his contributions of posters.

My wife, Joyce, has been my lifelong partner, but when all is said and done, the ones who made it all possible are Ruth and Barney Wein, whose love for a son who took an unconventional direction in life gave him the strength to realize that no matter how tough things got, he never had to quit.

# Foreword by Bill Cosby

Who is George Wein? What does he look like, and why did he write a book instead of getting his own talk show?

Well, George married a beautiful woman, which is part of the fairytale of George's life: the story of a fellow five-foot-something with two bad knees and no waistline. If he were a canary, he would be molting. But the man can sing. This is the definition of jazz. You can look like that and still get over.

The passages in this book are just beautifully written. Like passages in the Bible. For example, in Genesis they wrote the conversation between Eve and the snake, but never wrote about what Adam and Eve said to each other. This book George has written is like that. It's deep. It's jazz. It's love. The man is telling you how and why he chose to become what he is: a promoter.

What is it that George smelled and tasted that stopped him from becoming a bum? Certainly he could have sat at home and composed music. He's capable of that. He would've made a great thief. He knows good music, so why not steal?

Somewhere in George is the spirit of a *mandriano*. An Italian cowboy. With the life that George has had, he might have been six-foot-two when he started out. But George ain't afraid.

George would have drawn on John Wayne. And Wayne would've winged George, but George would've taken the Duke down.

George ain't afraid.

George would've pitched against the Babe for the sixty-first homerun, and George would've beaned the Babe.

George ain't afraid.

George would've tagged out Ty Cobb at second base with Cobb's spikes in his chest.

George ain't afraid.

George would've gone to Hitler's house and, with a voice like a canary that had too many sloe gin fizzes, called him out.

I'm telling you, George ain't afraid.

George would've taken on George Foreman, and George Foreman would've said, "I don't want to fight." Then George would've hugged George Foreman and said, "I love you, baby. You have a nice burger cooker there."

George ain't afraid.

I didn't say he wouldn't lie to you.

But George ain't afraid.

P.S. I forgot to mention George's wife Joyce. Be careful. Pay no attention to her smile. Just watch out if you mess with her man.

# PART ONE

# 1

## *Newton Boy*

WE PULL UP ALONGSIDE THE CURB and shift into park. Two hundred sixty-four Ward Street sits on the opposite side of the road, one house among many in the idyllic Boston suburb of Newton, Massachusetts. The window-panes and the front door are white, as I remember them; the clapboard walls have been painted a light grayish-blue. Tidy, rounded shrubs curve around the house on either side, like parentheses.

Suddenly, I'm not so sure about this anymore. I don't want to bother the people who live here. Maybe just having seen this place is enough. Maybe we should go home. I say this to myself as I watch the house from inside the car. I'm saying it even as I step out and begin, tentatively, to cross the street.

Reaching the narrow brick pathway, I glance at the front lawn, where I had often played touch football with the neighborhood kids. We used to go crashing through the bushes into my neighbor's yard, chasing after stray passes. My mother would often be out in the garden, kneeling beside her flowers. Instinctively, I look to that corner of the lawn—and there are her flowerbeds, exactly as I remember them.

I reach the front porch. How many childhood hours did I spend playing "baseball against the steps" in this spot? Where has all that time gone? My family lived in this house for twenty-one years—from 1929 to 1950. I haven't been back since we left it, more than a half-century ago. Who lives here now? What will I say to them? I pause for a moment and collect myself as I knock on the door.

A woman answers, opening the door just a crack. She is a young matron, and her features betray a cautious concern. Just beyond her, I spot a toddler moving across the hardwood floor. Another woman, a friend, stands nearby with another baby cradled in her arms. I try my best to appear harmless as I explain my reason for calling. Warily, they let me in.

Stepping inside is like entering a time warp. The foyer seems a little smaller but otherwise unchanged. There, just a few feet ahead, is the staircase leading to the second-floor bedrooms. To the right, the living room; I half-expect to see our six-foot Hallett & Davis grand piano in its usual corner. During my teenage years, I used to come home after a night out, sit down at the piano, and gently play a song or two. My folks—always eager to hear me play—would stir upstairs and listen, half-asleep.

The parlor seems to reverberate with long-forgotten voices. Standing there, I have a near-sensory memory of the dinner parties my parents used to throw. I can hear my mother gaily chatting with friends; the tinkle of ice in glasses; peals of laughter from Doc and his pals. I can remember clearly the times I brought Henry "Red" Allen and J. C. Higginbotham into this house for a midnight snack. I can almost see Frankie Newton stepping regally into the foyer and coaxing beautiful melodies out of a muted horn.

Walking into the kitchen, I encounter the tiny breakfast nook—my regular perch at five years of age. This was where I used to drink tea with Bridie Buckley, our Irish housekeeper. When I was older, my friends and I would gather in that corner after school and concentrate on answering dime-store trivia questions. The window above the kitchen sink overlooks a small and still-familiar back yard.

My hostess is kind, although still understandably nervous, as we talk about the house. She and her husband moved in just a year ago; he works for a computer company. They adopted their cherubic children from mainland China; she has her hands full taking care of them. I tell her a little about my life and career, about the jazz musicians who used to congregate in this house.

She interjects: "You know, there's a photograph of a musician in the basement; maybe you could tell me who it is."

She opens the door to the cellar, and I carefully test my weight on the stairs—the same rickety wooden steps, with flaking green paint, that I know from my childhood. The air in the cellar is stale. Bare cement floors and cracked plaster walls are illuminated by a single light bulb. On the far left wall, I spot the heavy door that leads to the garage; my father put it in, decades ago. In the opposite corner rests the heating system that we installed back in the early 1940s.

This musty space, too, holds a number of fond memories. I held my first band rehearsals here when I was thirteen years old. We used to gather in this basement every Sunday afternoon. It looks exactly the same as it did then.

When I turn to look at the staircase, I can almost see my pal Mark Rogers struggling down the stairs with a clarinet case in one hand and a tenor saxophone case in the other. I can practically hear the cacophony of the horns warming up; the rustling sound we made as we shuffled sheet music, settling down to play.

"Here it is," she calls out.

I walk over and direct my eyes to a dark rectangle over the doorway to the laundry room. It's an old photograph, all right; the cool darkness of the cellar has mercifully kept it from fading. But I still can't make it out. I move a little closer. There. The image is clear: a young kid—maybe fifteen, sixteen years old, wearing a suit and hunched over an upright piano. He's smiling proudly for the camera. Beside him is a poster-board sign: *Grant Wilson and the Stardusters.*

The hairs at the base of my neck begin to prickle. It's a picture of *me*, sitting at the piano with my pseudonymous junior-high band. That photograph has been here for sixty years without interruption, despite the succession of people who have lived in this house. Nobody has touched it. "I can't believe it," I mutter aloud. "I just can't believe it." I have no recollection of putting the picture there; I don't even remember posing for it. Yet I can't take my eyes away from it. Looking at that photograph is like peering into the face of a ghost.

"Should we try to take it down?" she asks. The photo is mounted on a piece of cardboard and stapled tightly to the wall.

It takes me a moment to shake out of the reverie. Finally I comprehend her question, and pause for a moment to consider it.

"Leave it," I say finally. I'm still squinting up at the rectangle on the wall, transfixed by my own grainy image. Then, decisively: "Leave it. It belongs here."

If there was ever an average middle-class, Jewish-American kid, as you can see from this short glimpse of my background, I guess I was it. Most biographies have something of the Horatio Alger theme—starting from nothing, an individual rises to the heights of his chosen profession. I didn't grow up in abject poverty in Limerick, Ireland. I wasn't an immigrant survivor of the Holocaust. My parents were not children of slaves who lived in a shack in Mississippi. Yet, somehow, I created a life for myself in a culture that was foreign to my Jewish heritage.

What I achieved was highlighted for me in the most complimentary way one evening at the home of my friend Lester Wunderman. Lester toasted his guests as individuals who made a difference in twentieth-century America. The invitees at this quiet gathering were Walter Cronkite, Don Hewitt, the producer of *60 Minutes*, Carl Reiner, one of America's foremost humorists, and Lester himself, an acknowledged pioneer in the advertising industry. My contribution was creating the Newport Jazz Festival in 1954, which forever changed the summer outdoor presentation of jazz and popular music in the world.

Because I never had any training or motivation to take my life in the direction it took, my story might be of interest to would-be entrepreneurs. It started in a simple enough way: Whenever I was not doing anything, I thought of something to do. My mind never stopped thinking. I guess the other attribute was that I was never afraid. We all have a fear of one thing or another. Like my father, I have a generic fear of heights. I have anxieties before every flight. But I loved football as a contact sport in my younger days. I wasn't afraid to not bail out on a right-handed pitcher's curveball. I have never been in an actual physical fight in my life, although I have never backed down from anyone. Maybe my stocky physical makeup has kept people from throwing the first punch. Maybe I've have just been lucky.

Fear of life is something else. For whatever reason, I don't have this problem. When the job that was supposed to be waiting for me in the family business was not available, I said never mind, I'll play the piano. At my mother's request, at the time of my marriage, I signed over to my brother what should have been my inheritance.

In my first business venture, I closed Storyville on one day's notice because of a sea of corruption that surrounded the club. I had no problem challenging the white governor of Ohio when we were involved in a prejudicial situation against African Americans; and, on the other hand, I did not defer from confronting the African-American mayor of New Orleans when there was a business bias toward me. Never did the demise of the Newport Jazz Festival deter me from attempting to create the grandest jazz festival in history in New York, the premiere city of the world. It didn't bother me to get the short end of a deal. I was never obsessed with winning.

In 1950, when I started dating my future wife as an interracial couple, holding hands walking down the street on a beautiful spring day was as natural to us as breathing. The fear of attack or criticism never entered our minds. In a time when intellectuals, artists, and kids were totally enveloped by drugs, I was not afraid not to be "hip." I had my own idea of what being "hip" was. I still do. The ability to make decisions and keep thinking of new ideas, knowing, but without fear of possible consequences, is really the basis of the story of my life.

\*    \*    \*

I was born George Theodore Wein in early October 1925; not in Newton, but in the township of Lynn, on Boston's North Shore. My father, Dr. Barnet Wein, maintained an ear, nose and throat practice there. Upon my arrival, the Wein family was complete and intact; he and my mother, Ruth, had been married for six years, and had a four-year-old son—my older brother Lawrence. We stayed in our cozy quarters in Lynn for two years, spending two more years in the nearby town of Brookline, and finally settling in 1929 at 264 Ward Street.

Newton was an old Yankee city that had gradually opened up one of its residential sections to a generation of successful Jews during the 1920s. The residents of Ward Street's bedroom community were doctors, lawyers, retailers, real estate entrepreneurs, and small manufacturers (of shoes, plastics, and textiles) who had left the tenement communities of West End, Roxbury, and Mattapan for better social climes. They lived on well-manicured half-acre plots, owned their own homes, and provided a standard of living well beyond that of their first-generation immigrant parents. This was certainly true of my father, who—after coming into the world on Manhattan's Lower East Side, growing up in Boston's West End, meeting my mother in Roxbury, and living briefly in Lynn and nearby Brookline—aspired to raise his family in Newton's suburban oasis.

In some respects, my father was a prime example of his generation's assimilation into mainstream American society. I knew very little about his parents; his father, Albert Wein, hailed from somewhere in Eastern Europe and died in the mid-1930s when I was just a few years old. Albert had made a living as a furrier in Boston's West End, until the depression put him out of business. The fruits of his hard work surfaced in his offspring, each of whom received a good education.

Throughout his youth, my father devoted himself to academic study; his straight-A average in Boston's High School of Commerce was a distinction that haunted my brother and myself during our less-glorious school days. After high school, Barney Wein earned a degree in dentistry from Harvard University and earned enough money through his dental practice to attend Boston University's School of Medicine. He received his certificate and, shortly afterward, became a fellow of the American College of Surgeons as an ear, nose, and throat specialist. He never again practiced dentistry.

In his younger days, Doc was an impeccable dresser. His Harvard Square suits wore like iron. This was, as he would occasionally point out, part of his profession; a smooth New England attire and well-trimmed moustache were key accoutrements for a physician in the 1930s. He kept the latter, if not the former, for the duration of his adult life.

My mother was also part of a second generation of immigrant Jews from Eastern Europe. Her father, Norton Ginsburg, had left the Lithuanian city of Vilnius in the late nineteenth century, settling in the state of Mississippi in the trading town of Meridian. He and a good friend had established a modest business there, peddling paper products to retail stores from the back of a rented horse and wagon. In 1897, Norton had sent for his fiancée, a woman named Etta Pinkofsky; they were married in Meridian, and would have raised their family there had it not been for an outbreak of yellow fever that fall. The epidemic forced Norton to send his young wife, who was now expecting a child, to Boston; he would join her later. It was there that my mother was born.

Soon after arriving in Boston, Norton joined Ginsburg Brothers Paper Products, the business that his brothers had established two years earlier. By the time my mother was a young woman, this company had developed into a prominent regional business, and the Ginsburgs had become one of Boston's principal Jewish families.

An interesting sidelight to the Ginsburg success was my grandfather's entrepreneurial involvement in an incipient motion picture industry. In 1915, Norton Ginsburg and a group of other Boston businessmen financed an ambitious young film producer named Louis B. Mayer, who was raising capital to purchase the rights to D. W. Griffith's film *Birth of a Nation* for eastern distribution. The financial support of these Boston backers enabled Mayer's great success with this now-controversial film. It was the first and only professional involvement in show business to occur on either side of my family, and it was rather short-lived. When Mayer asked his Boston backers to join him as investors in Hollywood, my grandfather, who had worked hard to establish a foothold in Boston, respectfully declined. Mayer found other investors, moved to California, and proceeded to make his mark as legendary head of production for the Metro-Goldwyn-Mayer studio empire. He amassed a fortune. Back East, Norton Ginsburg continued his respectable, conservative, and considerably less glamorous trade.

My parents had met in their high school years; courtship consisted primarily of dances in the bungalows that littered Roxbury and Mattapan. Whenever I asked my father about those days, he would shrug and say: "When I met your mother, she had a pretty smile and a cute little figure, and I liked her very much."

My mother was a reasonably attractive woman, endowed with the physical attributes of a typical Jewish matron of her time. As far back as I can remember she had a figure that could best be described as "pleasingly plump." She occasionally complained about her accentuated nose—a prominent and inescapable feature in the era before either rhinoplasty or Barbra Streisand. At any rate, my mother took justified pride in her appearance. She dressed smartly and usually had her dark, wavy hair done in the popular style.

Ruth was always conscious of the "right" thing to do. She made it a point to visit with all of our neighbors—even the Gentiles who lived down the street—because it was kind and proper to do so. She was diligent about my Sunday school attendance and bar mitzvah, for much the same reason. This was occasionally a sensitive point between my parents; my father, who had been raised in a highly Orthodox manner, resented organized religion. He called the Day of Attonement—the sacred *Yom Kippur*—a "farce." He would *kvetch*: "People sin all year, and they think they can clear themselves in just one day!" More to the point, I don't think Barney ever felt, nor wanted to feel, the need to atone for his sins. I can only remember seeing him in the synagogue on two occasions: at my brother Larry's bar mitzvah, and at my own. The bar mitzvah was one tradition that my mother insisted upon; after all, if the neighbors had parties for their children, why shouldn't the Weins? The gifts we would receive—pen and pencils and military sets with combs and brushes—would last us for years.

My mother would never have dreamed of serving roast pork in the house, but we did occasionally have ham or bacon for breakfast. I grew up thinking that shrimp and lobster were kosher. And at five years of age, my mother let me accompany Bridie Buckley to Christmas Mass at Boston College. As I look back upon Judaism in my household and in Sunday School, spirituality and religious doctrine took a backseat to cultural understanding. We were taught what it meant to be Jewish. Perhaps our training would have been more intense had we been less sheltered. The children of Newton, Massachusetts, were spared the discrimination that had plagued earlier generations. We were too young at the time to realize how fortunate we were in this regard. At times, it seemed that the only discernible division in Newton was a rivalry between members of the Pinebrook Country Club and those who kept a membership across town, at Belmont.

By the time I was in elementary school, my father had established an independent practice on Commonwealth Avenue, near Boston University. His clientele included people from every station in life—from State Street brokers to racetrack bookies, and everyone in between. He was always busy.

Even though he maintained his office in downtown metropolitan Boston, he continued making house calls on the North Shore. He would often leave the house at five o'clock in the morning to perform tonsillectomies on kitchen tables in Salem, Marblehead, or Swampscott. During an especially busy time of year, he could take out three or four pairs of tonsils in one day. He also performed mastoidectomies, although those required the patient to be hospitalized. He was a very good physician, and his patients were exceedingly loyal. It never crossed his mind to refuse services to someone who, for whatever reasons, lacked the funds to settle their bills. Sometimes he would receive payment in the form of goods: a box of smelts, or a wooden crate of halvah. Unlike many physicians who took pains to conceal their ethnic identities, Doc never shied away from treating immigrant Jewish patients; in fact, he took pride in his ability to converse with them in Yiddish.

Doc maintained what was even then considered an old-fashioned practice; this enabled him to make his house calls early in the morning, put in a few hours at the office, and then spend the waning daylight hours at the local racetrack. This was both an industrious and a leisurely lifestyle, indicative of my father's complementary impulses. He earned a good living, but he was never concerned with the idea of making money—that was the province of businessmen, not physicians. Part of this financial complacency was his perception that my mother had access to her family's funds. He always felt that if anything happened to him, the kids could count on the Ginsburgs for support. In fact, my mother's stake in the family business was rather modest, consisting of some preferred stock (which paid a fixed dividend but never grew) and dividends that yielded a few thousand dollars annually. Altogether, it was a nice sum for a woman in those days, but certainly not enough to live upon. But my father took her small income for granted, assuming that his financial obligations were somehow lessened. He never had a savings account. Instead of putting aside his excess income in real estate or investments, he devoted it to the horses. He was never contrite about this habit; during his later years, he would credit his longevity (he lived to be 97) to those afternoon hours spent at the track, while his colleagues had been hard at work.

He loathed the political maneuvering of the world of medicine, so he never made it as chief of the Ear, Nose and Throat Department at Beth-Israel Hospital—even though his uncle-in-law Albert Ginsburg had been one of the institution's founding members. No, Doc Wein was content with his easygoing way of life. He had worked hard to get there, and now that he was there he was going to enjoy it. This alleged contentment, however, didn't prevent him from complaining about those in his field who did climb the political ladder. He called them a bunch of phonies.

Doc was far more comfortable with the "little people" who visited his office, or the racetrack touts with whom he spent every afternoon. He was a long-shot better, and this habit probably cost him close to two hundred dollars a week—a lot of money in the hard-luck '30s. The denizens at the track loved his easygoing manner. They also loved the fact that he carried enough money in his pockets for a ten-dollar loan. There's one particularly telling photograph of my father and a half-dozen buddies outside the entrance of the track. They're a sharply dressed but obviously mischievous gang, loitering with devil-may-care attitude. Barney stands at the far right, torso angled away from the camera, face turned over his shoulder with a slight, inscrutable smile. When I look at this picture and think of my father's racetrack associates, I recall a piece of advice my mother offered me as a child: "When you lie down with dogs, you end up with fleas." This may not have been the exact wording of her proverb, but the gist of it was that one should always keep good company. Fortunately, Doc also had a large circle of friends beyond the racetrack—fellow physicians and professionals who crowded the living room whenever my folks threw a party. Even during the years of Prohibition, liquor was never scarce in my house. As a physician, my father had access to alcohol for "medicinal purposes," and he was always happy to offer an on-the-spot prescription to anyone who paid us a social call. Once, when I was a small child, he even attempted to distill his own bathtub gin.

My mother and father shared a love of show business—particularly the sort that had enjoyed a heyday during the vaudeville era. On their honeymoon, they had traveled to New York City, stopping at the famous Reisenweber nightclub to see Ted Lewis (of "When My Baby Smiles at Me" fame), who never performed without his trademark clarinet, top hat, and cane. They were no less enthusiastic about Al Jolson, Eddie Cantor, Harry Richman, or Rudy Vallee, all of whom were so familiar to me as a child that they might as well have been members of my extended family. We used to sit around the radio at night to listen to their shows. My father spoke of the vaudeville hoofers with a sort of awe; his own most impressive talent was a command of the "buck-and-wing," a rhythmic tap-dance step. He also sang, in the exaggerated, none-too-melodic delivery of the vaudevillian patter singers. He idolized Bert Williams, and my father used to warble the lyrics to "Nobody," Williams's signature tune:

*I ain't never done nothin' to nobody,*
*I ain't never got nothin' from nobody, no time.*
*Until I get somethin' from somebody, some time,*
*I'll never do nothin' for nobody, no time.*

My mother applied her passable skills as a pianist to the playing of popular sheet music. She encouraged my singing at an early age, and when we had parties, I was always summoned to sing to her piano accompaniment. At six years of age, I had a whole repertoire of Tin Pan Alley tunes; "I'm Stepping Out with a Memory Tonight," "Tie a Little String Around Your Finger," and "My Little Grass Shack in Kealakekua, Hawaii" among them. One of my personal favorites was "(When It's) Darkness on the Delta." Every once in a while, my mother would take me to Saturday morning radio auditions, where I could belt out my favorite tunes. I landed a spot on those kiddie shows a few times. I also successfully auditioned for a neighborhood production of Gilbert and Sullivan's *HMS Pinafore*, in 1933. I was happy to be in the play, but a little miffed to be stuck with the role of Boatswain; I wanted to play Ralph Rackstraw, the lead. I was a better singer than the kid who got the part, but he was better looking, and a Yankee to boot.

During these years I attended the Ward School, an idyllic grammar school nestled off a tree-lined avenue and surrounded by well-trimmed yards. Like the community that had created it, the Ward School was a cultural cocoon; its enrollment was probably 95 percent Jewish. As a learning facility, it reflected the high standards of the Newton school system, which was among the best in the nation. Boston University's School of Education often used the Ward School classrooms as laboratories for experimental or progressive curricula. Ours was one of the first primary schools, for example, to establish rapid advancement programs for talented students. The kids earmarked for high achievement were sequestered in a different section of the classroom and received more challenging assignments. During my grammar school years, I was always a card-carrying member of this elite group.

My first formal musical training began at age eight. I started taking piano lessons with Margaret Chaloff, a woman who lived across the street from my grandparents in Chestnut Hill. Mrs. Chaloff was married to the prominent piano instructor Julius Chaloff; their son Serge was two years my senior. She was a good teacher, and under her tutelage I developed an acceptable piano technique. But although I had an innate feeling for music, I realized rather quickly that I lacked God's gift of total musical understanding. It would take me weeks of practicing, for instance, to get Franz Liszt's *Liebestraum* down.

This was maddening, especially because I wasn't terribly enthusiastic about *Liebestraum*. Each year, Mrs. Chaloff would hold a recital of her students to show their musical progress. One of the most embarrassing moments of my life was when—after studying, practicing, and memorizing the insipid Liszt composition—I stopped in the middle of my performance. I had forgotten where I was and could not play another note. I finished to the chagrin of my father and the smug reaction of other students' parents by skipping most of the piece and finishing up with the pages of music that I remembered.

While attending Ward, my enthusiasm for music was rivaled—and occasionally eclipsed—by my love of sports. Baseball bordered on an obsession. Boston was a good place to be a baseball fan, and I worshipped virtually every player on Joe Cronin's Red Sox roster. Cronin, the Hall-of-Fame shortstop and playing manager of the Boston team, was a hero—despite his unsuccessful attempts to topple the reign of the New York Yankees. In those years, the Bronx Bombers fielded players like Lou Gehrig, Bill Dickey, and, later, Joe DiMaggio. The Boston stars, such as Jimmy Foxx, DiMaggio's little brother Dominic, and my boyhood idol Ted Williams, could never seem to overcome the insurmountable obstacle of those horrible Yankees. As kids we used to chant, without too much conviction, "Who's better than his brother Joe? Dominic DiMaggio!" Although I have lived in New York more than half my life, the Boston Red Sox remain my most frustrating passion.

If I could have pursued the path of a major-league catcher, I would have done so in a heartbeat. I could hit a baseball and could throw a football fifty yards down a field, but I was never a fast runner and I didn't have the build of an athlete. I compensated for this deficiency by developing a keen mind for strategy. There was no little league in those days, so I put together my own neighborhood baseball team (an early sign of my talent for organization). We used the Ward School playground for practices, and even bought team sweaters, emblazoned with the insignia *Beaver A. C.*—the moniker we had chosen for our athletic club. Before long we had sent a word of challenge to kids from other neighborhoods; we held informal games on the Ward School grounds and on their local turf. This continued, in more or less the same fashion, through my junior high and high school years.

In all of my endeavors—athletic, musical, academic, and otherwise—I could always count on the stalwart support of my parents. My mother was a pillar of unconditional love, and stood behind me in any circumstance. My father exhibited encouragement of a more volatile sort; he thought that whatever I did was the greatest, and he was quick to express this opinion freely. Anyone who disagreed with him was in for a rude awakening, since Barney's explosive temper was complemented by a remarkable ability to hold a grudge. When I think of the emotional climate of 264 Ward Street, I see my parents in these contrasting roles.

As for my brother, Larry, he was always a good friend. Although four years older, he never patronized me as the kid brother, and our relationship was free of the usual fraternal friction. This was remarkable, because I was clearly my father's favorite; I received better marks in school, showed more interest in sports, and played the piano, and Doc's pride in these accomplishments knew no bounds. Although Larry could easily have begrudged me this paternal favor, he never let it affect our interaction. He was not easily fazed. In this way, our personalities were distinct. Larry was disinclined to be the center of attention, and that was where I thrived. I was a perennial team captain and he was content to haunt the sidelines. He was neither an organizer nor much of a leader, so I never looked to him as a role model. He was a nice guy who got along with everyone.

When I was eight or nine years of age, I began to notice tension in my household. My mother had developed a tendency of crying almost every night, her tears persisting until late in the evening, when my father finally came home. Then there'd be desperate shouting matches, to which I listened, horrified, from my upstairs bedroom (where I was supposed to be asleep). Often these arguments would end with my father storming out of the house, punctuating his exit by slamming the front door behind him. This pattern of behavior was seldom discussed by light of day, but its presence was no less palpable, hanging over and around our family like a fog.

I don't know when I was old enough to realize what exactly was taking place. Doc had a mistress, a bright woman who was a divorcée, with children of her own. This situation was, to some degree, a public spectacle; in a community as insular as Newton, such secrets were never safe. Everyone knew about it, to my mother's great humiliation. To make matters worse, Doc's mistress called our house with some frequency due to her secretarial responsibilities. My poor mother would pick up the phone and find the "other woman" on the line.

My father's friends, who all liked my mother, would call him to task: "Barney, you have to stop doing this to Ruth." He did not take kindly to their advice; with every critical remark, he grew more obstinate and irate. He told his friends to go to hell. Before long our dinner parties dwindled, then ceased. Much of the joy had left our home.

Ruth was a woman of strong ideals, and among these the importance of family was primary. Family was sacred to her, and she would fight to preserve ours with every ounce of her being. This conviction—far more profound than a mere sense of duty—was what enabled her to endure my father's mistreatment.

She was steadfastly loyal to our family, even in the presence of gentleman callers (one of whom entreated her to leave my father and marry him). Today, conventional wisdom would most likely lead a woman in my mother's unfortunate position to leave her unfaithful husband. At the time, even Larry—who was in high school, and outraged by my father's behavior—was telling her to get a divorce. But my mother would hear none of it. The only time she ever spoke to me about the matter was when, after a particularly unpleasant exchange with my father, she turned to me with a tear-streaked face and said, "George, a man can do anything he wants—if he's just affectionate at home."

The affair came to a head one evening when I was eleven years old. Doc had been sleeping at his office for several days, refusing to come home. He had every intention of leaving; I suspect he had finally promised his mistress that he would marry her. As a last resort, my mother took me to see him at his office on Commonwealth Avenue.

"You can't leave," I cried, when I saw my father. "You can't leave." My mother knew that I was Barney's weak spot. Her decision to take me with her was probably much more calculated than I realized at the time. And she was right; my father came home.

It was a turning point, and a decision that may have messed him up for the rest of his life. I always suspected that Doc felt a sense of guilt for not marrying that woman. And he anguished about this guilt, because he still felt an allegiance and responsibility toward our family. He was torn. Unfortunately, he would unleash the bulk of this frustration upon my mother for years afterward. In his uglier moments, he would tell her that I had been the only reason for his return.

My father's mistress died years later—sometime during the 1960s—while vacationing in North Africa. My parents were in the car shortly after hearing this news. My father put his head against the steering wheel and began to cry. Without a moment's hesitation, my mother reached out to console him. This was her commitment—her man, father of her children. That's the way things were.

Through my parents' painful ordeal, they both continued to show me nothing but unconditional love. So while the marital conflict crippled our family, I didn't harbor much resentment toward Doc. Whatever his wrongs, I had to love him; he was my father. My tendency to forgive (if not forget) came from Ruth.

We all pick up certain characteristics from our parents. I picked up the habit of yelling at people around me, including my wife, from my father's stupid temper. But over time I learned several things. First of all, Joyce would not accept my yelling at her; and secondly, I did figure out how to contain myself, and once I exploded, I would immediately stop and apologize.

My sense of family came from my mother. Joyce and I have no children. So, in a sense, the people that have worked with me for many years have become family. It's very difficult for me to give someone notice unless flagrant abuses have been committed to the business. The employees of FPI have been with me for between 20 and 50 years. I guess I can thank Ruth Wein for creating this kind of company, with all its pluses and minuses. Good business sense dictates a different sense of management. We have managed to survive in spite of our antiquated approach.

My brother and I grew much closer during his high school years. What really deepened our relationship, as it turned out, was music. Although Larry had no musical abilities to speak of, he was an avid fan of music and musicians. Being four years older than I was, he also had a head start on the latest sounds. Such was the case, at least, when Larry started listening to the big bands. Despite his girth, Big Larry (as he was often known) was a good dancer. One fateful afternoon, he brought home a brand-new record player and a batch of Decca Blue Label 35-cent records. Louis Armstrong was on Decca, as well as Larry Clinton, Glenn Grey, and Jimmy Lunceford. The phonograph's crackling warble didn't filter out any of the kinetic excitement of those records—swing anthems like Lunceford's "White Heat," and Armstrong's "When the Saints Go Marching In." It was my first exposure to this kind of music. I was hooked.

In those years, every town in New England—from Portland, Maine, to Bridgeport, Connecticut—had a ballroom, glimmering like a palace in the desert. A typical ballroom would have an elevated stage, a mirrored orb rotating near the high ceiling, and a polished dance floor flanked by tables. Halls like these were much more than performance venues; they formed the center of local social activity.

The best of the swing and dance bands—those led by Jimmy Lunceford, Duke Ellington, Tommy Dorsey, Count Basie, and Glenn Miller—used to play the New England ballroom circuit for weeks at a time. Other groups—like Sam Donahue's band—might be lesser-known but were just as powerful as their marquee counterparts. Whenever a good band played a show somewhere in the region, Larry and I made it our business to drive out and see them. During my early adolescence, we saw dozens of fabulous shows, at such venerable ballrooms as Canobie Lake, Salem Willows, Salisbury Beach, and Nuttings on the Charles. This was a big part of my early musical education.

My formal education, meanwhile, took on a new character at around this time; I left the safe haven of the Ward School and moved on to Weeks Junior High, in Newton Center. Weeks was a short bus ride from Ward Street, but

it seemed a world apart. Its enrollment—consisting of a thousand kids between the ages of twelve and fifteen—was much larger than the Ward
School, and classes were nearly double in size. More significantly, Jewish kids
enjoyed no majority status at Weeks. For the first time, we encountered ethnic groups from other sections of town.

These were tough Irish and Italian kids whose families had at one point
moved to Newton from South Boston and the North End. Most of them came
from a lower economic class than Newton's Yankee natives and resident Jewish population, and like their parents, they had learned to channel their frustrations into racial prejudice. Because there were very few black residents of
Newton, we Jewish kids got it, but good.

This situation did wonders for our vocabulary. On my first day in seventh
grade, I learned two brand-new words when some punk called me a "fucking
kike." I had never heard the expression before in my life, but I knew it couldn't
be anything nice. It was a welcome to the real world.

Prejudice arises from fear, and people tend to be less fearful when a minority is small and contained. So there was never any major hostility—at least,
none that we could detect—directed toward the Booths, one of the only black
families in Newton. Mr. Booth was a postman, and had settled with his wife
and two sons in our town. His older son Wendell had earned the nickname
"Windy," for his remarkable speed on the football field at Newton High.
Allen, the younger Booth brother, was softer and more introspective. He was a
year or two ahead of me and also played the piano. Windy and Allen were both
well liked in the school, and I don't have the impression that they contended
with explicit racism from our community. Had the Booths been part of a large
and distinct African-American population in Newton—one that mirrored the
Jewish community—there would undoubtedly have been a great deal more
conflict. The Booth family, of course, may have a different story to tell about
being black in a white suburban town.

Weeks Junior High had a well-manicured baseball diamond, and each day
at lunch a student stood guard to keep kids from trampling it. This was usually a solitary and rather tedious task. But on the day that I was assigned to the
diamond, three or four of the tougher kids in my class decided to harass me. I
stood helplessly on the field and took their hazing, which involved a litany of
verbal abuses—most of them anti-Semitic. There was nowhere to go; I had to
stand at my post. All I could do was try to ignore the taunting.

Suddenly, a voice cut through the chaos: "Leave him alone!"

My tormentors turned to see Allen Booth, who must have spotted the
melee as he passed by the field. They looked at him for a moment, then be-

grudgingly walked away. Allen had defended me. He had told them to lay off, and they had split. Allen and I never became close friends, but I never forgot that afternoon. Allen and I would cross paths professionally, many years later.

The baseball diamond episode was not my last encounter with anti-Semitism in junior high, but life went on. In the eighth grade, I even summoned the confidence to run for president of the class. My friends Herbie Marcus, Sumner Mayburg, and Cyrus Harvey were running for vice president, treasurer, and secretary, respectively; we were the unofficial Jewish ticket. With my usual self-appreciation, I was convinced that I had the skills to lead our class. I wanted the opportunity to prove it to everyone else.

The campaign was an exciting experience. I remember speaking in the auditorium to the entire class; like most politicians, my speech consisted of smoke and mirrors. I thought I sounded very good. Herbie, Sumner, and Cy also made their pitches. We were quite confident as we left the assembly, because we just knew that we were better and smarter than the other candidates. We didn't have the money to make steel buttons, but we mimeographed sheets of paper extolling our virtues. We cluttered the halls with these flyers.

As Election Day drew to a fateful close, I entered my teacher's classroom, where she had just finished counting the votes. This particular teacher was especially fond of me, since I had recently scored 99 out of 100 on a citywide math exam. She had singled me out in class as the only student with such a strong performance; little did I know that it was quite possibly my last glorious academic moment.

I closed the door behind me and made a few hopeful steps in her direction. This was the moment of truth. "How did I do?"

She looked at me before she spoke. "George," she said gently, "I think you're a better math student than you are a politician. You got one vote."

One vote! I hadn't even secured the Jewish vote! Herbie Marcus had received more votes as vice president, because they had misspelled his name on the ballot; ten misguided students had cast their endorsement for some Irish lad named Herbie Moran. Sumner Mayburg's name was misspelled as Mayberry, so he got some WASP votes. Cyrus Harvey, whose name went unchanged, got four times as many votes for secretary as I did for president. So much for my calling as a natural leader of the masses.

So who had cast the single vote in my favor? Or had it been a facetious gesture, a practical joke intended to add insult to injury? I discovered the answer a few days later, when John Dorfman approached me in the hallway. John was a short, bookish Yankee kid with a somewhat rectangular build. He was the brightest student in our class.

Somewhat conspiratorially, Dorfman said: "I voted for you, George. I thought you were the most qualified candidate."

His words were like a salve to my wounded ego. I had always respected this kid, and it meant something to have this regard reciprocated. It was an important lesson, and one that would serve me well during many of my subsequent endeavors. Instead of feeling defeated, I was encouraged by the integrity of my solitary voter.

After a good five years under Madame Chaloff's instruction, I was ready for an instructor who would introduce me to basic chords, as they related to popular music. I began taking weekly lessons with Sam Saxe, a disciple and devotee of Earl "Fatha" Hines. Saxe had groomed some of the established pianists of the area (including such Boston big band luminaries as Bob Kitsis, Milt Raskin, and Arthur Medoff). Studying with Mr. Saxe, I learned some elements of the signature Hines style: the rhythmic touch, the tremolos in octaves, the tenths in the left hand. He taught me how to read lead sheets, and improvise over chords. He assigned homework: standards that I would have to learn in all twelve keys. Gradually, I began to develop an understanding of jazz piano. All that was left was for me to start practicing with a band.

Enter Grant Wilson, my adolescent alter ego. At fifteen years of age, I decided to organize a rehearsal group. I scoured the area for other young musicians, and managed to find four saxophones, three trumpets, two trombones, a rhythm section, and a vocalist—the standard big band configuration of the day.

I had purchased some stock arrangements; you could get them for thirty-five cents. I also owned some professional charts, courtesy of an entertainer named Belle Baker, who had met my mother at a "fat farm" in Tarrytown, New York, a few years earlier. Ms. Baker had begun her career in the Yiddish theater before graduating to the nightclub circuit and, eventually, introducing Irving Berlin's song "Blue Skies" on Broadway. She and my mother had kept in touch, and when Belle had learned of my aspirations as a bandleader, she arranged for me to visit some music publishers in New York City. With her note of introduction in hand, I had stopped at several Tin Pan Alley tuneshops, collecting an armful of arrangements free of charge.

I led rehearsals from behind a little out-of-tune upright piano in the cellar. At that age, it was the purest thrill to lead a band. I loved counting off the tempos, stopping to work on a tricky passage, handing out new stock charts. Our drummer, Buddy Harrison, used to labor valiantly (and vainly) to keep us in time. Myron Shain was our best improviser; he got all of the Bunny Berigan trumpet solos. Gus Signore, with whom I occasionally played the *Tarantelle* at Italian weddings, used to drive to the house in his father's oil truck. Sue Penn, our female vocalist, spent almost as much time warding off our unsolicited affections as she did singing at the microphone. We spent almost every Sunday afternoon in that basement, struggling with songs like Erskine Hawkins's "Tuxedo Junction," Tommy Dorsey's "Song of India," and Glenn Miller's "In the Mood." Our big hit was a thing called "The Johnson Rag."

But what were we to be called? I decided to concoct a stage persona, in the tradition of many popular entertainers of the day. Benjamin Kubelski had "Jack Benny"; Izzy Iskowitz had "Eddie Cantor." If I was to follow in their illustrious footsteps, I had to shed my Jewish birth name as well (this was, remember, many years before Simon and Garfunkel).

Because the band's headquarters—my house—was located on the corner of Grant Avenue and Ward Street, I briefly considered "The Grant Ward Orchestra." But it was too WASP-y even for show business. So I settled on "Grant Wilson" as my nom de guerre. Where the "Wilson" came from I have no clue. But at least my initials were the same. As for the band as a whole, I anointed them "The Stardusters"—after Hoagy Carmichael's sentimental hit.

We played one or two school dances, as I recall, probably earning no more than thirty or forty dollars for the whole band. But it might as well have been the big time. We purchased ten cardboard music stands for five bucks apiece, and had someone with artistic inclinations emblazon the front of each with a customized big band coat-of-arms: an elongated pentagon with a bold-faced GW.

For the most part, though, we were a rehearsal band (a diplomatic way of saying that we weren't actually very good). On more than one occasion we received help from more advanced musicians in the neighborhood. Serge Chaloff (Madame Chaloff's son) stopped by once to help the reeds with their phrasing and articulation. Just a few years later, Serge would establish himself as one of the preeminent baritone saxophonists in jazz. Another saxophonist, a high school girl by the name of Roz Kron, also came in to rehearse with us a few times. Roz would later become the only white musician in an all-female band called the Sweethearts of Rhythm, before settling down to become a wife and mother in California.

All in all, Grant Wilson and the Stardusters had a good run. During that time, I learned what it meant to rehearse a band. We all witnessed first-hand the joy and anguish of tackling big band arrangements and making them swing. We turned my cellar into a laboratory of musical exploration—and, like Dr. Frankenstein, the results were occasionally monstrous. But it was always a good time. We took the band seriously but also recognized the Sunday afternoon sessions as social gatherings. Our classmates would often crowd the basement steps and listen, tapping their feet; sometimes Larry would bring his friends. With a dose of imagination, it could have been a scene from a movie. Music was hard work, sure, but it was also supposed to be fun. I developed this conviction early on. It has stood me in good stead ever since.

This attitude was reinforced in high school, when I began to explore Boston's nightclub scene. There was always good music at the Savoy Club, then on Columbus Avenue, and the Hi-Hat, which sat on the corner of Columbus and Massachusetts Ave. I managed to catch a fair share of music in both clubs, despite my tender age. I also spent some time at the Vanity Fair on Newbury Street, and the Ken Club on Warrington Street, which ran a jam session every Sunday afternoon.

One of the mainstay groups at the Ken Club was a sextet led by the New Orleans trumpeter Henry "Red" Allen and trombonist J. C. Higginbotham. The group also included a hell of an alto player, Don Stovall; a fine pianist, Kenny Kersey; a soon-to-be-lionized drummer by the name of Kenny Clarke; and a bassist, Bennie Moten (not to be confused with the Kansas City bandleader of the same name). I saw this band at every possible opportunity.

In addition to his Ken Club gigs, Red Allen often led a Sunday afternoon jam session at the Hotel Bradford. The session was organized by a local disc jockey named Bill Ingalls; he would invite players up from New York City. On such occasions, Don Stovall would lie in wait for the saxophonists. He was like an undefeated local prizefighter jealously standing guard over his domain. I remember one afternoon when the alto saxophonist Pete Brown—who had recorded with Frankie Newton—rode into town. Perhaps he was sleepy from the train ride, but when Brown took the stage, Stovall completely destroyed him. It was something to behold; here was this Boston-based alto player coming out of left field, tearing the man apart. Pete Brown took his licking and went back to New York, but he made a point of returning a month later. This time, he was ready—he left Stovall, figuratively, lying on the floor. These were serious cutting sessions that were by no means exclusive to Kansas City or New York. The jazz aficionados of Boston would talk about such improvisational bouts all the time, in knowing tones; it's amazing that no one ever placed wagers on their outcome.

Well-known jazz musicians, like major-league baseball players, were otherworldly figures to me. As an aspiring musician, I idealized their improvisational ease and envied their casual, urbane manner. I often accompanied my brother, Larry (a high school graduate by this time), and one of his friends to a club. Even though we were all underage, they drank. Because I didn't, I invariably drove them home. It was a small price to pay in order to hear this music.

During one of Cab Calloway's six-week runs in town—at a nightclub on Warrenton Street called Southland—Big Larry managed to stop in almost every night. He quickly became friendly with the guys in the band. When I accompanied him to the club, he introduced me to Chu Berry, Hilton Jefferson, Dizzy Gillespie, Jonah Jones, Cozy Cole, and Milt Hinton. I was on cloud nine.

It was even more exciting when Larry first introduced me to Red Allen and J. C. Higginbotham, who were living icons to me. Both of them had played with Louis Armstrong; a credential that automatically bestowed an aura of glamor. Even the sound of their names was heroic; who had ever heard of anyone as audacious as "J. C. Higginbotham"?

Red was not as well known as "Higgy," as he had always played his trumpet in Louis Armstrong's considerable shadow. Red was a natural leader, a skillful showman, and a wonderful trumpeter; he was one of the few players at that time capable of taking a ballad and improvising skillfully on both the melody and the changes. Although he came from the same school of musicianship that Armstrong had popularized, Red was never paralyzed by slavish imitation to the Armstrong sound.

Needless to say, it was no small point of pride when Red Allen and his group would leave the Ken Club after their last set. My brother and I would drive them to my house in Newton for a late supper—as we did on several occasions. The first time they came, my mother was in the kitchen preparing an appropriate meal. She knew that Red Allen was from New Orleans, so she attempted to cook something that would make him feel at home. The resulting chicken and rice (her rendition of red beans and rice) became a staple of these visits. Red, Higgy, and the other musicians always followed this midnight snack with a jam session that lasted until two or three A.M.

Picture a carload of Negro jazz musicians in 1943 driving through our slumbering suburb after midnight and playing music there until the early morning hours. This sort of thing just didn't happen in Newton, Massachusetts. But, for whatever reason, my parents saw nothing unusual about the situation. They welcomed these musicians into our house as close friends. Musicians loved my mother for her hospitality. They also took an immediate liking to my father, even if he bored them with his continual questions about me and whatever little talent I might have.

One night, Benny Goodman's Band was appearing at the Totem Pole, a ballroom on the banks of the Charles River, in Newton's Norumbega Park. In order to preserve its upstanding reputation and prevent the development of a pickup scene, the Totem Pole enforced a strict "no stag" policy. If I wanted to see Benny Goodman, I would have to find a date. Well, at sixteen years of age, I was not exactly suave with the fairer sex. Whomever I brought would probably have been unhappy, as my attention was so unerringly focused on the music. Rather than subject one of Newton's fair maidens to this level of neglect, I decided to enlist some familial assistance; I strolled into the ballroom with my mother at my side. After we had cleared the door, she slipped out and drove back home.

Benny Goodman's big band, of course, was swinging. But what thrilled me most was to stand six feet from the Goodman sextet, listening to Cootie Williams. Cootie had left Duke Ellington's orchestra to play with this group—no small matter in the jazz world. Cootie leaving the Duke to join Benny was like Ted Williams leaving the Red Sox to play for the Yankees. A song was actually composed titled, "When Cootie Left The Duke." For the duration of the evening I stood alone, wide-eyed, at the foot of the stage—oblivious to the sea of couples swirling around the dance floor behind me.

There was nothing about high school that even remotely suggested the excitement of the jazz life. I did, however, make one attempt to incorporate music into my curriculum; I joined the high school classical orchestra. Since they already had a piano player, I was given the responsibility of playing the contrabass. But even this task proved to be incompatible with my jazz-inspired tastes. At one rehearsal, we played Schubert's *Unfinished Symphony*. One movement is in the key of G, and has a highly repetitive and monotonous bass part. Halfway through, I decided to make an adjustment. Knowing that we were on a G major triad, I played a B (the third) instead of the notated D (fifth). It was the simplest of note substitutions. But our teacher-conductor, a man named Jim Remley, stopped the orchestra. His face erupted into an alarming crimson color as he walked briskly in my direction. "Who do you think you are," he screamed, "changing Schubert's *Unfinished Symphony*?" I was henceforth banished from the orchestra.

My own musical explorations were confined to Stardusters rehearsals, and whatever rare gigs I could find around town. This latter prospect increased dramatically once I made my way into the seamy underside of Boston's nightclub scene. A nonunion booking agent named Duke Davis put together the entertainment for such spots as Ort's Grill, the Silver Dollar Bar, and Jack's Café. These tough little local bars—known smirkingly as "Buckets of Blood"—were inevitably located in the shady sections of town. They were just "joints." But there was always music, dancing, and ample cheap booze, from noon until midnight. Neighborhood blue-collar workers would hang out there, and transients would always be passing through.

Davis had a list of hundreds of musicians, many of them kids like myself. He got my name from somewhere, and before I knew it I was a part of the Buckets of Blood circuit. We were musical guns-for-hire, working for two bucks a night. Because Duke Davis hired individual players rather than intact bands, the music was always a bit haphazard. I would show up to a gig without any idea who else would be playing. Sometimes, I knew nobody else on the stand. We'd call out songs and hope that the other guys either knew the tunes or could fake it convincingly enough. As my own repertoire of songs was so slim, I spent a lot of time doing the latter.

One night on the stand at Jack's Cafe in Charlestown's City Square, I had the nerve to actually sing a number, accompanying myself at the piano. "Come to me," I crooned, "my melancholy baby." An unkempt barfly walked up to the stage as I was singing and then shot me a piercing, soulful stare. I saw the passion in his eyes and threw even more gusto into the ballad—my singing was really moving him! I was a big hit! But this hopeful train of thought was quickly derailed; the guy took a few more lurching steps and then proceeded to vomit all over the floor.

I was fortunate enough to have an older brother who set a precedent for underachieving. Larry had never wanted to continue his studies past high school, and his transcript reflected this fact. He saw no need for a college education; as a descendant of the Ginsburg line, he knew that he was headed for the family business. My parents, however, held fast to an unspoken code. Middle-class Jewish kids were not only supposed to go to college; they were expected to do well. Barney Wein, in his youth, had exemplified this tradition. But Larry simply wasn't the academic type. He did enroll at the University of Vermont, but came home after just a few weeks. He was only marginally happier after transferring to Boston University. Finally, Larry decided to try New York University.

NYU was an obvious strategic move; although Larry was technically enrolled in classes on campus, he actually matriculated at Café Society, the Village Vanguard, and a number of other Big Apple nightspots. I'd visit him as often as my own high school schedule allowed, each trip a smorgasbord of jazz. I saw so much music during those months that I have a hard time remembering one performance from the next. It's all one incredible collage of sights and sounds.

Larry and I had a routine, by which we could hit five or six different clubs in one night. We would start at around seven o'clock in the evening, with an inexpensive dinner at Child's Restaurant in Times Square, where the John Kirby Sextet had a regular engagement. Then we would head down to one of the clubs in Greenwich Village; one night we heard Benny Carter with a large band at Nick's, which was usually a Dixieland stronghold. Then off to the ten o'clock show at Café Society downtown—where, on different occasions, we saw performances by the Teddy Wilson Sextet (featuring Edmond Hall and Emmett Berry); the folksinger Josh White; Hazel Scott, the beauteous pianist married to Adam Clayton Powell; and a double-piano boogie-woogie act with Pete Johnson and the barrel-chested Albert Ammons. After Café Society, we'd hit 52nd Street, for performances by the likes of Art Tatum, Coleman Hawkins, or Ben Webster. We'd cap off the evening with a trip uptown to the Savoy Ballroom ("in the early one-hundred and forties on upper Lenox Avenue, the Home of Happy Feet," as they used to announce over the airwaves), where we'd brave the jitterbugging crowds to see the Erskine Hawkins Orchestra, Al Cooper and the Savoy Sultans, or the Chris Columbus Orchestra. The following evening, we'd start all over again, visiting the clubs we had missed the first time around.

The highlight of this circuit was 52nd Street; it was one of heaven's avenues of gold. A typical club on 52nd Street would consist of a plain storefront with a narrow interior space that barely contained a hundred and fifty people. There would be a bar on the right as you walked in, and a couple of particularly mean-looking guys at the door. Larry and I would have twenty dollars apiece—a charitable donation from my father. To make this pocket money last as long as possible, I would avoid the ubiquitous three- or four-dollar minimum charge by nursing a one-dollar ginger ale at the bar. There was no musical experience comparable to the feeling of walking in on a set by Oran "Hot Lips" Page, or Jonah Jones, or the Art Tatum Trio. Red and Higgy were headliners in those days, and we made sure to visit whichever club they were playing. I can recall a Red Allen–J. C. Higginbotham bill at Kelly's Stables, with the Nat King Cole Trio as a group who played at intermission. Billy Daniels (of later "That Ol' Black Magic" fame) and Thelma Carpenter were the house vocalists.

On a good night, you could walk into the Famous Door and see the whole Basie band crowded into the back of the room, swinging like mad. Around the corner from the Famous Door was the White Rose Bar, where the musicians would have affordable drinks between sets. Sitting there long enough, you might catch Ben Webster putting away a series of thirty-five-cent double-shots. After enough of them, he sometimes threatened to demonstrate his amateur boxing skills. Fortunately, the opponents who took up his challenges usually avoided hitting him in the mouth; they knew that Ben always had another set to play.

The first set at one of the 52nd Street clubs would start at ten o'clock, and the final set would sometimes last until four in the morning. Diehards like Larry and myself prized a closing set, because it was such an intimate experience. We could sit within ten feet of the musicians and have the room almost all to ourselves. At times, this seemed like the essence of jazz. Other fans enjoyed this unique experience; some of them would become future jazz critics. When I later started presenting jazz festivals and thousands of people began enjoying the music that some considered a private reserve, these critics voiced the requisite complaints.

New York was great, but Boston was still home. Larry enlisted in the army in 1941. With him gone, I spent more time with another older acquaintance—a Radcliffe graduate by the name of Ethel Klein. Ethel was the elder daughter of Dr. Ike Klein, one of my father's closest peers. She was more than fifteen years my senior, and had been my very first piano instructor, before Madame Chaloff. While Ethel had always been a sort of mentor to me, it was during these years that we really became friends.

Ethel lived with her parents on Blue Hill Avenue in Mattapan; their house sat directly across the street from the G & G Delicatessen, a hotbed of Marxist and Socialist activity. I don't know exactly how this affected Ethel's politics, but she did develop strong leftist views. Communism appealed to her, as it did to many people at the time, because it espoused the progressive idea of racial equality. At one of Ethel's parties, I found myself face to face with a huge black gentleman whose serene but striking presence I would always remember. She introduced him as Paul Robeson.

I was familiar with Robeson as the first black All-American football player at Rutgers University. He was also highly regarded as a baritone singer and theatrical actor. Seeing him in the flesh, I was overwhelmed by his majesty. A few years later, I would see a performance of William Shakespeare's *Othello* at the Colonial Theater in Boston, where Robeson shared the stage with Uta Hagen and José Ferrer. It was the most impressive theatrical experience of my life.

At another of Ethel's parties, in 1941, I met Lionel Hampton. At the time, the vibraharpist had just left Benny Goodman to form his own big band.

Ethel had thrown the party in his honor. Naturally Hamp spent the evening entertaining the guests; at one point he perched over the grand piano in Ethel's living room and played it in his percussive two-fingered style. Having been told that I played a little piano, he invited me to join him. So I sidled up and filled in a chordal accompaniment to "Lady Be Good."

I was elated. Hampton's work with the Goodman band was legendary, and here I was, sharing a piano bench with the man. I even followed this performance with a vocal number—singing a little song that I had heard over at the Savoy, a ditty called "Two Old Maids in a Folding Bed."

A few days later, my parents and I headed over to the Tic Toc Club on Tremont Street to catch Lionel Hampton's big band. He spotted us in the crowd.

"Ladies and Gentlemen," Hamp declared, "we have with us a famous Boston physician, the eminent Doctor Weems. And his son, George Weems, is a piano player." (He never did get our name right.) But Lionel did call me on-stage for our tandem rendition of "Lady Be Good." Here I was, sixteen years old, playing with Lionel Hampton and savoring the crowd's applause. Maybe my career in "showbiz" was born that night. Many members of this band became a part of my professional life in later years; Illinois Jacquet, Dexter Gordon, and Joe Wilder were among the superstars that Hamp fostered.

I was certainly indebted to Ethel for the experience of meeting Robeson and Hampton. But her most portentous introduction occurred when she started going out with a trumpet player who often headlined at the Savoy. She had fallen in love with him, and wanted me to get to know him as well. His name was Frankie Newton.

Although not a household name, Frankie Newton had already had a fairly illustrious career. He was a veteran of bands led by Cecil Scott, Elmer Snowden, and Charlie Barnet, and had been the original trumpeter in the John Kirby Sextet. He had also played for some time in the Teddy Hill Orchestra (leaving in 1937, only to be replaced by a young Roy Eldridge disciple named Dizzy Gillespie). Frankie had led the group that inaugurated Barney Josephson's Café Society. When I met him, in 1941, he was in the prime of his career; his best recordings, such as "The Blues My Baby Gives to Me" and "Please Don't Talk About Me When I'm Gone," were only a year or two old.

I had seen Frankie at the Savoy (with a superb small group that included the trombonist Vic Dickenson and saxophonist Ike Quebec), but it was at Ethel's house that we first met. He was a tall and strikingly handsome character, sharply dressed and exuding a natural charm. It was easy to see why Ethel was taken with him. Soon afterward we began having Frankie over to our house for my mother's late dinners. On one such occasion, he came with his drummer, Arthur "Mother" Herbert, in tow, and we had an impromptu jam session in my living room. Frankie muted his horn, and I sat down at the piano. "Mother" took out a pair of brushes and kept time on a piece of sheet music. Something about Frankie brought out my musicianship; on an impromptu version of "I Cried for You," I found my first creative moment in playing beyond what I thought I knew about jazz.

Before long, Frankie Newton had become my musical mentor. I would hear him at the Savoy, where he'd occasionally walk off the stand and stroll from table to table, quietly serenading patrons through a mute. His concern for subtle, lilting swing, intimate blues, and delicate improvisation would serve as a benchmark for my future musical tastes. I learned a lot about music just by being in his presence.

For most of the year, that meant seeing him in New York City; although he often worked in Boston, Greenwich Village was Frankie's home base. During my senior year in high school Ethel followed him there, finding her own apartment and a good administrative position at a private school. I paid each of them a visit whenever I went to New York; I'd usually crash on Frankie's couch.

Ethel was totally dedicated to Frankie, perhaps masochistically. I can remember having dinner with her in New York and consoling her as she cried. Her basic problem was Frankie's incorrigible independence. Although he appreciated the fact that Ethel loved him (and frequently supported him), he could never quite commit himself to her. He was a musician, and he liked to keep his options open. He had no qualms about approaching an attractive woman at a bar; his favorite line, delivered with a typical musician's charm, was "Whose little girl are you?"

Frankie was never much of a pedagogue; he had neither the temperament nor the skill of communication for that. But he'd say little things that stuck in my head. At Eddie Condon's club, Frankie leaned over and whispered: "Listen to Bud Freeman. He's playing more music than anyone else on the stand." I had never been particularly struck by Bud Freeman's tenor playing before, but those words of advice brought me around. I paid close attention to Bud after that, and began to understand what Frankie had meant. On another night we were talking about trombone players, and I noted my deep admiration for J. C. Higginbotham. Frankie shrugged. "Higgy's great," he said, "but Vic is the man." He explained how Vic Dickenson's rhythmic feel and melodic sense were unique, and quite modern. Frankie always tried to get Vic when he put together a combo.

This was the case in 1942, when Frankie got an extended engagement in Boston at the Vanity Fair. The band included Vic, Mother Herbert, the bassist Bill Pemberton, and a series of different saxophonists (including Franz Jackson, an alumnus of the Earl "Fatha" Hines Orchestra; and Ted Goddard, a good local alto player). I went as many nights as possible to the club. Frankie let me sit in with the band a few times, which was both a harrowing challenge and a big thrill. Each measure I played with those musicians was an education unto itself.

After hanging out in New York jazz clubs and playing gigs around Boston, my graduation from high school was a bit of an anticlimax. Adding to the ambivalence was the fact that I now faced the very real possibility of being drafted into the United States armed forces.

Larry had enlisted two years earlier, shortly after the bombing of Pearl Harbor in 1941. He had been anticipating the draft and had the good sense to leave NYU and return to Massachusetts, where he studied mechanics at Norwood Air Field. With a little bit of on-site training, he had gained the technical expertise to secure an assignment as a mechanic in the air force, a tactical maneuver that spared him from the risks of combat.

I had no such option, having been in high school during the first few years of the war. So holding my breath, I applied to Harvard University. Their inevitable rejection letter was appended with the suggestion that I apply again after the war. Thus spurned, I enrolled at nearby Northeastern University.

Northeastern was governed by hopelessly archaic regulations. For example: if you were two minutes late to class, you couldn't just slip into your seat. You had to go to an administration office and get a tardy slip. By the time you got back to the classroom, you had missed fifteen minutes of the lecture. It was a drag. This sort of vigilant, useless bureaucracy made Northeastern seem like an extension of high school.

To counteract the letdown of college, I took solace in familiar routines. I continued to play gigs in the city's Buckets of Blood circuit, and kept seeing whatever shows there were in town. I also got involved in neighborhood football games again—this time as a coach.

Despite my enrollment in Northeastern's freshman class, I was spending only minimal time in the classroom. The pre-med courses that I was taking to placate my father (who still imagined that one of his sons just might enter his profession) were pointless. I had no interest in the curriculum. My first semester transcript reflected this sense of apathy.

One morning the dean of the college called me into his office. "George," he said, after clearing his throat, "you've been missing a lot of classes."

"Well sir," I replied, "I'll be drafted into the army shortly, so I don't really care. I mean, I just turned eighteen in October, and I'm sure they're going to induct me."

"But don't you want to come back to school when you get out of the army?"

"No sir," I replied respectfully. "And if I did, I don't think I would come back to Northeastern. I don't like this school."

# 2

# *"That's a Plenty"*

THROUGH THE FROST-COVERED WINDOW of a troop bus at night, Fort Devens, the army-induction post in Ayer, Massachusetts, seemed especially charmless. Snow covered the ground and the roofs of the barracks. I was one of three thousand inductees assigned to spend a week at the Fort, for processing, before being sent out to basic training. It was early January 1944. I was only thirty-five miles west of Boston, but I had never felt further from home.

Morning came with the sound of a solitary bugle. I awoke shivering, tangled in a thin flannel blanket. To my left and my right, I saw dozens of other new recruits in varying stages of dress.

Within moments we were outside, freezing. Reveille. The sky was still dark; it was four A.M. We gathered in a clearing between barracks. I tried not to whimper in the cold.

Suddenly the metallic voice of a sergeant rang out.

"Does anybody here play the trumpet or the saxophone?"

There was a brief pause, as if no one had comprehended the words. Then a few scattered hands raised tentatively in the air. I lifted mine.

I played neither the trumpet nor the saxophone. But at least they were musical instruments; something familiar.

The sergeant spotted my outstretched arm and took note of my name. I received orders to report to Captain Prentice in special services the following morning.

We were directed to mess for breakfast. Three thousand people sat down to eat all at once. This drill was repeated for lunch and dinner. For obvious reasons, a daily tally of nine thousand meals made an unholy wreck of the kitchen. Cleanup was an unenviable responsibility. The pots in the kitchen were like barrels; you literally had to climb into them to scrub them. I was told that every recruit received kitchen patrol duty within a few days at the reception center. A towel at the edge of your bed, when you were jarred awake at four o'-clock in the morning, would indicate that you were chosen for K.P.

Not surprisingly, I awoke the following morning and found a white towel draped over the foot of the bed. I apprised a sergeant of my special orders with Captain Prentice.

"All right, get out of here," he growled. I reported to Special Services. The next thing I knew, I was holding a trumpet. Captain Prentice was organizing a small ensemble to substitute for the permanent reception-center band, which had gone on furlough. I was the only trumpet player there. He passed out stock arrangements for popular songs of the day, like "Careless." He counted off a tempo for the first tune. I lifted the horn to my trembling lips. I filled my lungs with air. I blew.

I wish I could relate an account of my natural genius; describe how the trumpet sang, how my embouchure produced a tone as clear as that of Frankie Newton or Armstrong. But the truth is that I sounded horrible. Worse than horrible. The other musicians exchanged glances and grimaces.

Soon the Captain called an intermission, to let us rest our chops and spare our ears. He cast a suspicious glance in my direction.

I began sweating. It was fairly obvious that I had lied about my trumpet-playing skills. But during the break I sat down at the piano and started to play. Captain Prentice turned in my direction. "You never mentioned that you played the piano," he said.

"Well, Sir," I replied, "you didn't ask for a piano player, you asked for a trumpeter."

Before long, they had found another trumpet player. I replaced the pianist, a refugee from Europe who was classically trained and had very little understanding of popular music. He became our conductor.

I breathed a sigh of relief. Even in the army, it never hurt to have a little nerve. After a few days of rehearsals, we began working at officers' dances, making twenty-five dollars a night. I was back on the bandstand. And no one ever called me for K.P.

Like many other high school graduates, I had been told that I would be enrolled in the Army Special Training Program. Joining the ASTP meant that I would go through thirteen weeks of basic training at Fort Benning, Georgia, and then go to college. After finishing my undergraduate education, I would enter Officers' Training School. A few friends of mine had already taken this path.

The train ride to Fort Benning was interminable; it seemed to me that Columbus, Georgia, in the heart of the red clay of this southern state, was at the ends of the earth. On our first day in camp they sent us through lines to receive shots in both arms. I had a reaction to these vaccines and developed a fever. When I woke up the next morning for reveille, I felt terrible. I had developed a mild case of pneumonia and spent the next two weeks in the hospital, after which I asked for and received a two-week sick leave.

And so I found myself back in Newton, Massachusetts; in full uniform, feted as a returning soldier. I had been away for three weeks—two of which had been in a hospital bed, and one which had been spent playing in a reception-center band.

When I returned to Fort Benning after my furlough in Newton, I discovered that the ASTP had been abruptly canceled. They needed bodies to put in the front lines, and canceling the ASTP provided that manpower by throwing a reserve of several hundred thousand hopeful students into the infantry on a moment's notice. What a double-cross of American mothers and their sons! Without the protective shield of the ASTP, a host of us were shipped out to Fayetteville, North Carolina—home of the 100th Infantry at Fort Bragg.

At Fort Bragg, I joined fifteen thousand other inductees on a huge, trampled parade ground. At the front of the mass, a general stood ramrod-straight on a high wooden platform.

"Gentlemen," he declared, "you will all start basic training again, as equals."

This was a noble proposition. But for me, it was impossible. As a soldier, I was *less* than equal to my fellow recruits. They had already received four to six weeks of training. I had spent those weeks in an army hospital and back in my own house on Ward Street. I was way behind the game.

That much was obvious as soon as we started training. I knew nothing. I couldn't break down a rifle, let alone fire one. I didn't know short-order drill. I was, as the army expression went, a "Number One Fuck Up." My ineptitude set me up for easy derision by my fellow recruits and, more significantly, by our sergeants. The army was enough of an ordeal for someone of my temperament; this problem made it even more insufferable. It was such an unpleasant situation that I retreated to sick call, feigning illness. At one point, I went to the doctor and told him that I had Osgood-Schlatter disease of the knees (which I had, when I was a kid).

"That's a childhood disease," he warily pointed out.

"Maybe it is," I said, "but my knees hurt."

Things were getting progressively worse in training, due to the malevolent aims of our presiding sergeant.

The sergeant in question was a tough Polish guy by the name of Kowalik. He had it in for me. He recognized my weakness and took every opportunity to exploit it. On one occasion, while we were ordered to stand at ease, he pounced on me for moving my right foot. I hadn't even learned to keep one foot in place.

"Alright, Wein," Kowalik snapped, "give me some pushups. Do them until you drop." So I did two push-ups and dropped. I wasn't going to go through that shit just because one son of a bitch was down on me.

He regarded me with disgust. "What's the matter with you?"

"I have a bad knee," I replied. "I *can't* do these things." (I had already learned never to say "won't" in the army.)

Without another word, the sergeant picked me up and dragged me over to the nearest officer. To a young recruit like myself, this was a terrifying experience. Officers were like gods on Mount Olympus; those bars on their shoulders were proof of an otherworldly sovereignty. I stood in horror as Sergeant Kowalik told his superior of my deficiencies—unmotivated; incorrigible; useless. The officer waited for an explanation.

Shaking, I tried to describe my situation. I had been in the hospital; I had been sent on furlough; I hadn't received any basic training. But each time I began to say something, the sergeant angrily interrupted me. "Stand up straight," he'd growl, or: "Say 'Sir' when addressing an officer!" It was impossible for me to get my point across.

Finally, I saw a flash of red. Throwing my rifle to the ground, I shouted: "Goddammit, you people don't give a guy a chance!" Tears were streaming down my cheeks.

Sergeant Kowalik was ready to kill me. I could see his face contorted in a violent expression. Fortunately, the officer spared me. "Take it easy, Sergeant," he said. Kowalik shot him a look, but eased off.

I was penalized for my outburst by having to carry my rifle everywhere I went and sleep with it, for a week. Given the circumstances, this was a lenient sentence. I could have been thrown in the guardhouse. I was extremely grateful for the understanding of that kind young lieutenant. Still, I knew that Kowalik would be looking for another opportunity to haze me. He was the only man who ever broke me.

In basic training, "recreation" usually meant some sort of calisthenics exercise. But one day they called tag football instead. This was good news; I had never been any good at somersaults or pull-ups or tumbling, but here was a sport I knew. I was happy to put my natural leadership skills—which had been forcibly suppressed by the rigidity of the military—to some use. Soon I was calling plays and throwing passes, and we were trouncing the other team.

Sergeant Kowalik saw this and went out of his mind. Here I was, the Number One Fuck Up, giving instructions: "You go out left and then come in this way, and I'll throw a pass."

Kowalik stopped the game and never let us play football again. And, as if to punish me for this show of individuality, he came down harder than ever during the next few days. Going through the drills, with his constant barrage of slurs, was hellish.

There was a Jewish sergeant in the next company who was a tough son of a bitch in his own right, and not very well-liked. But when he saw what was happening to me, he requested that I be transferred to his outfit. This might have been either a blessing or a curse; I never found out. Before the troops could be assembled, shipment-overseas orders came down to skim all the dead weight from the 100th Division. I was probably the deadest weight they had. So I was sent out, along with hundreds of other undistinguished recruits, to training at Camp Gruber, near Muskogee, Oklahoma. We were assigned to the 1275th Combat Engineers Battalion. Granted a fresh start, I applied myself anew to the task of becoming a soldier.

The Combat Engineers usually preceded the infantry into battle. They erected bridges over rivers and streams, so that troops and machinery could safely cross. This was obviously a harrowing task, and the training reflected that. I struggled to catch up on the drills and commands. It wasn't easy, but at least I had escaped the torturous clutches of Kowalik.

It just so happened that many army bands had been disassembled at around the same time as the ASTP Program. The demand for cannon fodder had outweighed the desire for entertainment, and some of the dispersed band members had entered our battalion. Not surprisingly, all the musicians found each other within no time. Soon we formed a small jazz band in the 1275th Combat Engineers.

In addition, the 42nd Division, the Rainbow Division, also stationed at Camp Gruber, had a near-professional big band. Their piano player was sick. Despite the fact that I wasn't a member of the 42nd, I was hastily recruited to play with the band. Alan Funt, who had worked for Ralph Edwards's CBS-radio show *Truth or Consequences*, organized shows at the PX once a week.

Soon I was getting paid to play Tommy Dorsey arrangements with a terrific-sounding big band—and at the same time, working officers' dances with the small group in the 1275th. Music had found me again.

But playing the piano couldn't rescue me from the rigors of training. I was still first and foremost a soldier.

One afternoon my company was out in the field, toiling in the excruciating Oklahoma summer heat. There were ten-minute breaks every hour, and at the beginning of each break the officer in charge (Sergeant Bradshaw) shouted: "Wein and Tannenbaum, set up the equipment for the next shift."

After three consecutive breaks like this, I complained: "What the hell, Sarge? Isn't there anybody else in the company besides Wein and Tannenbaum? I'd like to take a ten-minute break too."

I seemed to have a gift for pissing off sergeants.

My outburst earned me a company punishment: digging a four-by-four-by-four-foot seepage pit outside the mess hall. This was unendurable work. After several hours, I began to run a fever. By the time I convinced the nearest sergeant of my condition, I was barely able to stand. Finally I made it to the infirmary, where my temperature clocked in at 103 degrees. The doctor ordered that I be sent to the hospital.

As I was hoisting myself into an ambulance, our battalion commander, a Major Crawford, happened to walk by. He recognized me from the frequent gigs I played at the officers' club.

"What's the matter, Wein," he asked good-naturedly. "Is the training too tough?"

"The training doesn't bother me, Sir," I responded, "but this company punishment is killing me."

When my stint in the hospital was over, I discovered that the punishment had been lifted. I can only imagine that the commander had granted my pardon. Once again, the piano had served me well.

But my occasional outbursts had not gone unnoticed. One day a kid named Wasserman came up to me and delivered a message from one of our noncoms: "Sergeant Custer wanted me to talk to you. He says you're making it tough for the other Jewish kids in this company."

In fact, I wasn't really a wise guy; I only spoke up when somebody was giving me hell. I wasn't trying to shirk my duties as a soldier. I never did anything that warranted a trip to the guardhouse. But if someone was pushing me around, I asked why. I wasn't playing any games. So I told Wasserman: "I'm sorry, man. I can't accept that. I'm just being myself. I'm not going to allow people to push me around. If they're anti-Semitic, that's their problem, not mine. I'm not going to change who I am because I'm making it tough on the other Jewish guys in the outfit."

Despite the pervasiveness of such prejudices in the army, I was never inclined to befriend a fellow recruit simply because he was Jewish. That sort of group insularity held no appeal for me. Instead, I formed relationships based on common interests. This was the case with Elmer Wishnoff, a Philadelphia native who introduced himself one day while I was playing the piano. I discovered that he was an avid fan of show business and an intelligent guy. We quickly struck up a rapport; the fact that he was Jewish was incidental. At any rate, Wishnoff became my closest friend in the army. He's the only person I've kept in touch with in all the years since. And you might even say that this friendship saved my life.

Wishnoff and I were often assigned to the same field problem during our company's training exercises. One of these took place some distance from camp. We had slept overnight in sleeping bags and pup tents under the Oklahoma night sky. The following morning, there were several trucks waiting to take us back to our barracks. They were two-and-a-half-ton troop transport trucks, the kind with a canvas roof stretched over wooden struts. I hopped into the back of a truck loaded with guys. "C'mon, Wish," I said. "Get in here."

He called back: "The truck over here is empty. Let's take this one." So I clambered out and followed Wishnoff. Minutes later, after we had left the field, the first truck somehow turned over. Three men were killed; many others were injured.

These were the first casualties any of us had seen. They were just kids, young recruits like us. It was very sad; soldiers had to take the bodies home. If Wishnoff hadn't called me over to the other truck, I could easily have been one of them.

My fellow soldiers were a truly motley bunch. I met Ozark hillbillies with little or no education but possessing skills I could never dream of having. The Mormons and Seventh-Day Adventists in the company exposed me to new ethical and religious beliefs. And in a single barrack, there might be Native Americans, tramp athletes from Michigan factories, tough kids from Brooklyn, even a few other Jewish kids from Philadelphia and New England. Our company could have been cast in a Hollywood propaganda war film, demonstrating that Americans of every class and creed fought together in the war. Of course, this was a falsehood. The army, like the South, was legally segregated.

One of the guys in my division was a southerner, and he made no bones about his prejudice. He would often deride the black soldiers in Camp Gruber's segregated companies.

I confronted him once. "What's the matter with you? These guys are on our side. But you're talking about them as if you hate them more than the Germans. What if you're in combat and a black man is next to you, shooting at the enemy?"

"I'd shoot the German first," he said, grinning, "and then shoot the fucking nigger."

This same guy would walk over while we were both working and say: "Let me pick that up, pal. I don't want you to hurt your fingers." He liked the way I played the piano. It made no sense to me. He could seem like either a perfect gentleman or a raging bigot. I had never encountered anyone like this before. I soon realized that his sentiments echoed those of many other Americans.

My piano playing continued to serve me well. It seemed that everyone was fond of musicians, especially the officers who needed entertainment for their dances and parties. This was fortunate, since I had no other way of distinguishing myself in the service. Without the piano, I would have been Private G. Wein, just another guy in uniform with a dog tag and a number. So every time I sat at a piano and played, it was like a reclamation of my individuality. And I seemed to be playing constantly.

There just wasn't much of a jazz scene at Camp Gruber. Once in a while a band would pass through; I remember seeing the Benny Carter band, which was en route from California to New York. They set up on a basketball court in the campgrounds. Most of the buzz among jazz fans centered around Benny Carter's drummer, who was being touted as "the new Jo Jones." He was a skinny, handsome guy by the name of Max Roach.

But Benny Carter only came on one occasion, and similar diversions were few and far between. So I was understandably excited when I caught news of a Red Allen–J. C. Higginbotham club engagement in Chicago. Red and Higgy were not only musical role models; they also symbolized everything that I missed about civilian life. Eager to catch up with them, I applied for a three-day pass. It was granted mainly because my battalion would soon be shipping out for overseas.

A three-day pass literally meant seventy-two hours' leave. So I left the camp at the earliest opportunity, made my way to the train station in central Muskogee, and caught a steam locomotive headed for the Windy City. The train was noisy, filthy, and cluttered, with hard wooden seats and a gunmetal-gray smokestacks that belched soot and smoke. I changed trains in St. Louis. By the time I reached Chicago, nearly twenty of my seventy-two hours had passed.

I checked into a cheap hotel and caught a few hours of sleep before nightfall. When evening arrived, I cleaned up and headed for the club where Red and Higgy were billed. It was right in the heart of the city's downtown loop.

Both Red and J. C. were happily surprised when I walked into the room. They were far from Boston, and my appearance—in military garb—must have seemed like a distinct incongruity. I was invited to sit in at the piano during the next set.

I nearly fell over myself getting to the stage. They asked me to call a tune, and I chose "Rosetta," an Earl Hines piece. It was a ball being in a club again, playing with those masterful musicians. I stayed there until closing and returned the following evening.

Then I packed up and boarded the iron horse for the eighteen-hour ride to Muskogee. I made it back to camp with minutes to spare.

*     *     *

The 1275th finished training at the close of 1944. I had been in the army's employ for nearly a year. Now it was time to leave for the uncertain terrain of Europe.

Our troop ship landed in the U.K., where we set up camp in a wintry field near Warminster, a small English town on the Bath-Salisbury Road. There our unit went into constant training; we were practicing to build bridges across the Rhine. The Battle of the Bulge was under way. We didn't know it at the time, but this would mark the final turning point of the war. Allied losses were so severe that they were flying troops over from the States and dropping them directly into combat. Fortunately, the 1275th continued training in England. We were in a state of perpetual readiness, though; there was no telling when we would be ordered to head for the Continent.

One morning we read in the army newspaper, the *Stars and Stripes*, about the Remagen Bridgehead; the Rhine had successfully been crossed. One of the battalions involved in the Remagen effort was the 276th Engineers, which had trained with us at Camp Gruber. Warren Spahn, the Hall of Fame pitcher, was in that outfit. We offered many thanks to the 276th and the other units at Remagen. Thanks to them, the 1275th had been saved from combat.

In early April we received orders to leave England for France. The men in the 1275th boarded landing craft headed for Le Havre. This journey took a day and a night. After dusk fell, I clambered up onto a canvas stretched between the truck stays to sleep. In the middle of the night, I climbed down from my makeshift cot to relieve myself.

There was another soldier in the head, and as we stood there he delivered an earth-shattering pronouncement.

"Did you hear the news? Roosevelt died."

I was shocked. It was impossible to imagine the end of the Roosevelt Era. FDR had occupied the White House since I was seven years old. During his three-plus presidential terms, he had shepherded the nation through famine, the end of Prohibition, the Great Depression, and four years of international warfare.

The commander-in-chief was gone. What would happen to us? Who the hell was Harry S. Truman? How would this affect the war?

We didn't have long to ponder the implications. The following morning, we landed in Le Havre and drove eastward across France and into southwestern Germany. This was an eye-opening experience; the towns that we passed through were completely in ruins. One of them, Prum, was especially ravaged; most of the buildings had been reduced to rubble. We stayed there for a night, setting up temporarily in a bombed-out schoolhouse.

*     *     *

Soon we left Prum and set up operations in a medieval castle in Trier, the principal city of the Moselle Valley, one of the finest wine regions in Germany. In a happy coincidence, the castle where we were stationed had a magnificent wine cave. During our residence, the castle's German custodian offered many samples of wine, in exchange for cigarettes and candy. This was eye-opening. My exposure to wine up to that time was almost nil; in fact, my entire experience with alcohol had consisted of rye-and-ginger ale (at parties in Boston) and 3.2 percent beer (the only brew legal in Oklahoma). Suddenly here were these Moselle wines, with a rich complexity unlike anything that had ever passed my lips. I often trace my taste for fine wine back to this encounter.

We had been billeted in Trier for a little over two weeks when a special bulletin crackled over the radio. We gathered around and heard the voice of Winston Churchill—declaring that Hitler was dead. The Führer had killed himself, and the war in Europe was over. We rejoiced. The immediate threat was ended.

But Japan still maintained a stronghold in the Pacific, and the Army wasted no time in sending orders. Within a day or two we had packed up and traveled back to France to await deployment to the Pacific. The village of St. Vittoret, near Marseilles, was the site of our new cantonment. Tens of thousands of soldiers were billeted in a tent city that stretched across a huge open field.

With time on our hands while awaiting assignment to a ship, I began playing the piano again for USO shows in Marseilles.

One night Wishnoff and I were going to the movies, and we passed a crap game. So I said: "C'mon Wish, let's shoot a little craps." I put down $50, soon made $150, shot again and made $300, and then shot one last time. In just a few minutes I had made a $600 pass. So I picked up my money, turned to Wishnoff, and said: "Well, let's go to the movies."

I can't remember what film we saw. But on our way back we saw the same craps game. So I joined in. Before long I had done it again—another $600 pass. I took the money and went back to our barracks. That money—a staggering $1,200 earned in two brief craps interludes—I sent home the following morning, for safekeeping. This was the end of my winning gambling career. After that, I did nothing but lose. But when I got home, I was $1,200 ahead. When I went back to civilian life, gambling, in the gaming sense, had no appeal to me whatsoever. But I guess the instinct for risk has never left me.

There were other adventures as well. In Marseilles the army had marked all of the bordellos with bold yellow "Off-Limits" signs. This was a backward policy that had an unintended effect; it was as if the army had put up a flashing billboard over every whorehouse in the city. None of the soldiers would have known where the action was if it weren't for the signs.

I finally took it upon myself to visit one of these mysterious Off-Limit zones, making sure there were no MP's around. It was to be my first encounter of this sort; I was utterly inexperienced. Fortunately my hostess recognized that I was just a kid, and she treated me very kindly.

I left as stealthily as I had arrived. Returning to camp at St. Vittoret, I went to the medical center and got some ointment, a completely unnecessary precaution in my case. It felt like a hot poker in my "Johnson." But the Army had terrified me with its propaganda films about venereal disease. I made no more covert trips around the city.

I was still property of the United States Army: as a soldier yet untested in battle, I was destined for imminent deportation to the Pacific. I was painfully aware of the bloodbaths that had already occurred in the South Pacific islands, on the beaches of Okinawa, Iwo Jima, and Guadalcanal.

The harsh reality of war tainted every moment of each day I spent in St. Vittoret. Coincidence had mercifully spared me from combat on several occasions. One of the outfits I had trained with—the K Company 398th Regiment, 100th Division from Fort Bragg—had been decimated in combat. When I read an account of their losses in the *Stars and Stripes,* it aroused a painful mixture of horror, guilt, and relief. I could easily have been among their numbers.

We followed the events of the war with Japan through both the papers and the radio. It was through an article in the *Stars and Stripes* that I learned about the fateful mission of the *Enola Gay*, and the devastation of its atomic blast over Hiroshima in August 1945. A few days later, a second bomb hit Nagasaki. With it came Japan's surrender. The war was over.

News spread through the St. Vittoret reception center with incredible speed. I could hardly believe it. Stepping out into the heat of August, everything hit me at once. I was not going to die. The constant menace of combat had passed. When I received my next assignment and boarded a transport ship in Marseilles, it would be headed not for the Pacific but for the States.

I took a few steps outside before my legs gave out under me. I collapsed in a heap on the side of a dirt road and cried. The war was over. I was going home.

\*     \*     \*

I hated every minute I spent in the army. I've never been incarcerated, but some of the noncoms and officers I encountered could easily have exchanged uniforms with prison guards. I would never want to endure such an experience again. But having done it, I can also say that I wouldn't have missed it for the world. The Army had a huge impact on my life. I had seen no frontlines; no one had died in my arms. But I had enlisted in 1943 as an 18-year-old kid; I reentered civilian life in 1946 as a man.

Within no time, I looked up some of my old musical cohorts; we got together for an impromptu jam session in somebody's house.

"Let's do 'Groovin' High,'" the tenor player suggested.

"What's that?" I asked. I had never heard of the Dizzy Gillespie tune.

"It has the same changes as 'Whispering,'" he said.

"Alright," I said testily. "If we're going to play 'Whispering,' let's play 'Whispering.'"

A week or so later, I heard that Bud and Max were passing through town. I went to the club expecting to see Bud Freeman and Max Kaminsky. Instead, the bill featured Bud Powell and Max Roach. I was beginning to feel displaced and out-of-touch. I had only been away for twenty-five months, but it seemed as if the whole world had passed me by.

Meanwhile, I still had an army quota to fulfill. The war was over, but I hadn't been in service for the requisite number of months. Draftees with time left to serve were asked where they wanted to be for the remaining months of their army career. Faced with this choice, I told them to station me around New York City. I wanted to be close to 52nd Street.

I was assigned to a hospital at Fort Hancock in Sandy Hook, New Jersey—about two hours outside of New York City. I was asked to become a dietician. My primary duty was the coordination of meals for patients with special dietary needs.

My schedule was organized in such a way that I was on duty one day and off duty the next. A coworker was a kid from Mississippi who had just entered the Army. When I offered to pay him five dollars a day to take my shifts, he was glad to oblige. Under this revised schedule, he worked for three days straight, I was on call for one day, and he would work again for the next three.

With my hospital obligations limited to one day a week, I had free reign. I would hitchhike into New York City, where there was always a cot waiting at Frankie Newton's modest pad on Seventeenth Street, near Fifth Avenue. Frankie had a regular engagement at a Greenwich Village club called the Little Casino, with a trio that included Ram Ramirez on piano and Bill Pemberton on the bass.

To my great relief, Manhattan felt the same as it had before the war. It was a metropolis, brimming with promise and life. The sidewalks pulsed with people; the streets were full of cars. I loved it. I spent almost every night haunting the clubs on 52nd Street. There, I caught performances by the likes of Art Tatum, Roy Eldridge, and Charlie Shavers. I would sit through two or three sets, than take a brisk walk to the Brass Rail Restaurant on Seventh Avenue near Times Square. I had befriended an employee of the Brass Rail, and he would stash a piece of their famous cheesecake under the counter for me (cheesecake, like many products during the months after the war, was in short supply). So after a late set on "The Street," I would have my cheesecake and a roast beef sandwich, and then head back to Frankie's place for some shut-eye. It was like heaven; those were the most carefree days of my life. I began regaining the weight that I had lost during twenty-nine months of army cuisine.

As for the music scene, it was as if I had fallen into a Rip Van Winkle slumber, awakening to find my world of jazz inexplicably transformed. Bebop had not only infiltrated 52nd Street—it had taken over the idiom by storm.

I'd never even heard of Charlie Parker during the war years. But I learned who he was soon enough. In New York City in 1946, his name was a buzzword on almost everyone's lips. Kids in music school were memorizing Charlie Parker saxophone solos. I went to see his quintet at the Three Deuces on 52nd Street. The band featured Al Haig on piano, Tommy Potter on bass, Max Roach, whom I had first seen with Benny Carter's band in Camp Gruber, Oklahoma, on drums, and a young trumpeter by the name of Miles Davis.

I didn't especially like what they were doing. But I was impressed by Davis, who played most of his solos in the lower register; he reminded me of a bebop Bobby Hackett.

Bebop was truly a startling shift. I had cut my teeth on a different music; I was still trying to understand the styles of Teddy Wilson, Earl Hines, Louis Armstrong, and Duke Ellington. Swing was my bottom line. The thing I loved most about jazz was the way musicians improvised on a melody. But in bebop at that time, melody seemed to be beside the point. I was accustomed to hearing Bunny Berrigan play "I Can't Get Started." Dizzy Gillespie's rendition didn't reach me.

I wasn't digging bebop. Instead I sought out the music I loved. And there was still plenty of it in New York City. Who needed to hear "Fats" Navarro when you could go across the street and hear Stuff Smith playing the violin? Why watch Al Haig when next door you could catch Art Tatum?

My army discharge finally arrived late in 1946, and I returned to 264 Ward Street in Newton.

But one last reminder of the army arrived, unexpectedly. I received a telegram from one of the musicians I had played with on the troop transport ship during the voyage home from Marseilles. It said: "I have a job here in Green River, Wyoming, and we need a piano player. It pays about a hundred dollars a week, and we'll probably make another hundred by people feeding the kitty."

This gave me pause. In 1946, a two-hundred-dollar weekly income was good money. But where the hell was Green River, Wyoming? These were the days in which air travel was not yet generally available. Wyoming might as well have been the old Wild West; I thought I might have to take a covered wagon to get there. I seriously considered the offer. I was comfortable in Newton—but I had no plans, no ambitions, and less than a clue about the course of my future. I didn't go to Wyoming, but often wondered what would have become of my life had I taken the gig.

*     *     *

Having resided in and around Boston all my life, I held the Cambridge Ivy aloft as my golden ideal. Harvard's prewar invitation to reapply after the war demanded an aptitude test, which I knew I wasn't equipped to take. So I enrolled in Boston University, a distinct disappointment. It took me years afterward to realize that Harvard wasn't the alpha and omega of college education. In the meantime, I poked fun at my capitulation by singing a comically warped rendition of a Gus Kahn lyric: "It Had to B.U."

Out of respect for my father I embarked on a grueling pre-med curriculum, a terrible mistake. My first semester included college English, German, algebra, biology, and chemistry. I was studying harder than ever just to maintain decent marks. To my relief, I discovered that there were still musicians my age in Boston who hadn't tossed swing for bop. The trumpeter Ruby Braff and tenor saxophonist Sammy Margolis were the spirit and backbone behind a cadre of players inspired by Lester Young, Duke Ellington, Count Basie, and, of course, Louis Armstrong.

Working with Ruby, particularly, was an education. He was by far the best trumpet player in the Boston area (and, I would later discover, one of the finest swing-oriented trumpeters in the world). He knew what it was to play in a combo, and had an amazing ear that enabled him to pick up a tune and chord changes. While my musical training couldn't compare with Ruby's talent and knowledge, we were both anachronisms, and this brought us into musical contact.

Ruby and Sammy represented Boston's swing vanguard. But there was a separate contingent of musicians—epitomized by Harvard University's Crimson Stompers—who were dedicated to the Dixieland style. The first-call pianist in this circle was a guy named Ev Schwarz who ran a gas station at Coolidge Corner in Brookline. As I got to know some of the musicians in this crowd, Ev graciously took me under his wing. He taught me many of the Dixieland and Chicago-style standards of the '20s and '30s. By the time he was through with me, I was capable of working with any of the Dixieland bands in town.

Even with all of my musical activities, I was growing restless in Boston. So I decided to spend the summer after my sophomore year in New York City. In Manhattan, I found a room at the Hotel Empire, on Sixty-third Street between Broadway and Columbus, that cost sixty dollars a week.

I enrolled in a Russian history course at NYU. This would make my junior year at BU a little easier. I chose Russian history because of the influence of Ethel and Frankie Newton, who had become active members of the American Communist Party. This was summer 1948—an election year. The onset of the cold war under President Truman had mobilized the ranks of American liberals, including a growing number of Communists. Faced with a presidential race between Truman (the incumbent Democrat) and Thomas Dewey (the Republican challenger), liberals rallied behind an alternative and former vice president under Roosevelt, Henry A. Wallace, of the newly formed Progressive Party.

Wallace's Soviet sympathies made him a hero to American Communists, and much of his support during the 1948 presidential race came from their ranks. Wallace himself avowed no knowledge of this fact, but there was no mistaking it; in an internal report, the FBI denounced him as a "catalytic for Communism." This may have been an exaggeration in terms, but the statement was fundamentally true. Frankie and Ethel were staunch Wallace supporters, as were most of their Communist friends.

One of these friends, Laura Duncan, was a talented young vocalist. I met her through Frankie, and we immediately got along well. She asked me to be her piano accompanist. And just like that, I became an active participant in the Henry Wallace campaign because Laura, who was the official NY Communist Party singer, sang at Henry Wallace rallies. One evening I accompanied Laura on "Strange Fruit"—an anthem of the fight against racism ever since its Café Society debut (via Billie Holiday) in 1939—at a ballpark rally in Bridgeport, Connecticut.

In fact, it's for a performance of "Strange Fruit"—that July, at a Sunday afternoon Communist Party rally in Madison Square Garden—that Laura Duncan is most often remembered today. I was not her pianist on that occasion, for one simple reason: I was not a Communist. More to the point, I had second thoughts about getting onstage at such a prominent Party event. The Federal Bureau of Investigation carefully monitored all Communist activity, and I had no intention of getting on its list.

But Laura had asked me to play. I didn't want to say no. So I paid a visit to Jack Crystal, who managed the Commodore Music Shop. Jack ran the Sunday jam sessions at Jimmy Ryan's.

"Jack, I need you to give me a gig this Sunday afternoon. I don't care how much you pay me." This must have seemed like a strange request, but Jack complied. He hired me as intermission pianist for the afternoon, and paid me a nominal fee of $20. It was the excuse I needed. I told Laura that I couldn't make the rally because I had a conflicting gig.

Laura often asked me how I could be such a nice guy and not share the Communist ideology. My reservations about the Communist Party hinged upon the relative closed-mindedness of its members. I balked at the myopic assumption (held by almost every Party member I knew) that Communists were good and everyone else was bad. This idea seemed as wrongheaded to me as the ironclad distinction felt by many Jews to Gentiles.

The thing about Communism that held great appeal to me was its apparent stand against racism and discrimination. This explained the Party's initial success with African-American artists like Frankie Newton, Laura Duncan, and, of course, Paul Robeson. The civil rights movement as we know it was not to begin in earnest for another decade. Progress was made in small but significant increments; an achievement at that time was the capitalization of the word "Negro" in print. Because Communist ideology preached the equality and brotherhood of mankind, we embraced it. I had little interest in Marx or Engels, but I fervently believed that African Americans deserved equal treatment in our society in every respect.

Frankie imparted a good deal of invaluable information to me that summer, and I soaked it up like a sponge. During our trips to clubs around the city, he shared countless musical insights. Other lessons were of a more philosophic nature. One evening, walking south from Seventeenth Street, in the direction of Greenwich Village, Frankie was on edge; his eyes darted furtively around as we walked, and his mouth was a tightly pressed line. He wanted a drink.

We came upon a nondescript bar that was not one of his usual haunts, and I suggested that we stop there.

"I don't want to go in there," he snapped, spitting out the words. He was visibly tense.

"What's the matter, Frankie?" I asked innocently. "Why don't you relax? This place looks okay."

He said, "George, you've never been black one day in your life."

I've been trying to compose a proper response to that statement ever since. Frankie Newton was right. I had never seen the world through his eyes before. I had always embraced African-American culture; my heroes as a child had been Joe Louis, Bill "Bojangles" Robinson, and Jesse Owens. But as a white man—a kid, really—from a comfortable New England suburb, I had no concept of the crippling anxiety that many African-American citizens faced every day. Despite my devotion to racial equality, I was incredibly naïve.

While Frankie served as my unofficial guide and guardian, I received more formal tutelage from Teddy Wilson, another idol. Teddy shared the militant views on race that Frankie embraced; I had seen him a few times in Barney Josephson's Café Society. But it wasn't through politics that we met. I had asked Teddy for piano lessons.

Teddy Wilson had played in the Benny Goodman quartets and trios of the '30s. He epitomized small-group piano playing, and it was his sound that I had always tried to emulate. I owned a book of Teddy Wilson piano solo transcriptions, and could play some of the entries reasonably well. But to learn at the feet of the man—that was another story entirely. His students—there were perhaps eight or nine of us—gathered each week in a classroom at Juilliard (which was then located uptown, near Columbia University). Teddy would talk about a particular aspect of the piano, and then ask individual students to play. It was like joining a cadre of acolytes in a monastery, with Teddy as our sage. I knew from the start that he did not consider me the best student in the class; I wasn't even close. This hardly bothered me a bit. It was a privilege just to be in a room with such a legend. As far as I was concerned, Teddy was it.

But even full-blown idolatry couldn't prevent me from exploring other avenues. I had heard and read a great deal about the unique ideas of a modern pianist named Lennie Tristano, and curiosity brought me to his door. My youthful enthusiasm—and lack of knowledge regarding emerging harmonic approaches—had led me to believe that I could study with both Teddy and Lennie at the same time.

I was disabused of this notion very quickly. During a preliminary interview with the blind Tristano, the reclusive pedagogue asked me to play. I obliged him with a tune from my repertoire. When I finished, Tristano leaned forward in his chair.

"That's good," he said, nodding his head. "You have a freedom of improvisation that's very nice. You're not locked into patterns or clichés. But your style is pure Teddy Wilson. You're going to have to lose that if you want to move on to new things."

I was flattered by Tristano's praise, but this last bit of advice was unpalatable. Forget Teddy Wilson? Never! I left the apartment after that introductory lesson, and didn't return. For the rest of the summer, I was wholly devoted to the Wilson school.

That fall, the Ken Club hired me—along with a local bassist named John Field and a drummer from Washington, D.C., named Eddie Phyfe—to play a six-week engagement. We were backing Max Kaminsky, Charles "Pee Wee" Russell, and Irving "Miff" Mole.

It was awesome to be included in such illustrious company. Kaminsky had played trumpet memorably with Eddie Condon, Tommy Dorsey, and Artie Shaw. Miff Mole was the most prominent trombonist of his time; he had worked with Red Nichols, Paul Whiteman, and Benny Goodman. Pee Wee Russell, who had played with everyone from Bix Beiderbecke to Louis Prima, was one of the clarinet's true innovators, and already a jazz legend.

We worked seven nights a week, plus Sunday afternoons—a common routine in Boston that musicians referred to as "the eight-day week." Bands were expected to play five forty-minute sets during the course of the evening, with twenty-minute breaks in between. At the Ken Club, there was a floor show featuring Russ Howard, a stand-up comedian with a stale act. He told the same jokes every night: "You're the kind of a girl I can't get over . . . so please get up and answer the phone." After hearing this a few dozen times, it took great reserves of will to keep from groaning—or chiming in.

Ev Schwarz had primed me for the Max Kaminsky repertoire—tunes like "Fidgety Feet," "Clarinet Marmalade," "Muscat Ramble," "That's a Plenty," and "Sister Kate." I also had the benefit (a mixed blessing, really) of playing in a rhythm section with John Field. Johnny was a red-nosed Irishman who drove a taxicab by day. His expansive memory for tunes was rivaled only by his capacity for Pickwick Ale. John berated me for the songs that I didn't know or couldn't recall; when I made a mistake, he'd shout at me right there on the bandstand: "You're playing the wrong chord!" This added pressure kept me on my toes. If Max called a tune I couldn't follow, I did my best to have it down by the next time it appeared.

Among other things, the Ken Club engagement was a lesson in professionalism. I was earning sixty dollars a week to show up at eight o'clock (Pee Wee, Max, and Miff earned just twice that amount), play all evening, and maintain a high level of musicianship. It was a true learning experience.

It was also a bit of a hardship. For six weeks, I was committed to playing nightly until one in the morning—and then attending classes by day. Any studying that I couldn't avoid had to occur either in the early morning hours or during the afternoon, right before classes. The money was barely adequate to justify such a senseless pattern, but I didn't care. I was playing jazz with legends and enjoying another form of education.

I didn't hang out much with Pee Wee, Maxie, or Miff after the job; they were usually too tired or inebriated to go anywhere. I was shocked when I realized that these world-renowned jazz legends were forced to sleep in grungy third-class hotels. When the gig was over, they faced the prospect of an empty club, empty streets, empty bottles, an empty room. This was a continuing pattern for living. As for money, whatever a jazz player made in a week, that was it. If he couldn't scare up a gig—as was often the case—he was simply out of luck.

For the first time, I fully comprehended the fact that jazz was not a life of glamour. For guys like Max, Miff, and Pee Wee, music was life itself. As I played alongside them night after night, I noticed that Maxie tended to recycle the same choruses, but Pee Wee and Miff seldom repeated their ideas. Hearing them, I recognized a serious desire to play the best they could play, every time they picked up their horns. These men had given up most everything that life could offer in order to make their music. Sometime during the course of that gig, I stopped lionizing these musicians as icons and learned to love them as human beings. I also came to the realization that this career might not be right for my life. The jazz life demanded so many sacrifices, so much devotion. I had a suspicion that, for me, music itself might not be enough.

But I never gave voice to these thoughts, and for the time being Max, Miff, and Pee Wee treated me as one of their own. Their approval was an imprimatur, and I soon had quite a reputation among Boston musicians. My Ken Club run birthed many other gigs.

Several months later, I was visiting my army buddy Elmer Wishnoff in Philadelphia. We attended a concert at the Academy of Music. The featured attraction was Sidney Bechet with James P. Johnson. James P. Johnson failed to show up, leaving the band in need of a piano player.

Max Kaminsky was playing trumpet on the concert. He spotted me in the audience. The next thing I knew, I was onstage—filling in for the illustrious James P. Johnson. Bechet counted off a tempo. I was not exactly familiar with the band's repertoire, but somehow or other I managed to stay alive. The great Creole soprano saxophonist played with such power and authority that he seemed to pull the entire band along with him. I did my best; but I'm sure that Bechet missed James P. that evening.

Back in Boston, I was playing more and more often—and struggling to fulfill the obligations of an undergraduate. My academic ambitions were perpetually relegated to the back burner, and it didn't help that the other burners were blasting at high heat. The big diversion arrived that spring—the spring of 1949—when Steve Connelly, manager of the Savoy club, invited me to play a month-long engagement with a group led by the clarinetist Edmond Hall.

I jumped at this chance. Edmond Hall was well-known. After several years in the Teddy Wilson Sextet, he had led his own band at Café Society. Edmond Hall's greatest single asset as a musician was his irrepressible sense of swing. He was not an adventurous improviser in the manner of Pee Wee Russell, but his rhythmic powers were absolute. This was especially obvious in a pared-down quartet setting; the band consisted of Edmond and a local rhythm section (myself, a drummer named Joe Cochrane, and the ubiquitous John Field). We were working as an intermission band; the featured group was led by a young soprano saxophonist named Bob Wilber, who had a reputation among Dixieland fans in New En-gland. By the end of the job, the Edmond Hall Quartet had attracted its own considerable following.

The Savoy engagement was a lot of fun. Joyce Alexander stopped by a few times; we would sit together at a table with a group of friends. Nat Hentoff was an habitué, and on more than one occasion I joined him and a small crowd of club regulars in wide-ranging discussions about music, politics, art, literature, and anything else that crossed our minds. Nat and I had known each other for a few years, but it was here that we became friends. I found him to be an informed and impassioned thinker; in conversation, he could segue effortlessly and naturally from James Michael Curley to Bessie Smith.

The month passed in no time, and when our contract expired, Steve Connelly asked us to extend the engagement. I was handling all of the negotiations, at Edmond's request. Perhaps he recognized the business acumen that would direct the rest of my life. Under the original contract, Edmond Hall received a mere $120 for each grueling eight-day week. The rest of us got a paltry $60, the Boston minimum. We had proven our worth and I figured that it made sense to ask for a raise.

Steve was a nice guy, and he listened to my argument. Then he explained that even with a full house, the club was barely making it. At first I found this difficult to believe. But the numbers told the story; with no cover and no minimum, the Savoy relied entirely upon the sale of beer (sixty cents) and whiskey (ninety cents). I knew that many of the club's patrons spent all night nursing the same drink. "You deserve the raise," Steve said, "but it's out of the question."

Edmond and the band would have to sign on for another term at the same pitiful wage. I started thinking about other ways to sell the group. I remembered a conversation I had had in the club with Dick Mascott, who ran a Boston office of the Music Corporation of America. As an agent, Dick was always looking for a new attraction. He had mentioned that a group like ours would be a natural on the college circuit.

With this thought in mind, I made Steve Connelly a new proposition. We would continue to work at the same rate—but he would give us every other Saturday night off. I assured him we would pay for our substitute group. I knew that this was a painless arrangement; on Saturday nights the Savoy was mobbed regardless of who was playing. Steve agreed to the plan.

Dick Mascott started working on a series of New England college gigs. Dick did the booking, and I put together a band. In addition to the working quartet, I hired Ruby Braff and Dick LeFavre, a trombonist who had worked with Sam Donahue's band.

The resulting program, "Danceable Jazz: Edmond Hall and His Sextet," was a big success. We played in Middlebury, Vermont, and appeared at the Winter Carnival in Hanover, New Hampshire, on the Dartmouth College campus. Each night's fee was $750—much more than we could earn during an entire week at the Savoy.

We had a few other Saturdays open, so I called Charlie Shribman, who, with his brother Sy, had controlled virtually all of the New England ballrooms during their prewar heyday. By 1949, their business had diminished, and Sy had passed away. But Charlie still owned and controlled the venues, and he was kind enough to give us a gig at the Raymor Ballroom on Huntington Avenue, just down the street from the Savoy. He paid us something in the neighborhood of $400.

On another open Saturday, Mascott couldn't find a gig. I suggested to Edmond that it might be time to put on our own concert at Jordan Hall, the New England Conservatory's thousand-seat auditorium. I knew the quartet, or even the sextet, was not enough to fill the hall. We had to do something special.

I contacted Frankie Newton, and Edmond called the trumpeter Wild Bill Davison. We also corralled some of the stalwart players on the Boston scene. I organized a concert featuring this bevy of musicians in various combinations and a virtual catalogue of jazz styles. We printed a program book; Nat Hentoff wrote the notes, and Winnie Hall, Edmond's wife, solicited patrons for a "Friends of Edmond Hall" list on the back page. We plugged the show every night from the stage of the Savoy. Nat plugged it from behind his microphone at WMEX.

"Edmond Hall and George Wein Present: From Brass Bands to Bebop" took place on March 1, 1949.

To my great relief—since I had taken the risk and would be stuck with the hall rental and musicians' fees—and considerable surprise, we sold out Jordan Hall. The concert went off without a hitch. It was an extremely satisfying moment for me; I had come up with an ambitious idea and nursed it to completion. It was also a big night for Edmond; his biographer, Manfred Selchow, would later note that the concert was "the talk of the town for several days."

The concert made a profit of almost $1,200. I could hardly believe that we had pulled it off. It was my very first taste of producing and promoting a concert event.

The day after the show, I got to the Savoy early. Winnie Hall, Edmond's wife, walked in. She joined me at my corner booth. Winnie had an almost pensive look on her face. After some hesitation, she told me that she had been reconsidering my partnership with her husband. Winnie now suggested that since Edmond Hall was the "name" attraction, he should receive more than half of the spoils. She wanted a 60–40 split.

I was speechless. Certainly Edmond Hall had been the star of our concert, but we were partners. Edmond's name might have driven ticket sales, but my organizational work had been indispensable. The concert had been my idea and my onus; I had labored over every aspect of its production. I had undertaken the risk. But all of these thoughts were secondary to my emotional injury. I was a naïve and idealistic kid, and this was a crushing disappointment.

Winnie Hall was a good woman who had struggled for years to support her husband and make ends meet. I'm sure that she had negotiated on his behalf before, to keep him from being exploited. But I was not a promoter looking to take Edmond Hall for a ride, and I was hurt that she would treat me like one. She knew how much I valued Edmond's friendship, but what she was suggesting was wrong. I told her that I couldn't do it.

But Winnie was persistent. She continued to rationalize and argue and cajole. My protestations were pitiful: "No, Winnie. No, I just can't do that." She kept pushing the point. We sat at that booth in the Savoy and negotiated in that manner for over an hour. Finally, realizing that I simply wasn't going to change my mind, she came up with another plan. She and Edmond would keep the funds that she had raised for the patron's list. It was a few extra dollars. I was too worn out to argue. I said, "Okay, Winnie. Take the money."

The popularity of the Edmond Hall Quartet had prompted Steve Connelly to make us Savoy headliners. We were soon going to be working with Jimmy Crawford (former drummer with the Jimmy Lunceford Orchestra), Vic Dickenson (my trombone idol), and Ruby Braff (my man on cornet). I had been looking forward with great anticipation to this next run of gigs. But suddenly the whole experience was tainted. I felt lightheaded; my ears were ringing. A sudden wave of nausea overcame me. This must have been visibly obvious, because as I left the table Steve looked at me. "You look like you need a drink," he said. I wasn't much of a drinker, but when he poured me a double scotch, I took it.

A few minutes later, Edmond arrived. I didn't say anything to him about the deal. I wanted to forget all about it, but it was impossible. Before the beginning of the set, I walked over to Edmond and gave my notice. He didn't ask for any reasons and didn't attempt to change my mind. I agreed to stay on until the sextet started working. I played that night as if drugged. After the last set, I went home and broke down and cried.

Edmond Hall replaced me with a far better pianist—Kenny Kersey, a unique artist who had worked at the Ken Club with Red and Higgy. The group played on for weeks.

In the following years, I encountered both Edmond and Winnie a number of times, and we were always cordial. I kept my warm feelings for Edmond as both a person and a musician. Years after Edmond's death, when Manfred Selchow asked me what had prompted our parting of ways, I said: "I will never discuss why, except it was a great disappointment and shock to me." It would have been inappropriate to include the story in the biography of such a wonderful musician.

Nothing could erase the memory of that encounter; it was a jarring experience during my formative first steps in this business. Whereas I saw my relationship with Edmond as a venture between friends, Winnie saw dollar signs. The harsh realization of that night in 1949 has lasted, like a scar, throughout my professional career. I tell the story here for that precise reason.

I was relieved when my junior year finally came to a close. With the prospect of a long summer ahead, I made plans to join a couple of college friends, who were headed to France on what was then known as a "Youth Argonaut" trip—you flew out from Hartford, Connecticut on a chartered plane, and returned by way of military troop transport ship. The roundtrip package, available only to college-aged travelers, cost $250. I had been overseas during the war, but most of that time had been spent in army encampments. This time there would be no such restrictions.

A day or two before I was to embark on this voyage, we had a bon voyage party on Ward Street. We invited "Red" Allen, J. C. Higgenbotham, and a few other musicians we knew from the Savoy. Nat Hentoff came and offered some pointers on France, where he had spent some time the previous year. I also invited Joyce Alexander. Everyone had a terrific time.

*     *     *

Soon afterward, I found myself in Brussels, Belgium—the point of destination for our chartered plane. I blew more than a hundred dollars during that first night in Brussels, stopping at clubs and bars and picking up the tabs (as well as a coquette named Marie). I felt like a true cosmopolitan—I had saved up over a thousand dollars, most of which had been won during my freakishly lucky craps sessions in the army.

But there were stark realities that greeted me in Europe, even on so carefree a visit. On that first evening of carousing, we dined in a restaurant that had a violinist who serenaded patrons at their tables. He was an older Jewish man, a survivor from the war. As he approached our table, he studied my face for a long time, and then began to play "Maman," a popular song in France at the time. He knew, as I knew, that it had first been an American song. It was written by Jack Yellen for a Sophie Tucker Broadway production in 1925; its original title had been "My Yiddishe Momme."

This was Europe in 1949. I soon grew to understand that Holocaust survivors found ways to signal to other Jews without drawing any attention. Their lives were still stricken by fear. When that old violinist looked straight into my eyes and played that song, he wanted me to know that we shared something. That moment still affects me today.

Paris was next. I met a number of characters in and around the city, and even got a few club gigs with French musicians. There was an energizing spirit to Paris in those days. One night, after stumbling out of a club at five o'clock in the morning, my friends and I encountered a hip young African American at the corner of the Arc de Triomphe. We struck up a conversation, and I learned that he had played alto saxophone with Dizzy Gillespie. He had us practically rolling in the street with some of his stories; he was hilarious. I made a mental note to remember his name: James Moody. We talked for over an hour, as the sun rose.

While in Paris, I also looked up the legendary Charles Delaunay. The son of the important modernist painters Robert and Sonia Delaunay, Charles was codirector (with Hughes Panassie) of the Hot Club of France. They were exhaustive discographers and pioneers of jazz criticism. I paid Charles a visit at his home, and we became friends.

By this time, I had begun to part ways with my Boston traveling companions. When we finally separated, I headed alone for the south of France. My transportation during this journey was on the back of an open truck, nestled among stacks of wood; it was an old-fashioned truck and the wood was needed for fuel. I was one of a motley assortment of hitchhikers—Dutch, English, Scandinavians—on board. It was so incredibly cold that evening that I couldn't last the night. I hopped off the truck in Dijon and took a train the rest of the way to Nice.

Arriving in that coastal city, I got a room in a little hotel near the railroad station. This would serve as a base of operations, from which I could travel by train to nearby cities. Over the next few days, I visited Cannes and Monte Carlo. One afternoon in Cannes, I stepped into a club for a drink and noticed a grand piano on the terrace. I asked if I could play; it had been a while since I had touched a keyboard.

As I fooled around with a few old tunes, I was approached by several French kids my own age. They were brothers, and one of them spoke perfect English. He explained that they were Parisians renting a house for the summer in a nearby mountain town. They offered to let me stay there with them. It was a relief to check out of my grungy hotel. I could stop being a lone tourist and spend time with some friendly French kids.

I had never heard of St. Paul de Vence, the fourteenth-century hilltop village where they were residing. I could hardly believe my eyes when I got there;

it was like a fairyland. The valley was lush with vegetation, and the mountains to the north seemed to come alive in the crisp morning light. To the south, there was a panoramic view of the Mediterranean, a sliver of pale blue that faded seamlessly into the sky.

My new friends lived within the stone walls of the town, in a spacious apartment that had been owned by Americans before the war. There was a patio outside my bedroom, and I was awakened in the morning with coffee and croissants. I fell in love with the town. "Someday," I told myself, "I'm going to live in this valley."

After living in St. Paul for nearly a week, I joined my friends on a trip back to Paris; they had invited me to stay with their family. There I was treated with extraordinary courtesy and thoughtfulness. They arranged excursions to places of interest that I had never seen, like Versailles and Chartres. It was a lovely time; the warmth of this French family really touched me. I marveled to think that I would have missed out entirely if it hadn't been for a piano in a little café.

I left their home after a few days, and checked into a dollar-a-day hotel on the Left Bank. Still touched by the hospitality of my hosts, I wrote a thank-you note and sent it to their St. Germain address. Three days later, one of the sons returned to my hotel.

"My parents want you to come back this weekend," he told me. I asked why, since I had just left. He said, "They have had many guests in the past, and you're the first American who ever made the effort to write a thank-you note."

\*     \*     \*

My only other social engagement in Paris was with Louis Kronberg, a Boston-based painter (and first cousin of my maternal grandmother) who had for some years been my family's sole art investment. Doc purchased ten or twelve of his paintings over the years, and never considered buying anything else—a missed opportunity I would never quite forgive. Then again, my family's relationship with Louis was an opportunity in and of itself. He divided his time between Boston and Paris, and marked each return to Boston with dinner at our house (always in very proper attire). He was our family artist, and a good friend.

Born in the last leg of the nineteenth century, Louis Kronberg had an affinity for (some would say an obsession with) the style of Edgar Degas. Like Degas, he often portrayed ballerinas in interior spaces, and, to his great satisfaction, became known as the "American Degas." Louis received patronage early in his career from Boston's Isabella Stewart Gardner. Mrs. Gardner sponsored Louis's residence in Paris; he lived and studied there during an exciting period in the city's aesthetic history. But Louis might as well have been oblivious to the presence of the modernists, Cubists, or anyone else; he never strayed from the Impressionist painting that was his métier.

Kronberg was in his late seventies when I visited him in Paris. Given the extreme care he took in his personal appearance, I was surprised to discover that his living and working quarters consisted of a dingy unheated coldwater flat in Montparnasse, on the Rue Boissonade. It was one clue as to the downside of *la vie bohême*. The upside, of course, was the art itself. Louis was an invaluable guide in this regard. He took me to the Jeu de Paumes (at the time, a branch of the Louvre Museum) and introduced me to the Impressionists. We traveled by train to Antwerp, where he showed me how to tell the difference between a Reubens and a Van Dyck. ("Look for the hands," he told me, pointing out an elaborately realistic depiction of sinews and veins in one portrait. "Van Dyck loved to paint hands.") It was in this year that Louis Kronberg ignited a flame in me that has never diminished. The love of the visual arts and the aspiration to collect are important parts of my life.

I also learned that Louis was quite a lonely man. "It's terrible growing old," he told me once, "because your old friends die and your young friends get married. Either way, you lose them." He continued: "George, if you get married, I'll give you a painting. But if you *don't* get married, I'll give you two paintings." I never did take him up on the offer; he was still alive when I finally got married, but I didn't have the heart to tell him.

\*     \*     \*

Frankie Newton had moved back to Boston, and was occupying a small apartment on the corner of Massachusetts Avenue and Tremont Street. We would often hang out; I still considered Frankie a guiding light in the jazz world, and although he was never inclined to assume the role of an instructor, I learned by observation.

We occasionally played gigs around town, and he entrusted me to keep his pay. This was not exactly the great privilege it might seem. Frankie believed that when you went into a bar, you were bound by dignity to buy everyone a round of drinks. ("If people think you're down, they'll kick you.") When we were together, this obligation fell to me. By the end of the week, I had spent all of his money as well as my own—leaving us *both* broke. Such was the price of honor.

Frankie was also bitter. One night we were in my apartment on Peterboro Street, listening to a new record: Louis Armstrong singing and playing the pop tune "If." I thought Pops played that melody beautifully. All Frankie could do was shake his head, his face a proud mask. "Man, if I had the chance, I could do better."

Thinking both of Frankie's hard times and the beauty of his delicate muted sound, I came up with the idea of featuring him in a room for "quiet jazz." It was a rather original concept for that time. I scouted out some possible locations for such an endeavor and eventually met the owners of the Hotel Fensgate, on Beacon Street near the Charles River. They liked the idea and agreed to let me take over a guest suite. I made the arrangements along with a fellow named Rod Kennedy (a former Texan and Emerson College undergraduate, and founder of the Bob Wilber fan club). In fact, it didn't take much preparation. We merely brought in an upright piano and scattered cushions around the room. We started spreading the word.

Inspired by my recent trip to the Continent, I christened the room "Le Jazz Douxce"—what we thought was the French for "The Quiet Jazz." Frankie and Rod had no objections, nor did the hotel management. Our limited knowledge of the French language prevented us from recognizing that the title was a grammatical error. It should have been either "Le Jazz Doux" (masculine) or "La Jazz Douce" (feminine). I suppose that by employing the word "Douxce," we had inadvertently claimed jazz as an androgynous noun. (No one corrected us, so perhaps the blunder went unnoticed.)

Le Jazz Douxce involved a house trio: Frankie on muted trumpet, myself on piano, and a fine Boston bassist named Joe Palermino. People sat on the cushions that we had spread over the floor of the suite. The hotel had a liquor license and served drinks in the room—it was the only source of revenue, since we paid no rent.

The venture lasted only a few weeks, but it was a good experience. It gave me a chance to play more regularly with Frankie, who sounded as beautiful as ever. I gained my first taste of the nightclub business. Le Jazz Douxce was an ideal space in which to learn.

In the spring I graduated from Boston University. I had no idea what I wanted to do. Despite all of my musical experience in Boston, it had never occurred to me to pursue a career as a jazz musician. I was still a doctor's son from a middle-class Jewish family, and a college degree hadn't altered my situation or my outlook. I had no direction and no real goals. Like many young men and women upon graduating from college, I was adrift.

Without any better prospects, there was no recourse but the unthinkable: I decided to ask Ginsburg Brothers for a job. My brother had already been working in the family business for several years. For me, the paper products profession held not an iota of appeal. Nevertheless, I dutifully drove out to the company plant in Somerville, Massachusetts, to meet with Henry Nadell, an in-law who was president of the business at the time.

Henry told me: "I'm sorry, George, but I don't have anything for you right now. Come back in six months—there might be an opening then."

Rejection was never more of a relief. If there had been work for me at Ginsburg Brothers, however menial, I would have been obliged to take it. It was as if a massive load had been lifted from my shoulders. I had been spared from a career of selling toilet paper to regional grocery stores.

My mother naturally saw things in a different light. As soon as I returned home, she inquired hopefully about the meeting. I tried to suppress a grin as I delivered my report: "Ma, Grandpa just turned over in his grave. Ginsburg Brothers doesn't have a job for me."

She was devastated and quite upset that Henry hadn't found a position for me. Henry Nadell wasn't even a Ginsburg; who was he to keep me out of the business? She angrily picked up the phone to set things straight.

"Ma," I said calmly, "don't worry about it. I'll never go over there again as long as I live." I had no other employment options, but I knew that something—somewhere—would govern my future.

The first opportunity to cross my path was a nightly gig playing the piano at the China Rose, a restaurant next door to the Metropolitan Theater. It wasn't much of a job—I was supposed to be earning ninety dollars a week, but they didn't have enough money to pay me the full salary. So they compensated me with generous helpings of fried shrimp and lobster sauce. I ate there every night, and often invited groups of friends. Joyce Alexander was one of my occasional guests. But hanging out with me, as Joyce discovered, could be hazardous. One summer night she came to the China Rose and joined me for supper; she was leaving the following morning for Tanglewood to see the Boston Symphony. Her trip was nearly destroyed on my account—the food had made her ill.

I was more than a little embarrassed about this incident, and about my rather inglorious line of work. It came as a distinct relief when Mrs. Donahue—the owner of the Savoy, whose first name I never learned—asked me to work as the club's musical director. The primary responsibility of this post was putting together local rhythm sections to back visiting headliners. It was an effort described as "building the bands." This had been Steve Connelly's job in the past years, but he had moved on. Mrs. Donahue must have taken note of my Jordan Hall success.

It was easy for me; I would simply match a New York luminary with four or five local musicians, usually shouldering the piano duties myself. I brought in Wild Bill Davison, the Chicago-style trumpeter, for a few weeks. Joe Thomas, another trumpeter, appeared as well; his trumpet playing sometimes reminded me of Frankie Newton. Vic Dickenson also was a headliner. I learned much during this engagement. Some weeks were financially better than others, but we generally did well. I was happy to be hanging out at the Savoy again, and to have the opportunity to play the piano with some excellent bands. But the run ended after about three months, when a local agent persuaded Mrs. Donahue to book Phil Napoleon—a well-known Dixieland trumpeter in the Bix Beiderbecke mold—for a long-term gig.

*     *     *

I was so encouraged by the success of this brief assignment that I decided to take another crack at promotion. A friend of Frankie Newton's, a white guy named Ben DeCosta, had mentioned that there was a lot of money to be made in presenting rhythm and blues groups in Maryland, along the Mason-Dixon Line.

Ben DeCosta, though a nice guy, was a showbiz hustler; he went out on tours with different groups, sold program books, worked as a road manager, and in general earned his living on the fringes of the music business. And because he had been involved on concert dates with several rhythm and blues groups, he knew the terrain. So I agreed to join him in this venture.

From the Shaw Agency we bought three dates with Sonny Till and the Orioles, and Amos Milburn and His Chicken Shack Boogie Orchestra—two popular groups with hit records. Each group cost $300 per date, and promoters would usually charge one or two dollars admission per person. On a good night a promoter might draw as many as 2,000 people. Since the hall only cost a few hundred dollars, and the advertising cost even less, you stood to make a handsome profit. Ben and I bought a steel box in which to carry the money home.

We rented halls in Maryland at Annapolis, Cumberland, and Baltimore. In Baltimore we presented Milburn in a ballroom on Pennsylvania Avenue, in the heart of the African-American district. It was the equivalent of doing a concert on 125th Street in Harlem. We had bought radio time, put posters up on telephone poles, bought ads in black newspapers, and in general tried to make our presence felt in the community. But no one came; we sold maybe a hundred tickets. It was a washout.

Two nights after this fiasco, a local black promoter put on a concert in the same ballroom with Charlie Ventura and his band, featuring Jackie Cain and Roy Kral. He drew over 2,000 people, with a 90-percent African-American audience. This should have told us something. But we kept at it. We moved on to Annapolis and did just as poorly.

After Annapolis, there was just one more commitment—in Cumberland. But first we decided to accompany Milburn to a Petersburg, Virginia, concert that the Shaw Agency had sold to another promoter. This promoter was an African-American guy who owned a property on the outskirts of town. It appeared to be miles from nowhere. The performance was to be held in a cement-block building with two sets of doors on the front face. Ben and I checked out the space; it was too small to accommodate more than 250 or 300 people. Nearby, on the same property, this promoter owned a fried-chicken restaurant and a cluster of little cabin motels. We rented a motel room and waited for the show.

Amos Milburn started playing at nine P.M., and the people began streaming in. Ben and I watched the scene unfold: People would go in one door, get their hand stamped, hear some music, and get shepherded out the other door. The promoter had sold something like 700 tickets for this 300-capacity hall. Petersburg was a dry city at that time (alcohol was strictly prohibited), but the proprietor had a healthy supply of bootleg liquor, which his customers consumed gleefully. The fried-chicken restaurant was packed all night long. And at the same time, guys and girls were renting out cabins by the hour; what went on there one could only imagine.

Ben and I had rented our room for the whole night, but we were unable to sleep because the walls were thin, and nocturnal activities kept going on in the adjacent cabins until well past four. So we left the motel and went over to the restaurant, where the chicken was quite good. Ben and I got to talking about this scenario: with the combined income of ticket sales, homemade hooch, cabin rentals, and fried chicken, the promoter was making a killing. This was no mere concert event; it was a massive enterprise, a carnival of the senses.

The dance was just about over when we heard a woman outside say good night to the promoter's wife, who was working the restaurant's cash register.

"Good night, Mabel," the woman called out. "Are we going to see you at church in the morning?"

The proprietor's wife looked up and replied: "I don't think so, honey. I'll be up too late counting the money."

Knowing that we had no people coming to our concert in Cumberland the next night, I shot my business partner a resigned look.

"Ben," I said, "I think after tomorrow night I'm going back to Boston, where I belong. Maybe I have a life up there; I *know* I don't have one down here."

And return to Boston I did, no better (and just a little bit wiser) than before I had left. It was depressing to take stock in my situation. I had graduated from Boston University and been rejected from the family business. I had quit my job at the bankrupt China Rose and been relieved of my responsibilities at the Savoy. And now I had another failed business venture on my résumé. I was adrift once again.

\*     \*     \*

I loved playing the piano, and music was a crucial part of my being. But I had neither the confidence nor the desire to devote my life to being a professional jazz musician. The confidence was lacking because I knew my musical weaknesses; in my assessment, even years of intense study would not be enough training to overcome them. I had spent so much time digging the great pianists—Art Tatum, Teddy Wilson, Fatha Hines—that I was totally intimidated. My talent wasn't strong enough, I felt, to take me beyond the realm of mediocrity. Meanwhile, the lack of desire stemmed from my experience with Pee Wee, Max, Miff, and Edmond—who, even with all of their hard-earned successes, struggled constantly just to eke out a meager living. Yet I wasn't about to let music disappear from my life. I was continually listening, and as I listened, I learned. I kept playing, and kept getting calls from other musicians for work.

But what was I going to do? In these rudderless times, I began to seriously consider the words of Irving Levinson, a lawyer who frequented the Savoy. I had met Irving through Le Jazz Douxce; he was the attorney for the Hotel Fensgate. He was a nice guy who liked jazz, and he must have recognized both my organizational prowess and my boundless love for the music.

"You know, George," he had told me once, "I think you should open your own club."

# 3

# *Joyce*

THE BOSTON JAZZ COMMUNITY IN 1947 was small enough that diehard fans often attended the same events. So I was not surprised to run into writer Nat Hentoff at the Boston Opera House one evening, at a concert featuring James P. Johnson and Sidney Bechet. I had never seen either Bechet or Johnson in person before, and it was an impressive show. Afterward, I found my way backstage and spotted Nat across the room. He was conversing with two young ladies, one of whom I found quite attractive. When there was a spare moment, I managed to pull Nat aside to ask who she was. He told me that she was a junior at Simmons College who wrote a jazz column for the campus newspaper. Her name was Joyce Alexander.

Having gleaned this information, I approached the two girls and started what must have been an inane conversation. I offered them both a ride home, being sure to mention that I was driving a new 1946 Studebaker—one of the very first postwar models designed by Raymond Loewy. This was an exceedingly stylish automobile (the front hood and rear trunk were approximately equal in size), and driving it made anyone a focus of attention, as very few cars like it were on the road. It was my brother's car; I used it for my own purposes whenever I could. But Joyce and her friend were unimpressed. They declined my offer, opting instead for a ride on a city streetcar. The Studebaker and I drove off alone.

I would see Miss Alexander a few times after that evening, since we both spent time at the Savoy. We shared mutual acquaintances. On one occasion, I was sitting at a table in the Savoy with Joyce and some of these friends when she announced that Stephen Spender was giving a poetry reading at Simmons College; would anyone like to go? Without missing a beat, I gallantly offered to join her.

Who the hell was Stephen Spender, I thought? I'd heard his name before, but my exposure to English poetry at that time was limited to Shelley, Byron, Wordsworth, and Keats. No matter; Spender could have been a circus clown and it wouldn't have bothered me in the slightest. Poetry was just so many words to me; this was a chance to spend more time with a smart, attractive young woman. She even let me pick her up in Larry's car.

I'm not sure exactly what had specifically attracted me to Joyce at first sight. She was petite—a definite plus, since I was never particularly interested in girls who shared my rotund physique. I had noticed that her teeth were crooked; nevertheless I thought she had the most disarming smile—which conveyed both intelligence and innocence at once. I suppose I had recognized the same beauty in nineteen-year-old Joyce Alexander that the Boston artist John Wilson had captured a few years earlier, painting her portrait. His lovely, vibrant rendering suggests a young girl possessed of sophistication and self-confidence, along with the particular naïveté of youth.

But like oil on a canvas, beauty resides on the surface. As I spent time with Joyce, I recognized that she was a person of considerable depth. The first thing that struck me was her speaking voice, which was conspicuous by the absence of either a Boston accent or any typically African-American inflection. And unlike many self-consciously articulate Cambridge types, she sounded completely natural.

Our night with Stephen Spender was never designated as a "date," and I was careful not to make any unwanted overtures. We had a pleasant evening, and I drove her home. As far as I knew, I had made no particular impression. But a few months later, Joyce called my house and asked to speak with me. She had just purchased, for $200, a little green Plymouth coupe, and was preparing to take her driver's license exam. Would I accompany her to the registry bureau so that she could take the test in Larry's car?

Silently thanking Raymond Loewy and my Studebaker, I told Joyce that I would be happy to be of service. I picked her up, she passed the test, and our friendship deepened. We began seeing each other. I think that even after these short moments I thought that perhaps our lives would become permanently intertwined.

Having met Joyce in 1947, by the time I opened Storyville in 1950, our relationship had grown. I learned a lot about this remarkable woman who was to become so important to my future and my entire life.

Joyce had been raised in a brownstone at 23 Braddock Park on Boston's South End. The second-youngest of seven children, she had entered kindergarten when she was three years old (she was promptly sent home for being too young, but admitted a few weeks later, on her fourth birthday). At age nine she transferred to Boston Girls Latin School, one of the best public high schools in the nation (with a student body that was predominately white). She not only survived that institution's grueling curriculum; she was graduated at age fifteen, and matriculated at Simmons College, one of the finer women's colleges in the area.

Music had played a prominent role in her life. At the age of eight she began violin lessons at the South End Music School, an organization that provided music instruction at low cost. There she studied solfeggio and harmony, and played in small student orchestras and string quartets. Although she was definitely not a gifted violinist, this period of musical study—lessons once a week from age eight to fifteen—had a profound influence on Joyce. The South End School often had free tickets to Saturday night concerts at Symphony Hall; in addition, there were rush seats on Fridays for sixty cents. Because Symphony Hall was on Huntington Avenue within walking distance of her home, Joyce went often even as a young girl—seeing many performances by Serge Koussevitsky's magnificent Boston Symphony Orchestra. She was usually alone, since few of her neighborhood friends were particularly interested in classical music.

Jazz figured into Joyce's world; idols like Duke Ellington and Fats Waller were a natural part of her home life. While at Simmons College, she occasionally wrote a jazz column for the school paper. This brought her to the Bechet, James P. Johnson concert at the Boston Opera House. And so it was that she had entered my life. Our courtship moved at a very respectful pace. We were by no means a couple—but I felt something was happening.

Joyce came to my bon voyage party that was held the night before I left to summer in Europe for 1949. At party's end, I drove her home to Braddock Park. Arriving there, we sat in the idle car for a few minutes, exchanging pleasantries. Finally, I leaned across the seat and pressed my lips softly against hers. It was our first kiss. I don't remember exactly what I said, but it was probably something like, "I'm a Jewish kid from Newton, Massachusetts. I should probably be in love with a nice Jewish girl. But I think I'm falling in love with you." Joyce offered no reply.

Our relationship did in fact resume—and deepen—upon my return from France. I was intrigued by her intellectual acuity, her curiosity, her wit. She had a keener interest in aesthetic and cultural life than any girl I had known. Classical music and poetry were usually the stuff of a college curriculum; with Joyce, they also became social activities. One evening we went to Sanders Theater at Harvard University and heard Alexander Schneider perform a solo violin concert of Bach's "Partitas" and "Chaconnes." We saw the legendary pianist Vladimir Horowitz at Boston's Symphony Hall (sparking some rumors: George Wein had been spotted at a concert with Mary Lou Williams). We enjoyed John Gielgud in a rendition of the Chrisopher Fry play *The Lady's Not for Burning*. These were all things that I might never have experienced alone. The girls of my neighborhood fit the "Jewish American princess" mold of that time: they observed their mothers' materialistic agendas. In contrast, Joyce's wide array of cultural interests added a new dimension to my life. These interests may even have been even more important than our initial bond—a mutual love of jazz. But jazz was not a minor part of our agenda. While working at the Savoy, I would play "Sweet Lorraine" for her. Joyce's nickname appears in the first line of the lyric: "I've just found Joy. . . ."

Having graduated from Simmons College, Joyce had the opportunity to apply to medical school. This would have put a strain on her family's finances so she went job hunting instead, interviewing first at the Harvard Medical School laboratory at City Hospital. The personnel manager there wanted to hire her, but feared that the Irish girls working there might not like her. Hearing this, Joyce replied: "Maybe I wouldn't like them." She was accepted for a job at Gilchrist's Department Store, which had no history of hiring Negroes for anything other than menial work. She made a good impression and was recommended for promotion—at around the same time that Harvard offered her a position in the pathology department. She was torn for a few minutes because her employment at Gilchrist's was possibly breaking ground for further African-American job opportunities.

But Harvard won out as it usually does. She began working at the med school and soon transferred to the Harvard-operated Massachusetts General Hospital, where she became a technician in the laboratory of the renowned physician Dr. Fuller Albright. She was, in other words, on a trajectory that made my own course seem all the more rudderless.

At this time, we were both quite independent, and still far from becoming a bona fide couple. I was living in a one-bedroom apartment on Peterboro Street that cost a mere sixty dollars a month. My lifestyle was essentially that of a bachelor.

*     *     *

*But how Shelby, who could have had her pick of the best of breed in her own race, could marry outside her race, outside her father's profession, and throw her life away on a name-*

*less, faceless white man who wrote jazz, a frivolous occupa-
tion without office, title, or foreseeable future, was beyond
[their] understanding.*

**— Dorothy West, *The Wedding***

During the course of my friendship and courtship with Joyce, I had often heard about Oak Bluffs, the idyllic black resort on Martha's Vineyard where she had spent her summers since the age of twelve. In 1953, I visited her there. I can recall walking briskly along School Street to the Alexanders' house. It was my first trip to Martha's Vineyard, and my first meeting with Joyce's family.

Columbia Evans, Joyce's mother, was born in 1888 in Virginia, the youngest of thirteen children of Solomon Evans and Martha Lee, who were slaves. Two of Columbia's elder siblings—Joyce's uncle and aunt—were born before 1865, in slavery. How quickly we can forget! Joyce's mother had a childhood memory of attending a groundbreaking ceremony at Virginia's Gloucester High School at five years of age; Frederick Douglass was there as a guest speaker. Mr. Douglass was given a shovel, and young Columbia (along with two other tots) put her tiny feet on the blade of the shovel to break the ground. It was raining that day, so no photograph was taken, to the everlasting sorrow of Mrs. Alexander.

Columbia's maternal grandfather Jasper Lee had been a hardworking and enterprising man, a trait that would live on in his progeny. His master had allowed him to work on his own (in exchange for a percentage of his outside earnings). As a result, he entered emancipation with some savings. He used this money to purchase land for his sons and their families, becoming the first black to own land in Gloucester County. Columbia and nine of her twelve siblings attended Hampton Institute (now Hampton University), which was then primarily a trade school where girls would learn how to cook, sew, and run a household. There Columbia met a young man named Hayes Alexander, who was learning to be a bricklayer.

Their courtship was not immediate; after graduating from Hampton, Columbia Evans took a job in Philadelphia as a seamstress, and went to night school at Berlan College. She met the young bricklayer again in Atlantic City a few years later, and they were married. But white masons in Philadelphia wouldn't permit a black to work alongside them; Hayes's only option was to be a hod-carrier. So the Alexanders made their way to New York City, then on to Boston, where Hayes immediately joined the bricklayers' union and began to earn a reasonable wage. They raised seven children in two batches: Genie, Lee, Bill, Theresa and Mildred, each two years apart, and then a pause before Joyce and Theodora.

Thanks to a work ethic fueled by ambition, the Alexander family never suffered serious want, even during the lean Depression years. They purchased a townhouse at Braddock Park, where Joyce was raised. Columbia, who had inherited her grandfather's sense of resourceful industry, bought property in Brookline and Roxbury and took in boarders. This supplemental income helped support the education of seven children; Genie, their firstborn, graduated from Radcliffe in 1932. It also became the family's sole means of support after 1942, when a broken scaffolding tragically sent Hayes Alexander to his death.

The strength of character that had kept Columbia going during those years was still evident when I met her for the first time, that summer on Martha's Vineyard. Although I was a white kid entering a black community, the only thing she asked Joyce about me was whether I had received a college education.

The rest of Oak Bluffs was a bit more suspicious. The community was the perfect size for rumors: it wasn't so small that everyone already knew everyone else's business, and it wasn't so large that nobody cared. Naturally, all of Oak Bluffs buzzed that summer with the news of the Jewish jazz musician and nightclub owner who was visiting the Alexander girl.

One of Oak Bluffs's best-loved inhabitants at the time was the Harlem Renaissance author Dorothy West; she had moved to the Martha's Vineyard enclave in 1943. As a year-round resident, she probably had as much access to local rumors as anyone; she may well have heard about my stay with the Alexanders. In fact, it's highly plausible that Joyce and I provided the inspiration for Shelby Coles and Meade Wyler, the main characters of Ms. West's final novel, *The Wedding*. Shelby is the beautiful daughter of a highly esteemed African-American physician; Meade is a white jazz pianist visiting from New York City. The book opens on the morning before their wedding day, in Oak Bluffs, in the summer of 1953. When Oprah Winfrey produced and aired a movie adaptation of *The Wedding* on CBS a few years ago, Joyce's friends and family rang our phone off the hook, calling to tell us that "our story" was on TV.

Of course *The Wedding* is not really "our story." The novel posits a web of conflict around the interracial couple and introduces the character Lute McNeil, who vies against Meade for Shelby's affections. No such intrigue occurred during any of my time in Oak Bluffs. Joyce's mother was a proper lady and was always kind to me. The color of my skin had less significance in the Alexander household than the quality of my character.

Along with all her cultural interests, Joyce was also very active in the Negro community. She started as a member of the youth council of the NAACP and stayed active after our marriage, until we left Boston for New York City. She was not afraid to speak up and insisted on being heard at meetings.

She joined Delta Sigma Theta, a black women's sorority and went to the usual socials where she wanted to learn to jitterbug. Joyce can dance, but she is living proof that destroys the myth, especially after you hear her singing voice, that all Negroes have natural rhythm and can sing and dance.

Raised a Baptist, she stopped going to church during her college years. Her pastor asked her to give a talk one Sunday, which she did. His introduction didn't feel right to her. She left the church never to go back.

In Boston, the jazz scene featured Sunday-afternoon jazz sessions at the nightclubs. Even though underage, she was often in attendance drinking a ginger ale. The Savoy, Boston's most important jazz spot, was off limits. One night, Joyce and some friends decided it would be okay to go to the Savoy; who would know? As she entered the club, Jesse, the maître d', said, "Good evening, Miss Alexander." So much for who would know. On returning home that night, her brother, Lee, who had been working late at a pharmacy, said disapprovingly, "I hear you made your debut tonight."

\*     \*     \*

By the time I met Joyce, because she had gone to the predominately white Girls Latin High School, and then Simmons College, she was already comfortable in both worlds—black and white. I had worked both for and with black musicians, and my friendship with Frankie Newton was a learning tree. But I had not had as much of a social relationship with blacks as Joyce had had with whites. As our friendship grew, racial differences were not a problem. When Joyce said that some people might not like her personally because she was black, it didn't bother her. Remember, she was not the least bit naïve. I felt the same way about being Jewish and I certainly knew about anti-Semitism. To hell with the people who didn't like us.

Joyce moves about southern cities quite easily now. In New Orleans, she is treated like a queen. In Hampton, Virginia, we were given the key to the city. It's a far cry from when she first went to Washington, D.C., in 1944 and saw the shock on a girl's face when she asked for a dish of ice cream in a downtown store on a miserably hot day. She was told that she could not be served. They condescended to give her an ice cream in a paper cup if she would leave the store. On the same trip, she was refused a Coca-Cola in a five-and-ten-cent store. She cried.

Two of the last few times we were in Washington, D.C., we were honored guests at the White House.

*     *     *

My parents recognized the exceptional person I had found in Joyce Alexander. She was cultured, articulate, and respectful, and I had her over to the house quite often. But they didn't want us to get married. Using every ploy she could, my mother would warn me, "You realize what that would do to your grandmother; she would die." My grandfather had already passed away so she couldn't use his possible demise in her argument. But they never uttered a negative word about Joyce. They respected and liked her, and the issue wasn't with her as a person. It was the taboo, the invisible line that we would be crossing. It would be a *shanda* for the neighbors.

I put my parents' concern above my own desire. I had even tried once to break up with Joyce. I had met an attractive gentile girl with whom I tried desperately to fall in love. My mother was praying that we would marry—while this girl was a *shikse*, at least she wasn't black.

In what might have been the silliest day of my life, Joyce and I sat in my car in tears, overlooking the Charles River. The words we said to each other were like the corniest of soap operas.

That weekend, I went with the other girl to a bed and breakfast in Rockport, Massachusetts. She knew Joyce and the fact that I was still in love with her. It was supposed to be a romantic weekend, but it was a total drag. Joyce was ever-present in both our minds. On Sunday morning, I split as fast as I could and returned to Boston, where I immediately called the Alexanders' house. They told me that Joyce was at the ball game.

Fenway Park was filled to its 34,000-seat capacity. I went into the ballpark to find her. I knew she would be somewhere in the bleachers where a crowd of 10,000 were cheering and eating hot dogs. I scoured the aisles for her face. My heart was racing; everything else moved in slow motion. This would have been a great scene in a movie; I was only vaguely aware of the crowd's roar, the crack of the bat, the geometry of that familiar, manicured field—the green monster.

Then, amazingly, there she was. She saw me as I approached.

"Oh shit" was all she could say. We were off to the races again.

\* \* \*

We had wonderful times. One summer in Oak Bluffs, we walked a mile up a deserted beach and skinnydipped in the ocean. I can vividly recall the chills that traveled up and down my spine as we lay on the rocks, holding each other. The sun had already plunged over the edge of the horizon. As we charted the stars above us, the only sound was the rhythmic lapping of the tide. Joyce punctuated the stillness, very softly, but firmly. "I'll give you until I'm thirty years old." She was twenty-seven at the time and I was thirty. We had known each other for many years. There is no question that we would have married much sooner, except for the ridiculous attitude about racial differences.

When Joyce delivered her loving ultimatum, I had to respond; she was my life. We would get married.

I broke the news to my father at the club. When I told him, he walked over to Joyce and kissed her on the cheek. "Doc," I said, "I'm counting on you to take care of Ruth because she will be a little upset." We had planned to get married and take our honeymoon on a preparatory trip for the first Newport Jazz Festival tour of Europe in 1959.

It wasn't to be that easy. After speaking to me in the club, my father went home and had a long talk with my mother. The next time I saw him, he got right to the point.

"You can't get married," he said succinctly.

"What are you talking about, we're getting married."

"It will ruin your life. Live together, but don't get married."

I couldn't stand to argue that way so I put up a screen: "Alright, we won't get married for the time being." It wasn't exactly a lie; it all depended on your definition of the phrase "time being." Our plans remained unchanged. Joyce's mother didn't disapprove; she just insisted that one member of the Alexander family be there. Joyce's brother Bill accompanied us. We were planning on getting married in New York State, since all marriages in Boston were printed in the newspapers. We stopped at the first justice of the peace in some nameless town in March 1959. If Bill hadn't looked at a placard on the wall, we would never have known that our secret wedding took place in East Greenbush, New York.

Then we went to Europe to organize the first Newport Jazz Festival international tour. I had plans to return to the States and break the news to my folks. It's always easier to get forgiveness than permission.

\* \* \*

Unfortunately, our world was small, and news of this sort traveled faster than lightning. A truck driver who worked for Ginsburg Brothers was also friendly with Joyce's brother-in-law. From him, the driver found out about our marriage. Unwittingly, this employee offered his congratulations to my mother's brother, Uncle Joe. Uncle Joe went running to tell my mother.

In the meantime, Joyce and I were having an out-of-this-world time in Europe. We traveled by ship, on the ocean liner *Liberté*. Louis Lorillard managed a travel agency in Newport, and he made the arrangements. We had first-class accommodations. We became friendly with one of the ship's exceptional maître d's, who gave us an always remembered education in French cuisine and wine. I sang a few tunes with the orchestra at the ship's gala. We toured France with luxurious languor. We stopped in the Côte d'Azur, visiting the places I had seen during my last trip abroad.

After the *Liberté* pulled into the harbor in New York, I drove directly to Storyville in Boston. Doc was waiting for us. He didn't even give me a chance to greet him before asking, in an accusatory tone: "Did you get married?"

"Yes," I said simply, without malice or defiance.

"You lied to me," he said, "and I'll never speak to you again as long as I live."

\*     \*     \*

I had just been married, and to be unable to share that with my mother and father was a source of terrible frustration. Doc didn't come to the Newport Jazz Festival that year, which was excruciating for him. My mother begged me to come home. So every Friday night, I would visit them, alone without Joyce. I would fight with my father; when he refused to speak, I tore into him. I wouldn't let him get away with his idiocy.

"Who the hell are you?" I would shout. "You're like the old Jew in the village with the pais and the skull cap. You won't speak to me just because I *lied*?" You're not that kind of person. You can't disown your own son. I am what I am because of you." I kept fighting him for seven or eight months. His health was failing. It was horrible. Finally, he broke down one evening and started to cry. The family schism was over.

\*     \*     \*

We all got together as a family for the first time at Crane's Beach, where I was producing a summer concert series. Doc kissed Joyce and life normalized. He and my mother loved her as their own daughter, and Joyce accepted them as loving in-laws. After we moved to New York, Joyce took a job at Columbia Presbyterian Hospital in enzyme research in the department of neurology. She was the lead author on an important paper for the first time in her career. She used her maiden name, Joyce Alexander, and my father, in his newfound father-in-law pride, asked her why she didn't use the name Joyce Alexander Wein.

Although we were now a happy family, my mother asked me to give the stock in Ginsburg Brothers that she had already signed over to me to my brother Larry. Her excuse was that if anything happened to me it would not be right if "strangers" had a share of the family business. This was my life inheritance. I said, "Ma, if that's what you want, it's your stock, not mine." When I signed over the stock to Larry, I told him I was doing this because our mother had asked me. But I added, "Don't you forget to remember that this is my stock." Larry told me not to worry.

I'm happy that my life has been a success, so I never had to ask Larry to remember his words. My brother died too early, and Margie and Carol, my nieces, whom I dearly love, now own Ginsburg Brothers. Their life is secure.

It's obvious that marrying Joyce didn't ruin her life or mine. Our friends believed in us and in what I was doing. Perhaps they looked at us as some sort of an ideal that could possibly help to make this world a better place. Many of these friends went out of their way to help us. Marrying Joyce was the best thing I ever did in my life.

Joyce's sixty-fifth birthday party was an event to remember. Alan King, my partner in the Toyota Comedy Festival, held a mock rabbinical wedding. I had told him that we had not been married by a rabbi. I still haven't the slightest idea what he said; we were laughing so hard it didn't make any difference. Bill Cosby and his wife, Camille, were there. Dave and Iola Brubeck, John and Mirjana Lewis, Adolphus "Doc" Cheatham, and Jon Faddis paid their musical respects, as did Pete Seeger. More than two hundred people—friends and family—came to shower Joyce with respect and admiration. It wasn't loyalty to my friendship that brought them there. These were all people who loved Joyce—everything that she has been and everything that she has done. I am grateful to be able to count myself among their ranks.

At Newport in 1959, the first year of our marriage, a fellow approached me at the lobby of the Viking Hotel. He said, "I hear you are married to a black girl. So am I. Can you tell me where it is safe to go?"

I had a knee-jerk reaction and perhaps I was quite rude. "Man, you have a problem. Why don't you stop worrying and go wherever you want?"

# 4

# *Storyville*

*George's club has all the vitality—in a purely musical sense—of its namesake, the Storyville section of New Orleans where jazz was born . . .*

**—Nat Hentoff**

THE STORYVILLE SECTION OF NEW ORLEANS dates as far back as 1898. An alderman by the name of Sidney Story had decided to clean up the city of New Orleans. Mr. Story, a respectable, God-fearing gentleman, was concerned about the city's escalating levels of sin—and alarmed by rumors that a notorious Madam was setting up shop in his own neighborhood. So he introduced an ordinance banning prostitution throughout the city, with the exception of one confined area that included much of the French Quarter as it is known today.

Locals quickly began referring to the area as "Storyville," in honor of city Alderman Sidney Story who had unwittingly encouraged its creation. Story was mortified, but the moniker stuck, his name forever associated with this modern-day Gomorrah, a cesspool of rampant prostitution, gaming, corruption in every shape and form—and the sound that would later be known as jazz.

Half a century later, I would make the decision to open a reputable nightclub and call it "George Wein's Storyville: The Birthplace of Jazz." Whereas Sidney Story had balked, I had no reservations at all. Not that there wasn't opposition to the idea. I was, after all, the son of a highly regarded Boston physician; people of a background such as mine didn't usually get involved in the nightclub business. One of my father's patients, an accountant who had as a client the gangster Meyer

Lansky, advised Doc to protect me from this scene. The rest of my parents' friends were simply incredulous ("Georgie's going to do *what?*").

I must have kicked around dozens of names. My only steadfast requirement was that the name be a proper noun. For instance, I liked the name Birdland because it suggested a *place*. You would say: "Let's go to Birdland," instead of "Let's go to *the* Birdland." By these idiosyncratic standards, Café Society had a good name; the Village Vanguard didn't. In Boston, there was the Ken Club, the Hi Hat, and the Savoy. My club had to stand out from among this crowd.

The name "Storyville" dawned on me after conversing with Nat Hentoff. In fact, Nat came up with it first, and then changed his mind. But once I'd heard it, that was it. Storyville. And to prove that I wasn't ashamed of jazz's seamy origins, I put my own name right up there with it.

We had a prime location in the Copley Square Hotel, just west of Copley Square at the corner of Exeter Street and Huntington Avenue.

My arrangement with the hotel was ideal: I would pay no rent. I was to provide for the club's furnishings, sound system, decor, and operating expenses—and keep all of the earnings until I had caught up with my investment. After breaking even, I would split all profits with the hotel, which had a liquor license. I could buy liquor from the hotel stock.

I had five thousand dollars in my life savings (money that had been set aside for college but unspent, thanks to the GI Bill), and it had to go quite a long way. I became obsessed with things like second-hand cash registers. I found a number of used formica tables for twelve or thirteen dollars apiece; I bought two hundred chairs at five dollars each. I found a good second-hand piano. My sound system consisted of an amplifier, a couple of microphones, and two battered speakers—not quite state-of-the-art, but perfectly adequate. As for décor, I enlisted the help of a talented Boston artist, Danny Snyder. Danny, who recognized that his piece would never see the light of day, painted a striking black and white mural of a New Orleans street scene. This mural was a perfect accent to our dark interior.

The room sat just under two hundred people, banquet style. There wasn't a bad seat in the house.

The waitresses and bartenders were acquaintances from both the Savoy and the Hotel Fensgate. An old grade-school pal, Sam Brooker, offered to help with the books and the door. There was no elaborate hiring process; I just called up some friends and opened a club.

My only experience in this new world of business was as a frequent club patron, an occasionally working musician, and a onetime producer. I knew almost nothing about running a business. I just held my breath and jumped into the treacherous waters—hoping that I would stay afloat.

Knowing that my efforts would be fruitless without publicity, I contacted the only public relations man that I knew of: a veteran song-plugger named Harry Paul. Harry was a throwback to an earlier era of the music business; he had worked with Rudy Vallee in the '30s, and actually had a piece of a song called "Somebody Else Is Taking My Place." He hearkened from a time that was regarded as old-fashioned even in the '50s.

I entered Harry's office with some trepidation; he was a big guy, and a little rough around the edges. But Harry took a liking to me immediately. Here I was, a musician opening up a club on Copley Square. In terms of location, clientele, and the quality of the music, Storyville could be the first club poised to compete with the Savoy and the Hi Hat, both in an African-American neighborhood. Harry immediately began to plan a means of getting the word out to the press. "Well, don't get a big head, kid," he told me, "because you're going to get your name in the papers a lot from now on." Harry was my staunchest supporter from that moment on. He was like family.

Storyville opened in late September 1950, with the Bob Wilber Sextet. Wilber, a twenty-two-year-old white kid from Scarsdale, New York, was a soprano saxophonist and clarinet player who had garnered a reputation as Sidney Bechet's protégé. He had a good name in Boston, because of a Jelly Roll Morton–styled group that he had led for the past couple of years. For the six-week-long Storyville engagement, he put together a new sextet that featured Sidney and Wilbur de Paris on trumpet and trombone, respectively; Red Richards on piano; "Big Sid" Catlett on drums; and John Field, the sole Bostonian of the group, on bass.

"George Wein's Storyville" was an instant success and for the next six weeks would be crowded almost every night.

The real star of the Bob Wilber band was Sidney "Big Sid" Catlett, an ever-captivating drummer who originally hailed from Chicago. Big Sid was Louis Armstrong's favorite drummer; he had played in Louis's big band, and with the Armstrong All Stars. He was also a veteran of Benny Goodman's 1941 big band, and had recorded with Dizzy Gillespie and Charlie Parker in 1945. Sid was a charismatic musician. Magic coursed through the air when he played. Sid would build a tension in his solos; he'd crescendo to a deafening climax, then suddenly drop to a whisper. The audience would be in the palm of his hand. People came back night after night to see him. He was a phenomenon.

Probably the best portrait of Sidney's musicianship that I've ever seen was crafted by Whitney Balliett. "His solos had an uncluttered order and logic,"

Balliett wrote, "a natural progression of textures, rhythms and timing. He made them seem predesigned. One was transfixed by the easy motion of his arms, the pulse-like rigidity of his body, and the soaring of his huge hands, which reduced the drumsticks to pencils." This really captures the spirit of Sid. In fact, when this profile originally appeared in the *New Yorker*, I called Whitney to tell him how much I liked it.

"Well, it's understandable that you would feel that way," he replied. "I took those ideas straight from you when I came to Storyville. Sid wasn't there at the time. I had seen him play on other occasions, but I got the basic feeling from your description." I suppose I was effusive in my praise for Sid even then.

I got to know Sidney Catlett during his weeks at Storyville; we would often hang out. During our second or third week in business, I sent him on a mission. The Louis Armstrong All Stars were appearing in a concert at Symphony Hall. Sidney was an alumnus of that group. I told him: "Sid, I want you to take the night off. Go to Symphony Hall and get those guys to stop in after their show."

I had a Boston drummer fill in for Sidney during his absence. It wasn't long before he returned—with Earl "Fatha" Hines, my idol on the piano, in tow. I could hardly believe it. Red Richards gladly surrendered the piano chair, and Hines sat down to play. Sid commandeered the microphone and started playing emcee: "Ladies and Gentlemen, we are pleased to welcome Mister Earl 'Fatha' Hines. And now, here comes Barney Bigard."

Everyone turned in their chairs, craning their necks toward the entrance. Bigard came into the club, opened his clarinet case, and made his way to the bandstand. Sid spoke again: "Here comes Arvell Shaw." And suddenly there was the smiling bassist, maneuvering between tables and toward the stage. A minute later: "Here comes Jack Teagarden." And the legendary trombonist ambled in, looking stately and easygoing as he pulled out his horn. "Here comes Cozy Cole," Sid said, and the drummer took Sid's place on the stand. One by one, the All-Stars were coming into my club. I caught a glimpse of a few of my Boston friends, who looked at me as if to say: "how did you manage *this?*"

Then, as if rehearsed, in walked Pops. Armstrong entered the crowded club and headed straight for the stage. He hadn't brought his horn, but that was no problem; he sang, "When It's Sleepy Time Down South" in his inimitable style, and forever changed my life.

A few weeks earlier, Storyville at Copley Square had been little more than a promising idea. Now suddenly, as if by magic, the most eminent figure in jazz was in my club. That was it, as far as I was concerned. Life was very, very beautiful right there and then. When I saw and felt the electricity that Armstrong sparked just by walking on and singing a few songs, I knew that I had to be a part of his world. I knew that I had to work with the greatest.

Both my father and my mother were longtime Armstrong devotees, and I saw their faces when Louis walked in. Ruth and Barney simply *kvelled*.

\*　　\*　　\*

The week after our exhilarating Armstrong incident, Big Sid came through once again. Hoagy Carmichael, composer of "Stardust" and so many other standards, was working at the Copley Plaza Hotel across the square from Storyville. The Plaza had the most elegant music room in the city, and was charging a six-dollar cover for its show—steep by 1950 standards. Sid knew Hoagy, and when he went over to the Plaza, he was able to lure the songwriter back to Storyville, where to everyone's surprise and delight, Hoagy played and sang an entire forty-minute set. First Pops, and now Hoagy. Who, I wondered, would drop in next?

\*　　\*　　\*

One night, Big Sid started passing out invitations to a party at the house where he was staying. I thought this was a kind gesture; he'd been making decent money and was having a good time in Boston, and he wanted to throw a celebration to cap off his visit. On the night of the party Vic Dickenson came into the club, after playing a gig elsewhere in town, and asked me if I was planning on going to Sid's. We drove out to Roxbury together and found the address on the flyer. A dozen people or so were standing around when we entered the room, and we headed for a makeshift bar that had been set up in the corner.

After the bartender had poured our drinks, he said: "That'll be one dollar."

Vic and I looked at each other. "Well, kiss my wrist, man," Vic said. "Sid's having a rent party."

\*　　\*　　\*

By the end of the Bob Wilber Sextet's six-week engagement, I had already made back most of my investment on the club. We'd been grossing approximately five thousand dollars a week, which—after paying the band, the employees, and incidental expenses—left me with approximately eight or nine hundred dollars a week. Because of my arrangement with the hotel, none of this amount was earmarked for rent. As a result, we showed a considerable profit. Keep in mind that this music room had no cover charge and no minimum; our income came strictly from the sale of sixty-five-cent beers and ninety-five-cent whiskeys. Miraculously, we seemed to be cruising right along.

But soon a bump in the road showed up. Our waitresses began receiving numerous complaints about the liquor. I asked my bartender to check into it, and a few nights later he pulled me aside.

"We have a little problem, George," he said. "We've been paying list price for our liquor, but all the bottles are unsealed when they come in. I didn't tell you because I thought you knew. I don't know what we're getting, but it's not what we're paying for."

We were purchasing our liquor and beer directly from the Copley Square Hotel, at a cost of nearly a thousand dollars a week. The following morning, I met with the hotel owner, a smooth older gentleman in impeccable attire, and asked him to explain.

"Well, during the war, I had certain problems," he said rather cryptically, offering no further explanation. "George, I'd appreciate it if you would cooperate with me." What he was telling me, without saying it, was that wartime shortages had been so tough that in order to buy good liquor, he had been compelled to buy rotgut along with it. He was now attempting to unload this swill in my club. No wonder he didn't need my rent money; they had been pouring bad whiskey into top-grade bottles, and charging me top-grade prices, probably making more than $3,000 profit in less than two months.

At first I didn't realize the full scope of this situation, and I didn't know what to say to him. But after two more nights of complaints, I knew that something had to be done. I went back to the hotel office, where the owner was conversing with his brother.

"I'm sorry," I said, "but I'm just beginning in this business, and I don't want to start out with a dishonest reputation. I need to receive all of my liquor in sealed bottles from now on."

The hotel owner was furious. So was his brother, who said to me through clenched teeth: "I told my brother never to go into business with Jews, but I thought you were different."

I should have been upset by this statement, but at the time I was too perplexed. He thought I was *different*? What was *that* supposed to mean? Was he implying that Jews were typically crooked, and I was an exception? Or that Jews were typically honest, and I was a crook? Was he simply insulting me, or was he paying a backhanded compliment? To this day, I haven't figured it out.

My refusal to comply with their scam had dire consequences. The hotel owner informed me that my rent-free deal no longer applied. He now demanded payment of five hundred dollars a week. I knew that I would never be able to produce that sum every week, especially in the lean winter months.

That evening, I told the band and the employees that we would not open that night. We were closed. It was not a conscious decision; I merely acted on impulse, without a moment's hesitation. I couldn't continue selling cheap booze at premium prices and be able to live with myself. I didn't have to stop and weigh the options, or consider all the money I stood to lose. And so we closed our doors. It was the very end of November 1950. George Wein's Storyville had lasted six glorious weeks.

\*     \*     \*

That holiday season was lonely. But I didn't sit still long enough to let discouragement sink in. I had been bitten by the bug. The success of Storyville's first run motivated me to search for a new location. Somehow, I knew it had to open again.

Shortly after New Year's Day, I found a second home for the club: in the Hotel Buckminster on Kenmore Square near Fenway Park. I struck an agreement that everyone could live with: I'd pay minimal rent, along with a percentage of profits.

Like its predecessor on Copley Square, this room was located below street level and resembled a cavern. But it was almost one-third larger, with a seating capacity of about three hundred. There were booths along the perimeter of the room. I already had my tables, chairs, and sound system, so it wasn't hard to get things in order. For décor, I just had the walls painted black.

We opened our doors the first week of February 1951. Hoping to approximate our earlier success, I again hired clarinetist Bob Wilber as the headliner, but with a different personnel; the de Paris brothers and Sid Catlett had not been available. Johnny Windhurst on trumpet and Eddie Hubble on trombone joined Wilber in the front line. To spice things up, I also started up a Sunday afternoon guest-artist policy, bringing in luminaries like Ruby Braff, Vic Dickenson, Wild Bill Davison, Edmond Hall, and Mezz (Milton) Mezzrow.

But it didn't catch on. The crowds weren't coming in like they had before.

There were now four major rooms in Boston playing the same kind of music. It was too much. Although I had been careful to protect Storyville's name and location, the Copley Square Hotel had sidestepped the issue by opening the Music Room at street level in the same hotel, featuring Bobby Hackett's band. Meanwhile Steve Connelly, the former manager of the Savoy, was having cornetist

Jimmy McPartland appear in his new club, Jazz at 76, with his young wife, Marian Paige McPartland, on piano. And finally, the Savoy was still in business. In any case, Storyville at the Hotel Buckminster was not the unique presence that Storyville at Copley Square had been. I anticipated that Wilber's group would begin attracting crowds again in the spring, when Big Sid Catlett was due to return. In late March on Easter Sunday, I received a telegram from Sid. He wished me a Happy Easter, expressing how much he was looking forward to playing Storyville again. But our reunion never happened. That very night, Sidney suffered a massive heart attack, and died backstage at a theater in Chicago.

Sadness struck again a few months later when I brought Frankie Newton to Storyville at Kenmore Square. Frankie was a shell of his former self; he just couldn't keep fighting any longer. Once a proud, distinguished-looking man, he was now a confirmed alcoholic, and his posture and countenance were wracked with a feeling of futility. His playing bore similar signs of decay. My heart reached out to my friend and mentor, but there was little I could do. You can't help people who can't help themselves.

*     *     *

That June I received a call from Irving Siders, an agent with Shaw Artists in New York City. He suggested that I bring in Johnny Hodges, who had just left Duke Ellington's orchestra. Hodges had put together a group consisting of fellow Ellington expatriates Laurence Brown, Al Sears, and William "Sonny" Greer on trombone, tenor saxophone, and drums, respectively; and former Basie-ite Emmett Berry on trumpet.

I had had a soft spot in my heart for Hodges ever since seeing him play with Ellington at the Roseland Ballroom in 1940. The tone of his alto saxophone was a thing of beauty, and the thought of hearing that sound in my club was irresistible. So I agreed to present the Hodges band—even though their fee was twice what I usually could pay. (My basic budget for a group was under a thousand dollars a week; Hodges's asking price was $1,750.) But I was already in the hole; would it hurt to take this plunge?

My risk-taking was rewarded, in a musical sense; the band sounded terrific, and I had the opportunity to hear them every night and get to know Johnny. But I found out that his eloquence was restricted to his saxophone; a conversation with him tended to trail off into the distance.

Hodges's group did reasonable but uneven business; understandably I was discouraged. If I couldn't turn a profit with Hodges, what else was there to do? I was quickly learning how difficult it was to keep a nightclub going.

I closed Storyville for the summer season and made arrangements to open a "summer Storyville" in Gloucester, Massachusetts. Max Arnold, the former owner of the Ken Club, also owned a place in Gloucester called the Hawthorne Inn, a rambling, wooden seaside hotel that dated back to the turn of the century. I led a group that consisted of Buckminster regulars: Eddie Hubble, John Field, and Johnny Windhurst on trumpet. We lived together in a rented summer cottage and played music every night; it wasn't a bad way to spend a summer. During our run in Gloucester, Irving Siders contacted me again with another idea. He wanted me to open Storyville in the fall with George Shearing as a headline attraction. All I knew about Shearing was that he was a blind English piano player who had appeared at Birdland in New York. I wasn't sure if he had a following in Boston. When Siders told me Shearing's fee, I balked—it was $2,500 a week.

"Look," Siders told me, "this guy's got a hit record. You've never presented anybody with a hit record." The record in question was a single called "September in the Rain"; it appeared on the album *Lullaby of Birdland*. Shearing's group had a distinctive sound; he stated the melody on piano in block chords, while Chuck Wayne's guitar and Don Eliot's vibraharp tripled it in unison. The group was playing in a bebop manner smoother than Dizzy Gillespie or Charlie Parker. "September in the Rain" was probably the first successful effort to make bebop accessible to the general public.

I didn't see how I could possibly afford this group, but once again I took the risk. In the last week of August, I bought a modest one-inch advertisement in the *Boston Globe*, announcing Shearing's residence at Storyville beginning on September 10. And I crossed my fingers. If this didn't work out, I would find myself deeper in debt than ever before.

The phone started ringing almost immediately. Reservations began pouring in. Shearing appeared at Storyville for ten days, selling out every show. He was the biggest success ever to hit the Boston jazz scene. Because we had no air-conditioning and it was early September, the crowded room developed the humid, overheated atmosphere of a locker room. But no one complained; they still came in droves. I thought I was going to be a millionaire (in fact, I made just over $7,000 for the engagement). And, more than that, I had the pleasure of getting to know Shearing, who was an articulate presence both literally and musically. His sense of humor, however, was something else. I learned this after hearing him introduce custom-altered songs like, "I Don't Stand a Chance with a Ghost Like You" and "Lover Back Up to Me."

With my hope bolstered by the Shearing success, I bought every available name artist in the business. I spent countless hours on the phone in tedious negotiations with agents. (This was the real beginning of my business education.) I naïvely went after the people that I loved. One of the first such artists was the singer Lee Wiley; she came into the club on September 19, 1951.

Lee Wiley hailed from the era of Billie Holiday and Mildred Bailey. Her rendition of the Rodgers and Hart song "Manhattan," with accompaniment by Joe Bushkin and Bobby Hackett, had become a hit among the patrons of the Liberty Music Shop on Madison Avenue. I loved her records. The Eddie Condon gang—musicians like Hackett, Bud Freeman, and Pee Wee Russell—figured she was the best.

I booked myself as Lee's accompanist. During the first rehearsal, I don't know which of us was more nervous—because I didn't know if I could pull it off, and neither did she. But she had brought in some lead sheets, which made it easy for me. We got through it okay, and had a wonderful run.

There was a loyal contingent that returned to hear her night after night, including a Wellesley College graduate, Barbara Lea, a young vocalist who, fifty years later, still evokes musical memories of Miss Wiley. Another member of this admiring entourage was a dapper young gentleman, just a few years my senior, with the conspicuous appellation of Charles Bourgeois.

I didn't really know Charlie Bourgeois, although our paths had crossed a few times at Boston University. While at BU, each of us had dabbled in concert production; I with the Edmond Hall concert, and Charlie with a piano jazz concert featuring Lennie Tristano and Mary Lou Williams. Charlie was a jazz fan; this much I knew. The only other thing I could infer about him was that he was a stylish character. His attire was the epitome of Harvard Square fashion at its hippest and most urbane.

He and I didn't speak much beyond an occasional greeting, but I noticed that he was bringing classical music critics—like Cyrus Durgin of the *Boston Globe* and Rudy Ely of the *Boston Herald*—to the club, as there were no Boston jazz critics to speak of in 1951. Without being asked, he was boosting Storyville's publicity efforts. I asked some mutual friends if they could tell me about this elegant guy.

One mid-September evening, Mr. Bourgeois approached me in the club. "I don't know who you think I am," he said, in a clipped, direct manner that threw me off guard. "But I'm not a rich kid. I could use a job, just like anybody else."

Thereafter, Charlie was on the Storyville payroll. I started paying him fifteen dollars a week for his promotional assistance, in addition to generous credit in the club so that he'd never have to bring guests in at his own expense.

Charlie brought a certain quality to Storyville, a unique *savoir vivre*. He hailed from Island Pond, Vermont, the hometown of Rudy Vallee. He was utterly prepossessing; his weapons were a quick wit and a sense of gallant ease. Most important, Charlie's taste in music was as impeccable as his sartorial sense. Charlie Bourgeois has been a surrogate member of our family for more than fifty years.

Bourgeois's presence reaffirmed my vision of the club as a true music room. Storyville was never a joint. We had no floor show, no drug dealers or resident hookers. We kept things clean. There was no opportunity to purchase cocaine in the men's room. My parents were fixtures at the club; Doc especially. Nat Hentoff used to say that Storyville was the only jazz club with a resident physician.

As for the musicians, I treated them as artists. But I discovered that, no matter how friendly I tried to be, I could not help but be aware of a sense of distrust. To them, I was the Man.

*       *       *

There has always been a Man. In another era, he might have been called a king or ruler; the lord of the domain, the laird, or the boss. Today, the word has many different connotations. It can be a term of high regard ("Louis Armstrong is the Man!") or a casual greeting ("Hey, man"). Between friends, it's a term of endearment. In a profession, it can be a sign of status; during his entire musical life, Duke Ellington was the Man. A politician becomes the Man; so does the political system that he represents. When the draft came around, you'd hear people complaining: "The Man says I have to join the army." Anyone in a position of authority can become the Man, and be subjected to the criticism and wary recognition that goes along with it. To some, the Man is a friend; to others, he is the enemy.

I didn't know what it was to be the Man until opening Storyville. Suddenly, I was in the position of hiring musicians—most of whom were older than I was, and often famous. Many of these artists were African-American musicians who had an inherent distrust of whites—never mind white nightclub owners. In any case, I knew these artists by reputation and by record, and I loved them. I loved them for what they did and for who they were, even when they weren't necessarily easy to love. I would do anything for them. So it was difficult to understand that they usually perceived me in a different light. Not only did they not *love* me—they didn't even *trust* me. I hadn't yet realized that I had to earn the trust of the musicians who worked for me. Until then, I was just the Man with the bucks, the Man who signed the paychecks. I was the boss. Years later, I knew I had it made when cats would introduce themselves and say, "Hey, Man. You the Man, Man."

It took me many years to be able to handle this situation with any degree of ease. At Storyville, I was so young and inexperienced that I wore my authority tentatively, like a suit several sizes too big. This isn't to say that I was incapable of making decisions. At one point during Meade Lux Lewis's run, I found myself faced with a funny dilemma having to do with the club piano.

Because I played the piano, I prided myself on the condition of Storyville's piano, a secondhand, six-foot Steinway—not the world's greatest instrument, but good enough. Meade Lux Lewis was a terrific boogie-woogie piano player and a sweet little guy. But I found myself wincing throughout each of his sets. He was just killing the piano. I mean, he was practically breaking keys off the keyboard! After a few nights of this, I knew that I had to do something. I got Meade's agent on the phone.

"You've got to get Meade another gig," I cried. "He's pounding my piano to splinters! I have Art Tatum coming in next week; if things keep going this way, Tatum won't even have an instrument to play!"

Somehow, the agent found another gig for Meade in New England that paid more money. We didn't tell Lewis about this arrangement; I didn't want to hurt his feelings. So when the affable piano player asked me apologetically if he could cut short his Storyville run, I feigned surprise. "Take the other gig," I told him. "You've got to follow the money." Meade was relieved, and so was I. I couldn't afford another piano!

*   *   *

Working with Art Tatum was a dream come true. On this first Storyville engagement, he brought the bassist Slam Stewart and the guitarist Everett Barksdale. These particular musicians understood Tatum's complex harmonies. (Years later, Slam Stewart became a regular with my band, the Newport All Stars, and provided me with some of the most enjoyable musical moments in my life—he was one of a kind.) Art was a master of harmonic improvisation; he would play several choruses of a melody and change harmonic structures at will. At times, it appeared that he might not be following the tempo he had set for a tune he was playing; the beat seemed to disappear. Then: Bam! Without missing a beat, he'd come back in tempo; he'd been keeping perfect time all along.

Art had an affinity for Vladimir Horowitz; the two virtuosi often expressed their mutual admiration. Horowitz had perfected a run that he'd finish off with his left hand—while using the other hand to reach into his back pocket, pull out a white handkerchief, and ostentatiously mop his forehead. Art, who never *saw* this trick but must have heard about it, did the same thing. Genius had company.

Art was playing opposite the singer Maxine Sullivan, who was well known for her swinging rendition of the Scottish folk song "Loch Lomond." During the '40s she had recorded with her husband, the bassist John Kirby.

Joyce Alexander often dropped by during this run. Joyce was an enthusiastic jazz fan, and she was thrilled to be at a table with Art Tatum. On one such occasion, Joyce and Art were sitting together during the last set of the evening; there were very few people in the club. Maxine Sullivan finished her set, and Joyce expressed some disappointment.

"Oh, she didn't sing 'I'm Comin', Virginia.'" The tune was one of Sullivan's modest hits.

"That's alright," Tatum said, ever the gentleman. "I'll play it for you."

Joyce smiled. "Thank you very much, Mr. Tatum. But it's a very simple song. It doesn't lend itself to a lot of arpeggios or runs."

At this naïve suggestion, Art merely chuckled. In the middle of his next set, he played "I'm Comin', Virginia," stating the melody very simply. During his improvisational choruses, he did one intricate run, and immediately exclaimed: "Oh! I'm sorry, Joyce." From that moment on, we had a tradition with Tatum. Joyce and I would sit in the front of the club during his last set. He would play our requests, tunes like "What Does It Take?" and "Would You Like to Take a Walk?" that nobody else played.

After Tatum's last set of the evening, he and I would often go across town to an after-hours bar called the Pioneer Club. Art was always available to hang out, and we established a very personal bond. He never uttered a bad word about a fellow musician. The only time I heard him criticize anyone was one night at the Pioneer Club, when we were listening to a Stan Kenton record on the jukebox. Art tilted his head for a second to listen, and his features clouded over. He was visibly irritated. "That guy can't play any piano at all," he said.

Tatum was adversely affected by the dichotomy that had occurred in the jazz world after the war. Younger players had stopped listening to swing musicians. They were only interested in Bird, Bud, Dizzy, and Miles. Oscar Peterson, the talented young pianist who had wedded Tatum-esque digital dexterity to the bop idiom, was selling more records than his idol. Art never expressed perturbation about this phenomenon, but I'm sure that it bothered him on some level. It certainly bothered me; Tatum was a genius! Over the next few years, I would hire him at every possible opportunity. I loved the man.

\*    \*    \*

In mid-October 1951, in came the legendary Sidney Bechet. Like Tatum, Bechet was one of the artists I had wanted to bring into the club from the beginning. The soprano saxophonist dominated the history of his instrument as well as the history of jazz. He was as important a figure as Armstrong.

I had met Bechet a few times before; once, at a Boston Opera House concert in 1946, the night that I first met Joyce. Then, a few years later, I had actually played with him in Philadelphia (I silently hoped that he wouldn't remember this encounter). On both occasions, the thing that struck me most was the sheer strength of his sound. He was a giant.

\*    \*    \*

Stan Getz played Storyville in late October 1951. Stan's group was something of a happy coincidence; pianist Al Haig had just come out of a year-long sabbatical from music, and drummer Tiny (Norman) Kahn had joined after leaving Georgie Auld's band. The other members of the group—guitarist Jimmy Raney and bassist Teddy Kotick—hadn't been with Getz for very long, either. But this really was some band.

Roost Records, which had a contract with Getz at the time, set up shop halfway through the two-week engagement. The resulting double-LP, *Stan Getz at Storyville—Vols. 1 & 2*, stands as one of the freshest and most engaging items of his discography.

Incidentally, *Stan Getz at Storyville* was recorded on October 28, 1951. Stan Getz was recorded in the club again the following night—but not by Roost, and not with his quintet. Just as the first week of Getz's engagement had been a double-bill with Bechet, the second week overlapped with an appearance by Billie Holiday. Stan sat in during a few of Billie's sets, echoing the recordings she had done with Lester Young (Stan's idol and original inspiration). An air check from that night, consisting of several Holiday-Getz collaborations, has circulated as a bootleg recording for years.

Needless to say, I was thrilled to bring Holiday into Storyville. Bechet! Getz! Holiday!! I was in jazz heaven.

I was careful to make sure that Billie was comfortable during her time in Boston. She was very appreciative. As far as we were concerned, all rumors of unreliability were unfounded. She showed up on time every night, happily conversed with patrons, and even consented to do an extra set or two for a broadcast on WMEX.

Charlie Bourgeois and I took Billie out for dinner at Durgin Park, a restaurant near Faneuil Hall, which was well known for its enormous lobsters. We encouraged Billie to order one. She had particular instructions for the waiter—she wanted a *female* lobster. I was a bit perplexed: "Billie, can they even tell the difference before it's cooked?" But she was insistent. She wanted a female lobster, period. She had probably heard that a female lobster had more taste by virtue of its roe.

*　　*　　*

But even Holiday, Bechet, and Getz couldn't put Storyville's ledger in the black. Two months after my George Shearing windfall, I was in debt to the disastrous tune of twenty thousand dollars. It was obvious that nobody else had the appeal that George Shearing did in New England. At least, nobody except Erroll Garner.

Erroll drew crowds from the first night he came to the club. In addition to his national prominence, he had established a following in Boston after a number of appearances at the Hi Hat. Anyone who heard him play became an ardent fan. And for good reason; nobody could sound like Erroll, despite the hordes of pianists who tried. Erroll was like an entire orchestra; his piano filled the room. He would play these grandiose interludes and introductions before stating a melody, and no one ever knew what song he was leading up to. Then, when he finally launched into a melody—with that infectious 4/4 beat in his left hand—people applauded almost as a matter of course. It didn't even have to be a tune he had recorded. And when he did go into one of his hit songs, like "Laura" or "Misty," the recognition applause was huge.

Erroll Garner's manager, Martha Glaser, insisted that we break the standard forty-twenty rule: forty minutes per set, with a twenty-minute break. Instead of adhering to this schedule, Erroll would play three long sets, each lasting roughly an hour. The last set was often the least crowded, and Joyce, who was then working on cancer research at the Massachusetts General Hospital, would stop by after her shift. Joyce and I would sit down at a table near the stage and make requests, as we had with Tatum. Erroll knew the jazz piano so well that he could render impressions of other players, and still keep that unmistakable Garner touch. We would say: "play some Fatha Hines," and he would go into the Hines style. "Do a little Teddy Wilson," and he would play some Teddy. He would do the same with Fats Waller. But when we called out "Tatum," Erroll would just turn around and shoot us a comical look. It was a ball. Erroll loved it when people dug his music. Like George Shearing, he knew how to take the harmonic and rhythmic ideas of bebop and translate them into a language that the public could understand.

One of Garner's most loyal listeners was Ted Williams, the "Splendid Splinter" of the Boston Red Sox—and my boyhood idol. Years later, after Williams had retired and moved out of the city, he claimed that the thing he missed most about Boston was seeing Erroll Garner at Storyville.

Erroll Garner was a true original in the history of jazz piano. For reasons I do not understand, considering the high respect other contemporaries had for him, Garner seems to have been forgotten by younger jazz critics and jazz pianists alike. There was only one Erroll Garner and it would help every jazz pianist if they paid a little more attention to his talent and creativity.

\*　　\*　　\*

A lot of other ball players frequented Storyville on Kenmore Square, because of its proximity to Fenway Park, including Ellis Kinder, a twenty-game-winning all-star pitcher with the Red Sox. Kinder was originally from Arkansas, and he had some expectations that rubbed me the wrong way. The pitcher took issue with the fact that our maître d', a friend of mine by the name of Crawford Purnell, was black. Kinder complained to the management of the Hotel Buckminster about this indignity; how could they have a *Negro* at the front door of this establishment? One of the hotel managers, in turn, came to me and asked if I could fire Crawford. I couldn't believe his suggestion.

"How can you get up in the morning," I said to him, in an even tone, "and look at yourself in the mirror, and then ask me to do that?" Jackie Robinson may have already become a major-league star, but there were still seriously warped attitudes within the game. After my confrontation with the hotel, no one bothered me about Crawford again. He continued to work at Storyville until the day we closed.

\*　　\*　　\*

In early December 1951, I brought Sidney Bechet back for a repeat engagement. This time, Sidney left his regular group behind, and I had the task of assembling a band worthy of his stature. It consisted of Vic Dickenson on trombone, Claude Hopkins on piano, Jimmy Woode on bass, and Buzzy Drootin on drums. Again, Sidney played well. But he was ailing—he complained of persistent digestive problems. Partway through the engagement, we had to take him to the Massachusetts General Hospital for examination.

Fortunately, Joyce was working at Mass General, and could check up on him regularly. Sidney was happy to see her friendly face, because he had no family in Boston. He was clearly uncomfortable there.

When the doctors told Sidney that he needed an operation, he told them that he wanted the procedure done in France. This was a perplexing demand. There he was, in one of the premier hospitals in the world; Mass General was associated with Harvard Medical School. But Sidney was adamant—he didn't want to undergo surgery in Boston. He trusted the French more than he trusted Americans. Despite what must have been a painful flight, Sidney went back to France for the operation.

\*　　\*　　\*

In 1952 at a short-lived club I foolishly opened in New Haven, Connecticut, I presented a combo led by Coleman Hawkins and Roy Eldridge. Hawk was the undisputed father of the tenor saxophone. Roy was the most fiery of the swing trumpeters, commonly cited as a bridge between the continents of Armstrong and Gillespie. I had been a fan of Roy's style ever since hearing his performance on a Gene Krupa recording of "After You've Gone." There was a wildness and swing to his playing that surpassed anything I had ever heard.

It was natural to present Hawkins and Eldridge together. They had each played with the Fletcher Henderson Orchestra, among other groups. Their tandem sound was terrific; they seemed to bring out the best in each other. I figured that they were happy to work together. But one night, Coleman said something that gave me an insight into the mind of the master saxophonist: "Man, I don't know why everybody always books me and Roy together," he said. We were standing outside the club between sets. Bean had his hat tilted back on his head. "He's riding my tail, man. He can't get a gig by himself, so he tags along with me."

This came as a shock. Hawk might have been venting some longstanding resentment, or he might have just been having a bad night.

\*　　\*　　\*

I had begun to realize that double-bill appearances were exciting but hardly cost-efficient. So I put together a house trio for the purposes of intermissions and Sunday jam sessions. I played piano in this trio. My rhythm-section mates were the ubiquitous John Field and the inestimable drummer Jo Jones.

It was a treat to play with Jo, though it was also a little intimidating at times; Jo Jones was both a Hall of Fame drummer and a distinguished alumnus of the All-American Count Basie rhythm section (along with Freddie Green, Basie, and Walter Page).

Sometimes it was literally too much to handle. One week we played opposite the Billy Taylor Trio. I had seen Billy a few years earlier at Birdland, and I asked him to come to Storyville. He brought the bassist Charlie Mingus with him.

I had not met Mingus before this, but I had heard him at the Embers in New York with the Red Norvo Trio (which also included Tal Farlow on guitar). He was a fantastic bassist; I didn't know whether anyone had ever played the instrument with that sort of creative facility. And he loved to play. In fact, he loved it so much that, on one night of Billy Taylor's Storyville run, he asked to sit in with us. John Field left the stand, and Mingus came on. So there I was onstage with Charles Mingus and Jo Jones. I called the standard "I've Found a New Baby," and we started to play.

Things were going fine until, in the middle of a piano chorus, Charles Mingus and Jo Jones decided to stage a showdown.

"Man, you can't play fast," Mingus said, challenging Jo.

"I can play as fast as anybody," Jo countered.

"Oh yeah? You can't play as fast as me."

That said, Mingus started to accelerate—gradually at first, with Jo matching his every beat. I was able to keep up for a while. But they kept going faster and faster. Within a minute or two, the song was careening wildly out of control; Mingus and Jo pounded away at those quarter notes like a jackhammer laying into pavement. This was ridiculous—they were actually racing, egging each other on. I matched their pace as long as I could; but soon I couldn't even *follow* the tempo, let alone attempt to play it. What was I doing on the stand with these maniacs? Finally, we reached the finish line, ending the song with an unceremonious crash, with Jo and Mingus each claiming triumphant victory. I wasn't in a position to judge.

\*     \*     \*

Jo Jones had his own vocabulary—less extensive but no less cryptic than that of Lester Young. He used two choice phrases: "the vonce," and "the dingding." "Man, when I was with Basie," he'd say, "we'd come up on the vonce, and the man would put the ding-ding here." I hung out with him almost every night for six weeks; after a gig, we would head over to Slade's or Estelle's across town for some fried chicken, and then maybe hit the after-hours Pioneer Club for a jam session or a few drinks. We had a good time. But when Jo finally went back to New York City, I thought back upon our conversations and realized that I hadn't understood half of what he said.

This is not to imply that Jo was incapable of giving you a piece of his mind; Jo Jones knew a little more than anyone about almost everything, and he'd let you know it at all times. He was openly critical of my piano playing; he once told me disparagingly that my comping sounded like the "Charleston." I tried to take his criticism to heart, but no adjustments I made ever seemed to make him happy. Finally, Jo took decisive action, firing me from the house trio.

"George," he said one night, with the sort of grin that could connote either kindness or mischief, "you can't count the house and play the piano at the same time. I'm sorry, man, but I just can't use you." I was out of a gig in my own club. This was cause for a good deal of amusement. But Jo was right; I was too concerned with the club to focus on playing.

Fortunately, Jo Jones's advice didn't always result in my losing a gig. One night we were out drinking, and talking about the club. I had just received offers from the Shaw agency for Ella Fitzgerald and Sarah Vaughan; they were priced at $2,500 and $2,750, respectively. I wasn't sure whether I could afford to pay these princely sums. I asked Jo what he thought.

"You've got to go with the queens," Jo replied. It was all I needed to hear. I arranged to bring both Sarah and Ella to the club, in the first few months of 1952.

\*     \*     \*

Sassy came first. She was at that time the more popular artist; she had recorded a series of hit songs on Columbia Records. Sarah sang in a relatively straightforward style, with a purity of lyric, and few of the melodic embellishments and mannerisms that would later become her hallmark. She was also painfully shy in those days. If I asked her to sing for thirty minutes, she would do twenty-five. Getting her to perform an extra couple of songs was like pulling teeth. She eventually outgrew these inhibitions; years later, she would get into the habit of doing multiple encores and singing for two hours. I would often kid her about this turnaround: "Sassy, do you remember when you worked Storyville and we had to *fight* to get another tune out of you?"

\*     \*     \*

Ella Fitzgerald also made her Storyville debut in 1952. She was a wonderful lady, and her swinging sense of rhythm was absolute—she was like Erroll Garner in that regard. I developed a blister on my middle finger from snapping to the beat.

But Ella was not the hugely popular artist that she would later become. She had developed vocal problems and she would shortly need an operation. She was well known, but her commercial "A-Tisket, A-Tasket" heyday with the Chick Webb Orchestra was long past. In 1952, she didn't even have a serious manager; I had dealt exclusively with Shaw Artists for her engagement. On the morning after her final night, Ella came over to the club to pick up her money. She was dressed so plainly that I almost didn't recognize her. When I handed her the envelope of cash, she thanked me humbly and tucked it into her coat. I could hardly believe that this consummate artist didn't have someone to handle her money and look after her interests. Fortunately, Norman Granz soon took this great lady, who was just dying on the vine, and began protecting her as his artist. Jo Jones may have proclaimed Ella a queen, but Norman was the one who gave her the crown.

Another queen who worked Storyville around this time was Dinah Washington, the "Queen of the Blues." I was paying her close to $2,000 for the week.

But on opening night, Dinah played to an empty room. No one showed up. I was stunned, and realized that the gig would be a total washout. I was already deep in debt. So after three nights, I asked Dinah if she would agree to cancel the rest of the week. Although she didn't have much money herself in those days, Dinah voiced no objections; singing to an empty club would not be much fun for her. She let me out of the deal, and gave seven or eight hundred dollars back. She could have insisted upon playing the week and receiving her paycheck; but there was something in her heart that understood. Dinah was one of the few artists who ever made such a gesture.

I wanted to find a way to thank her. The following day, I went shopping for a gift. At Brooks Brothers, I found a nautically styled brass-bound barrel, with an inscription etched in the brass: "The Queen, God Bless Her." I bought the barrel for seventy-five dollars and gave it to Dinah. She loved this gift; it remained in her apartment for the rest of her life. From that moment on, we were friends. I loved Dinah, and I was happy when her next Storyville engagement, a year or so later, brought some fans to the club. At the end of every night, we would turn up the house lights, and Dinah would glide from table to table, singing "Don't Let Your Love Grow Cold." She would reach right into people's souls.

Another memorable incident with Dinah occurred in 1959, when I was producing a jazz festival sponsored by the Sheraton Hotel Corporation in Fenway Park, home of my beloved Boston Red Sox. It was a gorgeous summer evening. I had positioned the stage at second base with the music projecting to a possible crowd of 20,000. Standing beside the stage in short center field in darkening twilight, I slipped into reverie. I could feel the spirit of Ted Williams patrolling left field in the shadow of the "green monster." Suddenly I heard a voice in my ear. "I say I'll move a mountain, and I'll move the mountain. . . ." A shiver ran up the back of my neck. It sounded exactly like the ghost of Billie Holiday, who had passed away a few months prior.

I turned around to find Dinah leaning over me. "What are you doing to me?" I cried. "I thought I was dreaming." The Queen said, "I know you love the Lady. I just wanted you to know that there are others of us who loved her too."

\*     \*     \*

I had a less friendly experience with the majestic Ethel Waters. In the 1920s, Miss Waters had been a major trailblazer. Although she had come out of the race-record tradition of the twenties appealing exclusively to African Americans, she developed a more sophisticated manner of singing than the blues shouters of her day. In the years since, she had become a formidable presence both on Broadway and in Hollywood.

Ethel Waters was an influence on Billie Holiday, Lena Horne, Dinah Washington, and a host of other singers. But few ever acknowledged this debt. Billie, whose articulation and phrasing on early recordings clearly evoke Waters, always maintained that her sole influences were Bessie Smith and Louis Armstrong. I think the reason for this slight was Ethel Waters herself. If there was the possibility of another female vocalist sharing a bill with her, Waters would often make the proprietor or promoter take her off the program. She must have seen younger talent as a threat. Miss Waters's career had gradually diminished by the 1950s. A long and arduous path in show business had left her jaded and a bit suspicious. She was highly insecure, and she was mean.

I had heard rumors about Ethel Waters, but this didn't prevent me from presenting her in Boston. On Miss Waters's first night in Storyville, I welcomed her warmly and asked if there was anything I could do for her.

"I will let you know, Mister Wein," she replied, with flawless elocution and in a striking, resonant tone.

"Please call me 'George,'" I replied. I was twenty-six years old.

"I will call you 'Mister Wein,'" Miss Waters said decisively, and a bit forcefully. She was advising me, in no uncertain terms, that we were not yet acquainted. To her, I was not a friend or an appreciative fan, but the man running the club.

During her Storyville engagement, Miss Waters brought her own piano accompanist, and used the house rhythm section. Yet she all but ignored Jo Jones and John Field, as if they weren't sharing the same stage. Every night she would implore the brave souls in the audience to grant "a round of applause for one who so richly deserves it: our pianist, Mister Reginald Bean." She never once acknowledged Jo. This omission bothered me. One night I asked him how he felt about not being introduced.

"Ah, you don't understand Miss Waters," Jo said knowingly. "Don't worry, George, I'm not upset." His respect, in this case, outweighed his ego.

By the time Ethel Waters appeared at Storyville, her career was finished. She didn't make things any easier. When she arrived in Boston, she was invited to a reception on Beacon Hill; a group of people who appreciated her artistry had organized a party in her honor. Inexplicably, she had declined the invitation—an insult that her admirers repaid by assiduously avoiding her performances. Perhaps this was the main reason why Miss Waters's place in the history of jazz singing has been so sadly overlooked—she had few friends to help perpetuate her memory. She was so miserable that she just lashed out at everyone around her. By the end of the 1950s, she met the evangelist Billy Graham, and spent the rest of her life singing gospel songs at his crusades. This was a much-needed solace for her, and when I met Reverend Graham years later, I thanked him for giving her that precious opportunity.

*     *     *

Ethel Waters wasn't the only artist to come to Storyville from beyond the world of pure jazz. I took some cues from Barney Josephson's Café Society and Max Gordon's Village Vanguard—clubs that I had frequented in New York City during the 1940s—and presented the occasional folk artist as well.

I had seen Josh White at Café Society. By the time he came to Storyville in 1952, Josh White was a successful artist who played primarily in concert halls. His career had begun when he was a small boy, leading blind blues singers. At Storyville, he played the folk material solo with an acoustic guitar. For the blues numbers, he used a backing trio; I played piano in this group.

Josh White was a real heartthrob. He radiated a sexual charisma, and performed with an open shirt baring his chest before Harry Belafonte brought that image into the mainstream. In the early 1950s, this was considered to be slightly risqué.

The most intriguing thing about Josh White, for me, was the audience that came to hear him. It was different—a collegiate, folk-oriented crowd. Unlike the jazz audiences that talked quietly during sets by Erroll Garner or Ella

Fitzgerald, Josh White's following was unfailingly rapt. People held their breath when he sang. They wouldn't even dare to light a cigarette; it was as if they were afraid to strike a match and break the spell. I still can picture him crooning "The Riddle Song." When he sang the lines, "I gave my love a baby / with no cryin'" in his sensuous baritone, you could hear a collective sigh from the young girls in the room.

*     *     *

The college demographic was, unfortunately, not a regular part of Storyville's patronage. The music may have been a factor in this equation, but the biggest reason was the strict enforcement of Massachusetts's "Blue Laws." Boston was still a puritanical city, and the legal drinking age there was most decidedly set at twenty-one. One night, I was playing the piano with Wild Bill Davison's band when a dozen Princeton kids walked in and sat at a table right in front of the bandstand. They were in town for a Harvard-Princeton game, and this was their big night out. As I was playing, I overheard someone say: "Okay, we'll each buy a round of beer." In my head I started making calculations; twelve rounds for twelve guys was 144 bottles of beer. This was great! We were going to make some money! But then their waitress asked for identification, and they were under twenty-one. They hadn't even thought about it, because they were from New Jersey, where the minimum drinking age was eighteen. So the waitress apologized and told them they couldn't drink alcohol. Rather than ordering twelve ginger ales, they left immediately. And there I was with three empty tables. I can't remember what wrong chords I played as I watched them go.

Another stipulation of the Blue Laws was that all entertainment, music, and serving of alcohol had to halt at the stroke of midnight on Saturday night.

One Saturday night, three or four burly cops in uniform appeared in the club at ten minutes before midnight. City Hall had sent orders to check up on us. The officers just stood at the back of the room and waited for midnight to strike.

It so happened that we were packed that night; it was the Saturday evening set of Sarah Vaughan's second Storyville appearance. I was annoyed that the police were making such a menacing appearance. So I went to the side of the stage during a piano solo, motioned Sarah over, and whispered a request: "When I point to you, ring in Sunday morning by singing 'The Lord's Prayer,' *a cappella.*" This was a song she had recorded. She didn't know the reason for these instructions, but nodded her assent.

Midnight struck, and the police began a predatory walk toward the stage. I signaled to Sarah, and she started singing: "Our Father, which art in Heaven, hallowed be Thy Name . . ." It stopped the officers in their tracks. They stood numbly while Sarah performed her exquisite rendition of the prayer. You could hear a pin drop. When she had finished, she said good night, thanked the audience, and left the stage. The Boston Irish Catholic policemen were flummoxed. Perhaps they said a few Hail Mary's after leaving the club.

*    *    *

I was having a great time in Boston, spending every night of the week at Storyville, immersed in the music I loved. During the day, when I wasn't talking to booking agents or making other arrangements, I led a life of leisure. I took up golf, playing at public courses. It was satisfying to wake up every morning and feel no hurry, no pressing obligations.

This feeling was magnified as spring came to an end, and I closed Storyville for the summer. I had lined up a deal at the Hawthorne Inn in Gloucester for the second year in a row. This time, I assembled a group consisting of Ruby Braff, Eddie Hubble, Jimmy Woode, clarinetist Jack Fuller, and a young Boston drummer named Peter Littman. I shared the piano chair with Steve Kuhn, who was a Harvard student at the time. Charlie Bourgeois joined us. We rented a picturesque summer house on Pigeon Cove in Rockport. The house's owner, a friendly woman named Mrs. Dole, entrusted us with her keys. "Don't burn the house down," she said as she left.

It was in a gorgeous setting, with no pressures or concerns besides the music. Once again I was working with some of the best young musicians in the area, playing our brand of swing. We slept in, went swimming, hung out, and worked all night. It was a ball. But it all came to an unceremonious end after only a few weeks. Late one night, I stirred from sleep and noticed a crackling sound and the odor of burning wood. When I opened my eyes, I saw that the walls of my room were aflame.

I didn't even pause to grab my pants, which were crumpled on a chair next to the bed. I ran to the window, tore out the screen, crawled onto a porch roof outside, and jumped about twelve feet to the ground. I had enough sense to land on the balls of my feet and fall forward, avoiding injury. But I was stark naked. I ran around outside, screaming: "Fire! There's a fire!" I was like a satyr dancing at the gates of hell.

Peter Littman leapt out from the other side of the house. Jack Fuller catapulted from a window, hurt his back, and was hospitalized for a week. Hubble, whose room was on the third floor, had picked a fortuitous night to stay with a girlfriend in town. The others—Charlie Bourgeois, Ruby Braff, Jimmy Woode and Sarah Vaughan (who was there visiting Jimmy)—were out on the rocks near the beach, enjoying some herbal relaxation.

The house burned to the ground. Our instruments and clothes were incinerated long before the fire department arrived. I stood dumbfounded on the grass and watched the glowing embers, too shocked to realize that I was still nude. When the others rushed up from the beach, Charlie saw me in my immodest state and ran over.

"For Christ's sake," he said, handing me his jacket. "Put this on."

I put the jacket around my shoulders.

"Wrap it around your waist," Charlie suggested.

"Charlie!" I snapped, "I'm not bashful, I'm cold."

Fortunately, the firefighters were able to contain the blaze before it spread to the other houses of Pigeon Cove. They never figured out what had sparked the flames. We felt terrible for Mrs. Dole; she had lost a beautiful house.

And the guys had lost their instruments. So we decided to throw a benefit concert for the band. Rather than holding it in Gloucester, we returned to Boston, where we could raise more money. I asked Pee Wee Russell and J. C. Higginbotham to come up from New York.

Ruby Braff suggested that we get in touch with Leonard Bernstein, for whom we had performed a few months earlier at Brandeis University. Bernstein had organized a jazz symposium there with Lee Konitz and some other modernists. Knowing about the program in advance, Ruby and I had approached Bernstein at the Somerset Hotel, where he was practicing a Mozart piano concerto for a performance with the Boston Symphony later that week. After introducing ourselves, Ruby and I had suggested our services as a complement to his symposium. We offered to perform a capsule history of jazz (from Armstrong through Ellington and Basie) that would lead into his lecture. Bernstein had been thrilled by the idea, and it had been a success. Symposium panelist John Hammond heard Ruby Braff there for the first time. He loved his rendition of "When It's Sleepytime Down South."

Even with the glow of this recent collaboration, I didn't know whether Leonard Bernstein would be at all receptive to our plea for help. But there was no harm in trying. So I placed a telephone call to him at Tanglewood, and asked whether he would appear at Storyville for our benefit concert. To my surprise and delight, he immediately agreed. I hastened to place advertisements in the area newspapers, with his permission.

"Leonard Bernstein Plays Jazz at Storyville" took place on August 13, 1952. Bernstein was not yet the head conductor of the New York Philharmonic, but he was like a deity in New England. People were coming in from as far as Cape Cod. Everyone in a two-hundred-mile radius had seen the newspaper advertisement. We were charging a five-dollar cover; we probably could have asked for three times that amount. We packed 450 people into the club that night. It was pouring rain outside, and in mid-August this made it almost unbearable inside. The walls in the unventilated room were sweating.

"I hope you don't have the whole evening planned around me," Bernstein said to me when he arrived. He had driven down from Tanglewood.

"Absolutely not," I replied. "Just get on the stage and play whatever you want." Waiting for him was a rhythm section of Marquis Foster on drums and Jimmy Woode on bass with Pee Wee Russell on clarinet. They began to play the blues.

Leonard Bernstein was an important figure in contemporary music, but he didn't seem to know how to resolve a twelve-bar blues. He just played the piano with his concept of a jazz feeling. Pee Wee followed Lenny's lead, in his own angular fashion. The resulting collaboration was bizarre. Melodic phrases trailed off aimlessly, or met with other phrases in an incongruous fashion. Fortunately, a wire recording of this performance was made by a friend, Mel Levine. People came up to me after the set and asked, "Did you ever hear anything like that in your life?"

"No," I deadpanned. "I really haven't."

Bernstein's one-nighter netted three thousand dollars. We used these funds to purchase new horns for Ruby, Eddie, and Jack. We were all extremely impressed by Leonard Bernstein's generous spirit—if not by his command of the blues. He had saved the day.

*     *     *

In September I reopened the Boston Storyville, and said a silent prayer for this upcoming year's grosses. My hope would soon be rewarded; shortly after the Bernstein triumph, we welcomed an up-and-coming group led by the pianist Dave Brubeck.

Brubeck was not yet the major artist he would become. But he had made a splash with a club date in San Francisco, and word had traveled about his appeal. His agent called me to say that I should try this guy at Storyville; he was already booked in New York City, and a Boston stop would help defray the cost of the East Coast tour. His fee was a mere $800 for the week, and didn't cover transportation, hotel accommodations, or the commission for their agency. So obviously Brubeck and his guys were working for next to nothing.

In those early days, Brubeck and his alto saxophonist, Paul Desmond, looked disconcertingly alike. They had the same medium height and slender build; they wore similar suits and identical horn-rimmed glasses. For the first few nights that they were in the club, I couldn't tell them apart. But after a few days, I finally knew whom I was talking to—especially after I caught on to Desmond's dry sense of humor.

Paul was as sensitive and appealing a figure as anyone I ever knew. Keats or Shelley might have written a poem about him; he possessed a poetic romanticism to the people who knew him. He was quiet and introverted, but when he spoke, you listened, because he was just as talented verbally as he was with his alto saxophone. Paul never did a lot of prose writing, but he should have. What he did write—a few things for *Down Beat*—had the same fluid eloquence that marked his improvisation.

Charlie Bourgeois spent a lot of time with Paul and Dave while they were in town. He would take them to restaurants and bars, and out to see the sights. But Charlie's greatest contribution to the jazz world was sartorial. He was friendly with Charlie Davidson, the proprietor of the Andover Shop on Holyoke Street in Cambridge, and during the day he accompanied Desmond to the shop. Under Mr. Bourgeois's guidance, jazz musicians soon resembled denizens of Harvard Square. Brubeck and Desmond were hardly the only musicians to benefit from this service; Charlie Davidson's tailoring also fit right into the Modern Jazz Quartet's image. Miles Davis was known to visit the shop when he was in town. Roy Haynes became a customer, and before long he had been cited by George Frazier in *Esquire* magazine's "Best-Dressed American Performers," alongside the likes of Cary Grant and Fred Astaire.

Clothing aside, in a musical sense, Brubeck and Desmond were already stylish characters when they came to Boston. When the group started to play, their sound created a musical alchemy that everyone could feel. Brubeck's style and time were a little different; he had a dynamic sensitivity and a unique touch at the keyboard. And Desmond's lyrical, melodious sound borrowed from a number of sources but resembled no one else. They had a distinctive interplay. They swung, but with their own inimitable momentum. They were unique. Although they debuted to a small crowd, word quickly got around. After three or four nights into their engagement, the club was filled. This was the beginning of an association and friendship with Dave Brubeck that has lasted to this day. Dave and his wife, Iola, personified elegance and grace.

\*     \*     \*

Storyville's regular patronage included people from all walks of life. One of them was a man of the cloth. Father Norman O'Connor, a Paulist priest at the Boston University's Newman Club, had gone to school in Detroit with my brother's brother-in-law. This tenuous connection brought him into the club, and he was soon a regular presence. In those days, it wasn't common for a

Catholic priest to walk into a jazz club; in fact, it sounded like the beginning of a bad joke. But Father O'Connor was a true jazz fan. We became close friends.

Father O'Connor's acquaintance had happy consequences. At his urging, an academic organization called the New England All-College Conference, which was about to convene in Boston under the theme of "Arts in America," bestowed an honorary scroll upon Louis Armstrong. I had hired the Armstrong All Stars for a week-long engagement, and we held a special ceremony for Louis in the club one afternoon. Nat Hentoff emceed the program, which was broadcast on WMEX radio. Coincidentally, this was also the inaugural year of *Down Beat* magazine's Hall of Fame, and Nat announced that Louis had been unanimously chosen as its first inductee. Pops was awash in citations and distinctions as he took the microphone. He expressed his gratitude—and then began to tell a story about "this waitress in this swell restaurant":

> She was so fed up every day with this fella coming in every day—he had to have a hamburger, you know. So she got sick of that, and said, "I'm gonna scratch that off the list next time he come in." So as soon as he come into town, she starts scratching off the menu, and when he sat down, she went right to the table and said, "Good evening sir, I've just scratched what you like."
>
> He said, "That's alright, just wash your hands and give me a hamburger."

Pops's joke totally broke up the dry tone of the event. Suddenly, people were hooting and screaming with laughter; it was as if all their inhibitions had been lifted. Ironically, the only speaker who could get the room to settle down was not physically present.

The actress Tallulah Bankhead had agreed to participate in the event, but could not leave Hollywood at the last minute due to studio obligations. So she sent a recording of her speech instead. We had set up a phonograph onstage, and when the time came, we darkened the room and fixed a spotlight on the machine. Her disembodied voice wafted over the speakers and through the room. At one point, she quoted from an article that she had written for a recent issue of *Ebony* magazine:

> The genius of Armstrong, like that of Charlie Chaplin, is truly international. It reaches across land frontiers and oceans, obliterating man-made barriers of color and class. I believe in one world; so does Louis. I believe in one God; so does Louis. To me, Louis, like Chaplin . . . is a symbol of that one world. Their art is beyond nationality and language. It is universal in the greatest sense.

At this declaration, everyone stopped snickering and toasted Louis with warm applause. It was a proud moment for Pops.

*    *    *

A regal presence who came to Storyville at this time was the actor John Carradine. His command of language and theater was spellbinding. I learned more about Shakespeare during one meal with him than I had during an entire liberal arts education in college. He radiated dignity even though he was well past his prime, and had recently spent more time doing character acting in B-rate horror films than on the theatrical stage.

John Carradine was also a heavy drinker. This usually had no affect on his performance, but there was one evening that gave everyone a scare. He was onstage, perfectly poised before the microphone, and began a recitation.

"And though I speak with the tongues of angels," he started, his voice a resonant, powerful instrument. Then he paused, mid-sentence, and repeated the line. He stood puzzled for a moment, and uttered the words "excuse me" before falling over like a toppled stone pillar. The room froze; nobody knew whether he was dead or alive. We hurriedly picked him up off the stage, carried him into the kitchen, and stretched his body out over a steel table. I spread cold towels over his forehead. He lay there, virtually comatose, for almost ten excruciating minutes. A Storyville regular who practiced medicine tended to him.

Finally, he began to stir. I was relieved when he opened his eyes and, confused, asked me what had happened.

"John, you fainted onstage."

He shot me a proud glare. "I must have forgotten a line." Within minutes he had returned to the stage, finishing the show.

*    *    *

Around this time, I began to consider a move back to Copley Square. What facilitated a return to our old location was a change of ownership at the Copley Square Hotel. The new owner, Irving Saunders, had contacted me and offered a chance to reopen in our original home. I decided that the time was right.

I kept Storyville operating on Kenmore Square and opened a traditional jazz club in the Copley Square Hotel's old basement room. The modern, bebop sound had become almost *de rigueur* in the world of jazz, and this was my attempt to preserve a venue for traditional jazz. So I now had not one but two jazz clubs running at once, in two separate hotels. Storyville would move to Copley Square after the season was over and I had fulfilled that year's contracts. Meanwhile, I named the new basement club Mahogany Hall (after Lulu White's notorious Storyville-district bordello) and formed a house band called the Mahogany Hall All-Stars. This group featured Vic Dickenson, Doc Cheatham, Al and Buzzy Drootin, and myself. My cousin Jolf Wolfson became the club manager.

If ever there was a labor of love, this was it. There was always an audience for traditional jazz in Boston, yet I had no delusions about Mahogany Hall's potential for generating income. It was, instead, a haven for the music I loved. The All-Stars was a fun assignment; rehearsal was never needed, as we all knew the tunes. However, there were moments when I could have used some preparation. One winter night Vic Dickenson turned to me in the middle of a ballad medley and called: "'June in January'—E-flat." Lots of luck! I had probably last heard that song in 1935, when I was ten years old. Vic was a walking song library.

Vic liked to play the numbers, and had a regular numbers runner to whom he religiously allocated two dollars of his earnings every day. One day I asked him to play a couple of numbers for me. I gave him 602 and 6020; that was Joyce's phone number. The numbers were chosen from the daily handle at some racetrack. The following day I picked up the paper and saw that 6021 had come out; I had won six hundred dollars. Had 6020 come out, I would have won four thousand dollars. Elated that I had won anything at all, I said to Vic: "Hey man, get my money." He came back with $525. Where was the other seventy-five dollars? He had given it as a tip to his numbers runner. I said to him: "Vic, he's your numbers runner, not mine." It made no difference to Vic, who was as loyal as he was stubborn. I don't think he ever hit the numbers himself.

*     *     *

Back at the Hotel Buckminster, modern jazz held sway. In early March 1953, we welcomed Charlie Parker at his Storyville debut.

Bird came to Storyville as a solo. We put together a rhythm section consisting of Bernie Griggs on bass, William "Red" Garland on piano, and Roy Haynes on drums, who, of course, had worked with Bird before; the others were playing with him for the first time. I heard most of their sets during the engagement, and gradually, Bird's musical message reached me.

The countless copycats I had heard in Boston and New York didn't begin to capture his strength and brilliance. His ballad playing was especially revealing. Bird would improvise on the melody and not just the chord changes, which is what won me over. He was never just blowing notes.

I didn't get to know Charlie too personally. Our lifestyles were worlds apart. This was a persistent thread in my relations with musicians; certain players didn't take me into their confidence, because I wasn't a part of their world. Drug users—whether they were musicians or not—had a certain camaraderie, a brotherhood of addiction. Certain musicians had bought into the big lie—the idea that drugs would confer a sort of musical genius. I had no tolerance for this myth, and I steered clear of the narcotic subculture that enshrouded jazz like a toxic cloud. I didn't even want to know about it.

Bird, of course, was the original junkie—the man whose excesses and brilliance had turned on a whole generation of musicians. He was aware of this fact, and often seemed contrite about it. He would pay lip service to the virtues of staying clean. One night I was sitting at the bar in Storyville with a few friends, and conversation drifted to the lost element of professionalism in jazz. The big bands of the 1930s and '40s, someone argued, had been so much more responsible than the bebop groups. Something—a level of pride or decorum—had fallen away.

As we were talking in this manner, I heard a voice from behind: "Yes, you're absolutely right." I looked over my shoulder to see Charlie Parker, who had been walking by, and had overheard part of our conversation.

"Musicians nowadays really have no concern for professionalism," he said, seriously. "Half the time, guys don't even make it to the gig. It's terrible."

Then he walked off. The people I was with just looked at each other. Someone emitted a nervous laugh. Was Bird being earnest, or ironic?

Another story from this engagement illustrates Parker's gift for manipulative charm. He was staying upstairs in one of the Buckminster rooms, and he would hang out at the bar before his sets, often conversing with club patrons. There was a white numbers runner who was a regular at the bar, and he and Charlie struck up a friendly conversation late one afternoon. The bookie offered to buy Bird a drink.

"I'll have one of my regulars," Parker said to the bartender.

They talked for a while; Charlie was personable and quite eloquent. When he finished his whiskey, the guy bought him two more. Finally, Charlie excused himself, thanked his generous patron, and went upstairs to rest awhile before the first set of the night. The bartender brought the bill.

"What the hell is this?" the bookie said when he saw the total. "Twelve drinks? I only bought the man three!"

"Sure," said the bartender, "but he asked for his 'regular.' He orders double-doubles."

Although he was notorious for his habits, Bird never tried to con me. He was elusive, but gave us no problems. And his playing was marvelous.

Bird's first notable appearance in Boston was a success. I made sure to invite Charlie back to the club for our reopening in September.

\* \* \*

The year 1953 heralded a new era for Storyville. I moved the club back to the Copley Square Hotel in the street-level venue that had briefly been known as The Music Room. Now, both Mahogany Hall and Storyville were at the same address. The new Storyville was a beautiful room and could seat as many as four hundred. There were two parts to the room. In addition to our standard banquet-style setup, there was a bar in the back with some steel-framed couches and red foam-rubber cushions; it had a contemporary look.

The new and improved Storyville opened with Charlie Parker in September 1953. This time, I matched Parker with Boston trumpeter Herb Pomeroy, pianist Sir Charles Thompson, and bassist Jimmy Woode. Bird brought Kenny Clarke with him from New York. The band was recorded by John McLellan's WHDH broadcast dated September 22, 1953.

While Bird played upstairs, I held the piano chair with Doc, Vic, and the band in Mahogany Hall. That Sunday afternoon, we had our customary jam session; the Mahogany Hall band came upstairs to Storyville. Bird was happy to welcome the traditional players to the stand to play with him. He even called the tune: the classic "Royal Garden Blues."

With Doc on trumpet, Vic on trombone, Al Drootin on clarinet and Charlie on alto, the tune sounded as it should. Bird played in a highly traditional style. It seemed as if he had stepped out of the bebop persona for a moment. I'll never forget the energy of Bird's solo chorus that seemed to lift the whole song. We turned on the bandstand and gaped; Vic nearly dropped his trombone. Nothing could have prepared us for that power. Bird was reinventing the blues, but without stripping away their essence. And his rhythmic drive was enormous; from my perch behind the piano, I could feel him surging ahead on the homestretch like a thoroughbred horse. "Royal Garden Blues" was the only time I played with Bird, and the experience is etched in my memory.

History was made the next time I booked Charlie Parker for his third Storyville appearance; it was to be a weekend affair, beginning on March 9, 1955. Both of Bird's prior engagements at Storyville had produced remarkable performances and no serious problems, in spite of the fact that Charlie Parker was a less-than-reliable artist. It wasn't unusual for him to blow off a commitment without warning or excuse. So when the first night of Bird's Storyville gig arrived, but with no Bird, I was annoyed. We had a roomful of patrons, a rhythm section, and an absentee attraction. "Well," I thought to myself resignedly, "Bird goofed again."

I was pacing around the club, deciding whether or not to send the crowd home, when somebody came over and told me that Bird was on the phone. I rushed over and put the receiver to my ear. What I heard was a recorded message: "red-winged bobtail spotted this morning on the Ipswich marshes . . ." One of my employees had dialed the Audubon Society as a practical joke.

Bird never did show up that night. The next day, I picked up a newspaper and discovered that Charlie Parker had died in the Baroness Nica De Koenigswarter's Stanhope Hotel apartment. He was thirty-four years old.

I never had the opportunity to present him at Newport and to salute him as the genius that he was. In any case, Bird's excuse for missing his last gig was irrefutable.

*     *     *

As fate would have it, I found myself at the piano during Billie Holiday's third Storyville engagement. She was bringing her own accompanist, the pianist and arranger Carl Drinkard. But Carl got sick on opening night. Rather than canceling the date and sending people home, we decided to go with the next best thing: me. I faked my way through, but I can't say that I impressed Billie very much. Drinkard showed up the following night. WHDH broadcast the Tuesday night set, as usual.

Billie was not in top form during this engagement—in part because of an abscessed tooth that had been bothering her for weeks. One side of her face was swollen. Perhaps this accounts for her slurred articulation on air checks from this date. But it doesn't quite explain the tone of weary resignation that pervaded all of her songs. "Them There Eyes," which in 1951 had possessed a bright, swinging ebullience, now seemed flat. The joy in Billie's voice, and the resonance, were nearly gone. It was sad.

*     *     *

After Billie's week-long run, we welcomed Louis Armstrong back to the club. He played Storyville with the All Stars, which in this incarnation included the pianist Marty Napoleon. The band enjoyed a good week in the club, and then hit the road; they were opening the following night in Providence, Rhode Island. As it turned out, they got to Providence and Marty fell ill. They were stuck up there without a piano player. So the guys in the band called Storyville to ask whether I could fill in for the night.

Shelly Manne was opening at Storyville that evening. I usually tried not to miss opening nights in the club, but this was an extenuating circumstance. I left Shelly in good hands and took off for Providence. I must have broken every speed limit during the drive; I got there in just over an hour, on Route 1, making it just in time for the first set. There was no warm-up or rehearsal; thank God I knew most of the tunes. The songs I didn't know, I faked. I don't think Pops was particularly excited by my playing, but at least I didn't mess him up.

*     *     *

I had toyed with the idea of starting a record label for a while. Cecil Steen, a friend of mine, had a company that handled the distribution for a number of smaller labels, including Atlantic, Fantasy, Roost, and Roulette. With Cecil's help, I figured that it wouldn't be too difficult to press a small run of records and distribute them. I could keep production costs to a minimum by recording artists in the club and paying them scale (about forty dollars for a three-hour session) in addition to their performance fee. Sidney Bechet, who was making his third appearance at Storyville, was to be my first attempt at this experiment; he wasn't under contract to another American label, and he was more than happy to participate. So we arranged to tape a few of his sets on the Sunday afternoon of his engagement. I had put together the same group that had worked so well with Bechet the previous year: Vic Dickenson, Claude Hopkins, Jimmy Woode, and Buzzy Drootin.

On the afternoon of October 25, 1953, we set up the recording equipment and prepared for the session. But Claude Hopkins didn't show up—he either slept in or simply forgot about the session. I had an odd sensation of *déjà vu*; was there an epidemic in Boston that only affected piano players?

Without any other suitable replacements available on such short notice, I did the noble thing and performed the pianistic duties myself. Buzzy Drootin would claim, for years afterward, that I had somehow fixed it so that Claude wouldn't show. I can't lay claim to this ingenuity, although the thought of recording with Sidney Bechet was certainly tantalizing enough to drive a man to such measures.

*Jazz at Storyville* was an impressive record, featuring some very good Bechet, and some excellent Dickenson. Few people knew how to play with Bechet like Dickenson, and this record was ample proof.

My piano playing was not too shabby. Even as I listen to the record today, with a musician's self-critical ear, I'm fairly satisfied with my contributions. There was something that propelled my playing to greater heights on that occasion. That something was Bechet himself. Sharing a stage with the man was enough of an adrenaline boost to keep me on my toes, and Sidney raised the stakes by exhorting me, goading me on. During a piano chorus on "Crazy

Rhythm," you can hear Bechet saying: "Go, George!" He does the same thing during my solo on "Lady Be Good"—this time shouting: "One more, George, one more!" The excitement is palpable even on the recording. When a giant such as Bechet implores you to play, you *play*. I handled tempos on that record that I would never touch today.

The man other pianists called "god" was upstairs. While Sidney was playing Mahogany Hall, Art Tatum was working Storyville. During the Sunday afternoon jam session, I asked the two giants to play together. Their collaboration was mind-boggling. People who witnessed it—critic Dan Morgenstern was one of them—still talk about this momentous occasion.

Not long after the Bechet date, I recorded the second of our Storyville LPs; a duet session with Teddi King, whom Cecil Steen and I managed, and Beryl Booker. Teddi King was a twenty-four-year-old singer from Boston who had a lovely tone and impeccable articulation. Charlie Bourgeois and I both admired and liked Teddi, as did many jazz fans in Boston.

Beryl Booker had played piano with Slam Stewart in the late 1940s and with Dinah Washington in the early 1950s. Beryl came out of the Erroll Garner tradition in one respect—she was entirely self-taught and had never learned to read music. She came to Storyville at the helm of her first trio, which consisted of Elaine Leighton on drums and Bonnie Wetzel on bass.

This would be a "live" session, but without the distraction of an audience. It would be after hours. The club was empty except for those involved with the recording. Teddi and Beryl chose the repertoire—all ballads. Their rendition of Thelonious Monk's "'Round Midnight" became the title of a subsequent Storyville LP, which was released in early April of the following year, and *Down Beat* gave it five stars.

Duke Ellington worked Storyville shortly after *'Round Midnight* had been released, and we played the record for him. Duke appreciated the purity of Teddi King's voice, it seemed, as much as we did. But on the final cut of the record, "Prelude to a Kiss," he tilted his head ever so slightly as he listened to his own composition. I don't know whether Duke even heard Teddi's interpretation of the melody; he was too busy scrutinizing Beryl Booker's accompaniment. During the bridge, he looked quizzically at us and said: "What was wrong with the original chords for this song?"

I believe it was during this Storyville engagement that I noticed Duke had a different bass player on the stand every night. When I asked him about it, he told me that he was looking for a new bassist, and auditioning prospective players with the band. My house trio at the time included drummer Roy Haynes and bassist Jimmy Woode, and I suggested that Duke give Jimmy a listen. Jimmy was not only a good bass player, but also highly knowledgeable about Ellington's entire repertoire. Duke put him on the stand for one night, recognized that he fit right in, and gave him the gig.

Woode spent the next five years in the Ellington band. He might have lasted longer, if not for the fact that he was a bit of a con man. It always cost you something to love Jimmy. Duke's first words to me after dismissing him in 1960 were: "George, you've done many things for me over the years, but I want to thank you most for giving me Jimmy Woode." This was dry sarcasm, as only Ellington could deliver. Jimmy, after taking his leave of Duke's orchestra, moved to Europe, where he has enjoyed a fine career. Those of us who know him still love him.

As for my own life as a pianist at this time, it was completely tied up in the club. I was playing with the Mahogany Hall All-Stars on occasion, which was always a good time. Upstairs at Copley Square, I had played the piano (more or less adequately, depending on the situation) with Billie Holiday, Charlie Parker, Louis Armstrong, and Sidney Bechet. I was soon to add another illustrious name to that list: that of the president himself.

This was *Lester Young*, the president of the tenor saxophone.

The bebop era had influenced Lester to work with a number of fine bebop-oriented musicians. But for his Storyville gig, I hired musicians who hearkened from the earlier swing style. I asked Buck Clayton to come up from New York. I corralled a good Boston rhythm section. And, since there was a paucity of piano players in the area who weren't emulating Bud Powell, I took the liberty of putting myself at the piano.

Pres walked into the club in a manner that reminded me of his old tone—he seemed to float in, like a draft, from the street. We shook hands, and he asked me whom I had hired to work with him.

"We have Marquis Foster, a nice drummer from Boston," I told him.

"Oh, that sounds cool, Pres. Who's going to be on bass?"

"I've got a good kid, Stan Wheeler, he keeps good time. And Buck Clayton's coming up from the city."

"Oh, Lady Clayton. Well, that's beautiful, Pres. And who's playing piano?"

"Well," I said, attempting to sound nonchalant. "I thought *I'd* play piano with you, Pres.

He paused. "*You're* going to play piano, Pres?" Lester Young called the boss "Pres." I was the boss.

"I think it will be alright, Pres. I think I know your tunes."

Lester eyed me warily. "Well, if you say so, Pres." I could practically see the wheels turning in his head—he had come into Boston for a gig, and here was the boss of the club on piano. He knew nothing about me. He certainly didn't know whether I could play. Everyone in jazz knew that you had to have paid your dues to be able to play with the president.

At that moment Vic Dickinson happened by, and he stopped to say hello to Lester. Vic was crazy about Lester Young.

"Lady Victoria," Pres said warmly, "so beautiful to see you. How are your feelings?" Pres spoke with the gentle eloquence of a poet; Vic actually blushed at this salutation.

Soon it was a quarter past eight o'clock—time for the first set to begin. Marquis and Stan were ready. Buck Clayton was coming from New York City and had advised me he would arrive by nine o'clock. I approached Lester, who was sitting quietly at a table next to the stage. "Shall we hit it, Pres?"

"Why don't you start, Pres," he suggested, without moving from his seat.

"What tune should we play first?"

"Whatever you're feeling, Pres."

I suggested "Pennies from Heaven."

"That's cool, Pres."

"What key should we do it in, Pres?"

"Your comfort, Pres."

"How about 'C,' like the original?"

"That's fine, Pres."

"Do you want to set the tempo, Pres?"

"Your choice, Pres."

I counted off a tempo.

"Do you want the first chorus, Pres?" I asked.

"No, you have the first helping, Pres."

He was still seated, with his tenor laid out on the table. We started the tune. I played the melody, then took a chorus. I turned to look at Lester.

"Have another helping," he told me.

I went into a second chorus.

"Go again, Pres. Another helping."

One more chorus.

"One more time, Pres."

I began to wonder how long I'd be up there soloing. But as I finished my fourth chorus, Lester finally picked up his horn and took the stage. He looked over at me and gave his assessment before putting the mouthpiece to his lips: "You and me are going to be alright, Pres."

Lester Young made my life right then and there. If I hadn't measured up to his standard, he probably would have left the club that night and headed back for New York. Pres still had some dignity, and he wasn't about to wrap himself up in a bad situation for an entire week.

We had a wonderful run, and I handled the gig without any hint of a struggle. Pres was happy, and I was thrilled. I came to understand Lester's playing and even learned more of his vocabulary, which permeated the repertoire. "Indiana," for example, was one of our staple tunes. When Lester wanted that song at a faster tempo, he called for "Indianapolis." Other lines were less direct. He would say something like: "Let's give Lady Bass a chorus and then follow the Swallow back home." He was the Swallow.

When the band was really swinging, Lester would say: "We *must* get Lady Granz to record our little quintet." Unfortunately, no such effort was ever made. To my knowledge, there are no recordings of my gig with Pres. There is, however, one priceless photograph; a token memento of that unforgettable experience.

\*     \*     \*

By December 1953, we were busy making a few albums for Storyville Records. One of the artists we recorded was Lee Konitz, the alto saxophonist. Like his better-known contemporary, Paul Desmond, Konitz had taken Charlie Parker's innovations and absorbed them into his own sound. He was and is one of the most creative and individualistic of all jazz musicians.

Two days after recording Konitz, we recorded another group—the Bobby Brookmeyer–Al Cohn ensemble. Their set was later released as *Storyville Presents Bob Brookmeyer, featuring Al Cohn.* It was Brookmeyer's first album as a leader.

\*     \*     \*

There were occasional all-star concerts at Symphony Hall; I can remember one such show which featured trumpeter Oran "Hot Lips" Page.

Hot Lips Page was one of the finest of all swing trumpet players, a friend and disciple of Roy Eldridge. Like Eldridge, he was deeply influenced by the style of Armstrong; he also emulated Pops's singing and stage persona (his vocal rendition of "Gee, Baby, Ain't I Good to You?" is one of the most tender jazz recordings I know). Hot Lips had an early rhythm and blues band that recorded a few sides that weren't very good. But when he wasn't thinking commercially, he had a totally pure jazz approach. Every so often Lips would sit in at Eddie Condon's club with musicians like Bud Freeman and Pee Wee Russell. I had the good fortune to hear him on one such occasion. More than anyone I ever heard, he conveyed the genius of Armstrong while retaining his own distinctive voice.

This experience had such a profound impact on me that I recounted it to Page before the Symphony Hall Concert, when I met him backstage. "Man, I hope you play the way you did at Condon's," I said, "and not in your rhythm and blues bag." I can't remember his response. He alternated between both styles that night. I left the concert neither disappointed nor enthralled.

I thought nothing more of Oran Page until a few months later, when I saw him in New York. We were called to the same place by tragedy; Frankie Newton had died, and there was a memorial jam session at the Basin Street nightclub. Every musician who knew Frankie was there. I was saying my hellos when I came across Hot Lips Page. I tapped him on the shoulder: "Hi Lips, how are you doing?"

When he turned around to greet me, Page's smile dissolved into an expression of rage. "You," he scowled. "You're the son of a bitch who caused me to get drunk in Boston that night." This hit me like a ton of bricks. I offered some lame apology and slipped away. Oran Page had demonstrated, with no shortage of passion, the true sensitivity of the jazz musician who, for economic reasons, is forced to bury the soul of his music to make a living, at the insistence of club owners and record producers. Whatever my feelings about the results, I had neither the right nor the license to voice them. This would become an invaluable lesson in my life. It would take another misstep or two before I learned it in full.

\*     \*     \*

A few years operating Storyville had already cleared the way for learning through doing. Little did I know that there would soon be an even greater opportunity for growth. It was at around this time—during a cold Boston winter, as December 1953 gave way to January 1954—that the seeds were sown for what was probably the single most important event of my life. That event was the First American Jazz Festival in Newport, Rhode Island.

\*     \*     \*

My life changed after 1954. The Newport Jazz Festival, in addition to becoming the major public relations vehicle for jazz and making festivals a principal source of employment for jazz musicians, vaulted me into national and international prominence. However, for the next six years, Storyville was still my principal activity and learning tree.

I poured my energies into Storyville's perpetual maintenance: the booking of artists, the managing of nightly affairs. For this effort I received the appreciation of jazz fans from Boston and beyond. Sometimes I even managed to draw a week's pay. In any case, the club was going ahead full steam; the prestige of Newport had added hot coals to an already-burning fire.

But I was continually having financial problems; the artists who could make money were few and far between. Sarah Vaughan, Dave Brubeck, Erroll Garner, and George Shearing. Josh White had a strong following. But there were many wonderful artists who simply could not attract enough of an audience in Boston.

Even Dizzy Gillespie was a financial risk. During his first Storyville engagement, he received payment of eleven hundred dollars for the week, and we finished slightly in the red. Still, Dizzy was an important artist, and such a pleasure to work with, that I soon wanted him back. When I phoned Gillespie's agent a few months later, I was surprised to hear an asking price of *twelve* hundred dollars. The agent knew that we had lost money the first time; why had he raised the price? I protested, but he wouldn't budge. We went back and forth uselessly for several weeks.

I was still in negotiations when I was walking along Broadway one afternoon; I saw Dizzy loitering outside Birdland. I hailed him.

"Hiya, Diz."

He shot me a look. "You're some hell of a guy."

"What's the matter?" I asked, taken aback.

"Man, your brother just bought the Empire State Building, and you're fighting me over a hundred lousy dollars."

"Dizzy," I laughed, "you've got it all wrong." There had just been an item in the newspapers about a real estate mogul and philanthropist who had purchased the landmark skyscraper. I said: "Dizzy, that guy is Laurence Wien: W-I-E-N. My brother Larry spells his name the same way I do, and he doesn't have any more money than I do. If that other guy were my brother, I wouldn't have to fight you over the hundred dollars."

Holding out for a hundred dollars may now seem like unnecessary quibbling. Although that extra hundred dollars probably meant more to Dizzy—

who was responsible for his band's travel costs, payroll, and other expenses—it was also important for the club. We had to take in more money than we shelled out, in order to stay in business. Unfortunately, this model worked much better in theory than in practice, and Storyville seemed to be in a constant, purgatorial state of debt no matter what I did.

*     *     *

In addition to the club, I still kept trying with Storyville Records. This was an uphill struggle. While production costs for a Storyville album were minimal (roughly a thousand dollars), the record industry seemed to be rigged against us, which meant that distributors didn't pay for the records they received on consignment, unless they were hits. What kept us going was the hope that we might catch a Dave Brubeck or a Gerry Mulligan, as the West Coast labels had done.

We released the second volume of Sidney Bechet's performance, and made another LP featuring both the Mahogany Hall All Stars and the Jo Jones Quartet. We also recorded a date featuring Pee Wee Russell in the ranks of the Mahogany Hall band. And in early June 1954—in the midst of feverish preparations for the first Newport Jazz Festival—we had taken two fine saxophonists into the studio for a session that would later become *Serge Chaloff and Boots Mussulli, featuring Russ Freeman.*

Serge Chaloff was the son of my piano teacher, Margaret Chaloff, and was a year ahead of me in Newton High School. I didn't even know about Serge's jazz playing until he joined Tommy Reynolds's band in 1942. He gained celebrity status in the late 1940s as one of the four brothers in Woody Herman's saxophone section. His dominance was so pronounced that he monopolized the baritone saxophone category in *Metronome Magazine* polls from 1949 to 1953.

His mother was an important influence on my life. She taught me how to play the piano and gave me a fluid technique, which I still have. Unfortunately, I didn't learn enough harmony and voicings with her and it is lacking in my playing to this day.

Serge Chaloff became deeply involved in the drug scene of the bebop era. The best album he did for me was *The Fabel of Mabel*, with the title track written by Dick Twardzik. It was an ambitious work, well received by the critics. Twardzik and Serge's drummer Peter Littman joined Chet Baker's Quartet, and both died shortly afterward from drug overdoses. Serge lived a while, but his system had been destroyed by excesses of alcohol and drugs.

In the years since I had studied with her, Margaret Chaloff had become an in-demand piano instructor among jazz musicians and was associated with Berklee College. To some degree, this was odd, since to my knowledge, Mrs. Chaloff knew little about jazz. But many of the jazz piano players in New England studied at least part-time with "Madame Chaloff" (as she would become known). What she had was a personality that endeared her to her students, and an ability to teach pianistic technique that many jazz players lacked.

Mrs. Chaloff was devoted to Serge during the final, tragic years of his life. She asked me to use him at Newport. He was not in good shape. I gave him a forty-minute spot on an afternoon concert. Mrs. Chaloff was there with him. She was upset because she felt I hadn't given him a fair shot at the spotlight. This was a dedication of a mother to her dying son. I lost Margaret Chaloff at that time—somebody I loved dearly, someone who had been very close and influential to me as both a piano teacher and a human being. It was very sad because I could not just drop what I was doing to help her son. I had added him to the festival because she asked. I did what I could, but it wasn't enough. It couldn't be enough, because he was dying. And Mrs. Chaloff could not forgive me. I don't think I ever saw her again.

\*     \*     \*

It was just a week or two after the *Fabel of Mabel* session that the Count Basie band came to Storyville for the first time. Basie had just added the vocalist Joe Williams; together they had a hit song with "Every Day I Have the Blues." The city of Boston was waiting for the band when it rolled into town. What they heard was classic Basie, updated with arrangements by Neal Hefti and band members Ernie Wilkins, Frank Foster, and others. There were some terrific soloists in the band—including Clark Terry, Thad Jones, Frank Foster, Frank Wess, and Joe Newman.

Joe Newman was a talented trumpeter who had adapted Louis Armstrong's sound into an essentially modern vocabulary. Before joining Basie, he had played with the Lionel Hampton band. But Joe had never had his own album as a leader. So while he was in town with Basie, I scheduled a recording session. Joe agreed to get a small group together, from the ranks of the Basie band.

To my surprise, the Count showed up at the session. He played the entire record for Joe, without taking one note of a solo.

A few days later, I got a long-distance phone call from Norman Granz. As Basie's manager—and the head of Verve Records, Basie's label—Norman watched the Count's activities like a hawk. He told me that he had heard about the Joe Newman session, and it was a clear violation of Basie's exclusive contract. He forbade me to release the album.

"Norman," I protested, "I had no idea Basie was coming. Besides, he didn't take any solos."

"I understand that," he replied, "but does the album sound better with him at the piano?"

"I hope it does," I said. Then I used an argument that I figured would reach him: "Norman, come on. You know that there's a tradition of this in the business. Benny Goodman made records under the pseudonym 'Shoeless John Jackson.' And I believe you put out records with Nat King Cole, where he was referred to as 'A. Guy.' So why don't we say that I owe you one? I certainly won't use Basie's name."

Norman agreed. When Storyville released *Joe Newman and the Boys in the Band,* I listed the pianist as "Bill Bailey." In the liner notes I wrote: "In the distance, you can hear a plaintive voice calling: 'Bill Bailey, won't you please come home?'" I never heard any more from Norman about the session.

*　　*　　*

In early February 1955, we brought in a group that came to epitomize jazz refinement: the Modern Jazz Quartet. The MJQ had been formed four years earlier with John Lewis, Milt Jackson, Ray Brown, and Kenny Clarke. A variation of this unit (with Percy Heath on bass and Horace Silver, oddly enough, on piano) had played at the first Newport Jazz Festival. But the group's success was really just beginning. At the time of its first Storyville engagement, the Modern Jazz Quartet was still widely perceived as an emerging group. This week was the start of a lifelong friendship with John Lewis and, later, his wife, Mirjana.

John came upon the jazz scene at a time when some of the most talented people in the history of the music were emerging as the primary force in the musical revolution that became known as "bebop." The condition of the working life of a musician was more than difficult. It presented obstacles that many artists who were literally geniuses could not overcome. Drugs and alcohol were a way of life. John Lewis never succumbed to these destructive crutches that eventually led to incurable sickness. It was inevitable that with his training in classical music, and his knowledge and respect for the era of jazz in which he had become so involved, that he would end up doing his own thing, which, of course, was the MJQ.

While no one can ever diminish the contributions of Milt Jackson, Percy Heath, and Connie Kay who followed Kenny Clarke on drums to the MJQ, John was its heart and soul. It can be said that there would not have been an MJQ without the conception and writing of John Lewis. But, it was more than the music. John had a feeling for style and elegance that was a reflection of his personal life. He wanted jazz and jazz musicians to be treated with the same respect that the world of classical music treated its artists. The MJQ reached this pinnacle. It was not easy to work with the MJQ. The quality of the piano, amplification, hotels and backstage amenities all had to be exactly what the contract called for. The MJQ set new standards for the presentation of jazz that has left its mark to this day. Milt Jackson, of course, was one of the finest of all jazz musicians. With all of John Lewis's contributions, the MJQ might never have achieved its fame and success without the unique talent and sound of Milt Jackson's vibes.

*    *    *

Next came a new quintet led by Max Roach, which featured a young trumpeter who had become the talk of the jazz world. His name was Clifford Brown. Buzz from a tour the previous fall had spread like wildfire. This was their first gig in Boston.

The Clifford Brown–Max Roach Quintet was well received at Storyville. A WHDH aircheck from one of their performances, which has circulated for some time, reveals the group in top form. I heard the quintet every night for a week, but wasn't listening as carefully as I could have. For me, it was just another week in the club, with another bebop group—albeit a very good one. In a way, this was probably how the musicians approached it: as a gig. Boston was another stop on the perpetual tour. The only noteworthy occurrence during the trip, it seems, was Clifford's marriage to LaRue Anderson; they were already wed, but went through another ceremony (their third) in Boston, with LaRue's parish priest.

At any rate, I should have listened more closely. The brilliance—and brevity—of Clifford Brown's career have bestowed a precious aura to every one of his performances. The Storyville engagement of February 1955 may have been just a gig, but it occurred at the height of the trumpeter's powers.

In the 1950s there were hundreds of talented bebop trumpet players following in the directions set by Dizzy Gillespie and Miles Davis. But then, there was Clifford Brown. What music would he have played if he had not met such a tragic end in an automobile accident on the Pennsylvania Turnpike?

*   *   *

One evening, Charlie Bourgeois and I, along with columnist George Frazier, were invited to a fashionable soirée in a lovely apartment in midtown Manhattan. The room was filled with producers and other music-business folk—and equipped with a piano, at which several of the guests took turns. Herb Jeffries, Duke Ellington's esteemed vocalist, was there, and he treated us to a few numbers. The party's host played and sang a little. And after some cajoling, I myself sat down and delivered my rendition of "I'm Gonna Sit Right Down and Write Myself a Letter," with apologies to Fats Waller.

Later, just as I was about to take my leave—I already had my coat on—George Frazier nudged Ahmet Ertegun, the founder of Atlantic Records.

"Ahmet, why don't you record George Wein? He's got Storyville Records and you've got Atlantic. It'll be a good story—one record company records the owner of another record company."

In addition to amassing a pioneering catalogue of rhythm and blues, Atlantic Records loved to record the hip Café Society boîte singers. They had released albums by the likes of Mabel Mercer, Bobby Short, and Sylvia Sims. So Ahmet didn't dismiss Frazier's offhand proposal. The next thing I knew, I had a deal with Atlantic.

It was right around this time that Ahmet and Jerry Wexler were bringing Ahmet's brother Nesuhi into the company. Nesuhi Ertegun was to be Atlantic's jazz producer. He came to New York prepared to roll up his sleeves and devote his energy to ambitious jazz albums. But he discovered that his first two projects had already been assigned. He was to do one album featuring the Modern Jazz Quartet, and one featuring George Wein. I'm sure he scratched his head over the latter contract. How did he get roped into *this* one?

We began recording on an April morning in 1955. I walked into the studio with two horn players in tow—trumpeter Ruby Braff and tenor saxophonist Sammy Margolis. I wanted all the help I could get. Nesuhi forgave me for this presumption as soon as he heard Ruby and Sammy take their choruses. We cut eight sides that day—what would then constitute two-thirds of an LP. We agreed to complete the album at a later date.

Not long afterward, I found myself in the studio again—this time wearing the hat of producer. Storyville Records was recording another Café Society singer, Hugh Shannon—who, coincidentally, had previously recorded for Atlantic. Nesuhi stopped by the studio to listen.

Mr. Shannon played the piano well, had a good voice, and knew just about every song in the book. But he also loved alcohol. His wife came into the studio with a medicine bag full of spirits, and fed him drinks in between takes. He got so plastered during the session that he could barely stand, let alone record an album. So there I was, with a rented studio on my hands and an incapacitated singer. Jo Jones, Bill Pemberton, and Bobby Hackett were all waiting to play.

"Nesuhi," I said, shrugging. "I've got a studio and I've got musicians. Why don't you take over the recording, and I'll go ahead and do a couple of songs." We recorded four more tunes then and there, without any rehearsal. We did "I'm Through with Love," and "Why Try to Change Me Now?"—a Cy Coleman song that I had never sung before. Bobby Hackett played beautifully behind me. We couldn't use his name, because he was under contract with Jackie Gleason. So we called him "Wally Wales." He tried not to sound too much like Bobby Hackett, but he couldn't help it—he still sounded a lot like Bobby Hackett.

*Wein, Women and Song* hit the shelves and hardly sold any records. But everybody had a good time making it. The main thing was that Nesuhi and I became lifelong friends.

A brief sidenote: many years later, in 1972, the year I took the festival to New York City, I was sitting one night at the piano bench in Carnegie Hall during a rehearsal. I was just noodling. Suddenly a fellow came up to me and said: "I've hated you for years." A real nice guy.

I stopped playing and twisted around on the bench. "What did I ever do to you?"

"Remember when you came to a party in New York almost twenty years ago and played the piano and got an album contract out of it? Well, my name is Larry Carr. That was *my* apartment, and *I* set up that party so that Ahmet Ertegun could hear me sing. I wanted an album from Atlantic Records. That party cost me a lot of money—and you came in, sang one song, and stole my record deal!"


Larry Carr happened to be a masterful nightclub singer and pianist. He had an exquisite touch and a remarkable ear for harmony. His was a decent career, and he was well thought of and well liked. He deserved whatever success came his way. As for me, I assured him that my record contract had been serendipity rather than sabotage. (In 2002, Val Azzoli, president of Atlantic Records, generously gave me back the master tapes of *Wein, Women and Song*. Mat Domber of Arbor Records agreed to reissue the album with a few added tunes I had recorded thirty-five years later. I have mailed out more than 300 copies to my friends. How many will it sell this time? Take a guess.)

*   *   *

I had my hands full at Storyville as owner, proprietor, talent booker, and all-around manager. My partnership with Cecil Steen was still solid, although our record company was beginning to seem more and more like a losing proposition.

This assessment was purely from a business standpoint; artistically, Storyville Records was in terrific shape. We had recently recorded a fine album with Vic Dickenson—*Vic's Boston Story*—which included myself at the piano, Buzzy Drootin on drums, and Jimmy Woode and Arvell Shaw alternating on bass. True to form, Vic interspersed well-worn melodies (like "Yesterday" and "In a Sentimental Mood") with a few original songs, and some Tin Pan Alley gems of obscure origin. Vic even sang a vocal on "Willie Mae," sounding remarkably like his own trombone sound.

In fact, Vic Dickenson's biographer has cited it as the best record he ever made. I was moved to tears at Vic's funeral, as I walked into the chapel and heard the background music; *Vic's Boston Story* was the album they had chosen to play.

So Storyville Records was producing some quality product during these years. Our catalogue had expanded significantly, as we had made a live recording at the Boston Arts Festival featuring Vic with Ruby Braff; another Lee Konitz record; an album featuring the vocal duo Jackie Cain and Roy Kral; another Joe Newman small-group session; and a second album featuring Teddi King. In addition, Charlie Bourgeois had produced *Perfume and Rain,* a beautiful solo piano effort by Ellis Larkins. And then there was Rudy Vallee.

I met Rudy Vallee through my press agent, Harry Paul, who had been a songplugger for Vallee as far back as the mid-thirties. During that bygone era, Vallee had been a huge star; a romantic crooner and movie celebrity on par with Bing Crosby. His voice seemed to be on the radio constantly while I was growing up.

But by the mid-1950s, Rudy Vallee had been reduced to playing two-thousand-dollar week-long engagements at hotel venues. At that time, he was king of the has-beens, and had recorded an album of bawdy songs that no major record label would pick up. At Harry Paul's urging, I agreed to put it out. The result was *Rudy Vallee's Drinking Songs,* a rather embarrassing entry in the Storyville catalogue. We tried to create a moral outrage over the off-color humor of the songs, but nobody was interested; we couldn't even get it banned in Boston.

I found Rudy Vallee to be a nice guy, despite his well-deserved reputation for cheapness. Sometime in 1955, after the release of the album, we found ourselves in Paris at the same time. Surprisingly, Rudy asked me out to dinner. He picked a then-famous brasserie—the Café Royale on the Saint-Germain des Prés—where dinner was a prix fixe of twelve francs, including all the wine you could drink.

And we did just that; we drank all the cheap wine we could, and we both got very drunk. When the check arrived, Rudy left the exact amount, along with a pencil that was inscribed with his name. He reached into his pocket and showed me a handful of these customized pencils.

"There's a place in Paris Nord," he slurred, "where you can get a hundred of these for less than twenty-five cents each. I give them out as tips—people would rather have these than money." Then he added: "You know, you should do this too."

"Rudy," I replied, "nobody knows who the hell I am! In my case, I think they'd rather have the money."

We wobbled out of the Café Royale arm in arm, singing "The Whiffen-poof Song," a Yale anthem associated with Rudy's heyday: "We are poor little lambs who have lost our way. . . ." Then Rudy came up with a suggestion.

"Let's go hear some jazz," he said. "Since I paid for dinner, you can pay for drinks at the club."

"That's not fair," I protested. "Every drink at the club will cost eighteen francs, and dinner was only twelve."

He quickly replied: "Alright, we won't go." So we parted ways; I watched him stumble off into the night. That was the last time I saw Rudy Vallee. I returned to my hotel and spent the rest of the night bent over a toilet, sick as a dog.

By this time, Storyville Records was barely surviving. In 1955 the only thing keeping the company afloat was a loan from Louis Lorillard, the patron of the Newport Jazz Festival. So when Cecil Steen and I received an offer to sell the company, we decided to go ahead. We were bought out by the Sylvesters, an old New England family that had a record business; their specialty was recorded classical music, and they wanted to expand into the jazz market. We struck a deal: Cecil and I would collectively keep 20 percent of the company, and the Sylvesters would finance more jazz recordings. This would keep Storyville Records alive and solvent; we used the $30,000 they gave us to pay off our debts.

But we soon discovered that the Sylvesters were not savvy entrepreneurs. After spending a fortune to make yet another recording of Handel's *Messiah*—a work that had been issued countless times before—their enterprise slid into bankruptcy. Cecil and I were asked to give up our percentage, so that the Sylvesters could claim a tax loss. Without thinking, I conceded—thereby giving up the rights to the entire Storyville catalogue.

Many years later, a close friend of mine named Alan Bates, who owned Black Lion Records in London, asked me what had happened to the Storyville masters. He was interested in procuring them and possibly reissuing the albums. I suggested he call the Sylvester family in New Hampshire, and if he made a deal, we could become partners in the reissue.

Alan went to the Sylvesters and paid ten thousand dollars for the masters. I never heard anything about them again. In the years since that transaction, Black Lion Records has repackaged and resold the material. Bates hasn't made much money, but he owns my recording legacy. I would have split the venture with him in a second, but he must have decided that it would be preferable to work alone. My friendship over the years would have been much more valuable to Bates's career than the benefits he received from absconding with my albums.

Although Storyville Records was history, Cecil Steen and I continued to work as partners in management. Our clients included Toshiko Akiyoshi, a young Japanese pianist who had received a scholarship to Berklee College; Teddi King; Jackie Cain and Roy Kral; and Lee Konitz. But I soon discovered that management wasn't my true calling. A manager has to make an artist feel that he or she is the greatest thing since ice cream. If your client doesn't trust that you feel that way, you shouldn't be a manager. My problem was that I couldn't honestly tell my clients that they were "the greatest"—I was already working with the greatest artists as a promoter.

Fortunately, management was a side operation for both of us. I was drawing a week's pay from Storyville, and Cecil was earning a good living from his modest record distribution. The situation soon changed, however, when Cecil's business suddenly took off. It was a time when major entrepreneurs were buying out small record distributors in an effort to establish control of the music industry. Cecil made a deal for hundreds of thousands of dollars, which was a fortune in those days. Because I didn't have anything in writing, his good fortune marked the end of our relationship as partners. I never received a penny from his windfall.

I could have been upset about this turn of events, but it was clear to me that even this negative experience could have a positive effect in the long run. It was a shame that my partnership had to dissolve, but it was also a blessing. As a result of the split, I was broke, but I maintained my independence. This would be my most valuable asset over the years.

\*     \*     \*

The *Alcoa Hour* was a live, hour-long anthology drama series that ran from 1955 to 1957 on NBC. A particular episode, "The Magic Horn," ran in June 1956. It was the story of an elderly trumpet player who was having a problem until he got a magic horn that changed his whole career. Ralph Meeker played the trumpet player; Sal Mineo was the one who brought the magic horn to him.

I was asked by a record executive at RCA–Victor to put together a band for the show, consisting of musicians who could also act. It was also necessary to have two trumpet players ghosting for Ralph Meeker: before and after the transformation. Now, Jimmy McPartland was very happy to be in this show, but he didn't realize that I cast him as the horn player in decline, and I had Ruby Braff playing the parts with the magic horn. Jimmy was a wonderful musician, and a guy I loved very much. But he didn't have the clarity of sound that Ruby had at that point in his career. I don't think anybody paid attention to this except me; I'm sure Jimmy never thought about it in that light.

Bud Freeman had always wanted to be an actor like his brother, and he would have enjoyed being a part of this show. But of all the musicians I suggested to director Norman Felton—Ruby, Jimmy, Bud, Peanuts Hucko, Vic Dickenson, Buzzy Drootin, Milt Hinton, and Ernie Caceres—Bud was the only guy who didn't make the cut. Norman felt that Bud Freeman, a proper, impeccably dressed man with a little mustache, didn't look enough like a jazz musician. The show went on without him. It was one of the better jazz stories on television, because we had real musicians playing and portraying themselves. But I missed Bud.

\*     \*     \*

Around this time, Boston University asked me to deliver a series of visiting lectures on jazz. I responded by offering instead to write and teach an elective course on the history and evolution of the music, insisting that they make jazz a part of the curriculum. They agreed, offering me the position of Instructor in the History and Evolution of Jazz at a fee of $750 a semester.

To prepare for this experience, I immersed myself in every resource available, in an effort to present the most thorough history possible. I studied concepts of pitch, timbre, and the melismatic vocalization of African tribal singing. I examined African rhythms, and the call-and-response patterns that influenced American gospel music. I sought out the relationship between the music of Martinique and its cousin in New Orleans. I can't say that I became a scholar, but I certainly gained a thorough understanding of jazz's origins and development.

I had the advantage of being able to ask esteemed guest speakers, such as Dizzy Gillespie and Duke Ellington, to come in to the class. With two ninety-minute classes a week (for a three-credit course), I had to map out a lesson plan and a strategy, and implement it efficiently. I would never have imagined myself teaching a course at my alma mater, but jazz provided that opportunity. When I was called away for business reasons, Father O'Connor assumed my classroom duties.

My exams were thorough, and strategically designed to weed out slackers. I always left the room during an examination, and we had no proctors. I recall one of my old exam questions: "Who is Frankie Newton?" I had referred to Frankie several times during the semester, so it was clear that the students who had paid attention would know the answer. When the tests came in, there were three identical papers identifying Newton as a ragtime pianist in the tradition of Jelly Roll Morton. These suspiciously like-minded wrong answers are known to all professors. I didn't flunk those kids. I passed them—with D-minuses. I didn't have the heart to have a college student flunk jazz.

At the same time, the *Boston Herald* asked me to author a weekly jazz column in the Sunday paper. As is still typical of the newspaper business, I received very little compensation. In fact, they didn't pay me at all—but they did allow me to write about upcoming attractions at Storyville. The column was, in effect, a forum for my opinions. Some of the columns actually had nothing to do with my own affairs. I took the opportunity to sound off on a number of topics—while trying not to offend the artists who were appearing at the club.

\*     \*     \*

Storyville was still presenting the biggest names in jazz. Many of these artists were familiar to Boston audiences. Brubeck, Shearing, Miles, and Garner. Ella, Sarah, Basie, and Dinah. Duke Ellington. Josh White. Gerry Mulligan and

Bob Brookmeyer came in with a quartet and recorded a live album for Pacific Jazz. There were some first-time performances, too. The Woody Herman and Stan Kenton Orchestras both passed through at around this time. Bud Powell played a week-long engagement with a small combo, although his sicknesses affected the quality of his performance. Jonah Jones made an appearance at the peak of his Capitol Records success.

*   *   *

As usual, there were noteworthy developments in Storyville that didn't have to do with music. I had long been a fan of good comedy, and I made it a point to bring in the occasional stand-up comedian. Some people voiced mild objections to this policy, but it made perfect sense to me; it was an extension of the programming I had seen at the Village Vanguard and Café Society in the 1930s and '40s. There were often affinities between comedy and jazz. Mort Sahl—the West Coast comic with the rumpled appearance, rolled-up newspaper, and hip, improvisational style—was friendly with Paul Desmond. Meanwhile, Professor Irwin Corey took every opportunity to riff on his stage-mates. When he shared a bill with Dakota Staton, the Professor announced her name as if he were a speaker at the Democratic Convention: "North Dakota, South Dakota. . . . "

Of all the comics who passed through Storyville, Corey was my favorite. He was totally insane. I had seen "the World's Foremost Authority" at the Village Vanguard. "Many people think Bacon wrote Shakespeare," he'd say. "Actually, Shakespeare ate Bacon. Which was perfectly all right in those days, because all the bacon and the ham and the pork was kosher. They circumcised the pig. Very little waste, you know."

Shelly Berman offered a more polished approach. He would perch on a stool and calmly spin out deeply neurotic vignettes with practiced erudition. His monologues were little masterpieces of modern paranoia, nuggets of nervous angst hidden under a veneer of decorum.

My comedic choices were personal and idiosyncratic. I presented Myron Cohen, the Jewish dialect comic, despite the fact that his humor appealed to an older generation. I could relate to Cohen's humor. It wasn't the hippest thing around, but it was funny. On the other hand, I never pursued Lenny Bruce, although I could easily have hired him for the club. It wasn't that I had reservations about his controversy. I had seen the iconoclastic young comic in New York, and he just seemed to be floundering. His scathing tirades were seldom funny—a contrast to his earlier records in the mid-fifties, which were brilliant. If he had been performing like that, I would have hired him in an instant. He was too concerned with his image.

I never lost my interest in the world of comedy. Bill Cosby, Carl Reiner, Mel Brooks, Alan King, and Jerry Stiller are my good friends. In 1992, Alan, John Schreiber, and I started the Toyota Comedy Festival. Bill, Carl, Mel, Alan, and Jerry are all jazz fans.

Storyville was a respectable place. There was, however, an underage guest who frequented the club—a determined fifteen-year-old girl by the name of Stephanie Saltman. Stephanie lived a few blocks from Storyville. She came over almost every Sunday afternoon, and would sneak in on Wednesday nights under the pretense of studying at the Boston Public Library, which was right across the street. Mindful of the Blue Laws, we let her in the back door and kept her out of sight. During sets, she hung out in the kitchen, or backstage. She never attempted to get a drink; she was there for the music.

Inspired by Stephanie's example, a few people affiliated with Storyville—notably Father O'Connor, John McLellan, and Charlie Bourgeois—conceived of a way to make live jazz readily accessible to younger fans. Their solution was the Teenage Jazz Club, a group of high school students from all over Boston that convened in the club every Friday after school. Each meeting consisted of a brief jazz performance, often by a group headlining Storyville that week. Naturally Stephanie Saltman became the club's coordinator, and its most enthusiastic member along with writer Dick Sudhalter.

So Storyville was artistically thriving well into the late '50s. Unfortunately, the same couldn't be said for the business. Despite my status as the foremost jazz promoter in Boston, and the producer of the Newport Jazz Festival, there were still members of my extended family who routinely asked my parents: "When is Georgie going to get a real job?" The club was scuffling.

On one occasion when I needed a few thousand dollars that she didn't have, my mother, unbeknownst to me, was calling up relatives to borrow money. None of them would agree to lend her the money; they knew that she would give it to me. Winifred Glynn, an Irish Catholic church lady, had been our housekeeper for many years. She saved most of the salary she earned. She heard my mother making the telephone calls: "Mrs. Wein, stop calling and asking for money. I have two thousand dollars saved up, and I will give it to George." This was an act of human kindness that I never forgot. My relatives could have afforded to lend me the money, but they all had their reasons not to. Winnie Glynn, however, saw my mother making these agonizing calls, and something prompted her intervention. You can never fully understand the depth of feeling in someone's heart.

Although Storyville closed at the end of each spring, I had never given up the idea of a summer club. Many people, regardless of their economic status, maintained a summer residence on Massachusetts's north or south shore. My friend Paul Nossiter owned one such house on Cape Cod; Joyce and I had visited him and his wife there. Meandering around the Cape, I had come to the decision that it would make an ideal spot for a summer Storyville. Paul agreed to become my partner in this endeavor.

We found a place in Harwich, inland on a beautiful pond. It was a deserted restaurant and club that went back to the bootlegging days of the 1920s. We leased the building for very little money and secured an option to buy the land. Paul financed the venture, because I was broke as usual. But we created a nice club, enlarging it so it could handle as many as 300 people. In our inaugural season, the summer of 1957, we only served drinks. We were successful enough for the first year that we decided to keep it going for the next summer.

We opened Storyville in the summer of 1958 with a new policy. Paul Nossiter and I had decided to serve food, thereby competing with the good restaurants on the Cape. I hired a chef and a maître d', and went shopping for steaks in the Boston market.

If ever there was a fish out of water, it was me trying to run a restaurant. All of our friends on Cape Cod came to the grand opening and—due to the lack of kitchen management—waited three hours for their dinners. They never returned. Paul and I kept on with the food policy in the vain hope that it might get better. We finally stopped after a month, when Arnold London, my accountant and business associate, explained to me that the steaks we were charging five dollars for were costing us seven dollars to put on the plate. Our restaurant gambit was a resounding failure.

The music was another story. I had put together a schedule every bit as impressive as the one in Boston: Erroll Garner, Benny Goodman, Louis Armstrong, Duke Ellington, Sarah Vaughan, Ella Fitzgerald. But even with these stars, it was difficult to show a profit. We couldn't charge enough money, and the expense of running a ten-week operation was too much. We did, however, make money with the Kingston Trio. This should have told me something.

We had some good times, though. Benny Goodman and I went out to play golf once; those were my golfing days. Neither of us was a good golfer, but Benny was a little more consistent than I was. We played nine holes, primarily shooting bogeys and double-bogeys; I was in the woods half the time. By the time we reached the ninth tee, we had each won four holes. Benny, who was keeping the scorecard, and was at least four or five strokes ahead, had a look of disbelief on his face when he came to this realization. He was quite distressed. So I made sure that he won the ninth hole; I didn't want him to be depressed for the rest of the engagement.

*     *     *

As 1959 lapsed into 1960, I was devoted simultaneously to the Newport Jazz Festival, the Newport Folk Festival, the Sheraton Festival circuit, a seasonal Storyville club in Cape Cod, the Castle Hill concert series, and a newly minted corporation, PAMA—Production and Management Associates.

The only waning light was that of Storyville. At the end of the 1950s, I faced a tough dilemma. Our clientele was accustomed to Sarah Vaughan, Duke Ellington, Dave Brubeck, and George Shearing—musicians and performers of the highest caliber and commercial appeal. We could no longer afford to pay these artists. Their profile, greatly sharpened by exposure at Newport and the increased popularity of jazz in concert, had transformed them into major attractions. They had moved out of the realm of jazz clubs into the mainstream of American entertainment, commanding a far greater fee than a nightclub like Storyville could provide. I won't say that Newport killed Storyville, because people like Ella Fitzgerald, Louis Armstrong, and Erroll Garner were such talented entertainers that they would have eventually reached that level of success with or without a festival stage. But there's no question that Newport hastened the process. My club, which had served as a training ground, was withering on the vine. I decided to let it fade out. The club's staff moved on to other things; Charlie Bourgeois took to the road as Erroll Garner's tour manager.

Yet Storyville had become such a Boston institution that there were people who refused to let it go. A man named Ralph Snyder attempted to revive the club, with my permission, at the Hotel Bradford. But Mr. Snyder, a New

England old-timer, strongly felt that his patrons should adhere to a dress code. I brought an end to this policy when I received word that the legendary Ted Williams had been refused entry for not wearing a tie.

Without a club in business, I was suddenly no longer tethered to the city of Boston. I began to feel restless; the city of my youth no longer seemed compelling enough. With so many projects on the burner at once, I needed to be where the action was. So it was that Joyce and I, after careful deliberation, uprooted ourselves and headed for New York.

In 1917, Storyville–New Orleans, had been closed by the civil authorities because they were unhappy about having sin relegated to one section of the city. Jazz moved up the river. When Storyville–Boston closed in 1960, it was not because of too much sin, it was because of not enough gin—being sold. So jazz moved south, down the coast to Newport and New York.

# PART TWO

# 5

# *New Thing at Newport*

*To look at the white sails speckling the bay, at the wheeling of
a seagull in the cloudless sky and then the sweep of it over the
sea that, on such sunlit days as this, seems always splashed
with silver—to look at this, and, also, at the sailor joints and
the synagogue alike; to look at Bellevue Avenue, listening to
the stately silence beyond the high hedges where stand the castles that are called cottages—, to look at all this, you would
not think that this town could ever be a torrent of jazz.*

**—George Frazier**

THE WHEELS HAD BEEN SET in motion just six months earlier, on a wintry
evening in 1953. I was tending to my usual business in Storyville at the
Copley Square Hotel when Professor Donald Born of Boston University's English Department walked in. Professor Born was an ardent jazz fan. He visited
the club often.

On this occasion, he was with a handsome redheaded woman who had
been auditing his lectures at BU. She was clothed in stylish New England attire. A pair of horn-rimmed glasses perched on the bridge of her nose.

Elaine Lorillard, as Professor Born introduced her, possessed a charming
and extroverted manner. As the three of us took a booth and ordered drinks,
she began to relate tales of the exclusive resort enclave known as Newport,
Rhode Island—where she and her husband resided.

"Oh, it's terribly boring in the summer," she told us. "There's just nothing
to do." Mrs. Lorillard had helped organize a performance by the New York

Philharmonic at the famed Newport Casino the previous summer. The appearance had not been a success. The distinguished Bellevue Avenue residents underwriting the concert had lost nearly thirty thousand dollars. They had no intention of making the same mistake twice.

Mrs. Lorillard wondered aloud why there couldn't instead be some jazz in Newport to liven up the summer months. "That's why I introduced the two of you," Professor Born explained. "I thought you might come up with something, George."

Presenting jazz at Newport sounded like an interesting idea, but I was wary. I had heard enough late-night business proposals to know that most of them dissipated by morning, when the spell of music and cocktails had waned. Elaine, however, was insistent. She vowed to return in a few days with her husband, to discuss the matter further.

Elaine's husband was Louis Livingston Lorillard—a descendant of Pierre J. Lorillard, the founder of the Lorillard Tobacco Company. This was quite a noble lineage; Pierre Lorillard was not only a tobacco tycoon but also a Newport summer resident and the founder of Tuxedo Park. According to Cleveland Amory, it was within Pierre Lorillard's newspaper obituary that the word "millionaire" had first appeared in print.

Louis Lorillard had not inherited his great-great-grandfather's tobacco fortune; the enterprising Pierre had sold out near the turn of the century. Nevertheless, Louis and Elaine were considerably well off. They were leaders of Newport's formidable "younger set." Louis had a less dynamic presence than his wife, but he conveyed an air of competence. He was a member of most of Bellevue Avenue's exclusive clubs (including the Society of Cincinnatus, for descendants of the officers' staff of George Washington). He was a man who could get things done.

I was impressed by the fact that the Lorillards reappeared at Storyville so promptly. Although they knew little about jazz, they seemed serious about this venture. They invited Charlie Bourgeois, my secretary Terri Turner, and myself to visit Newport. We were to spend a night in their Bellevue Avenue home, "Quatrel" (perhaps named for the four 'L's in Louis Lorillard's name).

The air was cold but clear over Aquidneck Island when we arrived. We turned onto Bellevue Avenue, the main artery that ran through this summer playground of the Gilded Age. The storied mansions of this era flanked both sides of the street. Gothic cottages, Victorian Shingle-style houses, Italianate marble palaces, French chateaux. These "cottages" were stunning. I had seen my share of wealth and society, but nothing could have prepared me for this.

The heyday of the Gilded Age may have faded, but Newport still seemed to glow with its aura.

We rolled up to the high hedges of Quatrel. Louis and Elaine welcomed us warmly. Shortly after they gave us a tour of the distinguished town. In Touro Park, we saw the Old Stone Mill, a mysterious tower whose construction was attributed both to ancient Vikings and to Benedict Arnold. The Hotel Viking, a simple but stately red brick building, sat with quiet pride at the mouth of Bellevue Avenue. Just down the road was Touro Synagogue—the oldest in the country. And, at the intersection of Bellevue Avenue and Memorial Boulevard: the famed Newport Tennis Casino.

Wood-framed in forest green, the casino shut itself off from the traffic on Bellevue Avenue with a protective row of storefronts. We entered through a tunnel-like atrium that opened onto Horseshoe Court, a central croquet field. A latticed porch bordered the court's perimeters. The sun lit everything in varying shades of green.

The Newport Casino dated back to 1880; it was a sporting club for the opulent resort crowd. In all that time, the wooden trellises and Victorian shingles had gone virtually unchanged. The club had welcomed such tennis legends as Bill Tilden and Fred Perry. The first U.S. National Lawn Tennis Championships had been held there in 1881.

Looking out over one of the casino's courts was as disorienting a feeling as walking along the Thames Street waterfront; like stepping back in time. Some of Newport's streets were still cobbled. Much of the turn-of-the-century architecture appeared as it had in the previous century. The entire resort community hearkened back to the proud excesses of a bygone era. It was not a particularly jazzy place.

I left the company of Louis and Elaine Lorillard that winter night with the assurance that I would devise a means of bringing jazz to Newport. None of us knew exactly what such a proposal would entail. I thought at first that it would be appropriate to open a seasonal jazz club there, similar to my summer Storyville endeavors in the Massachusetts resort towns of Gloucester and Magnolia.

Something about the Lorillards' bold enthusiasm, however, led me to widen the scope of my ambition. I began to think about more substantial alternatives. There was, at the time, only one major musical event in New England in the summer—the Tanglewood Festival, a classical music event in Lenox, Massachusetts. A music shed had been built on the festival grounds so that Serge Koussevitsky, the legendary maestro, would have a summer venue in which to display the brilliance of the Boston Symphony Orchestra.

Was it possible to have a similar event at Newport with the backing of Louis Lorillard? Or did they merely want a series of weekly concerts that would alleviate the summer doldrums? I didn't know the answer. I did know a little about the jazz business and event planning because of four years at Storyville.

I also knew New England. Most every jazz fan in the region had been to Storyville at least once. During the summer months, though, they left for the north or south shores. Come summertime, the city of Boston resembled Paris in August. Nothing happened. People left the city for resort towns like, well, like Newport. My conclusion after weighing these various factors: why don't we produce a *jazz* festival?

I didn't even know what a jazz festival would consist of. Nevertheless, I presented a rough outline of my idea to Louis and Elaine. They gave me an enthusiastic green flag. Louis Lorillard instructed his bank to draw up as much as twenty thousand dollars on a line of credit, for the festival budget.

Twenty thousand dollars! I was petrified; I had never before had the responsibility of working with someone else's money. I remember driving at record speed from Boston to Newton, to report the news. It was nearly three in the morning when I pulled up to the house on Ward Street. My parents were both asleep when I barged in and breathlessly told them what had happened. I still wasn't sure whether I could shoulder the responsibility.

My mother, still bleary-eyed, dispensed the invaluable advice that I needed to hear: "George, this is a great opportunity. These people are placing their trust in you, and you can do something with it. You've got to produce something extraordinary."

What was a festival to me? I had no rule book to go by. I knew it had to be something unique, that no jazz fan had ever been exposed to. I remembered my nights in New York City when I had started off in Greenwich Village at 8 P.M., gone to Harlem, and ended up seven hours later at 52nd Street. I could never get enough jazz. I heard Dixieland, big bands, swing, unique singers, and modern jazz. If this is what I loved, then that was what should appeal to any jazz fan. I'm sure that that was what directed my concept of the first Newport Jazz Festival.

The vision of Elaine and Louis Lorillard was rewarded. They had wanted to "do something with jazz" in their community. I took that vague but earnest request and hatched the jazz festival. There is no doubt that the driving force and inspiration behind the festival was Elaine; without her visit to Storyville that winter evening, there would never have been a Newport Jazz Festival. Louis provided the necessary financial support and local influence. My role as producer was manifold. In other words, Elaine and Louis Lorillard were the proud founders of the jazz festival in Newport. I was a cofounder, and its creator.

Louis issued the official go ahead in mid-April and, leaving the entire matter in my hands, he and Elaine left for Capri a week later. They would not return to Newport until late June, just a couple of weeks before the date of the festival. Louis had set up Newport Jazz Festival, Inc.—a nonprofit corporation with a board of directors. He was president, and I was vice president. The board also included Elaine, several of the Lorillards' close advisers—including a lawyer and a banker—and Charlie Bourgeois.

We had the usual highly respected board of advisers, most of whom just lent their names. Others became very involved as the years developed the importance of Newport jazz to the business of jazz.

The use of the Newport Casino had also been Louis Lorillard's doing. It was no small feat, given the protectiveness of its president, James Van Alen. Mr. Van Alen was a mountainous figure in the world of tennis. It was his Van Alen Scoring System, or VASS, which later evolved into the universal method of scoring in use today. Mr. Van Alen—known to his peers as Jimmy—wasn't Irish, but he could have passed for a leprechaun. As if to make up for his diminutive stature, he was always impeccably dressed—in a white linen jacket, doeskin pants, and a "rep tie"—personifying the offhanded elegance of Newport in its most classic sense.

Jimmy Van Alen's generosity with the casino was due in part to the Lorillard pedigree; Pierre Lorillard had served on the organization's founding board. But there was another reason for Mr. Van Alen's lenience for the jazz festival—he fancied himself a performer. His great contribution to the world of entertainment was an annual recitation of "The Night Before Christmas" at Christmas Eve gatherings on Bellevue Avenue. Some years after our first meeting, Mr. Van Alen actually asked me if I would promote him as a performer—his ambition was to deliver the classic holiday poem at Carnegie Hall. I begged out of this obligation as tactfully as I could; I told Mr. Van Alen that I wasn't qualified to do him justice.

Jimmy Van Alen surrendered the Newport Casino for two nights at a nominal rate of $350. We had to set up thousands of folding chairs, number them as reserved seats, build a stage, and try not to step on the toes of the casino staff, whose chief concern was the preservation of the sacred center tennis court at the casino. An MIT-trained architect, Hsio Wen Shih, designed an attractive sheltered stage constructed of thick heavyweight cardboard.

We had to set up a publicity and advertising program on a regional basis, including New York, Connecticut, and Rhode Island, in addition to Boston, with which I was so familiar. One innovation we made has left a lasting impression. We cleared the area at the foot of the stage to create a photography pit, which would become legendary in the jazz world because it generated thousands of photographic images that are still iconic. This sort of media consideration had never touched the realm of jazz presentation before.

Outdoor sound and lighting were also a total mystery in 1954. We needed to project music with high fidelity to an open-air audience in a large field. The equipment available in 1954 was far from adequate, but we made the best of what we could get.

This was to say nothing of the actual booking of talent and organization of the program. No one knew what a jazz festival was about, but agencies were quick to detect a big payoff—despite the festival's nonprofit status. Agents were asking as much money for one or two nights at Newport as they would have for an entire week in a club.

*    *    *

Like a family man with a midlife crisis, the jazz world in the 1950s was heading in several directions at once. Musicians and critics alike were beginning to call for the acceptance of jazz as a legitimate art form. This was not an easy task, given jazz's outmoded image. It was even controversial within the jazz world, which was now steeped in conflict over "traditional" versus "modern." Critics and fervent fans had succeeded in creating a schism between bebop and swing.

I had no intention of steering the festival in any particular stylistic direction. I felt I had a responsibility to present the entire spectrum of jazz—"From 'J' to 'Z'." I believed—as a promoter, a player, and a listener—that there was as much artistic merit in a solo by Wild Bill Davison as there was in a piece by Lennie Tristano. Furthermore, I recognized that all these musicians were in fact a part of the same family.

After I had presented Elaine and Louis Lorillard with the concept of a jazz festival at Newport, they met with John Hammond in New York.

John Hammond had first become aware of me because of an article in *Down Beat* several years before. I had met him in 1951, at a gathering at his home in Wilton, Connecticut. We had also crossed paths during Leonard Bernstein's jazz symposium at Brandeis College.

In his autobiography, John writes: "They [the Lorillards] asked me if I knew George Wein, who ran a small night club in Boston and also played jazz piano around the Boston area. No, but I had heard good things about him. George, it turned out, was the Lorillards' choice to run the show." Although John didn't actually know me well, he knew enough about me to voice his endorsement. John had been the force behind the timeless Columbia sessions with Billie Holiday, Lester Young, and Teddy Wilson. He had been hugely influential in launching the careers of Count Basie and Benny Goodman. He was a worthy legend in the music business, and it was good knowing that I enjoyed his respect.

John was in a state of perpetual hurry. He was a man on the go. He always had a folded-up newspaper in his hand. He never stayed at a meeting to its conclusion.

By contrast, Marshall Stearns, another advisor to the board, was usually the last one to leave a meeting. He was almost the polar opposite of John Hammond; a pure academic. Marshall was a tall man with spectacles and a full head of hair. He was the perfect image of a college professor of the time, right down to the wool jacket with elbow patches. His book *The Story of Jazz* was for many years a definitive textbook; I used it in my course at Boston University.

Together, Marshall and John commanded more knowledge and contacts than I could pretend to possess. Although neither of them was heavily involved in organizing the first festival, I leaned upon their experience. I understood that I couldn't possibly know everything. And so, when I began to plan an afternoon panel discussion titled "The Place of Jazz in American Culture" for the festival, I enlisted the help of Marshall and John. I wanted the panel to reflect the concerns that had preoccupied the jazz community in recent years: jazz-as-an-art-form versus jazz-as-entertainment, and how jazz would fit into American society as a whole. Marshall assembled a panel consisting of himself, musicologist Henry Cowell of the Peabody Institute; Willis James, a folklorist from Spelman College in Atlanta; and Northwestern University's Dr. Alan Merriam. Each of these panelists was an important scholar in his respective field. It was only through the help of Marshall Stearns, who was their equal, that we were able to bring them all together for this occasion. This conference was not recorded, and papers were not formally presented. This is a shame, because such documents would have great historical significance today.

\* \* \*

The line drawn between jazz as an art form and jazz as a form of popular entertainment was nowhere blurrier than in the work of Dizzy Gillespie, whose singular artistry was balanced by a performer's instincts. Dizzy knew the business of entertainment because he had come up through the big band era, when jazz and show business were two parts of a whole. His onetime mentor Cab Calloway was simultaneously a bandleader and one of the big names in popular music.

Dizzy came into Newport at the helm of a quintet with Hank Mobley on tenor. The band played bebop, but also incorporated rhythm and blues. Dizzy was getting flak from critics for his irreverence and onstage antics. This worried me. So, shortly before his set began on Saturday night, I pulled him aside backstage and issued a request.

"Dizzy," I said, "please don't clown out there."

He looked at me as if I was crazy, but didn't say anything. He bounded onto the stage with the band, which wore a uniform of plaid blazers, skinny ties, and Bermuda shorts. Every time Dizzy started to do something funny he wiped the smile off his face because I was standing in the wings. Occasionally he looked in my direction and made a face.

Later I realized the foolishness of what I had done. I had advised an artist—a man whose comic genius was comparable to that of Charlie Chaplin—to stifle his natural performance. Dizzy was gracious enough to heed my request, even though it was highly misguided. Years later, he and I became friends, but he never forgot that encounter. Neither have I. At that moment, I recognized the stupidity of a producer telling a musician what or how to play. I may make suggestions from time to time, about the direction or format of a show, but the art itself is solely the artist's responsibility. I learned that if particular artists don't fit a certain program, I simply shouldn't engage them.

After a program that included Eddie Condon, Lee Wiley, the Modern Jazz Quartet (with Horace Silver shouldering the piano duties of John Lewis, who was on the same program but accompanying Ella Fitzgerald), the Lee Konitz Quartet, the Dizzy Gillespie Quintet, the Oscar Peterson Trio, and the Gerry Mulligan Quartet, we wrapped things up with a massive jam session.

I wanted to show, after presenting so many distinctive approaches to the music, that it was all one community. I knew that they could all play together, even if they weren't too happy about it. But they treated it like a party, and it was. Eddie Condon conducted a rhythm section consisting of Jo Jones, Milt Hinton, Milt Jackson, and Stan Kenton, who took a few choruses on piano. The horn section featured Dizzy, Wild Bill Davison, Lee Konitz, Bobby Hackett, Pee Wee Russell, and Gerry Mulligan. They delivered a momentous version of "I Got Rhythm."

After the show, Louis and Elaine hosted a party at Quartrel for the musicians, critics, and members of Newport's crème de la crème. It was a colorful collision of worlds. The soirée continued well into the morning hours. This was the first of many festival receptions at Newport.

The following night was, for me, the more memorable evening of the First American Jazz Festival. A noteworthy incident occurred before the show had even started: the sky, which had been growing increasingly dark and chalky, began to pour. Louis Lorillard and I stood in the Newport Casino office, which overlooked the sidewalk, and peered through a rain-beaded window. People streamed in through the narrow entrance below.

Louis sighed. "We're going to have to give all the money back."

"Louis," I protested, "we're not giving any money back. The stage is covered, so the musicians will be protected. These people are here for a concert, and we'll give it to them." We went ahead with the concert, establishing what would become an unwavering policy in my promotions. Unless the weather poses actual physical danger, the show goes on.

This "rain or shine" policy had an unexpected result during its inaugural year. On the morning after the festival, the pages of newspapers everywhere were emblazoned with a striking image: a sea of umbrellas gathered in front of the Newport Casino stage shell. The United Press International Wire Service disseminated that memorable image: people braving the elements for the sake of jazz.

One group I assembled was a sextet led by pianist Teddy Wilson, with Bill Harris, Gerry Mulligan, Ruby Braff, Milt Hinton, and Jo Jones. After playing with Ruby for years, I felt that he was almost criminally underrated. And I had an instinct that he and Gerry would hit it off. The combination of traditional and modern jazz musicians in this group was in keeping with my idea of unique programming. This set was, not surprisingly, a success.

The next featured artist was the famously elusive pianist Lennie Tristano, who seldom performed for an audience. His reluctance to perform was well known. But Lee Konitz had assured Lennie that it was a good situation, with the proper presentation and decent pay, and that they would go on before Billie Holiday and Teddy Wilson, whom Lennie respected. And so it was that that first festival included a rare concert appearance by Lennie Tristano.

The subsequent set represented a *raison d'être* for a jazz festival. I had orchestrated a reunion of Billie Holiday with Teddy Wilson, Lester Young, and Buck Clayton. The records they had made together on Columbia were dear to my heart, as they were to many jazz fans. Vic Dickinson, Milt Hinton, and Jo Jones rounded out the group; they had also played with Billie at one time or another. There was an additional element of anticipation surrounding this occasion, because Prez and Billie, who had once been inseparable, hadn't spoken to each other in years.

Billie walked out to the microphone and started singing "Billie's Blues." But Lester Young didn't take the stage. Stan Kenton had announced his name over the PA, and the set had started, but Pres was still standing in the wings next to me. I didn't know what to do. Finally, near the end of the first tune, I just turned to him and asked: "Are you going on, Pres?"

"I guess I'll have to go up there and help the Lady out," he sighed, stepping forward into the stage lights.

I was crudely jolted out of my reverie when I saw Gerry Mulligan go out to join them on stage. What the hell was he doing there? I was furious. I had worked so hard to put together this perfect set, a remembrance of things past, and Gerry was destroying that illusion. Mr. Mulligan always got a kick out of walking onstage unannounced; he did it a number of times during this and many other festivals. Usually, his enthusiasm was highly welcome. But this particular set was sacred; I felt his intrusion to be a sacrilege.

Later I realized that my negative reaction was even more inappropriate than Gerry's perceived misstep. I didn't know it at the time, but I was being hypocritical. I was working to dissolve the boundaries between different styles of jazz, and simultaneously trying to preserve them. At Gerry Mulligan's memorial service a few years ago, I admitted as much: "Gerry, I was mad at you in Newport in 1954, when you went up unannounced to play with Billie and Prez. But I was wrong. You *did* belong up there, and now you're all up in that Valhalla, playing together."

I remember the jam session that followed Billie's set primarily for what had happened backstage. I was running around at the last minute, trying to find a drummer. "Who wants to play drums? Any drummers want to do the jam session?" I was looking around to see who was there: Jeff Morton, Shadow Wilson, Bill Clark. I finally asked Jo Jones to stay on for the session. Then Gene Krupa called me over.

"Hey, I don't know if anyone informed you, but I also happen to be a drummer," he said angrily. "Why didn't you ask me to play the jam session?"

"Gene, you're the big star," I told him. He was closing the entire festival with his trio. His was a marquee name, and I didn't think it would be right to put him onstage before his own set.

"I don't care," he said, quite annoyed. "I play drums. When you need a drummer, you can ask me." He really did feel slighted, as if I doubted his qualifications as a capable musician. I remembered the incident a few years later, during a jam session led by Eddie Condon at the French Lick festival in Indiana. I made sure that Gene was on drums. He was happy to do it.

*     *     *

After the victorious second evening of the festival, when the final bars of the final song had ended and the casino had fallen silent, we began to congratulate ourselves. The crowd—which had totaled nearly 11,000 over the two nights— had exceeded our wildest expectations. The music had been fabulous. There had been some problems—a lack of adequate lodgings in the town and a backlog of traffic—but they were almost completely overshadowed by our success.

One of the spectators bowled over by the festival was Jimmy Van Alen, who had spent much of the past two nights warily eyeing the crowd on his casino lawn. He approached me shortly after the show with the announcement of an impromptu post-festival party at Avalon, his castle on Ocean Drive.

"I'd love to have some of these wonderful musicians over to the house," he said. It sounded fine. "But, ah, Mr. Wein," he added, "please try not to invite too many of the *African* musicians."

I was taken aback. Mr. Van Alen had voiced the mores of American high society in no uncertain terms. In the wake of our concert success, this was an ugly reminder of how deeply ingrained the prejudice was. Even after sitting and enjoying the music all evening, some of the Newport elite could not bear to welcome African-American musicians into their homes.

"Don't worry about a thing, Mr. Van Alen," I said. "I'll take care of it." And I didn't invite a single person. I went to the house myself for a few minutes, simply to put in an appearance. He had thrown a big party, at considerable cost, and there was a mere handful of people in attendance. Butlers stood scattered around the room, balancing trays of scrambled eggs. It was sad. After all the hours we had spent celebrating jazz in Newport, the specter of racial discrimination had not diminished.

There were other, much more encouraging exchanges with Newporters. The following morning, I was standing in front of the casino, where cleanup was underway. A tall gentleman emerged from the mansion next door and approached me.

In a deep Russian accent he asked, "Are you Mr. Wein? Did you produce this festival?" It was Maxim Karolik—opera singer, arts patron, and a very important collector of eighteenth-century American art. Today, he is best known as the namesake patron of the Boston Museum of Fine Arts's "Karolik Wing."

"What happened here is something we mustn't just think about," Mr. Karolik declared. "We must *ponder*." I never forgot that line. Maxim Karolik may not have been an authority on jazz, but he was perceptive enough to know that the past two evenings had been a portent of things to come.

\*     \*     \*

"Newport Rocked by Jazz Festival," proclaimed the front page of the *New York Times* the morning after the festival's close. A *Providence Journal* reporter wrote: "To say the whole affair was a success is a considerable understatement. The first Newport Jazz Festival was a sensation." There were similar reports from *Esquire, Newsweek, Time, Life, Mademoiselle, Our World, Seventeen,* and virtually every major wire service and daily paper. The following month's issue of *Down Beat* proclaimed that the festival had "opened a new era in jazz presentation." Lillian Ross penned a striking and vivid characterization in the *New Yorker* that captured, better than any other portrayal, the apparent incongruity of jazz musicians mixing with the privileged class.

In light of such an enormous positive response to the first festival, the board began to discuss plans for its sequel. The title "First Annual American Jazz Festival"—which I had insisted upon despite the board's misgivings—had been the right choice. There would unquestionably be a second jazz festival.

For its 1954 fete, Newport Jazz Festival, Inc., had earned a scant profit of $142.50, even with an oversold audience. What the books don't show is a producer's salary of five thousand dollars, which I didn't draw, so that we could emerge in the black. Although I certainly needed the money, I understood how important giving my fee back could be for the future of the festival. Louis was very happy about this decision, because it meant the difference between a profit and a loss. And it gave him the opportunity to boast, among the regulars at his various clubs: "Look what I did this year, and it didn't cost me a dime." That sacrifice made me a hero with Louis; we became close friends after that.

\*     \*     \*

Newport Jazz Festival, Inc., faced a new set of challenges as we set out to plan our second festival. The first of these was a decree from the Newport Casino Board prohibiting our use of its grounds. This was an understandable objection; no one argued with the simple fact that the festival crowds were too big for the casino's pristine courts.

As a result of that ruling, Louis Lorillard took an option to purchase Belcourt, a late-nineteenth-century, Moorish-styled castle with some sixty rooms, including a ballroom. The gray, U-shaped building was set back from Bellevue Avenue, on a large lawn with a towering wrought-iron gate. It had been built for Oliver Hazard Perry Belmont, heir to the American Rothschild fortune. In his time, the affluent heir and his outspoken suffragist wife had presided over the mansion and its armories, art galleries, and menagerie. After Mrs. Belmont's death in 1933, the cavernous dwelling had been abandoned.

It was a wreck. By the time Louis purchased Belcourt, it had been some twenty years since anyone had tended to it. Still, with a projected lawn capacity of 8,000 (versus only 5,000 at the casino), it seemed that Belcourt could make a tenable site for the festival.

Whereas the Newport Casino was located at the mouth of Bellevue Avenue, near a shopping district, Belcourt was embedded in the heart of the residential district. This fact ensured that our move would meet with opposition. A coterie of Old Guard Bellevue Avenue residents took up the charge. The festival, as they saw it, was a tumor that was now threatening to spread into their own backyards.

During the first week of June, the antifestival contingent presented its case before the city council and managed to have Belcourt ruled a no-concert zone. At the persistent complaints of Elaine Lorillard, the council agreed to let us use the mansion for afternoon panel discussions and evening receptions.

The festival was only weeks away, and we had neither the casino nor Belcourt for our use. Undaunted, the festival board made an arrangement with the city to use Freebody Park, a large municipal playground literally behind the casino. Freebody Park didn't have the cachet of the Newport Casino, but it was only a block away from Bellevue Avenue; close enough for jazz.

I was totally immersed in the planning of our event. In three evenings we presented a true smorgasbord of jazz. In addition to contemporary groups like the Lee Konitz Quartet and the Modern Jazz Quartet (this time with John Lewis at the piano), the program included traditional musicians like Bobby Hackett and Roy Eldridge. Four masters of the tenor saxophone—Coleman Hawkins, Lester Young, Ben Webster, and Bud Freeman—each took the stage. Louis Armstrong agreed to close out the opening night. There were two big bands—Woody Herman's Third Herd and Count Basie's Orchestra—and pianists Erroll Garner, Marian McPartland, and Billy Taylor. I booked Dave Brubeck's quartet, and a quintet fronted by both J. J. Johnson and Kai Winding. The cool school was well represented by Chet Baker's Quartet as well as Bob Brookmeyer and Al Cohn. The more fiery side of bop took the shape of the Clifford Brown–Max Roach Quintet. As for vocalists: I asked Dinah Washington and Teddi King to appear. Joe Williams and Joe Turner sang as guest artists with other groups.

Meanwhile, Madison Avenue had taken note of the unholy alliance between jazz and Newport. For a hot minute, jazz was hip and cutting-edge. Our program book for the second festival featured a series of jazz portraits by Vogue's maverick fashion photographer Richard Avedon (including an uncharacteristically stern impression of yours truly). There was a "Jazz Sketchbook" by Rene Bouché. There were also essays by Duke Ellington ("The Future of Jazz"), Nat Hentoff ("Variations on the Theme of a Jazz Festival"), Marshall Stearns ("Jazz

Is America"), and our own Charles Bourgeois ("What Time Is the Next Floor Show?")—a frustrated article inspired by personal experience answering the phones at Storyville.

As July 15 approached, we mobilized our forces and made our preparations. Willis Conover, who was the "voice" of the Voice of America, had accepted my invitation to join the festival board. This was important since it was arranged to have the Voice of America broadcast the entire festival overseas.

An article from the *Newport Daily News* on the morning of the festival touted our new arrangement for outdoor sound:

> More than 40 direct-driver loudspeakers will be used in the high-fidelity system. They will be driven by six 70-watt laboratory amplifiers, giving a total 420 watts of audio output. The speakers are all banked on top of the upward-sloping shell roof. Engineers tested the system last night in a 25-mile per hour wind and got a uniform 80-decibel reading even in the most distant parts of the arena.

It's funny to read this description in retrospect, since the sound that year was a catastrophe. But there was nothing funny about it at the time; it almost ruined the festival.

The festival found me running around like the proverbial chicken without a head. I was responsible for everything that happened. I stood in the wings ensuring that artists got on and off stage according to our time schedule. I walked around the entire outer perimeter of the field to check for sound problems and continually checked with our engineer. I was constantly involved with press and photographers. The artists looked to me for their paychecks. I also had to be available to Mr. Lorillard, if he was concerned about something. Because of the festival, I had become even more steeped in the role of The Man. John Hammond later commented on these demands in his autobiography: "George Wein tried to serve as a talent booker, producer, stage manager, artist rep and occasional pianist, and it became more than any one impresario could handle." John was absolutely right. Except I had no choice. I didn't have an experienced team. There was no cadre of people who had done these things, and we didn't have the time to form one. We were writing the book as we went along.

\*     \*     \*

I learned one valuable lesson from the 1955 festival. Because my earning capacity in Storyville and Newport was very meager, I was always looking at other facets of the entertainment industry. Managing artists and having Storyville Records became part of my business interests. Teddi King was a talented singer whom Cecil Steen and I both managed and recorded. She had won the Best New Artist award from *Down Beat* so I felt justified in putting her on the festival. But when the infernal sound system destroyed her performance and we put her on for a second appearance, I realized that this was a conflict of interest and it was not long before I gave up management of artists. After all, what good would I be as a manager if I could not put artists on my festivals?

I don't remember much of the closing set on Saturday night, but it was a jam session in which Max Roach insists that I also took part. A few years ago I had dinner with Max and I asked him to refresh my memory as to whether Clifford Brown had ever appeared at Newport. He told me: "Clifford not only played there—you played with him!"

The final night of the 1955 festival started with the elegant fugues of the Modern Jazz Quartet and ended with the swinging powerhouse known as the Count Basie Orchestra. In between were some fine moments, including Basie's reunion with Lester Young in a quintet that also included Ruby Braff, Eddie Jones, Jo Jones, and, on three tunes, a larger-than-life Jimmy Rushing. Brubeck reappeared with his quartet. Ben Webster and Bud Shank shared a stage with Bobby Hackett and Peanuts Hucko, Kai Winding, and J. J. Johnson.

The historic moment of the 1955 festival was the emergence of Miles Davis as a jazz icon whose fame would eclipse that of his bebop peers. We discuss this in detail in a later chapter.

\*     \*     \*

*In 1954 when we started out we got a lot more than we bargained for. We were rank amateurs—I think I can speak freely for most of us. . . . There is still plenty of room for improvement. It may take twenty years to run this festival smoothly.*

**–Louis Lorillard**

Media response to the festival's second year was almost universally positive. "America's jazz aficionados have a new mecca," proclaimed *Ebony* magazine. The *New York Times* cited our total audience of over 27,000 as a sign that jazz had "come of age," and commented with some mild surprise on the civility of our audience, which was "nearly as well behaved as a Town Hall audience listening carefully to Bach's 'Art of Fugue.'" The *Reporter* compared the atmosphere of Newport to that of Tanglewood and Salzburg.

Without any full-time jazz reviewers on staff, the *New York Times* had asked the esteemed opera critic Harold Schonberg, who happened to be in Newport at that time, to cover the festival. Schonberg was not terribly familiar with jazz, but he was intimate with the high-society atmosphere of Newport. He came to the festival and penned a piece that was largely favorable. It did, however, include this sour note:

> A pianist like Erroll Garner has as his stock in trade descending double thirds—not too fast and not too clean—with which he gets involved in vague impressionist ramblings of a Cyril Scott nature. It's not good music—or good piano playing, for that matter—and it certainly isn't jazz.

Mr. Schonberg may as well have committed blasphemy. How could anyone claim that Erroll Garner's music "wasn't jazz"? Erroll Garner was the *epitome* of jazz! The ink had barely dried on the newspapers when Martha Glaser, Garner's manager, organized a letter-writing campaign. The protest was so successful that the editors of the *Times* not only apologized; they hired John S. Wilson as the first full-time jazz critic on any major U.S. metropolitan newspaper. This set a crucial precedent for jazz coverage everywhere, and it was a direct result of Newport.

Race relations was an important issue in Newport, as it would have been in any American town of that time period. There were scattered but very real incidents of racial prejudice in Newport come festival time—some African-American fans had a hard time securing hotel and restaurant reservations. During the first and second festivals verbal insinuations, thinly disguised slurs, epithets, and insults had occurred. Given the Gilded Age aristocracy and heavy naval presence, Newport in the mid-1950s could be as tough for blacks as a Southern town.

During the course of the board discussion, several members had made the strong recommendation that the festival should leave Newport for less "insular" environs; Bridgeport, Princeton, Providence, and Randall's Island were each suggested.

One of the most vocal supporters of this idea was Alan Morrison, the editor of *Ebony* magazine and a member of our board of advisers. Alan felt that it would be pointless to confront racism directly in Newport. "I think [the festival] should be moved," he said. "[Racism] is an important reason—not the only reason. There have been arguments raised here against moving because of the universality of the prejudice. We know there is prejudice everywhere in the United States to a lesser or greater degree. But in a city like New York a Negro has a greater leeway in which to move and operate."

I was not convinced by this argument. Instead of recognizing discrimination in Newport as a reason to pack up and leave town, I saw it as problem to be corrected. John Hammond felt the same way. I iterated this position to Alan and the rest of the board. A transcription from the meeting, excerpted here, reveals how I felt at the time. It is, incidentally, how I still feel today.

GEORGE WEIN: If we decide to hold [the festival] in Newport I believe there is something we should do and something that could be done to solve the problem of racial prejudice. We can do it a little bit more quickly in Newport than it could be done in the entire country. Nobody has ever taken a stand editorially in the newspaper in Newport on the color question. Nobody has ever been made to feel ashamed of these different innkeepers and these housekeepers that they are being un-American by not having Negroes. This has never been done. I feel that this *can* be done. The first year the Viking Hotel showed prejudice. In the second year the Viking Hotel did not show prejudice. It is just a matter of hitting them over the head with it.

JOHN [Hammond]: That's right.

ALAN [Morrison]: I don't think that should be the function of the festival.

GEORGE: I think that should be the function of life. We are doing it by law in the south. What is the difference?

Several years after this meeting, the city elected Paul Gaines, an African American, as its mayor.

We did look into several alternative festival sites, but the fact remained that Newport was the true home of the Newport Jazz Festival. Louis Lorillard was still at the helm of the foundation. There was still considerable cachet surrounding the link between jazz and the *haute* enclave of American aristocracy. When Marshall Stearns rhetorically asked the committee what advantages Newport had as a site, John Hammond responded:

Could I tell you? You have the advantage of having had two festivals there which have had unprecedented publicity. It has done most for jazz as an art. Because of the Newport Jazz Festival, Louis Armstrong gets on the front page of the *New York Times*. . . I think if we had tried to have this festival anyplace else we would find that 80 percent of our publicity value from the past and our goodwill would be dissipated. This would be just another festival. It wouldn't be the Newport Jazz Festival. My feeling is that these two words are almost indivisible—festival and Newport. As far as the world acceptance of jazz is concerned, I think many of us who are on this advisory committee have been fighting for jazz for a long time. We have no particular love for Newport—I less than almost anybody here with family, relatives, and forbears all coming from Newport. It is a kind of society and a kind of life—everything I abhor. Yet in one sense of the word we have brought democracy to Newport, which was the last place in the world where it could have been expected to be found in America.

The festival would remain in Newport for all of these reasons—as well as the simple fact that Louis and Elaine Lorillard were our sponsors, and Newport happened to be their home. The Lorillards were the first of the so-called bluebloods to invest in jazz as an American art form. There had been some scattered support before—socialites occasionally hired musicians for private parties—but never had jazz and the upper crust enjoyed a working partnership like the Newport Jazz Festival, Inc. Jazz would come to depend heavily on such support; imagine the Jazz at Lincoln Center Program without its list of private donors. In this way, Louis and Elaine Lorillard have never received the credit they deserved; they were way ahead of their time.

\*     \*     \*

Opening night of the 1956 Newport Jazz Festival was best summarized by a garrulous Eddie Condon, who called it "the first jazz concert ever done under water." The rain had been falling in torrents without a pause since midmorning. At noon Louis Lorillard, now accustomed to the policy we had established the first year, made a public declaration that resembled a battle cry: "Rain or shine, typhoon or hurricane, the show goes on!"

Count Basie's Orchestra, which had closed the previous year's festivities, opened the undersea concert with a pair of anthems: "The Star-Spangled Banner," and "Jumpin' at the Woodside." We had arranged for this fanfare to lead into a brief introduction by Rhode Island's eighty-eight-year-old Senator Theodore Francis Green.

I stood on the wings of the stage while the band played, and surveyed Freebody Park. It was a mess out there. The field had become a sort of marsh. Wind was churning the rain around like a spin cycle. We still had a covered stage, but the wings and backstage area were exposed. Beside me, Senator Green upturned the collar of his raincoat in a futile attempt to keep from getting soaked; he looked like a basset hound. I was worried about the health of this elderly statesman, so I looked around for something with which to shield him from the elements. I soon spotted an umbrella, in the hands of Basie's valet—a young African-American kid standing at the edge of the stage. I approached him and asked if he could please hold the umbrella over the senator.

"I'm sorry," he said. "This is Count Basie's umbrella." It was only after some cajoling that the young man agreed to hold the umbrella for Senator Green until Basie came off the stage. This valet apparently knew all about pulling rank. He strongly believed that a Senator—no matter how distinguished or well advanced in years—should always defer to a Count.

*　　*　　*

Nineteen fifty-six was the Newport debut of the Duke Ellington Orchestra.

I had struck an agreement with Irving Townsend, Columbia Records's A&R man, earlier in the year. It would be good publicity to have some recordings from Newport. Our arrangement seemed like a good deal: for each artist recorded, the record company was to pay us an amount equal to that artist's performance fee. As it turned out, it was a terrible deal, because the record company got exclusive rights and all of the royalites. Columbia recorded the equivalent of four LPs during the 1956 festival: *Louis Armstrong & Eddie Condon at Newport* (CL 931); *Dave Brubeck & J. J. Johnson-Kai Winding at Newport* (CL 932); *Duke Ellington & The Buck Clayton All-Stars at Newport,* two vols. (CL 933); and *Ellington at Newport* (CL 934).

History, aided by this last LP, has rendered Newport '56 practically synonymous with Ellington. Like Miles Davis before him, Duke came to the festival in the midst of a discouraging critical and commercial slump. The band had not been faring well in recent years. Duke didn't even have a record deal at the time; he and Irving Townsend casually discussed the terms of a contract in a tent backstage. It was this festival appearance that launched the next highly successful phase of Ellington's career. Duke's victory, however, was uncalculated. He had not, as some reports have it, deliberately chosen Newport as the platform for his comeback.

On the opening night of the festival, Thursday, after we had changed out of our sopping clothes, everyone joined the Lorillards for a kickoff party at Quartrel. Louis and Elaine once again served the traditional Newport dinner party fare: scrambled eggs and champagne. At about two o'clock in the morning, there was a phone call for me. It was Duke. He asked me how things were going at the festival.

"Everything's fine," I replied. "What are you planning for your show on Saturday?"

"Oh, nothing special," he said casually. "A medley, and a couple of other things."

"Edward," I admonished gravely, "here I am, working my fingers to the bone to perpetuate the genius that is Ellington—and I'm not getting any co-operation from you whatsoever. You'd better come in here swinging."

Duke was comfortable enough with me to endure this sort of reprimand. I suspect that he considered Newport as just another gig, and he was prepared to treat it that way. But I was keenly aware of the need for new material and a strong showing by the band. Duke assumed that people wanted to hear "Mood Indigo" and "Sophisticated Lady"—hence their place in the medley. And, while a large portion of any audience probably would be happy with such a performance, an important minority wanted to hear new material. This minority included Duke's most loyal fans. It also included all of the critics who were poised to tear up any artist who appeared to be performing by rote. It would be disastrous if Duke and his men took the Newport stage and sleepwalked their way through the old familiar book.

I had commissioned or requested new works from a number of groups that year. The Charles Mingus Sextet had debuted two songs—"Tonight at Noon" and "Tourist in Manhattan"—on Thursday night. J.J. Johnson had composed a piece that would premiere on Friday night as "NPT." Teddy Charles was to play four new compositions on Saturday afternoon. Duke had promised something as well. He and Billy Strayhorn delivered with a three-part suite so hastily assembled that, as Duke announced: "We haven't even had time to type it yet."

The final concert of the 1956 festival began and ended with Ellington. The band took the stage promptly at 8:30, christening the affair with "The Star-Spangled Banner" before moving on to old favorites "Black and Tan Fantasy" and "Tea for Two." The set was then cut short; the band would not again take the stage until the last set. I had planned the evening in this fashion; I would never have opened a show with Ellington, unless it was a brief introduction. The first few songs were to be a taste of things to come, and the band was to come back to close the evening. This was the way I had programmed the show a few nights earlier, with Count Basie. And so the Ellington band whetted the crowd's appetite, then surrendered the stage to the Bud Shank Quartet, the Jo Jones Trio, Jimmy Giuffre, Anita O'Day, the Friedrich Gulda Septet, and the Chico Hamilton band.

For more than forty years, the only public document of the Ellington set was Columbia Records's *Ellington at Newport* (CL 934)—Duke's all-time best-selling album. And for all that time, overdubbed crowd noise and spliced-in Newport ambience masked the fact that over half of the album was recorded in the studio on July 9, the Monday after the festival. This included the entirety of "The Newport Suite."

Fortunately, the LP did include the now legendary live performance of Ellington at Newport in 1956: a medley of "Diminuendo in Blue" and "Crescendo in Blue," charts #107 and #108 in the Ellington book. More specifically, the climax was a twenty-seven chorus tenor solo interlude by Paul Gonsalves, linking the two tunes. This was the performance that put the Ellington band back on the map.

Most accounts have it that "Diminuendo" was a surprise call by Duke. One story has Duke assembling the band backstage and suggesting the number, and the band looking around at each other in bewilderment. Then Paul Gonsalves asks, "That's the one where I blow?" Duke answers, "Yes, and don't stop until I tell you." If this scene is to be believed, we might also consider Gonsalves's recollection, as reported by Phil Schaap, that he first played the "Diminuendo" interlude to an empty house at Birdland in 1951. Paul claimed that Duke promised to feature him on the tune again sometime, in front of a much larger crowd.

Whatever the case, the consensus has it that "Diminuendo and Crescendo in Blue" was a surprise to the band as well as the fans. It was to be the show-closer. Duke likely placed it in that spot in lieu of the *Newport Suite*, which had been recorded the day before in New York, but was still rough around the edges. I like to think that the decision could have been a direct response to my earlier admonition.

Duke kicked off the tune with three confident piano choruses. I was standing on the side of the stage during the performance, along with many of the musicians who wanted a better view. Jo Jones was sitting back there, egging Sam Woodyard on. The band barreled through the arrangement and the first movement reached its climax. Then Gonsalves took center stage.

Paul Gonsalves had been with Duke's band since autumn of 1950. He had stepped into the formidable shadow of his hero—Ellington's last great tenor, Ben Webster. Paul was in fact a devotee of Webster. But he had paid his own dues as well, working with Basie and Gillespie in the 1940s. He was a moving ballad player. In fact, it was for this talent that Paul was known—before his Newport appearance associated him with hard-blowing blues. His ballad playing reflected a bit of his personality: He was a diffident person, quite the introvert. He was also something of a lost soul. It was possibly only within the structured, organic setting of Ellington's band that Paul could achieve greatness.

At the proper moment, Gonsalves dug in with his tenor and started blowing. Somewhere around the seventh chorus, it happened. A young blonde woman in a stylish black dress sprung up out of her box seat and began to dance. She had caught the spirit, and everyone took notice—Duke included. In a few moments, that exuberant feeling had spread throughout the crowd. People surged forward, leaving their seats and jitterbugging wildly in the aisles. Hundreds of them got up and stood on their chairs; others pressed forward toward the stage. Sam Woodyard and Jimmy Woode kept driving the beat mercilessly. The power of that beat, and the ferocity of Paul's solo, is what stirred the crowd to those heights. Duke himself was totally caught up in the moment. The audience was swelling up like a dangerous high tide.

By the time Cat Anderson hit the final blast of "Crescendo," the sea of bobbing heads had whipped itself into a squall. The tune ended and the applause and cheering was immense—stronger, louder, and more massive than anything ever heard at a jazz concert before. I was concerned with the crowd, as was the festival security. Although several thousand fans had left the grounds earlier in the evening, there were still 7,000 people screaming for more music. Well aware of the situation, Duke wisely followed the powerhouse blues with something more precious and low-key.

"I'm sure if you've heard of the saxophone," he declared, "you've heard of Johnny Hodges." Hodges, who had rejoined the band in the fall of '55, was still one of Duke's most beloved sidemen. Hodges played "I Got It Bad and That Ain't Good," and the crowd relaxed. Then the band did "Jeep's Blues," once again with Hodges.

Seeing an opportunity to cut things short, I waved to Duke to stop the show and to get off the stage. But to my chagrin, he grabbed the microphone and reassured the crowd: "Oh, we've got a lot more, we've got a lot more, we've got a lot more." They ate it up. He called "Tulip or Turnip," a vocal feature for Ray Nance. Once Nance got on, there was no going back.

The years had wiped out my memory of the following sequence of events. The reissued concert tapes bring it all back. As "Tulip or Turnip" drew to a close, I ran out and seized the microphone.

"Duke Ellington, Ladies and Gentlemen! Duke Ellington!" The crowd was in a state of uproar. The band was exultant, willing to play all night. Listening to the recording, you can hear me telling Duke: "That's it!" End of story! You can also hear Duke pleading with me: "One more. We can do one more."

"Nope!"

"One more, George. They want one more."

"No, Duke!"

The crowd was demanding more Ellington. Angry boos mixed with cheering. I was without question the most unpopular person around at that moment. They wanted another song.

"No! No! I mean it now, Duke."

His eyes were looking blankly in my direction, as if through me. I could tell he was trying to think of the next tune.

"Let me tell them good night," he pleaded. "Can I tell them good night. . . "

"No more music, Duke. . . "

But I let him approach the microphone for a final adieu, one last "We love you madly" for the masses. They quieted as Duke stepped up and began to speak.

"Thank you very much, Ladies and Gentlemen." The roar began again. Duke continued over the din. "We have a very heavy request—for Sam Woodyard! And 'Skin Deep'!"

Heedless of my fruitless commands, Duke had gone right ahead—calling a *drum feature*! I shouted again, in vain. It was out of control, out of my hands. Woodyard drilled a barrage of syncopated eighth-notes and rolls. The horns came in again, swinging. It's much easier for me to enjoy this now than it was then. My heart was beating in my chest, keeping time with Woodyard's double bass drums. When would it end? Well, after "Skin Deep," the band slipped into something more comfortable: "Mood Indigo." And, over the dulcet sweep of his saxophone section, Duke spoke the final words of Newport '56:"Ladies and Gentlemen, we certainly want to thank you for the way you've inspired us this evening. You're very beautiful, very sweet, and we do love you madly. As we say good night, we want to give you our best wishes, and hope we have this pleasure again next year. Thank you very much."

What prompted Duke to play as much as he did that evening? It was not merely the allure of playing to his most responsive audience—although there's no doubt that this was a major factor. Duke's marathon performance was a masterful exhibition, not only of musicianship but also of his awareness of the power of music. Had the band left the stage after "Diminuendo and Crescendo," or even after "Jeep's Blues," it would have been wrong. The track after "Tulip or Turnip," which contains my argument with Duke, has been listed in the reissued CD as "Riot Prevention." This is a rather colorful exaggeration; jazz fans do not riot. Nevertheless, this was a crowd to be reckoned with, appeased. And so Duke Ellington gave them what they wanted. He gave them more than they could ever hope to absorb. "Skin Deep" was the final of several climaxes that evening, and he knew that eventually things would cool down. Duke taught me a lesson that night, one of many I would learn by his example. This particular lesson would come in handy on several occasions in the unforeseeable future.

It was an historic occasion; it was perhaps one of the first musical "happenings" of its kind. That sort of audience response would become more common in the soon-to-come rock-and-roll era; they have happenings like that all the time. But no one had ever witnessed anything like it in 1956, and no one could have predicted or expected it. It was purely a result of the power of that timeless, swinging music. In retrospect, the length of Gonsalves's tenor solo and its commercial appeal might have had a future influence on the willingness of producers to record lengthy solos by such giants as Sonny Rollins and John Coltrane.

I can't remember what I said to Ellington after the performance. I do recall that he was in a state of euphoria. He had just had the greatest performance of his life, and he probably suspected as well as anyone the impact it would have on his career. Columbia Records made a major record out of *Ellington at Newport.* And although the album was in large part a studio fabrication, the piece "Diminuendo and Crescendo in Blue" was the genuine article. It would have been futile to attempt to recapture that once-in-a-lifetime performance.

The success of the album was due to a simple fact: Duke at Newport was much more than the music. It stood for everything that jazz had been and could be. It was the story of Duke Ellington and the story of Paul Gonsalves. It was the story of the blues, majestic and low-down and utterly real. Duke's image soon graced the cover of *Time* magazine. Like Miles Davis the year before, Ellington had not only ended a long dry spell; he had used the stage at Newport to skyrocket to new heights. The slump was over.

# Interlude 1: Duke


*I was born at the Newport Jazz Festival on July 7th, 1956.*
**—Edward Kennedy Ellington**


DUKE NEVER FORGOT WHAT HAD TAKEN PLACE that night at Freebody Park. For the rest of his life, he not only credited the Newport Festival with his rebirth, but also singled me out as the Festival's impresario and founder. He fashioned lengthy, eloquent introductions for me at countless concerts, a gesture that gave me chills every single time. I had worshipped this man. To have earned his acknowledgment was no small honor.

It was at the Roseland Ballroom on Massachusetts Avenue that I had experienced the Duke Ellington Orchestra for the first time, on a late-January evening in 1940. I was fifteen years old, a sophomore at Newton High, still coming to terms with my jazz infatuation. I had already started leading rehearsals with the Grant Wilson band, and I was listening with rapt attention to every big band record and radio broadcast that crossed my path. Fortunately, the Roseland was lenient with its stag policy, so there was no pressure for me to find a date. I paid the two-dollar entry fee and made my way to the edge of the stage.

I understood the magnitude of the Ellington legend, but had not yet devoted myself to a study of the band's personnel, the individual colors on Duke's palette. Rex Stewart and Cootie Williams were both in the Ellington trumpet section at that time; I was aware of this because of a duet they had had recorded called "Tootin' Through the Roof." Both musicians were crucial facets of the Ellington sound—Cootie with his plunger mute (*a la* Bubber Miley) and Rex with his signature half-valve technique.

157

That night, I learned that Duke liked to answer requests. I confused Cootie with Rex and so I kept asking Duke to feature the chubby guy that was Rex Stewart. I thought it was Cootie. Half the night, Rex stood up and played his heart out and I kept shouting for more Rex. I thought Duke was ignoring my pleas. By the end of that night, Rex must have been worn out.

I had no such problem, however, recognizing Johnny Hodges's alto saxophone. He stood slack before the microphone, the mouthpiece of his horn dangling from his lips like an afterthought. He looked like his mind was in some distant place—anywhere but up on the Roseland stage playing the saxophone. But his sound was unquestionably present in that room. He was playing over a band arrangement of a rather inane pop song called "Whispering Grass"; in his hands, it was a song of love. I was mesmerized by the warmth of his tone, the way he caressed that melody. What might have been maudlin coming from another musician became, under Hodges' spell, an act of purest beauty. Johnny Hodges had opened a part of me that I had never felt before.

I encountered that sensation several times as the years went on. The first time I saw Margot Fonteyn dance Tchaikovsky's Nutcracker Suite in Paris, she seemed to glide above and across the burnished floorboards of the stage as if defying gravity. I sat transfixed.

Another time was when I heard Luciano Pavarotti in *La Boheme* at a jewel of an opera house in Nice, France. This huge Italian tenor sang "Que Gelida Manina"—what cold hands you have—to his dying Mimi with an expressiveness and power that brought me to tears. For some reason or other, Luciano singing opera reminded me of Louis Armstrong playing and singing jazz. I have been a devotee of opera ever since.

The Pavarotti experience instilled in me a desire to learn more about opera. Joyce and I went to see many operas and I became so involved with the music that I wanted to learn to play the well-known arias on the piano. Soon I was attempting, in a pitiful way, to sing. Luciano's manager at that time was Anna Marie Verde, who was a neighbor of ours in New York. We had become quite friendly and on a social evening, she heard me trying to sing Rudolfo's love song to Mimi; she thought it was the funniest thing she had ever heard. She exclaimed, "I want Luciano to hear you sing that." Shortly afterward, there was a party at an East Side brownstone following a Richard Tucker Foundation benefit concert, at which Luciano had been the master of ceremonies; Joyce and I were invited. Anna Marie asked me to play a little cocktail music on a new Hamburg Steinway piano that had been brought into the house that day. I played a few tunes and the next thing I knew, Luciano Pavarotti was standing by my shoulder and Anna Marie was saying, "Now, you have to sing for Luciano." I had had just enough alcohol to allow me to enjoy the moment. As I sang "Que Gelida Manina," just before I stretched to reach the high B-flat in the first part of the song, Luciano said, "Now, Georgio!" Somehow or other, I hit it. "Bravo, Georgio!" The bravo, Georgio that came from Luciano's lips etched itself in my heart and soul. Needless to say, I did not even try to hit the high C, which comes towards the end of the aria. Afterward I said to Luciano, "I have bravoed you till I became hoarse. To have you bravo me, just once, is something I will never forget."

I wouldn't go so far as to say that Pavarotti is the world's greatest tenor. I don't know whether Margot Fonteyn was the ultimate prima ballerina. I'm not even sure that Johnny Hodges was the numero uno of the alto saxophone (although he has always remained my personal favorite). Some artists offer a rare communicative power that transcends talent. Such moments are precious and rare for me, and it was Hodges that first awakened that part of my soul. That indelible experience fueled my inexhaustible search for a musical and personal attachment to Duke Ellington.

\*      \*      \*

It's not at all disrespectful to point out that this first striking experience with the Duke Ellington Orchestra had more to do with his featured soloists than with the man himself. Duke possessed, among many other things, a sharp ear for the individual qualities that each musician brought to his bandstand. He understood how to adjust the sound of the orchestra to the voices of his players. He also knew, conversely, how to get the players to make adjustments; musicians as fiercely individual as Johnny Hodges could sublimate their sound to the greater purpose of the band. Finally, Ellington knew how to take this intricately well-balanced organism and translate it into something that his audiences could comprehend and love.

I was a twenty-seven-year-old neophyte promoter when I first brought Ellington into Storyville. We rang in the New Year (of 1953) with a week-long residency by the Duke Ellington Orchestra. It was the fulfillment of a dream; my love affair with the Ellington band had only grown deeper with time. I was in total awe of this man.

But what I saw as a truly momentous occasion, Duke must have perceived as just another club on the circuit. "George Wein's Storyville" meant little to him, beyond a meager wage and a place in which to set down the band for a week. I could only afford to pay the band four thousand dollars for the typical Boston "eight-day week"—seven nights plus a Sunday matinee. I'm sure that Ellington, after settling his payroll and expenses, lost money.

Duke Ellington loomed so large in my perception of jazz that I expected to see a full house every night. But the band opened to a half-empty room. I was incredulous; I had no idea that Ellington's career had suffered ever since the demise of the ballrooms.

He always had admirers, even during this slump. One night, Frank Sinatra walked in for the late set. He was working at the Latin Quarter across town. Sinatra's career, like Ellington's, was languishing at that time; he had been dropped from Columbia Records. But the motion-picture branch of the Columbia company was kinder; they had just offered him the role of Maggio in a screen adaptation of James Jones's novel *From Here to Eternity*. Frank was excited about the part, but had some reservations; apparently, they weren't offering very much money. He mentioned this grievance while we were sitting in a booth in the club. Pearl Bailey, who was there because her husband, the drummer Louis Bellson, was onstage with Ellington, rendered her opinion: "You should do that movie even if you have to *pay* the studio." I don't know whether Sinatra took this advice to heart, but he did take the role. His portrayal of the wise-cracking soldier would earn him the 1953 Academy Award for Best Supporting Actor—re-invigorating his singing career (with a Capitol Records contract) and kicking off a *new* career, as a movie star.

I connected personally with Duke quickly. He seemed to listen attentively when I talked; he made me feel as if he was interested in everything that I said. On his part, I believe he recognized that I was a legitimate admirer of his music, and not just another nightclub owner. Instinctively, he must have understood that this first engagement at Storyville would not be his last. He could count on returning to the club for a brief but comfortable residence, a much-needed respite from the road.

More than once, I joined him in his room upstairs after the last set, to see if he needed anything. Each time, I encountered the same scene; I would find Duke on the telephone with his collaborator, Billy Strayhorn.

"Well, alright, I've got it through this first part—the second part, we developed that thing. You pick it up there, and then get back to me when you've got that done so we can get into the third movement. . . ."

This was quite a peek behind the curtain. After performing all evening, Duke composed until well into the morning. He kept a small electric piano in his room, and the hotel phone was practically an open line to Strayhorn in New York City. Strays had been with Ellington since 1939, and he knew Duke's musical language so well that they could work together from different cities; he was Ellington's alter ego.

Duke was never irritated by my appearance at his room. "George!" he would say warmly, his features brightening as he glanced up from his manuscript paper. Then: "Look, can you get me some ice cream?"

I would either send someone out or go myself to the all-night drug store and return with a quart of ice cream, which we would share as he took a break from the composing. I learned that Duke was quite adept at writing music in even the most adverse conditions. He had no problem concentrating in my presence.

Duke often mixed business and pleasure. He would reserve several rooms in the hotel, and use each for a different purpose. After the gig, he'd retire to his own room to compose. When he needed a moment of relaxation, he'd step out into the hallway and cross over to another room, to attend to one of several ladies-in-waiting.

*Q: Which of all your tunes is your favorite?*
*A: The next one. The one I'm writing tonight or tomorrow,*
*the new baby is always the favorite.*
**—Duke Ellington, Music Is My Mistress**

Shakespeare said that "the play's the thing." In Duke Ellington's case, the play was secondary to the process. Many of his band's performances were quite perfunctory; they would often play a medley that included "Sophisticated Lady," "Don't Get Around Much Any More," "Flamingo," and most of the other popular compositions. Duke could hardly wait for the evening to get through so he could go back to his room and labor over his current work-in-progress. His mind was always racing ahead.

Every once in a while, during a break in the action, I would sit at Duke's portable electric piano and play a few casual riffs.

"What's that," he would demand, looking up. "What are you playing?"

It wasn't anything, but Duke had been listening. His ears were always open. He listened to any riffs, ideas, or tunes that his musicians brought to him. As a result, collaborations were born; trombonist Juan Tizol supplied "Caravan," and clarinetist Barney Bigard "Mood Indigo." Throughout his career, Duke was drawing on the talents of his men in creative (and perhaps slightly exploitative) ways. Every musician has a melody in his head, and Duke knew how to coax that melody into something, give it a harmonic structure, arrange it for an orchestra, and make it into a good song. It all came from knowing how to listen—the same way he listened to my doodling on the keyboard in those various hotel rooms at the Buckminster and Copley Square hotels. I need not point out, however, that no Ellington standard ever came from my doodling.

\*     \*     \*

Duke's charm extended well beyond the bandstand. I wasn't the only person taken by his eloquence and cultured manner. Women flocked to him like bees to honey, and he took advantage of those opportunities. It was ironic, in fact, that Duke Ellington published his autobiography in 1973 with the title *Music Is My Mistress*, given the man's lifelong preoccupation with the fairer sex. He carefully avoided the mention of any woman in the story of his life.

Ellington was a marvelous sweet-talker; he could ease his way up to a lady and deliver an obvious line with sincerity. Beautiful or quite plain, they were all targets of his charm. He could spot a lady and immediately figure out which of her attributes to compliment. He would walk up to a girl and croon, "Are you this beautiful all the time, or just tonight?" Another favorite was "I'm sure you don't remember me, but I remember you." These lines, which would have been useless to a less formidable figure, were deadly weapons in Duke's arsenal.

At one Storyville press conference, there were quite a few women with eyes for him. One of them was a rather notorious character, a waitress from a restaurant across town whom we all knew as a "band chick." She approached Duke and greeted him with no small amount of flirtatiousness. He watched her walk away.

"Get me that girl's number," he said.

"Edward," I protested, "with all the lovely girls here, why would you want that one?"

"George," he replied with a slight smile, "we must all dig a little distortion every once in a while."

There was so much to learn from this master.

\*     \*     \*

Despite the gift of leadership, Duke Ellington exerted little order over his musicians. He admitted as much himself in his autobiography, when he claimed to "seldom have the urge or fortitude to be a disciplinarian." The band had been together so long that the players were almost nonchalant; they wandered onstage when they got around to it.

When Duke took the stage to begin a set, he would play his call to the bandstand: a series of ascending-descending half-diminished chords. Johnny Hodges showed me the voicings to those chords one night in the club, which is strange, since Hodges was usually one of the last guys to heed this call.

Duke was highly tolerant of his men and their problems, as long as they kept from interfering with the music itself. A perfect example would be the multitalented Ray Nance. Ray was a superb trumpeter, a fine violinist, a unique dancer, and a gifted singer. When Betty Roche left the band, he took over some of her responsibilities as vocalist, singing her "Take the 'A' Train" interpretation in his own inimitable way. And he fit right into Duke's trumpet section, with a style that owed much to Louis Armstrong. But it was on the violin that Ray's artistry was most evident. He played with near-perfect intonation. I never saw him tune the instrument, but his fingers always found their position on the strings, and it seemed as if they just couldn't play out of tune.

Had Ray not struggled so much with drugs and alcohol, he could have been a major star in show business. He was blessed with immeasurable talent, and cursed with the complacency that accompanies addiction. He could never get himself together.

But Duke had a place for him, as he did for every musician in his orchestra. A record like *Ellington Indigos* reinforces my awareness of Duke's influence over his surroundings and his musicians. That album consists primarily of standards, cast in unmistakably Ellingtonian hues. Paul Gonsalves delivers a breathtaking rendition of Cole Porter's "Where or When" that gently alludes to the tone of his predecessor, Ben Webster. Every measure that the ensemble plays behind him seems grounded in the sound of Harry Carney's baritone. Johnny Hodges's alto laments a tearful "Prelude to a Kiss."

The record ends with the Johnny Mercer composition "Autumn Leaves." Ossie Bailey sings the ballad in both French and English, with a gorgeous, plaintive violin chorus by Nance. Duke doesn't play a note on the piano until the last measures of the song, when he injects a taste of Willie "the Lion" Smith. It stands, to my mind, as the definitive treatment of that song.

Listening to the music now, it's easy to forget that guys like Paul Gonsalvez, Sam Woodyard, and Ray Nance were living in other worlds. When they played for Duke, those disparate worlds came together. Duke knew just how to utilize their artistry. At the same time, they probably wouldn't have survived without the guidance, direction, and control that Ellington exerted over their abilities. Many of the artistic contributions in our civilization have been made by people who could barely function within the accepted standards of society. I knew Paul and Ray very well, and loved them both. Would their lives have been any better if they had been sober and straight? I can't answer this question.

On one of our European tours, Paul was sick as usual, and I could see that he wasn't going to get any better. I told Duke that we had to do something or we would lose him. I suggested we send him to a detox or rehabilitation clinic, and that I would be willing to split the cost with Duke. Duke agreed. We were in the airport in Bergen, Norway, waiting to change planes. I went to Paul and told him what we wanted to do.

"Paul, you are going to die if you don't do this."

It was as sad a moment in my life as any I had experienced; when Paul replied he said something like: "George, I couldn't take that." He refused to go. He was dead within the year.

\*     \*     \*

Of course, not every Ellingtonian exhibited such unpredictable behavior. Take baritone saxophonist Harry Carney. Harry was the only member of the Ellington Orchestra with perfect time, in the temporal sense; he was always the first musician on the bandstand. Gonsalves and Hodges could be wandering off somewhere, but Harry was always exactly where he was supposed to be, at the moment that he was supposed to be there. It seems to me that Harry Carney had the same effect on Duke Ellington personally as he did on the bandstand; he was steadfast, providing a sturdy foundation for both the man and the music.

Johnny Hodges was from Cambridge, Massachusetts, and Harry Carney hailed from nearby Roxbury. What has always been a mystery to me is where they both learned how to play the way they did before joining the Maestro. Where was this school of jazz? I had never looked upon greater Boston as a northeastern Kansas City.

Harry owned a Cadillac, and used it to transport Ellington all over the country. They drove from one gig to the next, no matter the distance—a practice necessitated both by finances and by Duke's acute fear of flying.

What many people don't know is that, in addition to being a trusted driver, Harry was Duke's numbers runner. In fact, I would venture to say that he made more money taking his and band members' numbers than he did playing the baritone saxophone. He took bets and phoned them in, Ellington's included. Duke played the numbers nearly every day of his life.

As I spent more time with Duke, I recognized a natural intellect that had less to do with reading books than with living life. He had little time for literature—other than the Bible—busy as he was with the constant task of transcribing and arranging the sounds that filled his head and the world around him.

His primary love was his music, and the only way he could hear that music was to keep the band working. They were on the payroll fifty-two weeks of the year. When they weren't on the road, they were in a recording studio, or a rehearsal hall.

He had an attitude about his public that few musicians shared. No matter what was wrong with a gig—insufficient pay, out-of-tune pianos, inferior sound, bad lighting, inadequate hotel rooms—he never threatened to cancel. If the promoter was a crook, he would just remember that and never work for the guy again. He would tell me: "If I come to a town and people have bought tickets to see me, and that son of a bitch doesn't pay me, I'm still going to play for those people because they came to see me. I owe it to them."

Over time, Ellington's morbid fear of flying subsided, as economics made it impossible to turn down international tours. In 1963, Ellington's agent Joe Glaser had booked the band on a State Department tour, for a fee of roughly thirty-five thousand dollars a week. Duke felt that Glaser had sold him short. He called me to ask whether I would accompany him to a meeting with a State Department representative. I had never done business for Ellington before, aside from hiring him on festivals and in my club. He had no personal manager at the time.

Duke and I found ourselves sitting across a table from a well-dressed government official. I pleaded our case: "Mr. Ellington has to maintain an office while he is away. He has to pay arrangers. He has to guarantee his musicians specific fees while they are abroad, which is more than their usual rate in the States." I mentioned as many things as I could think of to justify a higher pay scale. By the end of the meeting, the fee had jumped from $35,000 to $75,000. Duke was elated.

The success of this exchange gave me the courage to ask Ellington whether I could become his manager. I had always felt that Joe Glaser treated Duke as if he were of secondary importance; Louis Armstrong would always be the star. Glaser and Armstrong were partners, and Glaser had complete control over the trumpeter's career and finances. With Ellington, he was only an agent earning a commission. I felt that Duke would do well to work with another manager, and based on my experience and our friendship, I thought I could fulfill that role.

Duke never directly told me that he didn't want me as a manager. Instead, he began an association with Norman Granz. Duke wanted someone with strong financial backing and solid connections, and Granz had both in abundance. Norman was more of an industry insider than I was, and Duke saw potential for harnessing those assets. There was one more thing: in his book, Duke calls me "one of the nicer guys." He didn't want a "nice guy" for a manager.

But he didn't mind having one as a friend. While we had always been on good terms, it was during this time—the early '60s—that Edward and I developed a relationship independent of our business. Every once in a while he would stop by our house on Central Park West, for dinner or a few drinks.

He once paid us an unannounced social call at around nine in the evening. "It's my birthday," he said. "I wanted to come over and have a drink with you and Jerce." Duke's pronunciation of "Joyce" was a playfully purposeful mistake. Jerce and I poured drinks; Duke had a cola. At this point in his life he had not touched hard liquor for quite a few years.

"Well, it's my birthday, I'm 46 years old," he said when we lifted our glass. Then, with a touch of sadness, he corrected himself: "Turn that around. I'm 64 years old."

We sat and conversed for a little over half an hour. Then Duke rose and asked whether I had a back door to the apartment. Our place was on the corner of the first floor; the entrance was at 50 Central Park West, but our kitchen opened out onto West 65th Street. I let Duke out that way without asking why.

I imagine that Duke was dodging someone. Because his wife Evie drove him everywhere, it's not unlikely that she could have been parked outside in the Cadillac. Truth be told, I didn't even stop to wonder about Duke's possible evasion, or his next destination. Mystique was his way, and this was merely a flickering instant in "the many lives of Duke Ellington."

A similar situation arose a couple of years later, when Joyce and I were awakened by an early-morning phone call. Joyce rolled over to answer the phone and heard a voice: "Hello, Jerce, this is Eddie."

"I don't know an Eddie," she mumbled, half-asleep, before hanging up the receiver.

The phone rang again. "Jerce, this is Duke."

"Oh, Duke," she said, waking up. "It's wonderful to hear your voice. Some damn fool named Eddie just called a minute ago and woke me up—Oh my God, *you're* Eddie!"

Joyce handed me the receiver. I knew the call must be fairly important, since the Ellington band was then on tour in Frankfurt.

"Edward, what compels you to call us from Germany?"

"Well, I'm writing the music for a Broadway show called *Pousse Café*," he told me. "They're rehearsing it in Toronto and they need more music. Tom Whaley is there in a hotel. Will you take a trip to Toronto and have Tom play a few things for you? You choose the music you think fits and bring it to the producers."

Tom Whaley was Ellington's copyist and music librarian. Duke was asking me to meet with him and make some choices for the play. It was an outrageous request. There was no question that the play's producers would balk at my appearance as Ellington's go-between, especially if I came bearing recycled material.

"Edward, I really would do anything for you," I said, "but I'm not ready to die. You're the composer. They're looking for new music for their show. If they see some schmuck coming in with music that Tom Whaley has pulled from your trunk, they'll kill me. I hope you'll forgive me for passing on this one."

There was no question that I was Duke's pupil in matters of music and the art of leading a band. Duke had seen me in action on that front, usually with the Newport All-Stars. We had shared a bill on more than one occasion, on and off the Newport stage. One such evening was a benefit concert at the Village Gate. The All-Stars were scheduled to open for the Ellington band. I thought it would be nice to set the stage for them, so for our last song I called "Take the 'A' Train," Duke's theme.

When we finished, I saw Duke backstage. Without smiling, he said: "What am I going to play, now that you've played that?"

It hadn't occurred to me that he would feel that way. I had intended the tune as a tribute. But in his mind, we had stolen his theme song. Duke's reaction taught me a golden rule about concerts featuring several groups: never tread on the other guy's turf.

This was an attitude forged during the highly competitive heyday of the big bands, and I had witnessed it once before. At Newport in 1968, I asked Duke to play an extra set featuring two great alto saxophonists with the Ellington rhythm section. The altoists were Johnny Hodges and Benny Carter, a legendary bandleader in his own right. I was surprised to see that Duke didn't treat Benny very well on the stand—he featured Johnny on his regular repertoire, then stuck Benny with songs with which he was not necessarily familiar. He also gave Johnny more numbers than Benny. Afterward, I told Duke that he hadn't been very fair to Benny. Duke responded in a manner I never could have imagined, "Never let the other band's guy show up your guy," he said.

It was Duke's toughness, along with his genius, that kept his band going all those years. Pay in the Ellington band, as in all big bands, was far from generous. But Ellington's musicians rarely let economics tarnish the image of their leader. I've worked with a number of Ellington alumni, including Harold Ashby, Clark Terry, Laurence Brown, Louie Bellson, Shorty Baker, Ray Nance,

Norris Turney, and Butter Jackson. With the possible exception of Laurence Brown, these men possessed a love for Duke so real as to be nearly tangible.

Laurence Brown's reservations were personal in nature. When he had first joined the Ellington band, Laurence had been married to one of the most beautiful women in America, the movie actress Freddy Washington. Freddy had preceded Lena Horne as a featured African-American woman in a Hollywood movie; she conveyed a sense of glamour that brought her squarely into Ellingtonian orbit. It's been said that the first of the "sophisticated ladies" was Freddie Washington. Of course, this distinction has been claimed by more than a few ladies.

At one point in the '50s Laurence Brown joined a band led by Johnny Hodges, who had just struck out on his own. But Hodges's group was short-lived; both he and Laurence, like errant housecats, inevitably returned to Duke. In the interim, though, I was asked to form a band to play Easter week at the Embers nightclub in Manhattan. The group I assembled included Shorty Baker on trumpet, Laurence Brown on trombone, Pee Wee Russell on clarinet, Mickey Sheen on drums, and Bill Crow on bass. It was one of the best bands I ever put together. Laurence and Shorty, of course, knew the Ellington harmonies, and the way Pee Wee fitted his notes over theirs was fascinating. Bill Crow later told me that Laurence Brown, after a particularly exhilarating set, exclaimed: "We should keep our band going so I won't have to go back with Duke."

This band, unfortunately, was never recorded, but a few weeks later, we played a concert at the Museum of Modern Art with Tyree Glenn replacing Laurence Brown. Bethlehem Records happily recorded this live performance and it features beautiful work by Pee Wee and Shorty Baker.

In the winter of 1960 I received a call from Associated Booking's Joe Glaser. At the time, Duke was in Paris with Billy Strayhorn writing the soundtrack and score for United Artists' jazz-oriented film *Paris Blues* (in which Louis Armstrong appeared).

Glaser sounded quite irritated over the phone. "I don't know what the hell is going on," was his brusque salutation. I had no idea what he was talking about. He went on: "That crazy nigger Duke Ellington just called me and told me to put the band in the Jazz Gallery—with you as the leader."

I was astonished. Duke Ellington personified all that was elegant, gracious, and beautiful in my world. How his agent could label him with the pejorative N-word was incomprehensible. I hadn't heard the word in years; except when one African American used it, either jokingly or angrily, in reference to another black. I knew Glaser well, and had no delusions about his tactlessness; but I could hardly bring myself to realize what he had just said.

Glaser's crude verbiage was only half the shock. I also couldn't believe that Ellington had recommended me as a surrogate leader of the band. Duke had received word of an opportunity for the band at the Jazz Gallery, an East Village club, and he had decided it would be a good place for the guys to work while he was abroad. Duke had heard me play the piano at Storyville, and I had even sat in with his band from time to time. He had also seen me leading various groups over the years, and must have respected my organizational abilities. But to suggest that I could sit at the piano and lead the Ellington Orchestra for a week was an incredible overestimation of talent. I've never quite been able to figure out exactly what made him think that I would be up to the task. It was both a preposterous misjudgment on Duke's part and a moving statement of his trust. I hastily declined. It couldn't happen. But what a dream!

An indication of Duke's artistry and how he worked with others happened on the Thursday evening of the 1958 Newport Jazz Festival, which was a tribute to him. Mahalia Jackson was to close the evening, singing the "Come Sunday" section of *Black, Brown, and Beige* with the Ellington Orchestra. They had recorded the entire suite six months earlier, in late January (CL 1162).

All afternoon and into the evening Mahalia kept asking me to find Duke. She hadn't rehearsed with the band, and wanted a run-through. I informed Duke of Mahalia's worries several times, and every time he fluffed it off. He appeared unconcerned. Mahalia, in the meantime, got more and more anxious with each passing minute. She was almost a wreck by the time Duke's band took the stage. She was going to have to wing it.

When Mahalia finally walked out into the stage lights, a hush descended over Freebody Park. Duke grinned at her from the piano. The band went into "Come Sunday," floating on the sophisticated voicings of Billy Strayhorn's new arrangement. Despite her nervousness, Mahalia took to the task as only she could. It was breathtaking. Duke knew all along that it would work; his confidence in her artistry surpassed her own. She was not only capable of this performance; she was the only person on earth who could pull it off. It was magical, as Duke must have anticipated. Why mess things up with a rehearsal?

*     *     *

The 1959 festival also featured a Benny Goodman tribute, which Columbia Records was recording. In addition, they were recording the Duke Ellington Orchestra that year. Because Benny's performance was such a major production (requiring special contracts and rehearsal provisions), his fee was more than Ellington's. Irving Townsend, who as Columbia's A & R man had access to both artists' contracts—actually mentioned this to Duke. It was a highly un-professional thing to do. Irving had access to privileged information and he used it in a way that was harmful to me.

I didn't find out about this for a couple of years; but during that time, I detected a degree of coldness from Ellington. We finally got it straightened out when I asked him about it. After I explained the reason for the disparity in fees, Edward understood and all was forgiven. I was somewhat less forgiving of Irving Townsend, whose indiscretion and unprofessionalism could easily have destroyed my relationship with Duke. This was my only rift with Ellington in all the years we worked together.

\*    \*    \*

Duke was concerned with another major project. He had premiered his second Sacred Concert, a two-hour program of religious music, in New York's Cathe-dral of St. John the Divine early in 1968. A year later, as we sat down to dis-cuss the possibility of an international tour, he had expressed his desire to present the Sacred Concert in Europe. I came up with an ambitious idea: we would produce it in Paris, at the Cathedral of Notre Dame.

I called Father Norman O'Connor to ask whether he could get Cardinal Cushing, the archbishop of Boston, to write a letter introducing me to Cardi-nal Marty in Paris. Father O'Connor did just that, and Cardinal Cushing agreed to his request.

I flew to France to make arrangements, and was met by my European liai-son Simone Ginibre. I had met Simone a few years earlier at the Blue Note club in Paris; we were introduced by the club's patron, Benny Benjamin. Si-mone had had a career as a jazz singer, under the name Simone Chevalier. She was still singing in the mid-'60s, but looking for additional work opportuni-ties. She had heard I was bringing Cannonball Adderley to Europe, and asked if I would pay a commission for a few dates in Italy, which she could set up. I was grateful for any available dates so I agreed. It was not long before Simone had booked the entire tour for me.

Simone knew many people in Europe with whom I was only vaguely acquainted: Anders Steffensen in Copenhagen, Alberto Alberti in Italy, Al-fredo Papo in Barcelona, and Julio Marti in Valencia. She knew seemingly all of the expatriate American musicians. And Simone spoke Italian and Spanish fluently—in addition to English and French. On more than one occasion I saw her handle four successive phone calls, each in a different tongue. It was only a matter of time before we opened a full-time office in Paris called ATLT—an acronym for "a thing like that," a statement I always used when I couldn't explain matters clearly.

Simone was pessimistic when I asked her to get me an appointment with Cardinal Marty. It would be impossible to get. At best, it would take weeks to procure. And he would never say yes.

Unfazed, I insisted that she call the archbishop's office and explain, in her most elegant French, that there was an American with a letter from Cardinal Cushing about an important sacred music project that would surely pique his interest. Simone reluctantly made the call. Soon after, she came to me with a look of combined puzzlement and astonishment. "You have an appointment this afternoon at three o'clock."

I met with Cardinal Marty and delivered my letter of introduction from Cardinal Cushing. He was receptive, and introduced me to a monsignor who could handle the project. "The only problem is this," Cardinal Marty told me. "I have no jurisdiction over Notre Dame, and I highly doubt that you can secure permission from the brothers in control there."

The Monsignor suggested the Cathedral St. Eustache in Les Halles. But I explained that I had lived in Paris for a few months in 1949, and had been impressed with L'Eglise St. Sulpice, a large church on the Left Bank. I had walked past the church almost every day that I was in Paris, awed by its elegance. The organist and composer César Auguste Franck had served there. I don't know whether the cardinal and the monsignor were surprised at my forthrightness, but in any case, they made arrangements for the performance.

The Sacred Concert took place in L'Eglise St. Sulpice on November 16, 1969. The performance was televised. It was a huge success. The following morning, the front pages of every Parisian newspaper bore an image of Ellington standing like a saint before the church's enormous cross. In addition to 3,000 people in the church, there were thousands more in the square outside, listening to the concert over loudspeakers. Featured with the band was the thrilling soprano of Alice Babs and the young son of Phil Woods.

Duke was thoroughly exhausted after the concert, but we had scheduled a post-performance reception. Getting Duke to receptions was often difficult; he was rarely interested in them. Fortunately, I had learned by that time that it was best not to ask Duke whether he would go to such an event—he would never give an answer. The best strategy was to get into the limousine with him and simply head for the engagement. This was what we did in this case. As soon as we arrived, he turned on his usual charm. We stayed at the reception just long enough to make the requisite appearance.

On our way back to the hotel, Duke asked where Joe Turner was playing. The legendary stride pianist had lived for many years in Paris, and had a long-term gig at a small club on the Avenue Georges V. I knew that Duke was tired, but he wanted to see Turner. It was two o'clock in the morning when we reached the club. We stayed there for an hour. Joe Turner's playing brought Duke to life; it was as if his fatigue dissolved in the face of those stride choruses.

The Ellington band played three regular concerts in the French provinces before taking the Sacred Concert to the cathedral in Barcelona late in November. I had other commitments and couldn't join them for that leg of the trip, but Joyce was there. On the night of the performance, they sat down to dinner and were pressed for time. "*Bon appétit*," Joyce urged, and picked up her fork—conscious of their impending appointment and eager to get the meal over with.

"Jerce," Ellington said, "are we in such a hurry that we don't have time to say grace?"

Duke was a religious man. The only time I saw him flustered was at his last concert in Berlin at the Philharmonie on the Berlin Jazz Festival. (The Berlin festival had been created by Rolf Schulte-Barenberg.) The Duke was scheduled to do two concerts in the same evening. At that time, there was a rebellious spirit among young people and they didn't appreciate romantic or sacred music. When Tony Watkins sang, "Come Sunday," they booed. Duke finished the first concert and came off the stage, mumbling, "They booed a hymn. They booed a hymn." In truth, he found it difficult to believe. I told the producer Joe Berendt that I would not let Duke play the second concert in such an insulting atmosphere. Duke would have done whatever I suggested. Berendt begged me to reconsider. He made a speech to the audience prior to the concert, explained what had happened and admonished and requested at the same time that the audience respect the artistry of Duke Ellington. The second concert went on without incident. Duke featured Tony Watkins on two-thirds of the concert.

\*     \*     \*

In the first year of the New Orleans festival, I commissioned Duke Ellington to write a "New Orleans Suite." For the week before the concert, we arranged for the Ellington band to play nightly at Al Hirt's club on Bourbon Street. Duke used this stretch of time to work on the suite—which, typically, he had not yet finished composing.

I stopped in at the club every night, but rarely spoke to Duke, since he was busy orchestrating the suite and I was busy orchestrating the festival. I do remember one thing he said about the New Orleans Suite: "I'm going to let Cootie play his boy." He was referring to Cootie Williams's love for Louis Armstrong. Duke also told me that he was trying to coax Johnny Hodges into playing soprano saxophone, in honor of Sidney Bechet.

It was during this week that Tom Whaley, Ellington's longtime copyist, was badly scalded in a hotel shower. He was admitted to the hospital's emergency ward with serious burns. Johnny Hodges, whose usual mien was that of vague disinterest, took personal responsibility for Tom's recovery. He went to the hospital every day, usually more than once; his concern was touching. It was a side of Johnny that not many of us had ever seen. He probably saved Tom Whaley's life. Sadly, it was only a week later that Johnny himself passed away, suffering a heart attack in the dentist's chair. A deeply saddened Duke recorded his "Portrait of Sidney Bechet" two days afterward with Paul Gonsalves on tenor; Johnny Hodges was never recorded on the Bechet segment of the suite.

Nor did he play it on the New Orleans concert; Ellington's performance that Saturday night included the suite's five movements, but none of its biographical portraits. Still, the concert was by no means incomplete; I was thrilled by the new material. It was a triumph.

*       *       *

My association with Ellington was very important to my business after the "music should be free" sickness in society closed down the Newport Jazz Festival in 1971. Fortunately, we had already scheduled a massive Duke Ellington tour for the State Department. We had also planned tours of Australia, Japan, and Europe for various other artists.

Ellington's longtime business association with Norman Granz had ended in 1969. When I asked Duke why, he told me that Granz had spoken curtly to his sister Ruth on the phone. This offense may have been one of a number of reasons, but this is the reason Ellington personally gave me. At any rate, he replaced Granz with Cress Courtney, former head of the William Morris agency's band division. Courtney and Ellington had done business in the '40s; the agent had even served as Duke's personal manager for a few years, before the advent of Joe Glaser. When Courtney reentered the picture in 1969, the price for the Ellington Orchestra abroad suddenly doubled. I couldn't figure out how Courtney could have the audacity to impose such an increase. But Duke's new manager was absolutely clear that the band would not work for less.

My office had previously booked tours of Europe directly with Glaser. I wanted to continue as Duke's international impresario, and Courtney was happy to oblige—as long as I could get the money. I was astonished when Simone Ginibre, who ran my Paris office, told me that everyone was willing to pay the increased fee. This lesson in selling was never forgotten.

Ellington's 1971 tour began in mid-September, with a month-long residence in the Soviet Union.

After exiting the Soviet Union on October 12, Duke and his men performed in Germany, France, England, Belgium, the Netherlands, Poland, Yugoslavia, Hungary, and Romania. They played in a different city every night, and, occasionally, two or three concerts on the same day. After Vienna, they were scheduled for Denmark, Norway, Sweden, and Spain. For Duke, this was business as usual.

The Ellington band left Europe for America after playing a concert in Barcelona, Spain, on November 14. But not North America. Along with Buenos Aires impresario Alejandro Szterenfeld, I had coordinated a twenty-four-day tour of South America. The band flew directly from Barcelona to Rio De Janeiro, where they played three concerts in the Teatro Municipal. I joined them there. But I wasn't on the same flight. While they had been playing in Barcelona, I had been with Miles Davis in London. I flew from London to Madrid, and then headed for Brazil.

After Rio, I accompanied the Ellington band to São Paulo. But business compelled me to return to New York late in November; São Paulo would be my final date with the band. When I broke this news to Duke, he looked at me with an expression of bemusement. Here was a man who had been on the road for over two months. He still had concerts ahead in Uruguay, Argentina, Chile, Peru, Ecuador, Colombia, Venezuela, Puerto Rico, Panama, Nicaragua, and Mexico; the tour ran until December 10. Although he lived for the road, the bags under his eyes (heavier than usual) told me that Duke was tired. He allowed himself a wry smile, and said: "You're going back to New York? This must be when the tour gets tough."

Part of the reason I had to return home was the massive amount of planning required for the band's six-week tour of the Far East—scheduled to begin shortly after the New Year. I left São Paulo on November 20, only weeks before that next tour.

Beginning in Tokyo on January 5, 1972, this tour kept as grueling a pace as the last. It began with two weeks of concerts in Japan, without a day off. Then the Orchestra went to Southeast Asia, in a circuit very similar to the one traveled by Count Basie the previous year. But this tour was more extensive, as it included dates in Calcutta, India; Colombo, Ceylon; Kuala Lumpur, Malaysia; and Jakarta, Indonesia.

I accompanied the band on the first two weeks of travel. It was quite an experience; Ellington got a splendid reception wherever he went. There were no major mishaps (although we came close, when several airport buildings in Manila burned to the ground the day after our departure).

In Bangkok, we had an appointment to meet with the king of Thailand. Duke was particularly excited about this performance. We had been asked to check in at the theater an hour before His Majesty's arrival, and we were running late. I can clearly recall the scene in the hotel room: Mercer Ellington was administering B-12 shots to his father, a ritual that had become increasingly common during Duke's later years. Ellington Sr. was obviously concerned about the time, and he tried to get Mercer to rush the injection.

"Don't worry, we're going to get there," Mercer said, in an effort to calm his father. "There's no rush."

"But there is," Duke countered. "You must never keep a king waiting."

We made it to the theater in time, and the Orchestra delivered a characteristically graceful performance. Afterward, they met the king in the theater lobby; he decorated Ellington with a garland of flowers. It was difficult, during that momentous meeting, to tell which of the two distinguished gentlemen present was true royalty—the Duke or the King.

In the fall of 1973, one of the more significant items was another European tour with the Ellington Orchestra, which as usual involved much foresight and planning.

Duke had expressed interest in performing a third Sacred Concert, and I made arrangements to present it in Westminster Abbey. My contact was my close personal friend, Gerald Lascelles, son of the Princess Mary. As the first cousin to King George VI and the Duke of Windsor, Gerald was in the position to get access at Westminster. We scheduled the performance for October 24, 1973. On that evening, the Abbey was lit up like a jeweled crown—a condition usually reserved for royal functions. It was an unforgettable scene.

Don George, one of Duke's personal friends, later wrote an account of the evening:

> Seeing Westminster Abbey on the night of Duke's third sacred concert was the most extraordinary experience ever. The abbey had never been opened at night and lit up except for coronations and state funerals. The entrance was lined with elaborately uniformed guards standing at ramrod-straight attention, enhancing the pomp that only Britain can maintain. Limousines were pulling up, one Daimler after another, one Rolls after another. All the klieg lights were on, and there was a huge crowd milling about behind a human wall of London bobbies watching the great and famous arrive.

I witnessed none of this pomp, because I was stationed as usual behind the scenes. The sad irony was that, amidst the decorousness of the occasion, Ellington was very ill; his cancer had begun to take its toll. To make matters worse, he had characteristically neglected to prepare adequately for the concert, and was attempting to write music up to ten minutes before curtain. In fact, he was writing music for the concert's second half during intermission.

After the concert, Duke was exhausted; I had never seen him in such a state. He had no choice but to decline an invitation to a reception at No. 10 Downing Street offered by the Prime Minister.

The next morning, we went to the airport to leave for Copenhagen to appear at a concert in Malmo, Sweden. For the first time, Duke Ellington used a wheelchair on the tarmac. When we got to Copenhagen, we took a ferry to Sweden. On board, breathing the sea air, his life seemed to return. He greedily devoured the shrimp sandwiches so popular in Denmark, and topped it off with Danish pastries—his favorite.

That evening, he played a concert that will remain in my memory as his last hurrah. After the final number, the band left the stage, but Duke was exhilarated. He came back and sat down at the piano. The rest of the musicians weren't thrilled with the idea of returning to the stage, but a few of them came back. They were onstage for another forty-five minutes; Duke played and played. It was one of the last glimmers of life and spontaneity that I saw in him. This concert was recorded, and in 1999 a Swedish record label acquired the rights and issued a CD. To my surprise, as part of the encore, Duke introduced me and asked me to sit in at the piano. I eagerly played "Take the 'A' Train" with the band. So there it is, a part of history: yours truly, captured forever on disc with the Duke Ellington Orchestra, and receiving a royal introduction from the Maestro himself. I personally had no recollection of playing that evening until the producer of the CD called to request permission. He even sent a check for my participation.

Exactly seven months after that concert, Joyce and I were vacationing in a spa in Brittany when we heard news of Duke Ellington's death over the BBC. It was May 24, 1974. I turned to Joyce and said, "I have to go back." I flew from Nantes to Paris, then to New York City.

I don't know what I was expecting to feel as I walked into the darkness of that funeral home on Madison Avenue. I was completely unprepared for the wave of grief that shuddered through me. There was the face of Edward Kennedy Ellington, frozen in death. I found a chair and crumpled into it. The only other time I would experience such grief was some twenty years later, at a funeral service for my mother. To have spent time with Duke, working together, was worth everything else I've done in this business. I had never known anyone who touched me in quite that way before, and I have never encountered anyone since.

Duke Ellington, as a celebrity and world-renowned artist, was as warm and generous of spirit as any man I've ever met. His favorite stage expression to his audience, "We love you madly," was sincere. He loved women and had dozens of female friends around the world. Yet the title of his autobiography, *Music Is My Mistress*, told more of a story than was apparent. I didn't know Duke personally before 1953. But in the time I was with him, with the exception of a steadfast devotion to his sister Ruth, I never knew of any one woman with whom he was in love. Was this the case his entire life? Perhaps he was continually searching and seeking that special "sophisticated lady" and never found her.

Duke Ellington has become an icon in our culture. I've heard and read the words of musicians of many styles, from traditional to the so-called avant-garde, say that he was a primary influence. Unfortunately when I hear a lot of guys play, they don't sound as if they ever heard any of Ellington's music.

In reviewing my association with Duke, I found that in the last twenty years of his life, 1955–75, I worked either for or with him over 365 days, the equivalent of one full year of his career.

# 6

# *A Long Step Forward*

*Dear Gentle Folk of Newport,*
*—or maybe I should say "Heps and Cats"—*
*I want you to lend an ear*
*because, well, I want you to hear*
*some really shimmering sharps and flats.*
> **– Bing Crosby, *High Society***

IF THERE'D BEEN ANY DOUBT that the Newport Jazz Festival was the nation's leading musical event, Ellington's 1956 performance tore that to pieces. The association of Newport and jazz—once thought of as a novelty—was now an ineluctable fact. Duke's *Time* magazine cover story heralded Newport as the site of the Maestro's comeback. In a *Holiday* magazine feature story, Cleveland Amory described the high society pressures that had plagued the festival; he summed up by pointing to "the realization, after three long years, that the Festival had, after all, made Newport, as it was wont to be in happier social climes, front-page news again all over the uncivilized world." Elaine Lorillard penned a piece for *Collier's* similarly focused on Newport's newfound mixture of jazz and snazz. "It's actually as though jazz has helped to break down class and racial barriers," she wrote.

\*     \*     \*

Louis Armstrong had played the previous two festivals (1955 and '56); we invited him back again in '57. I was well aware of the problems involved in a repeat performance. Louis's "act" had gone unchanged for years. *Down Beat* had reviewed his first Newport performance in 1955 by comparing it to a vaudeville show. In *Saturday Review*, Whitney Balliett had complained that Louis had become "a caricature of himself."

My love for Louis was enormous, and I wanted to keep presenting him at Newport. But we couldn't have him playing the same show again. I said as much to Joe Glaser, Louis's longtime manager, and told him about an idea I had. The 1957 festival was beginning on July 4—Louis's then-acknowledged fifty-seventh birthday. What if we organized a birthday tribute featuring many of the artists who had been associated with Louis? Glaser knew even better than I how badly Louis needed a boost to his career. But I was still surprised and grateful when Glaser—who otherwise never agreed with anything I said—not only approved of the plan, but told me he would personally come to Newport to see that things went smoothly.

The arrangements involved bringing in Ella Fitzgerald, Kid Ory, Red Allen, Jack Teagarden, and J. C. Higginbotham; each would play his or her own set during the night, and then they were all going to come back for the finale with Louis. Songwriter Johnny Mercer, who worshiped Louis, would come up to Newport for the occasion. A huge, three-tiered birthday cake with icing and candles would be wheeled out at the finale.

The only tricky part was working all this into Louis's set. Ella Fitzgerald's presence was particularly significant; she had agreed to sing a few duets with Louis, as they had on numerous popular Columbia recordings. Because Ella was scheduled, we figured that it wouldn't make sense to also feature Velma Middleton.

But Velma was a permanent part of the Armstrong entourage. She was family. So when Joe Glaser, at my request, told Velma not to sing, she went straight to Louis. And he wasn't happy. Backstage, I heard him telling Velma: "Who's your daddy? Haven't I been your daddy all these years? I'll take care of you." (His language was actually much more vituperative than that.)

Louis made his frustration clear during his set without saying a single word. He raised his horn and began blowing his usual show with the All-Stars, completely ignoring the special plans we'd made. Red Allen, Jack Teagarden, Kid Ory, and Ella were all standing in the wings. It was apparent that Louis had no intention of bringing them on stage with him.

A lot of effort had been put into this affair and we weren't going to let it pass. So, after about forty-five minutes, we interrupted the set. In between songs, Willis Conover announced the trumpeter's birthday, and as the cake was wheeled out onto the stage, Louis grew angry and he knew just how to stop the show: He raised his trumpet, played the "Star-Spangled Banner," and then walked offstage.

Backstage, he raged: "I'll kill him! That Goddamn motherfucker! That son of a bitch!" His voice cut through the sudden hush. No one knew the whole story, and the jazz magazines printed several speculative accounts. Some writers thought Louis was upset that Velma had arrived late. More popular was the rumor that Louis was mad at me. It would be more than fifteen years later that Louis himself would tell me about the true source of his anger that evening. Apparently, Armstrong and Glaser had made an agreement at the start of their long association: Louis would handle the music, and Joe would stick to the business. Joe's intervention that evening was a betrayal of Louis's trust. If I had been aware of this mutual understanding, I would have spoken about the program directly to Louis myself.

\*     \*     \*

We made the same agreement with Norman Granz and Verve Records in 1957 that we had made with Columbia the year before: The fee for recording an artist was equivalent to that artist's performance fee. Granz was to record the entire festival. It was a win-win situation. The festival won because Granz essentially underwrote our artists; Verve won because they had the opportunity to record a stunning array of performers. Norman Granz even got into the spirit of Newport's old guard by throwing a lavish party at the Viking Hotel on the same night as the official festival soiree. Many of the festival musicians showed up at Granz's party instead of the Lorillards; they even played a jam session there. Norman liked to do things like that; upstaging the Lorillards helped reinforce his feeling that the jazz world revolved around him, like planets around the sun.

That year, Verve recorded George Lewis, Eddie Costa, Red Allen, Jack Teagarden, Kid Ory, Ella Fitzgerald, Billie Holiday (in her last festival appearance), Toshiko Akiyoshi, Teddy Wilson, Gerry Mulligan, Oscar Peterson, Sonny Stitt, Roy Eldridge, Coleman Hawkins, Ruby Braff, Don Elliott, Pee Wee Russell, Bobby Henderson, Dizzy Gillespie, the Gigi Gryce–Donald Byrd Jazz Laboratory, Cecil Taylor (a daring presentation, for 1957), Count Basie with Lester Young, Illinois Jacquet, Mary Lou Williams, Joe Williams, and the Drinkard Singers. And this list only includes artists who were released on LP! Many performances went unreleased (including sets by Cannonball Adderley,

Bobby Hackett, Carmen McRae, George Shearing, Erroll Garner, Stan Kenton, Jimmy Smith, Jackie Paris, Horace Silver, Chris Connor, Dave Brubeck, Jimmy Giuffre, and Sarah Vaughan).

Norman Granz put the Newport LPs on the market. Norman felt they didn't sell quickly enough, and he buried them. Verve still has all of these historically significant albums. With the recent trend of CD reissues, we might yet have the opportunity to hear these sets.

Perhaps the most important feature of the 1957 festival was John Hammond's visionary idea of presenting gospel music. Gospel sounds of the African-American church were quite alien not only to the Newport crowd, but to white America at large. I was moved when years later I saw a television documentary on Gospel music; Cissy Houston (Whitney's mother) was describing how nervous her group, the Drinkard Singers, were before their Newport appearance. They had never performed for a white, nonchurch audience before.

In addition to the Drinkard Singers, John corralled the fifty-member Back Home Choir and Clara Ward and the Ward Singers, and got the important gospel disc jockey Joe Bostic to emcee the program. Both Hammond and Bostic tried to convince Mahalia Jackson to participate. Mahalia was the reigning queen in the world of gospel. Furthermore, she was one of my favorite singers of any style. If the angels' voices could be heard by the human ear, I always thought they would sound like Mahalia Jackson.

Mahalia was skeptical because she still associated jazz with the bordellos of New Orleans, her old hometown. To her, jazz was "devil music." She had never performed for a secular nightclub audience, and she wasn't about to start. The deciding factor was an invitation from Newport's Trinity Episcopal Church to sing during the Sunday morning service. She agreed to come.

Before the show the entire gospel entourage was to pose *en masse* for publicity photos. Everyone showed up at a tent we'd assembled backstage, but the performers' propriety frustrated the photographer. They were all like marble statues, frozen in solemn composure. Try as we did, they couldn't let down their guard.

"C'mon ladies, relax," coaxed the photographer, exasperated, in vain.

Finally Mahalia Jackson, who was in the middle of the congregation, shouted: "Mother Ward, do you still owe me any money?" Everybody broke up, and that was the picture. Mahalia knew just how to break the ice. Her performance that afternoon was even more rousing, and she sang a total of thirteen songs. History tells us that Mahalia's reference to Mother Ward's debt had a ring of truth to it.

The Newport Jazz Festival, meanwhile, reported its first substantial profit. We emerged with a $30,000 surplus, which was the opportunity I'd long been waiting for. I'd been toying with an idea in my head, and for the first time the board was in a position to consider it. Taking the concept to Marshall Brown—who'd been the musical director of the Farmingdale High School band that had made such a hit in the '57 festival—I wondered if he'd be interested in assembling a youth band made up of jazz musicians from all over Europe to play at the following summer's festival.

Marshall was highly receptive. The idea had the potential to be not only a sensation at Newport, but a diplomatic mission the likes of which the music industry had never seen before. Europe in 1957 was still pulling itself out from the shadow of war. Jazz had both an audience and a following among musicians in Europe, but jazz was still far from any cultural mainstream. Seeking out and bringing together young players from different countries would foster a sense of cross-cultural unity, employing the universal language of music. The project could also greatly increase the international exposure of the Newport Jazz Festival.

The board enthusiastically approved the proposal, objecting only to my suggestion of naming the group "The Tower of Babel Band." In any case, the ball got rolling. It was a mission of innumerable details, logistical challenges, and correspondences. We were to embark in late winter and travel through early spring. We sent letters to a list of known jazz critics and aficionados on the Continent: Arrigo Polillo, publisher of *Musica Jazz* in Milan; Esteban Colomer Brossa, an occasional promoter in Barcelona; Pat Brand, of *Melody Maker* magazine in London; Joachim Berendt, of *Sudwestfunk* in Germany; Eric Wiedemann, of *Orkester Journalen* in Stockholm; Jozef Balcerak, with *Jazz* magazine in Poland; the Baron Carlos de Radzitzky in Belgium; and several others, including my friend Charles Delaunay in Paris. Delaunay introduced me to a man who later became a longtime friend and the producer of the North Sea Jazz Festival—Paul Acket (he conducted our auditions in Holland). These men were all a part of the intricate jazz network; they were known as jazz authorities in their respective countries, and, to some degree, in America. A few had even been to Newport.

All of them were excited about our upcoming tour. In every country, we were met at the plane with flowers. The promoters arranged our hotels, taking care of us from the minute we landed until the minute we left.

Quite a few artists showed up for auditions, as many as twenty to thirty musicians in some countries. Marshall ran the proceedings like a true professional. First he would give out sample charts to test a musician's sight-reading ability. Once he found that they could read the music, we then set up jam sessions where they could blow. Marshall and I would also play a little bit; Marshall played decent valve trombone, although he never really had a trombone lip.

Several of my *Boston Herald* columns reported our progress for the folks at home. Describing our session in Lisbon, I wrote:

> Unfortunately, interest in jazz is very recent in Lisbon. It is only in the last five years that Luis Vilas-Boas, the acknowledged spokesperson for jazz in Portugal, started playing it over the airwaves. The club was loaded with enthusiasts but most of the musicians were too shy to try out for the band. After a while they relaxed and we finally had our pick from about fifteen candidates. We heard a good drummer but our choice will probably be either a pianist or a trumpeter who did not even bring his trumpet to the audition. We had to go to a club where he was working where he played for us a beat-up old trumpet that looked like it came through the Spanish Civil War.

Despite huge logistical obstacles, we found some good musicians. Most of the players in the International Youth Band went on to achieve success in their home countries; some went on to become world-class musicians: Dusko Goykovich was a fine trumpet player from Yugoslavia; Albert Mangelsdorff, the German trombonist, has since become an important international figure; Ronnie Ross was our baritone saxophonist from England; Gabor Szabo, a guitarist from Hungary, became well known in America.

However, occasional snags and quandaries did show up. Despite the help of our Swiss contact, Demetre Iokamidis (who worked a day job as a nuclear scientist), we could find no suitable musicians in Switzerland, one of our target countries. Fortunately, we did eventually find a good Swiss pianist by the name of George Gruntz—in Milan. Our problem seemed to have been solved, but another arose when we discovered a more desirable pianist in Austria, a young man by the name of Josef Zawinul. What could we do? There were a number of good musicians in Austria, but only one capable player from Switzerland. And so it was that we chose George Gruntz over Joey Zawinul for the International Youth Band. As it turns out, Gruntz went on to become a serious impresario and producer of the Berlin Jazz Festival—as well as a talented bandleader, arranger, and composer. Meanwhile, Zawinul came to the States a year or two later. I signed his immigration papers so that he could accept a scholarship at the Berklee School of Music. He didn't stay at Berklee very long. I also hired him as intermission pianist at Storyville—where he came to the attention of Maynard Ferguson, which kicked off an illustrious career. He soon became one of the major figures of his generation in jazz, playing with Miles Davis and Cannonball Adderley, and organizing Weather Report with Wayne Shorter.

With the ever-present tension of the cold war, our time in Yugoslavia, Hungary, Poland, and Czechoslovakia was poignant. Flying into Prague from Vienna was, as I reported in my column, like stepping into a Hitchcock movie. Marshall and I boarded an airplane with the not-so-reassuring moniker of "O.K. Lines." Prague was leaden and sunless, shrouded in soup-like fog. The cityscape was austere, conveying the feeling of a vast military camp, an impression only confirmed by the ubiquity of armed and uniformed guards. But the quality of musicianship in Czechoslovakia was as high as in any other country in Europe. The musician who impressed us most was a trombonist named Zdenek Pulec, a near-virtuosic player adept at both traditional and modern jazz, and with award-winning classical ability. In the end, though, we were unable to get the Czech government's permission to spirit Pulec from behind the Iron Curtain. He was the only musician we wanted but failed to get.

Fortunately, Czechoslovakia had a brighter side, and it was brought to my attention by Marshall's wife, Judy, who had accompanied us on the trip. Judy Brown was a talented sculptor. The spires of the churches and castles in the town communicated to her, and influenced her later work.

While in Warsaw, Poland, I received a visit at my hotel from Jozef Balcerak, our Polish contact and one of our hosts. Jozef was obviously a bit troubled. He wanted to talk to me, but he wouldn't say a thing in my room, so he led me outside. It was 10 o'clock at night and five degrees above zero. The streets were slick with ice.

When he felt that we were far enough from the hotel, Jozef confided to me that he was Jewish. He wasn't living as a Jew. He wanted to leave Poland, and asked me if I could I help him. The war had ended a decade before, but the fear had not subsided. Jozef had a partner in a jazz magazine, and while he thought that his associate was Jewish, it was never discussed. I regretted my powerlessness to help him.

Despite these occasional dark moments, the experience was priceless in terms of my cultural awareness as well as the friends and contacts I made. Many of the promoters, critics, and musicians I met on that trip would later be key players in my forthcoming international career.

\* \* \*

*The [1958] Newport Festival took a long step forward.*
*Throughout its four-day session there was constant evidence*
*of programming aimed at bringing some area of jazz into*
*focus, of ventures that made provocative use of the resources*
*available to an organization such as the Newport Festival.*
**—John S. Wilson, New York Times**

Friday afternoon of the 1958 festival was notable for the much-anticipated debut of the Newport International Youth Band. The planes had touched down just a few weeks before, amid some fanfare. The U.S. State Department, recognizing the value of our goodwill tour, had requested a performance of the International Band at the Brussels World's Fair, which was to occur later that summer. Vice President Richard Nixon wrote a letter to the festival board commending the project as "an outstanding example of what can be done by private citizens and groups in furtherance of the concept of 'people to people.'"

Like an Olympic coach in the weeks leading up to competition, Marshall Brown rehearsed the group with feverish intensity. As befitted the grandiose vision of the project, Marshall had commissioned arrangements from the likes of John LaPorta, Jimmy Giuffre, Bill Russo, and Adolphe Sandole. While these men were all accomplished writers and talented musicians, their material was quite "far out" for the time. This might not have posed a problem for established New York musicians, but the International Youth Band had little time to prepare, and furthermore had not been exposed to the progressive sounds that were becoming commonplace in the States. Add to this a language barrier, and you have a major challenge. Marshall's ambition, which had always served him so well, was in this case a few steps ahead of reality. In a sense, that ambition destroyed the International Band.

Despite an inauspicious performance and horrible reviews, the International Youth Band was in many ways a success. The project did accomplish an unprecedented collaboration among international musicians and solidified the nascent global jazz community. Members of the band went back home to their respective countries and were celebrated as musical heroes. More important, they would soon become a generation of innovators on that continent, spurring the growth and evolution of a distinctly European take on jazz.

\*　　\*　　\*

Friday night was another special occasion: an evening with the "King of Swing." Although Benny Goodman's heyday of the 1930s and '40s had passed, his legend, talent as a clarinetist, and celebrity were all untarnished.

Because Goodman did not have a working band, I put together for him a strong group of Goodman alumni: Doc Severinsen, Taft Jordan, Eddie Bert, Vernon Brown, Buddy Tate, and Kenny Burrell on guitar. Martha Tilton, his old vocalist, agreed to sing, as did Jimmy Rushing. I even managed to get Billy Butterfield—a longtime Goodman associate and the best lead trumpeter in the business. All of these musicians had endured the rigor of the Goodman Orchestra, an experience often likened to boot camp. Benny could be a real taskmaster and a difficult boss. The stories of Goodman's "Ray"—his cold, evil eye—were legendary. But he was one of the most important names in jazz; no single jazz artist had ever achieved the public acclaim and popularity that Goodman did in the 1930s. The sidemen, whatever their personal histories with the man, were here to take part in that spirit once again.

It was an emotional rehearsal. The band sounded inspired. There was a sense of elation, as if they were reliving the glories of the swing era. Benny seemed satisfied; we were all excited. Then Benny asked, "Who's going to introduce me?"

"I don't know, Benny," I said. "Either Willis Conover or myself."

"What if my brother-in-law introduces me?"

I was shocked. Benny Goodman's brother-in-law was none other than John Hammond. It was known in the industry that they hadn't spoken in years. And when I went to John and told him what Benny had said, he couldn't believe it. Benny was a strange man, and this gesture of reconciliation was totally uncharacteristic.

Those who knew the history of their conflict were amazed by the fact that John was going to introduce Benny. Billy Butterfield, Goodman's favorite lead trumpeter, was so moved that he went out for a celebratory quaff. In the meantime, we had made preparations for the big performance; we set up a ladder so that John could come up out of the audience to introduce Benny, as a sort of staged surprise.

By the time the band took the stage, Billy Butterfield was so drunk that he could barely play a note. He clammed on all the arrangements. Goodman's theme song, "Let's Dance," sounded as if it had been arranged by Archie Shepp. Butterfield's playing completely messed up the band. Benny didn't know what was happening. It was quite a shambles. Plans to record the show were thwarted. As *Down Beat* reported, "The Benny Goodman band made mincemeat of Benny Goodman night."

I witnessed this meltdown from the wings with a sickness in my heart. Dave Brubeck sidled up to me and, gesturing toward a precariously swaying Butterfield, said: "You know, sometimes it takes years for a guy to get back at you—but when he does, he really gets you good."

We had decided to produce a Saturday night blues show. John Hammond insisted on including a handsome and highly charismatic singer-guitarist named Chuck Berry. John was concerned with Chuck's position as a rhythm & blues performer and a pioneer of rock and roll.

John also recommended Big Maybelle, the powerful blues shouter. At the same time, I was made aware of Ray Charles, by my friends Nesuhi and Ahmet Ertegun at Atlantic Records. I appreciated Ray Charles. He had fast become a major figure in American music, and he had his own sound, which has since influenced thousands of performers. Atlantic recorded and released Ray's set that year, as *Ray Charles at Newport*. It was one of the largest-selling albums ever recorded at Newport.

But I was dead set against Chuck Berry. Rock and roll, in my mind, and in the minds of jazz critics and fans that I knew, did not belong on the Newport Festival any more than Guy Lombardo did. Despite the fact that Chuck Berry sang with the jazz-slanted Newport Blues Band (which included Jack Teagarden, Buck Clayton, Buddy Tate, George Auld, Rudy Rutherford, Pete Johnson, and Jo Jones—totally the wrong musicians to play with Chuck, as I later realized), there was no disguising his act as jazz. When he went into his duckwalk during "School Days," I literally cringed. I could almost feel the knives that the critics were going to hurl in our direction. Needless to say, the crowd loved it.

The grand irony lies in the fact that putting Chuck Berry on at Newport was a daring move that opened the door for similar presentations all over the world. So I get credit for being a visionary. I'm always careful to point out that John Hammond was responsible for this decision. John deserves the credit, and I'll take the blame. Incidentally, I've grown to like Chuck Berry's music. In future years, I would present Chuck on all the major European jazz festivals.

Mahalia Jackson was due to close the Saturday night blues program. As usual, she was worried about appearing on such a secular bill. Our solution: we programmed her set to begin after midnight, to let her ring in Sunday morning. At 12:01 A.M., Willis Conover announced: "Ladies and Gentlemen. It is Sunday—and it is time for the world's greatest gospel singer—Miss Mahalia Jackson."

Mahalia walked out and delivered some of the most stirring music heard that year. By this time rain had come pouring down over Freebody Park, but the crowd stayed put. They were captivated. Mahalia's voice carried every ounce of her heartfelt convictions. When she delivered a hand-clapping and soulful rendition of "Didn't It Rain," the rain, as if chastised, stopped falling. When she left the stage, the audience's applause was more deafening than it had been all night. Mahalia returned and, almost bashfully, said, "You make me feel like I'm a star."

We are fortunate enough to have this moment preserved on film, in Bert Stern's movie *Jazz on a Summer's Day*. Stern and Aram Avakian had come to Newport with the intention of making a film short; what they ended up with was a full-length documentary feature. They had cameras set up in the wings, at the foot of the stage, and in the audience, and covered almost all of the music that year.

Because of the huge amount of footage they shot (reportedly over 100,000 feet of exposed negative color stock), along with various financial problems and the challenge of finding distributors, *Jazz on a Summer's Day* was not released until 1960.

I saw the film for the first time at a theater in Boston. A feeling of eager anticipation grew as the lights dimmed and the screen lit up. There was Newport Harbor, the pier reflected on the undulant surface of Narragansett Bay. The soundtrack for the opening credit sequence was a pointillist recasting of the blues, as rendered by Jimmy Giuffre, Bob Brookmeyer, and Jim Hall. The title appeared, followed by the names of its featured stars, Louis Armstrong and Mahalia Jackson receiving top billing. The credits then listed all of the accompanying musicians in the film—players like Peanuts Hucko, Henry Grimes, and Dave Bailey who would otherwise have gone unsung.

There was footage of a pre-show Freebody Park, thousands of wooden chairs assembled in formation, workers putting finishing touches on the stage shell. The film then cut from the Newport stage to arranged shots of a jalopy driving through town, carrying a boisterous Dixieland band. During a segment depicting Thelonious Monk playing "Blue Monk," it cut away to shots of the 1958 America's Cup Trials: white-sailed yachts skating over the bay, an announcer's voice superimposed over Monk's piano solo. The technical aspect of it was sensational, and the color photography was striking. This sort of documentary was still a new thing in 1958, and jazz had never been presented this way on screen before.

It was rewarding to see excerpts from Louis Armstrong's set in the movie, since Louis and I had planned it together. We both knew that it was important to eliminate the bad aura of his blowup the year before. So I asked Louis to do a special program—which included a guest appearance with the International Band, as well as a few numbers with Jack Teagarden and Bobby Hackett. Louis was not only compliant; he was enthusiastic. He played more trumpet than I had heard from him in years.

Seeing the opportunity for a more spiritual conclusion, the editors of *Jazz on a Summer's Day* followed Louis's segment with footage of Mahalia Jackson. I sat in the theater and held my breath throughout the duration of Mahalia's screen time. The movie ended with "The Lord's Prayer," and Mahalia's voice resonating: *"For Thine is the Kingdom / and the Power / and the Glory / Forever—Amen."*

On the final "Amen" a title appeared on the screen: "End of a Summer's Day." My eyes were on the brink of tears. The film was marvelously shot and skillfully edited. Aside from some obviously staged audience shots that were filmed in New York, the movie stuck to Newport. It was, for the most part, a good piece of work.

Then the closing credits rolled, over a backdrop of the jalopy as it approached First Beach. Credits for Cameramen, Script and Continuity, Assistant Cameramen, Assistant Editors, Script Girls, Sound, Optical Effects. And, as the car whizzed by the stationary camera, the credit read: Musical Director—George Avakian.

The credit only lasted a second, and for a moment I thought my eyes had played tricks on me. My name hadn't been mentioned anywhere. Not one credit. Not even a special thanks or an acknowledgment. I literally could not bring myself to believe that they had cited Avakian for musical direction—when I had produced every minute of music on that stage. Giving George Avakian credit for the musical direction of the film was more than a slight; it was an insult. I left that theater livid.

I was so offended that for years I didn't extend a hand of friendship to George Avakian. I would see him and say hello, but I never told him how I felt. He found out through someone else thirty years later, and he wrote a letter explaining that Bert Stern had made the decision to leave my name out of the picture. I wrote a letter back, explaining to George that I was sorry it happened, because we might otherwise have been good friends all those years.

The incident, unfortunate as it was, taught me another hard and valuable lesson. No one will give you credit for something unless you make sure they give it to you. No one else is looking out for you. And there are people out there who are always more than eager to claim credit for your creative work.

\*     \*     \*

The 1959 Newport Jazz Festival season kicked off with all the hysterical drama of a soap opera. The Lorillards were in the process of splitting up, and Louis was drumming Elaine off the board of directors. To Elaine, this resembled a coup, since the idea of having jazz at Newport had been hers. But because Louis was the president of the board, and because we were still reliant upon his financial support, the board unanimously took his side. Louis was integral to the festival's operations; Elaine, at that point, was not. So she was ousted. She didn't take this lying down, and proceeded to file a lawsuit against the entire board of directors. No one enjoyed this process.

The 1959 festival was huge. Aquidneck Island, now happily resigned to a massive annual influx of visitors (and tourist dollars), prepared for the festival in a number of ways. Newport's police force was marshaled for the weekend, to maintain order and regulate traffic. The Newport Chamber of Commerce regulated room rental in private homes, at an average price of five dollars a night (ten dollars for a double). The local bars and pubs, which had gradually slackened their last-call policies over the past few years, were now staying open all night long.

On Saturday night, the bill consisted solely of Erroll Garner's trio and the Duke Ellington Orchestra.

The army of photographers in attendance, spoiled by several years of almost unlimited access, were sore that night because Erroll requested a ban on photography. It was basically an issue of flashbulbs; Erroll had been in an auto accident not long before, as a result of blinding lights. But the photographers were vocal in their complaints. No one seemed to realize how well we had been treating them all along. One of the biggest mistakes we made at Newport was not getting the rights to photos. Some of the most enduring images in jazz were taken at Newport, and my company has relatively few archival prints.

Duke's performance on Saturday night was one of the highlights of the festival. The new material included "Idiom '59," composed for Newport, and the brand-new score from *Anatomy of a Murder*. The band itself was driving as hard as ever, a phenomenon that could be easily traced to Duke's augmented percussion section. Sam Woodyard had rejoined the band, and Duke was using both him and Jimmy Johnson onstage at the same time. I thought this was odd, and I asked Duke about it: why the two drummers?

His answer was revealing: "With the left hand that Erroll Garner's got, you need all the help you can get." And Duke really meant that. That was the level of his respect for Garner.

Newport had been accused of commercialism almost from the start, but the allegations reached a fever pitch this year. Critics foamed at the mouth over the fact that the Four Freshmen, Pat Suzuki, and the Kingston Trio were all booked on the festival.

The Four Freshmen were a vocal group that had a place on a jazz festival because of their Kenton-influenced harmonies. Pat Suzuki, on the other hand, was a mistake. I honored a request from RCA–Victor, which I should not have done. Pat Suzuki was not a bad artist, but there were a lot of jazz singers in America who could have benefited from such an appearance.

The Kingston Trio was another story. I had worked with them just weeks before, at Storyville on Cape Cod. Their agents, Larry Bennett and Bert Block, were friends of mine who had formerly worked with Joe Glaser. With the Kingston Trio, Storyville–Cape Cod did better business that week than with any of our jazz artists. They were the biggest group in the country, and I was happy when they had agreed to appear on a folk afternoon I was planning for the Newport Jazz Festival.

It was shortly after confirming this booking that the folk afternoon expanded into a full-fledged Newport Folk Festival, and I asked the Kingston

Trio to shift their appearance from one festival to the other. Bert responded: "They'll play the Folk Festival, but they also want to keep their spot on the Jazz Festival." The Kingston Trio had no place on a program with Dave Brubeck, Red Allen, and Bobby Hackett. But because I felt that the group could be a key factor to the success of the first Newport Folk Festival, I went along with their request. Their set at the Jazz Festival wasn't terrible, but it provided just the ammunition the press needed to sound the cry of "commercialism at Newport." In the long run, though, the Kingston Trio's presence at the Jazz Festival was a small price to pay; it did secure their place on the Folk Festival. My decision was a mistake, but not unconscionable.

While the festival was having its problems with the cultural policemen who decried the commercial programming, Newport itself was becoming chaotic. People had caught on to the fact that Newport pubs were staying open until 4 or 5 A.M. during festival week, and the additional fact that few bars and stores were checking for ID. These people were coming in from all over New England and beyond, many of them college kids out for a good time. They boozed, made out, and generally caused a ruckus. They slept wherever they could find space: on the beaches, in Touro Park, in their cars, or on cots in the firehouse and police station. They bought cases of beer, or brought them, and left their refuse strewn all over town. In his Boston newspaper column, John McLellan accurately surmised that these kids "[had] begun comparing Newport at festival time to Ft. Lauderdale during spring vacation."

Little of this ruckus entered the festival gates, because few of the troublemakers had any feeling for jazz. Inside the park, the only sparks flying were generally on the stage. This was our sixth festival, and we had grown more capable and efficient with each year. Stage waits were getting shorter, programs were less rushed, and the ground crew knew exactly what they were doing. The visibility of festival security seemed to keep the crowd in order. There were still occasional awkward moments, but by 1959 we ran a tight ship. One reporter noted "signs that the annual affair is getting more sedate every year."

Nevertheless, we recognized the rowdiness of the kids outside as a threat to the festival. Louis Lorillard had met with Newport city officials and had stressed the importance of better enforcement and control. If we kept the kids who weren't attending the festival from causing unnecessary trouble, the problem would be solved. But the chamber of commerce stubbornly refused to address the issue. The problem, they insisted, was ours. We were to be responsible not only for the goings-on inside Freebody Park, but also the activities all over town. This position might have been a result of sheer complacency on the city's part. Or it might have been the influence of Newport's shopkeepers and tavern owners, who made a killing off those weekend revelers. Whatever the case, our board attempted to work with the city, and got nowhere. Unchecked, the problem would return the following summer, with direr consequences than even the most ardent pessimists could have anticipated.

\*　　\*　　\*

In fall 1959, I experienced my first business venture in Europe under the title "Newport Jazz Festival in Europe," featuring Dizzy Gillespie, Dave Brubeck, Buddy Tate, and Jimmy Rushing. We had a financial flop and our trip home on the *Liberté* was filled with anxieties about what we might encounter on our return. As our voyage drew to its conclusion, the *Liberté* moved gracefully up the Hudson River, and the city skyline sparkled in the morning sun. As soon as Joyce and I stepped off the gangplank onto the docks, we encountered Jay Weston, the Newport Festival's public relations man. We weren't expecting a welcome party.

"George," Mr. Weston said. "You're in trouble."

Within a few days, I found myself reporting the dismal financial news to my colleagues on the festival board. Their faces told the extent of their disappointment: grim, serious, unsmiling. Someone coughed just to break up the uncomfortable silence. Then the Newport Jazz Festival Board called for my resignation as vice president and producer.

My blood ran cold. What was I going to do? Everyone else on the board had a career apart from the festival; they were lawyers and record businesspeople and so on. But the festival was almost my whole life and livelihood. Aside from Storyville (which was beginning to show signs of decline), and side projects like PAMA (still in its infant stages) and French Lick, Newport was all I had. The Newport Jazz Festival was my life.

I sat numbly in my chair. The board made a swift motion to nominate and elect John Hammond, who had been second vice president, as my successor. No one was asked to fill John's V.P. position.

Before I had the chance to collapse into a state of abject depression, John showed what he really thought of me. "I make a motion," he said, "to rehire George Wein as producer of the festival."

I looked up. John recognized that I was doing all of the work. He understood the board's anger towards me, so he accepted my dismissal as first vice president. But he also knew that I was the only board member who could run the festival. And so this dark hour actually only lasted a few minutes. Joyce and I remained close friends with John and his wife, Esmé, for the rest of their lives.

\*　　\*　　\*

A new development on the festival was the Newport Youth Band, whose members had been culled from New York City's high schools. Marshall Brown and I had first started scouting for the group in 1958, and they had done some recordings. After the disappointment of the International Band, Marshall was happy to demonstrate his leadership skills; working with high school kids, he was back in his element. Perhaps even more impressive than the Youth Band's strong showing is the fact that so many of its members became professional musicians. Clarinetist Eddie Daniels, trumpeter Jimmy Owens, baritone saxophonist Ronnie Cuber, pianist Mike Abene, and bassist Eddie Gomez all went on to become well-respected professionals. Larry Rosen, the group's drummer, later founded GRP Records. When Rosen hosted a fortieth reunion party at his house in New Jersey late in 1998, almost all the musicians showed up. They toasted me as having made possible their big debut.

Although some critics approved of the programming and production that the festival offered, anti-Newport sentiment was at its highest peak. Leading the charge was my old friend Nat Hentoff, who had accused the Newport board of being racist in the *Village Voice* the previous year. Now in *Rogue* magazine, Hentoff labeled the festival a "prototype of the insensitive, grasping commercialism the jazz creator has had to combat from the beginnings of jazz." Given this opinion, it wasn't surprising that Hentoff was responsible for bringing Charles Mingus and Elaine Lorillard together.

Mingus at that time had decided that Newport embodied everything that he detested about the jazz world. He felt that he wasn't receiving compensation for his effort; he couldn't accept the fact that Dizzy Gillespie or Dave Brubeck commanded more money than he did. So Charlie decided to start his *own* Newport jazz festival. He asked Hentoff for advice on how to get one started, and Hentoff directed him to Elaine.

She had been a vocal opponent of the festival since her dismissal the year before. She had spent much of the past spring hanging out in Manhattan jazz clubs and grumbling about the festival to whoever would listen. When she and Mingus got together, they each found a sympathetic ear and, more important, an ally.

Elaine contacted Nick Cannarozzi, the owner of the Cliff Walk Manor, a restaurant and inn on Memorial Drive overlooking First Beach. They made plans to hold a festival there; the musicians would split the admission receipts. As for talent, Mingus drummed up a roster of players who weren't booked for the Newport Jazz Festival that year. Among them were Max Roach, Ornette Coleman, Jo Jones, Arthur Taylor, Kenny Dorham, Wilbur Ware, Kenny Drew, and Coleman Hawkins. Most had been regulars on the Newport Festival in years past.

The press were drawn to the Mingus festival like moths to a flame. Some referred to it as the "rump" festival, while others called it the "rebel" festival. Because of the highly publicized Lorillard split, one New York columnist dubbed the respective festivals "His" and "Hers."

Elaine and Mingus coordinated their fete to run concurrently with ours. On opening night at Freebody Park, we featured the Newport Youth Band, the Cannonball Adderley Quintet, Nina Simone, the Art Farmer/Benny Golson Jazztet, the Dave Brubeck Quartet, and the Maynard Ferguson Orchestra. Down the road, the rebel festival hosted extended jam sessions, with Mingus and Coleman taking the lead. Despite a drenching rain, our small but intent audience stayed put. Our opening night had drawn a crowd of about 5,000; the rebel festival's had attracted a small crowd of several hundred.

The real masses started to descend upon Newport on Friday. By Friday afternoon, the cars were backed up for miles, literally inching their way into town. The festival ran smoothly on Friday afternoon and night and Saturday afternoon. The Saturday-evening attendance reached record-breaking proportions, peaking near 15,000.

I wasn't aware of the dangerous situation brewing in the town. What I do know about the events outside Freebody Park I gleaned mostly from eyewitness accounts. Apparently, the madness that had been brewing in the streets for hours finally came to a head shortly after 7 P.M., when the police, learning that the show was sold out, attempted to clear the crowd.

Many of the kids were already drunk from private stashes of beer. Among the visitors were college kids looking for kicks, and despite Louis's attempted negotiations with the city, no attempt was made to keep them under control. Bars and liquor stores, ignoring a mandate from the governor of Rhode Island, stayed open as long as the money kept coming in. A large mob of inebriated kids—estimates ran anywhere from 3,000 to 12,000—began charging the Newport police force, hurling full cans and bottles of beer at them like grenades. The conflict erupted into a full-scale riot on Middleton Avenue, behind Freebody Park. Some of the kids tried to storm the festival gate, but were repelled; others tried scaling the stone walls surrounding the park. Firemen vainly attempted to disperse the crowd with hoses. The violent throng moved onto Memorial Boulevard. The mob then curled around onto Bellevue Avenue, smashing store and car windows along the way. Governor Christopher Del Sesto, informed by phone of the situation, ordered the deployment of state troopers.

Not everyone in the audience knew what was happening outside, but there was definitely something sinister in the air. Onstage, Horace Silver played a blistering set—and kept playing at my request, because the police had asked me to keep the concert going until they had cleared the streets.

After spending the previous seven years getting musicians to abbreviate their sets, here I was getting them to play *longer*! Oscar Peterson closed the terrifying evening at 2:15 A.M. The musicians left in a phalanx of cars, with a police escort, the fans streaming out onto streets littered with broken glass, beer cans, overturned cars, smashed windows, and the lingering, diffuse odor of tear gas.

The following morning, the city council held an emergency meeting that would last two hours. The chief of police basically shrugged his shoulders at accusations that the police had inflamed the situation. Council members decried the disastrous turn of events. At the end of the meeting, the council voted 4–3 in favor of revoking Newport Jazz Festival, Inc.'s entertainment license.

The Newport Jazz Festival was dead. We weren't even allowed to put on the Sunday-night, Monday-afternoon, or Monday-evening performances. Louis Lorillard and the rest of the board immediately protested, charging that the mêlée was the fault of the city. Louis declared that the festival would sue the city for damages and lost revenue. Even the mayor of Newport opposed the council's ruling.

I knew that the council would happily take this opportunity to shut down Mingus's Cliff Walk festival as well. I begged Louis Lorillard: "You go tell them, do *not* close down that other festival. Whatever else happens, make sure they're still allowed to play." I harbored no ill will toward the rebel festival; I respected these musicians, and they had every right to do what they were doing. It really was a shame that the rioting had to happen. Because if both festivals had continued, the other festival might have, in time, flourished. Eventually, it could have been incorporated under the umbrella of the Newport Jazz Festival.

Louis did manage to get an exemption for the rebel festival, but not before rumors of its cancellation began to circulate. On Sunday morning, I got a cautionary phone call from Max Roach: "George, Mingus is on his way to your hotel. And he's going to kill you."

Joyce, who had overheard this conversation, responded with typical coolheadedness. She ordered English muffins and coffee to be delivered to our room in the annex of the Viking Hotel, so that when Charlie arrived we could receive him warmly and diffuse his temper. But Mingus never did come; he must have heard that his festival would be allowed to continue.

Like an executioner offering one last cigarette, the city council consented to let us hold our Sunday blues afternoon. The show was to be narrated by festival advisory board member Langston Hughes; it featured Jimmy Rushing, violinist Butch Cage, pianists Sammy Price and Otis Spann, and guitarists Willie B. Thomas, John Lee Hooker, and Muddy Waters. This last artist had been recommended to me by Nesuhi Ertegun, now a member of our board of advisers. Nesuhi had heard Muddy in the blues joint Smitty's Corner on the South Side of Chicago; he felt that Muddy belonged on any blues show at Newport.

Muddy, however, had almost decided against coming. He had never heard of Newport, and he wasn't happy with his fee. Muddy "couldn't imagine even taking this gig," his drummer, Francis Clay, has recalled. "I had to convince him what it would do for him and his career and the band . . . That's the one that really exposed the blues to the whole world." A further challenge was the fact that Newport would introduce Muddy to a predominantly white audience for the first time.

Muddy Waters's band featured Clay, James Cotton on harmonica, Pat Hare on guitar, Otis Spann on piano, and Andrew Stephenson on bass. They were uniformed in white jackets and black bow ties, while Muddy himself wore a gray suit. They played some of their Chess Records hits, starting with "I Got My Brand on You." When they left the stage after "Got My Mojo Working," the crowd demanded an encore of the tune. A recording of that song would soon become a popular single for Muddy, and it would bring about his first Grammy Award nomination. Chess would release the whole set on the now legendary album *Muddy Waters at Newport, 1960*.

As Muddy's band walked back out for their encore, Willis Conover informed the crowd of the Newport Jazz Festival's fate. The council had ruled the festival's demise. "Instead of treating the sickness," Willis pronounced, "they shot the patient."

Then, Langston Hughes handed Muddy a Western Union envelope on which he had penned an elegiac blues lyric. But Muddy Waters—this magnificent, nearly regal performer—had never learned to read. So the lyric was passed to Otis Spann, who improvised a melody as he began, like a mourner at a wake, to sing:

> *It's a gloomy day at Newport,*
> *It's a gloomy, gloomy day.*
> *It's a gloomy day at Newport,*
> *It's a gloomy, gloomy day.*
> *It's a gloomy day at Newport,*
> *The music's going away.*

# 7

# *Brother, Can You Spare a Dime?*

I'VE NEVER BEEN POOR, but I've been broke. In the wake of Newport's demise, I found myself in New York City, with nothing going—no horse to ride. The festival was history and Storyville was finished. I did have a brand-new corporation with an office on Central Park West, but the company had no visible means of income, and no real prospects. It felt hopeless. Up to this point, I'd been a big fish in the little ponds of Boston and Newport. Now I was lost in the ocean of New York City.

*       *       *

I had always had other things going besides Storyville and Newport. Only a few weeks after the 1958 Newport Jazz Festival I joined Sidney Bechet in Europe for a week-long engagement at the Brussels World's Fair. This was at the behest of the U.S. State Department; they had asked the Newport Jazz Festival and me to present a jazz program representative of America's most vibrant musical art. I had put together "a package" consisting of Sarah Vaughan, Teddy Wilson, the Newport International Youth Band, and Sidney Bechet. All of these artists were to perform at the American Pavilion; the Benny Goodman Orchestra, which had been booked through other channels, had appeared a few weeks prior.

After almost every concert, I'd hang out with Sarah Vaughan and Johnnie Gary, her road manager at the time. One night, at about one o'clock in the morning, we went to a bar to have a drink, where we received some antagonism from a group of intoxicated Americans who voiced their disapproval of having a black man and woman drinking at the same bar as they did. It looked as if there might be some serious trouble. I'm not a fighting man, but I joined

Johnny in standing up to challenge these drunken jerks. They backed down and left the bar, to my great relief.

Events such as this strengthened my relationship with Sassy—which was a good thing, as she could be difficult to work with. I worshiped Sarah as an artist. No one could emulate her supreme musicianship and quality of voice; she was to vocalists what Art Tatum was to pianists. Sarah was already a star, but I felt that she could reach an ever greater audience. This fact, and the promise of our developing friendship, inspired an interesting idea. "Sassy," I said one night in Brussels, "why don't you let me be your manager?" I sincerely felt that I could do for her what Norman Granz had been doing for Ella Fitzgerald.

Sarah shot me a quizzical look. "How can you be my manager?" she asked. "Aren't you still going with that girl in Boston?"

I was indeed in love with Joyce; we would get married the following year. But it surprised me that this was a deciding factor. I never had eyes for Sarah Vaughan. But she had grown so accustomed to having romantic relationships with her managers that it was hard for her to imagine the arrangement in strict business terms. As a result, she was robbed and cheated all her life. Perhaps more unfortunately, she was mismanaged and never realized her full career potential.

During the World's Fair, the group I'd hired to work with Sidney Bechet for the occasion featured Vic Dickenson on trombone and Buck Clayton on trumpet, who knew how to play with Sidney and avoid a conflict on the melody lead. Bassist Arvell Shaw, drummer Kansas Fields, and myself rounded out the sextet.

It was a memorable week—one of the high points of my musical life. Once again Bechet was pushing me to my musical capacity, making me play my best. One of the sets from our engagement was caught on tape and later issued on Columbia Records under Sidney's name, as *Brussels Fair '58*. It received five stars in a *Down Beat* review.

The poet Hayden Carruth, who was not at the concert, but had the recording and had never heard Vic Dickenson in person, has written about the music on this album. I called Hayden and asked him if I could use his words. Despite my deep love for Vic, nothing I could write could match Hayden's description. One of his poems, a response to Vic's solo on "Society Blues," includes the following passage:

> *Dickenson, no other could sing as you, your blasts, burbles,*
> *and bellowing, those upward leaps, those staccato descensions,*
> *Your smears, blurs, coughs, your tone veering from muted to*
> *stentorian, your confidences, your insults,*

*All made in music, musically. Never was such a range of*
*feeling so integrated in one man or instrument.*
*How you made farts in the white mob's face at the Belgian*
*International Exposition and Mr. Bechet laughed out loud.*
*You were the Wagner of tonal comedy, you were the all-time*
*King of the Zulus, you were jazz.*
*Thanks be to St. Harmonie for the others, yet next to you*
*they are extraneous to the essence, a throng milling outside.*
*I learned it all from you (and from a few dozen others),*
*evinced so incompletely in these poems, yet in my mind*
*A bliss for fifty years, my resource, my constance in*
*loneliness or loving. Now you are dead.*
*You grew old, you lost your teeth, you who had seemed*
*Indestructible have been destroyed, and somehow I survive.*
*Not long, however. Hence from aged humility I dare to*
*speak. May these words point to you and your recorded*
*masterwork forever.*
*Which means as long as our kind can endure. Longer than*
*that, who cares? Thereafter will be only noise and silence.*

Reading Mr. Carruth's reaction to a recording in which I participated in 1958 gave me a profound thrill. Sometimes we think playing jazz is a casual thing, and hope that someone somewhere likes what we do. This poem, called "What a Wonder Among the Instruments is the Walloping Trombone!" confirms the meaningfulness of our endeavor, and eloquently conveys the feeling that many people must have in listening to jazz. We played "Society Blues" at Brussels in 1958; there are now few living witnesses to that gig. But as long as there are people like Hayden Carruth who find meaning in recordings and recollections, the music will endure.

\*     \*     \*

Another opportunity knocked in the form of a phone call from Al Banks, the entertainment director of the Sheraton Corporation. Mr. Banks had a problem. He was desperately seeking a way to resuscitate a dying Sheraton resort in the midwestern town of French Lick, Indiana. Today, French Lick is renowned as the home of Boston Celtics hero Larry Bird; in 1958, it was a stone's throw from oblivion. I had never heard of it. No one I knew had heard of it. Nevertheless, Mr. Banks sounded like a trustworthy character and I knew that the Sheraton Corporation had capital. In fall 1958, I set out to examine the premises.

Sheraton had purchased an early-twentieth-century wood-framed hotel with hundreds of rooms and an adjoining golf course. There was a spa at French Lick with hot sulfur baths; the pungent odor permeated the air constantly. This hotel was an aging oasis in the heart of a midwestern wasteland. Talk about a "white elephant"; this thing even *looked* like a white elephant. In my mind's eye I could almost picture tumbleweeds blowing across the lobby. But Al Banks's offer did give me pause; he was prepared to surrender the entire hotel for my use if I could organize and produce an event similar to the Newport Jazz Festival. Sheraton would provide all of the facilities, as well as advertising and publicity. I'd pay for the artists and keep all of the receipts. It would be a calculated risk.

I told Al that I'd consider his proposal. I visited the towns that bordered French Lick's lonely periphery: Cincinnati, Louisville, Dayton, and others with less-familiar names. I visited music shops and record stores and radio stations and what few clubs there were, and asked everybody the same question. If there were a major jazz festival at French Lick—which was, depending on the city, anywhere from fifty to seventy-five miles away—would people come? The answer, surprisingly, was always yes.

And so it was that, from August 15 through 17—a little more than a month after Newport had ended—the "Midwest Jazz Festival" breezed into French Lick, Indiana. We set up a stage on a corner of the golf course, and staged a three-day program including such legends as Duke Ellington, Gene Krupa, Erroll Garner, Eddie Condon, Gerry Mulligan, Stan Kenton, Miles Davis, Dave Brubeck, Dizzy Gillespie, and the Four Freshmen. The talent, in other words, was on par with what we did at Newport.

Roy Eldridge's comment when he first heard about my plan to mount a jazz festival in French Lick was: "You mean you're really going to do a festival in Cotton Curtain Country?" Even though it was in Indiana, French Lick was near the Kentucky border. Its culture was highly southern, and Jim Crow was still an official policy in the South. The musicians were wary of this fact; Art Farmer and Dave Bailey of the Gerry Mulligan Quartet expressed some doubts about using the hotel swimming pool. They lost all hesitation, however, when Dizzy Gillespie, arm in arm with Jimmy McPartland, dove right in—thereby integrating French Lick's untested waters.

With nothing else to do in a fifty-mile radius, all the musicians spent their time on the hotel premises. The gig devolved into a bacchanalia. On opening night, I had a few musicians over to my suite, and before I knew what was happening, it turned into an impromptu party. Soon there were nearly fifty people in the room: Jazz musicians as well as festive hotel guests whom I'd never seen before. We were all talking, drinking, playing a little music, just having a good time. At one point, Miles Davis slipped into the john.

A while later, a gorgeous blonde woman came out of the same door and triumphantly declared: "I just made history in your bathroom."

\*    \*    \*

With the success of French Lick, Al Banks asked me to produce festivals for Sheraton in Boston and Toronto. My producer's fee for these events was a staggering $40,000, more money than I had ever received at one time before. Unfortunately, neither event caught the magic of French Lick. We lost money in both cities.

Soon, however, it was time for the Newport Jazz Festival European tour. First stop: London. Dizzy Gillespie, Buck Clayton, Jimmy Rushing, and a coterie of sidemen were met there by promoter Harold Davison, a valuable partner and already a good friend. Harold had been helpful to Paul Robeson during his expatriation in the United Kingdom. As a result, he was well regarded by the ultra-left-wing English Musicians' Union, which was a tough organization. The union often made it difficult to get groups into England, with their equal exchange policy; for every American musician who came to England there had to be an English musician appearing in America (and in 1959, before the rock invasion, nobody in America was even vaguely interested in British musicians). Fortunately, through Harold Davison we had an "in" with the union. They allowed our group to enter the country without any hassles. Our Newport package was augmented there by Dave Brubeck, who was then on his second UK tour.

England was successful, but the Continent was another story. In Sweden, I was working with the promoter Nils Hellstrom, who had hosted our audition for the International Band. He loved the idea of the Newport tour. He arranged for us to play many towns in Copenhagen and Sweden that had seldom, if ever, presented jazz before. We found ourselves in places like Sundsvall, Aalborg, Aarhus, Gothenberg, Malmö. Nils and I were both taking a risk. We lost money because business was terrible.

In Germany we were met by an old-time classical and popular-music promoter called Frau Gunderlach. I never knew her first name. Frau Gunderlach wouldn't give us a guarantee, so I worked out a deal: We'll give you the band, and after you pay the hall, just give us what's left. A fair deal, except for the fact that there was never anything left! There were laws in Germany providing for a reduced student-ticket price of four deutsche marks—which equaled about one dollar. Every night it seemed that there were more tickets at the student rate than there were at full price. In addition, there was every kind of tax imaginable, which we knew nothing about. I would think we were getting five marks, and then find out about a tax of a mark and a half: over 20 percent. We played Frankfurt, and Berlin and Munich, and instead of collecting compensation for even a fraction of our expenses, I found myself shelling out a thousand dollars a night to pay for the hall—a total economic disaster. I was shouting at Frau Gunderlach: "It's costing *us* money to play! How do you expect us to keep doing this?"

"Alright, alright," she said. "I'll pay—just leave the country! Get out of here!" Frau Gunderlach was a decent person, but she hadn't clearly described these problems in advance. I was going out of my mind.

In France, the tour was involved with a promoter named Marcel Romano. Part of our deal involved a concert in Algeria, which at the time was in the middle of its war for independence. People were getting killed every day. I don't know how he came up with this gig, or why I decided we should take it. But there we were, flying out of France on a French army plane. When we landed, they ushered us onto a bus, accompanied by two soldiers armed with machine guns, who spent the entire ride kneeling on the floor, out of sight. We, however, were sitting up in plain view, fully exposed. (We would be *their* protection if anyone shot at the bus.) When we arrived at the theater, they let the people in and then locked all the doors; we needed special permission to get back to our hotel. Bombings occurred while we were in Algiers. We all breathed a sigh of relief when our plane lifted off the tarmac of the French army base, and headed back for France.

In Italy, our promoter, Francesco Fior, took us all over the country, wining and dining us like royalty. Our concerts fared well, but in the end, we didn't get the money. Fior owed us about three thousand dollars, and after the last concert he suddenly disappeared. I went to his office in Florence; it was dark and boarded up. He wired me with instructions: meet me at this café at such-and-such-a-time. When I got there, he failed to show. This happend repeatedly.

A beneficial thing for my career occurred on this tour because Joyce, who had joined us in Scotland, was spending a lot of time with Dizzy's wife, Lorraine. One night, Dizzy and I were talking, and he said, "Lorraine tells me you're alright." It was a turning point; Dizzy Gillespie—who had always regarded me warily ever since my gaffe at Newport, in 1954—now gave his stamp of approval: I was alright.

This was a milestone for me, with implications far beyond those of my relationship with Dizzy. It was the first time that I had gained the complete trust of a major artist. This would occur with many other musicians after Dizzy, and although I never understood how to create this sort of bond, I always recognized when it happened.

The financial disaster of this tour taught me a lot about European culture, food, and people; and about the dangers of promoting concerts abroad. It was a lesson learned by trial and error. This time around, the "error" cost Newport Jazz Festival, Inc., over $30,000.00.

*   *   *

Another idea I had was forming a company called Concert Jazz Productions for the purposes of promoting jazz in small towns in New England and New York State. My first venture was the Dave Brubeck Quartet. Most of the touring occurred in towns like Utica and Watertown, New York, and Trenton, New Jersey, which rarely heard jazz. But there was no audience out there, and no community concert subscription to bring people to the halls. Rather than beat a dead horse, I let the idea drop. Concert Jazz Productions was mercifully short-lived. But fond memories of the tour with Dave, Paul Desmond, Joe Morello, and Eugene Wright remained.

*   *   *

Having made the move to New York City, I realized that in order to see the growth I envisioned I would need help. I formed a three-way partnership with Albert Grossman and Eddie Sarkesian, a jazz promoter from Detroit. Our company, with the self-explanatory name of Production and Management Associates (PAMA), seemed clearly slated for great things. Albert and I had already proven our ability as a team in producing the first Newport Folk Festival, and Eddie had a good jazz festival going in Detroit. We were confident in our ability to make things happen, and the opportunities were there.

Just before I moved to New York, I entered into a partnership with folk impresario, Bostonian Manny Greenhill. Manny worked as an occasional promoter and manager for various folk and blues singers, and printed a folk newsletter out of his small South Station office. He approached me with the idea of converting Mahogany Hall into a folk café, and after the success of the Folk Festival his proposition seemed timely. We became equal partners. Inundated as I was with projects, I left the operation and management of the club to Manny. He booked the room with familiar artists from among the Boston scene. Naturally, he was interested in featuring Joan Baez, the new darling of the folk world and the first Cambridge coffeehouse singer to stir national interest. But Joan was noncommittal, Manny told me, and difficult to persuade. He couldn't get her to agree to perform at the Folk Room.

Manny was not the only party interested in Baez. Albert Grossman was courting her as a potential client; he wanted to be her manager. He had worked with her not only on the folk festival, but also in Chicago at the Gate of Horn nightclub. But as Joan had rebuffed Greenhill, she evaded Grossman. I told Albert that I would try to talk to her. Joyce and I invited Joanie over for dinner at our apartment. We had a wonderful time. I played the piano, Joanie sang, and we sat and conversed about her music as well as her concern for nonviolence and peace. We talked at length about segregation; as a statement of protest, Joan had joined the black musicians' union in Boston instead of its white counterpart. We found that we had a lot in common with this young woman, in terms of our social philosophies and approach to life.

"Joanie," I said at one point, "why don't you work for us at the Folk Room?"

"Well, Manny and I don't get along. He wants me to stop working at Club 47, but I don't want to. And he's only offering twenty dollars a night." She was working at the folk room on Mt. Auburn Street twice a week. They had just increased her fee to twenty-five dollars a night.

"Why don't you continue working at Club 47 on Tuesdays and Fridays," I ventured, "and work for us on Wednesdays, Thursdays, and Saturdays? We'll match their twenty-five dollars a night." She agreed.

We parted in good spirits. I felt that Joyce and I had connected with Joan, and that we had a mutual sense of trust and respect. Beyond that, it seemed that we had reached her as human beings. I genuinely liked this talented young singer, not only as a musician and performer, but as a person. I appreciated her perspective and her ideals, which were not identical, but highly similar, to my own.

I spoke with my PAMA partner the next day: "Albert, we had a nice dinner with Joanie Baez, and I think I can talk to her about management. Should I try?"

"No," Albert said, "let me take care of it. I want to manage her." Grossman had, in fact, approached Joan Baez several times before, without success. She was young and perhaps a bit naïve, and Grossman's aggressive manner alarmed her. He did, however, set a record deal for her with Manny Solomon at Vanguard, a small classical label.

In the meantime, Joan's ongoing engagement at the Copley Square folk café brought her into regular contact with my other partner, Manny Greenhill. In Manny, Joan found an older promoter in the folk world who was far less intimidating than Grossman. Although they weren't entirely on the same wavelength—Manny being a somewhat anachronistic remnant of the Old Left, and Joanie being part of a new, hopeful generation—they struck up a friendship, spending a lot of time together at the club. Before long, Joan Baez had chosen Manny as her manager. Although they signed no contract, they worked together for years.

\*    \*    \*

With PAMA we hoped to produce more jazz festivals. But because of the riot at Newport, city administrations looked at us with a wary eye. Wherever we went, we had to overcome a fear generated by the incident at Newport, which had been blown up to major proportions in the national media. We did manage to do a festival in Wakefield, Massachusetts, in an amusement park called Pleasure Island. At the same time, we did a three-day festival at the Connie Mack Stadium in Philadelphia. Both of these had only a slight degree of success and we didn't consider their continuation. In the meantime, the Sheraton Corporation had unilaterally canceled a third French Lick Jazz Festival in Indiana, and I had to sue them to get back the money I had already expended in its preparation. The suit was thrown out of court when the judge told the Sheraton lawyers, "You owe this man money. Pay him, but I won't give him damages." It seems that in the eyes of the court, festivals didn't equate with normal businesses, and even though I had made a profit in two previous festivals, their unilateral cancellation was not considered damaging to me. Years later, my friend and attorney, Herb Baer, who agreed with the court at that time, told me that he had never stopped thinking that, perhaps, we were wrong and we should have fought that decision. It was the only time in my career that I have been involved in a lawsuit.

The summer of 1960 ended on these notes—the closing of Storyville and the end of Newport, French Lick, and other festivals. I had nothing going. What else was there for me to do? Joyce took a job at a hospital so that we would have enough money to eat and pay the rent. I spent most of my days alone in the apartment, seated forlornly at a Scrabble board—trying to see how high a score I could get by playing two hands at once.

Within months we were no longer alone. Albert Grossman finally took my advice, selling his club in Chicago and moving to New York. Without any other New York City contacts, he was obliged to stay with us. It wasn't long before Grossman began to show his genius as a manager. For over a year, he had been working to assemble a folk trio with one female and two male singers. He had tested different performers in different combinations; just months earlier, the trio had included Bob Gibson, Carolyn Hester, and Ray Boguslav. When that group failed to gel properly, he tried another combination consisting of Noel Stookey, Mary Travers, and Peter Yarrow. The group, then in its infancy, had not yet recorded. I can remember evenings when we sat around playing bridge with Nesuhi Ertegun and his wife at the time, Belkis, and Peter would pull out his guitar to sing "Brother, Can You Spare a Dime?"— one of his favorite songs. As I recall those months, it seems as if we were all biding our time, living day to day.

Yet we were hardly down and out. As newcomers to the Big Apple, Joyce and I made it a point to make friends. People often stopped by our house for dinner or drinks. Once we had a knock at the front door at two o'clock in the morning, and there was Peter Brook, the brilliant theatrical director. Someone he knew had just asked him: "Are you going to George Wein's house? He's having a New Year's party tonight." We were indeed throwing a party, in collaboration with the sculptress Judy Brown (Marshall Brown's wife)—but not for another twenty hours. Peter's friend had been too literal in his designation of time. Our party was scheduled for New Year's Eve, December 31. Technically, it was the early morning of December 31 at the time of Mr. Brook's visit, but to all of us it still seemed like Dec. 30. At any rate, the most celebrated director of the modern English stage was standing on my doorstep. We knew each other from Boston; he had stopped into Storyville a few times. "Peter," I said, "it's wonderful to see you. You know Joyce and I got married." Silence. Finally I prodded him: "Peter, aren't you going to congratulate us?"

He sniffed: "To think that forever you've lost the thrill of illicit love."

I invited him in. It was then that I noticed he wasn't alone; he'd brought along the actor Richard Burton and his wife, Sybil. We sat around until four or five in the morning talking. At one point Richard Burton looked around and said: "This is a nice room. Are you really having a party here tonight?"

"Yes," I said, "why don't you come back?"

He looked at Peter. "Why don't we see what the others are doing?" The English theater was in town at that time, to full effect.

"Look," I said, "bring whomever you want, but come at around 12:30 or 12:45 because by that time some of the people will have left."

That night we threw a grand New Year's Eve party; there were maybe thirty or forty people in attendance, half of them friends of Judy Brown. I think I had Ruby Braff and Pee Wee Russell playing. Joyce cooked dinner at

10 o'clock. At midnight everybody kissed each other, and most of Judy's friends said goodnight; the party half dispersed. I didn't tell anyone about our special guests. They simply arrived: Richard Burton, Sir Laurence Olivier, Peter Brook, Clive Revill, Elizabeth Seal, a whole coterie of stars from the English theater. People were coming up to me and whispering, "I thought I just saw you walk in with someone. Was it?" I replied, "If it looks like who you think it is, it probably is." The electricity was palpable. Yet no one was a prima donna; the actors just fell into the party. Joyce cooked again, this time forgoing hors d'oeuvres for early-morning ham and eggs.

It was a festive time for theater in New York. Peter Brook had opened a New York production of *Irma la Douce*, a show I had seen with him in London a few years back. En route to London on that trip, Charlie Bourgeois and I realized that Tammy Grimes, an up-and-coming New York actress, was on our flight. During a layover in Newfoundland, I said to Charlie: "Let's go and say hello to Tammy. She's supposed to be from Newton, Massachusetts." We had an hour or two to kill and thought she might be happy to have some company. This turned out not to be the case; she didn't want to be bothered. We got the hint and left her alone. The following evening I was sitting in the audience with Peter Brook, watching Elizabeth Seal play the lead in the play *Irma la Douce*. In those days I had a wristwatch with an alarm, and, of course, like today's cell phones, it went off during the show. Heads turned, and there I was sitting with the show's director. What an embarrassment.

Backstage, I told Peter: "You know, that girl Elizabeth Seal is wonderful. Are you going to bring her to America for the show?"

He looked thoughtful. "Well the truth is, we're auditioning other people. In fact, there's a girl by the name of Tammy Grimes coming over."

"I know who Tammy Grimes is," I said. "She's very good. But this Elizabeth Seal is tremendous." I would never have said a bad word against Tammy, but I might have been a little more enthusiastic if we had talked for an hour and were friendly.

Brook did bring Elizabeth Seal to New York for *Irma la Douce*. Tammy Grimes, meanwhile, got the lead in a smash hit called *The Unsinkable Molly Brown*. As it turned out, Tammy was one of the people who showed up at our New Year's party. Richard Burton, who had heard my story the previous night, took her by the hand and said to Joyce: "Where's George? I want Tammy to meet the man who kept her out of *Irma la Douce*!" He thought it was amusing. I don't think it was quite as funny to Tammy Grimes.

But the party was such an unqualified success that we held one again at the end of 1961. As I recall, Duke Ellington and Gerry Mulligan came with

Judy Holiday; Barbra Streisand (who was then not yet a star) attended as well. It was a fine time, but I noticed that we had several crashers. Afterward I told Joyce: "I think we'd better stop these New Year's parties; they're getting too big." The following New Year's Eve we went to Cape Cod to spend a quiet week with our friend Paul Nossiter. When we came back, our doorman said, "You know, it was the strangest thing. These people kept coming around and looking for a New Year's party in your apartment."

Social events like these made Joyce and me feel like we had met up with a community—a hard thing to come by sometimes, in the big city. It also helped deflect our thoughts away from the fact that, professionally speaking, nothing was shaking.

*     *     *

My only substantive work of the season took place at the Crane estate in Castle Hill, a gorgeous expanse of land on Massachusetts's northeast shore. Formerly the sprawling estate of Gilded Age plumbing magnate Richard Teller Crane, the grounds had since become a public trust managed by area residents (some of whom lived in posh homes on a country lane called Argilla Road). The residents had, for some years, presented a summer concert series in the gardens, consisting almost exclusively of classical music. In the summer of 1960 I had taken over as producer at the organizers' behest. Under my direction the series had spanned eight weeks and touched upon many facets of music. We had presented concerts in an Italian garden, and I had received a fee of several thousand dollars—the equivalent of manna from heaven, in the aftermath of the Newport Jazz Festival's unexpected end.

The endeavor had been such an obvious success that the Castle Hill board asked me to expand in 1961. I responded by moving some of the series to the main lawn on the premises and bringing artists like the Duke Ellington Orchestra and Lambert, Hendricks and Ross. I made a lifelong friend of Arthur Fiedler by asking him to conduct a thirty-piece string ensemble; he was amazed that anybody would ask the conductor of the Boston Pops Orchestra to tackle Mozart. The renowned classical pianist Leon Fleisher performed a solo recital; so did the famed Spanish flamenco guitarist Carlos Montoya. Mahalia Jackson, Odetta, Josh White, and Nina Simone also performed.

Suddenly the Crane Estate, which had probably never seen a crowd of more than a few hundred people at a time, was drawing audiences of six or seven thousand on the lawn. The crowds were quite diverse; some of them were far removed from Castle Hill's rarefied social milieu. But almost without exception, everyone was well-behaved.

The one exception occurred at series' end—after the Ellington/Lambert, Hendricks, and Ross concert—when most of the audience had already dispersed. Joyce and I were leaving the seating area with two friends and walking in the direction of the mansion when I spotted two men engaged in fisticuffs. A single police officer was wedged between them, trying unsuccessfully to break it up. Without thinking, I rushed over, grabbed one guy by the collar of his shirt, and flung him backward onto the grass. He went down like a piece of wheat. In an instant I was on top of him, my knee in his chest, and two fingers poised over his eyes. "Don't move or I'll put your eyes out," I said. The poor fellow froze. The fight was over—the two men had been fighting, predictably enough, over a girl—and the cop thanked me for jumping in. He let the two guys go. I was surprised at my own instinctive and uncharacteristic reaction, because I had never been in a fight. But I'd had a Newport flashback. I wasn't going to let my life be needlessly ruined all over again.

This altercation aside, the series was a learning experience. It was the first time that the Castle Hill concert series had garnered a significant profit—money that went directly to the upkeep and maintenance of the estate. This was good news for the trustees, as they usually paid those expenses out of pocket. It was just as good for me, as I received a percentage of profit in addition to my fee. This percentage yielded a handsome $12,000 bonus, on top of the $6–7,000 that was my guarantee.

Concert committee president Richard Russell—a tall, distinguished elder gentleman who had served both as mayor of Everett and as a U.S. Representative—had publicly expressed his wish to create "a program of music for the many." Clearly, I had met this goal. But now, Mr. Russell was concerned that we had attracted a few *too* many. "The neighbors are complaining," he said, "so I think we should go back to the way things were."

I shrugged. "I'm sorry the series was such a success."

Mr. Russell said, "We would like to see you continue as producer, Mr. Wein. What if we bring you back next year, and you don't take your $12,000 bonus?"

I wondered whether I had heard him correctly. "Mr. Russell," I said slowly, "are you asking me to *buy* my job back?"

"I wouldn't put it that way exactly, but yes, that's the idea."

"I don't think that's right," I said. "I think you should give me the bonus, which I earned, and if you want to hire me next year, I'm available."

I received no further invitations to produce the series.

*   *   *

Meanwhile, Production and Management Associates was taking its formative steps. Grossman's folk trio was working on a record contract, and their sound had quickly evolved. In the winter of 1961, after hearing a test recording, I knew they were ready. "Albert, you have a hit song there," I said. The song was "Lemon Tree," and the group, of course, was Peter, Paul and Mary, three of the nicest and most interesting people I have met in this industry. Their demo immediately landed them a contract with Warner Brothers. The resulting debut album shot to the top of the charts, sold over two million copies, and scored them a Grammy Award.

Grossman was not the only one playing his hand at management. I was now managing a group I had noticed at a café in Paris the previous fall. They were three young singers—siblings—from Newark, New Jersey. The two older sisters were named Salome and Geraldine, and their younger brother, who also played the piano, was a polite young man by the name of Andy. They called themselves Andy and the Bey Sisters.

I was fascinated with this group. They had a unique style that incorporated the blues feeling of Ray Charles. At the same time, they could do a personal rendition of "Smooth Sailing" and get a whole room swinging. They had their unique interpretation of "Bye, Bye Blackbird." They did a musical version of Joyce Kilmer's poem "Trees." Because of their distinctive sound, I had no problem securing a recording contract with RCA Victor. This was encouraging, to say the least. I felt that we were on our way—Grossman with Peter, Paul and Mary, and myself with Andy and the Bey Sisters.

But my partnership in PAMA was losing its luster. Grossman was still living with us at 50 Central Park West, and had shown little intention of finding his own place. He brought with him a lifestyle not entirely compatible with ours. On numerous occasions Joyce and I would come home to discover Albert sitting on the floor with a friend, passing a pipe or makeshift hookah between them. This provoked some consternation from my wife. I wasn't exactly thrilled with it, either. Another problem was Albert's callous concern for the people to whom he owed money. These unwilling lenders figured that 2 or 3 A.M. was the only time they could catch Grossman at home. So the phone would ring at all hours of the night. Grossman never picked up the receiver. It didn't take long for Joyce and me to grow tired of answering these calls.

There were other problems as well. Although Andy and the Bey Sisters had been promised full support from RCA's promotional machine, we saw scant results. The label's other new artists, among them the trumpeter Al Hirt and a folk group called The Limelighters, were receiving massive amounts of publicity. And my group had none. So I went to see Bob York, who was head of the recording division at that time, and asked what had happened. Why had Andy Bey and the Bey Sisters been excluded from the paid advertisements? Mr. York had a hangdog look on his face when he sighed: "George, don't you think that they're too black?"

It's quite possible that Bob York didn't personally feel that way, but was merely following the lead of RCA's promotional department. This was the very early '60s, and major labels featured very few black artists. Those artists who were fortunate enough to have major-label contracts were usually light-skinned, "acceptable"-looking blacks like Harry Belafonte or Johnny Mathis. The typical young African-American artist who was interested in a music career had better be accepted by Atlantic, Imperial, Chess Records, or another independent. They didn't have a chance on a major label. It's hard to fathom what the record business would be now if this attitude still prevailed.

\*      \*      \*

I didn't lose faith in Andy and the Bey Sisters. But I had to make a living. Having hit a brick wall with management, my thoughts returned to Europe. Having learned from the disastrous Newport package of 1959, I was confident in my ability to set up a successful tour. Although a number of prominent jazz artists were touring Europe, Thelonious Monk had no offers. His reputation for bizarre and erratic behavior scared promoters off. It alarmed me a bit too, but when I contacted Harry Colomby, he assured me that the stories were exaggerated.

Monk commanded a nice fee in Europe, although promoters were fearful of his reputation for strange behavior. I sold the dates rather easily because I took complete responsibility for each performance; promoters had my guarantee that Monk would appear and perform. Harry Colomby and I had many talks about Thelonious's behavior patterns, we settled all the business arrangements, and I was off to Europe with Thelonious Monk, a circumstance that ushered in one of the most beautiful associations in my professional life.

Before I left, I arranged for Andy and the Bey Sisters to appear for six weeks at a club on Sixth Avenue in Greenwich Village. The money was sufficient; I believe it was $1,200 a week, which was not bad at the time. Although I was not in the city during their engagement, Andy and the Bey Sisters were still very much on my mind.

\*     \*     \*

I returned to the United States after the Monk tour in good spirits. I grew even happier when, during the drive home from Newark Airport, Joyce and I heard a familiar tune on the radio—"Bye, Bye Blackbird," as recorded by Andy and the Bey Sisters. This made me excited; the group just might have a hit song in the making. Maybe things were looking up again. First thing the next morning, I called Geraldine Bey. "Why don't you come over? I'm back from Europe, and anxious to talk about the next move."

To my utter amazement, the three of them came in that afternoon carrying an armload of LPs I had loaned them: Billie Holiday, Bessie Smith, Ella Fitzgerald, and Louis Armstrong. They deposited these records on my desk, and announced that they wanted to be released from their management contract. "We want a manager who has a lot of money," they told me. They didn't say it, but I could tell that they also considered my tour with Monk to reflect a lack of concern for them.

I would never have held Andy and the Bey Sisters to a written contract against their wishes, despite my managerial hopes and aspirations and my affinity for their sound. Since none of us was making any money to speak of, our parting was simple; I tore up the contract and let them go. Out of sheer curiosity, I rifled through the records on my desk after they left. Everything was there except the Ray Charles LPs.

Suddenly my prospects were nil again. This blow, along with my ongoing roommate conflict with Grossman, was enough to dissolve Production and Management Associates. I told Albert that it wasn't working out, and we parted ways. He went on to become one of the most powerful men in the music business, managing not only Peter, Paul and Mary, but also Bob Dylan and Janis Joplin. Ending our partnership was a huge financial mistake on my part, and Grossman never failed to remind me that *I* had ended the association, not he.

I assumed that Albert's newfound security and stature would encourage him to settle his debts. I was one of his many creditors; I had borrowed $15,000 to pay for PAMA's office expenses, and Albert owed me half this amount. To my chagrin, but to no one's great surprise, Albert never paid me back. It didn't make sense; $7500 was like nothing to someone with Grossman's means. On one of the few occasions that I saw him in the following years, I kidded him about it.

"Albert, why don't you pay me the money you owe me?"

"Listen George," he said, "you've been telling everybody that I owe you money. That's why I haven't paid you."

"But Albert, you *do* owe me money! If you pay me, I'll stop telling people about it."

This exchange perfectly illustrates why we were never meant to work together.

In any case, I was back—again—to Square One. No income, and nothing happening. The tour with Monk had marked a beginning, not an end unto itself. PAMA had come and gone. I wasn't sure where to turn next. But I derived consolation from the words of a friend. During our travels in Europe, I had grown close to Charlie Rouse, Thelonious's longtime tenor saxophonist. We spent many nights talking, over drinks in anonymous pubs, taverns, and bôites across the continent. On one such evening, I was particularly down.

"Charlie," I complained, "I've always had a horse to ride. But with Newport finished, and Storyville closed, I have nothing. I don't know what I'm going to do."

Charlie Rouse's response still resonates with me. He said: "George, I'm not worried about you. You're a good hustler."

His assessment helped me to keep faith in myself during the long, fruitless days that passed.

It was especially hard for me knowing that there was in fact a jazz festival in Newport in 1961. My colleague Sid Bernstein had managed to get a license to present music there, with a group of Newport businessmen who had formed a for-profit corporation. Despite complaints, the town still wanted the economic shot in the arm that a festival could provide. Sid presented a festival that included appearances by Judy Garland and Bob Hope, as well as a number of important jazz figures. Sid knew how to put on a show; a few years later, he would organize the Beatles' first U.S. tour. But the operation in Newport was grossly overbudgeted in every department. Despite a sizable attendance, "Music at Newport" reported a loss of $60,000.

I made this discovery over the radio. Joyce and I were sitting in the apartment when a newscast caught our attention. Included in the segment was a brief interview with Sid Bernstein—who announced, in response to a question, that he had no intention of returning to Newport in 1962.

"No, no, I'm not going back next year," he said. "The only person who really knows how to handle what goes on up there is George Wein."

I looked at Joyce. "He's right. We're going back."

# Interlude 2: Monk

LATE-AFTERNOON SUNLIGHT STREAMED THROUGH the window of a tea house on the London–Bristol Road, bathing her high cheekbones in a manner reminiscent of Georges de La Tour's portraits in candlelight. This waning light created the impression of a halo. Sitting across the table he regarded her and, in his typically clenched voice, said, "You look like an angel."

Witnessing this moment of tenderness, I began to understand the depth of love and feeling—combined with a touch of genius—that enabled Thelonious Monk to compose "Crepuscule with Nellie" for his devoted wife.

\*     \*     \*

Communist organizations provided a lot of work for jazz musicians in the late 1940s; the Party often hired bands to play social engagements. I remember accompanying Frankie Newton to a function at Irving Plaza, near East Fourteenth Street. The band that evening included a bearded piano player who, as Frankie observed in a tone of admiration, was "doing something different." I always listened to my mentor's pronouncements, but this one threw me for a loop. The guy at the piano was just playing some bad Teddy Wilson. My curiosity was hardly sated when I tried to talk to him after the gig, and discovered that this tall, bear-like musician wasn't interested in conversation. It was my first encounter with Thelonious Monk. I had no inkling of his genius, and not the faintest idea of how close we would later become.

\*     \*     \*

I have little recollection of Storyville for the latter half of the 1950s. I missed many of the club's engagements because of travels in Europe and working on my increasing festival agenda. But I remember well the Storyville debut of the Thelonious Monk quartet in spring 1959.

I had worked with Monk at Newport in 1955 and 1958. But we had no personal relationship at this time. So I didn't know what to make of it when Thelonious came to Boston in an agitated state. I wasn't there when he arrived at the Copley Square Hotel and was refused a room; he had alarmed the hotel staff by scrutinizing the lobby walls, with a glass of liquor in one hand.

The first set that night was scheduled for 8 o'clock. Thelonious didn't show up until 10. The fact that the audience stayed put for two solid hours without complaint amazed me. They had such love for the music of Monk that they were willing to sit patiently, even though it was entirely possible that their man might not even make the gig.

When Thelonious did arrive, he went straight to the bandstand, where his sidemen were waiting. He played two songs, then walked off—and wandered aimlessly around the room, picking imaginary flies off the walls. The audience watched him in silent bewilderment. I got him to return to the stage at 11:30, and he played the same two songs again. Then he sat at the piano without moving for some time. His bandmates eventually left the stand. I had no idea what to do. I had tried talking to Monk, with no response.

After what seemed like an eternity, Thelonious stood up from the piano, shuffled around for a few minutes, and left the club. I later found out that he went to the Hotel Bostonian, where his sidemen were registered, but disliked the room and left. He then tried the Hotel Statler, and was refused. So he took a taxi to the airport in hopes of catching a flight to New York. By the time he got to the airport, the last flight to New York had departed. He wandered aimlessly there for some time. Finally a state trooper apprehended Thelonious and, not being able to communicate with him, took him to Grafton State Hospital for observation.

I knew nothing of this, however, when I called both his manager, Harry Colomby, and Nellie Monk the following morning to ask whether Monk had gone back to New York. When they realized that his whereabouts were unknown, they grew frantic. Harry hired a private detective, who questioned Boston's Finest (but not the state police). A week passed before they discovered that he was at Grafton State near Worcester.

Although Monk's Boston breakdown achieved near legendary status, I presented him a few months later at the 1959 Newport Jazz Festival and also that summer on a Sheraton-sponsored jazz festival at Fenway Park. These appearances were critical successes for Thelonious with no untoward incidents.

\*     \*     \*

I'd been hesitant about investing the time and energy necessary to arrange a concert tour of Europe for  Monk. My experiences in the previous five or six years had been both rewarding and bizarre. In 1955 there was the famous appearance at Newport in an all-star jam session with Miles Davis, Gerry Mulligan, Zoot Sims, and others where Miles had played, "'Round Midnight." Miles came out the hero of the festival, and it gave his career an incredible boost, even though there was a musical conflict between Miles and Monk.

In 1958, Monk had appeared at Newport with a trio in an afternoon session that was filmed for the Bert Stern movie *Jazz on a Summer's Day*. His set was one of the highlights of the film. Then, of course, there was that incident at Storyville.

I still believed in Thelonious. However, I had mixed feelings when I approached Harry Colomby about the possibility of taking Thelonious to Europe. I knew Thelonious was looking forward to a European tour. The fee he was getting for each night was as much or more than he would receive in a week at a night club, and the money meant a lot to him and Nellie.

Nineteen sixty-one was the year of my first concert tour of Europe with Thelonious. We were having a lot of fun. I rented a Rolls-Royce in London at the suggestion of the Baroness Nica de Konigswasser. Thelonious enjoyed riding around and having people stare at him in his huge luxury car. As he returned their gaze, he blessed them much as would the pope from his pope-mobile. T. loved grandeur. He was always impeccably dressed. I experimented with taking him to the finest restaurants. He responded with a ravenous appetite and was trying exotic continental dishes that to my knowledge had never been part of his diet. He liked London and when we played the provinces like Birmingham, Leicester, and Manchester, all within a few hours' drive of the capital city, Thelonious and Nellie after the concerts would choose to drive back with me to London. I drove the car and these two- and three-hour late-night, early-morning rides gave us the opportunity to get to know each other on a more intimate basis.

On tour, I catered to Thelonious's every whim and spent a lot of personal time with him. I treated him as a professional. Thelonious seemed to like me and my concept of working with him. He made every show on time and played the required full-hour set each night. Charles Rouse was on tenor,  Frankie Dunlop was the drummer, and John Ore was on bass.

No matter how well you get to know a musician or an artist it's never easy to gain his trust. Monk had a keen mentality that went along with his musical genius, which allowed him to see whether anyone that he was associated with was for real or was just flattering him in order to benefit from the relationship. As close as we had become in the few days that we were in England, I had not yet gained this trust. However, Thelonious had become quite relaxed on the tour. One night at a concert in Manchester, he was drinking a little brandy before the performance, and conversing quite eloquently with a group of friends. Monk was usually quite taciturn, but when he felt like talking, it was difficult to get him to stop. His monologues could be interesting and amusing. On this particular evening he was due on the stage at exactly eight o'clock. To get to the stage from the dressing room in Manchester you had to climb about ten stairs. After entering Thelonious's dressing room, I said, "T. you're on" and went back up the stairs to check what was happening. No Thelonious appeared. After running up and down the stairs several times, I finally lost my cool and went to his dressing room and yelled, "Thelonious, get the hell on the stage!" He looked at me, walked up the stairs, sat at the piano, played a chorus of one of his songs and proceeded to feature the drummer for approximately forty-five minutes of the sixty-minute performance. As he was returning to his dressing room with little or no response from the crowd, he had the defiant expression on his face of a sulking little leaguer who purposely struck out because his coach yelled at him. I said, "What was that all about?"

With his teeth clenched even harder than usual he said, "You hadn't oughta yelled at me."

I replied, "Thelonious, I had to run up and down those stairs six times to get you on the stage and I'm getting too old and fat to do that." I was thirty-five years old at the time.

"You mean you ran up and down those stairs six or seven times?"

"Yes."

"Then I don't blame you for yelling at me."

At that point I gained the trust of Thelonious Monk. We established a relationship that lasted for the rest of his active years.

*     *     *

*Webster's Dictionary* gives eight different definitions of the word "genius." The one that applies to Thelonious Monk reads, "an exceptional natural capacity of intellect especially as shown in creative and original work in science, art, music, etc. e.g. the genius of Mozart."

There's no question that Thelonious fits this definition. I believe his schizophrenia kept him from realizing the full potential of his enormous creativity. For whatever reason, I always relate Thelonious Monk's artistic life to that of Duke Ellington, as they were so similar in many ways. Thelonious came out of the pure traditions of jazz. His piano style was derived from the stride pianists of the early 1930s such as James P. Johnson, Willie "the Lion" Smith, and Fats Waller, as was Duke's. Each had pride in his appearance and loved a sense of grandeur. But Duke carried his genius to different levels. He wrote extended works, he composed scores for Broadway shows, he wrote many popular songs, and he created works that his band could play with symphony orchestras. Monk obviously thought of having his works played by groups larger than quartets or quintets. He needed musicians like Hall Overton to score these arrangements. I'm sure if Thelonious was more in control of his life that he could have experimented with other musical forms. As time went on however, he seemed content to stick with the small-group format and rely upon his original songs for his repertoire. I often wonder what musical heights he might have reached if he had had the opportunity to think in more ambitious terms.

Many critics and fans alike feel that Thelonious's contributions were perfect as they were.

Many of Monk's songs were based upon the blues, or like Parker's melodies, utilizing chord patterns of established standards. Yet, the complexities of his melodic lines caused many problems for musicians who treated them in a casual manner—whether they attempted to play by ear or simply read the notes. It was difficult, if not impossible, to play Thelonious's melodies unless you fully understood and studied the rhythm, time, intervals, and phrasing that Thelonious had instilled in each song he wrote. Yet, once you absorbed the content and the meaning of his music, the songs unfolded to the listener like a beautiful country road opens up after the driver has maneuvered difficult turns and hills and finds a calm and clear highway to the end of his journey. No song is simpler than "Blue Monk"; it derives from the oldest blues melody in jazz lore. But until you master its rhythmic twists and turns, you don't get it right.

Thelonious was known as "the high priest of bebop." Yet, his own phrasing as an instrumentalist on piano did not reflect the articulation and improvisations of Charlie Parker or Dizzy Gillespie. Where they had a relationship and where his influence was most felt was in his harmonic structure and voicings of chords. These unique musical innovations affected the playing of all boppers. Yet, when the average bop musician would play with Thelonious, it did not sound right. Soloists playing with Monk's groups have to relate to Monk's intervals and time when leaving the melody and beginning their own solos. In other words, while Monk would compose a thirty-two-bar or twelve-bar melody, his comping behind the soloist and what he expected from his featured sidemen had to become part of the composition to work. I learned this on the Giants of Jazz tour when I realized the difficulty that Dizzy Gillespie had in playing Monk's melodies.

Another example was the 1963 Newport Jazz Festival, when I invited Pee Wee Russell to join the Monk Quartet.

I had long felt that Pee Wee, despite his established identity as a Chicago-style clarinetist, used intervals in a way that suggested the most modern approaches to improvisation. A few years earlier, I had made this exact point in an interview with a British jazz magazine:

> He has that same melodic approach that Thelonious Monk has—they are both concerned with intervals. Pee Wee, you will have noticed, never uses an interval you will be expecting, which is part of the great appeal of his playing. Monk is the same. He is, of course, more concerned with the harmonic concept, but his intervals are usually where one would least expect them to be. Although Monk is a little more "out" than Pee Wee, their approach to jazz is in many ways very similar. They both play what to many people are dischords, they are both always looking for that note—that note that is right yet different.

It seemed natural to me, then, that I would want to put Pee Wee and Thelonious on the same stage. Pee Wee had shifted his style away from the traditional sound; his recent album with Marshall Brown featured some songs by Coltrane. So he wasn't averse to my programming idea. In fact, he had even taken an opportunity to see Monk's quartet at the Five Spot. From that repertoire he had chosen two songs on which to play.

What transpired onstage at the festival on July 3, however, wasn't quite what I had hoped for. On both pieces ("Nutty" and "Blue Monk"), Thelonious strolled during the majority of Pee Wee's solos—a common practice that, in this case, yielded strange results. Jazz critic John Ephland would later summarize the effect:

> When Monk lays out part-way through both tunes, Russell takes the music to a decidedly different place, bringing Warren and Dunlop with him. It's as if he recasts Monk's alternating dark colors and playful melodies by simply upending them, the sound of his thin clarinet voice literally a reed in the wind.

Critics turned in both positive and negative reviews of the pairing. While Ira Gitler praised Pee Wee's "personal poetry," John Wilson asserted that "the meeting [had] amounted to little more than their presence on the same platform at the same time." Listening to the recording now, and remembering everything that had been involved, I find myself agreeing with both opinions at once. I still feel that Pee Wee and Thelonious had the same feeling for intervals in their playing. But without so much as a single rehearsal, their affinities were dwarfed by idiosyncratic differences. This is unfortunate, because even a few hours' preparation might have had a substantial effect on their performance.

*     *     *

Joyce joined me on several of the tours with Thelonious and Nellie. Thelonious seemed to recognize the special qualities in my wife that maybe reflected his background and youth. Although she was many years younger than him, he appeared to look up to her as he might have to a mother image. He said to me once, "Your wife is some lady. I had to know her a long time before I would say motherfucker in front of her." I said, "What makes you think you can say it now, Thelonious?"

Thelonious and Nellie's apartment, when they were getting ready to pack for a tour in Europe or Japan, was similar to a current-day sitcom where everybody is running around like crazy; total chaos reigned. Nellie would be screaming in her high-pitched voice, "Thelonious, Thelonious, I can't find your cufflinks." Thelonious would be muttering that he couldn't go on the tour without his cufflinks. At this point, Joyce would interfere. She would question, "You are Thelonious Monk? Do you mean to tell me that Thelonious Monk has only one set of cufflinks?" Quickly another set of cufflinks would appear, and Thelonious and Nellie would finish packing and then be on their way to the airport. Something about the way Joyce talked to Monk allowed her to relate to him in a way few people did.

Thelonious had a mannerism in public of dancing or pirouetting the way he did on the stage when Rouse might be strolling without piano accompaniment. This movement could be quite intimidating in a small room to someone who had never experienced it. Thelonious liked to test people and Joyce was no exception. One day while standing next to Joyce he did a serious pirouette and landed on one foot within inches of Joyce. He asked, "Did that scare you?" Joyce calmly replied, "No."

Shortly after his visage had appeared on the cover of *Time* magazine, wearing an English sporting hat, we went to Europe. Everybody recognized Thelonious there. He wore the same hat every day for three weeks. One morning, he appeared in the lobby of the hotel with a different chapeau. I asked him why he had changed his headgear. His answer was simplicity in its purest form. With usual clenched teeth, he said, "You can't wear the same hat every day."

In Milan we went to a well-known eatery. In the early 1960s most Americans knew only Neapolitan or Sicilian Italian cuisine, which featured pasta with tomato or meat sauce. Fettucine Alfredo with its delightful cream sauce was not yet widely known in America. I picked Thelonious's menu and I explained to him what the first course was and how it was a unique dish that everyone who came to Northern Italy experienced. After he enjoyed the fettucine, we had a second course of saltimbocca. Then they brought the dessert tray and I asked him what he would like from this very appetizing display of sweets. Thelonious wasn't ready yet. He said, "You mean it's time for dessert?" "Yes." "Can I have some more of those noodles?" I understood Thelonious's feelings because years before, when I had first encountered fettucine Alfredo, I had also devoured a second portion of this miraculous pasta.

On tours it's necessary sometimes to take an early morning plane. You might have a seven o'clock flight and arrive at your destination at nine thirty or ten A.M. Usually hotel rooms are not ready for occupancy until noon. This can be very upsetting to tired artists who played a concert the night before and probably had, at the most, two or three hours' sleep—if any sleep at all. This happened as we checked into a hotel in Copenhagen, and I could sense trouble brewing. We were told our rooms would not be ready until noon, a two-hour wait. I had to do something about this problem because I knew it could affect the performance that evening. I went into an improvised act. I started screaming and yelling in the lobby of the hotel, about this famous man who was on the cover of *Time* magazine, a great artist, who comes to Denmark to play a concert and his room is not ready. I carried on in such a way until I saw Thelonious and Nellie start to laugh. At that moment, the pressure point passed. The manager assured us that the room would be ready as soon as possible and Thelonious and Nellie sat in the coffee shop and had breakfast. An hour later they had their room.

Thelonious gave up joining me in my dining adventures; he had begun to put on a few pounds and this bothered him. He did not want his suits to be the least bit ill fitting. His vanity and pride outweighed his enjoyment of food. On the first few tours, I was with the Monks continuously, and he never played a concert without my being there. A rare jazz concert was scheduled in the town of Lyons, France. About twenty minutes from this central French city, there is a smaller town, Vienne, which was the home at that time of the most famous restaurant in France, Fernand Point's "Pyramide." I told Thelonious that I wouldn't be at the concert that night, that I had always wanted to go to Pyramide and that he wouldn't see me before or after his performance. He calmly stated, "Now I know why you booked us to play here." When he wanted to, Thelonious could always be short and to the point.

Thelonious never lost his love for stride piano. In Zurich, he and I went to see Joe Turner, the pianist, not the blues singer, who had established himself in both Paris and Switzerland as the leading exponent of this unique style of piano playing. When Joe Turner saw Monk enter the room he began to turn it on, playing "Carolina Shout" and other standards of the stride repertoire. I said to Thelonious, "T., why don't you go after him? You can stride like that." T. looked at me, thought about it for thirty seconds, and said, "Not me. You take him on." We both sat down, had a few drinks, and enjoyed Joe Turner.

Several books and many articles have been written about Thelonious Monk—his life and his musical contributions. Much of this writing acknowledges that after 1961, I became his international impresario and that the association with me was a great help financially to Monk and his family. What no one has mentioned is what working with Monk meant to my life and career. Nineteen sixty-one was a very difficult year for me. Both the 1960 riot in Newport and the closing of Storyville in Boston at the same time had left me without a business base.

Joyce, who had given up working in cancer research in Boston at the Massachusetts General Hospital shortly after we married, took a job at Columbia Medical School that paid $7,000 a year, which put food on the table. I borrowed $15,000 to pay the rent and keep the office with one employee working for a year. Although I made little money on the first tour of Europe with Thelonious, the facts that Thelonious acted so professionally and that the promoters showed a profit on the concerts helped serve to establish me as someone that European impresarios could work with and trust. I had previously toured Dizzy Gillespie and Dave Brubeck in 1959, but it was the Monk tour that established my European business.

I had a yearning to go to Japan. Knowing Toshiko Akiyoshi had piqued my curiosity about a Far East culture that could produce such a talented young woman. I also found that in 1963 there was interest in Monk in Japan. But the strict Japanese currency laws made it difficult to do business there. Getting work visas required each individual to go to a Japanese consulate. With little else on my plate, I had time to take on these difficulties. Japanese promoters had severe restrictions in leaving Japan to come to America and negotiate deals with agents and artists. Thelonious and Nellie and the group were eager to see Japan, but getting them together at one time to go to the Japanese consulate and get the work visas was not easy. I finally corralled all of them and we went to the office of the consulate in midtown Manhattan. We found the place shut tight with a sign, "Closed for the Emperor's Birthday." After seven or eight months of ridiculous red tape, we finally surmounted all the obstructions; and in May 1963, the Thelonious Monk Quartet with Charlie Rouse, Butch Warren, and Frankie Dunlop did its first tour of Japan and opened up a career for me of doing business with the Japanese that has lasted to this date.

Joyce and I loved Thelonious; he knew this. We told him any time he felt like relaxing or playing my piano, to please drop by the apartment. Occasionally, usually at 1 A.M., the doorbell would ring and there would be Thelonious impeccably dressed, coming to pay us a visit, which often lasted as long as two hours. We would open a good bottle of cognac, and have short conversations about nothing in particular. Then he would sit down and play the piano. There were not many of these occasions; but they were memorable and meant a lot to us.

My professional involvement with Thelonious continued to deepen, as I scheduled an extensive European tour for early spring 1964. Due to some conflicting commitment, however, I was unable to accompany Thelonious and Nellie on the first leg of this trip. Joyce took the helm.

On the evening of Monk's scheduled departure, Joyce arrived at the Monks' house to discover that they hadn't even packed. Thelonious was lying in bed, agitated, and Nellie told Joyce that he was too sick to go anywhere. Joyce stepped into Monk's bedroom and asked him what was wrong.

"My hand hurts," he said.

Against her natural inclination, Joyce held his large hands in hers like a caring mother. "I'll kiss it and make it better," she said in a soothing voice, kissing both hands. Then, more firmly: "I think you can go to Europe now, Thelonious." He got up and went to the airport.

\*      \*      \*

The Giants of Jazz were an all-star group that I had put together in spring 1971. From the start I had envisioned a band featuring Dizzy Gillespie and Thelonious Monk. I had also hoped to include Sonny Rollins, J.J. Johnson, Ray Brown, and Max Roach. But for various reasons, some financial, these artists were unavailable. So I approached Sonny Stitt, Kai Winding, Al McKibbon, and Art Blakey—and a band was born. We agreed that there would be no leader of this group, although Dizzy did most of the emceeing. Everyone contributed tunes, and each received a share of stock in the group (including income from future recordings, films, and so forth). And although they were accustomed to flying first class on their own tours, Dizzy, Monk, and Blakey joined the rest of the band in coach, to reduce costs.

The Giants of Jazz began their Australian tour in September 1971, with concerts in Sydney, Melbourne, Adelaide, and Perth. After Australia, the Giants spent the first half of October in Japan. This trip was memorable largely for Sonny Stitt's visa problem. Because of his arrest record, they wouldn't let him into the country. There was nothing we could do. Sonny cooled his heels at the Tokyo airport, then flew to Europe and waited two weeks for the tour to catch up with him. He was temporarily replaced by Japanese tenor saxophonist Sleepy Matsumoto. We all felt badly for Sonny. He missed ten gigs, and lost a lot of money because the Japanese promoters docked us for his absence. So when the Giants left Japan in mid-October, they volunteered the earnings from their next performance (a U.S. State Department concert in Israel) so that Sonny wouldn't be short at the end of the tour. It was a beautiful gesture, exemplifying the respect and love among the musicians in this group.

But, in retrospect, I'm not sure that the Giants ever really cohered as a unit. The band generally played well; but they weren't carrying out the motivation of a single musical mind. I can't help but feel as if I did Thelonious Monk a particular disservice by asking him to join this group. He did it because he trusted me, and he never complained. But neither Sonny nor Kai were accustomed to playing with Monk; they veered closer to Dizzy's musical universe. Only Blakey and, to some extent, McKibbon really understood Monk's music. So it was as if the Giants were governed by two very distinct personalities. I remember noticing Dizzy's astonishment at the recognition and applause that Thelonious's tunes evoked.

Of course, my critique comes only after the fact. At the time of their tours, the Giants of Jazz received untarnished praise, doing business wherever we went. The group's first album, recorded in mid-November at the Victoria Hammersmith Theatre in London, was released on Atlantic and became a minor classic. The experience was positive for everyone involved; it certainly didn't hurt anybody's career. But it wasn't the glorious musical success that I'd hoped it would be.

On the last tour at a recording session in Switzerland, Monk, apparently bored, left the studio and went for a walk. After years of being with him, I recognized the symptoms. He was going into one of his spells. I was afraid he might get lost in the strange Swiss town so I left the studio myself and joined him. We talked and had no problem communicating. He returned to the studio and finished the session. I knew he would never be the same. I didn't realize that this would be Monk's final recording.

*     *     *

By 1971, Monk was living in Weehawken at the home of the Baroness Nica, where he spent the rest of his life. I presented him in the only public appearances he made in New York after that.

In 1974 I created the New York Jazz Repertory Company. We scheduled a concert of Monk's music on April 6. We had commissioned special arrangements, and Barry Harris rehearsed on piano all week with the band. I know he was looking forward to playing the concert. In one of the most unselfish acts I have ever seen by a musician in showing his love for a mentor and an idol, Barry called Thelonious, told him about the concert, and asked him to come and play. No one expected it, but Monk appeared and, without a rehearsal, played the entire concert. Tears were in the eyes of those who loved Monk, and though he did play at the Newport Jazz Festival–New York in 1975 and 1976, to me, this NYJRC concert was his last hurrah. After the concert I told him that I thought it was time for him to come out and get back on the road. He asked why I felt that way. I answered, "The whole world wants you, Thelonious." He looked at me with a slight smile and said nothing. I didn't know at the time that whatever his illness was, he had the problem of containment and he was embarrassed about appearing in public. It was quite amazing that he did play again in 1975 and 1976. At the concert in Carnegie Hall in June of 1976, T. S. Monk, Jr., was playing drums. I had become friendly with T. S., Jr., and in 1997 the Thelonious Monk Foundation gave me a lifetime award.

Between 1955 and 1976, Monk appeared at the Newport Jazz Festival twelve times; with all-star groups, once with the "Giants of Jazz," with a trio, but most often with his quartet. We toured Japan in 1963, 1966, and 1970. We did many tours in Europe, and Thelonious was a regular at the other festivals that I presented in America. Whatever sickness destroyed Thelonious's health, he always showed Joyce and me the greatest of love and respect. It was a privilege to have been a part of this man's life.

*     *     *

Riding in the car one day with Thelonious, I asked him if he had any aspirin. "Why do you want them?"

"I have a headache."

He admonished me and said I could get rid of the headache by strength and will. For the next hour or so, I tried to take his advice. I did everything—holding my breath, closing my mind to every thought except losing that pain in my head. Finally, I stopped the car and got two aspirin out of my luggage, and in fifteen minutes, the headache was gone.

Thelonious's funeral was held at St. Peter's Church on Lexington Avenue. (Monk died on February 17, 1982.) The church was packed with fans who had come to pay last respects to the master. I had been asked to be one of the speakers. It was not a memorial service, it was a funeral. Where was the casket? Twenty minutes after the congregation had assembled, from the back of the church a harried group of pallbearers rushed in carrying the casket and put it in place as quickly as possible so that the ceremony could begin. Believably, Thelonious was late to his own funeral.

# 8

# *The Festival Is Me*

*No matter what else I've done, I feel best about the festival.*
*The festival is me.*
**—George Wein, press conference, April 1962**

GOING BACK TO NEWPORT was like reclaiming my identity. Without the festival I had been lost, adrift. Newport gave me a purpose. I had already survived rioting, near-bankruptcy, and character assassinations. This move would resuscitate not only the festival, but also my career.

As soon as I had made the decision to return, I called every member of the former festival board of directors, offering an opportunity to invest with me in a new, profit-making corporation. With the exception of Charles McWhorter, their responses fell into two categories: either conspicuous silence or outright refusal. The Newport Jazz Festival was dead, as far as they were concerned. The only board member I couldn't contact was Louis Lorillard; he was living out of the country, as a result of problems with his divorce.

Without Louis's clout and connections, I faced the somewhat unfamiliar task of negotiating with the city of Newport. Fortunately, there were no major hurdles. Newport did want the festival back. Most of the residents enjoyed the glamour, the excitement, and the economic boon bestowed by the event—despite the accompanying inconveniences.

I later considered the possibility that my position as an outsider might have been an advantage. There was a chasm separating Bellevue Avenue society from Newport's working class, and I was a member of neither group. Now that my endeavors were no longer entwined with the Lorillard name, the rest of the city may have felt more inclined to claim the Newport Jazz Festival as its own. However, I made sure that the "Newport Jazz Festival," as a trademark, was registered and owned by me personally.

It made no difference to the public that the festival was no longer a non-profit event. This was an intriguing discovery. People pay attention to what you accomplish. If your work is important, and good for the community, they'll support you; if it isn't, they won't.

And so it was that Newport welcomed the festival back, like the father greeting his prodigal son. In early April, Mayor Charles Hambly signed a contract for a license with Festival Productions, Inc.

I now faced artistic and economic freedom; I was on my own. There was no foundation, no institutional encumbrance.

With invaluable assistance from Charlie Bourgeois, who handled our publicity *in toto*, the festival's resurrection began turning into a major news event. Newport '62 came with a subhead: "The Meaning of Jazz." This subtitle was an attempt to evoke the tone of the early festivals, with an emphasis on presenting the world of jazz in its broadest (but purest) sense.

"The name 'Newport' is synonymous with jazz, and signifies the most important single event in the history of jazz," I declared at a press conference in April, with some bravura. "Success at Newport did more to help jazz and increase the prestige of jazz than anything else in the world." I held a press conference in Newport to which I invited Charles Mingus, whose "rebel festival" had generated so much interest: "Mingus, who once threatened Wein with violence, has 'made his peace with Wein,'" a newspaper article read. "Last night he was seen arm in arm with the new festival promoter." My talent for generating publicity was second only to that of Mingus himself.

In addition to Charlie, I relied upon Arnold London, my longtime accountant, who served as treasurer. Although his home was Boston, he became my contact man, local representative, and protector in Newport. Arnold wasn't a jazz person, but he enjoyed working on the festival; he ran the company's newly christened Newport office on Memorial Boulevard. Gordon Sweeney, who had worked on previous festivals, took charge of the field crew. Marie St. Louis, Joyce's closest friend from childhood, was also a member of our production team and had become my invaluable assistant. As for our technicians, we had the best in the business. Chip Monk and Bill Hanley, who handled our lighting and sound, respectively, would later form the nucleus of the technical team at Woodstock.

Joyce stepped into what would become her perpetual role—that of hospitality coordinator. Her involvement created a new social atmosphere. The festival parties with scrambled eggs and champagne were no longer held in mansions; they now took place in the houses that we'd rented for our summer residency, with Joyce's home-cooked food. This helped create a stronger affinity between the musicians and the festival.

My Newport All-Star band, which had toured the Midwest during much of the long, cold winter of 1961–62, now began to serve a handy promotional purpose. When Rhode Island's U.S. senator Claiborne Pell, a former Newport Festival board member, invited us to play a concert in the rotunda of the old Senate Office Building in Washington, it made news. The group—which consisted of Ruby Braff, Pee Wee Russell, Marshall Brown, Eddie Phyfe, Billie Taylor (the bassist, not the pianist), and myself—played a lunch-hour show on Monday, June 18, to some 500 senatorial staff members. It was the first such concert in the rotunda; the occasion was noteworthy enough to prompt an AP Wire Service photo that was distributed to newspapers across the country. We appeared the following morning on NBC's *Today Show*. We also made a series of appearances leading up to the Newport Festival—the first at the Boston Arts Festival on July 2. For the following week, we played nightly at Nick Cannarozzi's Cliff Walk Manor in Newport, the former rebel-festival site. We shared this engagement with "Charles Mingus and the Newport Rebels," which featured Toshiko Akiyoshi (then Mariano) on piano.

The Bellevue Avenue elite had mixed feelings about my return. Those who hated the festival continued to hate it. Most were just waiting to see what would happen. But some of them helped me, and were happy that I was back. Senator Pell belonged to this latter category; he not only advanced our cause in Washington, but also requested the honor of delivering the festival's opening remarks. Senator Pell's enthusiasm spoke volumes about the validity of a jazz festival in Rhode Island. Another interesting development involved a member of the Royal Family of England. Gerald Lascelles, the first cousin of Queen Elizabeth through his mother Princess Mary, came to Newport as my guest. Gerald and I had met during my travels in Great Britain. He was a jazz fan; this was to be his first visit to the Newport Jazz Festival. Not surprisingly, Gerald was invited to a series of parties on Bellevue Avenue. While he did manage to go to one or two of them, he turned down several other invitations—politely explaining that he was the guest of Mr. George Wein, and had made a prior commitment to attend the Newport Jazz Festival. This opened the eyes of some nonbelievers. Gerald understood the significance of his endorsement. He knew that by associating with me, he enhanced the image of the jazz festival—and in doing so, he supported the music he so intensely loved. We became lifelong friends.

When the 1962 Newport Jazz Festival finally arrived, it had the distinction of being perhaps the most highly anticipated event in jazz since Benny Goodman's 1938 appearance at Carnegie Hall. After a warm-up set by a Providence-based Dixieland group and a welcoming address by Senator Pell, Roy Eldridge opened the concert with his quartet. There were some murmurs, since Eldridge was supposed to have shared the group with Coleman Hawkins. Eldridge worshiped Hawk. He had patterned his trumpet playing on Hawk's tenor improvisations.

But Hawk only arrived at the very end of the set, claiming that he had been caught in traffic. I thought at the time, as I do now, that he missed the set intentionally. I couldn't help but remember the conversation I had had ten or eleven years before on the street in front of Lillian's Paradise in New Haven, Connecticut, where he complained about people always booking Roy with him.

Friday night also featured the Dave Brubeck Quartet, with Paul Desmond. In keeping with my idea of creating different programming, they were later joined by Carmen McRae on vocals and Gerry Mulligan on baritone saxophone. It was a pleasure to have Carmen on the festival. She never quite received her due because of the immense popularity of Sarah Vaughan and Ella Fitzgerald. I was sad when Carmen fell ill shortly after Sarah's passing. If Carmen had remained healthy for just a few more years, she could have amassed the greater fame that she deserved.

The following afternoon included perhaps the most important development of the 1962 festival. I had decided to reinstate the tradition of afternoon panel discussions at Newport, and no one was more capable of spearheading this effort than Professor Marshall Stearns. With my enthusiastic approval, Marshall organized a workshop entitled "A History of the Tap Dance and Its Relationship to Jazz."

Tap dancing, which had been a mainstay of American entertainment for so many years, was withering as an art form. Floor shows were rapidly disappearing from nightclubs, and vaudeville was nonexistent. Those few remaining luminaries of the art of tap had an increasingly difficult time finding work. Honi Coles, one of the leaders of that generation, had been working for years at the Apollo Theatre—as house manager, as there was little work for him as a dancer.

The workshop featured not only Honi, but also Baby Laurence, Bunny Briggs, and Pete Nugent; they performed to the accompaniment of both the Roy Eldridge Quartet and the Toshiko Mariano Trio. They all danced with an elegance too difficult to describe, along with dignity, athleticism, and creativity as well. Each of those dancers had his own style: Bunny Briggs, Duke

Ellington's favorite dancer, reflected Duke's refinement and grace; Baby Laurence, a pioneer in adopting the language of bebop, employed the intricate rhythmic innovations of Dizzy Gillespie and Charlie Parker.

Bud Freeman had once told me that he loved to work on shows with tap dancers, because he took their rhythms and applied them to his improvisation. By bringing jazz and tap dancing together so deliberately, Marshall emphasized this thriving relationship. He also helped inject new life into a dying art. The popular and critical response to this event had a major impact in the resurgence of tap dancing; an impact that resounds to this day, through the work of such artists as Gregory Hines and young Savion Glover.

On Sunday evening, Duke Ellington made his second appearance on the festival; this time with Thelonious Monk as his honored guest. Thelonious played on a Billy Strayhorn arrangement of his "Monk's Dream." Monk's admiration for Duke was unlimited, and quite obvious; you could hear it in his playing. There was also his Ellington album for Columbia, the only time Monk recorded an album consisting entirely of another composer's songs. As for Duke, I was never quite sure what he thought of Thelonious—but he must have had regard for Monk, because he agreed to this special programming. Maybe they just agreed to do it because I was so close to both of them. Whatever the case, it was an interesting experiment; but to my knowledge, it never went further than the Newport stage.

John Hammond's influence surfaced during the next set: a performance by a new young singer named Aretha Franklin. John had recently signed Aretha to Columbia; at his recommendation, I presented her at Newport. At the time, Columbia was attempting to mold her as a popular singer, and the true measure of her talent was not yet apparent to the uneducated ear. But she was a gem, and she did a fine job. Over thirty years after that debut, at a JVC Newport Jazz Festival in 1996, Aretha called upon me to take a bow—announcing to our audience of ten thousand fans that it had all begun for her on that magical night.

The final set of Newport '62 was billed as our "Discovery of the Year." I'm surprised to see this title; I never claimed to "discover" artists, but merely provided a stage on which they could be heard. In most cases, new jazz artists are found by other musicians, who then spread the word to record companies or critics. Rahsaan Roland Kirk was one such artist. Kirk had the ability to play several saxophones at one time. Yet he was no freak; Roland Kirk was a musical genius. I worked with him as often as possible.

The 1962 Newport Jazz Festival broke even, to my great relief. I had financed the festival with the help of my mother, and the support of my friends

Charles McWhorter and Freddie Taylor. Freddie, who had opened a jazz club in Boston called Palls Mall, was relieved by the return of his investment, and decided to withdraw his funds. As is often the case with casual investors, he was not prepared to wait for long-term growth. I gave him his money back. Once again, I was independent. As for Charlie McWhorter, he never asked for his money back, and wouldn't accept equity in the festival. He believed in me, as he believed in jazz, and our friendship grew as the years went on. Eventually I paid him back by contributing to nonprofit musical programs that he supported.

The festival was a major artistic success. I had a sense of accomplishment, coupled with a feeling of personal triumph. I was once again producer of the Newport Jazz Festival—and now I was also in charge.

\*       \*       \*

In late spring 1962, Art Talmadge—the head of United Artists Records—asked me to produce some albums. I first recorded Howard McGhee, whom I felt had always received short shrift from the jazz press. The resulting album, *Nobody Knows You When You're Down and Out*, included an exquisite rendition of Leonard Bernstein's "Lonely Town." I also made a vocal LP featuring Dakota Staton, which was buried by the record distributors. At the time, Dakota was married to a Muslim preacher who had made public statements denouncing Israel—a bad idea, since most of the record distributors in the music industry were Jewish.

United Artists had made a deal with Charles Mingus, who wanted to record a big band album in front of an audience. In September, record producer Alan Douglas had produced the session with Mingus, Duke Ellington, and Max Roach, which would be released as *Money Jungle*. Alan asked me to write the notes for this album. My opening line was: "One of the greatest trios ever assembled." Joyce edited this to read: "Ellington! Mingus! Roach! A triumvirate, not a trio."

Mingus's live-recording session had originally been scheduled for mid-November, but UA bumped it up to October 12, to be held at Town Hall, with Alan Douglas as producer. I had nothing to do with the execution of this recording, but I had been asked to organize the concert. My office rented the hall and took care of the advertising; UA financed the event.

Like Ellington, Mingus was writing for this concert right up until the last minute. He had to prepare charts for an orchestra of thirty pieces: a band that included seven trumpets, six trombones, four alto saxophones, two tenors, two baritones, an expanded rhythm section, an oboe, and a bass clarinet. Some of the musicians involved—like Buddy Collette, Eric Dolphy, Danny Richmond, and Britt Woodman—were veterans of Mingus's Jazz Workshop. But others were unfamiliar with the bassist's somewhat unorthodox methods. This fact, combined with the unique instrumentation of the group, left the bassist with a monumental challenge. It was too ambitious a project for so short a span of time.

Pressure began accruing weeks before the concert. Mingus enlisted trombonist Jimmy Knepper to help with the task of copying charts; for more than a month, Knepper worked with several other arrangers to get the music on paper.

The day before the concert, Knepper went to Mingus's apartment and the two had words. Charlie punched Jimmy in the mouth. This was the ugly side of Mingus; he was as unpredictable a human being as any I have known. He could be cooperative, gentle, extremely friendly—and then, without warning, suddenly irascible, annoying, even violent. But those closest to him found a way to forgive him. Despite a painful broken tooth, Knepper showed up to a rehearsal late that night to drop off the last of his charts for the band.

The concert was chaotic from the start. Before curtain call, Mingus went out and told the audience: "This is not a concert, it's a recording session. Blame George Wein—he didn't give us time to rehearse." He promised refunds to anyone who didn't like the show.

Things went from bad to worse. The musicians were struggling to make sense of the arrangements. Jerome Richardson, the evening's concertmaster, was trying to keep it together. Mingus was storming and seething. Copyists were set up at a table in the wings of the stage, frantically writing charts for the next movement.

I spent this time in the front lobby, so I missed much of the music. But I was aware of the use of my name as an excuse for the utter bedlam onstage. At intermission, I saw Charles as he came out to get some air and I confronted him.

"Charlie, what the hell are you doing up there?"

In his usual hurried cadence, he said: "George don't worry man, you and I are going to make a lot of money, just let me take care of things."

I had no choice but to leave it at that. I had long since grown accustomed to Mingus's shenanigans.

The fiasco cost UA well over its original $35,000 projection. And the company was stuck with nearly three hours of material on tape, much of it inscrutable. A few days after the concert, I received a call from Art Talmadge:

could I help them edit the music for release? I said I'd try, on the condition that my involvement on the project be kept a secret.

I entered the studio at midnight with an engineer, and listened to the tapes over and over again until I could understand the structure of what Mingus was trying to do. He was writing in more or less traditional twelve- and thirty-two-bar choruses. Some of these choruses were muddy and made no sense to me; others were clearer and easier to comprehend. I spliced and edited with the engineer for nearly five hours straight—from two to past six in the morning. We ended up with about thirty-six minutes of music, barely enough for an LP. United Artists released this edited product as *Town Hall Concert*. It received five stars in a *Down Beat* review, and later won the *Down Beat* International Critic's Poll as album of the year.

Purists may still feel that I tampered with the music. Whatever the case, it's clear that the results of my tampering had no adverse effect on the career of Charles Mingus. Still, I never wanted Charlie to know that I had edited the album, and my name was withheld from the release. I only mentioned my role in the recording to Sue, Mingus's widow, after his passing. I do appear in the credits of a recent CD reissue, on which the music from the concert has been reassembled and remastered.

* * *

Many highly successful collaborations took place during the 1963 Newport Jazz Festival. One such example: Sonny Rollins invited Coleman Hawkins to join his group on stage. It was a rare summit of talent. Sonny had long idolized Hawkins. His sound had first emerged as a bebop translation of Hawk's broad, expressive tone and harmonic prowess. But by this time, Sonny was exploring new territory. Hawk hadn't stood still, either. Although his heyday had transpired decades earlier, he was still an undisputed giant on his instrument. He had been one of the few swing-era musicians to embrace and encourage the development of bebop, and he now fostered a similarly open attitude toward the freer forms of expression. All the while, he remained steadfastly true to his own sound. The tenor pairing at Newport was so rewarding that it inspired Rollins and Hawkins to record together later that year.

Looking back upon a half-century of festivals presented all over the world, I'm hard-pressed to name one particular moment that stands above the rest. And yet, if there was ever a "golden age" of the jazz festival, it would have to be Newport in the 1960s. After the litmus test of 1962, the Newport Jazz Festival had blossomed into an event that was as lean and focused as it had ever been in the best years of the previous decade. Any mistakes were my mistakes; I alone answered to the musicians, the public, and the critics.

It helped that this was an extraordinary time for jazz as a whole. Most of the great figures from the 1930s and '40s were still alive. The 1950s had produced a new crop of stars, like Gerry Mulligan, Dave Brubeck, Cannonball Adderley, and many others. Record companies were very active in promoting both established and emerging artists. Simultaneously, there was a bold, incipient movement taking shape, known variously as "the avant-garde" or "the new thing," spearheaded by such visionaries as Cecil Taylor, John Coltrane, and Ornette Coleman. Despite a considerable range of styles and sounds, most jazz musicians were still confreres; they liked one another and respected one another's work.

The John Coltrane Quartet, perhaps the most prominent group to span the modern jazz divide, closed the festival on July 7; it was their Newport debut. Coltrane was at a sort of peak in his career, and had garnered widespread critical accolades as well as a rapt and quickly expanding public. He was at the helm of what would later be called his "classic" quartet, with McCoy Tyner on piano, Jimmy Garrison on bass, and Elvin Jones on drums. In summer 1963, however, Elvin Jones was unable to perform with the group. So Coltrane used Roy Haynes, who was already playing on the program.

Many of the reviewers at the time were turned off by Coltrane's marathon-length modal improvisations. As had been the case with Charlie Parker, I recognized this brilliance before I developed an affinity for it. Whether I liked it or not at the time, Coltrane's music—rooted in the traditions of jazz yet stretching far beyond them—provided the perfect summation to the 1963 Newport Jazz Festival.

\*     \*     \*

My involvement in the Far East—which had burgeoned after a successful Thelonious Monk tour of Japan in May 1963—was another source of work. In September the Sonny Rollins band traveled to Japan on a tour I had organized. I was not able to join them on this trip, but Joyce volunteered to go. Charlie Bourgeois and I went to Idlewild Airport (presently JFK) to see everyone off. The band—Hugh Lawson, Roy McCurdy, and Henry Grimes—checked in and boarded the Eastern Airlines flight to San Francisco en route to Tokyo.

There was one problem: no Sonny. We waited near the gate and there was no sign of him. All of the flight's passengers had boarded, and the crew was preparing to shut the door to the plane. Finally the tenor man showed up.

I hailed him: "Sonny, what happened?"

He shook his head. "I was over at Western Airlines. I didn't think Eastern Airlines flew to the West Coast."

I didn't stop to ponder the logic of his assumption. "Well, you've got two or three minutes to make the flight. Let's get you on that plane." We hustled Sonny through the checkpoint; Charlie and I couldn't go through because we had no boarding passes. So we stood by as Sonny turned a corner and walked in the direction of the gate.

I said to Charlie: "Let's wait a while to be sure he makes the plane." We waited eight or nine minutes before Sonny Rollins came back into view.

He shrugged. "They shut the door on me."

"You had time! What happened?"

"Well," he said, "I stopped to get some insurance on the way." He had paused at a vending machine to purchase a flight insurance policy.

We hurried Sonny to the nearest ticket counter, and booked him on another flight due for San Francisco. He arrived safely. Joyce was with the band there; and her mother, who lived in California, had come to the airport to say hello. When she met Sonny Rollins, Columbia Alexander offered a motherly salutation: "Oh, you're the young man who missed the flight in New York." I don't think she fully realized the stature of the Saxophone Colossus.

A month later, another group toured Japan under my auspices: the Max Roach ensemble featuring Abbey Lincoln. Max was performing his *Freedom Now Suite*, a seven-part composition commissioned by the NAACP to commemorate the centennial anniversary of the Emancipation Proclamation. The suite, which had debuted in 1960, was perhaps the boldest statement on race ever made by a jazz musician. At this point, in 1963, it was right in step with the times; the battle for civil rights was reaching its zenith.

I traveled with Max and the band on this tour. I regarded the *Freedom Now Suite* as a major work. It combined the rhythms and pulses of Africa with the sound of modern jazz, in an effort to emphasize the roots of jazz, our music. More important, it captured the energy of the Civil Rights movement. I noted that Japanese audiences responded positively to the piece, even though they may not have been entirely familiar with its social and political message.

\*     \*     \*

The 1964 Newport Jazz Festival began on July 2 with a program called "Great Moments in Jazz." The concept was to bring together important jazz musicians who, for one reason or another, had been lost in the shuffle, and to have them play the songs that they had made famous. Trombonist George Brunis did "I Wish I Could Shimmy Like My Sister Kate," and Bobby Haggart played

"Big Noise from Winnetka." The program also included guys like Lou McGarity, "Wingy" Manone, Bud Freeman, Peanuts Hucko, and Max Kaminsky. It was a night tailor-made for those fans, like myself, who had fallen in love with jazz long before bebop.

The pianist I had hired for this occasion was the legendary Chicago stride player Joe Sullivan. Joe had played with the Bob Crosby band for years; in the 1930s, he had made a hit record called "Little Rock Getaway." He had also worked with everyone on this program at one time or another, so he was a natural choice for the gig. But Joe had a bit of a drinking problem; during the afternoon rehearsal, he collapsed and had to be rushed to the hospital. I found myself filling in for him, playing piano on the program. Fortunately, I knew most of the tunes; they brought back memories from all my nights at the Ken Club and the Savoy. This illusion was encouraged by the fact that I was sharing a stage with Edmond Hall and J. C. Higginbotham, two of my earliest musical heroes. I hadn't played with either of them for over ten years.

*     *     *

One of the most interesting sets was that of the Stan Getz Quartet, which in 1964 included Gary Burton on vibraphone. I had briefly been Gary's manager, so I was happy to see his career taking off in such meteoric fashion. The group brought a studied intensity to the stage. Stan had agreed to include guest artists, and I had managed to secure an appearance by Astrud Gilberto. Their album, *Getz/Gilberto* (Verve) had been released the previous year, and had quickly ascended the pop music charts. But it was quite a promotional achievement to get Astrud to perform with Stan. By this time, the two didn't exactly get along, to put it mildly. But perform she did, to the delight of a capacity crowd. On a different note, Getz's quartet was also joined by trumpeter Chet Baker. This, too, was a coup. Baker was living out of the country. His various afflictions made him a less-than-dependable artist. Somehow, it all went off without incident. Baker showed up on time, wielded his flugelhorn, and revisited his glory days with Getz's piano-less quartet. Baker had received his first recognition with the Gerry Mulligan piano-less quartet.

*     *     *

The first World Jazz Festival in Tokyo was the brainchild of my Japanese contact, the impresario Tokutara Honda. Mr. Honda had made provisions for a full-scale festival at Shibuya Park on July 10, 1964. Headlining the festival was the Miles Davis Quintet, which included the saxophonist Sam Rivers. The package also featured such artists as Carmen McRae, J. J. Johnson, Dakota Staton, and Edmond Hall. I was apprehensive about this venture, primarily because Mr. Honda had broken his promise to pay us in advance. He assured me that he would have the money—in U.S. dollars—when I arrived in Tokyo. I took him at his word.

In Tokyo, Mr. Honda informed me that the money had cleared, but the bank could only release ten thousand dollars per day. I went to the bank to retrieve the first installment. The attendant at the window handed over a bundle of cash; ten thousand dollars wrapped in brown paper and elastic bands. I signed a form authorizing the transfer of these funds to my bank in New York, and then handed back the bundle. It was a comical transaction—made all the more so when, the following morning, I performed this task again, and noticed that it was the exact same bundle from the day before. Ten thousand dollars was a lot of money in 1964, and Japanese banks only had a limited amount of United States currency. Since Honda-san owed me something like fifty or sixty thousand dollars, I returned to the bank every day for almost a week. Each time, they handed me the same stack of bills ("Hai, dozo. . . "); I signed it over for transfer to my bank; and ("Hai, dozo. . . ") I handed it back.

Nineteen sixty-five began with a bang, as I embarked on my second drum-battle tour of Japan. This time the featured artists were Buddy Rich, Louis Bellson, Charlie Persip, and Philly Joe Jones. Philly Joe was the only holdover from the previous year; he had been such a hit that my Japanese promoter requested his presence again. We all flew together, along with trumpeter Blue Mitchell, saxophonist Junior Cook, bassist Gene Taylor, and the jazz tap dancer Baby Laurence.

Baby Laurence was a phenomenal talent, a dancer whose routines often caused master drummers to shake their heads in admiration. The drummers on this tour had a lot of respect for him; Buddy Rich and Philly Joe Jones had been tap dancers themselves, and Louis Bellson often said that he based his playing on the rhythms of tap. I remember sitting with Baby, Buddy, Louis, Philly, and Charlie Persip at 40,000 feet over the Pacific Ocean, swapping stories; it was a lot of fun. At one point, the conversation turned to drug use among jazz musicians. Someone noted how Charlie Parker's habit had led an entire generation of musicians to heroin. At that moment, Baby Laurence proudly chimed in: "And I was the one who turned on Charlie Parker!" He explained that he had introduced Bird to junk in Kansas City, years before the alto saxophonist moved to New York. There's no way of knowing whether this story is true. Baby Laurence believed it to be, wearing the dubious distinction like a badge of honor.

At another point during the flight, Buddy and Louis conferred with Philly Joe; they knew he had done the drum tour the previous year, and they wanted to hear how it would go down. Philly Joe, who had respect for both Buddy and Louis, explained that the concert would open with all four drummers onstage without the horns; they would establish a beat in unison, then take turns playing brief solos. Then each drummer would play a featured segment with the band.

Our first concert took place in Tokyo. After the opening segment, Charlie Persip played a few tunes with the horn players, and took his featured solo. Then Louis Bellson came out to close the first half with his dynamic double bass drum exhibition.

After intermission, Philly Joe came on to do his segment. He went through his whole repertoire, whirling his brushes in frenzied circles like a chef whipping eggs into a froth. He finished to a huge round of applause; he was the champion. As he came off the stage—still wearing his drum shoes, and with a towel draped over his neck like a prizefighter—you could almost hear his thoughts: "Go ahead, Buddy. Follow that."

Philly Joe stood in the wings beside me as Buddy Rich walked out and sat down at the drums. Buddy started with a roll on the snare drum—quiet at first, then gradually building in volume and intensity. What took place over the next ten minutes or so was a sort of magic. Waves of applause ran through the auditorium as people marveled at Buddy's solo. I cast a sidelong glance at Philly Joe. His shoulders drooped, and his chin had fallen to his chest. Finally he turned away in disgust, muttering the only word that could express his mixed feelings: "Motherfucker!" He left the auditorium in a huff. Tokyo had a new champion.

We did a television broadcast the next day. It was not a live-concert taping, and there was no studio audience. So during a half-hour break, while Louis Bellson and Charlie Persip were cooling off, Philly Joe started to toy with his set. Offhandedly, he played a few rhythmic patterns; it was just a master drummer fooling around with his instrument. Buddy perked up his ears and when Philly Joe paused for a moment, he delivered his own statement. The next thing we knew, we were witnessing one of those incredible moments that jazz can offer. The two of them went at each other in a drum battle. They went back and forth, like sparring partners, for over fifteen minutes. It was astounding. When it was over, they finished the television show.

The following day, in Kobe—in spite of many warnings—Philly Joe Jones and Charlie Persip got busted for buying marijuana in a bar that was known to be monitored by the Japanese police. Buddy and Louis completed the tour with two Japanese drummers.

None of this was making me rich. My friend Sid Stiber, who had come along in order to film these drum battles, happened to ask how much money I was making on the tour. I told him I was getting a commission of about $200 a night.

He shook his head. "How the hell do you do it? You've got an office in New York with rent and expenses. That's crazy—you're losing money before you even start."

"Sid," I said, "what else am I going to do? This is what I do." And I kept doing it, and doing it, in the hopes that my efforts would someday bear fruit.

Back in Newport, there was another set of circumstances awaiting my attention—the complex political web of Newport, Rhode Island. Although I was now inarguably the most experienced jazz festival promoter on the planet (having produced nine Newport Jazz Festivals, four Newport Folk Festivals, two Sheraton festivals in French Lick, three Ohio Valley Jazz Festivals, and a festival each in Boston, Toronto, Pleasure Island in Orlando, and Philadelphia), I knew very little about this side of things; Louis Lorillard and his lawyers had shouldered much of the city council negotiations in the 1950s.

It had been relatively smooth sailing during the past two years; Newport had taken the festival back without complaint. But the welcome mat was getting a bit threadbare. The city council had issues with the festival. So it was at this time that I began to learn an important lesson. If I was going to keep presenting festivals in Newport, I would have to assume more responsibility in the community. It was a new approach to being a producer—taking initiative for everything that happened, beyond the festival itself. I had spent a decade writing the book on how to produce a festival. Now it was time to write the next book: How to deal with the big picture, the totality of an event.

My team and I still had a lot to learn. We started by responding to the council's ruling banning festivals at Freebody Park. The ban didn't exactly take us by surprise; the festival had clearly outgrown the municipal football field and its adjacent narrow streets. Residents were complaining about the noise level during concerts. Parking was virtually impossible. Traffic was horrendous, and getting worse by the year. Newport simply couldn't support such an influx in its downtown area.

We had already begun to consider possible alternate sites. After the council decision, we finalized this search, settling upon a thirty-five-acre open field located off Connell Highway—about a mile north of downtown Newport. It was a half-mile from the city dump, and just opposite the Newport Naval Base. This property, which had previously served as a stop for traveling circuses, was owned by a commercial fishing company. When Gordon Sweeney and I drove over to see the field, there were enormous nets spread out to dry. Dead fish were scattered about on the grass, lending the air a primordial odor. It took a good deal of imagination to envision this as the home of the Newport Jazz and Folk Festivals.

Fortunately, imagination was one of our most abundant resources. We knew that the Connell Highway site had great potential. The abundant acreage was perfect for parking. The field's position made it possible to project sound away from the city, so that no homes would be affected. It was close to Newport's downtown area, but far enough to alleviate traffic congestion. We reached an agreement with the fisherman who owned the property—a burly, amiable guy named Mariano Bucolo, who is one of the unsung heroes in the history of Newport Jazz.

Beach sleeping was a thorny issue, and it formed the axis around which that year's conflicts revolved. At the time, thousands of festival-goers resorted to the beaches and parks of Aquidneck Island for both carousing and repose. They weren't given much choice in the matter, since the accommodations in Newport and neighboring Middletown were fully booked, often months in advance. Some of Newport's residents perennially registered with the Chamber of Commerce and opened their homes to visitors, but that only did so much to alleviate the problem. It was simple fact that many of the people who came to the festivals—especially those of collegiate age—did so with the intention of roughing it. But officials in Newport and Jamestown frowned upon this tradition. As far as the authorities were concerned, festival season heralded an insidious transformation on the island's beaches.

But a popular voice was opposed to a ban; many in Newport wanted to keep the beaches open. As early as January 1965, the *Providence Journal* ran an editorial criticizing the cities of Newport and Middletown for not considering such compromises as better lighting and patrol on the beaches during night hours. "Closing city and town beaches for sleeping will be another manifestation that festival fans are not wanted," the article sensibly stated.

The banning of the beaches was approved by the city council. I have mixed thoughts about camping and sleeping. Today rock festivals in Europe and some "jam" festivals in America where music continues twenty-four hours a day have camps where fans can sleep right on the property. Some small communities allow these type of events because they have a certain economic impact. The Philadelphia Folk Festival has a camping area, which is family oriented. There is no question that having camping facilities available makes a music festival more attractive to the young people who can't afford hotel rooms or rooming houses. The ideal festival site, in my mind, would have a monitored camping area with all the necessary amenities for decent living—available food, free water, showers, and toilets.

At the time, I never considered this whole mess to be my responsibility as a festival producer. I began to realize that when you go into a city with the intention of attracting thousands of people, you need to know what sort of accommodations are available. You must examine traffic and parking issues, and the general effect this influx will have on the community. And you should do it all in cooperation with administrators in the city. When we present festivals in Newport today, we work with the city to ensure they run smoothly. But in 1965, we had yet to learn this lesson. We felt that, whatever happened, we were right. How could we be wrong, when we were presenting marvelous music? To borrow a line from one of our Folk Festival's favorite performers, we felt that God was on our side. The problem was that we didn't give God any help.

Earlier in the year, I had been doing business with Count Basie's manager, Willard Alexander, about a possible European tour. At the time, he was on his way to Las Vegas. "I'm going to see Frank," he said. He always liked to drop names. In this case, he was talking about Frank Sinatra. So I told him to ask Sinatra if he would be interested in working at Newport. It was a wishful request, but I wasn't about to hold my breath.

After returning from Europe, I received a call from Willard. He told me that Frank was interested. I asked, "Frank who?" I had forgotten about our previous conversation. And that was it. Sinatra had agreed to appear at the Newport Jazz Festival with the Basie band. Sinatra was at his peak of popularity. As soon as we finalized the contract and issued a press release, the newspapers picked up the story.

One paper reported: "The news—Sinatra is coming!—started a gold rush matched only by teen-agers in search of seats to a Beatles bash." Even though our other programs featured major attractions, nothing could compare to the demand for Sinatra tickets. There were 12,000 reserved seats in Festival Field, and they were going as fast as we could sell them. At a certain point, I announced a new policy: Anyone buying a ticket to the Sinatra show had to purchase tickets for another night as well. It was the first time we had made any such request, but nobody complained. I could have scalped tickets for five times the price, but this was a no-no with both my treasurer, Arnold London, and me. Our advance sales, for Sinatra as well as the rest of the festival, were unprecedented.

The Connell Highway property turned out to be an even better site than we had planned. In June, the press came out to take photographs of our empty field. It was three or four weeks before the festival, and the place was still quite unkempt. More than one paper commented on the maritime stench. "We've got to get all these dead fish picked up," Gordon Sweeney was quoted as saying. "It really kills you when the wind isn't blowing." In addition to this task, Gordon's team along with Charlie Bourgeois had to erect over a mile of snow fencing, drape thousands of yards of bunting over it, and set up 12,000 folding wooden chairs in twenty-eight sections. Each chair had to be numbered. In an interesting coincidence, many of the folding wooden chairs we used had just come from the Cassius Clay–Sonny Liston prize fight in Lewiston, Maine.

When the newspaper reporters came back to the field for the festival, they could hardly believe their eyes. We had four entrances, all facing Connell Highway. Our new stage, consisting of structural aluminum and heavy plywood flooring, was more than one-third larger than previous festival stages. The thirty-five-acre property proved to be adequate for this stage, our 12,000 chairs, and 2,500 cars. There was room enough even for a helicopter landing (more on that later). We had shaped a rugged, expansive mound into an outdoor concert arena worthy of Sinatra. Some reporters called this transformation "The Miracle on the Hillside."

The first night of the festival was a program entitled, "The Family of Jazz." The Muddy Waters Band was opening the show. At the previous Folk Festival, I had been listening to his band when I was struck by a sudden idea: Dizzy Gillespie with the Muddy Waters Band! I could just hear Dizzy blowing his trumpet over Muddy's blues. So I had asked Dizzy whether he would do this. He had responded: "It's the blues, man. Why not?" During Muddy's set, Dizzy and James Moody sat in with the band. I had suggested the pairing as a personal request. Moody, and Muddy—playing Mississippi Delta blues together, in seamless accord. A Voice of America tape reveals that while the music wasn't exactly off target, it would have been better with a little rehearsal.

The following afternoon consisted of a highly controversial program: a study of the so-called jazz avant-garde that I had titled "The New Thing." There was a distinct movement happening in jazz, and I felt an obligation to feature some of these artists at the festival. I had done programming of this sort in the past—Cecil Taylor had played Newport as early as 1958—but never before had I given these sounds their own featured show.

The afternoon started with the Jazz Composers Orchestra, which was led by trumpeter Mike Mantler and pianist Carla Bley, and included in its ranks was trombonist Roswell Rudd, alto saxophonist John Tchicai, drummer Milford Graves, bassist Steve Swallow, baritone saxophonist Charles Davis, and multi-reedist Ken McIntyre. The music was certainly a challenge for listeners; one paper labeled it an "exercise in cacophony."

Before Cecil Taylor and his quintet closed the afternoon program, other artists who appeared were Archie Shepp with a quartet and Paul Bley with a trio.

It was a rousing afternoon of "new music." Only a few hundred people bought tickets to the event. And while I feel it is crucial to expose this music, a promoter must have adequate subsidies. The obligation to present artists just because they are "new" is not high on my list of priorities.

The meaning of the term "mainstream" changes all the time. In classical music, Stravinsky, rejected at first by the academy, soon became a permanent part of the artistic flow. It is the same in every art form. If the work of a given artist has validity as accepted by contemporaries and students, it invariably, perhaps against its own objections, becomes part of the mainstream. The modal music of John Coltrane, the experiments of Ornette Coleman, and many elements of Free Jazz, which rocked the jazz world in the '50s, '60s, and '70s and had to overcome negativity from jazz traditionalists, have become part of the mainstream and must be recognized as such. Unfortunately, the sales of jazz records seem to diminish every year. It appears that musicians' acceptance of "new things" is far ahead of that of the jazz public.

*　　*　　*

The Saturday afternoon was a workshop of master drummers including Jo Jones, Elvin Jones, Louie Bellson, Roy Haynes, Art Blakey, and Buddy Rich. Dan Morgenstern noted in *Down Beat*, "the audience's standing ovation for Rich seemed a modest tribute. (Elvin Jones showed his appreciation by hugging Rich and lifting him off the ground.)"

Ironically, Buddy Rich might not have even appeared, had it not been for some shrewd bargaining. Buddy had longstanding problems with the Internal Revenue Service; he had failed to file federal and state taxes for fiscal years 1961–63. An IRS agent caught up with him at Newport and threatened to block his performance by seizing the money he was to receive. Father O'Connor and I accompanied the agent to the Newport police station, where they had Buddy in a holding cell. I had to produce a $1,000 bond in order to get him out.

Sunday night was Sinatra, from beginning to end. He had put the show together. Sinatra had decided upon the Oscar Peterson Trio to open and the Count Basie Band with Quincy Jones as musical director. Frank's fee for this entire package was $40,000.

Sinatra's contract had many stipulations. He was to have tea in his air-conditioned trailer backstage. We were to set aside 250 box seats in the front area, for Sinatra's entourage. Photographers would be allowed only ten minutes of shooting. He was going to fly to Providence via his own private airplane, then take a helicopter to Newport—where he would touch down right in Festival Field. We had to set up a landing pad behind the stage for two helicopters, one each for Sinatra and Quincy, and a few bodyguards. This landing would take place just before he was due on stage.

When the dual aircraft landed at 7:45 P.M. there was a mild ruckus. No one was performing at the time, since the concert was scheduled for 8 o'clock. The hatch opened, and Sinatra emerged. There could be no better way to describe it than this: He became, for that moment, the festival's deus ex machina. A god stepping out of the machine. Frank walked from the landing pad to his trailer by way of a lane that had been fashioned out of double rows of snow fencing flanked by bodyguards.

It was the most heavily attended concert in Newport Festival history, up to that point. All twelve thousand seats had been sold. Scores of people were gathered on the hillside of Miantonomi Park, across Girard Avenue from the east side of our field. A few zealots attempted to break down the barricade that marked the perimeter of Festival Field; they were swiftly dispersed by an attentive police force.

Sinatra's manager at the time was a lawyer by the name of Mickey Rudin. Mickey had come to Newport a day in advance, to make sure that everything was in order. He had provided the list of friends and press who were to be included in the reserved box seats. He had specified what other preparations needed to be made. He spent hours with the members of my team, and we accommodated him perfectly. We had absolutely everything done, to a T. But just moments before the concert was ready to start, Mickey Rudin asked me: "Now, where's my box?" He had asked for everything except his own box. I hadn't reserved one for him.

"You can have my box, Mickey," I told him. He was incredulous; he couldn't believe I hadn't secured a box for him. I had been so preoccupied with every little detail that it hadn't even occurred to me. That was the first mistake. The second mistake, the one I could learn from, was not thinking on my feet. I should have just said, "Oh, I have your box right here," and given him my box without telling him. Whatever I had done that was positive in his eyes was completely shattered. I could have saved face if I had been quicker on the recovery.

The Basie band, which was augmented that night at Sinatra's request by trumpeter Harry "Sweets" Edison and drummer Sonny Payne, played until 9:20 P.M. At that point, Count Basie stepped to the microphone for an announcement. People thought that he was just giving the name of the next tune. Instead, he intoned: "Ladies and Gentlemen, The Chairman of the Board." And Frank Sinatra came onto the stage. Before anyone had time to react, the band had hit with "Get Me to the Church on Time," and it was swinging. The applause was deafening.

He sang eight songs with the band; they revisited hits like "Fly Me to the Moon," "Street of Dreams," and "I've Got You Under My Skin." Then he took a break, during which he drank some tea onstage and delivered a monologue littered with corny one-liners. "With all those beards out there," he said famously, "it looks like a state home for the hip." When the talk segued back into song, he did "You Make Me Feel So Young," "Where or When," and "My Kind of Town," among others. His program was heavy on swing and short on ballads. He was just swinging. He was at Newport, at the Jazz Festival. The audience would have loved a few more ballads with a feeling of love and emotion.

Still, it was a glorious performance. Frank Sinatra performed eighteen songs that night, in an hour-long set. He waved goodnight at 10:20 P.M. As he left the stage, he said: "Thank you, Father O'Connor, and thank you, George," and walked straight toward one of the helicopters. Two minutes later, he was airborne. Both choppers lifted out of the park as suddenly as they had arrived; their landing lights blinked a wistful farewell. Sinatra was off to New York where he wanted to be in Jilly's restaurant by midnight and tell everyone what had happened at Newport. It was the most dramatic exit he could possibly have made. Even as the birds disappeared into the night, thousands of people just stood silently and watched, transfixed. Frank had literally come down from the heavens to bestow his gift, and now he was making his ascension.

I was always grateful to Sinatra. Despite all the stories about his temperament, Frank was a total gentleman each time I encountered him. Once, I was in England with Sarah Vaughan while he was opening at the Palladium and his management wanted to use Sarah on the show with him for a week. Sassy was in Europe on my contract, but Frank's people could easily have gone to her manager directly, leaving me high and dry. But they came to me, and offered compensation for the dates that I was giving up on her tour. That courtesy reflected the respect that had been forged at Newport.

# 9

# *Conflicts and Concerts*

B Y AUTUMN 1965, I HAD PRESENTED eleven jazz festivals and five folk festivals in Newport. Those festivals had featured hundreds—perhaps thousands—of artists, representing a stimulating range of styles. Jazz history had been made again and again, in one way or another. The festival had seen some triumphs, along with a few disasters. And as I looked ahead, there was no end in sight.

It made sense, then, that Joyce and I would look for a house on Aquidneck Island, finding it in Middletown, the next town north of Newport. The town's seven miles of rocky shoreline—bordering Narragansett Bay, the Atlantic Ocean, and the Sakonnet River—secured its status as an attractive resort. Private landowners prized the area for its placid seclusion; and to them, Middletown was a rural setting, even though downtown Newport was only five minutes away by car. Our house, a lovely old two-story wooden structure, was one of several hunting and fishing lodges that had been originally built for wealthy summer residents from across the bay. It was situated right on the water; sitting on the back porch, you could clearly see some of the mansions on Ochre Point Avenue. We had a better view than had the Vanderbilts. They looked across the bay at us.

My bid for permanence in Newport extended to the festival grounds as well. I had a vision of creating a major entertainment facility on Aquidneck Island, a complex that could serve as home to the Newport Jazz and Folk Festivals, and whatever additional festivals or special events I might choose to produce. Why couldn't Newport have a performing arts center, like those in Saratoga or Tanglewood? Such a site, invested with the prestige of our various festivals, could transform Newport into a world-class destination for the arts.

The first thing needed was a site. No appreciably large piece of property was available in Newport, but Middletown had quite a bit of undeveloped land. I found a large, L-shaped plot near the Middletown-Portsmouth border that was rustic enough to support an impression of real country. I paid the site a visit on a clear morning in early autumn; clouds were drifting across the sky, and the grass was the most brilliant shade of green. Shiny-coated black goats grazed there, belonging to the tenant farmer who was then leasing the land. A small, ancient cemetery sat on the premises—probably the family plot of the property's original owners, the Coggeshall clan. To the east, the land was flanked by a dairy farm and a huge expanse of cornfields, beyond which ran the highway. To the west, there was crystalline Narragansett Bay, separated from the property by a rarely used naval base access road. Half of the property ran alongside this road.

Coggeshall Farm was tailor-made for a festival; it could solve every logistical problem we had encountered. The site consisted of 104 acres—more than enough land to accommodate a music shed, a dressing-room facility, concert seating, and parking. The field's incline, which gently sloped down to the bay, was almost a natural amphitheater; a stage could be set up with its back to the water, with the seats facing west toward the bay. A primary entrance could be constructed on West Main Road; a private backstage entrance along a small perpendicular road called Green Lane was available as well.

The farm was on the market for the price of $140,000. While I didn't have the million dollars necessary for construction and development, I knew I could get it. The state would help me; both Rhode Island U.S. senators were supporters of the festivals, as was the state's governor. In addition, there was private investment money available. My mother gave me $40,000 for the down payment—a considerable sum of money, and the bulk of her life savings. The remaining $100,000 I obtained through a mortgage with the bank. All I needed was a permit from the Middletown town council. The land was zoned for farming and residential use, and we would have to get a zoning change approved. This would require some effort on our part, but it didn't appear to pose an insurmountable problem. We scheduled a public hearing on the matter for a mid-January evening.

Our most serious obstacle arose from an unexpected source. The area surrounding the Coggeshall Farm was pastoral in more than one sense of the word. Adjacent to my property, on the north side, was another green plot of many acres sloping down to the water. It was owned by a Catholic mission, and housed the favorite novitiate of Bishop McVinney, the archbishop of Providence. When word spread that I had purchased the land for a possible festival site, it quickly became apparent that Bishop McVinney, concerned about his novitiate, would come out against me. I met with the auxiliary bishop, the Reverend Bernard Kelly, and disclosed my intentions in detail. Actually, he was sympathetic and polite, but in no uncertain terms he said, "We're going to have to come out against you." My dream was about to become a nightmare.

Controversy exploded early in the new year. During the first week of 1966, "The Middletown Voice," a four-page newsletter, suddenly appeared; it had been mailed to every Middletown resident. The front and back sides of this newsletter contained editorials about the festivals' proposed relocation. One article stated, without any documentation, that the majority of Middletown residents were opposed to the plan. Another article consisted primarily of quotes from various town residents who had reservations about our move. One of these people expressed concern over the building of a "circus site" in Middletown, ignoring the fact that our proposed zoning amendment especially excluded circuses and amusement parks. Another letter suggested that property values in the area would plummet as a result of the festivals, despite the fact that prices for property near Freebody Park had actually risen during our tenure there. Someone else charged that police costs to the city would be high if the festivals were in town, even though Festival Productions, Inc., was contractually bound to shoulder all of these costs. Another letter stated that I'd failed to post a bond in Newport the previous year, which was simply not the case. The litany went on and on; each of its charges was unfounded, misguided, or just plain false.

But these editorials were only the tip of the iceberg. The newsletter's inside pages unfolded to reveal a lurid, tabloid-style collage of newspaper headlines. Almost every one of these headlines dated back to the summer riot of 1960. In the center of this ugly antifestival propaganda were the words: "Lest We Forget."

I couldn't believe it when I saw this. During all the years of the Festival's existence, we had never been subjected to such a blunt and crooked attack. It went far past mudslinging; this was a character assassination. It went beyond the realm of argument to the realm of conjecture and insinuation. My first reaction—pure disbelief—was quickly supplanted by rage. I was incensed.

Both regional newspapers rallied to the festivals' defense. The *Providence Journal* called the flyer a "shocking investment in fear-mongering," and elaborated: "to invoke the ugly headlines of six years ago while ignoring Newport's record since 1960 in handling the festivals is sheer demagoguery." The *Newport Daily News* opined that "such a vicious tactic was uncalled for and the shame should be borne by those who conceived the idea and published it for town-wide distribution."

But who were these vicious demagogues? Neither paper claimed to have any idea who was behind the mailing. The newsletter listed as its publisher the

Middletown Community Committee, but no such organization could be accurately identified. However, I felt I knew who was responsible, and it made my heart sink. Examining the Middletown Voice, I noticed that it had been postmarked on a Providence postage meter; this was unusual, given the paper's alleged status as a Middletown product. The meter in question was registered to the Providence Visitor, the official diocesan newspaper of Rhode Island. The newsletter had been printed and mailed at the expense of the Visitor. I was sure of it, and I made my suspicions known. In a speech delivered to the Middletown Rotary Club the week after the newsletter's appearance, I criticized the Catholic Church for attempting to control Middletown residents from the outside. I called attention to the opposition's irresponsible tactics. I defended the integrity of the festivals, and reiterated my position.

The following day, the Reverend Edward Flannery, managing editor of the Providence Visitor, responded. "I can deny categorically Mr. Wein's alleged implication that the Middletown Voice was 'printed and mailed at the expense of the Providence Visitor,'" he was quoted as saying, in one newspaper article. Reverend Flannery went on to explain that the printing shop that published the Visitor had received a contract for the job; such special projects were not uncommon. The Visitor, he emphasized, had "no initiative whatsoever in the composition or distribution of the Middletown Voice at any time."

The day after this disavowal, the truth came to the surface. The Most Reverend Bishop Bernard Kelly, auxiliary bishop of Providence, admitted that he had been on the committee that prepared the newsletter. My suspicions were confirmed. As the *Newport Daily News* reported, "neither the Visitor nor Bishop Kelly denied Wein's implication [that] the postage meter used in mailing the papers was registered to the Diocese of Providence."

Bishop Kelly attempted to explain himself in an editorial in that day's Providence Visitor. "It was our sole purpose," he wrote, "to bring to everyone's attention certain facts about the festival and the pending petition which have been glossed over by the friends of the Jazz Festival." This didn't address one of the most serious problems with the Middletown Voice; that its "facts" were highly suspect. Bishop Kelly concluded his column by reminding his readers that Roger Williams had founded the state of Rhode Island in order to provide a space for the free practice of religion. "Apparently," the bishop wryly added, "his descendants have developed a more sophisticated set of values."

The Visitor that day also ran an article stating its official position. In it, Bishop McVinney spoke publicly regarding this matter for the first time. "This type of entertainment," he said, referring to both jazz and folk music, "is incompatible with the religious life of prayer and silence that prevails in the Mother of

Hope Novitiate. The noise and confusion and traffic congestion caused by the crowds would not only be a general nuisance but would indeed negate the entire purpose of our Novitiate." Elsewhere in the paper, an editorial likened the festivals to a "cancer," and warned that their continuing existence threatened to bring "a decline in moral and spiritual values" to Aquidneck Island.

An attempt to counteract this negative campaigning was made by Friends of the Festival, a group of Middletown business residents who, at their own expense, paid for a full-page advertisement in the *Newport Daily News*. The ad consisted of block quotes from several prominent sources. One of these quotes was from the Board of Directors of the Newport County Chamber of Commerce, declaring that it was "convinced that developing [the proposed Middletown location] as a cultural center is worthwhile." Another quote, from a past *Daily News* editorial, lauded the Middletown site as an "excellent choice." The most striking words, however, were those of Newport's men of the cloth:

Dear Mr. Wein: The Newport County Clergy Association wishes to make it known to you that it will go on record favoring the continuing of the festivals because of their cultural and economic advantages. We further commend you and the entire management of the festivals for the efforts made to eliminate the moral problems; and for improving the festivals with the proposed upgrading of the quality of the programming.

Meanwhile, the opposition was circulating petitions against the zoning amendment. The integrity of this process was called into question after several festival backers were approached at their homes and pressured into signing. During a Middletown Council meeting the night before the public hearing, one man described his petitioner's pitch: "'If you don't want junkyards, pigpens or circuses in your back yard, you'd better sign this.'" Dozens of other residents complained of similar encounters.

All these conflicts reached a dramatic climax on the night of January 19, at the scheduled public hearing in Middletown. The meeting had been moved from the claustrophobic Council Chamber to an auditorium at Middletown High School, with a seating capacity of 500. Even this precaution had proved insufficient; despite a light snow and slick roads, Middletown residents flocked to the meeting. They had been bombarded with impassioned arguments, opinions, and propaganda for weeks; this was their chance to hear both sides of the issue, and to be heard. Police stood guard at the entrance to the building, checking identification to make sure that only Middletown residents were admitted. By the time they closed the doors at 8 P.M., there were about 800 people crammed into the auditorium. More than sixty cars were turned away as they approached the parking lot.

The zoning amendment wouldn't exactly be approved or rejected on this occasion; that was for the town council to decide at a later date. But all five council members were present at the hearing, and supposedly the arguments they heard this evening would influence the outcome of their vote. They had already received more than their share of harassment, rhetoric, and threats from various citizens of Middletown.

The format of the meeting was roughly similar to that of a courtroom trial; each side would be allowed thirty minutes with which to argue its case. Then the floor was opened to comments from Middletown residents in the audience, each of which was limited to five minutes. It was like one of those Andy Hardy movies. Andy Hardy was played by Mickey Rooney, and he was always faced with some crisis of opposition, along with his plucky girlfriend du jour (usually played by Judy Garland). Each of these movies reached a climax in a courtroom of some sort; invariably, there was a kindly judge, played by Lewis Stone, who would grant permission to do whatever it was they were trying to do. Of course, I was no Andy Hardy and no kindly Lewis Stone character was anywhere in sight in the room. Instead, I faced a sea of faces, most of which were unfamiliar and many of which were openly hostile.

We presented a sound argument. My attorney, Joseph Macioci, pointed out that a faction in Middletown had opposed a zoning change several years before, when the town was first presented with the proposal for a new shopping center. That center, he emphasized, was now a substantial taxpayer and an integral part of the area. A spokesman for the Newport Kiwanis Club attested to the community fundraising that resulted from each festival's concessions. A Newport businessman spoke to the notion of progress, noting that "one cannot walk backwards into the future." The Reverend Carl Saunders, pastor of the Middletown Methodist Church and a spokesman for the Newport County Clergymen's Association, gave his endorsement of our plan.

Then three Catholic priests—each of whom had traveled to Newport at his own expense—addressed the crowd. The Reverend Andrew Marinak went first, attesting to my character. Father Marinak was the chaplain of the federal penitentiary in Lewisberg, Pennsylvania, and he explained how I had helped him to rehabilitate convicts in that state through musical productions. My moral integrity, he emphasized, was "beyond reproach."

The Reverend Michael Williams followed suit. Father Mike and I had become close personal friends while I was producing a festival in Pittsburgh. He spoke eloquently of the work I had done for the Catholic Youth Organization there, and described how Cardinal Wright, the archbishop of Pittsburgh, had supported our festival. He gave me the highest of recommendations.

Then came Father O'Connor, one of the closest friends and allies I ever had. He directly answered charges that the festivals would spoil the peace and solitude of the Mother of Hope Novitiate, and did so in his own personal way. We were fortunate enough to get his words on tape:

> I want to talk about just two points. I speak in my own experience in this sense; that if the priesthood has meant anything to me—and it means my life—then it has meant the fact that I can belong to you, the men and women of the world. And I belong to you because you are black, or green, or brown, or square, or anything; and you may play silly-looking guitars and you may have long hair hanging down the back of your neck, and you may walk with a limp, or you may speak with the best of English or you may have a strange name—but this is what we are. And this is where we're supposed to be, and this is where we're going to be. And we thank God for the Vatican Council for assigning some of the good reasons why religious—and this includes us all—should be involved in the world in which we live. That this should happen to be with nuns, little nuns who are always, I suppose, the little ladies who live on the hill. Well, you know the movements that are amongst the sisterhoods of the East and the Midwest and the West, and the feeling that they know that this is their world, too. The little kid who may be the funny-looking guitar player is a youngster who they may have to deal with in the time to come. I am quite sure that in the nuns' hearts and my heart, and all our hearts, is the fact that as religious, and I speak now in terms of that—just religious, and if you're Protestant or Jewish, bear with me in your indulgence—this is our task. This is where we belong, this is what we were ordained for, this is what we take our vows for, this is where we are, and this is where we shall ever be—no matter what the words may be that come of sarcasm, or bitterness, or anger or shunning off or turning away, or giving strange glances. And the Novitiate, in my sight, could be a better place because artistic things take place beside it, with kids who sometimes speak loud, and sometimes make mistakes. That's what we are, Gentlemen, Ladies.

The second point is: I want to live and I want you to live. And the life that we lead, Gentlemen, is in Middletown here. All across the nation excitement and dangerous living, in a sense, is happening; and the arts are becoming something that, spiritually, we can express ourselves in because it tells a lot about what we are. I'm talking about me, you, human beings. And if it's jazz that's trying to help a group of musicians who perhaps in many instances are Negro in background, trying to talk to you; and folksingers bringing up the tales that are part of our woes in the times in which we live. In the opera, in the theater, in the art that's impressionist and abstractionistic, and pop art. This is our life. This is where we are, and you need it as much as I need it; all of us need it. I don't care whether you live in the most sheltered of homes; why can't we have it, Middletown? Is there any reason why you can't all come? And we'll all go together, and may it be a success. And if George Wein is the leader, who cares? As long as we get the right type of direction; and the right type of direction will come, because the right people are behind it, and the right people are you. You could be outstanding. We talk about Tanglewood and Aspen and the other festivals all across this kind of wonderful world in which we live. Why can't Middletown do that? Middletown was nothing to me until the day that I came here for the festival; and it has become something that's deep within my innards and deep within my heart and deep within my memory. I look for those familiar faces.

So . . . short and inarticulate, maybe a little emotional, but it is said from my heart. And I suspect that all of us would like to have that same kind of feeling. We love you, we want you to help, we're with you—not here to fight with you, not here to be angry with you, not here to be sarcastic with you, not here to be preaching to you. We came here to love you. Like Duke Ellington says: "It's good for him, it's good for me." Thank you.

When Father O'Connor stepped off the podium, the auditorium erupted in applause. Members of the Town Council stood up and cheered. I was completely choked up. Looking across the table, I could see Bishop Kelly stiffening with anger. He was clenching his fists so hard that the knuckle under his ring whitened. Here he was, representing the archbishop of Rhode Island, and having to contend with three priests—men of the same calling—who aligned themselves with the festival and its Jewish producer. He must have felt as if I had orchestrated a mutiny aboard his ship.

The catharsis of Father O'Connor's speech closed our portion of the proceedings, and we yielded the floor to our opposition. Bishop Kelly took the podium. He wasted no time in referring to the riots of 1960. "We are asked to gamble the security of the sisters for the next ten, twenty, or thirty years on the idea that a huge crowd will always be orderly and that police control will always be firm," he said. "Gentlemen, I wasn't born yesterday, and my answer is 'no.'" He reiterated the diocesan position that the music, traffic, and general activity surrounding each festival would "liquidate the spiritual benefits of the novitiate." Responding to our rousing pro-festival presentation, he said: "Mr. Wein's reputation is not the issue at stake." Then, his voice entirely flat and devoid of expression, he added: "As for the good deeds he has done—God bless him."

The opposition continued, with speeches by several attorneys and former Rhode Island governor Dennis Roberts. Their line of argument was familiar to anyone who had seen the past few issues of the Providence Visitor.

To an extent, the gibes of the anti-festival contingent could do no more harm than had already been done. The public hearing had been a thrilling and dramatic confrontation; it hadn't changed anything as far as our position in Middletown. But having Father O'Connor, Father Williams, and Father Marenek go to so much trouble to support me—that left an indelible impression. These gentlemen had devoted their entire lives to the church, and yet they had the courage and conviction to take my side, in total disagreement with their superiors in the church establishment. I'd like to think that they made this decision because of my association with them; they were my friends. But in actuality, they did it because they believed in the music, and in the festivals, and what they stood for. They felt that it would only benefit the church if the bishops supported these events. In my mind, it is wrong when religion— whether it be conservative Christianity, Islamic fundamentalism, or Orthodox Jewry—attempts to exert political influence upon a society. In Middletown, this brought me in direct conflict with the Catholic Church. And yet my most ardent defenders were Catholic priests. Their eloquence and support touched me deeply. When I left the Middletown High School Auditorium that night and a reporter asked for my impression of the hearing, I responded: "Win, lose, or draw, I have won."

But the Middletown council decision was not to be announced until February 7, and I wasn't about to sit idly while awaiting its ruling. Various Rhode Island towns spoke up and examined the possibility of holding the festival. The Providence Journal ran an editorial urging that we consider a move to that city. Governor Chafee voiced his endorsement of a proposal to hold the festivals in Kingston, on the University of Rhode Island campus. All these people recognized the economic boon that came with each festival. So did the business-men and women of Newport, many of whom expressed concern over the thought of losing the festivals to a town across the bay. A group of these residents, including the manager of Newport's Hotel Viking, announced their intention to help find alternate festival sites on Aquidneck Island.

Around this time, an objective fact-finding committee commissioned by the Middletown Town Council presented the results of its study. It was highly favorable to the idea of establishing the festivals permanently in Middletown. Their conclusion read as follows: "Properly managed, controlled and supported, the festival park, as proposed, could become one of the finest festival sites on the East Coast, if not in the entire United States and perhaps one of the cultural centers of the world."

The report was an obvious endorsement, but you can't fight the church in a Catholic town, which Middletown most certainly was. So, after examining a number of sites in other areas of Rhode Island, we found our solution. I called a press conference just a few days before the Middletown Council's scheduled decision. Scores of curious reporters came to the Hotel Viking conference room to hear what we had to say.

"The future of the Newport Jazz, Folk, and Opera Festivals has never been more secure," I announced, as the cameras whirred and clicked around me. "We will have our festivals in Newport, regardless of the decision of the Middletown Council Monday night." Mariano Bucolo had agreed to give us a ten-year lease on his Connell Highway property; he had also consented to let us build our permanent facilities there. It had always been my desire to keep the festivals on Aquidneck Island. For whatever reason, Mariano Bucolo had a sympatico feeling for Joyce and me. Perhaps it was a concern for the "underdog," which related to his own life. His decade-long commitment to me saved us. The hillside property had served its purpose during the 1965 festivals. With some investment in long-term stage, dressing-room, and restroom structures, it could be almost as good a site as what we had envisioned for the Coggeshall Farm.

When the Town Council of Middletown convened for its decisive vote, the results turned out as I had imagined. They voted four to one against the zoning petition. The lone festival supporter, Herbert Grant, argued for the amendment despite the catcalls of his hecklers. It so happened that Herbert Grant was the only Protestant on an otherwise all-Catholic council.

Today, the Coggeshall Farm area consists of identical, pre-fabricated housing. I eventually, and reluctantly, sold the property to the United States Navy for that purpose. I had no choice, since the taxes and mortgage on the land were far more than I could afford.

But when asked by a reporter at the aforementioned press conference what I would do with this $140,000, 104-acre Middletown property, I confessed that I had no idea.

"I'll probably go out there some nice, warm spring day," I surmised, "and walk around, and think what a lovely place it would be to have a festival."

\*     \*     \*

*We Newporters are glad that our first inhabitants were so tolerant and understanding and permitted the frivolities of music and dancing to flourish. They recognized then that times do change.*

**—Leonard Panaggio,
1966 Newport Jazz Festival Program**

My Middletown dreams trampled, I wasted no time in applying for a festival contract back in Newport, where there was a predominantly friendly feeling with the council. We were anxious to finally put the political maneuvering behind us and focus once again on putting the festivals together. But, as we soon discovered, our headaches were not yet over.

Like fundamentalist zealots, our opponents never really went away. The mayor, Dennis Shea, was a noted festival objector on the council. Our enemies in Middletown had friends in Newport and urged them to come out against us. Several months of time were wasted attending useless town meetings where anything having to do with the festival contract was tabled by the mayor. Finally, at a city council meeting in April, the Newport Jazz, Folk, and the proposed Opera festival licenses were approved with one dissenting vote—that of Mayor Dennis Shea.

Construction commenced at Festival Field immediately. Our designer, Russell Brown, envisioned sleek, modern structures made primarily of concrete and steel. The stage would be much larger than in previous years: 120 feet long and more than 50 feet deep. Its wings would curve around on either end; its canopy and support beams would consist of over thirty tons of steel. The stage would connect—via a twelve-foot-high, fifty-foot-long bridge ramp—with a two-story backstage performer's edifice that included dressing rooms, lounges, permanent showers and restrooms, and a control room. There would be a separate administration office building (with six offices and a conference room), a building dedicated to the press, and a box office near the highway. A permanent restroom facility would be located toward the rear of the seating area.

The construction crew had a tight deadline for so massive a project; the Jazz Festival was due to kick off on July 1. We had over 500 men off and on in the construction crew, working more than ten hours a day on the site. Somehow they finished it on time. Standing there before our mammoth stage, it was hard to believe that the space had been an open field just six weeks prior. There were two hundred stage lamps, connected by nearly four miles of electrical cables, and 16,000 feet of underground sewer lines, all at a cost of approximately $200,000, which I had received from the bank with collateral of real estate owned by Arnold London and myself; a sum that, all things considered, was a bargain. We christened the site "Festival Field" just a few days before the onset of the Jazz Festival. We were ready.

\*     \*     \*

Mid-January 1966 marked our first jazz festival for the Boston Globe. This event had been born through collaboration with Globe editor Tom Winship, a jazz fan who appreciated the music—and recognized the promotional benefits of sponsoring a festival. We also had the enthusiastic approval of John I. Taylor, the paper's esteemed publisher.

A few months before the festival, I happened to see Mr. Taylor at a black-tie charity dinner at the Waldorf-Astoria Hotel in Manhattan. Benny Goodman was also in attendance, and Mr. Taylor asked him if he would like to play at the Globe festival that winter. Benny, who recognized the Taylors' influence and social standing in New England, agreed without hesitation.

When Benny showed up at Veterans War Memorial Auditorium for his concert, however, he was far less accommodating. He made himself miserable, bitching and complaining about everything. "I thought you told me this wasn't a jazz festival," he said. I didn't know what he was talking about; I had never tried to conceal the fact that this was the Boston Globe Jazz Festival.

"Benny," I asked, "don't you want to play at jazz festivals?" He had worked at Newport only once, in 1958—a train-wreck performance that I took pains not to mention.

"No, I don't," he replied.

"That's alright Benny, I just won't ask you." He played that night, reluctantly. It was a few years before we worked together again. This was just one sour note in an otherwise auspicious festival debut.

Our emcee on opening night was the Reverend Alvin Kershaw of Boston's Emmanuel Church—yet another man of the cloth who supported jazz. We had a good lineup: Dizzy Gillespie, Dave Brubeck, Joe Williams, and Herbie Mann, among others. The Newport All-Stars played, as did the Duke Ellington Orchestra (led by Mercer Ellington, since Duke was in Hollywood working on the soundtrack to the 1959 film *Anatomy of a Murder*). We sold more than 5,000 tickets each night: a sellout. This resounding success ensured the event's future; I would continue producing Boston Globe Jazz Festivals (with a few interruptions) until 1996.

\*       \*       \*

A few weeks after the Globe festival, Dino Santangelo and I produced a concert in February at Detroit's Cobo Arena. Our headliners for this event were the John Coltrane and Thelonious Monk Quartets.

On the day of the engagement, there was a blizzard in the area, making transportation difficult. Nellie Monk, who by this time had worked with me on many concerts, wisely checked the weather forecast and rerouted the bands' flight to Toledo, Ohio; there they rented a van and made it to Detroit in time for the concert. John and Alice Coltrane were already in Detroit; they had arrived the day before, probably to visit with Alice's family. But Coltrane's rhythm section was unable to get out of New York City due to the snow in Detroit.

John Coltrane was at the height of his popularity at this time, with his *A Love Supreme* having been released the previous year. But his music was changing; he was exploring atonality and pure sound; a few months earlier, he had hired a second drummer, Rashied Ali. By January 1966, McCoy Tyner and Elvin Jones had both left the band. Coltrane's quartet now included Ali, his wife, Alice, on piano, and Jimmy Garrison on bass.

We had a reasonable crowd in spite of the heavy snow, and I knew that many of the die-hards had come specifically to see Coltrane. But without Garrison and Ali, John had no group. I knew it was important that he perform, so I asked if he would sit in with Thelonious Monk's group. John readily agreed.

Coltrane, who had not played with Monk since the Five Spot in 1957, blew like he was glad to be back home. And I never saw Thelonious more enthusiastic; having Coltrane with the band seemed to make him feel years younger. The energy they exchanged was obvious; they were on the same wavelength. The people cheered the triumphant set, and the evening was saved.

I thanked John as soon as he left the stage, telling him how much it had meant to the success of the concert. And I added that I was almost glad that his group hadn't shown up, because it gave me a chance to witness the reunion of these two giants. John half-smiled and said he knew that I might feel that way.

"You know, George," he continued, "sometimes I don't know exactly what to do—whether I should play in my older style or do what I'm doing now. But, for the moment, I have to continue in this direction."

Although it was only a few sentences, this was literally the most vital conversation about music that I ever had with John Coltrane. It didn't help to clear my mind. But it indicated the thought that John devoted to his music. He never mentioned the spiritual concerns that have since become such a part of his legend.

\*       \*       \*

*The early festivals were fashioned out of orange crates and baling wire, and at night a lot of their illumination was provided by the moon. But permanence has arrived at last.*
**—Whitney Balliett, The *New Yorker***

After the struggle of the past months, I was hungry for the joyous feeling that the 1966 Newport Jazz Festival was all about. So I did an opening-night set with the Newport All-Stars—which, this year, featured not only the usual cast of Bud Freeman, Jack Lesberg, and Ruby Braff, but also Gerry Mulligan and Buddy Rich. I had never played with either Buddy or Gerry and I was looking forward to it. We started with "Rose Room," my piano leading into the tune.

From the first few measures, it was clear that Buddy was steering the ship. His drumming was so exacting and propulsive that it took us all to another level. It brought things out of the group that surprised everybody. It seemed to inspire Ruby in particular. He "played as if he might never play again," Whitney Balliett later wrote.

Gerry was another revelation. His baritone saxophone swung through "Out of Nowhere" with a lightness; like a soft-shoe tap dancer with an intricate, delicate routine. And Gerry surprised everyone when, counting off "Bernie's Tune," he switched to alto, an instrument he had not played publicly in nearly twenty years.

Gerry and Buddy were on the gig because they had asked to play with us. Playing the piano may not have been my main calling in life, but it was surely my raison d'être. I never would have done anything in this business had I not been a musician. I'm grateful that our performance was recorded and later released in Britain. The moment's excitement is audible even on the recording; there we were in front of 8,000 people, scaring everybody! John Wilson of the *New York Times* noted with some surprise that our little band had been the "stars" of the program.

On Sunday afternoon, we presented a concert devoted to Woody Herman's Herd. This was a treat since we were able to corral a number of former Herdsmen for the performance. Stan Getz, Zoot Sims, and Al Cohn—three of the "Four Brothers"—took the stand once again to play the popular arrangement (with Gerry Mulligan playing Serge Chaloff's baritone part). The band also revisited "At the Woodchopper's Ball" and "(Wild) Apple Honey"—two of Herman's hits from the 1940s—and "Early Autumn," on which Getz soloed. Buddy Rich, joined the band as well; he went into a routine with Woody that capitalized on their common vaudevillian experience. Another highlight—this one a surprise—was the appearance of Tony Bennett, who joined the Herman band for several songs. He was in fine voice and the audience fell under his spell.

The rest of the festival was no less compelling, with performances by the Duke Ellington Orchestra (alone and with Ella Fitzgerald), star-studded guitar and trumpet workshops, the Count Basie Band, and many others. Miles Davis appeared with Wayne Shorter, Herbie Hancock, Ron Carter, and Tony Williams. I had already booked several European tours with this quintet; Charlie Bourgeois was their road manager. Miles, who had always been an enigma to some degree, was now honing the elusive and vaguely hostile persona that would be a calling card for the rest of his life. For this festival appearance, he rented a boat so that he wouldn't have to hang out with the other musicians backstage. He sailed into Narragansett Bay, docking in Newport Harbor. Then he came to the field, played four songs, retreated back to the boat, and split.

Overall attendance at the '66 Newport Jazz Festival broke all records; we easily surpassed the previous season's high of 43,000, even without the drawing power of a Sinatra. It was a testament to the festival's quality and maturity, and it gave us a feeling of immense satisfaction. We had fought to preserve a place on Aquidneck Island, and our persistence had yielded this triumph.

*     *     *

I felt further vindicated when, on July 12, 1966, Festival Field received the imprimatur of the Metropolitan Opera Company. This was the debut of the Newport Opera Festival—an event against which even our most committed antagonists on Aquidneck Island could utter no reproach.

The Opera Festival had been in the works for over a year. In those days, the Met took up an annual summer residence at Lewisohn Stadium in New York City. In summer 1965, they had asked me to bring some Newport Jazz and Folk Festival performers to the stadium, to augment its series. I had gladly obliged, producing a night of folk music (with the New Lost City Ramblers, Theodore Bikel, Pete Seeger, and others) as well as a jazz night (with the Dave Brubeck Quartet and the Duke Ellington Orchestra). The success of both concerts had encouraged me to entertain a new thought; if the Metropolitan Opera Company could bring the Jazz and Folk Festivals to New York City, why couldn't I take opera to Newport? I discussed the idea with my liaison at the Met, a young man named Glenn Sauls who worked as assistant to the organization's artistic administrator. Glenn was in charge of the company's summer programming, and together we devised a plan that would bring the Metropolitan Opera to Rhode Island.

After some negotiation, Glenn and I confirmed that the Metropolitan Opera Company would present concert opera (that is, performances without costume or sets) for four nights in Newport the following summer. At the same time, Lewisohn Stadium would host performers from the Newport Jazz and Folk Festivals. It was a cultural exchange program of sorts.

Glenn and I agreed upon a total fee of $100,000. This figure had to cover four nights of performances and an entire company. It probably didn't cover the salaries of the Met's 100-piece orchestra, seventy-voice choir, and star soloists. In this regard, the Met was in fact cutting me a deal.

After signing the agreement, I left the Metropolitan Opera House—then located at Broadway and Fortieth Street—with Joyce on my arm. It was a clear fall afternoon, and as we walked home, we talked excitedly about what had just transpired. Not only would Newport have an Opera Festival; it would sponsor the most illustrious opera company of its kind in the world.

We were so wrapped up in this reverie that we paid scarce attention to where we were heading. Before we knew it, we were standing on one of the triangular median strips in the heart of Times Square. Traffic swept past us on either side. With Joyce's hand in mine, I looked up at the buildings, and the bright advertisements that hung over their facades. I made an expansive movement with my free arm, "Well, kid," I said, "I just bought you the Metropolitan Opera. What do you want next?"

My original intention was to have presented the Opera Festival in Middletown, at a permanent structure. Although this plan had been thwarted, the stage we erected on Mariano Bucolo's Connell Highway site—with its broad wings—was more than adequate for our purposes. Its massive dimensions could accommodate both an orchestra and a full chorus.

It served an additional purpose on the festival's opening night, when we presented a gala supper for Rhode Island's patrons of the opera. Joyce, who had mastered the art of serving multitudes at each Newport Folk Festival, took charge of planning this event. Of course, the guests at this formal supper were a different sort of group than the unassuming folk crowd. But with a little help (most notably from Mrs. John Watkins, wife of the *Providence Journal* publisher), Joyce translated the communal spirit of her Folk dinners into the dialect of the opera's dignified social set.

Ten tables were set up right on the stage, each with floral pieces and decorative fans. Flags and buntings disguised the stage's support beams. Large, modernistic decorative panels served as partitions. Mexican rose trees were arranged around the stage platform, which was also littered with loose red roses. The menu, which had been prepared by Manhattan's fabled 21 restaurant, included Senegalese soup and Long Island duckling. We served Korbel Brut champagne. Licia Albanese, the star of that evening's concert, mingled with the patrons, all of whom were bedecked in elegant formal attire.

Those members of Bellevue Avenue's elite who attended the supper were duly impressed; the Boston Globe later proclaimed it a "spectacle of social magnitude" on par with Cornelius Vanderbilt's best efforts. But far more impressive than the spectacle, at least from a production standpoint, was the fact that we ended the repast at 7:25 P.M. and managed to start that evening's performance by 8:30. In one hour, our crew was able to clean up, pull the tables and partitions down, and set up the orchestra.

I had insisted that the Met present the same programming that they would in Lewisohn Stadium; I vetoed a suggested Rodgers and Hammerstein night. That evening's concert was a production of *La Bohème*, with Licia Albanese portraying Mimi, Barry Morell filling the role of Rodolfo, and George Schick conducting the orchestra. The audience, numbering just over 4,000, was spellbound and even included a number of previously staunch festival opponents. Newport mayor Dennis Shea attended nearly all of the performances; when cornered by a reporter, he admitted to "thoroughly enjoying" them.

There was a lesson to be learned in operatic sound. We had a new system, provided by Hanley Sound of Boston. When the first movement of *La Bohème* began, I walked over to Bill Hanley. "Bring out that chorus," I advised him. He amplified the chorus, and the heavens just exploded with these voices. Within a matter of minutes, opera lovers from the audience and the Met staff came storming back to us, absolutely furious. They wanted as natural a sound as possible; the outdoor amphitheaters of Europe usually go with natural acoustics. And here I was blowing out the speakers with sound! It shows how little I really knew about opera at the time.

The remaining three concerts of the festival were *Carmen*, *Lucia di Lammermoor*, and *Aida*, respectively. There were stellar performances by Regina Resnik, Richard Tucker, Jan Peerce, Lucine Amara, Roberta Peters, and Robert Merrill. The orchestra was superb. The twenty-two recitals and workshops that we presented on the field during the afternoons—ranging from "The Art of the Conductor" to "Ballet Movement"—were also successful.

Unfortunately, the weather (which had been insufferably hot during the Jazz Festival) took a turn for the wetter. During each evening's performance, it rained.

Those devotees who braved the elements were rewarded by the music, their umbrellas forming a phalanx across the seating area. On one night, we were forced to stop a performance during a particularly nasty squall. We had phoned Providence for the weather report from the airport—this was standard practice during a festival—and were informed that the rain would let up. So, when we stopped the concert, I walked out to reassure the audience: "Ladies and Gentlemen, please be patient. We're going to stop the opera for a few minutes. But the rain will stop shortly, and we will continue." Later I found out that people laughed at this pronouncement. How did I know the rain was going to stop? It appeared as if I were God's messenger.

There's no question that the inclement weather adversely affected our box office, especially since the opera drew an older crowd. Carmen drew only 4,500 people. The other operas fared marginally better. Although the *New York Times* reported the Opera Festival's total attendance at just over 28,000 people (about half that of the 1966 Newport Jazz Festival), I believe that even this anemic figure was inflated. Whatever the case, we sold nowhere near enough tickets to hit our break-even point.

*   *   *

The first Newport Opera Festival chalked up a loss of approximately $100,000. It was a financial disaster. There was also some critical disdain for the event; one reporter opined that the festival presented opera "in a musically ruthless manner and in an acoustically disagreeable one." But I wasn't discouraged by these setbacks, and the Metropolitan Opera Company felt the same way. Glenn Sauls told newspapers that the company was "having a marvelous time" in Newport. He even publicly announced the Met's wish to return the following summer, for a longer stretch. A two-week residence would be more logical from a financial standpoint; it would allow the company to distribute its operating expenses over more concert dates.

Shortly after the close of the festival, I received a call from Herman Krawitz, the Metropolitan's administrative director. I was pleasantly surprised when he told me that the company wanted to return to Newport the following summer for an even more ambitious series of concerts. The Met would organize the Festival, and shoulder the financial onus. I would be involved as producer, working closely with the company's artistic directors and staff.

I owed the Met $50,000 as a result of the 1966 festival. Mr. Krawitz told me to pay $20,000 of this amount; the remaining $30,000 would be considered a producer's fee for the 1967 festival. This was a kind proposition, and I was grateful. The Met understood that it took time for an event of this magnitude to grow roots. They were willing to give me the benefit of the doubt. I was touched and flattered by this gesture.

In 1967 the festival sprawled over ten days and literally dozens of separate events. The Met devoted the festival to the work of Giuseppe Verdi, and our evening performances—seven magnificent Verdi operas—reflected that homage. There were also a number of afternoon chamber recitals, in such appropriately elegant surroundings as Marble House and The Elms. Rogers High School served as the setting for studio performances and miniature operas. There were opera-related film presentations, readings, and tape performances. A children's opera was staged at St. George's School. For that ten-day stretch in mid-to-late August, it seemed that opera was ubiquitous; as integral a part of Newport summer life as sunshine, or the ebb and flow of the tide.

The breadth of this effort was no accident. The Metropolitan Opera Company put hundreds of thousands of dollars into the event. In its program book, General Manager Rudolph Bing expressed his hope that "at Newport we are on the threshold of a festival that will take a prominent and permanent place among international musical events." Mr. Bing was, in fact, present for the duration of the festival. It was an honor to work with him; since taking his position as general manager nearly two decades prior, he had accomplished much for the Met. Shortly after taking the helm, he had broken the company's color barrier. He had continued to bring the organization into the modern era, while keeping the company's past glories intact. At that time he was probably the world's most important living opera impresario.

Mr. Bing was a striking figure. His relatively tall stature was all the more impressive with the accoutrements of a slim build, silvery hair, and a thin, gaunt face. His attire befitted that of a man in his position; he resembled a character from the heart of London's Saville Row. Although he was not unpleasant during our brief partnership, he conveyed a definitive sense of stern authority. It was the manner of a man accustomed to getting things done his way.

I encountered this professional stubbornness firsthand, on an evening in which we had a rather sparse attendance. Shortly before the start of the concert, Mr. Bing looked out across Festival Field and noted the scattered seating. He suggested that we ask the audience to move forward, filling the empty seats near the front of the stage.

"I'll make the announcement," he said. "I'll tell the people to move down."

"Mr. Bing," I replied, "please don't do that. They will move down after the concert begins. But don't ask them to move down, because those are reserved seats. Someone might come in late and find that his or her seat has been taken."

But it was no use. Mr. Bing dismissed my concerns, stepped onstage, and announced his request over the microphone. Audience members from various corners of the field began streaming down to the front section. It seemed to work well enough. But a mere ten minutes later, a man arrived and followed an usher to his reserved seat, only to discover another man sitting there.

"This is my seat," declared the latecomer, brandishing his ticket stub.

"Mr. Bing told us to move," the seated man protested. "This is my seat now."

The usher didn't know how to resolve this conflict, and before he could stop them, these two elderly, well-dressed men were hitting each other over the head with their umbrellas! It was like something out of the Marx Brothers movie *A Night at the Opera* (which we screened later that week as part of our festival).

On another night, there were heavenly stirrings that suggested rain. That evening's presentation of *Aida* had only sold a few thousand tickets, despite the heavyweight presence of Martina Arroyo and Richard Tucker (as Aida and Radames, respectively). The nearby Newport Naval Base had a hall with a large enough capacity to hold this audience, and Mr. Bing decided to relocate the performance there.

"Mr. Bing," I said, "please don't move the concert. The weather isn't really that bad. Those people will stay out there." It wasn't even raining. Even if it did rain, past experience had proven that the audience would stay put.

But Mr. Bing objected. "The grass is wet. We can't have Mrs. Ryan getting her feet wet walking through the grass." He was talking about Mrs. John Barry Ryan, a woman of considerable repute and resources. Her grandfather, Otto Kahn, was a German Jewish industrialist who had made a fortune and founded the Metropolitan Opera. But Mrs. Ryan was quite an unaffected lady. Years later, when she was ninety-two years old, my friend Robert Pirie brought Mrs. Ryan to my last jazz festival in Nice. She wouldn't have minded walking through the grass at all. It seems strange to me, now, that Mr. Bing didn't voice objections to performing in the rain because the dampness might hurt his singers' voices.

Nevertheless, we moved *Aida* to the indoor hall. The concert went well, but it wasn't the same feeling. I was disappointed that we hadn't held the concert at Festival Field. But Mr. Bing was immovable. This was, after all, the man who had dismissed Maria Callas. He certainly wasn't going to back down to me.

Members of the Newport City Council were so impressed by the artistic triumph of the Metropolitan Opera Festival that they voted unanimously to make me an honorary citizen. But the 1967 festival was both the first and last of its kind. There simply wasn't enough response to keep it going. The Met lost $300,000 on the venture; I had lost $100,000 the previous year. There was no choice but to count our losses and abandon the project. It was to be my last involvement with opera at Newport. However, a group of resident Newporters decided to resurrect one aspect of the festival: the recitals at The Breakers, The Elms, and Ochre Court. These opera enthusiasts set to work establishing an annual event consisting solely of these small-scale concerts. And so the Newport Music Festival was born, out of the ashes of our ambitious but unsuccessful enterprise.

*    *    *

With the 1966 Newport Jazz, Opera, and Folk Festivals over, I turned to other activities. Having gone to such lengths to erect a permanent structure at Festival Field, I was interested in using it for individual concert events. Though our new stage did not have a proscenium or a curtain, we had lighting, sound, and space worthy of any major artist in America. We put this to the test that August, with a special appearance by Barbra Streisand.

Streisand was on tour, and the comedian Alan King and a partner of his, Walter Hyman, had made arrangements with her management to present her in several cities. They approached me about doing so at Newport; Frank Sinatra's otherworldly reception at the previous year's Newport Jazz Festival had not gone unnoticed. While Barbra was not yet the goddess that she is now, she was already an important artist. I can't recall the exact deal I made with King & Hyman, but I believe they took the risk and paid me some percentage. I provided certain elements of a production for my share in the profits.

The first word we received from Streisand's management was that she was flying in from California and landing in Boston. Ms. Streisand was pregnant, and there was a concern that she not get too fatigued during her trip. Her management wanted to know where she could stop to rest during the trip from Logan Airport to Newport. This was a funny inquiry; Boston is only seventy miles from Newport, and there really isn't a place to stop en route. Joyce jokingly said, "Tell her to stay in Fall River." I'm glad she never told Streisand's people that; if they had taken this advice, we would never have seen the singer again! Fall River at that time was an industrial wasteland, just over the bridge in Massachusetts.

Part of Streisand's show called for a scrim. A scrim is a sheer screen that, depending on the direction of the lighting, can be either opaque or translucent. I wasn't aware of this element of the production, but on the afternoon before the concert, Walter Hyman and I were conversing in the administration office on the field. Looking out through a window that overlooked the stage, I saw this workmanlike exercise underway. The festival production team and Streisand's guys were hanging this enormous scrim across the expanse of the stage. It was obvious that this was an expensive process; the festival had never done anything this elaborate.

I said to Walter Hyman, "Wow, you're really doing a first-class production. This must be costing you a fortune."

Looking at me in surprise, he said, "I thought you were paying for it."

You never heard a banshee wail like I did. I tore out of the office and onto the field, and nearly assaulted Chip Monk, my lighting coordinator. How could they do this without telling me? This was a lesson in dealing with stars: You'd better get every detail worked out. In the end, we managed to get Streisand's people to pay for it.

The concert didn't draw as many people as we had anticipated, which should have clued us in to the fact that it would not be easy to stage successful one-night programs at Festival Field. We had similar financial problems in later months, when we presented Harry Belafonte and Herb Alpert's Tijuana Brass.

\*     \*     \*

Obviously, Newport was the center of my universe throughout most of 1966, but I was also involved elsewhere. That spring, before the onslaught of summer festivals, I organized tours of Japan for the Modern Jazz Quartet, the Jimmy Smith Trio, and the Thelonious Monk Quartet. In the summer months following the festivals, John Coltrane and Cannonball Adderley each brought his group to Japan under my aegis. And that November, three drummers and a handful of other musicians embarked on the third drum-battle tour.

The drum tour featured Art Blakey, Elvin Jones, and Tony Williams. The band consisted of Jimmy Owens, Wayne Shorter, McCoy Tyner, and Ben Tucker. I was unable to go along this time, so my accountant Arnold London served as road manager.

Remembering the previous year's fiasco—whereupon Philly Joe Jones and Charlie Persip had been arrested for possession—Arnold and I had told the guys to stay away from anyone offering any kind of substance. This advice was futile; on the very first day of the tour, someone approached Tony Williams in the hotel lobby and sold him some drugs. Special agents then followed Tony to his hotel room and busted him. They asked him where he had gotten the stuff, and he offered a reply: "From Elvin Jones." Why Tony indicted Elvin, we will never know because our investigation did not reveal that Elvin Jones, in any way, was involved with Tony getting the drugs.

I received an international call from Arnold London that afternoon. "What the hell am I going to do?" he asked. "The tour's just starting, and the police just took two of them away to jail!" Both Elvin and Tony had been incarcerated. We contacted Kenny Clarke, who flew to Tokyo from his home base of Paris. Klook and Blakey did the tour with two Japanese drummers and Klook and Blakey both behaved themselves throughout the trip.

I was not able to make the tour with John Coltrane that summer. In my place, I sent my attorney and friend Elliott Hoffman, who had never been to Japan before.

Throughout this tour, Elliott and his wife, Nancy, usually stayed in the room adjacent to the Coltranes. They noticed that John and Alice kept their own counsel, eating alone and distancing themselves from the band. They also noted that John rose at six or seven every morning to practice. But it was never the saxophone. John had brought a violin with him, and was teaching himself to play pieces by Mozart. On some mornings, Mozart would also turn up during John's practice sessions on the flute.

The band performed in Tokyo, Kyoto, and a host of other major cities. Every concert was sold out in advance; the Japanese were fanatic about Coltrane's music. Elliott observed that audience response to each performance was reserved; they entered and left the hall silently and in an orderly fashion. But after the concert, out on the street, they blocked every stage door, clamored for autographs, and had to be moved aside by the police so the band could leave.

The only negative incident of the tour took place in Nagasaki, where a local promoter had arranged for a limousine caravan to take the entire group to the site of the 1945 atomic blast. At ground zero a monument commemorated the people who had died. The concert promoter asked if John would pose in front of the monument to be photographed by the local press. He obliged, kneeling in front of the monument and striking an appropriately spiritual pose, with hands together in prayer. He knew that this image would be reprinted in the local papers. What they hadn't told him was that the accompanying story would claim that John had begged the Japanese people to forgive him and his country for the barbaric injustices committed twenty years earlier.

The tour was a success, and in spring 1967 I called John to ask if he would like to do it again. He said he wasn't making any plans, because he was fasting. I asked, "What kind of regimen are you on? What kind of diet?"

He said, "I'm not dieting. I'm just not eating."

I told him this was dangerous; he couldn't do it. He had to sustain himself with at least some minimal nutrients. Why would he want to stop eating? He told me that he felt his system needed a complete cleaning out. I think he saw the hand of God, and was looking for a way to save himself from the inevitable end. I had arranged to present John again at Newport that summer, but it was not to be. He died of liver cancer in mid-July 1967.

*     *     *

That same year I was involved with a number of major tours, in the States and abroad. This included a massive Newport Jazz Festival tour of Europe with an aggregate of artists as diverse as Sarah Vaughan, Thelonious Monk, Miles Davis, and Archie Shepp. I accompanied the tour on every date, heard most of the music, and spent time with the musicians. This was especially illuminating because I got to know Archie. Archie was playing free jazz. One night I was hanging out with him backstage, talking about music. I said: "Archie, you keep talking about making the music 'new,' free, and continually different. But I've been listening to you play night after night, and it always sounds exactly the same to me." I wasn't trying to arouse a response; this was just how I felt about the chaotic sound of six musicians playing whatever came into their heads and out of their horns. Archie looked thoughtful for a moment, then said: "You know, you may be right."

In addition to a Newport tour of Europe, the spring 1967 brought the first "Newport Jazz Festival in Mexico"—an event produced in conjunction with that nation's leading concert agency, Conciertos Daniel. American Airlines had chosen to sponsor the festival as a celebration of its 25th anniversary of service to Mexico. In effect, American Airlines wished to make the festival a contribution to Mexico's cultural life.

We presented two concerts in the city of Puebla, two concerts at Belles Artes (a lovely 2,000-seat opera house in Mexico City), and one at the National Auditorium in Mexico City (which had a capacity of 14,000). The festival was a huge success; our concerts in Puebla and at Belles Artes sold out, and we drew 10,000 people to the National Auditorium.

For me, the only thing more exhilarating than the success of the festival was the fact that I was musically a part of it. I played at each of the concerts with the Newport All-Stars, which then consisted of Bud Freeman, Pee Wee Russell, Ruby Braff, Jack Lesberg, and Don Lamond. The music of this group was timeless. Dizzy Gillespie, one of the festival's better-known attractions, later confessed to me that he had wanted to walk out onstage to join us in Mexico City. I told him that he should have.

A handful of selections from the All-Stars's concerts in Mexico were later compiled and released on a Columbia Records LP called *George Wein Is Alive and Well in Mexico*. It's a fine album, with good playing by Ruby, Pee Wee, and especially Bud Freeman. Bud plays a gorgeous solo on "Have You Met Miss Jones?"—his tenor singing with the tone of a fine cello.

\* \* \*

The average jazz fan in talking about tenor saxophonists will first think of Coleman Hawkins and Lester Young and then, Sonny Rollins and John Coltrane. Those of us that are a little deeper into jazz history know about Bud Freeman. Bud was a contemporary of Coleman Hawkins. Lester Young often said that Bud was one of his influences.

Bud Freeman was a magnificent musician. Like Pee Wee Russell, he understood the music of both Bix Biederbecke and Louis Armstrong and developed his own musical style from the two of them. Bud's technique and melodic concept and swing were unique. "The Eel," Bud's composition, like many of Monk's works, can't be played by ear; you have to study it because the phrasing is so difficult. It takes a lot of practice to play "The Eel." Bud's solos were like his compositions; he loved his solos so much that he played them over and over again. He had a first chorus and a second chorus to every standard. When we were working together, every so often, the spirit moved him and you could get him to play a third chorus. Then you would hear the most thrilling of improvisations by the master; and Bud Freeman was the master of the tenor saxophone.

I had lots of fun with Bud Freeman. Playing gin rummy with him was a lesson; you couldn't beat him. He had a mathematical mind. The same mathematical mind he gave to his tenor saxophone. He wasn't a good golfer, but he was such a competitor that he wouldn't lose if you and he were in any way comparable in the skill needed to play this difficult game. I found that out once when we had a day off after playing a concert in Manchester, Vermont.

Bud was a musical soul mate to Pee Wee Russell. But he never ceased to be embarrassed being on the same bandstand. Bud was always impeccably dressed, and looked like he would be right at home at a fashionable London cocktail party or as a character in a play by George Bernard Shaw. He didn't want to be seen with Pee Wee. Bud always had this feeling even though they had worked with each other for many decades all over the world. To him, Pee Wee was a drunkard and looked like he was ready to fall on his face. Freeman stood up straight and even if Bud had imbibed a bit, one would never know it. It was a unique relationship.

Yet, whatever Bud Freeman's embarrassments were about Pee Wee Russell, when he was interviewed by Jean Bach in the 1994 film that she produced, *A Great Day in Harlem*, Bud said that he feels Pee Wee Russell will be remembered for his musical contributions more than will Benny Goodman. Let's not forget however, that Bud Freeman worked with Benny Goodman for quite a while and, like many other musicians who suffered Benny's employment, didn't have fond memories of him.

*     *     *

The most significant aspect of the Newport Jazz Festival in Mexico, at least in the long run, had been its reliance upon corporate sponsorship. Jim Ragsdale was my liaison at American Airlines; he was a member of the company's promotional team. Without American's support, the festival would never have happened; it was one of the first examples of corporate support for jazz, along with Pan Am (which sponsored the Newport Jazz Festival in Europe). That summer, we even received substantial financial support for the Newport Jazz Festival in Rhode Island.

For years, Narragansett Beer had bought the back cover of our program book. The most they ever did for us besides that was to arrange interviews for me with announcer Curt Gowdy between innings during the broadcast of Boston Red Sox baseball games. I would trudge up to the broadcast booth at Fenway Park and be allotted about one minute to talk about what was happening at Newport. I was such an avid Red Sox fan that I regarded this experience as a treat rather than an obligation.

However, the publicity efforts of Narragansett Beer were limited. We were fortunate enough, in 1967, to receive far greater support from a rival beer corporation—the Joseph Schlitz Brewing Company. Schlitz's public relations advisor, a man named Ben Barkin, had come to Newport in 1966; Schlitz beer was being sold at the concessions, and he wanted to see what was happening. Ben had been sufficiently impressed to arrange for Schlitz to buy the back cover of the following year's program book. More important, he had managed to procure a $25,000 sponsor subsidy, which would be applied to festival programming. This was the beginning of a fruitful association with

Ben Barkin, who proved to be one of the most important people in the course of my career.

A popular program that year was a reunion we organized with Lionel Hampton. Hamp had been working with small groups and playing in clubs. When I approached him with the idea of putting together a Hampton alumni big band, he was excited. The band that took the stage at Newport included Frank Foster, Joe Newman, Al Grey, Benny Powell, Illinois Jacquet, and Snooky Young, among many others. It was a big night for Lionel. After that memorable concert, he refused to play with any configuration other than a big band. For several years, I organized groups for him and arranged European festival tours. I've never seen a man happier than Lionel Hampton when he's standing before a roaring group, pounding out "Hamp's Boogie" or "Flyin' Home."

A poignant moment to this festival was a unique vibraphone workshop that we presented on a Sunday afternoon. Each participant was an important voice on the instrument: Hampton, Milt Jackson, Bobby Hutcherson, Red Norvo, and Gary Burton. To my knowledge, this was the only time a vibraphone concert of this order has been produced. For years, whenever I ran into Milt or Gary or Lionel, they reminisced about that program. It meant at least as much to them as it did to their modest but attentive audience.

\*    \*    \*

Summer 1968 found us in a pioneering event with Ben Barkin. Schlitz sponsored a nationwide "Schlitz Salute to Jazz" tour—a package featuring Dionne Warwick, Cannonball Adderley, Wes Montgomery, Thelonious Monk, Gary Burton, and Herbie Mann. They played in twenty-one cities over a two-month period—opening in Winston-Salem on June 21, closing in Memphis on August 18, and covering thousands of miles in between. The tour played primarily in arenas with an average capacity of eight to ten thousand.

The amount of work my company, FPI, put into organizing and producing this tour was staggering. It paid off; the program was a success. But as often happens with corporations, Schlitz changed brand managers in 1969, and the new guy was more interested in sponsoring sports than jazz. In just one year, however, this venture had an impact not only on my career, but also on the entire field of entertainment.

The innovation was in the sponsorship. In calling our tour the "Schlitz Salute to Jazz," we acknowledged our corporate patron to an unprecedented degree. It was the first time an entertainment event had been so designated; no sponsor had ever been associated this closely with the name of an event. Up until this time, sponsors of the arts were acknowledged in the fine print, almost as an afterthought. Here we essentially branded the event with the Schlitz identity, in boldface, up front.

Nothing is original; I had derived the idea from the old radio and TV broadcasts of my youth, like the "Texaco Star Theater." But by bringing the practice into the realm of concert events, we set the tone for increased sponsor involvement in the arts; today, corporations commit billions of dollars toward every facet of the entertainment industry. The Schlitz Salute to Jazz was a foretaste of things to come in my own career, and in the broader field of music and the arts. If ever I was a pioneer, I was a pioneer in that.

\*    \*    \*

In 1968, FPI produced the first annual Hampton Jazz Festival in Hampton, Virginia. As is often the case in my life, this event started with a gig—a Newport All-Stars engagement the previous year at what was then called the Hampton Institute. The band included Ruby Braff and one of the finest tenor saxophonists in the history of jazz, Illinois Jacquet. It was lovely working with Jacquet; he was playing our repertoire, which consisted of many songs he had not performed in many years. It was with some reluctance that he revisited his signature song, "Flyin' Home," when I called it as the closing number to the concert. Jacquet's only other engagement with the All-Stars would not occur again for nearly thirty years—when he joined fellow guests Clark Terry, Al Grey, Flip Philips, Warren Vache, Kenny Washington, Howard Alden, and Eddie Jones for a Columbia recording session, yielding probably the most musical of all Newport All-Star recordings.

At first I had suspected that our invitation to play at Hampton was a personal matter. Joyce's mother and father had met at Hampton as students, and her family had resided in Gloucester County prior to emancipation. In addition, Hampton Institute President Jerome "Brud" Holland was married to a Boston girl, Laura Mitchell, a close friend of the Alexanders. As it turned out, these coincidences had nothing to do with our hiring. The faculty member in charge of entertainment funds for the school had received the Newport All-Stars's brochure, "The Golden Age of Jazz." Being a jazz fan, he had signed the contract to bring us to Hampton in '67.

As I drove to our motel in Hampton, I was intrigued by the surroundings. Hampton is a navy town, situated on Chesapeake Bay. Newport rests on Narragansett Bay in Rhode Island and houses a naval war college. I was struck by the similarities between these two locales, and had an idea. Seeing Brud Holland the next morning, I suggested that maybe I could produce a jazz festival in association with the school. He was enthusiastic about this prospect, and thus was born the Hampton Jazz Festival.

Brud Holland was an all-American end at Cornell and, after leaving Hampton, was asked by President Nixon to be ambassador to Sweden.

The first two Hampton festivals, in 1968 and 1969, were held in an outdoor football stadium on the campus grounds, and featured a program similar in tone and content to the Ohio Valley Jazz Festivals of that era: jazz mixed with R & B, gospel, and soul. One of our headliners in 1968 was Ray Charles. My natural inclination would be to put Ray Charles on as a closing act, but his agent had informed us that Brother Ray wanted to open the festival at the scheduled starting time of two P.M. As a precaution, I sent them a contract with 1:30 P.M. as the scheduled performance time—figuring that the band would need an extra half-hour to prepare for the show. This was not the case. The bus arrived, the band set up, and Ray called us to his room to say that he was going on at 1:30, as stated in the contract. I told him that we weren't beginning the concert until two P.M., and pleaded for him to wait another half-hour for the people to arrive. In a reproving tone, he explained that I should never send him a contract without specifying the precise time he's due onstage. In the dozens of occasions when Ray has since played for us, we have been careful to remember this lesson. I was grateful that he didn't pack up and leave at 1:30, because it would have destroyed the Hampton Jazz Festival before it even got started.

My business arrangement with the Hampton Institute was simple: I took all the risk, and we split all profits equally. Of course, there were no profits the first two years, and after witnessing the erratic weather patterns in the Tidewater area (which made even Newport seem like a pillar of stability), I told Brud Holland that I was no longer in a position to underwrite the festival. This would have been the end of the Hampton Jazz Festival if not for an interesting development: the city of Hampton had recently constructed a coliseum, and wished to keep the festival alive there. So the school and city, together, volunteered a new arrangement with me. They would take 50 percent of the risk; we would be partners, presenting the festival in the new coliseum. The festival has continued without interruption ever since—thanks in large part to the school administration, the city of Hampton, and, for many years, the tireless efforts of John Scott and Bill Cope, two Hampton students who began as volunteers in

1968 and quickly became instrumental in producing the event. Cope and Scott are no longer with the festival, but the school and the city work closely with us to see that the festival flourishes.

\* \* \*

In light of all of this activity, it's easy to forget that Joyce and I resided primarily in New York City. My professional experience in the Big Apple was limited; I had never produced a major event there. This changed in mid-May 1969, as I presented a stand-alone concert at Town Hall featuring the incomparable Mabel Mercer and the inimitable Bobby Short.

Mabel Mercer was not well known in jazz circles, although her career had intersected with the jazz world more or less continuously since the 1930s. Amidst the many jazz clubs on 52nd Street in its heyday—the Famous Door, the Onyx Club, Jimmy Ryan's, Kelly's Stable, the Hickory House—sat one club on the North side of The Street (between Fifth and Sixth Avenues) that featured Miss Mercer. I don't know how many years Mabel Mercer sang on 52nd Street, but I do know that I never went to see her. I've been sorry about it ever since. I had first encountered the artistry of Miss Mercer through Charlie Bourgeois, who played me a ten-inch LP of hers on Atlantic Records. I was not the only person who received this tutorial; Charlie once played Miss Mercer's recording of "Les Feuilles Mortes" for Stan Getz. Stan would make his own recording of the song "Autumn Leaves," thereby introducing a new jazz standard.

Joyce and I fell in love with Mabel Mercer, and with her stories in song. I can still feel the yearning in Mabel's interpretation of a woman sensing the fading of her youth in "The End of a Love Affair." I was enraptured by the way she expressed the joy of adult love when she sang, "You are not my first love / I've had other charms / But I was just rehearsing / In those other arms." I was just as in love with the way she conveyed the emotion of an older woman realizing she could "still be the belle of the ball."

In the 1950s, Joyce and I occasionally drove down from Boston to see Mabel in person, at some small nightclub on the East Side. After moving to New York in 1960, we saw her more often, reveling in her tales of loves gained and lost. But then, for some odd reason, she had no place in which to perform. By 1969 I realized that we hadn't seen her for quite some time. So I said to Charlie and Joyce: "Let's bring Mabel Mercer back. We'll call Bobby Short and ask him if he'd like to do a concert with her at Town Hall."

We visited Mabel at her home in upstate New York, and happily discovered that she was eager to sing again. I made a partnership with Mabel and Bobby, and they performed together on May 18, 1969. Response to the concert was electric; all of New York's old café society bought the tickets as fast as we could put them on sale. The concert was wonderful, a true reflection of uncommon artistry, and it effectively brought Mabel Mercer out of retirement. Clubs once again presented her under the best possible conditions: sans microphone, accompanied only by a pianist. We eventually did a total of three concerts—two at Town Hall and one at Carnegie Hall. Atlantic has released a CD of material from two of these concerts.

Another by-product of the concert was my deeper friendship with Bobby Short. I had known Bobby casually since the late fifties, when he came to Storyville. Over the years, we had crossed paths a number of times—especially since Nesuhi Ertegun, Bobby's producer at Atlantic, was a mutual friend. This concert paved the way for a more intimate rapport. Bobby and I would work together a number of times over the ensuing years.

The Town Hall concert with Mabel Mercer and Bobby Short still stands as one of my proudest achievements. Bobby, Mabel, and I split the profits—realizing afterward that we should have charged more for the tickets.

Unfortunately, such ventures were rare; an oasis in the ever-widening desert of a rock-and-roll culture. Although I had always rejected rock personally, it was becoming clear to me that resistance was futile. In 1969 I crossed the threshold, and began presenting rock groups alongside the usual jazz artists.

Fearing that the jazz festival was becoming lost in the muck and mire of the media explosion of rock and roll, I asked my friend Joe Boyd—a record producer whose first job had been with Festival Productions—about potential rock artists for the 1969 Newport Jazz Festival. I didn't want rock for its own sake. "Joe," I asked, "which of these people can really play?" The list that he gave me included such musicians as Ian Anderson, the flutist from Jethro Tull who had been influenced by Roland Kirk; Jeff Beck, the remarkable English guitarist; Lew Soloff, whose trumpet playing was one of the distinctive characteristics of Blood, Sweat and Tears; and several others.

I soon discovered that all of the major rock artists we contacted were eager to perform at Newport. The Newport Jazz and Folk Festivals were still undisputed as the most important outdoor music events in the country, and the response from rock artists and agents was a deluge. From dozens of offers, I carefully selected a handful of popular and promising rock acts that I hoped would be appropriate for Newport. Even after I had made my choice, there were those who wanted in. One afternoon the telephone rang, and it was Jimi Hendrix, calling to ask whether I could fit him on the festival. I had to tell him: "Jimi, I already have too many people. I don't have room to put you on." Nobody believes this, but it is true that Jimi Hendrix called me personally, and that I turned down his request to perform.

Of all the new groups I had booked on our program, I was most interested in Blood, Sweat and Tears. They had a monstrous hit with "Spinning Wheel," and were fast becoming one of the hottest groups in America. More important, for me, was the fact that their sound was somewhat close to jazz. I could relate to their music.

Blood, Sweat and Tears was managed by Mort Lewis, an industry veteran who had previously worked with Dave Brubeck and was managing Simon and Garfunkel and the Brothers Four. Mort and I were good friends; we had toured Europe together with Brubeck, and he often came to Newport. Columbia Records had asked him to take over Blood, Sweat and Tears because they needed management. I was surprised when Mort called me, just a week before the festival, to tell me that Blood, Sweat and Tears might not make it.

David Clayton-Thomas, the band's lead singer, had been involved in some illegal activity in Canada (his home country), and was now having problems with his work visa. Because of his criminal record, officials in the United States were blocking his reentry. "We've got people working on it," Mort told me, "but I don't know whether we can get him in." Blood, Sweat and Tears had a massive American tour booked that summer. After their Newport Jazz Festival appearance, they had a string of thirty or forty dates lined up, at ten or fifteen thousand dollars a night. They were a hot group, and this was to be their first major tour.

"Mort," I said, "let me know if you need any help. I think I might be able to help you."

On the week of the festival, Mort called me again. "They won't let him in," he said despondently. This was a Tuesday afternoon; the band was supposed to play Newport that Friday. I called my friend Charles McWhorter, who had been on the original Newport Jazz Festival board. Charlie had worked as an aide to former Vice President Richard Nixon in the late '50s, and was, by this time, involved with the National Endowment for the Arts. Charlie made a few calls, and the next thing we knew, Clayton-Thomas was in the country. Mort was extremely grateful for my intervention; we all breathed

Doc and Ruth, George and Joyce—a happy family. *George and Joyce Wein Collection*

Hayes Alexander, Joyce Alexander, and Columbia Alexander. *Alexander Family Collection*

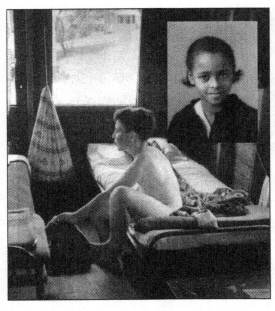

Camp Winneshe-wauka. The little girl must be saying, "Is this what I'm going to marry?" *George and Joyce Wein Collection*

The 1934 Mme. Chaloff recital: "Will the kid in short pants on the left grow up to play with Lester Young?" *Courtesy of Richard Stedman*

Nice, 1945: "Look, Ma, I'm a soldier." *George and Joyce Wein Collection*

Le Jazz "Douxe"—Hotel Fensgate, 1949: Frankie Newton, Joe Palermino, and George Wein. © *Bob Parent*

George Wein, John Field, J. C. Higginbotham, Howie Gadboys, Frankie Newton, at Jordan Hall, Boston—first concert. © *Bob Parent*

Brass bands to Bebop, 1949—
"The Promoter Bug Bites".

Edmond Hall Quartet: John Field on bass, Joe Cochrane on drums, 1949.
© *Bob Parent*

Storyville, 1950—Hotel Copley Square. Louis Armstrong and Friend, and Bob Wilber: "The night that changed a life." © *Ira Kaye*

Storyville, 1950: Sid Catlett, George Wein, and Hoagie Carmichael. © *Bob Parent*

Storyville, 1951. George Wein, Charles Mingus, and Jo Jones: "This is one nobody will believe." © *Bob Parent*

Charles Bourgeois, Johnnie Mercer, and Lee Wiley at Storyville, 1951. © *Bob Parent*

George Shearing, Muggsy Spanier, and George Wein at Storyville, 1951. © *Bob Parent*

George Wein and Lester Young: "You and me are going to be alright, Pres." *George and Joyce Wein Collection*

Newport. Louis and Elaine Lorillard with George Wein, 1954: "The Co-founders." *George and Joyce Wein Collection*

An edition of the Newport All Stars: Pee Wee Russell, Bud Freeman, Ruby Braff, Jack Lesberg, and George Wein, 1958. *George and Joyce Wein Collection*

Backstage at Newport. Three piano players: Duke Ellington, Erroll Garner, and George Wein! *George and Joyce Wein Collection*

New Orleans Jazz and Heritage Festival, 1970: Joyce with
Mahalia Jackson. © *Michael P. Smith*

New Orleans Jazz and Heritage Festival: Sister Gertrude,
George, and Joyce. © *Jules Cahn courtesy of the Jules Cahn
Collection at the Historic New Orleans Collection.*

Newport All Stars, 1966: Ruby Braff, Gerry Mulligan, Bud Freeman, Buddy Rich, Jack Lesberg, and the piano player. *George and Joyce Wein Collection*

Miles Davis at Newport, 1969, following me and rock. © *David Redfern, Redferns Music Picture Library, Ltd.*

Bringing the Big Apple back home.

Newport comes to New York City in 1972: George with Dizzy, Mayor Robert Wagner, and Vernon Jordan. *George and Joyce Wein Collection*

White House, 1978: Dizzy sings "Salt Peanuts." Jimmy and Rosalynn Carter, George Wein. *Courtesy of White House photography*

George Wein and Sarah Vaughan: "I'm still going with the girl up in Boston, Sassy." *George and Joyce Wein Collection*

Nice: George Wein outsmiling Hamp (not easy to do). © *Pierre Lapijover, F–06700*

Welcome to Madarao: Kunio Ogawa and staff, 1981. *George and Joyce Wein Collection*

Backstage Hall of Fame, Waikiki, 1977: Benny Carter, Larry Wein, George Wein, Joe Venuti, and Earl 'Fatha' Hines. © *Milton J. Hinton*

Marie St. Louis, Charlie Bourgeois, and Bob Jones's daughter Nalini Jones. © *John Abbott*

George Wein and Luciano Pavarotti: hitting a B flat in Que Gelida Manina—singing for God. © *Walter Karling*

White House, June 10, 1993: John Phillips arranges a photo with President Bill Clinton. *Courtesy of White House photography*

Ed Bradley, Wynton Marsalis, and George Wein. © *Bill Cunning-ham/The New York Times*

Legion D'Honneur: Minister of Culture Jack Lang, Miles Davis, and George Wein. *George and Joyce Wein Collection*

George Wein and Norman Granz. © *Lee Friedlander*

a sigh of relief. But this wasn't to be the last of my problems with Blood, Sweat and Tears.

> *The better rock kids have the enthusiasm and the drive that many young jazz musicians seem to lack. They know there is a public out there and they go get it. They improvise, jam, play with a beat, play the blues and have many of the characteristics of jazz. But is it JAZZ?*

> **—George Wein,**
> **1969 Newport Jazz Festival program**

The Thursday-night opening program was a typical jazz festival evening, featuring artists like Freddy Hubbard, Anita O'Day, Phil Woods, the Bill Evans Trio, Sun Ra, and introducing a young guitarist beginning to make his name, George Benson.

Shortly after the Friday afternoon session ended, the field filled up for our Friday evening concert, which featured Jethro Tull, Ten Years After, Jeff Beck, and Blood, Sweat and Tears. The only jazz that evening was played by Roland Kirk and tenor saxophonist Steve Marcus, who was playing jazz-rock. So that night's program was a rock concert. We had sold out the field, and an indeterminate number of kids managed to jump the fences. In all, there were nearly 22,000 people packed onto the grounds (well over our maximum capacity), and another 10,000 on the adjacent hillside. It was hard to look out at this massive audience and not feel a bit apprehensive. Inside the field, kids were climbing over chairs to get closer to the stage. Outside, they were leaning against our wooden snow fences, trying to get in. At one point, a section of fence collapsed, and the perpetrators poured into the field. My pleas for some sense of order over the microphone had no effect on the crowd.

Saturday afternoon was calmer, probably because jazz and rock were doled out in equal parts. The concert began with the Newport All-Stars; this season's crop included Ruby Braff, Red Norvo, Tal Farlow, and Larry Ridley. Because our drummer, Don Lamond, was unable to make the gig, we called upon the services of Miles Davis's drummer, Jack DeJohnette.

After the All-Stars came John Mayall, whose group owed much to the blues of Muddy Waters. Miles Davis followed, in a group that included DeJohnette, bassist Dave Holland, and keyboardist Chick Corea; although he was scheduled to perform, Wayne Shorter didn't arrive at the field until after the set. There was no overt rock influence to Miles's work just yet; his group played a series of sketches, linking them together in a swirling, continuous suite. The show ended with Frank Zappa and the Mothers of Invention, playing their bold and purposefully ridiculous material. When Zappa's entourage took the stage, a previously orderly crowd rushed forward.

It was becoming increasingly obvious that I had no control over the kids in the audience, who by their sheer numbers held a sort of power. But we went ahead with the program as scheduled. Saturday night's concert began with a Finnish ensemble that had won a Montreux Jazz Festival contest. Dave Brubeck followed, with special guest Gerry Mulligan. Art Blakey's Jazz Messengers came next, followed by the Gary Burton Quartet. And then there was Sly.

Sly and the Family Stone was a young band—they had been around for less than two years. But they were big; their album *Stand!* (Epic) contained several hit singles. Sly Stone, the erstwhile San Francisco disc jockey and record producer, had created a sound that incorporated funk, soul, rock, and '60s psychedelic music.

Sly stood on the stage at Newport before a sea of faces. The sight intoxicated him. He went into a sort of crazed rapture. The audience went berserk right along with him. As the band's allotted time came to an end, and I signaled to them, they kept on playing. It was a mess; people had spilled over the box seats and into the photography pit. The snow fence had collapsed in several places. Field security and police officers were forced to form a human barricade at the foot of the stage in order to keep people from climbing up. The fans who weren't charging forward were standing on their chairs, screaming.

Pandemonium was like a drug to Sly Stone, and instead of calming his fans, he incited them. "I want to take you higher!" he sang, his body convulsing. He screamed: "Higher! Higher! Higher! Higher!" He was whipping those kids into a fever pitch. It's a miracle that we avoided a riot.

We finally got Sly off the stage, and I begged the crowd to settle down. Rather than canceling the rest of the show (a move that would surely have had consequences), we went ahead with the program. The next scheduled group was the World's Greatest Jazz Band, consisting of Bud Freeman, Bob Wilber, Lou McGarrity, Carl Fontana, Ralph Sutton, Bob Haggart, and Gus Johnson. They were joined midway through their set by Maxine Sullivan. If these musicians were unnerved, they certainly didn't show it. After they left the stage, we brought on the violinist Stephane Grappelli, in his American debut. It's a wonder that in all this chaos Stephane didn't disappear into the land of Django, wherever that might be.

Given what had happened during the Sly Stone debacle, I had serious reservations about letting any more rock bands perform on Sunday night. Led Zeppelin, which had gone from obscurity to stardom in the course of a few short months, was no exception.

After making my feelings known, I found myself face to face with Peter Grant, the heavyset mug who served dual roles as the band's manager and strong-arm man. I didn't realize the extent of Peter Grant's reputation as a thug and his propensity for violence. He relayed a message: "The guys wanted to come to the Newport Jazz Festival," he said, "and now they find out that it's just another rock concert."

"If you don't let them play," Grant continued, "they're going to set up their equipment in the street outside."

This of course would have been impossible given the state of rock-performance logistics. I said. "Maybe I will let them play. But first I want to talk to them personally. Alone." Grant led me to the band's dressing room. They were a bit surprised to see me, but they listened to my pitch.

"Listen, guys," I said. "When Duke Ellington played here in 1956, he created a happening. And he kept the situation under control through his music. When Gonsalves finished his twenty-seven-chorus tenor solo, Duke played a slow blues. Now, you guys are going to get that crowd excited. And if you do what Sly Stone did, we might have a riot. So if things start to get out of hand tonight, I'm going to give you a signal, and I want you to go into a slow blues. That's how we'll get through the night."

They must have thought I was crazy. But they voiced no protests, and I accepted their tacit agreement as a matter of faith.

That evening featured the Newport Jazz Festival debut of B. B. King (who had been one of the highlights of the previous year's Folk Festival). B. B. not only delivered a stunning set of his own; he also sat in with the young white blues guitarist Johnny Winter. According to the underground music press, Johnny Winter was the greatest thing to ever happen to the blues. B. B. was kind to him, but it was clear who was the source. Winter never seemed to resolve his twelve-bar blues, while King played with his usual economy and soul.

Led Zeppelin's performance was a wall of raw energy and reached its climax with an explosive drum solo. The kids started to rush the stage. I signaled to Jimmy Page, and he went into a slow, dirge-like blues. His Delta-influenced guitar was hopelessly distorted through the speakers. But the people who had been running out of their seats now stood in place and swayed to the beat, or sat back down. This precaution—and Led Zeppelin's cooperation—got us through that last evening concert without incident.

Total attendance for the 1969 Newport Jazz Festival—85,000 people—broke all previous records. By almost any standard, it had been a huge success. At that point, I could have shifted gears and gone into the rock business; I had the field wide open to present rock concerts in Boston, Connecticut, all of New England. I had the experience, the organizational staff, and the connections. No one had broken into this field yet. There were fortunes to be made.

But I never gave this scenario a second thought. The 1969 Newport Jazz Festival had been four of the worst days of my life. Jazz—the music I loved—was being poisoned and stamped out, and I had served as an unwitting, but willing accomplice in the murder. The rock bands that played the festival were in another league and in another world, and their scene had nothing to do with my passion as a promoter or as a musician. So while it's possible to look at the 1969 Newport Jazz Festival as a pioneering step in programming (probably the only time Led Zeppelin shared a bill with Buddy Tate), I still consider it the nadir of my career. I agreed wholeheartedly with Dan Morgenstern when he wrote, in *Down Beat*, that "the rock experiment was a resounding failure."

Several years later, after a meeting at Atlantic Records, Ahmet Ertegun offered me a ride uptown in his Rolls-Royce; a fellow passenger was Mick Jagger. Ahmet, half jokingly, said to Mick, "Why don't you have the Rolling Stones play for George at Newport?" Before Mick could answer, I responded, "Please, no. If Mick and the Rolling Stones came to Newport, that would probably be the end of the festival. Mick, I love you. Thanks, but no thanks." I'm sure Mick Jagger never gave a passing thought to the Rolling Stones playing at the Newport Jazz Festival.

\*     \*     \*

Although I was thoroughly fed up with the rock world, the bad trip wasn't over just yet. My company had committed to producing several pop festivals around the country, in addition to jazz events. I was working once again with a number of the same rock artists that had played Newport.

One such rock-oriented venture was the Philadelphia Pop Festival, which took place on July 11 and 12 at the Spectrum, the massive sports facility that housed both the Philadelphia Flyers and the Philadelphia '76ers. We had embarked on a trial partnership with the owners of the Spectrum. One of the important conditions in our contract was a time restriction; it would cost an extra eight thousand dollars if the show went past midnight. Attendance was disappointing.

By this time, I had realized that my usual way of communicating with artists was ill-suited to the rock world. So I took Jimmy Sullivan, one of the kids who was working with me at the time, and made him my representative. Jimmy was basically a hippie; he had the long hair and the dungarees, and fit right in with the rock bands and their entourages. Whenever a group exceeded its time limit, I sent Jimmy out onto the stage. He would go up to one of the musicians and deliver a simple message: "George says to get the fuck off the stage." It usually worked.

In Philly, however, I had to take care of some details personally. Led Zeppelin was a powerhouse, and an extremely difficult act to follow, but they didn't want to close the show. They had asked me to put them on earlier in the program. This ran contrary to my instinct as a promoter—but because they had done me a favor in Newport, I consented. Led Zeppelin played its set, finished on time, and left the stage. And the audience went nuts. Jethro Tull was the next band on the schedule, so I ran into their dressing room and said: "You guys are on."

They looked at me. "We want to wait until the applause stops."

"Wait until the applause stops?" My jaw dropped. "You guys get out there and start while the applause is still going! Don't you know anything about show business? Do you want to let the crowd die? When they're screaming and focused on the stage, before they go to the goddamn concessions—that's when you go on! Get out there!"

The guys in the band were shocked. They just looked at me dumbfounded. So I restated my request, more forcefully: "Get the hell on the stage!"

They went on. But while they were playing, their manager Terry Ellis, who became one of the most important figures in British rock, came to me and asked me to apologize to the group. Nobody had ever talked to them like that. I did apologize. But showbiz is showbiz, and we had a schedule to meet. That audience would have cheered Led Zeppelin for another ten minutes.

A few days after Philadelphia, we had a festival in Detroit that was a bit more jazz-oriented. Sly and the Family Stone was one of the only rock acts on the bill. I called Sly's agent and said that I wasn't going to use him on the show. I was still infuriated about what had happened at Newport.

The agent protested: "You can't do that to Sly." Those agents and record companies never questioned their artists. If the musicians were drug addicts,

their managers would get them drugs. It made no difference. The industry ti-
tans were milking their artists for everything they could get. Nobody gave Sly
Stone advice; he did whatever he wanted.

"I can't use Sly," I said again. "If he does what he did at Newport, we'll
have a riot. I can't afford to take that risk."

"No," the agent argued, "you've got to let him play."

So I made a condition: "If he plays, he's got to open the show."

He countered: "Sly doesn't want to open the show."

Exasperated, I said, "Where's Sly, I want to talk to him." Reluctantly, the
agent gave me Sly Stone's phone number, and I called him.

"Yeah," he answered when he picked up. He was stoned.

"Sly, this is George Wein. Look, I'll let you play Detroit if you promise me
you'll stop when I tell you."

"Man, why are you talking to me? Why don't you talk to my manager?"

"Sly," I said, "you're a man, and I'm a man. I can pay you not to play, and
you don't have to play. But you want to play, and I've got problems. Now, I
want you to forget that you're a rock star. Forget that you're a recording artist.
If you give me your word as a man that you will listen to me and stop when I
tell you to stop—then I'll let you close the show."

There was a silent pause before he grunted his assent. And that night, he
went on and closed the show. He did his thing, and the people were screaming,
but when I gave the signal he took it out. It was perfect. Sly Stone's father was
there that night, and he came up to me after the show. "You know, Mr. Wein,"
he said, "I wish more people talked to Sly like you talked to him."

*    *    *

Despite its unprecedented ticket sales, the 1969 Newport Jazz Festival had generated negative revenue because we were slapped with massive fees from the city
for police protection, cleanup, and a chain-link fence. We had presented two
nights at the Spectrum in Philly and lost money. We had lost money as well in
Detroit, at the Laurel Pop Festival in Maryland, and at the Rutgers Jazz Festival
in New Brunswick, New Jersey.

New Brunswick was the setting for a memorable musical incident that
summer. At the last minute Nina Simone canceled her appearance, leaving us
with a slot to fill. So I decided to allot more stage time to a young singer
who had come on the recommendation of Vic O'Gilvy, a former festival employee. Her name was Roberta Flack. I had originally told her to do two

numbers, but as the crowd kept screaming, I'd say, "Do one more." She ended up doing seven or eight. She was phenomenal; a star from the beginning. To this day, Roberta Flack acknowledges the effect of that concert on her career. She usually dedicates "The First Time Ever I Saw Your Face" to me.

Despite such occasionally bright moments, the summer of love was a disaster in every sense. Financially, it was the worst year I'd ever had. It was like I had the reverse Midas Touch; everything I touched turned to shit. As a last resort, I called Mort Lewis—my friend who managed Blood, Sweat and Tears. Mort had told me to let him know if I ever needed anything, and I now found myself calling in a marker. This was uncharacteristic of me, but I could see no alternative. Blood, Sweat and Tears had played in Philadelphia, and I told Mort that I didn't have the money to pay them.

Mort called me back. "I spoke with the group," he told me, "and they don't want to give you a reduction."

I said: "I don't think you heard me, Mort. I didn't ask for a reduction. I literally don't have the money to pay you. This was a terrible summer for me."

Mort was my friend, and he replied: "Well, you don't have the money to pay me. That's it." He let me off the hook. But a year later, when Mort Lewis broke up with the group, they made him pay a settlement of ten thousand dollars—the amount I owed the band. When Mort told me this, I was incredulous.

"Mort, did you ever tell them that I was the one who got them back into the States? They could have lost hundreds of thousands of dollars that summer!" He had never told them. It was another unfortunate experience in the rock business—a lesson in trust and in greed.

Ironically, it was just a few weeks after my dismal rock promotions that the Woodstock Music Festival drew more than 300,000 people to Bethel, New York. I remember standing on the sidewalk in Manhattan that Friday afternoon, and seeing scores of kids walking down the street wearing backpacks. It was a literal exodus. I had no idea where they were all going.

Most of the major artists who had played Newport appeared at Woodstock, along with many others. What differentiated my rock promotions from the Woodstock event was the fact that I sold tickets to my concerts, while Woodstock was free of charge. But this was not the result of altruism so much as necessity; the organizers of Woodstock fully intended to sell tickets, for profit. But they were outnumbered by the hordes. The notion that "music should be free" had become a slogan for the youth generation—a cry that would come back to haunt me.

Following the near-mayhem of 1969, the Newport City Council voted to outlaw rock and roll from all future festivals. They needn't have gone to such efforts; I was finished with rock. The headaches of that summer were too great. More important, I was ashamed of myself. It was one thing to make mistakes on the festival—for example, presenting the Kingston Trio—but the "rock experiment" was a step too far. I vowed never to present a rock-centric event again.

It wasn't the fact that I was a purist. I may have been conventional in my personal tastes, but my scope in presenting jazz festivals had always been quite catholic. It went deeper; I couldn't work with these people. They were not my life. I love jazz artists, as difficult as they might be. Monk had problems, but he was a genius and a wonderful human being. Dealing with Mingus was a challenge, but Mingus was a peerless musician and an incredible talent. To deal with Miles and all of his arrogance was not a picnic—but he was Miles Davis. It was a privilege to know these people—to go to war with them and to become friends with them. It was a privilege to have them trust me. I was doing something important, and I did not want to lose that. No matter what problems and setbacks I encountered with this "dead" art form, I was determined to continue my journey.

\*     \*     \*

*The Newport Jazz Festival? Oh man, that was one of the greatest thrills of my life.*
**—Louis Armstrong, 1970**

I approached the 1970 Newport Jazz Festival with renewed vigor. There was still antagonism from the local anti-festival contingent. The City Council made us fight for our license again, and levied penalties, fees, and restrictions.

Their most adamant stand was a moratorium on rock groups. The 50,000 rock fans who had jammed the city in 1969 had sparked no serious incidents, but their presence had scared the hell out of everybody. The council reasoned that excising rock music from the festival would keep this undesirable element out of Newport. I agreed with their decision in practice (I had already vowed to keep rock off the festival), but not in theory. By codifying their prejudices in an official ruling, they practiced a form of institutional repression. They undertook the role of censor.

In reality, the council's restriction had no effect on my vision for the festival. I was concerned with showing the jazz public that we were still dedicated to its music, but I made a few concessions. I made plans to present Ike and Tina Turner—who had proven during previous Ohio Valley Jazz Festivals that they were powerful performers, and had a wide audience. We received no complaints about Ike and Tina; they played soul music, not rock and roll, and suited Newport well. Roberta Flack and Nina Simone also reached beyond a jazz audience. Critics voiced no objections to these artists; quite the contrary. In a Festival review for *Down Beat*, Dan Morgenstern wrote of Ike and Tina Turner: "It's good to have them at Newport."

The 1970 festival program was peopled with the likes of Dizzy Gillespie, Gary Burton, Keith Jarrett and Don Byas. Dexter Gordon came from France. An interesting feature was a drum workshop with Jo Jones, Philly Joe Jones, and Elvin Jones, plus Chico Hamilton.

On a Sunday afternoon show, we presented Badfoot Brown and the Bunions Bradford Funeral Marching Band—a twelve-piece band led, organized, and conducted by stand-up comedian and *I Spy* television-show celebrity Bill Cosby. This group consisted of experienced, professional musicians (Monk Montgomery, Kenny Barron, and Jimmy Smith among them), and their music, a blend of soul and progressive jazz, was not bad. Despite the ridiculous name, this was not a joke. Cosby was serious about conducting the band; he didn't do any comedic routines or deliver any lines. Badfoot Brown didn't have much of a career beyond Newport. But their appearance gave me an opportunity to become friends with Cosby; our relationship would grow and deepen over the years. It was clear, even after just meeting the man, that he loved jazz—and jazz musicians.

The climactic conclusion of the festival was twofold: a driving Buddy Rich Orchestra performance, followed by Ella Fitzgerald with the Tommy Flanagan Trio. This was a jazz festival, any way you looked at it. And it was a good one. Yet this was only the tip of the iceberg; all of these artists were preceded by a special Friday evening concert that just might have been the finest single program I ever produced.

July 4, 1970, marked Louis Armstrong's ceremonial seventieth birthday; he had come into the world on Independence Day, at the dawn of the twentieth century. At least, that's the story that he maintained (and probably believed) throughout his life. In fact, Louis was born on August 4, 1901—a detail that surfaced when his baptismal certificate was discovered by Gary Giddins, more than a decade after his death. During Pops's life, however, the legend was unchallenged.

For some time, I had been hoping to produce a tribute concert in honor of Louis's seventieth year. But Louis had recently been ill. His heart and his kidney were weakening, and he had been in and out of the hospital. Early in 1969, he had undergone an emergency surgical procedure to drain his lungs of fluid. After a two-month hospital stay, his doctors released him with much cautionary advice. His lungs were frail, and he couldn't risk overexerting himself. His doctors' most adamant plea: Louis could no longer play the trumpet. But they said that he could still sing.

It is generally conceded that the three most important jazz figures of the twentieth century are Louis Armstrong, Duke Ellington, and Charlie Parker; for me, Armstrong was the greatest of the three. Even the musicians who found it necessary to renounce the Armstrong persona recognized his genius. He may not have composed with the prolific sophistication of Duke Ellington, but his contribution was, ultimately, more profound. Louis Armstrong created the jazz language.

This isn't to say that Armstrong invented "jazz"—he didn't. Nor did he create the concept of improvising on a melody. He was, however, the first person to play with the loose swing feeling that distinguished jazz from other forms of music. There was ragtime before Louis, but that was a composed exercise in syncopated four-four time in which the notes were mostly played as written. What Armstrong did was infuse ragtime with the rhythmic and melodic flexibility of the blues. And as the first true soloist in jazz, he became the source from which everybody inevitably flowed.

It was late in Louis's life when I got to know him well enough to ask: "Pops, how is it that you were the first one to play 'behind the beat,' and swing the way you did? To my knowledge, nobody did that before you came along."

Louis replied: "I just played the way I sang." This answer was as clear as it was concise—except he never told me where he learned to sing that way. His vocals were almost as significant a contribution as his trumpet playing. Ethel Waters, Billie Holiday, Lena Horne, and Ella Fitzgerald were all deeply indebted to Louis. So was Bing Crosby; when you listen to Crosby's early work with the Paul Whiteman Orchestra, you don't hear the relaxed phrasing that came in the thirties—after he heard Armstrong.

The program I envisioned for Louis's birthday tribute at Newport would salute his instrumental genius as well as his accomplishments as entertainer and worldwide ambassador of jazz.

The concert's official title was "The Schlitz Salute to Louis: A New Orleans Tribute to Louis Armstrong." It was unfortunate that my skirmishes with the Newport City Council had pushed the festival from July 4, the day Louis celebrated his birth, to July 10 but it ultimately didn't matter. I set out to create a concert that would do justice to Pops's legacy. I spent a lot of time thinking about the direction and tone of such a concert, and how it could be produced.

I had a strong feeling for the spirit of New Orleans, Louis's hometown. I arranged to bring the Preservation Hall Jazz Band, the Eureka Brass Band, and the New Orleans Classic Ragtime Band to Newport—three quite different sides of traditional New Orleans music. I also asked Mahalia Jackson to perform a gospel mini-concert, to show Louis's clear, lifelong ties to church music. Like Louis, Mahalia originally hailed from New Orleans; you could detect that city's distinctive accent in her pronunciation of certain words.

And certainly, an all-star trumpet tribute was necessary in any salute to Louis. The most obvious choice, to me, was Bobby Hackett. It wasn't so much that Bobby's style was wedded to Armstrong's (he had actually been influenced just as much by Bix Beiderbecke) but that he loved Louis as a friend. There was a relationship there. Then I picked Wild Bill Davison because he came from the Chicago style of trumpet playing—which was patterned after Louis's Hot Five and Hot Seven recordings. Joe Newman was my next pick; he was an example of a big band trumpeter whose playing reflected the boldness of the Armstrong sound. Ray Nance was another natural choice; like many of the Ellington trumpeters (Bubber Miley and Cootie Williams especially), he was a pure Armstrong disciple. Dizzy Gillespie was a representative of the post-Armstrong school. And finally there was trumpeter Jimmy Owens. Although Jimmy's style was the product of another generation, he had admiration and respect for Armstrong.

When I gave Louis a list of the trumpeters on this program, he said: "I bet Dizzy is going to do that imitation of me that I hate." He was referring to a rendition of "I'm Confessin'" that Dizzy had performed during a U.S. State Department tour of South America. I knew that Dizzy was going to use this number because I'd requested it; I never imagined that Louis would take offense. I told Louis: "If you don't want Dizzy to do it, I'll ask him not to." On the day of the concert, though, Louis greeted Dizzy at the afternoon rehearsal with a big smile on his face, and the first thing he said was: "Hey man, you going to do that 'I'm Confessin'' that I love so much?"

My friend Sid Stiber, who had often asked me whether I would consider shooting concert footage at Newport, saw the Armstrong tribute as a perfect opportunity. Together we formed a company, Festi Films Inc., and made plans to shoot and edit a 16-mm documentary of the performance. As partners we each put up half the money (where I got my half is a mystery lost to time). In

1970, it was not a common thing to film live performances, and we were able to squeeze by without major funding. We paid the musicians scale; Louis and Mahalia received slightly larger fees.

Filming began during the afternoon rehearsal that preceded the concert. The resulting footage, which we dubbed "The Anatomy of a Performance," turned out to be some of our rarest and most interesting material. We got Louis greeting Joe Newman backstage, and meeting other friends on the grounds. Pops leads the house rhythm section in rehearsing some of his tunes; at one point he tries to teach pianist Dave McKenna the changes to "What a Wonderful World." Another scene depicts the New Orleans musicians striking up a second-line beat and legendary clarinetist Willie Humphrey, playing the part of Grand Marshall, proudly parading around the stage. Louis stands amidst all this happy noise, beaming.

While Louis was in fragile condition, he was in good spirits and in surprisingly good health, considering the problems of the past months. If Louis emitted an aura of frailty in rehearsal, it was because his guard was down. He was not an entertainer during those moments; he was among friends. His presence was not tragic, but triumphant.

Before his grand entrance that night, Louis took in the whole tribute from his chair on the side of the stage. He later explained: "I had to sit in the wings, so I could catch everybody—and see what they were doing."

There was a lot to catch. The concert began in true New Orleans fashion, with the Eureka Brass Band. They emerged in standard uniform; clad in white caps, white short-sleeve shirts with skinny black neckties, and black pants. Leader-trumpeter Percy Humphrey and alto saxophonist Captain John Handy each soloed over the subtle, undulating rhythm of Cie Frazier and Booker T. Glass (on snare drum and bass drum, respectively). The band's polyphonous take on "St. Louis Blues" evoked the old New Orleans sound as if it were happening right then and there. Willie Humphrey, festooned with a Grand Marshall's red-and-gold sash, demonstrated a series of steps, turns, and flourishes that signified the pomp and pride of the second line.

After Eureka, Bobby Hackett came out with trombonist Benny Morton, pianist Dave McKenna, bassist Jack Lesberg, and drummer Oliver Jackson. Bobby's trumpet was understated and graceful as ever, especially during a muted solo on "Someday." Bobby's mini-set, which lasted only three songs, was a teaser for the trumpet smorgasbord to come.

The New Orleans Classic Ragtime Band, organized by the Swedish musicologist and pianist Lars Edegran, was resplendent in elegant formal attire;

they resembled a classical chamber group. On this program, Edegran ceded his leadership duties to special guest William Russell, the venerable musicologist and fine violinist (and member of the New Orleans Jazz and Heritage advisory board). If anything was going to transport the listener to another era, it would be the beauty of ragtime as played by Bill Russell. The Ragtime Band played such old chestnuts as "Creole Belles" and Scott Joplin's lovely "Ragtime Waltz." Their performance was fresh, refined, and, as Dan Morgenstern later put it, "redolent with late 19th century charm and grace." It perfectly illustrated the sophistication of old New Orleans society, a sound almost as important to Louis's early experience as the blues.

Many bright moments during the trumpet tribute followed. Bobby Hackett played a tune I loved, "Thanks a Million," and declared it a gesture of gratitude to Louis. Joe Newman revisited "Way Down Yonder in New Orleans." Wild Bill Davison, in his usual irreverent manner, introduced "Them There Eyes" by saying, "If I told you what I really thought about Louis Armstrong, you'd probably call it indecent exposure." Jimmy Owens played a hard-boppish "Mack the Knife" in waltz time, and a flugelhorn rendition of "Nobody Knows the Trouble I've Seen"—one of the prettiest, most simply stated moments of the evening. Ray Nance did "I'm In the Market for You" with both trumpet and vocals inspired by the master. And Dizzy prefaced his hilarious take on "I'm Confessin'" with a sincere introduction. "Louis Armstrong's station in the history of jazz," he declared, "is unimpeachable. If it weren't for him, there wouldn't be any of us. I want to take this moment to thank Louis Armstrong for my livelihood."

It was during the first few bars of "When It's Sleepy Time Down South" that Louis made his first appearance onstage, unannounced. Bobby Hackett and Tyree Glenn had started playing the song, and out walked Louis, to tumultuous applause. This moment, which seemed spontaneous, was actually well-planned. I wanted Louis's entrance to be a surprise. Originally, I was planning on bringing him out during "Pennies from Heaven." But Louis was more comfortable opening with "Sleepytime" ("That's my theme song!" he had protested, during the rehearsal), so that's what we did. The song order ultimately didn't make a difference; Louis came out unannounced and broke up the whole house. "Blueberry Hill" closed the first half.

After intermission, the Preservation Hall Jazz Band, under the direction of Allan Jaffee, struck up their first tune. Willie Humphrey—who had momentarily replaced his Grand Marshall costume with a white shirt and black tie—played clarinet. Captain John Handy delivered a bold alto solo on "Bourbon Street Parade" (quoting liberally from John Phillip Sousa). DeDe Pierce not only played trumpet, but also did some rousing singing on both "Bourbon Street" and "Little Girl." Meanwhile Jim Robinson—the dean of New Orleans trombonists—blew heartily. Allan Jaffee puffed away at his bass horn, and Billie Pierce left the piano at one point to sing a blues. The whole set was carried by the drumming of Josiah "Cie" Frazier, who defined the ultimate rhythmic feeling of New Orleans drumming. To me, Frazier was one of the great drummers of all time. There was a depth and intensity to his beat that I have never experienced with any other New Orleans drummer and with not many who represented other eras of jazz.

Then, out walked Mahalia Jackson, dressed in a lovely baby-blue gown and looking like a queen. It was her first time in Newport since 1958—the year Bert Stern had filmed *Jazz on a Summer's Day*. We were fortunate to have cameras on hand once again, because we got what I believe is her finest filmed performance. Mahalia had suffered some poor health in recent months, but her performance that night was matchless in its grace and inspiration. She did a powerful, deliberate version of the old hymn "How Great Thou Art," and a majestic "Let There Be Peace." On the gospel number "Elijah," she held the microphone stand with one hand and gently swayed back and forth in time. At other moments, she stood as still as a monument, lifting everyone with that miraculous voice.

Any misgivings Mahalia had once felt about appearing at a jazz festival were now gone. She introduced her last song by thanking Louis Armstrong for giving us jazz, "one of the great arts of the world." She went on to describe Louis as "a man with the warm smile. A man that everybody loves. And if you don't love him, I don't think you really know how to love." And with that, she went into a gospel favorite, "Just a Closer Walk with Thee."

It began gently. "Just," Mahalia sang, "a closer . . . walk with Thee." Her words rang with quiet conviction. She went through several choruses, each rising and falling like successive waves. And gradually, as the song came around, her performance grew more intense. She nodded vigorously with each accent, loosing several strands of her elaborate coiffure. She squared her feet and held her mic stand at a severe angle. She began punctuating the verses with shouts and brilliant exclamations. And then, as if taken by the spirit, she left the microphone and strutted across the stage, still testifying in full voice. Her hair now hung over her face. She pointed her arms to the heavens as she sang. It was an unforgettable climax; people cheered. She returned to the microphone, but only for a moment. Then she headed straight for the wings, as the organ kept churning.

Louis and I were waiting when she walked off, and we then took the stage together. Everyone was euphoric during that moment. Louis's face was illuminated by a huge smile; he was moved. He applauded vigorously, and kept clapping even as I eased Mahalia back out to the microphone. She greeted Louis with an enormous hug, and kept one arm around his shoulder as they went into the song again, together. Louis took the mic in hand and began to sing.

But he didn't know the words! So Mahalia spoke them, one phrase at a time, and he repeated what she had said. Of course, some things were lost in translation—Mahalia's "Please keep me from doing wrong" became Louis's "Oh, please keep me . . . all wrong." It was the same thing Louis had done all his life with Tin Pan Alley songs—but Mahalia was visibly frustrated. Then it began to rain; umbrellas began popping up in the crowd, with some people fleeing for cover.

Louis, concerned that there would be no one left to hear his own finale, decided that he had to bring the gospel bit to a close. "We won't keep you in the rain," he said imploringly to the cheering crowd. But the song kept going, like a train clinging to its tracks. So while Mahalia repeated "Just a closer walk, just a closer walk," he butted in with the line: "Oh, hello Dolly!" This was a not-too-subtle hint which Mahalia either didn't catch or just plain ignored. So Louis tried again, half-singing and half-speaking: "Oh, look at 'em trucking on out that gate!" But the song kept going. Then seeing that I'd better get to the finale, I sent out the Eureka Brass Band and Bobby Hackett, augmenting the gospel accompanists. Louis grew more exasperated. "Look at all them New Orleans cats," he said exuberantly to the crowd, before turning around and waving his arm at the musicians in an attempt to stop the tune. Finally, he got the attention of Bobby Hackett, who brought "Walk With Thee" to a halt.

Louis was happier with the next selection, "When the Saints Go Marching In," which I had asked all of the groups to avoid, so we could save it for this finale. I called out "Saints," I then sat down at the piano, and the whole band laid into it. Willie Humphrey, back in Grand Marshall mode, took Louis by the shoulder and paraded him around the stage, while Mahalia sang wordless variations on the melody. And then Louis came to the mic to sing it once through, and took it out. By this time, the crowd was up. Louis held his hands up like a heavyweight champion; the applause was deafening. Without missing any time, we did an encore: "Mack the Knife," which Louis sang. We finished, and Louis left the stage with Mahalia on his arm. It was a glorious moment.

Our tribute was over, and it was more spectacular than even I could have imagined. This concert meant all the more to me because I had produced it number by number. The evening had been as carefully planned as possible, without the encumbrance of either a script or a dress rehearsal. Louis himself said it best: "George Wein—I think he really knows us well to put us together like this. Every time he does a concert, he knows who to get, and where to place 'em." The fact that I was friends with these musicians—and that I had played with many of them—gave me the flexibility and understanding to work with them. And I was able, that evening, to run a tight ship—while keeping a loose, relaxed feeling. The result had been a thrilling success, especially coming on the heels of 1969's rock invasion.

If you ask me what night I remember most from all the years in Newport, The salute to Louis Armstrong tops the list. In *Down Beat*, Dan Morgenstern praised it as "the kind of night festivals seem to be made for."

\*     \*     \*

After the festival, I sat down with Sid Stiber to view hours of concert footage. I had an idea: Why not shoot an interview with Louis at his home? I would ask him questions in reference to what was happening in the film (which, of course, he had not yet seen). My questions would later be edited out, so that the only voice and image onscreen would be those of Louis himself.

I had interviewed Louis in the past. The first time was when he played Storyville in 1952. Our conversation had taken place onstage and was caught on a recorded disc. But at that time, Louis gave me the same stories that he was giving everyone else. He was such an old hand at interviews that he had an arsenal of readymade answers; it was like he was reading from a script.

This time it was slightly different. Sid, Joyce, and I went with a cameraman to his home in Corona, Queens, two weeks after the festival. Louis was very proud of his house, and showed us his collections. Then we sat down and started talking. The camera was trained on Louis; I sat across from him. Our interview lasted all day. We returned a few days later, and picked up where we had left off. We were amassing hours of interview tape.

We talked about everything from second-line New Orleans parades (he recalled carrying King Oliver's cornet at every opportunity) to the Beatles (he pointed out that the Paul McCartney/John Lennon song "Let It Be" was "church music if there ever was"). He recounted how the melody of "Someday You'll Be Sorry" had occurred to him in a dream, on a cold early morning in North Dakota. He explained how he had found his theme song "Sleepy Time" from Joe Glaser (who had probably found it at a music publishing house). He recalled listening to the radio as a young boy, and hearing Bessie Smith singing W. C. Handy's "St Louis Blues." He related the story of "how scatting was born," during an Okeh Records recording session for "Heebie Jeebies."

Many of these anecdotes were familiar Armstrong-isms, but there were also stories and opinions that I'd never heard before. I got Louis to talk about meeting Wild Bill Davison in Chicago in the 1930s. He offered his opinion of Bobby Hackett ("he's always been my favorite trumpet man, as far as intonation and phrasing"), Ray Nance (who played with "a beautiful tone"), and the rest of the musicians on the concert.

Off-camera, Louis was even more candid, especially when I brought up the subject of his former manager, Joe Glaser. Louis's high regard for Joe was well known. In 1943, he wrote that he "admired Mr. Glaser from the first day I started working for him." Most official accounts paint a picture of friendship and mutual admiration between them; Glaser, despite his idiosyncratic gruffness and mob affiliations, had done more for Armstrong's career than anyone else. Louis often recounted how King Oliver advised him to find a white manager who could run interference and navigate the business. His relationship with Glaser, which had first begun in Chicago in 1926, seemed a paradigm of successful cooperation—and a miracle of longevity in the inconstant world of show business. The only time I had witnessed any serious conflict between them was at Newport in 1957, when Glaser, at my request, had interfered with Louis's act.

Fate landed both Louis and Joe in Beth Israel Hospital in Manhattan at the same time, in the fall of 1969. While Louis was there recovering from lung surgery, Joe Glaser suffered a serious stroke. Louis didn't even know that anything had happened until Dizzy Gillespie, paying a visit, mentioned that he was preparing to give blood for Joe. Louis, shocked by news of his manager's stroke, had the hospital staff wheel him to the intensive care unit—where Glaser was in a coma. Biographer Laurence Bergreen has noted that Louis, shaken by this sight, wrote a memoir in his hospital bed and dedicated it to Joe Glaser, "the best friend that I've ever had." A few months later, after Louis had left the hospital and Joe had left the mortal world, Louis wrote: "It was a toss up between us, who would cut out first. Man, it broke my heart that it was him. I love that man, which the world already knows. I prayed, sick as I was, that he would make it. God bless his soul. He was the greatest for me and all the spades that he handled."

As Joyce and I spoke to Louis a year later, though, he told a different story. "When we started," he said, recalling Chicago in the 1920s, "we both had nothing. We were friends—we hung out together, ate together, we went to restaurants together. But the minute we started to make money, Joe Glaser was no longer my friend. In all those years, he never invited me to his house. I was just a passport for him." Louis was also offended by the fact that Joe Glaser's will bequeathed Associated Booking, Glaser's company, to my friend Oscar Cohen and several other people in the company. To Louis, he had only left the rights to his own publishing. "I built Associated Booking," Louis said angrily. "There wouldn't have been an agency if it wasn't for me. And he didn't even leave me a percentage of it."

Louis also described his bedside visit with Glaser in the hospital. Joe Glaser was indeed in a coma, unable to communicate. Louis, quite ill himself, seated in a hospital-issue wheelchair, leaned in to whisper a message. It turned out to be the last words between them. What Louis said was this: "I'll bury you, you motherfucker."

Joyce, Sid Stiber, and myself were present when Louis spoke these words. I don't doubt that his feelings of resentment, which had many years to accrue, were sincere. In a sense, Louis may have felt unburdened when Joe died; he was no longer under Glaser's managerial yoke. With precious little time left in his own life, Louis may have simply decided to air long-suppressed emotions.

No such catharsis was anywhere in our film, but because Louis opened up to us, our footage stands as probably the most intimate portrait of Louis ever captured on film. The Louis you see onscreen here is without question a show business icon, but his guard is down. He's comfortable and relaxed, and, despite a large sty in his right eye, he has a certain vibrancy. This wasn't the case a few weeks later, when Sid and I returned to his house for some additional voiceovers; by then, Louis's voice had deteriorated quite a bit. We used only a few seconds of this weak voiceover material at the very beginning of the film.

When we edited our material into a final product, Sid and I interspersed interviews with concert footage. As a result, Louis's reflections on "I'm Confessin'" lead straight into Dizzy's funny performance of the song. Louis's recollection of King Oliver and Bunk Johnson playing "Panama" in the street serves as an introduction to the Eureka Brass Band's performance of that tune. The entire documentary proceeds this way, with concert and interview engaged in a sort of call-and-response. Through some skillful and painstaking editing, we managed to have Louis Armstrong narrating his own film.

It ended up costing Festi Films, Inc.—Sid Stiber and me—a little over $100,000 to complete four forty-five-minute segments on 16-mm film. Although we tried mightily, we never could sell that film in the United States (though it was seen overseas). The Public Broadcasting System did offer to pay us to use some of the footage; they were doing their own Louis Armstrong documentary and needed excerpts of our material  rather than using our complete film. Sid and I were extremely reluctant to do this, but we desperately needed the money. We gave them a few shots of Louis in his home, which they used on their program; they paid us roughly $60,000 for this privilege. Meanwhile, in order to break even, Sid and I shopped the film all over Europe; we ended up selling onetime rights to television in Germany, Austria, Australia, and a few other countries. The film still occasionally surfaces, with overdubbing, on German cable television. Fragments of our footage can be seen in PBS's Louis Armstrong documentary, and in Ken Burns's *Jazz* film. But aside from one screening at Columbia University in Armstrong's centennial year, the film has never been seen in its entirety by an American audience. Because of the rapid decline of his health in 1971, I don't think Louis ever saw it.

*     *     *

In January 1971, I embarked on a month-long tour of Europe and the Far East with the Count Basie Orchestra. The band spent two weeks in Japan before passing through Southeast Asia (with dates in Okinawa, Taipei, Manila, Hong Kong, Bangkok, Rangoon, and Singapore), then Australia and New Zealand.

My father accompanied us on that tour; it was his first trip to the Far East. Doc was seventy-seven years old, and still practicing medicine in Boston. I thought this was remarkable, and I said words to that effect to a newspaper reporter in Hong Kong. Afterward, Doc told Basie that he was annoyed I had mentioned his age. He thought it would hurt his business; who would want to see a doctor that was seventy-seven years old? Basie replied: "Dr. Wein, you shouldn't be upset. Your son is proud of you. It means a lot to him that you're here, and that you're still practicing at your age." This thoughtful response was typical of Bill Basie. He didn't mention the fact that my comments were printed only in Hong Kong—halfway around the globe from Doc's nearest patient.

Count Basie was a joy to work with; he was always cooperative, but I was puzzled by his attitude toward encores—he wouldn't take any. Audiences surged to their feet at the end of each performance, shouting for more. This happened all over Japan, and in Taipei, Bangkok, and Hong Kong. But no matter how great the ovation, Basie never went back onstage. Puzzled, I asked Eddie Lockjaw Davis—Basie's straw boss—about this policy. He shrugged. "Why don't you ask Basie? I try to get him to do encores, but he won't." We were in Rangoon, Burma, at the time. That afternoon, I approached Basie with the question: "Bill, I've been wondering why you haven't taken any encores. The people are crazy about you. They would be thrilled to get just one more number."

His explanation: "Well, I learned a lesson at Birdland: You've got to leave an audience hungry for more, so they come back the next time."

"That's very good," I said. "Because you were working Birdland every night. But Bill—when's the next time you'll be in Rangoon?" That night, Basie played an encore. In fact, he played encores after that on all of his foreign tours.

After Burma, the band was scheduled to play a one-nighter in Laos. Now, neither Burma nor Laos were typical stops on a tour itinerary; the Vietnam War had plunged the whole region into a state of unrest. But we had arranged to penetrate this territory on behalf of the U.S. State Department, in spite of the fact that it was a danger zone. Over a decade later, Basie would recall that this leg of the tour "was no sight-seeing trip for me. All I was concerned about was when we were going to get the hell out of there."

Basie's contract stipulated that he would travel only on commercial flights. But there were no such flights from Burma to Laos; the only transportation available was a chartered U.S. army plane with bucket seats along the walls. When I told Basie about this arrangement, his eyes widened. It was bad enough flying into war-torn Laos; taking a paratrooper transport was too much. Basie knew that military planes were prime targets. "Man, I'm not going," he declared. "Unless you go, too."

"I'll go," I said. I hadn't planned on it, but I didn't hesitate. If going to Laos meant the difference between Basie making and missing a gig, I knew I had to do it.

I showed up at the airfield at daybreak the following morning. The army plane was stretched out like an enormous slug. Basie was standing there with all the guys in the band. As I walked over, he said: "What are you doing here?"

"You said you weren't going unless I came with you. So here I am."

He looked at me as if I were nuts. "Is your father back at the hotel?"

"Well, yes."

"Get out of here; you go back to your father and stay with him."

Basie's concern and respect for my father touched me. He was like that—considerate, cooperative, and unfailingly polite. In his autobiography, he recalls this incident slightly differently:

> I told him I was not going anywhere else over there in those war zones, and when we came down, we went on talking about it, and I told him to count me out. But old George could dig it. "Well," he said, "I guess I'll have to take your place. Don't worry about it. I'll go."
>
> George himself is a good piano player, and he was actually getting ready to fill in for me on the next gig. But that's when I said to myself, I ain't gonna be that chicken. If the rest of the guys in the band were going, I had to go, too. And besides, George had his father along with him on the trip, and he needed to stay with him.

I actually like his version better than mine, because it has me playing the piano with the Basie band. In any case, Bill and I solidified our friendship during that tour, and the plane incident reinforced our mutual respect. Not only in Burma, but all throughout the tour, it was a pleasure to work with him. Basie hardly ever complained about the tour. Like Ellington, he was a road rat accustomed to the grueling pace of the road.

And he had to be, on a tour like this. The band was playing in a different city almost every night. I used to tell musicians: "If you're looking for an easy tour, don't go. There's no such thing as an easy tour of Europe or Asia." Because you have to get up early in the morning, go to the next town, and play the gig. Basie's guys were champs; in Australia, they did four concerts in three days (in the cities of Perth, Adelaide, Melbourne, and Sydney). Then, after playing in New Zealand, they flew to Honolulu for a gig at the Hilton Hawaiian Village. I had set it up so that the band played a concert in Auckland, left that evening, arrived at Honolulu at 6:35 A.M., and played the Hilton gig that night. Because of the change in time zones, they actually performed in both New Zealand and Hawaii on the same day.

These engagements wrapped up the tour. The following morning, I had breakfast with Basie in the Hilton Hawaiian Village. It was nice to relax for a moment before parting ways; Basie's band was heading for San Francisco later that day. As we were sitting and conversing, a worried-looking Freddie Green walked up to our table. Green had played rhythm guitar in the Count Basie Orchestra since 1937; his subtle but steady four-four time was an integral part of the band's sound. Over the years, Freddie and Basie had become like one musician. It was almost impossible to imagine one without the other. Freddie's mere presence created an atmosphere of peace and tranquility wherever he went. But he was also quite a shopper. Upon arriving in Honolulu, he got slapped with a $500 or $600 customs duty for purchases he made in Japan and Hong Kong. This was what Freddie had to talk to Basie about. With his eyes focused on the ground in front of his feet, he mumbled something about a loan.

Basie waved him away. "Yeah, yeah. I'll see you later." He appeared irritated. After Freddie had left, Bill looked at me and shook his head. I'll never forget his words: "Just because a guy's been with you for over thirty years, he thinks he can ask you anything he wants!" I'm sure Count Basie did in fact lend the money to Freddie, but that line was priceless. The love Freddie Green had for Basie was reflected in his tearful eulogy at Count's funeral.

*    *    *

*The festival has become a symbol of the survival and re-silience of jazz itself—with all its faults and occasional strayings from the path. There will always be a Newport, somewhere, somehow.*

**–Dan Morgenstern**

Like an encroaching storm front, the crowd on the hill seemed to grow more and more menacing by the hour. Their presence had transformed Miantanomi Memorial Park into a sort of freaked-out refugee camp of thousands. Lacking food or water, they survived on wine, liquor, amphetamines, acid, and dope. They were taking uppers to get up and downers to get down. They were stoned completely out of their minds.

On the festival grounds, all was calm. Fans listened appreciatively to the Dave Pike Set and the successive big band performances of the Stan Kenton, Buddy Rich, and Duke Ellington Orchestras. But I was hardly aware of the music; my attention was diverted to the hillside, where dozens of bonfires burned ominously. I could see our unwelcome neighbors clearly even from Festival Field; their encampment was only about a hundred yards away. The only thing separating my world from theirs was a chain-link fence, an access road, and the gradual slope of the hill.

This was Friday, the first night of the 1971 Newport Jazz Festival. Some of the kids on the hill had arrived as early as Thursday morning, filtering in like pilgrims seeking an unholy Mecca. Their clothes and hair were disheveled;

most of them had hitchhiked onto Aquidneck Island from far afield. They had quickly found their way to the outskirts of Newport, occupying the park. Their numbers had grown as kids kept pouring into town; there were now thousands of outsiders on the hill.

How could this have happened at the Jazz Festival, with nary a rock band in sight? Although I had gladly obeyed the Newport City Council ban on rock acts, there had been one crucial oversight. While programming the festival in January, I had asked Ahmet Ertegun to come up with a young white band for a Sunday night blues concert. I wanted to illustrate the universality of the blues, the way John Hammond, Jr., had done at the Folk Festival a few years back.

"But I don't want anybody popular," I had emphasized. "Make sure they don't have a hit record." Ahmet had been more than happy to help out; he offered me a relatively unknown white blues group that he had signed to Atlantic not long before. But in March, the Allman Brothers played a series of concerts at Fillmore East that drew lots of attention. In early summer, they released tapes from these concerts as a live album, which immediately became a hit. So the Newport Jazz Festival came at the crest of their wave of success.

There were almost no rock festivals anywhere in summer 1971; after Woodstock and Altamont, no promoter would take the risk and no town would allow one. But the youth culture would not be denied. In June, a concert in McCrea, Louisiana, billed as the Celebration of Light, had drawn nearly 50,000 people. And the underground press had singled my festival out as another destination. "There are some good sounds at Newport," the papers had advised. "Hang out on the other side of the fence and you can hear the music for free."

And on Friday, that's exactly what they did. Several times during the night, I left the stage and walked nervously over to the edge of Festival Field to check out the scene. It was like observing lemurs at the zoo; they were zonked. Some kids stumbled around on the access road; others were sprawled out on the hilltop. By the time Roberta Flack closed the evening, it was apparent they were just cooling it. But there was some reason for concern—a few of the ragged lot had announced their intention to take the Festival stage by 9 o'clock the following night.

The concert ended and the audience streamed out of Festival Field to their cars. Joyce and I drove to the Hotel Viking, where we had planned a buffet in the ballroom for the artists and our many visiting friends. But I couldn't get my mind off the hillside, and I knew that I had to do something about it. The horde on the hill could reach critical mass at any time.

What was especially frustrating was the fact that I had taken precautions against this situation. Earlier in the week, the Newport Police Department had agreed to keep the kids away from Miantanomi Park for a fee of $8,000. This was in addition to the then-exorbitant $20,000 sum that I paid them just for basic services. It had soon become clear, however, that the police had failed to fulfill their side of the deal.

Earlier in the day, on Friday afternoon, I had conducted an experiment. Jimmy Sullivan, a kid who worked for me on the festivals, my resident hippie, went downtown to pose as one of the incoming visitors. "Go up to a police officer," I suggested, "and tell him you're in town because of the festival. Ask him where you can go to hang out." Jimmy did what I asked and returned with an incriminating report. Instead of advising him to get out of town, the cop had sent him directly to Miantanomi Park. The Police Department had double-crossed me.

Hearing this, I called Coles Mallory, the City Manager. "Coles, didn't I make a deal with you earlier? What's this about the police sending the kids to the hillside?" Coles was upset; he said he'd call me back.

When he did, he said: "The police changed their minds. Those kids were starting to congregate downtown."

"We're going to have a problem."

"I'm sorry, George. But that's the way it is."

And so the kids gathered on the hill, nearly seven thousand strong. After the party at the Viking, I asked Father O'Connor to accompany me to the site.

We walked along Girard Avenue, the narrow access road that ran along the base of the hill. What we witnessed there was a feverish oblivion. Kids were strung-out and sprawled across the road. The scant illumination of a few streetlights showed that their eyes were glazed over. We stepped gingerly around them; no one seemed to notice. This surrealistic spell was only broken momentarily when one kid staggered over to pay his respects to the clergy: "Hiya Father! How are ya, man?"

There was no reasoning with these kids. All we could do was let them loll about, and hope that they lacked the skills of organization to cause much of a disruption. I returned to our house in Middletown at around 4 A.M. to find Joyce and our houseguests (a handful of friends from New York and Boston) waiting up for me. I told them what we had seen. We all retired and caught a few hours of fitful sleep.

By midmorning I had returned to the field, discovering to my dismay that even more kids had arrived. The mass on the hill now looked like a mercenary army; some estimated their numbers near 10,000. But they stayed up there as our audience filed into the field, and we proceeded as planned. The weather was ideal: clear skies and a perfect temperature.

That afternoon we presented one of the unique daytime concerts of the festival's history.

An eighty-eight-year-old Eubie Blake played some vintage piano rags, including his own "Memories of You" and "I'm Just Wild About Harry." He could scarcely believe the standing ovation that met his final bar. "You don't know what this applause means to me," he marveled, surveying a sea of twenty thousand fans. It was a hard act to follow, but Willie "The Lion" Smith handled the task with style. The remainder of the afternoon had a more contemporary flavor, with sets by Charles Mingus, Freddie Hubbard, an impressively precise New York Bass Violin Choir (led by Bill Lee, Spike Lee's father), and the long-awaited Newport debut of Ornette Coleman. The program was a virtual panoply of styles, and it went over well.

The weather was still beautiful as our evening set approached, but there was a sense of foreboding in the air. As our audience filtered in, they had to endure a gauntlet of young hecklers. Pockets of kids loitered outside our front entrance, chanting: "Liberate the main gate!" Others, tripping on acid or amphetamines, terrorized Girard Ave. Every breeze that swept across Festival Field carried the pungent aroma of pot.

Shortly before curtain call, I tried to reason with a large group outside the fence.

"We don't have the money for the festival," they shouted. "Music should be free!"

Inside the field, the concert began. Almost as soon as the music started, a swarm of kids—in groups of hundreds—converged on several different segments of the eight-foot-high chain-link fence that flanked Festival Field. It was as if Bill Chase's piercing trumpet had sounded the call for Judgment Day. As Chase's powerful jazz-rock band played inside, the mass of kids leaned its collective weight on the fence. A few of them managed to scale the fence and run into the field.

Our audience stayed in their numbered seats just dozens of yards away, aware of the bedlam but not overly concerned. Meanwhile, the festival staff did what they could to maintain order. Joyce patrolled the interior of the fence, swatting out small bonfires with her pocketbook.

Father O'Conner and I went over to the fence, and I addressed one group of them.

"Don't you know you're going to destroy this festival?"

"Fuck the festival!" they shouted back.

"Why are you doing this?"

One kid stopped pushing to answer me: "We want to get on the stage."

"Why do you want to be onstage? You don't have any talent."

"Man, you don't know me. How do you know I don't have any talent?"

I leaned in close, my face inches from his, separated only by the quivering chain links. "You wouldn't be out here trying to break this fence down like a silly motherfucker if you had any talent!"

He looked at me through the fence, considering my statement for a moment. Then he shrugged. "Man, maybe you're right," he said, and went back to his task of pushing down the fence.

By now, Gerry Mulligan and Dave Brubeck were playing. They probably couldn't wait to get the hell out of there.

When Mulligan and Brubeck finished their set, Dionne Warwick—the star of the evening—came on. She went into her Burt Bacharach repertoire, which the audience enjoyed. But things were heating up at the perimeters of the field. The fence was beginning to buckle; it was only a matter of time.

What was the point of so much wasted energy by so many stupid kids? What were they trying to prove? My mind flashed back to the riot around Freebody Park eleven years earlier. But the booze-riddled gang of 1960 was naïve compared to this crowd in '71. The rock-and-roll generation had come into power and Woodstock had given them a voice. They were obsessed with protest, intoxicated by their collective strength.

I decided to deny them the satisfaction of a confrontation. If the police went into action, there would surely have been bloodshed. They would have come in with riot gear and tear gas; it would have been a disaster. We couldn't afford to incite this mob, especially with thousands of innocent people around. So I swallowed hard and passed instructions along to the staff and security: Do Nothing. We didn't know it at the moment, but the police had already made this decision.

Onstage, Dionne Warwick continued to sing.

"What the world needs now . . ."

A thirty-foot-wide section of the fence began to fold over . . .

". . . is love, sweet love . . ."

. . . and with one last creaking sigh, it fell flat.

The gatecrashers poured into the field like angry wasps. I rushed onstage; Joyce followed me. From that vantage point, a panorama of the mayhem unfolded. I grabbed the microphone from a confused Miss Warwick and cleared the lump from my throat.

"Ladies and Gentlemen," I said, in as calm a voice as I could muster, "the city of Newport has ordered us to close the festival, at least for the night. Please file out of the park as quickly as possible, and in an orderly fashion. This action is being taken for your safety." I repeated variations of this statement over and over, keeping a watchful eye on the dispersing crowd.

No one panicked, despite the band of hostile youths now running rampant through the grounds. Some of the kids made a beeline for the foot of the stage and began shouting obscenities in my direction. Joyce stood implacably at my side; for years afterward, Eubie Blake would say that her presence on-stage beside me had saved my life. Meanwhile, Mary Lou Williams, the next artist due to perform, was standing in the wings, not believing what she saw. Jimmy Smith, Dizzy Gillespie, and Illinois Jacquet were all backstage with their bands.

I attempted to reason with the intruders over the microphone: "We're trying to do a thing here. This is the only town that lets us in, and you can wipe us out. The whole thing is in your hands!" Gerry Mulligan and Father O'Connor voiced similar pleas. But it was no use. We were shepherded off the stage by the police.

About seventy or eighty of the maniacs mounted the stage. They smashed lighting fixtures and music stands, and tossed wooden chairs around, breaking them into splinters. They set sheet music on fire. They climbed up onto the frame of the stage shell and tried to dislodge the floodlights. They tore the lid off the concert grand piano. While this was happening, 20,000 loyal jazz fans filed peacefully out of the park without incident.

The mob had promised to take the stage by nine o'clock Saturday night. It was 9:30 when the fence crashed; they were only half an hour late.

Meanwhile, I stood behind the stage with Joyce and our houseguests, in a state of shock. Finally a guard suggested we leave the field, for our safety. We piled into two cars, and spent what seemed like an eternity inching our way home, through the unruly throng.

Back on the grounds, the insanity persisted until after midnight, with nearly 300 kids eventually crowding onto the stage. Ironically, the raiders never got to see the Allman Brothers, the group they had come for; they never had a chance to perform.

It was like a wake at our house in Middletown that night. People came to pay their condolences. Nobody could believe what had happened. At around two A.M., we received a phone call from the City Manager: the rest of the Festival was to be cancelled. Other calls came in, from musicians who were just arriving in Newport. I had to tell them what had happened.

It was nearly dawn when I finally got to bed. But Joyce and I were soon awakened by a telephone call from the Newport police. They had approached the field at daybreak with bullhorns, evacuating the area in less than an hour. If similar action had been taken on the hillside even one day earlier, none of this would have happened. But the police were calling not only to report the successful field-clearing, but also to inform me that a disgruntled mob of festival-goers had gathered outside my box office on Festival Field, demanding their money back.

I wrestled into my clothes and stumbled out of the house. I must have been more nervous and upset than even I realized, because I bit the inside of my cheek on my way over. By the time I reached the slope above my box office, blood was running down my chin and neck.

I joined a group of policemen there. We looked down on the protesters; there were about a hundred of them. They were angrily chanting: "Rip-off! Rip-off!" It was not a pleasant scene.

"Alright," I sighed, "let's go down there."

"We're not going down there," the cops replied. I just looked at them wearily. By then, I had learned to expect little from Newport's Finest.

"Fine. I'll go down by myself."

One cop finally agreed to go with me. We walked down to the box office, which was just a shack on the grounds. The crowd saw me coming and intensified its shouting.

"Rip! Off! Rip! Off!"

I stood on the porch and held up my hands. Finally they grew quiet.

"You people know me," I said. "I've been putting on this festival for almost twenty years. We've always run every show the way it should be run. Now, you know as well as I do that there's no money in this box office. We've put it in the bank. We can't give out refunds until the bank releases that money." I told them that there would be refunds for the Sunday and Monday afternoon and evening programs; but not for Saturday, since Dionne Warwick had performed. I told them to send us their ticket stubs, with names and return addresses. "It's going to take some time," I said. "We have to refund thousands and thousands of tickets. But we'll do it. You have my word."

Somewhat placated, the disappointed ticket-holders gradually dispersed. I returned to the house to well-wishers and friends. T-Bone Walker and Eddie "Cleanhead" Vinson were there; they were supposed to have played on that evening's concert. T-Bone shook his head and mused about how long he had waited to play Newport.

Then the reporters arrived, armed with notepads and television cameras; John Chancellor, of NBC Nightly News, was among them. I sat down in the living room to give a statement. "What happened out there," I said, "is something only America can explain." I continued: "Don't lay the blame on kids in general. This can be laid directly to narcotics freakouts, hundreds of them, who were there to destroy the festival. Every kid I talked to up there at the fence, when they were breaking through, was out of his head and high on something." I added: "These are the same kids who invaded the festival in 1969, only they're two years deader, two years more into walking zombies. . . . Their purpose in being here was to get stoned and raise hell. They had no concern for jazz, no concern for the festival. They are America's disgrace."

Then the topic turned to the city's handling of the whole matter. Joachim Berendt, who had flown in from Germany for the festival, posed a rhetorical question: "Are the people of Newport aware of what 'Newport' means to the whole world, that it is a symbol and image of music festivals?"

Asked about the city-ordered cancellation, I attempted to deflect blame away from the city council, the city manager, the chief of police. But who was I kidding? As I spoke, my voice gave out. "This is foolish," I croaked, my eyes filling with tears. I asked someone to get me a glass of water. And then, with cameras whirring and clicking around me, I broke down and wept.

That afternoon, more people crowded the house. George Shearing, who had driven up from a gig in West Virginia with his manager, stopped in and tried to cheer us up. Shearing was to have played Monday night, on a bill with Miles Davis, Phil Woods, Weather Report, Gene Ammons, Sonny Stitt, Louis Bellson, Dizzy Gillespie, Billy Eckstine, Cannonball Adderley, and Herbie Mann.

Nesuhi Ertegun came over and noted that Aretha Franklin was especially sorry about the canceled performance, as she had rehearsed four new songs. Aretha would have performed that afternoon, along with the Les McCann Trio, the King Curtis Orchestra, and Rahsaan Roland Kirk.

By that evening, the well-wishers had drifted off, and it was just Joyce and our guests in the house. It was the Fourth of July, and someone suggested that we lighten the atmosphere by commemorating Louis Armstrong's seventy-first birthday. Someone put Ella and Louis on the turntable and we drank a toast to Pops.

Calls kept coming in; Joyce's eighty-year-old mother phoned from Berkeley, offering to send a check for $2,000. Joyce cried.

Later that evening, Charlie Bourgeois took Joyce, our guests, and me to dinner at a small restaurant in Newport; he wanted to get us out of the house. The pianist at the place recognized me, and asked me to play. I sat down and sang "Nobody Loves You When You're Down and Out," and I meant it.

Tuesday arrived, and with it came more saddening news: Louis Armstrong had died. No one knew what to say. I went out to the rear porch and listened to the lapping of the water against the rocks. Louis was gone. Just two nights earlier I had drunk a toast to his health. And the festival, which had seemed so promising this year, was gone as well. There were many reasons to be upset, but the thing that rankled most was the timing. Pops had died, and I didn't even have the chance to mourn his loss. My deep sadness mingled with frustration, anger, and despair.

An insight into the love fellow artists had for Louis Armstrong occurred a few days later at his funeral. At the church, Ella Fitzgerald sat in the row in front of Joyce and me. Peggy Lee had been asked to sing. I asked Ella if she would also be singing a song for Louis. Her answer was simply, "No, I didn't come here to sing, I came here to mourn."

# 10

# *The Newport Folk Festival*

*Newport can be seen as the first and certainly the most influential festival of the urban folk revival.*

**–Robert Cantwell**

MY ENTRÉE TO THE SO-CALLED folk revival had come during a Storyville engagement in 1958 by the so-called Queen of Folk, a young woman known simply as Odetta. Her sobriquet was well deserved; she had the appearance and benevolent, regal bearing of a tribal African queen. She was revered in the folk world. While business was less than sensational during the nighttime performances, on Sunday afternoon I found the place completely packed. The crowd consisted entirely of young people. What was happening here? Though Boston was the base of my life in jazz, I was not aware of the folk movement evolving on the Cambridge side of the Charles River; college-aged kids from all over New England were converging upon the coffeehouses of Harvard Square. Cambridge haunts like Tulla's Coffee Grinder and Club 47 were becoming platforms for local folk music enthusiasts. The brightest face among them belonged to young Joan Baez, an occasional Boston University student who sang traditional ballads in a clear, delicate soprano.

I began to consider the possibility of a folk afternoon embedded within the 1959 Newport Jazz Festival; a program similar in scope and tone to the highly successful blues and gospel shows of the previous few years. I asked Odetta, Pete Seeger, and the Weavers to perform on this afternoon in addition to the Kingston Trio. In 1959, Pete Seeger was a father figure to many in the folk revival.

Not surprisingly, as I did more research and conferred with more people in the folk community, it grew abundantly clear that one afternoon program would not even begin to scratch the surface of this folk explosion. What Newport needed was a full-fledged Folk Festival.

I had more than six months in which to make preparations. Aware of my own limited experience in the folk world, I turned to Albert Grossman, the owner and proprietor of a well-known folk club in Chicago called the Gate of Horn. I knew Albert because he was Odetta's manager. We had hit it off, hanging out every night of Odetta's engagement in Storyville.

I was impressed by Grossman. He was bright, witty, and familiar with the folk world. I learned something almost every time he opened his mouth.

When I asked him to produce a festival of folk music in 1959, he eagerly accepted, and with the enthusiastic approval of the Newport board—which was as taken with Albert as I was—we began to work together on a program. The first Newport Folk Festival was roughly modeled after its jazz counterpart, with both evening and afternoon concerts and reserved seating. Grossman's talent roster emphasized the wide variety of material that thrived under the banner of folk music. Robert Shelton later lauded the program as "a catalogue of current trends and styles in American folk music."

Pete Seeger, introduced by emcee Studs Terkel as "America's Tuning Fork," opened the Newport Folk Festival with "Bells of Rhymney." Telling stories, he was almost theatrical, and completely captivated the audience. Seeger was a masterful communicator; his personal passion was as responsible for the folk revival as any other factor. He was such an emblem of the movement that his image—onstage, alone, banjo hoisted forward—would emblazon the cover of the Folk Festival program book the following year.

There were dozens of other performers—including John Jacob Niles, who was armed with a dulcimer—covering the blues (Sonny Terry and Brownie McGhee), spirituals (Odetta, then Leon Bibb), country (guitarist Frank Hamilton and banjoist Frank Warner), and traditional folksongs of many nationalities. The New Lost City Ramblers—Mike Seeger on fiddle, Tom Paley on banjo, and John Cohen on guitar—embodied the tone of the folk revival, specializing in mountain music of the 1920s and '30s. All told, there were more different sounds and styles in one place than you could absorb. But it was all a part of the same idea, part of the folk movement. An unspoken feeling was in the air, a sense that folk music was approaching a threshold. The music at the Newport Folk Festival that summer constituted more than a revival; it was a transformation. A synthesis of traditional sounds with new ideas and perspectives was put into motion in Newport.

This merging of folk worlds was captured by the surprise debut of eighteen-year-old Joanie Baez. Although she hadn't been listed on the program, Bob Gibson brought her on during his set; they had worked together at Grossman's Gate of Horn club in Chicago. Together they sang "Virgin Mary Had One Son" and "We Are Crossing Jordan River."

"I looked like the Original Bohemian," Baez later recalled, "wearing knit tops from Latin America or India, nondescript skirts or blue jeans, dangling earrings like my heroine, Odetta, and sandals with thongs that laced up to just below the knee." Her gift was immediately apparent. She was an exceedingly talented vocalist, the Sarah Vaughan of folksinging. Perhaps more important, with her modest but alluring stage presence, her dark eyes and long hair, no makeup, her "Bible sandals" and religious songs, she conveyed a visual impression of purity to match her singing voice. Instantly she became not only the great discovery, but also the living symbol, of the first Newport Folk Festival.

Though the choice of artists was primarily Grossman's responsibility, I still coordinated the production of each show—in what order the artists appeared, and how they were presented. Albert and I sat down with the list of performers, and when I wasn't familiar with a particular artist, he described his or her style and importance. I put a lot of thought into the pacing and content of each program.

The Kingston Trio was a pop act with elements of folk music. I felt that they would give a crucial boost to the fledgling festival; and they did, drawing more people to Newport than any other single group. Kingston Trio fans knew little or nothing about the folk revival; many of them were teenagers. Many parents had brought their preteen children to the festival. The true folk enthusiasts at the festival accepted the presence of the Kingston Trio begrudgingly. I had scheduled the group to close.

As the Sunday evening show blazed on, people from the audience approached Louis Lorillard to ask that we give the Kingston Trio an earlier slot. Midnight was approaching, and many of the younger fans who had come for the popular group were up past their curfew. There were dozens of requests: "Could you get the Kingston Trio on earlier? I have to take my kids home."

Preceding the Kingston Trio was five-string banjo virtuoso Earl Scruggs. Scruggs, who had been born into a banjo-playing family in North Carolina, was an alumnus of both the Grand Ole Opry and Bill Monroe's Blue Grass Boys. He had been so influential on his instrument that his three-finger technique became known as "the Scruggs style."

At Louis's urging, I flipped the order of the two groups. The Kingston Trio would play the penultimate slot, and Earl Scruggs would close the show.

But when the Kingston Trio finished their set of hit songs and left the stage, the audience went crazy, unleashing what the *Newport Daily News* later called "an unquenchable burst of protest." They refused to quiet down, despite the considerable efforts of emcee Oscar Brand, who stood at the microphone for over ten minutes. Finally, Dave Guard of the Kingston Trio came back out and asked the crowd to give Scruggs his due. Earl Scruggs played a brief set before the return of the Kingston Trio for a final encore.

I lost a lot of friends in the folk world because of that slipup. It was an insult to Earl Scruggs, one of the most revered figures in bluegrass. Twice, I had been led astray by the Kingston Trio. I had permitted them to play on the Jazz Festival a week earlier, and now I had unwittingly allowed their popularity to obscure the light of a greater talent. I'm not particularly contrite about including the Kingston Trio in the Jazz Festival, but I'm very sorry that I put them on before Earl Scruggs. For some folk purists, it would take years for me to achieve redemption. Insulting Scruggs, who could be considered the Louis Armstrong of the banjo, was like insulting "Pops" himself.

This was one unfortunate incident in what was otherwise a successful festival. The atmosphere that prevailed around the Folk Festival was notably different from that which held sway over the Jazz Festival. The folk world was not as defined as the jazz world; there was not much of a machinery in place to handle the business of folk music. There was no sense that the critics were out there sharpening their claws and waiting to pounce. There was less backbiting, complaining, and carrying-on. The performers believed not only in their music, but in a message: the message of their songs as well as the message of simply being there, in Newport, together.

\*     \*     \*

*The term "folk music" itself has become so broad that it covers an incredible variety of music. Thus among the many thousands attending the Newport Folk Festival of last summer were devotees of Elizabethan ballads, honky tonk blues, southern mountain banjo and fiddle playing, and songs in many different languages.*

**—Pete Seeger**

The 1960 Newport Folk Festival was expanded to include three nights, and preceded the Jazz Festival by one week. There was an even greater degree of musical diversity this year. We had performers from Africa, Scotland, Spain, Israel, and Ireland. Professionals like Will Holt, Theodore Bikel, and the Gateway Singers performed alongside more "authentic" performers like Jesse Fuller and Frank Warner. John Lee Hooker performed his mysterious blues.

Robert Pete Williams, a singer-guitarist who was born into a sharecropping family, had been paroled from the Louisiana State Penitentiary in Angola, where he was serving a life sentence for murder. Folklorist Harry Oster had discovered Williams during a research expedition in the prison, had recorded the thirty-six-year-old inmate, and by sending the record to the Governor and parole board, had arranged for Williams's release. Oster named Williams "a likely successor to Leadbelly," who had also been discovered at Angola.

It was a thoroughly mixed bag. Writing about the folk revival, and Newport in particular, Pete Seeger said:

> One can see now that no one sector has charge of the situation, not the right nor the left, the cynic nor the romanticist, the purist nor the hybridist, the scholar nor the fan, the money-maker nor the money spurner. And perhaps this is the best thing one can say: everyone, but everyone, is more free than ever to decide what he likes best, what he feels is most meaningful and honest.

It was clear that the folk festival audience—mostly college age—found such meaning and honesty in the songs themselves. Every night after festival's end, many of these kids would take their sleeping bags to the beaches, setting up little bonfires and trading folk songs well into the early hours of the morning. They "sat huddled in little groups as if drawing warmth from each other," wrote a reporter in *Mademoiselle*. "Their faces were solemn, almost expressionless, while they were singing, and they moved quickly from song to song without talking very much." This scene reflected the true spirit of the folk revival, and stood at the very heart of the festival.

\*　　\*　　\*

*A real folk festival should present, side by side, the oldtime ballad singer, the young aspirant, the nationally famous, the good unknown performer from both rural and urban cultures; in short, the best of everything.*

**— Jean Ritchie**

The original Newport Folk Festival had been curtailed after only two seasons—before it really had time to take off. But it had been obvious from the start that, given enough time to develop, this festival could achieve something significant and altogether new. After 1962, the original Newport board was defunct, and I had the freedom to bring the folk festival back in whatever way I chose.

Albert Grossman and I were no longer partners; our company, Productions and Managements Associates (PAMA) had dissolved in 1961, and Albert was busy managing Peter, Paul, and Mary, among other groups. As folk music grew more and more popular, the older folk community was becoming increasingly wary of the commercial element that was creeping in. Furthermore, Albert Grossman had been too much of a control person for the folk artists; he was a promoter. He was such a powerhouse in the business that "the business" governed most of his interactions.

To create the kind of festival that would faithfully represent the folk world, I needed someone who would uphold—even embody—its ideals. I needed a prominent figure whose own interests were indistinguishable from those of the folk movement. This person had to have the respect of traditional musicians as well as contemporary songwriters, and the ability to work just as easily with more commercial acts. In other words, I needed Pete Seeger.

In the autumn of 1962, Joyce and I drove out to the Seegers' home—literally a log cabin that they had built on a mountainside overlooking the Hudson River, in Beacon, New York. Toshi Seeger had forewarned us about the "primitive" state of the cabin, which was apparently not quite finished. "I hope you two will be able to rough it," she had fretted repeatedly, over the phone. Toshi was putting us on. When we arrived, we found our room located over a barn. It was the warmest, coziest space you could imagine. That evening after dinner, Joyce and I sat down with the Seegers and discussed the possible future of the Newport Folk Festival.

Pete recognized the value of Newport. He agreed to work on reviving the festival. "But I would like to do it differently," he said. Pete and Toshi then explained their idea for a nonprofit, musician-run folk festival. In choosing the content and format of each program, this foundation would consider not only the best interests of the festival itself, but also those of the entire folk world. And under this system, Pete emphasized, all festival performers—no matter how famous or obscure—would receive the same fee of fifty dollars, plus travel expenses, housing, and food. Profits from the festival would be applied to fieldwork, folk library endowments, research, and similar endeavors.

These ideas were consistent with Pete Seeger's personal philosophies. For Pete, the music was a message rather than a business; his concern was with reaching people. In 1960, he had asked that his performer's fee for the Folk

Festival be used to bring the French Canadian fiddler Jean Carignan to Newport. Pete's decision hadn't been fueled by ideology, but rather the desire to help a fellow musician. I recognized the depth and sincerity of this generosity. The "flat fee" idea echoed his own personal selfless spirit. The proposal was also in seamless accord with my own vision for the festival.

In the weeks that followed, Pete, Toshi, Joyce, and I set about outlining a proposal for a nonprofit Newport Folk Foundation. Theodore Bikel joined us in planning the organization's structure. Together we decided that the board should be a rotating committee of seven members, three of whom would be replaced by new appointees each year (thereby maintaining "a mixture of old blood and new"). In its first year, the board would consist exclusively of folk performers; subsequent boards could include non-performing members of the folk world (folklorists, historians, and collectors). In all cases, directorships would be unpaid.

Both Pete and Theo were members of our first board. The rest of our appointees were chosen with careful consideration as to their place in the folk community and what contributions they could make to the festival. We asked leader of the Dixie Mountain Boys Bill Clifton, the pianist/guitarist/singer, to coordinate our country and bluegrass efforts. Clarence Cooper, a member of the Tarriers, agreed to supervise our blues and gospel. Erik Darling, who had succeeded Pete Seeger in the Weavers before playing guitar in the Tarriers and forming the Rooftop Singers, was chosen for his wide-ranging experience. Jean Ritchie, who had sung and played at the first Newport Folk Festival, was to curate our southern Appalachian music. And Peter Yarrow was recognized not only for his prominent place in the popular folk arena, but also for his knowledge of (and enthusiasm for) an enormously diverse array of both traditional and contemporary material. Those were our first seven members.

The Folk Festival could rely upon its established jazz cousin for support; my company had the staff and experience to get the project off the ground. The Folk Foundation borrowed the legal counsel of Elliott Hoffman and the financial expertise of Arnold London. I was designated the nonvoting chairman of the Folk Foundation Board. In no time we had an organization in place. Together, my staff and the new board began to discuss the blueprint for a 1963 Newport Folk Festival, which would follow the Newport Jazz Festival in July.

\*     \*     \*

In the two weeks that transpired between the jazz and folk festivals, we had much to accomplish. Compared to the jazz festival, which usually involved a network of booking agents and managers, the folk festival was a homespun affair. We not only had to give our performers food and a place to stay; we also arranged for their transportation.

No one contributed more to this arrangement than Joyce. She oversaw the artists' housing, transportation, food, and general well-being. This last item was especially important; many of the musicians who came to the festival had never performed before large audiences, and some of them had never even left their hometowns. Joyce, and others among us (notably Toshi Seeger and Helen von Schmidt), saw to it that they would not only feel welcome in Newport, but also comfortable and at ease. Joyce had the uncommon ability to shape order out of chaos, and still maintain a sense of caring and warmth.

The inner workings of the festival were like those of a small city. Joyce supervised an army of volunteers, many of whom were relatives of the performers. They worked as bed-makers, food servers, grocery shoppers, chaperones, and in many other capacities. The most diligent and devoted of these volunteers was Bob Jones, an aspiring young folksinger. Bob would soon become an invaluable asset—not only as a member of the folk festival staff, but for the next forty years, an indispensable member of the hierarchy of Festival Productions, Incorporated.

Bob helped Joyce with the task of artist lodging, which involved renting houses around town, and utilizing some of the dormitory facilities at Newport's Vernon Court Junior College. Joyce rented sheets, pillowcases, and towels for our many guests; she bought blankets from a local army-navy store for two dollars apiece. She had to install a temporary kitchen in one of the rented houses, as we were responsible for breakfast, lunch, and dinner—and a massive party every night. She was lucky enough to find a local chef named Curly Dufault, who, along with dozens of other helpers, contributed to the food preparation. We set up tables on a lawn behind one of the houses, and there we fed hundreds of people three times each day. The Folk Festival was organized in such a way that the artists not only appeared on the same stage; they lived together, like a family.

Even in its first year, it was clear that the spirit of the Folk Festival was something new. Here in Newport, Rhode Island, a stone's throw from the nation's most lavish mansions, we had gathered some seventy-five folk performers and their families. Backstage, there was a calliope of folk artists: country fiddlers, itinerant guitar pickers, Greenwich Village folksingers, Southwestern Native American dancers, topical songwriters from every part of the country, and blues singers from all over the South. These performers—and the multifaceted crowd that had come to hear them—were united by their devotion to the folk world.

The folk people themselves were the message of the Folk Festival. But there were other, more concrete ideas that held sway in 1963. The boldest of these related to the Civil Rights Movement, which was in full bloom. The folk world embraced this cause. "Freedom songs"—which fell under the wide banner of folk music—were playing an integral role in the civil rights battle. Old spirituals, hymns, and gospel songs helped keep the fires burning. Bernice Johnson (later Reagon) and Cordell Reagon, two young members of the Student Nonviolent Coordinating Committee (SNCC), had formed a gospel vocal quartet named the Freedom Singers to spread the message. To some extent, they had taken a cue from the Weavers's success in advocating the labor movement. In 1962, Pete and Toshi Seeger had helped the Freedom Singers organize a cross-country collegiate tour. These students from SNCC were in the front-line of the Civil Rights Movement. Many had been victims of police brutality and some had served time in jail.

It was natural, then, for the Freedom Singers to be at the Folk Festival in 1963. They performed on the first night of the festival. On the second night, Joan Baez joined SNCC activists—and some 600 festival-goers—on a march through Newport. The crowd walked past the Bellevue Avenue mansions and into Touro Park, where SNCC's executive secretary James Forman and Freedom Singers leader Cordell Reagon delivered speeches, rallying support for the March on Washington scheduled for the following month.

Integration and civil rights were my way of life. I hadn't participated in street demonstrations or lunch counter protests; I had been at the forefront of the fight in a more personal, less confrontational sense. For this reason, the Folk Festival's activism was extremely important to me. It provided an opportunity for me to know and relate to brave individuals who staked their lives and freedom for the cause. The festival was a platform and a forum. My role as festival organizer was just another part of the continuing struggle. It's difficult to ascertain the extent to which the Folk Festival affected the bigger picture, but it was certainly a contributing factor.

If the civil rights cause had a rallying cry at that time, it was Bob Dylan's "Blowin' in the Wind." Peter, Paul and Mary's version of the song, released one month before the Folk Festival, had sold 320,000 copies in just over a week. They were, without question, the biggest "name" on the festival. And unlike the Kingston Trio, they had a meaning beyond commercial success.

I had planned on scheduling Peter, Paul and Mary as the final act on Friday night's program. But Grossman, who was at Newport as manager of P.P. & M, persuaded me to put them on before intermission; he insisted that the final set of the evening be given instead to Dylan, whom he was also managing at the time. It turned out to be the best possible decision. When Peter, Paul and

Mary finished their set to tumultuous applause, we announced that they would reappear at the end of the evening. The audience responded warmly to the authentic grassroots groups that followed—Bill Monroe's Bluegrass Boys, Jean Carignan, and Doc Watson, among others.

It may have seemed incongruous to some observers to give Bob Dylan the closing set. This skinny kid with the nasal voice and the iconoclastic, oddball demeanor had certainly made a splash in the folk world; he had performed a solo Town Hall concert that April, garnering critical raves. He had aroused more industry attention the following month by turning down an Ed Sullivan appearance after a conflict with the CBS censors (over a topical song about the John Birch Society). And he had been prominently featured in both *Broadside* and *Sing Out!* as a promising and prolific songwriter. But Dylan was not a nationally prominent artist. He was nowhere near the league that Peter, Paul and Mary were in. For his debut Newport appearance with Joan Baez on Friday afternoon—at a "talk session" which included words from Theo Bikel, Pete Seeger, and Clarence Cooper—fewer than a hundred people were in attendance.

Dylan's solo performance that evening, however, was another story. He sang a program of uncompromising, vivid topical songs: "Bob Dylan's Dream," "With God on Our Side," "Talkin' John Birch Society Blues," and "A Hard Rain's A-Gonna Fall." The audience was less demonstrative than they had been during Peter, Paul and Mary's set. Instead, they were quiet, taking in Dylan's every word.

Peter, Paul and Mary returned and performed their encore of "Blowin' in the Wind." Then, amidst a deafening roar of applause, they brought to the stage Dylan, Joan Baez, Pete Seeger, Theo Bikel, and the Freedom Singers. The eleven singers stood in a single line facing the audience with crossed arms and clasped hands. The group began to sing a variation on the old Baptist hymn "I'll Overcome, Someday." The song's new incarnation—"We Shall Overcome"—had become an anthem for the Civil Rights Movement. The unaccompanied blend of voices onstage gave heft to the song's plaintive chorus—as did the 15,000 voices beyond the stage, throughout Freebody Park and out in the surrounding streets.

Writers say it was the apex of the folk revival. To me, it was a moment never to be forgotten. I still get emotional when I think of it. There was never anything close to it in the jazz festival.

It would seem that, with such a momentous opening night, the Folk Festival had no further to go. But further it went. We knew the evening had been special, but we didn't know we had hit an apex. That realization always comes much later. So the following afternoon, without fanfare or pretense, we held a blues workshop at the Newport Casino that nearly equaled the Friday finale in folk world significance.

Like all of our afternoon folk workshops, this one had a less formal presentation than the evening concerts. Instead of an audience of thousands, a few hundred people were on hand; they sat on the grass instead of on folding chairs. On this particular Saturday afternoon, the program included blues legends Brownie McGhee, Sonny Terry, and John Lee Hooker and a twenty-year-old white kid by the name of John Hammond, Jr. Yes, this was the son of Columbia Records's John Hammond. As Lightnin' Hopkins had pronounced in our festival program: "Blues dwell in everyone. It's all in the soul."

The highlight of the afternoon was seventy-one-year-old Mississippi John Hurt, the self-taught blues guitarist and singer whose recorded output (a dozen sides recorded for Okeh Records in 1928) had long been a sought-after prize among collectors. The understated subtlety of his vocal style and the distinctiveness of his guitar technique had made him a legend among blues aficionados; the obscurity of his whereabouts and personal life had made him something of a myth.

In spring 1963 (a few short months before our festival), a blues collector from Washington, D.C., named Tom Hoskins had managed to conjure up Mississippi John Hurt, seemingly out of thin air. Acting on the slightest of tips he had found him in a Mississippi town formerly known as Avalon.

This was like a folklorist's fairytale. John Hurt, who had long been presumed dead, was there among us at Newport. His creased, dark face was set against a white shirt, open at the collar. A weathered brown felt hat sat atop his head. Yet underneath his modest exterior was a source of deep inner calm and confidence. Those of us who heard him perform marveled not only at the distinctiveness of his music, but also at the fact that it had gone unheard for so long. If John Hurt could live in obscurity for thirty-five years, how many other hidden treasures were scattered across American soil? His presence at the Folk Festival was a confirmation of every impulse that ran through the folk collector's psyche.

Over a dozen other afternoon workshops went on during the course of the 1963 festival, ranging from "Fiddles" and "Old Banjo Styles" to "Collecting Folk Music" and "Folk Music and Copyright Law." Predictably, the most popular of these was a session devoted to "Topical Songs and New Songwriters"—it attracted some 500 people to the Newport Casino lawn on Sunday afternoon.

The Freedom Singers once again portrayed the urgency of the civil rights effort; "Fighting for My Rights" left little room for misinterpretation. Other performers touched upon the same nerve; Phil Ochs delivered his memorable

324 / MYSELF AMONG OTHERS

"Ballad of Medgar Evers," and his "Talking Birmingham Jam" evoked the afternoon's only standing ovation. There was an equal rights message in some of the songs of Bob Dylan, as well. Dylan, whose star had risen considerably since his performance two nights earlier, closed the workshop by performing his tune "Playboys and Playgirls" as a duet with Pete Seeger. At Seeger's prompting, the audience joined in.

After each night of the festival, everyone—the performers, their families and friends, the festival staff and volunteers—headed for one of our rented houses, where Joyce and company had prepared ample food and drink. These get-togethers were nothing like the Bellevue Avenue soirees of the old Jazz Festival era; they served to bond the folk world to Newport and what it had come to mean.

One night, Mississippi John Hurt gave an informal concert, sitting on a stoop in the backyard. A group of kids were sitting on the grass, and Hurt was there singing and playing. I went out on the porch and stood listening for a while, and said to myself: "this is musical heaven." In the living room, Odetta was singing in her powerful alto. A bluegrass group was parked on the front lawn.

Joan Baez and Bob Dylan disappeared into a room by themselves. So much was happening that no one noted their absence. But after a while I stuck my head in the room and saw that they were trading songs. Baez and Dylan, the virgin queen and crown prince of the folk revival. Moments like these were what the Folk Festival was really all about.

\*     \*     \*

The Newport Folk Foundation had been in a state of constant activity in the fall of 1963 and winter of 1964. Everyone on the board was keenly interested in making contributions beyond the festival itself. Almost every decision that our board made was reached by consensus. This was remarkable, considering the diverse perspectives that coexisted on each successive board. In our first year, there wasn't much potential for conflict. But later versions of the foundation directorship included numerous contradictory voices. I presided over this board and chaired meetings, and it's a testament to the openness of the folk community that they let me do so. Though I didn't have a vote, my input—as producer of the festival—was always taken into consideration.

My suggestions to the board often pertained to the box office. But we would be hard-pressed to support the festival and its foundation without presenting a few artists who could generate income. Fortunately, there were artists at the time who had achieved popular success. The board heeded this advice, even when members were more inclined to focus strictly on more grassroots fare.

After the success of the first Newport Folk Festival, the board had allocated several thousand dollars in grants to individuals and schools dedicated to research on America's folk music. One of these grants went to Guy Carawan for the establishment of folk song festivals on John's Island, off the coast of South Carolina. Carawan had devoted himself to the indigenous culture of the Georgia Sea Islands for the past several years. There were scattered vocal groups throughout the islands—like the Coastal Singers of St. Simon's, which had been organized in the 1920s by the wife of the visual artist Maxfield Parrish—who still practiced a traditional antebellum style of Negro singing. This unique music had been represented on the first folk festival by the Georgia Sea Island Singers, featuring Bessie Jones.

But the traditions of these old-fashioned singing styles were on the decline. With the funds he received from the Folk Foundation, Carawan established a series of musical and cultural festivals on the islands. It was his attempt to resuscitate the region's indigenous music and culture, and provoke a sense of local pride. To everyone's delight, it worked.

Recognizing Carawan's success as a possible model for other community-based cultural revivals, the Folk Foundation board promptly earmarked $5,500 for a special field project. Alan Lomax and Mike Seeger, who had been appointed to the board at the beginning of 1964, then recommended that a representative be hired to travel extensively across the continent, seeking out traditional performers who might perform at the festival. More than a talent scout, this individual would prepare the performers—many of whom had no stage experience—for the shock of Newport. This individual would also find places where local festivals were "needed," as they had been in the Georgia Sea Islands. He or she would, in other words, be an advocate for local musical traditions.

Ralph Rinzler, as a former member of the Greenbriar Boys and an organizer of the Friends of Old-Time Music, was well suited to the task. He was appointed in February 1964, and he spent the following months trekking through eight states, as well as Nova Scotia and French Canada. He logged some 12,000 miles that spring, accompanied at times by Bob Jones.

During his travels, Rinzler corralled an impressive cast of grassroots performers for the 1964 Folk Festival. Among them were the singing high-school principal Jimmy Driftwood; North Carolina banjo player and mountaineer Frank Proffitt; Ozark ballad singer Almeda Riddle; bottleneck guitar hero

Mississippi Fred McDowell; Arkansas cowboy-folksinger Glen Ohrlin; and sixty-five-year-old country fiddler-bandleader Clayton "Pappy" McMichen. Rinzler managed to import Cajun musicians from Mamou, Louisiana, as well as Sacred Harp Singers from northern Alabama. The local festivals that he arranged with Dewey Balfa in French-speaking Louisiana were instrumental in reviving a languishing Cajun culture.

Most of these artists appeared on the opening night of the 1964 Folk Festival. It was billed as "A Concert of Traditional Music," meticulously produced by Alan Lomax. No one alive knew this topic more thoroughly than Lomax, and his production was appropriately wide ranging and well informed. Ticket sales were slim, but attendance for our other evening concerts—which included such performers as Joan Baez, Bob Dylan, Judy Collins, and Peter, Paul and Mary—attracted record crowds. Fans swarmed into Newport on Friday night, and stayed in town through Sunday. Never was there so clear a contrast between the "authentic" folk audience—a small, devoted band of aficionados—and the wider public. We were learning firsthand that the so-called national "folk boom" had more to do with celebrity than with any deep grassroots interest.

Nevertheless, we persisted in presenting lesser-known artists alongside their marquee counterparts. Baez, Collins, and Dylan appeared on programs with country fiddlers, banjo pickers, and autoharpists. A nineteen-year-old José Feliciano performed on the same afternoon program as Nubian oud virtuoso Hamza El Din. A workshop on guitar styles featured not only North Carolina guitar legend Elizabeth Cotton and blues giant Muddy Waters, but also Hawaiian guitarist Noelani Mahoe. Old-time fiddler Clayton "Pappy" McMichen played on the same evening concert as the Chad Mitchell Trio and country star Johnny Cash. All told, there were over two hundred artists.

The list of blues artists we presented in 1964 was historic. Tennessee country bluesman Sleepy John Estes performed with Hammie Nixon and Yank Rachel on Friday night. Jesse Fuller and Mississippi John Hurt were both featured on a Saturday morning concert.

A Saturday afternoon workshop hosted by blues expert Sam Charters and our friend Willis James featured first-time performances by Mississippi Fred McDowell and his wife, Annie Mae; Virginian banjoist/fiddler Hobart Smith; and young white blues artists Dave Van Ronk, Judy Roderick, and Koerner, Ray & Glover.

There were even two "rediscoveries" on the program, echoing the Mississippi John Hurt debut of the previous year. Eddie James "Son" House, the gutbucket guitarist of the 1930s and early '40s, had been brought out of obscurity just a month earlier; several Cambridge blues enthusiasts had found the sixty-two-year-old bluesman living quietly in Rochester, New York. Another sixty-two-year-old blues singer was rediscovered in June 1964: Nehemiah James, better known as Skip James. This Delta blues legend had been tracked down so recently that his name wasn't even printed in our program book. This workshop was Skip James's first major performance since his reemergence, and he floored everyone with his keening, still-potent falsetto voice and his unique, personal guitar style. Joyce got to know most of these blues artists quite well. When Peter Yarrow wanted Muddy Waters to perform in the blues workshop, Muddy said he would have to ask "Miss Joyce if it was alright."

All of these blues artists—and others featured on the festival, including Muddy Waters and Otis Spann—stayed together in one rented cottage in the middle of Newport, away from Bellevue Avenue. Joyce had found this house and furnished it with borrowed beds from Vernon Court. The resulting residence, which we dubbed the "Blues House," was something to behold. These timeless blues legends were having a ball. It seemed that the house was full of song at all hours; informal jam sessions would start in the afternoon and persist until late evening. Some of these artists hadn't seen each other in years; others had never previously met. Having them all together under one roof was a joyous arrangement. It probably would have become a Folk Festival tradition if the board hadn't received a letter that fall from folklorist Ethel Raim's husband, complaining that we had set up a "segregated" house for blues singers.

The next summer, when SNCC member Julius Lester arrived at the festival, the first thing he asked Joyce was: "Where's the Blues House?" Joyce, looking at him uncomprehendingly, replied: "Blues House? There's no such thing." We had scattered the blues singers among the rest of the performers.

Our sensitivity to the ongoing battle for civil rights was once again evident in the festival programming. Guy Carawan organized a vocal ensemble that included members of the SNCC Freedom Singers. He called it the Freedom Group. In addition to Cordell Reagon, Bernice Johnson Reagon, and James Peacock, the Freedom Group included several members of the Birmingham Movement Choir, and Mississippi civil rights activist (and congressional candidate) Fanny Lou Hamer.

Our strong political views must have seemed strange to some of the performers who hailed from the rural South. In 1964, there were many artists in this category. I can recall an incident involving two choirs that perfectly illustrates this collision of worlds.

On the first night of the festival, we sent a shuttle bus around Newport, taking performers to Festival Field. By the time the Georgia Sea Island Singers were picked up at their temporary residence, this shuttle was completely full. As it turned out, the front of the bus was occupied by a group of Sacred Harp Singers from a small town in Alabama—all of whom were white.

As Bessie Jones and the rest of the Georgia Sea Islanders boarded, they saw that there were no available seats. There was an awkward silence; both of these groups came from places where blacks and whites had no interaction whatsoever. The Sacred Harp contingent was a fundamentalist Christian group; they were accustomed to segregation as a way of life.

The tension on the bus was palpable. Then, without anyone saying a word, one of the men from the Sacred Harp Singers stood and offered his seat to a woman from the Georgia Sea Island Singers. After a moment's hesitation, she gratefully took it. Soon another Sacred Harp gentleman offered his seat, then another—until all of the Georgia Sea Island women were seated.

This atmosphere certainly pervaded the festival behind the scenes. Our army of staff and volunteers resembled that of a large family—a family with some problems, perhaps, but a family nonetheless. Everyone would meet in Newport at the end of June and stay until the Folk Festival was over in mid-July. This group included Joyce and myself, Ralph Rinzler, Marie St. Louis, Charlie Bourgeois, Bob Jones, and Bob's sister Helen Von Schmidt, among others.

Helen Von Schmidt was Joyce's biggest asset during the Folk Festival. She helped with travel and housing arrangements for the performers—a task worthy of Sisyphus, since conditions kept changing all the time.

In addition to the adult staff, Joyce always had lots of young people in her employ. Going to work for Joyce Wein at the festival became a rite of initiation for the children of our friends, when they became too old for summer camp. Most of these young recruits came through with flying colors. After a few days of hauling blankets, pillows, toilet paper, and guitars, they gave up their hopes of hearing all of the music at the festival. Quite often, they would approach Joyce during the evening parties and ask to be excused; they had to get a few hours' sleep.

They weren't alone in their exhaustion. Working at the festival was hard, hard work for everyone—physically, mentally, and emotionally. By the time Joyce, Helen, and the others pushed out the last partygoers and got all the houseguests to bed, the first country Texans would be awake and looking for breakfast. One of the Irish fiddlers might be looking for his Guinness. Then there was the matter of transporting the artists and their families to the field along with lunches; feeding everyone; answering question from members of the board; getting musicians back to the field after their workshops; sending off the nighttime performers; keeping track of stragglers; and generally looking after an army of ragtag musicians, staffers, and volunteers. All this without walkie-talkies, pagers, or cellular phones.

It's hard to imagine that we managed to keep the festival operating at all, especially with an unprecedented influx of 70,000 people to Newport. The town was saturated with kids who had no place to stay. They slept on beaches, in parks, in cars, on porches—wherever they could find refuge. Congestion in the downtown area was omnipresent; all business in Newport essentially came to a halt. Not surprisingly, this left an unpleasant aftertaste among locals. Just 48 hours after the close of the 1964 Newport Folk Festival, the city council voted unanimously to ban future festivals—jazz as well as folk—from Freebody Park. Once again, our success was causing problems.

The banning by the city council of the use of Freebody Park for music festivals caused us to search for another location in Newport. The new site on Cornell Highway, which later became known as Festival Field, is where the council approved the 1965 jazz and folk festivals.

\*     \*     \*

*An them two simple sides that was so easy t tell apart bashed an boomed and exploded so hard an heavy that t'day all 'ts left and made for us is this one big rockin rollin COMPLICATED CIRCLE—*

**– Bob Dylan**

The 1965 Newport Folk Festival featured as diverse an array of performers as its predecessors, but history has chiefly remembered it as The Year Dylan Went Electric. A great deal has been written and said about this event, and the effects—for both ill and good—that it inflicted (or bestowed) upon the face of American music. A few historians have argued that the brouhaha over this perceived betrayal was unwarranted. The Folk Festival wasn't Dylan's first foray into rock territory; his most recent album, *Bringing It All Back Home*, had featured several songs with a plugged-in accompaniment. He came to Newport in late July of 1965, just over a month after the release of a single called "Like a Rolling Stone." The new song was an "electric epic"; it clocked in at over six minutes (almost unheard-of in pop single terms), and featured Dylan backed by electric guitar, organ, bass, and drums.

But there was a significance to Dylan's Newport appearance. The folk community had always attempted to distance itself from the trappings of popular music, and their strongest objections were reserved for rock and roll. This prevailing mind-set among the folk faithful kept young listeners from buying into the rock phenomenon; the purest among them wouldn't even touch the Beatles.

By 1965, though, anyone could see that there was dissent in the ranks. The first indication that there was something amiss at the Folk Festival took place during a Friday afternoon blues workshop. "Blues: Origins and Off-shoots" drew from yet another Folk Festival lineup of legendary blues artists: the Reverend Gary Davis, Willie Dixon, Memphis Slim, Lightnin' Hopkins, "Son" House, and Mance Lipscomb. Among such company, the young, racially mixed, amplified Paul Butterfield Blues Band may have seemed out of place. But the upstart Chicago group had the endorsement of blues scholar Sam Charters and the managerial backing of Albert Grossman. It seemed harmless enough to present them.

Alan Lomax, who was still on the festival board, served as the workshop's emcee. After lavishing considerable praise on each of the "authentic" blues-men, Lomax introduced the Butterfield band with a tirade that Paul Rothchild later recounted:

> Used to be a time when a farmer would take a box, glue an axe han-dle to it, put some strings on it, sit down in the shade of a tree and play some blues for himself and his friends. Now here we've got these guys, and they need all of this fancy hardware to play the blues. Today you've heard some of the greatest blues players in the world playing their simple music on simple instruments. Let's find out if these guys can play it at all.

When Lomax left the stage, Grossman angrily confronted him about this caustic introduction. This was no surprise; Grossman backed the Butterfield Band. In the past couple of years, Albert's tastes had changed. The man who had formerly maintained a sharp, conservative wardrobe and a close-cropped hairstyle now resembled a freaked-out Benjamin Franklin. He still wore a jacket, but no tie; his gray hair was down to his shoulders and pointedly un-kempt. He looked less like a member of the folk community and more like a Greenwich Village con man (which, some might argue, he was). All of these things must have occurred to Alan Lomax, who was offended by the Butter-field Blues Band and by Grossman himself, both of whom he perceived as in-truders. So when Grossman snapped at him, Lomax snapped back. The next thing we knew, the folk world's most venerable figure and its most powerful businessman were physically brawling. Lomax and Grossman: two middle-aged, un-athletic men literally rolling in the dust. They had to be separated by onlookers. It was quite a scene.

We didn't realize it at the time, but the message of this backstage spectacle was larger than the incident itself. Lomax symbolized the sacrosanct traditions of folklore; Grossman was the power broker whose very existence threatened to corrupt those traditions. For the first time, the tension that had lurked beneath the placid surface of the folk revival erupted in plain sight. The conflict was personified, there in the flesh.

Fortunately, there were performances during the festival that transcended these tensions. Dick and Mimi Fariña played to a Saturday afternoon audience so captivated that even a sudden deluge couldn't break the spell. On another program, we heard a moving performance by a prison work-song group from Texas. Ralph Rinzler had found them and arranged for their temporary parole. They sang while chopping wood onstage. Later, during a festival party, these prisoners mingled with the rest of the performers and kin. And the whiskey was flowing (not very quickly, though, since at Joyce's instructions our man Leroy was probably the slowest bartender in Newport). At any rate, someone came over to Joyce and said: "Mrs. Wein, I think I'd better take so-and-so home—he's murdered three people while he was drunk."

On Saturday night, we presented Spokes Mashiyane, a tin whistle player whom Pete Seeger had heard in South Africa the previous year. The mere fact of his appearance was a small miracle. At the urging of the board, we had written to Gallo Records in November; that was the only way we knew to reach Spokes. We never heard a word in reply until the day before the festival, when the doorman at our house in New York phoned Newport to tell me that a musician had shown up looking for us. We arranged for someone to find Spokes and put him on a bus to Newport. We never did figure out how he had gotten to the States. In Newport we lost him every day; he would disappear into one bar or another, and never made any rehearsals. On the night of his scheduled performance, he was nowhere to be seen, and the Seegers were despairing. Spokes finally did turn up, with only minutes to spare.

Despite the limitations of his instrument, Spokes Mashiyane swung like a jazz musician. His phrasing and articulation evoked the sound of Lester Young. He was amazing. At first, he played with no backing musicians. Then Pete walked on to lend his accompaniment on twelve-string guitar. A few moments later, I sat down at the piano and joined them. We played some "rhythm" changes and some blues, and through each measure of every song Spokes kept up a lightly swinging sound that wafted over the crowd of 15,000.

Nobody knew who he was; here was this quiet, diminutive black man creating some of the festival's most stirring music. The beat was infectious. Spokes was dancing gaily with the tin whistle in his mouth, like an African pied piper. His music made everyone forget about the infighting in the folk world. After Newport, Spokes traveled to London, and I believe it was there that the man they called King Kwela was stabbed to death.

The final night of the 1965 Folk Festival had the potential to convey the same communal feeling that Mashiyane had so masterfully evoked. Pete Seeger opened the concert by playing a tape of a newborn baby crying. He asked the audience, rhetorically, what sort of world this child would grow up in. The singers on the program that night, he implied, would sing about that world—and by singing, would make that world a better place. For the most part, they fulfilled Pete's wishes. Ronnie Gilbert sang "Masters of War," the compelling, highly personal antiwar song penned by Bob Dylan just a few years earlier. Obviously, Dylan was the linchpin in the topical songs movement. We all must have expected that he would deliver more of these poignant set-pieces that night.

We had no way of knowing what he actually had in store. Dylan hadn't brought a band to Newport—but upon arriving, he had assembled one by borrowing musicians from the Butterfield Blues Band. Late one night during the festival, he rehearsed this pickup group in secret in a Bellevue Avenue mansion. Dylan had obviously made a decision; perhaps he recognized the Beatles' musical contribution to the world and he wanted to be a part of it. This could have been either a shrewd business move or a genuine musical statement. In Dylan's case, I believe it was a little of both. He felt that he could better express himself and reach more people by going electric; and he felt it necessary to tap into the pulse of popular culture.

Halfway through the evening, after a few songs by the traditional country-folksinger Cousin Emmy, Bob Dylan mounted the stage. He was clad in a flamboyant orange shirt and black leather, and carrying an electric guitar. His bandmates, unexpected guests, followed him on. They kicked off with a rock-and-roll version of his song "Maggie's Farm." The audience, which was shocked into silence for a moment, quickly began to register its disapproval. People began booing; there were cries of "Sellout!" Others shouted about the sound quality, which was poor, since the sound system was designed for acoustic performers. The prevailing feeling among the crowd was a sense that they had been betrayed.

There was just as much pandemonium behind the scenes. Pete Seeger, Theo Bikel, Peter Yarrow, Albert Grossman, and I were standing on the far left side of the stage when Dylan's band began playing. At the sound of the first amplified chords, a crimson color rose in Pete's face, and he ran off. The rest of us were just as shocked and upset—except, perhaps, for Grossman, who must have relished the moment. This was a sacrilege, as far as the folk world was concerned.

After a few excruciating minutes, someone tapped me on the shoulder. "Pete's really upset. Maybe you should talk to him."

I found Pete sitting in a parked car in the field behind the stage.

"That noise is terrible!" he cried. "Make it stop."

I said: "Pete, it's too late. There's nothing we can do."

Several accounts of this fateful night have suggested that Pete threatened to cut the power cables with an ax. This wasn't the case. At any rate, Pete wasn't carrying an ax that day (although he often did carry one, for wood-chopping purposes), and he didn't go looking for one. What he did—what all of us did— was wait, helplessly, while Dylan's entourage played.

The band made it through two more songs. "Like a Rolling Stone" elicited some scattered applause, along with the heckling. Dylan and his band evacuated the stage, and then the menacing rumble of thousands of hostile fans could be heard. When Dylan came off the stage, I confronted him.

"You have to go back," I told him. "You've got to play something acoustic."

"I don't want to. I can't go back." He spoke stubbornly.

"Bob, we're going to have a riot on our hands if you don't."

"I don't have a guitar."

I turned to the assembled folksingers backstage. "Does anyone have a guitar?" About twenty acoustic guitars went up in the air. This was the Newport Folk Festival; it was a sea of guitars. Peter Yarrow grabbed one and handed it to Bob. We ushered him back onto the stage.

There were shouts for "Tambourine Man," and Dylan obliged, prompting his first unequivocal applause of the night. Then, maybe with tears in his eyes, he sang "It's All Over Now, Baby Blue." The song, with its longing to "strike another match, go start anew," was more than Dylan's adieu to Newport. It was a farewell to the idealism and purity of the folk revival. There was no turning back—not for Dylan, not for anyone. The young figurehead of the folk movement, the songwriter who had given us "Blowin' in the Wind" and "With God on Our Side," had remade himself into a rock star. The repercussions were huge; no longer was there the semblance of a pure folk community that resisted corruption by outside forces. Instead, distinctions were blurred. The young idealistic folk fans, who had valiantly resisted the mainstream tastes of their friends, no longer had to hold out. Rock and roll was no longer taboo; if Dylan could cross that line, so could they.

Several other artists followed Dylan onstage, but the night had been derailed. Everyone was exhausted. When the finale finally came, people began a weary exodus from the field. And, without any warning or announcement, Mel Lyman, leader of the Fort Hill folk community in Boston, was onstage playing "Rock of Ages" on his mouth harp. This plaintive, beseeching sound came through the loudspeakers, gently wafting over the masses. He played the old spiritual over and over again, with hardly any variation. Broadside reported:

> It was a plea, a hymn, a dirge, a lullaby. Twenty times, thirty, more, and always the same beseeching, stroking, praying, pleading; then slower, softer, and as the supplication trailed away, the park was empty and people were on their way home.

\*     \*     \*

After Bob Dylan's controversial performance of 1965, the Folk Festival board had decreed its intention to eschew show business presentation. Mike and Pete Seeger, along with Ralph Rinzler, urged that we consider the festival not only as a showcase for folk music, but also a sort of massive, organic workshop of folk life.

We designated a portion of Festival Field as a crafts area, and invested a lot of energy into its operation. All day Saturday and Sunday, this area was the site of cloth weaving demonstrations, led principally by weavers from Cape Breton Island (in Nova Scotia) and Johnson County, Tennessee. There was also woodcarving, pottery making, basket weaving, and quilting. A group of Seminole artists demonstrated their patchwork sewing, and some Alaskan Eskimos taught the intricate process of ivory carving. But it was Rinzler's passion rather than widespread public interest that drove the crafts activities at Newport. The influence of Rinzler and his love of crafts is now seen at many festivals throughout the world, including the New Orleans Jazz and Heritage Festival.

As for the music, the 1966 Newport Folk Festival consisted mostly of "authentic" artists. This isn't to say that there weren't any big names on the bill (Chuck Berry appeared on a program called "The City"), but the roster consisted primarily of grassroots performers. The blues were well represented (by Son House, Skip James, Delta rambler Bukka White, and Chicago legend Howlin' Wolf), as was gospel (the Original Gospel Harmonettes, the Dixie

Hummingbirds, and the Swan Silvertones), country (Virginia banjo player Dock Boggs, North Carolinian fiddler Clark Kessinger, bluegrass musicians Alice Foster and Hazel Dickens), and plain folksinging (Jack Elliott, Judy Collins, Carolyn Hester, Phil Ochs). There was also a small but noteworthy concession to the folk-rock trend; we presented the Blues Project (a group that included Al Kooper on organ and Danny Kalb on electric guitar), and the Lovin' Spoonful (which hadn't yet adopted the rock and roll edge of "Summer in the City").

That Sunday afternoon, we presented the first of our "New Directions" programs, designed to feature an array of performers—"some of whom are new to folk music performing and others who, though they are seasoned performers, represent a new trend." In 1966, this mini-concert profiled Greenwich Village folksinger Richie Havens alongside Cambridge blues revivalist Tom Rush, Mormon folksinger Rosalie Sorrels, and Bangladeshi sarod virtuoso Ali Akbar Khan, among others.

Overall, the 1966 Folk Festival was true to its mission; it featured the real aspect of "folk," in its various forms. But the absence of commercial attractions took its toll on sales figures. Attendance was hardly anemic, but it was less than impressive. For the first time, the Newport Folk Festival lost money.

At the end of 1965 the Folk Foundation had reported a surplus of approximately $80,000. The board felt it was rich, but they soon found out that $80,000 was not a lot of money. The loss on the festival, combined with the exhilarating way field projects were paid for, resulted in a deficit $15,661.49.

The sudden shift from surplus to deficit raised some red flags among the board. How could this have happened? Alan Lomax and Ralph Rinzler were particularly suspicious, and together they mounted an investigative campaign. Of course, I was the only person on the board who could have committed any indiscretion, as my company handled the Folk Foundation's accounting. I was prime suspect number one. Lomax and Rinzler questioned my handling of the books. It didn't take long before they had convinced the board to request an audit.

As long as I've been in business, I've been careful with money—especially when it isn't my own. So this development was irksome at best. I recognized that both Lomax and Rinzler might have seen an opportunity to bring me down; they were ambitious men, and they would have liked to have more control over the festival. After all, Lomax and Rinzler had put in much of the hard work that made these events possible. And yet the festival's producer, supposedly a watchdog, was an outsider, a jazz man. It wasn't difficult to see why they might come to resent this.

I received news of the audit while conducting the third drum-battle tour in Japan. I picked up the phone and called Pete Seeger.

"It appears to me," I said, "that Alan and Ralph are trying to get control of the festival, and they're using the deficit to arouse suspicion and a lack of trust within the board. This attitude could destroy the festival. Do you want me to try to save it?"

"Yes," Pete replied. "The festival is worth saving."

At the next board meeting, I proposed a compromise. An audit would show only that the money was deposited and spent and every dollar would be accounted for. Whether those funds were spent wisely was a matter that couldn't be ascertained by an auditor. I suggested that individual board members recommend people that they knew and trusted to be on a committee that would study the books.

Pete Seeger asked his manager, Harold Leventhal, to be in charge of this impartial committee. Jim Rooney, former Club 47 owner, and Jac Holzman, president of Elektra Records, were included in this group. They pored over all of the Folk Foundation's financial records with an accountant. They saw detailed information about our income and expenses—including my producer's salary, which amounted to roughly $7,500 per year. After a month or two, the committee presented its findings at a meeting. Harold Leventhal spoke on their behalf.

"I wouldn't take George Wein's job for $50,000 a year," Harold said. "Our only criticism of George is that he's too lenient with the board. He lets them spend money too freely, and in a manner that could endanger the festival."

\*     \*     \*

The 1967 Newport Folk Festival was the first to last for nearly a week. Once again, we featured a wide-ranging mix of performers. Balfa Freres, a group of five brothers in the Balfa family, performed Louisiana Cajun songs. We presented an impressive selection of country artists—among them, Maybelle Carter, Grandpa Jones, May Gadd, Jimmy Driftwood, Dave Dudley, and Merle Travis.

Arlo Guthrie, a "new face" who had been singing professionally for about a year, was clearly on the rise. When he performed his new song "Alice's Restaurant" at a Saturday topical songs workshop, the audience responded with a massive ovation. Guthrie performed the song again the following afternoon at a workshop called "Songwriters & the Contemporary Scene;" it also featured Judy Collins, a Canadian songwriter named Gordon Lightfoot, and the young poet and folksinger Leonard Cohen.

The Folk Festival maintained its activist stance with regard to civil rights; in addition to presenting groups like the Freedom Singers and encouraging topical songs, tents were set up where groups such as the Student Nonviolent Coordinating Committee (SNCC) and the Congress of Racial Equality (CORE) could each distribute their literature. From 1966 to 1967, we appointed a SNCC officer—the folk and blues scholar Julius Lester—to our Folk Foundation board. Lester's involvement brought SNCC and the Folk Foundation together more closely than ever before. During the 1967 festival, the SNCC booth was manned not only by Lester, but also by two of the organization's militant new leaders: Stokely Carmichael and H. Rap Brown.

Located at the far edge of Festival Field, this booth was in a position that put the group in close proximity with police officers who were standing by the fence. The police weren't bothering them. But the officers' mere presence was enough to provoke the SNCC members. They soon took up a chant: "Black Power over Blue Power!" This taunt was ubiquitous and continuous.

The police didn't say or do anything in response. But when the festival was over for the night, they couldn't resist the temptation to flex some of that "Blue Power." They approached the SNCC booth and told them to pack it up and leave the grounds.

"Hey, we can stay," they protested. "We've got a tent, we're part of the festival."

"Sorry, it's closing time." And when they wouldn't move, the police used their infamous "nudging" tactic to push them out of the field. The SNCC members were furious. That night we had an emergency meeting in the house where Joyce and I were staying. Five or six SNCC people, including Carmichael, Rap Brown, and Lester, presented their complaint to assorted members of the Folk Foundation board.

"Is this a police brutality case?" I asked. "Has anyone been hurt?"

"No, but they pushed us out of the park. You've got to do something."

I tried to explain that theirs was a difficult case. The situation was surreal, and even a little amusing, to me. These people had been on the frontlines, at lunch counter sit-ins and countless protests in the South. A few of them had served time in prison; many of them had suffered beatings at the hands of the police. But in this situation, there was no serious offense. Their taunting had created a situation. I advised them to let it pass.

But they would hear none of this advice, and kept insisting that I do something. Finally, I attempted to defuse their anger. Flippantly, I exclaimed: "What do you want me to do—call the NAACP?"

They couldn't believe what I had just said. I thought they were going to kill me. So, seeing that they weren't going to let it go, I proposed a course of action. Elliott Hoffman's partner, Mike Beldock, was at the festival that weekend. Mike was a civil rights lawyer; he later became known as the attorney who took on a pro bono case representing former prizefighter Rubin "Hurricane" Carter. I knew that he would agree to help out in this situation.

"I'll go down to the chief of police in the morning," I told the SNCC members, "and try to get him to put together a lineup for you. Then you can identify who pushed you out and you can register a complaint. You know that even if you single out somebody, he'll protest his innocence. He'll say, 'I wasn't even there; I was on the other side of town,' and there will be another cop who swears by it. But maybe the Police Department will cooperate."

They liked my idea, so I went to the station the following morning with Mike Beldock and relayed the incident to the Chief. "These SNCC people weren't really doing anything wrong," I explained, "and the police officers should not have pushed them. Could you put together a lineup of officers who were at the festival, so that SNCC could pick out the ones who pushed them?"

We were pleased when the Newport Chief of Police agreed to do this. All over the country at this time, police departments were consciously trying to clean up their image; this was the turbulent '60s, and the authorities were tired of being vilified by the press.

We went out to the hillside behind Festival Field that morning, and met up with the SNCC members. It was early—around 8 A.M. When we got there, twenty or thirty officers were assembled about a hundred yards away, at the bottom of the hill. There I was, with Mike Beldock and the leadership of SNCC.

The organization's members were full of nervous energy. "You mean the police are going to line up for us? You mean it's really going to happen like that?" They couldn't believe it. These people had been mistreated by cops all over the South; they had been imprisoned and assaulted. The thought of turning the tables—lining up the police for a change—was an intoxicating idea.

But as we watched the congregation of police officers, one of them began to climb the slope and head toward us. He was a plainclothes detective, and we could see that there was something amiss. When he reached us, we realized that he was drunk out of his skin.

"It's not going to happen," he told us. As he slurred these words, the cops below began to disperse. They weren't going to go through with it, despite whatever orders they had received. It had all been a façade. We didn't have the power to keep them from leaving. Our lineup had evaporated.

The SNCC kids were suddenly scared stiff. "They're going to kill us," I heard one of them murmur. They seemed to deflate before my eyes. Within a couple of minutes, they had all jumped into their cars and left town.

*    *    *

*This has not been a year Americans shall reflect upon with much pleasure or pride. At times the anger and frustration and isolation and desolation seemed more than we were geared to bear, and like an insane Gothic novel there was always another chapter to prove we could in agony contain yet more.*

**—1968 Newport Folk Festival Program**

The bizarre outcome of SNCC's police protest at Newport soon seemed like a quaint reminder of innocence lost. Over the ensuing months, the nation slid into a moral quagmire. There were widespread protests against the Vietnam War, which by this point had an American death toll fast approaching 30,000. Martin Luther King, Jr., was assassinated, and the race riots that ensued across the country resulted in over 20,000 arrests and more than forty deaths. Robert F. Kennedy was shot in Los Angeles after celebrating a presidential primary win. Protests and violent police confrontations at the Democratic National Convention in Chicago shocked the nation. And SNCC activists joined members of Students for a Democratic Society and the Society of African-American Students in taking over Columbia University for an entire week.

Against this tumultuous backdrop, both jazz and traditional folk music seemed hopelessly out-of-date. The new era of plugged-in protest—which Bob Dylan had officially inaugurated at the Newport Folk Festival in 1965—now had enormous strength in American society. This was more than a musical change; it was a transformation, a tidal shift that affected every aspect of American life. Youth, which had always deferred on some level to authority, was now the supreme commodity. People who were over thirty-five were worrying about their careers; many of them were being summarily replaced by recent college graduates. The baby boomers had come of age, rejecting and dismantling the value systems of their elders. Rock and roll was their rallying cry.

An underground press had arisen out of the chaos, and I began to read what they were saying. Jazz, I learned, "was dead." According to these alternative papers, Ginger Baker was a better drummer than Elvin Jones. Jimmy Page had rendered the Kenny Burrells and Tal Farlows obsolete. That year's Newport Jazz Festival, which featured an array of big bands (Ellington, Basie, Herman, Gillespie) as well as modern jazz groups and crossover stars (Dionne Warwick and Ray Charles), was sparsely attended, and lost money. I was coming to the unfortunate realization that the youth of America were no longer interested in jazz. In 1968, we had to fight just to get the Newport schedule printed in the newspapers. They weren't interested anymore. Record companies were no longer clamoring to record at the festival; columnists weren't scrambling to cover the event in their columns. For the first time, the Newport Jazz Festival had lost its relevance to the cultural mainstream.

The 1968 Newport Folk Festival also seemed to keep its distance from the turbulent center of American youth culture; it bore no resemblance to that summer's "Festival of Life" in Chicago's Grant Park, which featured bombastic rock bands, an impenetrable haze of marijuana smoke, draft card bonfires, beach nude-ins, and public lovemaking.

But the Folk Festival did reflect the spirit of the age through topical songwriters like Richie Havens, Arlo Guthrie, Tim Buckley, and a fifteen-year-old Janis Ian. Songs about civil rights were ubiquitous. So were songs in protest of the Vietnam War. In fact, the pervasiveness of political dialogue during the festival prompted at least one performer to voice discomfort. "I don't want anything to do with tearing down America," complained Buell Kazee, a sixty-eight-year-old Kentucky banjo picker and Baptist minister. "I don't know why these folks don't do the honest thing and admit that this is ideology and not just music. If I'd known it was goin' to be like this I'd of stayed in Kentucky."

Yet despite the Folk Foundation's emphasis on authenticity, sincerity, and political activism, the festival still bore a lingering reputation as a star-making platform. We were continually reminded of this fact. That year, a young Nashville country-folksinger named George Hamilton IV came to Newport with fifty dollars in hand; he thought that the festival's flat-rate fee was collected from the artists, like the entry fee in a talent show. On the opposite end of the spectrum was B. B. King, whose management just couldn't understand how a festival as prominent as ours could have the audacity to insult him with a paltry fifty-dollar fee. Joyce had the insight to carefully rephrase the offer—adding estimates for B. B.'s travel, expenses, and hotel arrangements onto the amount, so they wouldn't feel like they had been undersold.

Rock and roll was still anathema to many of the Folk Foundation board; Julius Lester even prevailed upon B. B. King to perform without an amplifier during an afternoon workshop. But the spirit of the age was such that we had no choice; rock music made the difference between a financial catastrophe and a self-sustaining box office. And so it was that the 1968 Newport Folk Festival was saved from ruin by a single group—a San Francisco psychedelic rock band managed by Albert Grossman that had performed to great acclaim the previous summer in Monterey. They were called Big Brother and the Holding Company, and their lead singer was Janis Joplin.

Whatever her reputation, Joplin conducted herself like a perfect lady for the duration of the festival. She went to all of the parties, and never displayed any signs of the self-involvement or excess for which she was seminotorious. She showed respect for the festival and what it stood for. And this respect was mutual; the board had approved Big Brother's inclusion because the band had roots in folk music and southern blues. Joplin was a good singer, and she understood music. Her presence that year brought thousands more people to the festival, putting us in the black.

In this climate, we continued to tread on thin ice with our opponents on Aquidneck Island. That fall, they managed to put a nonbinding referendum on Newport's presidential election ballots. The questions were: "Do you approve of the Jazz Festival?" and "Do you approve of the Folk Festival?" The presidential election that year was Richard Nixon vs. Hubert Humphrey, and Nixon won by a wide margin. But even with these conservative results, the ballot produced good news for the festivals. Seventy-five percent of Newport voters approved of the Newport Jazz Festival, and more than 65 percent approved of the Folk Festival—in spite of the latter event's decidedly progressive political agendas. This was great encouragement. Knowing that we had majority support made life a little easier for us—for a little while.

\*     \*     \*

Though I was letting the 1969 Newport Jazz Festival capitulate to the pressures of a rock-and-roll generation, the Newport Folk Foundation remained admirably steadfast to the purity of its mission. There was nary a rock group in sight on the '69 Folk Festival—only city and country-folk music, international traditional music, blues, gospel, bluegrass, and various offshoots. The program was as strong, as pure, and as diverse as anything we had put together in the past. Among the artists performing at Newport for the first time: Cape Breton guitarist John Allen Cameron; country duo the Everly Brothers; Atlanta blues guitarist Buddy Moss; Texas-based songwriter Jerry Jeff Walker; Swedish fiddlers Bjorn Stabi and Ole Hjorth; and Big Mama

Thornton, the blues singer whose record "Hound Dog" had been covered by Elvis Presley.

Pete Seeger sailed to the festival that year in the Clearwater, a sloop that he and Toshi had built in an effort to promote environmental consciousness along the Hudson River. During the winter, Pete and other folk artists had toured the Hudson River Valley to raise funds for their cause. Eventually—buoyed by private donations, a $10,000 loan from the Folk Foundation, and several large grants—the project had become a reality. The sloop, which had set sail in May, came into Narragansett Bay and docked in Newport. Pete led a vocal ensemble from the deck of the Clearwater; he called this group (which included Don McLean, Jack Elliott, Len Chandler, and a half-dozen other folk artists) the Hudson River Sloop Singers. This was a perfect example of the positive idealism that Pete still practiced, despite growing cynicism on all sides.

The "New Faces" on the 1969 Newport Folk Festival were particularly impressive. Judy Collins brought in a young songwriter from Canada named Joni Mitchell; she was just beginning to build a reputation with the song "Both Sides Now." In much the same manner, the Irish folk-rock artist Van Morrison was on an upward trajectory when he came to the festival. But the biggest surprise came when we presented a twenty-year-old songwriter who originally hailed from North Carolina. This kid knew one of our festival volunteers (who happened to be the daughter of Professor Irwin Corey). She said: "You've got to put him on the New Faces program," and I'm glad that we did. He was a good performer. His name was James Taylor.

This festival—aesthetically, one of our strongest—was a financial train wreck. James Taylor, Van Morrison, and Joni Mitchell had not yet become stars and audience turnout was poor. Making matters worse, it had been an expensive festival. Despite the uniform performer's fee (which was still fifty dollars), we spent a lot of money on transportation. A case in point: bringing the noted songwriter Jean-Bosco Mwenda to Newport from Africa cost us $2,000. Unexpected expenses as well came up; the previous week, after a scuffle at the Jazz Festival, the Newport City Council had hurriedly passed strict edicts that greatly increased our costs. Police fees rose from $15,000 to $25,000 overnight. The chain-link fence that we were required to build around Festival Field, an expense shared with the jazz festival, cost the Folk Foundation another $14,000.

Due to the financial problems, the Folk Foundation decided not to put on a festival in 1970. But the foundation did not want to let the festival die; one was scheduled for 1971, a week after the jazz festival. But it was in that year that the mob of kids, demanding that the music be free, broke the fences down and forced the cancellation of the last two jazz concerts (see chapter nine for more on the Newport Jazz Festival, 1971).

In the interim week, the Newport City Council voted to cancel the license for the upcoming Newport Folk Festival. It was the end of an era.

What did working on the festival all those years mean? The creating of the folk festival is as important to me as anything I have ever done in my life. Because I was not directly involved with the music, my position historically is somewhat vague. This doesn't bother me. The story of the folk festival belongs to folklorists and musicologists.

The Cajun music of Louisiana, the Georgia Sea Island singers, the rediscovery of so many blues artists, and bringing Spokes Mashiyane from South Africa are just a few examples of potentially lost music that were presented on the huge national stage that the Newport Folk Festival had become. The echo of this work by the Folk Foundation is still being felt by the world of folk music.

The Folk Festival gave me the opportunity to know and to work with two people who have made a difference: Alan Lomax and Pete Seeger. Alan Lomax, even though he caused me many problems on the board, was one of the important minds of the twentieth century. He contributed as much to the study and discovery of American folk music as any human being. (The day after these words were written, in July 2002, he died at the age of eighty-seven.) Pete Seeger is another story. He is not a genius, in the way Lomax was. But Pete has a quality that surpasses genius. He has the greatness of communication that brings out the best in people. He's not a preacher; he has never had any desire to control people. Self-aggrandizement is not part of his dedication. For Joyce and me to have associated with him and his wife, Toshi, is a highlight of our lives.

Pete was the spirit behind the exercise in idealism that was undoubtedly the reason for the success of the festivals between 1963 and 1969. Idealism, by itself, does not have much meaning unless it works. For four or five days at the Newport Folk Festival, it worked; for six or seven years, it worked. Most of the artists on the folk festival earned their living through the music—they could be called "entertainers." But they had put aside this need for the week that was the folk festival so that what they could bring to the table would make it possible to hear many other artists that were forgotten and who may have been lost forever to obscurity. The idealism worked because these artists and myself had a streak of pragmatism. We didn't have our heads in the clouds. Whether it was Peter, Paul and Mary, the Clancy Brothers, or Mississippi John Hurt, they were people who got paid for making music. But they gave up their professional lives for these three or four days that were the festival.

The folk festival was at the right time and in the right place. The battle for civil rights was the prime focus of most Americans in the 1960s. The spirit of the folk festival was more than a footnote. The power of fifteen or twenty thousand people, holding hands, swaying, and singing "We Shall Overcome" spread throughout the country even to the point where our president, Lyndon Johnson, quoted these words in a speech broadcast over national television.

One thing I haven't mentioned: Back when I was partners with Albert Grossman, I was concerned with artist management. In my job as producer of this festival, I could have chosen to make the folk world part of business life. I chose not to do so because I considered my position a privilege and I wouldn't take advantage of that privilege. If there was any benefit to what I was doing, it was that having the folk festival helped the economic structure of the jazz festival by splitting some expenses. At the same time, it might have been the problems that the jazz festival incurred that brought about the end of the folk festival; it's a double-edged sword. We couldn't have had the folk festival without the jazz festival; the folk festival was a child of the jazz festival. Perhaps it is just another example of the wilderness, where some animals devour their young.

\*     \*     \*

The day after Louis Armstrong's death, on July 7, 1971, I appeared before the Newport City Council to address the issue of the festivals. I remember that I had no speech prepared; I just made a conscious effort to compose myself, and spoke from the heart. So the following text—transcribed verbatim by a court stenographer—reflects my thoughts at that turbulent time in more vivid detail than I could ever summon today.

I want to thank the people of Newport for the tremendous expressions of sympathy that have been extended to me and my wife about the misfortune of last weekend. The response and concern are overwhelming and we are grateful. But in truth, sympathy is a sad word. It implies that something or someone is dead. And the Newport Jazz Festival has never been more alive. Sympathy is gratifying but action is necessary. In 1968, the citizens of Newport gave the Jazz Festival an incredible favorable plurality in a referendum. All of the business community has continually endorsed the festivals. The chamber of commerce is one of our biggest supporters. The hotels want and need us. The State continually expresses its pride in the festivals. And in granting the license for the Jazz Festival last October, each of the seven councilmen expressed his appreciation and support of the Jazz Festival.

All of this is wonderful, but unfortunately it means very little. Because I wonder if anybody really meant it. You see, an attitude has continually permeated the relationship between the city and the festivals—the attitude that the festivals are a business that belongs to George Wein and George Wein must pay for everything in relationship to the festivals.

Well, it is of course true that I am the owner of the Jazz Festival and chairman of the board of the nonprofit Folk Festival. But this still does not excuse or fully explain this attitude. Because it is this attitude that is the reason for all the problems that continue to occur between the festivals and the City up to and including the cancellation last week. Cities help build stadiums for football and baseball teams. Industry is continually given tax advantages as inducement to moving into communities. Newport has never even authorized a few hundred dollars to put a banner across Broadway to say, "Welcome Newport Jazz Festival." A festival study committee appointed by the city council several years ago came up with many positive suggestions, all of which we implemented on our side. The City chose to ignore all recommendations of its own festival committee pertinent to any monetary expenditures on the city side.

Yet if you as citizens of Newport want something, you must be willing to pay for it whether it is an education, sewage systems, or tourist attractions. Yet never in the ten-year history of my being in control of the festivals has a councilman stood up to say that Newport should share in the costs of insuring the safety and comfort of the people that are invited to this city when it grants George Wein a license to put on the festivals.

It's not that I think that the festivals shouldn't pay their way in the city. We should pay as much as is practically possible. But the city should share this responsibility with us. "Why is this necessary?" you might ask. Because if the city has a direct involvement, the police wouldn't have the excuse that what happened last weekend was because I didn't want to pay for enough police. You see, if the city had a financial and moral interest in the festival the city manager and the chief of police wouldn't have been so quick to cancel the Sunday and Monday concerts after everybody had been cleared out of town early Sunday morning. While I stated at the time and now do so again that I felt the city manager made a correct decision in stopping the festival on Saturday night, I also say now that little or no thought or concern was given to the possibility of continuing the festivals after the situation was cleared up. The police attitude was "good riddance." Yet if the city had an interest, the police would not have had that attitude and the city manager would have waited until Sunday morning daylight to make a final decision. Several alternative steps could have been taken. But nobody consulted me. Nobody called the councilmen for an emergency meeting. No one thought of the thousands of dollars the hotels and restaurants would lose. Least of all none of the powers that were in control cared about the festival. The only consideration was get the trouble over, let the jerks tear the park apart, and then kick them out and end it all. Yet it turns out that it really didn't have to be that way. Because if, on Saturday night, aid had been sought, not to quell a disturbance, but to insure the festival's staying open, perhaps something positive might have been done.

What I am trying to say is that if the police and the city manager knew that the responsibilities of the festival also belonged to the city and its people, and if they had been instilled with the attitude that the festivals were an integral part of life in Newport, then I feel that the concerts would have been allowed to continue Sunday and Monday, at least on a concert-to-concert basis.

It cannot be denied that once the police decided to clear the hills with a show of force on Sunday morning that it was a relatively easy police action, and little or no violence was necessary.

This fact might also be taken to consideration in an examination of why the hill was allowed to be occupied in the first place. But this can wait for a later discussion.

You see, if all of our friends who express sympathy, and all the businessmen and councilmen who say Newport needs the festivals really want them, the festivals can still survive in Newport. We have been putting on the festivals for eighteen years without any help. Think how long we could last if we really had your help. And I'm not absolving the state of Rhode Island for its responsibility in this matter. We thank Governor Licht for providing State police to help in the traffic, but the colonel of the State Police was involved in the decision to cancel the Jazz Festival. If the state was more actively involved and believed its own publicity about the wonderful music festivals in Rhode Island, the colonel would also have been looking for ways to save the festival.

What we have just opened for discussion is important for the entire community to think about, particularly with the election coming up shortly. Because after the election I am going to apply once again for a license to put on the Nineteenth Newport Jazz Festival at Festival Field unless the State has condemned our field by that time.

At this moment I owe the city of Newport approximately $22,000 for police protection per a contract signed last week. The reason I owe this money is that checks I gave the city last Friday were returned for insufficient funds due to the cancellation of last week's festival. The city does have a $3,000 certified check of ours and I have another certified check here for $5,000 which I wish to give to the city treasurer now as a show of faith that this bill will be paid in full. We want to state publicly that we signed the contract in good faith and will live up to the letter of the agreement and pay our bill. But we must ask the city to wait until we get our finances in order. We request the cooperation of the council in this matter. The money we do have available to us now is a public trust and must be refunded to the people that bought tickets. This money must be refunded quickly and efficiently and we request that the city in no way interfere with this process. The friends we have in the jazz world are aware of our problems and are at present formulating plans to help solve our financial difficulties. As soon as this is done the city will be paid in full. I live in Middletown; I own a house there and am a resident voter. I hope the council takes this into consideration in replying to my request.

Now as to the Folk Festival about which everyone is concerned. I have informed the board of directors of the Newport Folk Foundation that if the festival is canceled at this time, they will have liabilities of some $20,000 to $25,000. If we are granted the license to continue, then the projected loss at this writing is at least $40,000 to $50,000. Nevertheless, the board has directed me to say that they wish to have the Newport Folk Festival on July 16, 17, and 18, and further request that there be minimal police costs. We did not expect crowds of more than 5,000 people per night. Now I have revised these estimates downward.

At this writing, the city council of Newport has a glorious opportunity—an opportunity to prove that a violence-prone minority in this country cannot tell an American city that it must give up something that means so much to so many people in the community.

Now is the time to prove that all these years Newport has not just been paying lip service to the festivals.

It is my feeling that if you as a council revoke the license for the Folk Festival, then you are bowing to the elements in our society that all of us abhor.

I cannot stress how important I feel your decision is to all of America. I feel the community is still behind us and the people of Newport will let you know this by their response to an affirmative vote for the Folk Festival.

Later that week, the Newport City Council voted 5–2 against the Folk Festival. With that decisive action, they not only killed the event, but also effectively terminated my connection to their city. I had presented nine folk festivals, two opera festivals, and eighteen jazz festivals (or seventeen-and-a-half, depending on your math) in Newport, Rhode Island. I had fought, more than once, to keep them alive. And this was how it ended.

I had somehow picked up the pieces after the disruption of 1960; could I do it again? I wasn't sure. All I knew was that Newport was finished.

# PART THREE

# 11

# *New Orleans*

NINETEEN SIXTY-NINE HAD DESTROYED ME financially, putting me deep in debt. Festival Productions had lost money in Newport, New Brunswick, New Jersey, Columbia, Maryland, and Philadelphia. My response to these insurmountable problems was characteristic: I scrounged around for a gig.

I managed to get some bookings for a veritable all-star band consisting of Red Norvo, Barney Kessel, Ruby Braff, Larry Ridley, Lenny McBrowne, and myself on piano. Later that fall, we worked a week at the Plaza Hotel in Manhattan, and one night Frank Sinatra stopped by; he and Red Norvo were good friends, having worked together in the 1950s. After the set, Sinatra walked over and greeted me: "Hello, George. How's the festival?" Although it felt a lifetime ago to me, his big night at Newport was still a vivid recollection for him.

Shortly after our Plaza gig, I took the band to New Orleans for a four-week engagement at the elegant Royal Sonesta Hotel. Over the past few years a friendship had developed with the hotel's manager, Jim Nassikas, and his successor, Archie Kasberian, both of whom were connoisseurs of fine wine and international cuisine. During earlier trips to New Orleans, we had spoken at length about gastronomical matters, and they were interested in the various culinary adventures that I'd had in France and elsewhere. I believe it was Archie who hired my band to appear at the Sonesta, in December 1969, playing at Economy Hall, a club in the hotel's basement.

This four weeks constituted the longest stretch of time I had ever spent in New Orleans, and I took on the task of exploring the city. I got to know the French Quarter and dove into the local jazz scene. It was at this time that I first met Ellis Marsalis, who was then the pianist with Al Hirt's band in Hirt's Bourbon Street nightclub.

One night during our Economy Hall run, I was approached by Durrell Black, a successful New Orleans businessman who loved Louis Armstrong and presided over the board of the city's jazz festival. For a number of reasons, I had not been involved with this festival during its first two seasons, in 1968 and 1969.

I joined Mr. Black for a drink, and he wasted no time in delivering his message.

"George, we want you to take over Jazz Fest," he said. Jazz Fest was to become, under my aegis, "The New Orleans Jazz and Heritage Festival."

*     *     *

The story of the New Orleans Jazz and Heritage Festival begins in 1962—the same year I reestablished myself as producer of the Newport Jazz Festival. One fall day of that year, I received a phone call from Olaf Lambert, manager of the Royal Orleans Hotel, asking me if I would come to New Orleans to discuss the possibility of producing a jazz festival.

My fascination with the so-called birthplace of jazz stretched back as far as my introduction to Red Allen and J. C. Higginbotham. I had named my club Storyville: The Birthplace of Jazz after that city's zoned red-light district. I had worked with such New Orleans icons as Louis Armstrong, Mahalia Jackson, and Sidney Bechet—and had toured with Papa French and his band in Europe. Yet I had never been to New Orleans. So I was more than happy to accept Mr. Lambert's invitation; at the very least, I'd see this historic city for the first time.

I had reservations, though; the fight for civil rights had heated up in the South in recent months, as white supremacists who saw their traditions faltering began fighting back. The previous May, an angry mob had viciously beaten the integrated "Freedom Riders" at a bus terminal in Birmingham, Alabama. In the fall, a riot had broken out at the University of Mississippi when James Meredith showed up for classes, prompting President John F. Kennedy to send in federal troops. I was extremely concerned with the movement and its progress, and was apprehensive and not without fear. Naturally I didn't bring Joyce with me to New Orleans; we wouldn't have been able to register in the same hotel, or even eat in the same restaurants. The greater part of my life had consisted of interaction with jazz musicians. I wasn't sure how I'd react if confronted with any prejudice or threats.

Even though I realized that New Orleans was typical of the South in some regards, it was certainly atypical in other ways. Historically, there had been more mingling of races there than in any other city in the Deep South. Before the Civil War and through the mid-twentieth century, Creoles of color had often interacted with white society, and blacks in New Orleans enjoyed more "freedom" (a relative term) than most of their northern counterparts. In the early 1960s, this was clearly no longer the case—but vestiges of an unusual past remained. I'd heard stories of staunch white segregationists encountering their colored relations at family funerals. I wondered if the city's complicated cultural life would seem completely foreign to me.

I was greeted at the airport and then taken to the Royal Orleans, a fine hotel in the French Quarter. Olaf Lambert had arranged a meeting for me with the city's power structure, including Mayor Vic Schiro, Trade Chairman Harry England, local musical legends Harry and Doc Souchon, several members of both the Chamber of Commerce and the Hotel Association, and the Roosevelt Hotel owner, Seymour Weiss (an old-line segregationist who had been an associate of the legendary populist Senator Huey Long). We adjourned for lunch in the Royal Orleans's private dining room, the Pipken Room.

It was an auspicious introduction to the wonders of New Orleans cuisine. Moreover, everyone was affable, proud of the jazz traditions of New Orleans, and eager to plan a possible event. They were brimming with ideas. I listened, and then offered some insight into even more advantages that New Orleans would reap from a major festival. But I knew that the festival they had in mind was impossible to present in the South. Without adopting a confrontational tone, I itemized a few of the obvious problems.

"You know, Duke Ellington is accustomed to being treated as royalty wherever he goes. He stays in the finest hotels. But I understand that your hotels are segregated and will not accept blacks as guests."

They couldn't refute this fact, and it was further confirmed by Seymour Weiss, who, thank heavens, was nearing the end of his long life. He emphasized that no "nigras" would ever stay at his hotel.

I went on to note that most groups had clauses in their contracts stipulating that they would not play before segregated audiences. My lunch companions pondered this for a moment. Then someone brought up the fact that President Kennedy had addressed an integrated audience outdoors during a recent New Orleans visit. Because a precedent had been established, they reasoned, the audience could be integrated as long as the festival was held outdoors.

Then I raised the fact that many jazz bands included both white and black musicians, citing, as examples, the Duke Ellington Orchestra (which then featured drummer Dave Black), the Cannonball Adderley Sextet (featuring Joe Zawinul), and the groups of Dave Brubeck and Gerry Mulligan, among others. According to established segregationist laws, it would be possible to present a black group and a white group in succession, but no mixed groups could appear.

Here was a group of prominent Louisiana figures sitting together and valiantly trying to find a way around the laws that they themselves had helped to create and enforce. The irony of the situation wasn't lost on me, outsider that I was. We finished our lunch and concluded that the time had not yet come for a jazz festival in the South. They advised me that maybe things would change, and they would call me if there were any developments. We parted on good terms.

I wasn't sure if my nonconfrontational stance had been the correct way to work. I recognized that I was a stranger in a strange land; these people had grown up in a society whose social mores were alien to me. I certainly stood no chance of altering this way of life in one visit; change like that doesn't happen unless the law is on your side. In a culture steeped in white supremacy, racism becomes a personal thing. An individual in such a place will never see racism as immoral unless he begins to feel it in his heart and soul (and—let's face it— his pocketbook).

I'd never been the type who marches in the streets and gets thrown in jail. But I had cemented my commitment when I married Joyce. The way we conducted our lives, and the people we influenced, would be as significant a factor in the battle against racism as any action of those brave souls who risked life and limb in demonstrations.

Time passed quickly; I returned home, successfully resurrected the Newport Jazz Festival, and got deeply involved in European promotions with Thelonious Monk, among others. It was a couple of years before Olaf Lambert called me again, in March 1964.

Spring 1964 was a memorable time in America. Lyndon Johnson had recently been sworn in as president following the assassination of John F. Kennedy. Johnson, a Texan, had become involved in the fight to pass civil rights legislation proposed by the Kennedy administration. At the time, we didn't realize just how dedicated to the integrationist cause Johnson had become. The predominant talk in the media was whether the legislation would be passed—or blocked by southern segregationist congressmen.

Olaf Lambert, however, had little doubt as to the outcome. His first words to me were: "George, they're going to pass the civil rights bill at the end of May. Come down. We want to discuss the festival again." Within days, I was back in New Orleans. Once again I met with a group of powerful businessmen and politicians. This time, we talked about the jazz festival with certainty, as if the civil rights bill had already been passed. These pragmatic leaders were eager to explore the financial future of a desegregated South.

We decided that the inaugural New Orleans jazz festival would be held in the city's Municipal Auditorium in the spring of 1965. I was to receive a salary of five thousand dollars—which, believe me, I needed desperately in those years. Transportation and expenses would be paid. A Newport Jazz Festival–style event was about to be realized in the South for the very first time.

During that exciting trip, I renewed acquaintances with Allan Jaffe, the tuba-playing mastermind behind Preservation Hall, and his wife, Sandy. I met the writer Thomas Sancton, whose clarinet-playing son Tommy, Jr., would later help out on a few of my festivals before accepting a job with *Time* magazine. I got to know Dick Allen, knowledgeable curator of the Hogan jazz archives at Tulane University. And I met numerous others—musicians, scholars, and devoted jazz fans—who would become part of my New Orleans future.

My trip coincided with a convention of the Catholic Youth Organization, which drew several thousand priests from all over the country. I had an affiliation with the Pittsburgh CYO through Father Mike Williams, with whom I had worked for several years on a jazz festival inspired by Pittsburgh native Mary Lou Williams. It was only natural, then, that Father Mike and I would meet in New Orleans, hang out, enjoy a good meal, and see a bit of nightlife.

Father Mike was accompanied by ten young priests from Pittsburgh. The next thing I knew, I had reserved a private room at Antoine's, the famous French-Creole restaurant established in the mid-nineteenth Century. The priests had a grand old time. As they marched through the main dining room they burst out singing the Battle Hymn of the Republic: "Mine eyes have seen the coming of the Glory of the Lord . . ." It was a fascinating evening for me; I was the only non-Catholic (indeed, the only noncleric) at the table. My dinner companions—many of whom had just been ordained—eagerly bombarded me with questions. I felt like a bishop holding a meeting of his young charges. They were concerned with the public image of Catholic priests, especially among Jews. The friendship and respect they showed me was overwhelming.

After dinner, I suggested going to Preservation Hall. But one of the priests had heard of Pat O'Brien's, the nightclub next door. I had never wanted to go to this tourist spot, but I agreed to accompany them. The maître d' there informed us that the main room was full and we would have to wait to enter. In the meantime, I was approached by a black waiter who said, in a brusque manner: "You don't want to go in there. Come over here and sit in the court-yard; I'll serve you."

I figured this waiter was trying to drum up some business for himself. At any rate, we all needed a place to sit while waiting to get inside, so we entered the central courtyard and took a table. Most of the priests did partake of alcoholic beverages, and our interesting conversations continued. After being notified that there was room available in the club, I summoned the waiter for our check. I was surprised when he said, firmly: "There is no check for you."

No check? Perhaps he was a Catholic? I asked him why we weren't being charged.

"You can't buy a drink from me," he said. "I know you, but you don't know me."

"What do you mean, you know me?" I replied. "I've been in New Orleans only once before in my life, and that was two years ago."

"I know," he said. "I was the waiter at the Royal Orleans the day you met with the mayor and all those other bigwigs. What you said to them did more for integration in this city than any man who ever came down here. So you can't buy a drink from me. I want to buy you a drink."

I was suddenly transported. This waiter—supposedly deaf to the conversation at our table like a serf at the table of a sovereign—had not only heard every word, but also recognized me after two years. Certainly he had an inflated perception of my role in New Orleans's civil rights struggle. But my words had reached him without my ever knowing.

I spent the rest of the evening in a fog. The priests and I went to Preservation Hall, heard some music, and eventually said good-night. All I could think about was the encounter I'd just had; emotionally, it had wiped me out.

The civil rights bill was passed in May 1964, and the New Orleans Jazz Festival committee scheduled a press conference for late January. I was to appear in New Orleans for this historic announcement. I spent that fall booking artists for the festival, and making countless other arrangements.

Meanwhile, the newly desegregated City of New Orleans wasted no time in planning other events of national interest, in the hopes that the increase in tourism would boost a weak economy. Working with the National Football League, they scheduled an all-star game for Christmas Day. This was to be New Orleans's first fully integrated major sporting event.

About ten days before Christmas, the NFL all-stars (both black and white) descended upon New Orleans. But the league's many black players quickly realized that although the laws had changed, the city was not yet socially ready for integration. Famous athletes found themselves stranded on street corners, ignored by taxicabs, rejected for tables at restaurants. Overall, it was a thoroughly unpleasant experience for them, and they collectively decided that they could not play the game in New Orleans. It was canceled, and rescheduled for Phoenix.

As these events transpired, I was in Japan on the second of my drum-battle tours. Buddy Rich and Louis Bellson were playing a series of concerts with two Japanese drummers (after the arrest of Charlie Persip and Philly Joe Jones). I was planning on flying from Japan to New Orleans for the press conference; I had canceled a trip to Sydney, where my friend Kym Bonython wanted to discuss the possibility of an Australian tour for Thelonious Monk.

Just before Christmas, my hotel phone rang in the middle of the night. It was Joyce. She told me about the cancellation of the football game, and said I might as well go to Australia after all. The NFL imbroglio was an embarrassment to the City of New Orleans. City officials feared that, after losing a hefty sum of money over the aborted game, a similar situation might occur if African-American jazz musicians were ill-treated. This was probably an overreaction on the part of the city. Jazz musicians would not have come into town ten days before the gig. Furthermore, the artists needed the money more than professional football players. And the older jazz musicians, who had toured the South extensively under Jim Crow, were more accustomed to the racial prejudice of that society. But there was no discussion of these factors; in a heartbeat, the festival was canceled. I flew from Japan to Australia.

I didn't hear from New Orleans again for another four years. Nineteen sixty-eight was this city's bicentennial year and there was talk once again of mounting the first jazz festival. A foundation had been established for this purpose. I received a call from Durrell Black. Mr. Black told me about their situation; it was obvious, he said, that I would be the most appropriate person to serve as producer. We began to talk about preliminary arrangements. But soon after I had become involved, he apologized and told me not to come down. The mayor and his advisers had just learned that I was married to an African-American woman. The consensus was that it might be a political embarrassment for Mayor Schiro if I were given the job.

My response was low-key: "Fine. When you're ready to do business with me, give me a call." To my recollection, this was the only time in more than forty years that my relationship with Joyce adversely affected a business opportunity. The festival board in New Orleans, having decided that my appointment would be too controversial, offered the position of producer to Willis Conover, who accepted the job.

Willis and I had worked together in various capacities since the mid-1950s, when I nominated him as a member of the Newport Jazz Festival board. He had served as emcee on many Newport concerts, and his Voice of America broadcasts had carried the music and image of Newport across the globe.

I never really forgave Willis for taking the job. He was aware of the years I had spent trying to make a festival happen in the New Orleans. But in his heart, Willis wanted to be a producer, and he jumped at this chance. So Jazz-Fest, the given name of the 1968 New Orleans festival, took its first steps in 1968 as a Willis Conover production. It was moderately successful. In a review of the event in *Down Beat,* I read that the festival committee granted Conover a ten-year contract. This obviously obliterated any future I might have had as a festival producer in Louisiana.

Life went on. Nineteen sixty-nine found me struggling in vain to reconcile jazz and rock. In New Orleans, the festival went on again without me, and was somewhat less successful than it had been the previous year. Unbeknownst to me, problems were brewing among the festival organizers; Conover, with his Washington, D.C., background, had mounted an internal campaign to wrest control of the board from President Durrell Black. This was a mistake, since Black was the man who had raised the money necessary to finance the festival.

And late in 1969, it was Black who approached me during a set break in Economy Hall in the Royal Sonesta Hotel, where I was playing with the Newport All-Stars, and offered me a contract as producer of Jazz Fest.

I was puzzled. " Durrell, how can you do that? I read that you gave Willis Conover a ten-year contract." Mr. Black assured me that this would not be a problem. They would dissolve the present foundation and set up a new one. I blinked at such an easy solution to what I had perceived as an unsolvable problem.

Then I added: "You know, I'm still married to Joyce—and if I come down here, she will be with me."

"It's all right now," he said. "I've checked with the mayor, the Chamber of Commerce, and the Board of Trade. They all said it's not a problem." I suppose I should have been flattered that so many legislative officials were interested in the details of my marriage.

I accepted Durrell Black's offer, marveling at the thought that after almost a decade of stalled initiatives, I would finally be producing a jazz festival in New Orleans with my wife at my side. This realization lent an exuberant feeling to the remainder of my Economy Hall engagement. We'd finish playing at 2 A.M. and hang out afterward at bars or restaurants, often until sunrise. One of our favorite hangouts was a bar with a Ping-Pong table; I frequently found myself batting a little white ball across a net with other musicians, bar waitresses, or other assorted characters.

One night after work, one of the waitresses in the place, a lovely, light-skinned Creole girl, invited me to hear some jazz in a nightclub in Mason's Hotel on the other side of town. We took a taxi to the hotel and entered the club, which was packed. The entire clientele was black; I was the only white person. As we walked in the door, a guy approached me with fists clenched.

"Who do you think you are," he snarled, "coming in here with a black girl?" This guy was "calling me," with an animosity I had never encountered. He was ready to fight.

Without even thinking, I said, "Man, I'm not interested in that shit. Let's have a drink."

The next thing we knew, I was at the bar sharing a couple of drinks with my newfound friend. There was a piano, and I sat in with the band. After I had finished playing, my new friend came up to me and said: "Man, I didn't know you were a musician. I really didn't care that you were in here with a black chick, but baby, she's a fox!"

Joyce came to New Orleans for Christmas, and we met with Durrell Black. A contract was drawn up, and we celebrated the foundation of a new festival—to which I bestowed a cumbersome title, "The New Orleans Jazz Festival and Louisiana Heritage Fair." We scheduled this event for the last week of April and first week of May 1970. It truly was a Merry Christmas.

In the eight years since my first trip to New Orleans, the world had changed. With the passing of the Civil Rights Bill of 1964, the South had opened up, and there was a desire on the part of Southern cultural establishments to join the mainstream of American art and entertainment. Just as significant were the developments in musical presentation provoked by a nationwide youth rebellion. After Woodstock, it had become clear to me that young people would no longer sit in reserved seats at an outdoor concert event. They wanted the freedom to move around and be part of what was happening. I had seen this firsthand at the Newport Folk Festival, during the afternoon workshops.

My first job, then, was to convince the board of directors in New Orleans that the Newport Jazz Festival model was no longer valid. We needed a different approach to presentation and format. The festival that I envisioned for the city where jazz was born had to be unique; it had to reflect the entire spectrum of Louisiana's musical heritage. I wanted to use New Orleans and Louisiana artists exclusively, to showcase this wealth of local culture. And tickets had to be inexpensive, so that people from every economic level of New Orleans life could attend.

Before I could continue, I had to build a team. The board of directors of the New Orleans Jazz and Heritage Foundation had little or no relationship to music, with the exception of early-jazz enthusiast Harry Souchon. I assembled a board of advisers, consisting of archivist Richard Allen, musicologist William Russell, art dealer Larry Bornstein, Preservation Hall guardian Allan Jaffe, and pianist Ellis Marsalis. This was as fine an advisory board as could be assembled; each member brought his own expertise to the table.

The late William Russell understood the intricacies of the New Orleans music world better than anyone; he was the Pete Seeger of Louisiana. He was also, incidentally, an erstwhile contemporary classical composer and violinist (and former pupil of John Cage).

Allan Jaffe was an invaluable adviser, as well as a good friend. There was an affinity between Allan and me, as he was a Jewish kid from Pennsylvania who had come to New Orleans in 1960 because of his love for the music—and I was a Jewish kid from Boston who was coming to New Orleans ten years later for the same reason. I quickly recognized that he was an organizer, a natural publicist, a good businessman, an artist, and a musician. Over the years, Joyce and I grew close to him and his wife, Sandy. Through Allan, I got to know the veteran Preservation Hall artists: among them, the legendary Jim Robinson, Kid Thomas, Billie and Dede Pierce, and Cie Frazier.

Allan's polar opposite in temperament was his close friend and supporter Larry Bornstein, another of our advisers. Larry was a confirmed iconoclast, and not necessarily easy to get along with. But it was his art gallery on St. Peter Street that later became Preservation Hall in the 1950s, and he was an important figure in the revival of New Orleans music. In addition, he was a central personality in the local art community. He made me aware of the folk art of Sister Gertrude Morgan and the brilliant, explosive Noel Rockmore.

Ellis Marsalis, was a guide to the contemporary scene; he showed me the paths that the younger New Orleans musicians were pursuing. This was a full decade before he would become famous as a jazz patriarch; for now, he was simply the best pianist in New Orleans.

As for Richard Allen, he was a committed historian who curated the jazz archives at Tulane University; his knowledge of New Orleans music was vast. It was Dick who introduced me to a kid who was working at the William Ransom Hogan Jazz Archives on a part-time basis; jazz was not this kid's forté, but he was deep into the New Orleans blues, funk, and folk scenes. This young man's name was Quint Davis, and he became instrumental in the festival's operations. We also came to depend on Quint's girlfriend Allison Miner, whose dedication to New Orleans music matched his. Both Quint and Allison also became members of the advisory board.

Each of my many advisers took me to his or her favorite restaurant. The results varied: everything from Antoine's in the French Quarter to Buster Holmes's soul food restaurant on the corner of Orleans and Burgundy Streets. With all these culinary adventures and my various musical discoveries, I was having a fabulous time; preparing for a festival had never been this much fun. I probably spent a total of six weeks in New Orleans that spring, spread out over three or four different trips. Fortunately the Royal Sonesta Hotel gave me a free room whenever I came down, so the expense wasn't too much to bear.

Festival time came quickly. We kicked off the Jazz and Heritage Festival on Wednesday, April 22, with a Mississippi River cruise on the steamer *S.S. President*, with the legendary New Orleans clarinetist Pete Fountain. The following day, we started at noon with a street parade by the Eureka Brass Band.

After the parade, Harry Souchon hosted a program called "New Orleans Potpourri" featuring such fine "white jazz" players as pianist Armand Hug, bassist Sherwood Mangiapane, and my favorite New Orleans clarinetist Raymond Burke, whose playing style and personal demeanor both reminded me of Pee Wee Russell. Later that afternoon Dick Allen hosted a separate concert called "The Musical World of French Louisiana," featuring such artists as Adam and Cyprien Landreneau, Clifton Chenier, and the Creole Jazz Band. Both of these concerts took place in the Municipal Auditorium, a large multi-purpose indoor facility that still serves as a sometime opera house and concert hall (and had been the site, in 1968 and '69, of Jazz Fest).

But the Heritage Fair, which I deemed every bit as important as the music, could only work outdoors. My simple solution was to hold the fair outside the Auditorium—at what was then known as Beauregard Square. There was no small amount of historic import to the area. During the nineteenth century it had been a gathering place for blacks, both slave and free; it had then been known as Congo Square.

Beauregard Square was not a large area, but we managed to erect four stages—one at each corner, and each one featuring a different style of New Orleans music (blues, cajun, gospel, and street). The artists who appeared on these stages personified New Orleans's stylistic gumbo: Snooks Eaglin, Roosevelt Sykes, the Mardi Gras Indians, the Olympia Brass Band, the Zion Harmonizers, and Reverend Johnny Youngblood, among dozens of others. Also in the square was a cover serving as a tabernacle, under which Sister Gertrude Morgan presided—telling stories, making drawings, and singing folk and gospel songs.

This being New Orleans, food played a crucial role in the festivities. More than twenty booths dotted the premises, serving everything from shrimp Creole and crawfish étouffée to raw oysters and crabmeat jambalaya. Buster Holmes was there serving his red beans and rice. We had Vaucresson's sausage po-boys. And there was even a booth serving my personal favorite: Begue's praline ice cream pie. We had a little bit of everything.

Everything, that is, except people. Despite considerable grassroots promotional effort, a cornucopia of talent, the unique character of the festival, and an admission charge of merely three dollars, attendance was shockingly sparse, with only about 300 people at the square. Joyce went across the street to an orphanage and came back with a gaggle of children in tow. Even with the extra mouths, we finished the day with mountains of unused food.

The New Orleans Police Department had sent a dozen plainclothes men to the fair, to mingle with the crowd and see that nothing went awry. But their "plain clothes" made them stick out like sore thumbs. At one point, Joyce walked up to one African-American gentleman in a green gabardine suit and asked him why there were so many police on hand. Surprised, he replied: "How did you know I was a policeman?" After explaining that it was all too obvious, Joyce talked with him about the festival. This officer, a Sergeant Francois, was so impressed by Joyce and the attitude of all of us affiliated with the festival that he became one of our closest allies. Over the years, the police department worked with festival producers to ensure that there were no problems. The same holds true today.

The first nighttime concert at the Municipal Auditorium featured the Young Tuxedo Brass Band, the Pete Fountain Orchestra, Sharky Bonano and his Kings of Dixieland, Papa Albert French and the Original Tuxedo Jazz Band, and the original Dukes of Dixieland with Frank Assunto. Other evening concerts included a performance by the "New Orleans Modern Jazz All Stars" (Ellis Marsalis, Earl Turbington, Johnny Vidocovitch, and several others); the Onward Brass Band; saxophonist Al Belletto; the Al Hirt Orchestra; the Meters; and many others. In addition, we presented Mahalia Jackson—who had been born in New Orleans. And Saturday night saw the official premiere of the Duke Ellington Orchestra's *New Orleans Suite*, which I had commissioned. Duke was the only artist on the festival without personal ties to New Orleans; I figured that the contribution of a new extended work would more than compensate for this fact.

The following afternoon, Duke Ellington made a second appearance at the Municipal Auditorium, this time for a concert of sacred music. It was a fitting close to my first New Orleans Jazz and Heritage Festival, which had been an unqualified artistic success.

Financially, however, the New Orleans Jazz and Heritage Foundation was in sad shape; it lost over $40,000, a far greater sum than anyone could have anticipated. Durrell Black came to me and said: "George, let's not do the fair next year. I think we should just present some evening concerts."

"If that's the case," I replied, "then you don't need me." The prospect of just having a few concerts at the Municipal Auditorium did not interest me. I had no idea what the future held with regard to the Heritage Fair, but I did know that a Newport Jazz Festival–style event would not make it in the South. There were a lot of jazz festivals around the country by this time; in 1970, Newport was already in decline. I knew that I couldn't just bring jazz names to New Orleans and expect people to come. The rock generation was now in full bloom, and unless the event had some appeal to American youth, it was destined for failure.

But I never pushed this message with any board members; I was not about to launch either a campaign or a crusade. Instead we had one meeting, at which I outlined my conviction that the future of a New Orleans festival relied upon the promotion of New Orleans and Louisiana culture. Name artists would come and go, but the core of the festival had to be the culture itself.

I don't know why, but the board voted against Durrell Black's proposal for change, and in favor of continuing with my concept of production. Perhaps, being businessmen, they knew that success and innovation were often intertwined. In any case, Black accepted their decision and agreed to raise money for the 1971 Jazz and Heritage Festival. After that, he said, he would resign. So Mr. Black's involvement with the foundation was brief, but hugely significant; without him, there would not have been a New Orleans Jazz and Heritage Festival.

\*     \*     \*

As 1970 marched forward into 1971, I continued to immerse myself in the culture of New Orleans. That winter, I even trekked down for my first Mardi Gras, alone. Although I knew many people in the city by this time, I felt I could never capture the unadulterated flavor of Fat Tuesday unless I wandered the streets by myself and observed firsthand what was happening. I made my way onto Bourbon Street, and was quickly swept up in the crowds—a frightening experience. In that mass of people, I felt engulfed, with no control of my movement; the crowd was a huge organism with a life and a motion all its own. I escaped this situation as fast as I could, heading for Rampart Street, where there was a typical Mardi Gras parade underway.

I don't know what had developed before I arrived, but I surmised what must have happened. There was a young, good-looking black kid—no more than sixteen or seventeen—who weighed approximately 130 pounds. He had come early to the parade to claim a coveted curbside space; the crowd behind him was four or five people deep. Among them was a white guy who had asked the kid to let his wife and baby take his place in front. Apparently, the kid had replied: "Yes, but give me a few minutes." He had arrived early, and wanted to see the parade. This must have irked the white guy, and soon some strong words passed between them. I arrived in time to hear the kid say "I told you I would move. I just asked you to wait a few minutes." The guy swore at him, saying he should let the wife and baby up front.

The white guy was twice the size of this kid, and they were now getting ready to fight. I overheard the words: "I'm not going to take any shit from no white man." From behind, I could just see the white guy's flushed neck tensing up, like a cat preparing to pounce. It was by no means an even match; the guy outweighed the kid by nearly seventy pounds.

There were some older black ladies standing around. They started saying things like "Son, don't get yourself messed up," and "Don't ruin your whole life." The kid was paying them no heed.

I didn't want to see this fight break out. I went up to the kid and put my arm around his shoulder—a dangerous act, since he might have been inclined to swing at me. I whispered something in his ear: "Man, this guy is a mother-fucker. He's not worth it."

The kid turned around, looked at me, and split. That was it; I had spoken to him in a language he understood. I backed away from the crowd, walked across the street, and started crying like a baby. There was a drama to the scene that affected me on a personal level. It was as if the entire tableau of racist America was included in that one scene.

That was my only Mardi Gras. But I spent many more weeks in New Orleans that spring, in preparation for the second Jazz and Heritage Festival. One day I was hanging out with Quint Davis, Allison Miner, and Dick Allen in a little bar on Magazine Street. The jukebox was playing a swinging rhythm and blues record I had never heard before: "Go to the Mardi Gras." Quint told me this was Roy "Professor Longhair" Byrd, one of the founding fathers of New Orleans R&B.

I asked: "Is he still alive?"

"Yeah, he's still around."

"Does he still play?"

"Yes."

"Where does he live?"

"Right around here."

I shook my head. "Don't you guys realize that this is what our festival is all about? Let's find Professor Longhair and bring him back!"

Quint and Allison did just that—they found Fess, and we presented him on that year's festival. Professor Longhair was such a big hit at the fair that his long-lost career took off. Atlantic Records reissued an anthology of his early sides, and he recorded a number of new albums in the last decade of his life before finally passing away in 1980. Allison Miner looked after him like he was her father, and at one point served as his manager as well.

Professor Longhair aside, the 1971 Louisiana Heritage Fair was a near-facsimile of the year before: It spanned three days at Beauregard Square, which we now referred to by its original name, Congo Square, and featured a slew of New Orleans artists and tables of local cuisine. In addition to the brass bands and other assorted artists that had appeared in 1970, the fair this year included Louisiana bluesman Robert Pete Williams, cajun fiddler Allen Fontenot, and jazz saxophonist James Rivers. To our relief, there were a few more people on hand this time—in fact, it seemed that we were already outgrowing Congo Square.

We divided the evening concerts between several venues. In the Main Ballroom of the Roosevelt Hotel, we presented the Original Young Tuxedo Jazz Band led by Papa French along with pianist Armand Hug, Punch Miller's New Orleans Jazz Band, and a number of other artists—including Bobby Hackett, the program's sole Yankee. The following night, Dizzy Gillespie appeared at the Jung Hotel on a concert that also featured Al Belletto, Kid Thomas and the Preservation Hall Jazz Band, and the New Orleans Ragtime Orchestra. Our pièce de résistance was a tribute to Louis Armstrong at the Municipal Auditorium.

This concert was noteworthy for a number of reasons—not the least of which was the long-awaited New Orleans homecoming of trombonist Edward "Kid" Ory. I had hoped to reunite Ory with Louis, but Pops was too ill at this point to preside over the concert. Nevertheless, we staged a warm tribute, with musical contributions from such local favorites as the Dukes of Dixieland, Sharkey and His Kings of Dixieland, and the New Orleans Trumpet Choir. The concert also featured several out-of-towners: Gillespie, Hackett, and the Galvanized Jazz Band, a New Haven–based traditional jazz unit featuring the clarinet playing of Woody Allen. Woody was a surprise guest, not listed on the program. His love for New Orleans jazz was not yet common knowledge.

Later, at the Heritage Fair, I asked him if he would come to the festival the following year and let us advertise him. He asked me why. I explained that since he was a national personality, his name would help to focus attention on the festival; these were our formative years, and we needed the publicity. I was sorry when he politely turned us down.

The second New Orleans Jazz and Heritage Festival ran a deficit, but nothing as disastrous as the previous year. There was some indication that the food, crafts, and music were beginning to catch the fancy of New Orleans. But what were we to do now that Durrell Black had tendered his resignation? Who would raise the money for subsequent festivals?

My answer came to me one afternoon at the fair. I was approached by a gentleman in black-rimmed glasses who said that he was indebted to me. When I asked him why, he said: "I'm Arthur Davis. You seem to have given my son Quint a direction in life."

I had learned by this time that Arthur Davis was one of America's leading architects. Now here he was, declaring himself indebted to me. With my usual reserve of boldness I told him that I would have to draw upon that debt. Durrell Black was resigning, I explained, and I needed new people on the board of directors. Arthur Davis agreed to this plan. He would be instrumental in keeping the Heritage Festival alive.

After its sophomore season, the New Orleans Jazz and Heritage Festival seemed to have found some solid ground. Meanwhile, things were going well for Dino Santangelo and me in the Midwest. And the festivals in Newport had become institutions unto themselves. I was busier than ever, and happier. What could possibly go wrong?

\*     \*     \*

That fall and winter, I spent many weeks in New Orleans putting together the 1972 Jazz and Heritage Festival. The previous year's festival had been a major step up; Quint's father Arthur Davis had accepted membership on the board of directors, becoming its president. We had held the event on the infield of the Fair Grounds Race Track—the third-oldest racetrack in the country (in operation since 1872). George Rhode, a member of our board of directors, was the venue's catering manager; with his help, we worked out a leasing arrangement with Louis Roussel, the Fair Grounds's owner (and, later, owner of a Kentucky Derby winner).

The Fair Grounds infield was a better site than Congo Square in terms of area. In 1972 we had erected five separate stages: Soul, Gospel, Jazz, Country/Cajun, and Blues. The Jazz stage showcased both traditional and modern styles. The Country/Cajun stage, true to its dual moniker, featured not only Louisiana artists like Allen Fontenot and the Country Cajuns, and the Mamou Cajun Band, but also the bluegrass Meyers Brothers. On the blues stage, it was Roosevelt Sykes, Robert Pete Williams, and Clifton Chenier—who had all appeared at the Newport Folk Festival—among others. And the Gospel stage, organized by Zion Harmonizers' leader Sherman Washington, featured the Harmonizers as well as Sister Gertrude Morgan, the New Orleans Spiritualettes, the Ott Family, and a number of others.

The evening concerts, meanwhile, had assumed a more national profile. We had presented a "Night of Stars" concert at the Municipal Auditorium featuring Nina Simone, the Giants of Jazz, Jimmy Smith, Kenny Burrell, the Young Tuxedo Brass Band, the Mardi Gras Indians, and—in the first of many festival appearances—B. B. King.

Kid Ory came back to New Orleans in 1971; in 1972, it was Barney Bigard, the celebrated clarinetist formerly with Duke Ellington, who came "home." Barney, who had thought he would never return to New Orleans, had been happy about the way he was treated at the festival. He had appeared on a concert called "Jazz at the Ballroom" at the Jung Hotel, along with Wild Bill Davison, the Louis Cottrell New Orleans Jazz Band, and "Sweet" Emma Barrett. I had asked each group to dedicate a song to Joseph "Sharkey" Bonano, the New Orleans trumpeter who had died just one month prior to the festival. Murphy Campo, a fellow Italian trumpeter from New Orleans, had saluted his friend with a rousing rendition of "When the Saints Go Marching In." In the audience, Sharkey's widow applauded. Later, trumpeter Percy Humphrey and the Preservation Hall Jazz Band took over, and Narvin Kimball sang "What a Friend We Have in Jesus." It was beautiful; pure New Orleans. At the song's end, Mrs. Bonano, who was sitting at a table in front of the bandstand, collapsed with grief. Everyone was moved; Percy and Narvin understood what it meant to reach out and give solace to someone who had lost a loved one.

An interesting sidelight to the 1972 Jazz Fest was the fact that politicians had begun to pay attention to what was happening. Louisiana governor-elect Edwin Edwards gave a welcoming speech on Friday, while New Orleans's mayor at the time, Moon Landrieu, addressed a Sunday afternoon crowd. Former governor Jimmie Davis, who wrote the song "You Are My Sunshine," sang it at the fair on Saturday. When politicians want to be seen at your event, then you know that you've arrived.

The festival, however, was still not in the black, but losses were manageable, and it was clear that we had a future. In fact, the event had grown so quickly that it was now necessary to maintain a quality staff on a full-time basis. To support this expense, I asked Arthur Davis to sign a note at the bank for $30,000. He agreed to do this, as long as I cosigned. I had no money; the only thing I could stand to lose was my reputation. But Arthur knew how important this was to me. I signed. This was not the only financial help Mr. Davis offered in 1972. He had also agreed to cosign a bank loan for $50,000, in order to support the inaugural Newport Jazz Festival–New York. It was the most significant source of funding for this gargantuan event, and it was instrumental in our success.

The New York festival was so consuming that I was happy to delegate much of the New Orleans work to Quint Davis and Allison Miner; they were recognized respectively as director and executive secretary of the festival, and shared credit as musical directors of the Heritage Fair. I was still producer of the event; Dino Santangelo, my Cincinnati partner in the Ohio Valley Jazz Festival, was assistant producer.

The 1973 Heritage Fair was bigger and better than in previous years, and still featured New Orleans talent almost exclusively: local heroes like Professor Longhair, Papa French, Allen Toussaint, Robert Pete Williams, and the Meters. The Mississippi River boat cruise, once again featuring Pete Fountain, seasoned the festivities with an unmistakable New Orleans flavor. Evening concerts at the Municipal Auditorium, meanwhile, were beginning to reflect the influence of Festival Productions' two other big festivals—in Cincinnati and New York City.

"The Soul of Jazz," which took place on a Friday the 13th, could easily have been an Ohio Valley Festival program. The Staple Singers and B. B. King appeared on the concert; so did Dave Brubeck, Gerry Mulligan, and Joe Newman. "Night of Stars," the following evening, followed a similar tack: Stevie Wonder and Kim Weston were the soul headliners on a bill that also featured Herbie Mann, David "Fathead" Newman, Rahsaan Roland Kirk, Ramsey Lewis, and the Olympia Brass Band. This evening was notable mostly for the surprise presence of Ella Fitzgerald, who was appearing across town at the Fairmont Hotel. Ella joined Stevie Wonder onstage, and the two performed a showstopping duet.

"Blues and Roots," meanwhile, featured legends Taj Mahal, Howlin' Wolf, and Albert King, along with the Como Mississippi Fife & Drum Corps and the Mardi Gras Indians. That evening, during Albert King's set, he spotted me in the wings and called me out to jam on Hammond organ. I had never played this instrument before; I ignored the pedals and used it as a keyboard. The next day, on the Fair Grounds and up and down Bourbon Street, kids approached me with wonderment in their eyes and said: "Man, you played with Albert King last night! You were great!" I gratefully accepted their praise, but made no plans to abandon jazz piano for blues organ.

The "purest" jazz concert of the series was an opening-night "Salute to the King of Swing," featuring the Benny Goodman Sextet and the Preservation Hall Jazz Band. This program would have fit right in at Carnegie Hall, and in fact we did present Benny on the New York Festival that summer. We were happy to present him in New Orleans.

In New Orleans, there were ongoing festival preparations; the 1974 Jazz Fest was to feature such artists as Gladys Knight, Herbie Hancock, and Stanley Turrentine, along with the usual staple of New Orleans greats. We had long wondered why the festival had such a dismal lack of support from the local media in general and the New Orleans *Times-Picayune,* in particular. Larry Bornstein volunteered to help in this regard. As an art dealer, Larry had acquired many works of pre-Columbian art from Mexico and Central America. We never asked him how these works came into his possession; he seemed to have a continual source of supply. Through this activity Larry Bornstein knew pre-Columbian art collector Si Newhouse, Sr., the newspaper tycoon who owned the *Times-Picayune.* Larry spoke with Mr. Newhouse, and they arranged a meeting in New Orleans between me and the paper's publisher, Ashton Phelps.

I told Mr. Phelps about our growing festival, and wondered aloud why we weren't receiving more support from the paper. I explained that New Orleans had international heroes walking the street everyday, men and women who were glorified in Europe and Japan—and the *Times-Picayune* only acknowledged them in obituaries. Mr. Phelps heard what I said, and the response was immediate. Thus began a new era in coverage; that year the paper printed interviews, feature articles, diagrams of the field, directions to the Fair Grounds and reviews. This overdue media attention was a boon to the festival. The *Times-Picayune,* now published by Ashton Phelps, Jr., still supports Jazz Fest in this fashion. The press had adopted the name "Jazz Fest" from the 1969 festival and applied it to the more cumbersome "Jazz and Heritage" title.

\*   \*   \*

The New Orleans Jazz and Heritage Festival became an unstoppable force. Sometime around 1975 or 1976 I told Arthur Davis that we had turned a corner financially, and the time was right, if we so desired, to convert the non-profit New Orleans Jazz and Heritage Foundation into a private business. He, Quint, and I stood to make some money from this decision. Because we were financing the festival, the board would not be a problem. I also knew that we were the type of people who had our own ideals. If we made money, it was understood that we would put much of it back into the community.

But as we discussed the matter, our festival staff—who were so devoted to the festival and had earned so little compensation—pleaded with us to keep Jazz Fest nonprofit. We went along with their pleas. It was probably the biggest financial mistake I ever made. At the same time, this decision created the beginning of an experience that became an interesting part of my life.

The board of directors of the Jazz and Heritage Festival has grown since 1977. It now represents many segments of the community. Prior to this, a judge, Gerald Federoff, was president. Edgar "Dooky" Chase, owner of the most popular soul-food restaurant in the city, was vice president. There were more than thirty members on the board, including Johnny Jackson, Jr., an African-American member of the New Orleans City Council. But the board was predominately white. Quint, myself, and the various producers were dedicated to New Orleans music. We were proud of what we were doing; our audience was integrated, to a large degree. Pete Seeger came down and was amazed to see, in his time, such an open event happening in the Deep South. We knew we were doing something important.

But during the 1977 Jazz Fest, as I drove through traffic on Esplanade Avenue en route to the festival grounds, something happened to raise a few doubts. Parading in an adjoining field was the cutest group of youngsters, ranging in age from eight to eleven years old, dressed in green Mardi Gras costumes with brimmed hats and white sashes slung diagonally from shoulder to waist. Reaching the festival grounds, I went to Quint and asked him why those kids were not part of the fair; they certainly reflected a colorful part of New Orleans folk culture. I learned that these young black children were organized by a man named Jerome Smith. He would not allow them to be a part of Jazz Fest. He felt we were ripping off black culture, that the African-American community was not sharing in our success. I told Quint that we had to do something about this. I wasn't aware that there were movements in motion already; we wouldn't have to do anything, as things were being done without our help.

Jerome Smith was, and is, a community activist—a street-fighter—whom I have come to know and respect. He was a friend of Jimmy Baldwin's. He was telling us something that was to affect the future of the festival in a way never before seen in any American city. Until then, I had thought that I knew something about the guts of New Orleans. I soon found out that I knew very little. The surge of publicity in the newspaper, and the fact that so many African Americans were part of the festival in the Gospel tent, food booths, and countless other aspects, had finally drawn the attention of prominent figures in the black community, who were more politically and socially involved in its problems. A community committee had been formed, and its members demanded a meeting with the Jazz Fest board—in the Saint Bernard housing project, deep in the bowels of New Orleans's black ghetto. Our board asked me to attend this meeting.

A cloud of violent energy hung in the air as I entered a small cement-block room. Thirty or forty African Americans, mostly male, were standing about. Seated at a table was a burly guy in a dashiki; he was obviously the spokesman. I don't recall knowing anybody in the room, but that might not be the case. And I don't remember who else was with me representing the Jazz and Heritage Festival. After a few forced greetings, the conversation started in earnest.

The man in the dashiki spoke: "We're going to force you to take more blacks onto the board of directors. You have been ripping off black culture. The community is not benefiting nearly enough by what's happening."

Simply, I replied: "You can't force us to do what we want to do in the first place."

The man didn't hear what I was saying. He repeated himself, more forcefully: "We're going to force you to make us part of the festival. We want more control over what happens."

"I don't think you heard me. You can't force us to do what we want to do in the first place."

This conversation went on in similar fashion for a few more minutes before the group understood that I was extending an open invitation. I learned that this man in the dashiki was Kalamu ya Salaam, a writer and newspaperman. Kalamu, whose impassioned views were well matched with a levelheaded intellect, would later accept a nomination as executive director of the Jazz and Heritage Foundation.

This group in the concrete room represented people who have since become my closest friends in New Orleans and taught me more, in a few years, than a person could otherwise learn in a lifetime. Bill Rouselle, Tom Dent, Emilo "Monk" Dupree, and Reverend Herman Brown became members of our board of directors in 1978. Rouselle and Dupree each served a two-year term as president. Tom Dent followed Kalamu as executive director.

Sadly, Tom Dent passed away in 1998. He was a friend whose loss leaves a void in your life. I still look for him every time I'm in New Orleans. His father had been the president of Dillard University. Tom was a writer, whose last book was an oral history of the civil rights movement in the South.

Bill Rouselle and Monk Dupree and some others, who eventually became part of our board, had been strong fighters for civil rights. When Jimmy Baldwin died, Tom Dent asked me to speak at the memorial service at Dillard. The other speakers were all African Americans who knew Baldwin when he came to

New Orleans prior to 1964. Lolis Elie, Sr., Jerome Smith, Rudy Lombard, and a young woman named Susan Smock (an artist who had done a woodcut of Jimmy that I am happy to possess), Tom Dent, and I were the speakers. I was very moved that I was asked to be part of the evening that meant so much to these dedicated friends.

Joyce and I were quite close to Jimmy Baldwin. He had a home in St. Paul de Vence, and we had a house in nearby Vence. We saw a lot of Jimmy and shared many good times. There are few people who are unforgettable. Jimmy Baldwin, like Duke Ellington, was just that.

\*     \*     \*

The new faces on our board of directors joined with Arthur Pulitzer, Sarah Meltzer, and roughly twenty-five others who had been regular members for several years. This signaled a transition in the board. Previously, our governing body had been friends of Arthur Davis or Durrell Black. They had little interest in running the festival; Quint and I were never questioned. That era, we soon learned, was over. The activists on the board were making their presence felt. The largesse that Quint and I had always enjoyed in producing the festival was now challenged. The new board members accused me of being a dictator. I never thought of myself in that way, but I suppose there was an element of truth in the allegation since I ran the show. At any rate, it was back to square one; once again, we were writing the book as we went along.

Interestingly, many of the white board members joined in the militant energy on the board. Those that did not, resigned. The board members who had never worked closely in any organization with blacks showed sympathy, support, and, in some cases, a patronizing tone. Soon the board had a black majority.

This was an adventure that I welcomed, but at times it was a stressful situation for Quint and our New Orleans staff. The board was attempting to exert its influence on the festival itself. Most of the demands put upon us were reasonable and important, and it was necessary to put them into effect as soon as possible. Quint's staff, for example, was mostly white. They were people he had known as members of the musical community of New Orleans. The few blacks on staff, like Dodie Simmons, were not part of the new activist movement. That began to change. Quint, who is a perfectionist, did not fight this—but he found it difficult to incorporate new people into his daily work.

It took some time, but now Quint Davis's personal staff is predominately black. E. J. Encalarde is his right hand, invaluable to him. Karlton Kirksey, the festival's financial manager, learned from my longtime accountant Arnold London. Louis Edwards is our chief of public relations. Charlie Bering was a producer of the jazz tent; after his death, the task fell to Gregory Davis, creator of the Dirty Dozen Brass Band. Badi Murphy produces our workshops. The entire Festival Productions, Inc.–New Orleans office is integrated. But it didn't happen overnight. Quint's concern for excellence in production, in the handling of transportation, in the coordination of food booths, in stage managing, and in income generated by souvenir sales made it difficult for him to make immediate changes. Our staff had become quite expert at the minute details of running the festival. I was urging Quint to move as quickly as possible. But he had fears I did not have. In his nightmares, which were quite real in his mind, he could see the board attempting to replace him. To reassure him, I continually repeated a phrase: "Stop worrying; I'll tell you when it's time to really worry." Quint was young; he hadn't had the experience of working with volatile characters like Miles Davis, Charles Mingus, and the rest. Nor had he experienced the pressures of dealing with nonprofit boards like the Newport Jazz Festival and the Newport Folk Foundation. I had learned what it was to have my personal integrity ambushed, my honesty questioned, and my motivations examined. I knew that I had to gain the trust of this new element on the New Orleans board that had every reason to perceive me as a white (Jewish) promoter from New York looking to milk their city for a buck.

I have earned their trust. In 1991, Louis Edwards published his second critically acclaimed novel, N. In my copy, he penned an inscription that packs an emotional wallop whenever I read it. He wrote: "To George T. Wein, a . . . man whose work in music is widely known but whose contribution to race relations has the subtlety and importance of a great work of art."

From some members of the board, there were intimations of racism toward Quint and me. It got to the point where someone actually suggested that I only brought Joyce to New Orleans as a shield for my prejudice. This reminded me of the 1950s, when Nat Hentoff and Alan Morrison of Ebony flayed Louis Lorillard and me in print for our decision to keep the festival in Newport. Using an old debating trick, they had written something to this effect: "We do not mean to imply that George Wein is racist, but . . ." The atmosphere grew toxic.

The mounting tensions so upset Quint that in 1982 he disappeared, without leaving notice of his whereabouts. We heard at one point that he was in a motel in Memphis; then somewhere in Florida. No one spoke with him for many months. He was trying to escape. He couldn't take the constant badgering of a board that had not yet learned to allow us to do our job. It was an enormous credit to Quint's organizational abilities that when he left, his associate producers under my direction, Dodie Simmons, Joanne Schmidt, Nancy Ochsenschlager, Anna Zimmerman, and Charlie Bering, and staff were able to put on the festival without a hitch. It was a credit to his character that when he returned after a year's absence, they all welcomed him back as their leader.

The entire board was dedicated to the message of the festival, which was the preservation of New Orleans music and culture, and that its own motivations were not to be questioned. Certainly the majority of the board shared a commitment that I greatly admired. This was perhaps best exemplified in 1982, when I told them that the cigarette company Brown & Williamson (which produced KOOL cigarettes) had offered us a contract for a million dollars for name sponsorship of the festival. I felt that Brown & Williamson's offer—nearly enough money to underwrite the entire festival—was too good to refuse. With that kind of financial security, we could ensure the festival's future. The Jazz and Heritage Foundation, however, had serious objections. Given KOOL's brand-name clout in the African-American community, some of our black board members felt that it would be exploitative to transform Jazz Fest into a KOOL New Orleans Jazz Festival. They turned down the offer. I might not have made this decision, but it perfectly illustrates the board's direction. My respect for our governing body escalated in the wake of that decision.

But the board was not without its faults or problems, and we had an argument over another sponsor that nearly prompted my resignation. I had a long-standing relationship with Schlitz through Ben Barkin, and the beer company had become one of our New Orleans sponsors; they gave us money in exchange for primary vendor's rights at the Fair Grounds. It was a good arrangement. But one of our board members owned his own beer company locally, and he began lobbying other members to change the contract in his favor. His argument—that Jazz Fest would do better to support a New Orleans–based company—was mitigated by self-serving motivations. Add to this the fact that my relationship with Schlitz had preceded Jazz Fest by many years—and the even more salient fact that Schlitz was economically stable (whereas the local company was far from it). It would be far too easy in a city as small as New Orleans for people involved with the festival to corrupt its operation by giving contracts to unqualified individuals. So I was against this movement; it was good-ol'-boy cronyism, plain and simple. But I could feel the board going his way. Things finally came to a head, so to speak, during an evening board meeting. The vote was obviously going to go in the local brewer's favor. Never one to hold my objections in reserve, I told the board that I would rather resign than see the decision approved. And with that, I walked out of the meeting. Then-President Bill Rouselle tabled the decision that night, giving the board time to realize what a mistake it was about to make. The local brewer went out of business soon afterward, proving my point. I was saved from resigning and I think the board learned a lesson.

Of course, many other conflicts did occur over the years, most of them insignificant in the long run. We had skirmishes with vendors, arguments with artists, infighting among board members. As an outsider with an acknowledged track record, I was ideally suited to serve as mediator—between different factions in the foundation, or between the board and Quint's staff. And my outsider status actually served as a plus, since I was not a part of New Orleans's southern white establishment. As a result, despite the foundation's many conflicts with FPI–New Orleans, my own personal integrity was hardly called into question. It was obvious to everyone involved that I was committed to Jazz Fest. My original vision had been achieved, and the new constitution of the board had ideas of its own. The job Quint and I had was to put on a festival and raise money for the board; the job of the board was to spend the money. (They have never realized that the function of a board is to raise money in addition to spending it.)

My concern now is that the board has not yet learned to make its money grow by applying for grants from major foundations. I think they believe that the money tree of Jazz Fest will never wither and die. I know differently, as I have lived through successful festivals that no longer exist. I also disagreed with the board's decision, made several years ago, to grant themselves automatic lifetime membership. Any organization needs turnover every year, allowing for an infusion of new blood. I believe there are many influential individuals in New Orleans who could, and would like to, contribute to the work the foundation does. I would like to see them as part of our family.

Quint no longer fears for his job. I think the element of trust that is so necessary among people of different races and backgrounds working together has been established. The board reflects a wide range of professions: we have the chief of the fire department, judges, businessmen from the Hispanic community, professors and administrators from local colleges, and employees of the city.

As for Jazz Fest, it has evolved into the largest, and perhaps most significant, outdoor festival of music and culture in the world. Every spring it brings a massive influx of people to New Orleans, almost all of them more interested in the music than in Mardi Gras–style debauchery. At the festival they get more of it (the music, that is) than they could possibly hope to absorb. With ten separate stages, we can simultaneously present traditional jazz, contemporary jazz, New Orleans funk, African music, Gospel, zydeco, blues, country, and pop. National artists appear alongside local legends and promising new faces. Food vendors, carefully chosen by the board (and dutifully taste-tested by my friends Elliot and Nancy Hoffman), offer a staggering variety of culinary choices. Quint's team literally erects a city on the Fair Grounds, a living organism capable of accommodating over 100,000 people at once. There may be an emphasis on pop (the festival would fold without it), but it never comes at the cost of genuine artistry. And I can say with confidence that no other festival in the world has a sharper, more focused, or more capable staff. Without it, Jazz Fest could never be possible.

New Orleans is a city of musical families. A wealth of young jazz musicians has emerged since the festival's inception in 1970. Terance Blanchard, Donald Harrison, and Nicholas Payton are just the tip of the iceberg.

Lionel Hampton appeared on Jazz Fest in 1979. We organized a big band for him with several local musicians. I was on piano. In the trumpet section sat a sixteen-year-old kid whose playing was little short of sensational. His father's name was Ellis Marsalis. It was my first encounter with his son Wynton. It was later that I met another brilliant progeny of the Marsalis family who played tenor saxophone. His name is Branford.

At approximately the same time that I met Wynton, the district attorney of Orleans Parish was bugging me about his son, who was a child prodigy on the piano. He played jazz, blues, funk, and whatever. I wasn't interested in a ten-year-old "wunderkind jazz pianist." What a mistake! The D.A.'s name was Harry Connick, Sr.

The closing evening of the festival has become a tradition. Aaron Neville, in his unique soft tenor voice, sings "Amazing Grace." The warmth and togetherness of the massive audience at the end of the ten-day Heritage Festival always reminds me of the group chorus of the 1960s Newport Folk Festival audience with voices ringing, "We Shall Overcome" or, in some years, Woody Guthrie's "This Land Is Your Land."

# 12

# *Newport Jazz Festival–*
# *New York and the NYJRC*

> *The comeback of jazz is clearly the top American music story of 1972.*
>
> **–Albert Goldman, Life**

ALTHOUGH THE NEWPORT JAZZ FESTIVAL had been demolished during the gate-crashing of 1971, its spirit would not be quelled. In the months after its demise, I kept recalling the words of my father, the morning after all hell had broken loose. He and my mother had come into our house—where the prevailing atmosphere was gloom—and upon seeing me, Doc had said: "What happened here last night is making national and international news. You have to take advantage of this." I had been worried about the well-being of my parents, who were seventy-eight and seventy-four years old, respectively. But they were the ones who first saw the light at the end of a dark tunnel.

Inspired to some degree by my father's exhortation, I had told newspaper reporters that there would be another Newport Jazz Festival the following year. To everyone who saw this, I must have seemed not only defeated, but also deluded.

But the Newport Jazz Festival had to continue. Jazz had really taken a backseat by 1971. If jazz had disappeared, it's questionable that anyone in the industry would have cared; certainly not the record companies, the radio stations, or the newspapers. But there were those who still did care—jazz fans as well as musicians. For these people, Newport was important. Joyce tells me that even as the walls of the festival site were being torn down around us, I was talking about how it might be possible to keep the festival going.

Without question, the rural resort outdoor non-classical music festival idea—which had started at Newport in 1954—was dead. The fatal blow had been struck at Woodstock in 1969, and it had taken two years for the victim to expire. But what the kids had created and destroyed at Woodstock was a rock festival. What they had buried at Newport in 1971 was a jazz festival and an institution. No matter how often the press had tried to write jazz's obituary, their pronouncements had always been mitigated by the fact that thousands of people flocked to Newport every Fourth of July. As long as Newport thrived, jazz could not be dismissed.

So how could I resurrect a festival from the dead? Although I was personally in debt many thousands of dollars, my company was making some financial headway. Our European and Japanese businesses were growing. The events that we were producing in Cincinnati, Atlanta, New Orleans, Oakland, Houston, and Hampton, Virginia, were accomplishing varying levels of success.

I recognized that if the Newport Jazz Festival was to be revived, it would have to follow this lead and relocate to an urban area—someplace with a large and diverse populace, where the festival could come under tighter control. I was not alone in coming to this realization. In his *New Yorker* review of the Newport fiasco, Whitney Balliett suggested that the only place the Newport Jazz Festival could now be held was Radio City Music Hall. Whitney intended this as a facetious comment; ironically, it turned out to be a prophecy. If I was going to take the festival to a city, there was no other choice but New York.

By late autumn 1971, I was dead set on this idea—no matter how improbable the odds. One night, I sat down and sketched out ideas for a hypothetical New York jazz festival. I had presented jazz concerts at New York's Lewisohn Stadium and at Boston's Fenway Park; why not try a massive event at Yankee Stadium? I had experimented with multivenue presentations at the Newport Folk Festival and in New Orleans; why not replicate that concept in New York City? We had done Mississippi River boat rides in New Orleans, with traditional Dixieland music; why not create the same feeling on the Hudson River, using the Staten Island Ferry?

Most important would be evening concerts, but evening concerts at Carnegie Hall and Lincoln Center's Philharmonic Hall. Afternoon workshops, concerts, and panel discussions. A spiritual concert at St. Peter's Lutheran Church; late-night big band swing dances in hotel ballrooms; street fairs in midtown Manhattan. And yes: even something at Radio City Music Hall. When I finished brainstorming, I had before me a dizzying nine-day schedule of events, and a massive list of participants. We would take over the city. For my scheme to succeed, it wouldn't be enough to merely take a bite of the Apple; I would have to eat it all.

I knew nearly all of the city's jazz writers, musicians, agents, managers, and record label people—and they knew me. But I was still slightly intimidated by the New York cultural hierarchy and power structure. Would New York deliver the kind of help that this festival needed?

New York cultural organizations suspended operations for the summer season; Carnegie Hall and Philharmonic Hall were empty during most of July and August. I approached the management of both institutions, and asked whether they would consider opening their doors for an extra week in July. I would pay the full cost of each hall. To my relief, both of them agreed.

I discovered that people wanted to help. The New York Yankees administration made every effort to accommodate my needs at Yankee Stadium. The Staten Island Port Authority consented to doing the Hudson River jazz rides. The management of Rockefeller Center agreed to let us use its plaza, as did the Brooklyn Museum. We received an early pledge of promotional support from the New York Convention and Visitor's Bureau.

Mayor John Lindsay took the time to accept honorary chairmanship of the Committee for the Newport Jazz Festival–New York. Former New York mayor Robert Wagner became the active chairman of this committee. Having Wagner's endorsement opened many doors. We had former mayor Wagner on our team because of Joyce's friend Mary Nicholas, who had worked for him for many years.

Other members of the committee included old friends (Father O'Connor, Nesuhi Ertegun, Elliot Hoffman, and Charles McWhorter) and new acquaintances (Julius Bloom of Carnegie Hall, the Rev. John Gensel, Senator Jacob Javits, and many others). The outpouring of support and enthusiasm I received in New York formed a stark contrast to the antipathy I had so often encountered in Newport. Instead of laying down obstacles, people smoothed the path ahead of me. The festival would still be a logistical nightmare, but I at least had some help.

When F. M. Flynn, publisher of the New York *Daily News*, accepted an invitation to be on the festival committee, he had his managing editor, Floyd Barger, relay a message to me. I was most welcome to New York, Flynn said, and the *News* was behind our efforts. But Lord save us if I didn't put on a festival of which New York could be proud; they would run me out of town on a rail.

The musicians were anxious for the event to succeed. Jazz was at a low ebb in 1971. New York City, the club scene was rather anemic at that time. Most of the city's clubs—Bradley's, The Cellar, The Cookery, The Gaslight—were piano rooms. Only a few venues—the Village Gate, the Half-Note, Slugs, and the Village Vanguard among them—were full-fledged jazz clubs, and these would book one group for long stretches. Gone were the Embers, the Hickory House, Birdland, Basin Street East, Eddie Condon's, and the glories of 52nd Street. Jazz was still a part of New York's life, but it had clearly lost some ground. Musicians sensed that this festival could make a difference. As a result, everyone cooperated; nearly all of the artists on my wish list came through at reasonable fees. Dozens of players agreed to play at midnight jam sessions for union scale.

I officially announced plans for the Newport Jazz Festival–New York during a press conference in early January 1972, at the Rainbow Grill atop Rockefeller Center. By that time, I had elicited some corporate sponsorship. The Schlitz Brewing Company sponsored two of the Carnegie Hall concerts. American Airlines put in a subsidy of $17,000, and served as the festival's official airline. Various corporations took out advertisements in our program book, for a total of $30,000. These and other donations accounted for approximately one-sixth of the festival budget. Percentage-wise, this was not a massive sponsorship; but every bit helped.

I made a decision to donate fifty percent of the festival profits to the National Urban League. I made this commitment for several reasons. First of all, I felt that it was our corporate duty to contribute to the community. We were serious about making the festival more than an entertainment event. I had become interested in the work of the Urban League in particular because Bill Simms, the organization's fundraiser, was married to one of Joyce's close friends. The Urban League's dedication to social services and civil rights mirrored my own personal concerns. So I made a deal with Vernon Jordan, the executive director of the organization. Festival Productions may have been a profit-seeking corporation, but I wanted it to practice a sort of pragmatic idealism that would echo the feeling of a nonprofit.

What I didn't anticipate were the ramifications of my announcement. Shortly after making public my Urban League involvement, I began receiving phone calls from CORE and other groups—they wanted contributions as well. And in those days, the militancy of CORE could be intimidating. I called Vernon Jordan and explained my situation. "I'm being hit upon here," I told him. "Is there anything you can do to help me?"

I was surprised by his response: "If CORE is hitting you up, that's your problem, not mine." He distanced himself, and the League, from the scenario. It taught me a lesson. If I wanted to support the Urban League, I should have simply made a donation. Sometimes a public gesture can cause more problems than it's worth. I knew nothing about these sorts of complications. But I was learning all the time.

The symbol of the Newport Jazz Festival–New York was a shiny red apple. Historically, jazz musicians knew New York City as "the Big Apple"; the term had been forgotten. But thanks to the Loew's Corporation, there were Newport cigarette ads welcoming the Newport Jazz Festival to New York on buses and subways all over town—each bearing the apple insignia. To my knowledge, we were the first organization to use that logo in this fashion. A few years later, Charles Gillette of the New York Convention and Visitor's Bureau adopted the apple in conjunction with the city of New York, kicking off an ad campaign that has continued to this day. Mr. Gillette always credited us with the inspiration for this trademark.

After our January press conference, the *New York Times* reported on the festival's relocation, as did *Down Beat* and dozens of other publications. The coverage was astounding. The local and national press buzzed with anticipation. At one point, the Broadway producer Alexander Cohen asked me how I had wrangled such monstrous publicity. He usually spent thousands of dollars on public relations and received a mere fraction of the coverage. I was forced to admit that I didn't even have a professional PR firm in my corner; I had Charlie Bourgeois and Joe Morgen.

The reason for the enthusiasm went far beyond any efforts on my part; it even went beyond the scope of the festival. The editors, reporters, publishers, and radio and television producers who provided coverage were my age or older; they were in their 30s, 40s, and 50s. These people were jazz fans, or at least remembered what it had been like when jazz was around. They had seen 52nd Street, or they had hung out in Greenwich Village. They had spent time in Eddie Condon's club, and had dined at the Hickory House. In some measure, jazz had been a part of their lives. They jumped on this festival, because it was a highly tangible way for them to spark a resurgence of the music they loved.

At the same time, it was more than nostalgia that drove them; this was also a sort of protest against the influences that had turned their world upside down. Rock and roll had radically altered the face of advertising, the form and content of print and televised media, and the whole concept of musical presentation. The rock generation had taken over everything: food, dress, style. Rock had created a culture that glamorized youth. Corporations were laying off scores of experienced workers and replacing them with barely-qualified twentysomethings, hoping to tap into the pulse of the new generation. Since jazz was part of the era that had been overthrown, its resurrection was like a coup. We were leading a charge, and the media were quick to pick up our cause.

I was renting a staggering number of music halls. My headlong involvement in the city's venues did not go unnoticed. That spring, I was invited to speak at a convention of New York City hall managers. Sol Hurok was also speaking at this conference. Hurok, 84 years old by this time, was the world's most renowned living concert impresario. In their more charitable moments, critics had occasionally likened my work in jazz to his in classical music.

When I found myself alone with Mr. Hurok for a moment, I introduced myself and told him about the magnitude of the impending festival. In nine days, I was presenting over thirty concerts with some 600 musicians. I explained my budget and break-even point to him.

"Mr. Hurok," I said after enumerating these details, "do you think I have a chance?"

The old man looked thoughtful for a moment. "You just might," he finally said. "You just might."

Hurok suggested that we have lunch or dinner sometime. I didn't take him up on this invitation for several years. When I finally did, he invited me to lunch at La Cote Basque. We had a fascinating conversation. He was very impressed by the fact that Joyce and I were going to see Artur Rubenstein that week in a concert at Carnegie Hall. He congratulated me for that, and said that I should see Mr. Rubenstein, because he was quite old. To this I replied: "Mr. Hurok, how old are you?" Quickly on the defensive, he said: "Oh, age doesn't make any difference. You have to keep working."

*     *     *

The 1972 Newport Jazz Festival began with a bang, as both Philharmonic Hall and Carnegie Hall presented "Schlitz Salute to Jazz" concerts on Saturday, July 1. The Philharmonic concert featured performances by the Giants of Jazz, Billy Eckstine, Sarah Vaughan, and Max Roach. The Carnegie concert showcased the Modern Jazz Quartet, Pharoah Sanders, and Stan Getz. There were two performances of each concert at five and nine P.M., and there were many fans who attended an early concert in one hall and then strolled over to the other hall for the later show. Columbus Circle—directly between Carnegie Hall on Fifty-seventh Street and Lincoln Center on Sixty-second—was transformed into a pedestrian route, as hundreds of people walked across between shows, program books in hand. Upper midtown Manhattan took on the atmosphere of a jazz *feria*.

We held a midnight jam session at Radio City Music Hall. All of the musicians on the bill (dozens, including Roy Eldridge, Dizzy Gillespie, Gene Krupa, Jim Hall, and Max Roach) had accepted a minimum wage of $150 for the night. More than an hour before show time, a line began to form outside the hall. Gradually, it grew, and grew, until there were six thousand people wrapped around a city block. We had sold out the show. At ten dollars a head, this meant a $60,000 gross—enough to clear the cost of the hall and all expenses. For those who had declared jazz a lifeless art, this must have seemed an unlikely turn of events.

The next morning found Kid Thomas's Preservation Hall Jazz Band and Papa French and the Original Tuxedo Jazz Band on the Staten Island Ferry—both groups authentic staples of the Crescent City. The first ride, on the ferryboat *John F. Kennedy*, left its Battery Park berth at 10:30 in the morning and chugged northbound on the Hudson River for an hour. Reaching the George Washington Bridge, it turned around and headed back, gliding down the entire panoramic West Side skyline. "Jazz on the River," Joyce's idea, was a success.

On the Fourth of July we presented a major concert twice at Philharmonic Hall. It was a pairing of two progressive minds. Charles Mingus brought his orchestra for a set of his risk-taking music. And Ornette Coleman premiered "Skies of America," an ambitious and unprecedented attempt to write a jazz symphony.

Originally, I had booked Ornette to play with his quartet. But his cousin James Jordan had approached me and told me Ornette's wishes. To fund such an endeavor, we received a small grant from the New York State Council of the Arts. We engaged the American Symphony Orchestra with conductor Leon Thompson. The orchestra surrounded Ornette's core group, which consisted of Dewey Redman on tenor, Charlie Haden on bass, and Ed Blackwell on drums.

I heard "Skies of America" twenty-five years later at Lincoln Center, with Kurt Masur conducting. I was not sorry to have presented Ornette's symphony; it was an important historical moment.

The second Radio City jam session was another sellout. "When a ticket-holder got to the Music Hall's wraparound marquee," reported McCandlish Phillips in the *New York Times*, "he followed a line stretching toward Fifth Avenue. He traced it all the way to Fifth, then up Fifth and all the way back to the southern side of the marquee, a few yards from where he had started."

On Saturday afternoon, at Carnegie Hall, I had paired the Ellington band with Terumasa Hino, Japan's top trumpeter, at the request of my friend Koyama-san at *Swing Journal*. Practically every jazz critic in Japan came to

New York for the festival. They were extremely proud to have Hino opening for Duke.

The Ellington Orchestra convened for a rehearsal onstage at eleven A.M.; the concert was scheduled for one P.M. Alumni Barney Bigard and Ray Nance were there, as well as Bobby Short—who was paying tribute to the late Ellington vocalist Ivie Anderson. Duke also had a Rumanian singer named Aura Rully. The band sounded fabulous. As the rehearsal ended, Duke pulled me aside.

"I want to open," he said.

I was taken aback. "Open? Duke, you can't open! Hino is opening the show; you're the featured performer."

"George," he replied, *sotto voce*, "if I let these guys go now, and they come back for our set at two or three o'clock, they'll all be drunk. The band sounds good *now*, and I want to get them on right away."

When Duke Ellington tells me he wants to open, he opens.

The Duke Ellington Orchestra was sensational. They performed the *Toga Brava Suite*, along with old favorites like "Rockin' in Rhythm" and "East St. Louis Toodle-Oo." Then Duke surrendered the stage to Bobby Short, who performed his elegant tribute with the orchestra. After Bobby left the stage, the band went into "Mood Indigo," with Tyree Glenn playing his muted trombone over the sweet, slow melody. Then out walked Aura Rully, picking up the melody in a soprano voice that caught everyone by surprise. The audience was enthralled. The Ellington Orchestra hadn't sounded this good in quite a few years. They finished their set to a massive ovation; people brought bouquets of flowers to the foot of the stage.

After the band had cleared out, I took the microphone and asked the audience to remain in their seats. Terumasa Hino, I told them, was Japan's finest jazz musician. He deserved our attention and respect. I spoke in this fashion for some time, and it worked. Everybody stayed. A few moments later, Hino's band took the stage.

They played one song. As soon as the song was finished, ninety percent of the hall cleared out, *en masse*.

The exodus was a scandal. The Japanese critics were sitting in their seats and looking around in disbelief. They were astounded that American jazz fans would do such a thing.

The following morning, I had all of these critics headed by Koyama-san in my office. They were outraged. "You're finished in Japan! Hino was disgraced, and so were we! How could you let this happen?" All I could do was tell my story, and beg their forgiveness. What was I going to do—incur the wrath of Ellington? If I had the decision to make again today, I would do the exact same thing. It was only after writing numerous letters of abject apology to the Japanese magazines that I was forgiven.

On the festival's final day, a Sunday, we presented a morning gospel concert at Radio City Music Hall. The show was conceived and produced by a gospel scholar named Tony Heilbut, who had written the book *The Gospel Sound: Good News and Bad Times*. Our roster for this program included several of the artists who had worked at Newport in the past: the Dixie Hummingbirds, Dorothy Love Coates, and Marian Williams. The concert also featured a number of important gospel artists whom I had never met before, like Willie Mae Ford Smith, The Consolers, The Jesse Dixon Singers, and R. H. Harris and His Gospel Paraders. The highlight of the morning was an unscheduled appearance by Thomas A. Dorsey, composer of "Precious Lord" and a number of other gospel standards. His presence, and the rousing performances of the other artists, made this a momentous occasion.

All told, the festival hadn't turned a profit. We had essentially cleared our costs. I had no official net to share with the Urban League, but I gave them a check for $6,000.

Breaking even was encouragement enough for me to declare the Newport Jazz Festival–New York an annual, permanent event. With more hard work, some increased sponsorship, and a little luck, I was convinced that we could make the New York festival into a lasting success.

\*　　\*　　\*

I had worked with Benny Goodman several times in the past (most closely during the 1958 Newport Jazz Festival), but our personal relationship was a fairly recent development. I knew all about his enigmatic and often abrasive personality. I was on the plane with Benny during a flight from New York to Jazz Fest in New Orleans. We sat together and talked most of the way. It was fascinating for me to hear his thoughts on music and musicians. At one point, the conversation veered toward the subject of drummers. I mentioned a list of names; Benny acknowledged some of them as good, some as not-so-good. He didn't put down all of them.

Just the day before, I had been talking with Bobby Rosengarden, Benny's drummer in the sextet. Bobby had told me how much he enjoyed playing with Benny; he had heard all the stories about how tough Benny was with musicians, but he himself had never had a problem. Benny had treated him very well. So when Benny and I got to talking about drummers, I mentioned Bobby's name. It was an innocuous remark. "Bobby Rosengarden is a good drummer," I said.

Benny's response was vehement: "He can't play the drums!" That evening, in the Municipal Auditorium, Benny Goodman treated Bobby Rosengarden intolerably; he shot "the ray," he did everything he could to demoralize the poor drummer. After the show, Bobby came up to me and exclaimed: "I don't know what happened! Benny never treated me like that before. He fired me!" I offered some words of consolation, and inwardly kicked myself. I had tried to put in a good word for Bobby, and it had caused one of the most miserable nights of his life.

In New York Benny had a spacious apartment on the fortieth floor of a white brick building on the Upper East Side. In the weeks leading up to the Newport Jazz Festival–New York, I went there often to discuss the program. Sometimes he called to question me about musicians he might be able to hire; he was a brain-picker, and I was on his list of brains to pick. We would talk about the state of jazz, and which musicians were good players. As a rule, Benny didn't think anybody was a good musician. One afternoon I was in the apartment and our conversation was going along these lines. I said: "C'mon, Benny. Louis Armstrong, Duke Ellington—these guys were not great musicians?"

Benny stood up, walked across the room, and opened his clarinet case. He put the clarinet together, and with me sitting there on the couch, proceeded to play a movement of Webern's Clarinet Concerto from memory. I couldn't believe what was happening. Here I was on the fortieth floor of a Manhattan skyscraper, and Benny Goodman was exhibiting his prowess for me alone. He finished the solo, put the clarinet down, and triumphantly crowed: "Can any of them do that?"

"No, Benny," I meekly replied. "I don't suppose they can."

That summer's Newport Jazz Festival–New York included a reunion of the original Benny Goodman Quartet. Benny hadn't played with Lionel Hampton, Gene Krupa, or Teddy Wilson in years, and the concert sold out Carnegie Hall. It was an exciting evening. The opening salvos were delivered by a Ruby Braff–George Barnes quartet, which easily kept everyone's attention. Then out came Benny, with his old compatriots in tow; the last time they had stood together on that stage was for their historic concert of 1938. They were joined by a fifth member, the bassist Slam Stewart.

Benny was quite relaxed during this evening. In fact, he sat in a chair at one point and propped his feet up on Lionel Hampton's vibraphone (an act that did not go unnoticed by the press). I asked him about this incident. With perfect elocution, Benny mused: "I don't know why I do such things." He paused. "Then again, perhaps I do."

I believe this was the last time Benny's quartet played together; Gene Krupa had cancer. It was only a month later that Eddie Condon died. At Condon's funeral, Gene spoke eloquently about their friendship, as well as their musical bond. He finished with these words: "Eddie, get the guys together up there. Because I'll be joining you soon." It was the most moving eulogy I've ever heard. Gene passed away that October.

\*     \*     \*

Another major event on the 1973 Newport Jazz Festival–New York was the "The Hallelujah Chorus's The Life and Times of Ray Charles, Written by James Baldwin and Performed by Ray Charles." I had received sponsorship from Schlitz for this concert, and a subsidy from Pan Am airlines for Jimmy's travel from France to the United States. At my request, Jimmy had visited Ray in California to discuss the program. I was prepared to put the show entirely in their hands. I had only one request as a producer. I wanted the concert to begin with Jimmy at the podium and Ray alone at the piano. I knew that Ray would object to the idea, but I felt that this intimacy was crucial to the spirit of the concert. They could begin by talking about their common ground in the church, with Ray playing a little gospel music. "If you can get Ray to do this," I said to Jimmy, "anything that happens after that will be a perfect evening."

Ray Charles had a strong personality. When Jimmy met with him in California, they quickly came to an understanding: Ray would open with the band. That was that. Jimmy didn't press the issue. As a result, the concert fell short of my hopes. Jimmy read a lyrical passage at the beginning of the show, and later presented some material from his play, "The Hallelujah Chorus," with Cicely Tyson and other actors. Otherwise, it was a fairly standard Ray Charles show—which was a treat, but not the personal program that it could have been.

Jimmy's fee wasn't terribly high, but his expenses were phenomenal; they consumed all of the Schlitz sponsor money. We paid for his trip to the West Coast; he flew from New York to California first class, and stayed in a suite at New York's Plaza Hotel. Jimmy Baldwin was totally irresponsible when it came to finances; it was one of those frustrating traits that endeared him to you. After the concert, I paid Jimmy $5,000—a sum that he went through in one night, entertaining friends in Paris. Although Jimmy and I grew very close in the ensuing years, I never told him that I had been disappointed with the concert.

Jazz had changed dramatically since the forties. In the late fifties and sixties, one of the most important innovations was a widespread interest in modal improvisation. Everywhere I turned, musicians were playing modally (modal improvisation is improvising on a fixed scale as opposed to improvising on harmonic progressions). So I decided to put together a group that would explicitly address this style; if all my musicians were playing modal jazz, I figured I'd better learn what it was all about. I teamed up with bassist Larry Ridley, drummer Al Harewood, saxophonist/flutist James Spaulding, and our teacher, guitarist Ted Dunbar. While I led and managed the group, Ted was our *de facto* musical director. We had played a number of gigs, including one week-long engagement at the Half Note Uptown, and a series of concerts at black colleges in the south.

The Half Note engagement was especially memorable because we shared a bill with Sonny Rollins. After we had played our first set on opening night, Sonny took the stand with his quartet. He played "God Bless the Child," and it was breathtaking. During intermission I went up to Sonny in the dressing room and said: "Sonny, couldn't you at least have waited until the second set before you completely wiped us out?"

For me, modal playing proved to be restrictive; I couldn't access the "infinite possibilities" that were at the disposal of any facile jazz musician. My harmonic concept was too rooted in chord changes and progressions. I did, however, have a good time playing in the modal vein for a while. The Newport Ensemble played a concert under an outdoor tent in Utica, New York. We had a decent crowd, and played a good first set. But Joyce, who was sitting in the audience, told me that my piano wasn't amplified enough. I couldn't tell; we didn't use monitors in those days. So during the second half, I turned the piano mic way up.

When it was time for my solo, I really cut loose. I can't remember what song we were playing; it was basically a vamp over an E-flat seventh mode. And I threw in everything but the kitchen sink: fast tempos, slow moods, Latin, blues, and anything else I could think of. The rhythm section picked up whatever I was playing and went along with it. I could have gone on forever.

When I finished, I got the biggest round of applause of my life. People cheered over the nothing that I had played. I stood up, took a bow, and never touched that music again as long as I lived. It was meaningless to me. Of course, the advanced modal musicians know voicings and progressions and can apply them to any situation. I could not. Recognizing that fact, I gave up modal exploration and returned to the art of the 32-bar chorus (a format that still poses manifold mysteries for me).

I learned an unhappy lesson in Harlem that summer. I had received some help from the Harlem Cultural Council, the Department of Cultural Affairs, the New York State Council on the Arts, and a few corporate sponsors to produce a series of concerts at the Apollo Theatre. This was a treat, since the previous year's New York festival had been centered around the midtown Manhattan area. To bring part of the Newport Jazz Festival to Harlem was a step in the right direction. The shows that I produced were as ambitious as anything happening downtown; for instance, an evening with the Dizzy Gillespie Quintet, the Kenny Burrell Trio, Irene Reid, the Charles Mingus Quintet, the Junior Mance Trio, and the Rod Rodgers Dance Company. Another night we had Carmen McRae, Rahsaan Roland Kirk and the Vibration Society, the Roy Haynes Hip Ensemble, the Jazz Opera Ensemble, and Louis Jordan's Tympani Five. Our closing night featured groups led by Max Roach, Ruth Brown, Robin Kenyatta, Stan Getz, Elvin Jones, Charles Earland, and dancer Eleo Pomare. Each concert's admission was a mere two dollars. We barely sold any tickets. It took this discouraging experience to teach me that the artists who could fill Carnegie Hall were not necessarily marquee attractions in Harlem. Aretha would have sold out. But our jazz artists floundered.

A downtown innovative concert, the theme of which still resonates, was "A Jazz Salute to the American Song," featuring the Modern Jazz Quartet, Rahsaan Roland Kirk, Al Hibbler, Mabel Mercer, Stan Getz, Teddi King, Gerry Mulligan, Dave Brubeck, Jimmy McPartland, and a number of others. The concert had been produced in cooperation with Alec Wilder, the composer whose book *American Popular Song: The Great Innovators, 1900–1950* defined a songwriters' canon. The unique moment of this evening was Getz playing with Mabel Mercer. It was marvelous.

Nineteen seventy-three was the year in which the city of New York decided to change the Singer Bowl in Flushing Meadow Park to "Louis Armstrong Stadium." At the city's request, we produced a jazz extravaganza at the stadium, in Louis's honor. I corralled dozens of musicians for this event; everybody wanted to be a part of it. All the participants, musicians and festival staff alike, donated their services. The proceeds went to the charities of Lucille Armstrong's choice: the Queens Child Guidance Center, and the Corona-East Elmhurst Community Corporation, a group formed by citizens of the area with the purpose of erecting the Louis Armstrong Cultural Arts Center and Memorial Plaza.

The stadium's renaming took place on Wednesday, the Fourth of July—what would have been touted as Louis's seventy-third birthday, had he been alive to celebrate with us. The festivities began at one in the afternoon, and went on until the evening. We filled the stadium. The list of participating musicians was staggering:

Count Basie, Eubie Blake, Darius Brubeck, Dave Brubeck, Cab Calloway, Barbara Carroll, Al Casey, Doc Cheatham, Cozy Cole, Eddie "Lockjaw" Davis, Wild Bill Davison, Vic Dickenson, the Drootin Brothers. Roy Eldridge, Ella Fitzgerald, Stan Getz, Dizzy Gillespie, Tyree Glenn, Al Grey, Tiny Grimes, Herb Hall, Elvin Jones, Max Kaminsky, Emme Kemp, George Kirby, Gene Krupa, Ellis Larkins, Yank Lawson, Howard McGhee, Dave McKenna, Jimmy McPartland, Marian McPartland, John Mayall, Turk Murphy, Ray Nance, Marty Napoleon, Joe Newman, Anita O'Day, Larry Ridley, Sam Rivers, Jimmy Rowles, Arvell Shaw, Archie Shepp, James Spaulding, Sun Ra, Billy Taylor, Clark Terry, Sarah Vaughan, Eddie Vinson, Grover Washington, Bob Wilber, Cootie Williams, Joe Williams, and Reggie Workman.

Having all of these musicians on one program presented a logistical challenge. It was a miserably humid summer day, and we wanted to keep the show moving. I told every band to play for no longer than ten minutes. Period. Most of the artists had no problem with this directive, and we presented five groups an hour for four hours. Sun Ra, however, had some qualms about the time limit. "Man," he said, "I can't play for just ten minutes." I told him not to worry about time; I would come up and signal when the ten minutes were up.

Sun Ra performed on an electric piano with a few of his Arkestra members. His music was so personal; he just projected this otherworldly sound. After ten minutes, I walked up and tapped him on the shoulder. He turned around, nodded his head, and stopped playing. And that was it. I don't know whether this shows a lack of respect or a true understanding of that music. But it worked out okay, there were no complaints, and he was a highlight of that celebration. The airplanes that kept flying overhead, which were an irritation and a distraction for other artists, didn't seem to faze Sun Ra at all.

I learned several other hard lessons that year. A Monday night at the Roseland Ballroom featured the orchestras of Duke Ellington, Count Basie, and Woody Herman. Called "A Thirties Ball," it was a dance as well as a concert. Part of the program also involved a fashion show sponsored by the Wool Bureau and *Harper's Bazaar*, and choreographed by the Arthur Murray Dance Studio. The guest of honor was Andy Kirk, the leader of a band called "The

Clouds of Joy" from Kansas City, who was still alive and an official of Local 802, the musician's union. It was fun. Duke, Basie, and Woody had all worked on many festival programs in the past. I had asked Woody to play some music during the fashion show, and he did. Afterward, though, he pulled me aside.

"Don't take me for granted," he said, visibly upset. "I respect Basie and I respect Duke, but I'm Woody Herman, you know. You didn't ask them to play the fashion show; you asked me. And I did it. But that didn't show respect for me. You took me for granted."

He was right. Instead of getting the three of them together and asking who would be willing to play for the fashion segment—in which case Woody would have happily volunteered—I just assumed that he would do it. I apologized. I had not handled that situation well.

A most exciting concert was a salute to Ella Fitzgerald at Carnegie Hall. I recreated the Chick Webb Orchestra, the band with which Ella got her start. We gathered a number of Webb alumni, including Taft Jordan, Dick Vance, Garnett Brown, and Panama Francis. With this reunited Webb band, Ella sang some of her material from the thirties—"A-Tisket A-Tasket," "Stairway to the Stars." The charts were good, and Ella was fabulous. Next we presented her in a more intimate setting—accompanied solely by the pianist Ellis Larkins, with whom she had recorded. Their rendition of "I've Got a Crush on You" left the audience breathless. Finally, Ella finished the concert with her working quartet, which featured pianist Tommy Flanagan and guitarist Joe Pass. The evening was a living retrospective of her forty-year career.

John Hammond had asked for permission to record this concert for Columbia Records; in exchange, Columbia would pay me for the concert. Norman Granz agreed to this arrangement. Norman, who protected Ella as if she were a virgin daughter, appreciated our concept. He recognized that the program showed an enormous amount of love and respect for Ella Fitzgerald. I have always been grateful to both John and Norman for their cooperation; *Ella Fitzgerald Carnegie Hall 1973* (Columbia) is a timeless recording, and it is still in issue.

\*　　\*　　\*

*By playing Jelly Roll Morton and Armstrong and early*
*Ellington freshly and intelligently, they lift the music from*
*the tombs of the twenties and thirties recordings. What had*
*sounded ancient and strange so long on the old 78 r.p.m.s*
*becomes brand-new again.*

**—Whitney Balliett**

Jazz fans in 1973 embraced a precarious art. Although two years had transpired since Louis Armstrong's death, we continued to mourn his absence. Johnny Hodges had died a year before Louis, in 1970; Coleman Hawkins in 1969. The demise of these and other irreplaceable legends, and the precipitously worsening condition of Duke Ellington, prompted me to consider the state and future of our music. The masters of jazz would all pass on. But why should their music die with them?

There were a number of incipient movements in jazz at the time. In addition to the musicians who were immersed in modal improvisation, others were continuing the exploration into the territory of free jazz and the avant-garde. Fusion and jazz-rock were making strong inroads into the mainstream.

Yet all this stylistic diversity somehow seemed to diminish, rather than expand, the jazz legacy. Young musicians were so quick to adopt the latest trend that they failed to contend with the history of the music. Even bebop, which had emerged just a few decades before, was becoming old hat. Swing was even more marginal. It wasn't far-fetched to envision an encroaching future in which traditional jazz would be little more than a quaint footnote; the dim recollection of those few, like myself, who were there when it happened.

I formed the New York Jazz Repertory Company with the basic assumption that jazz was an art form that deserved to be treated as such. The practitioners of any art, if they are serious, begin at point A, and not at point Q or X. In other words: to understand the music, you need to start at the beginning: with early blues, spirituals, and ragtime. This viewpoint, now a basic tenet of music education, was relatively foreign to young jazz musicians in 1973. The formation of an active repertory company—like those in the classical arena—could keep jazz traditions alive. At the same time, it could bring together the numerous, disparate schools of jazz under one banner; the work of past, present and future. As I described the project in our first program book:

> The NYJRC may be all things to all people in a musical sense. Critics and observers should be careful before they attempt to define exactly what the NYJRC is. If they think it is a museum where great music of the past can be put on display, they may be right, but only up to a point. It is a living museum where a young artist can seek an outlet for his original work, but not to the exclusion of already established contemporary and traditional jazz.

The idea hit a good nerve. Julius Bloom, then executive director of Carnegie Hall, made it possible to rent the hall at a reduced cost. The New

York State Council on the Arts and the National Endowment for the Arts provided some financial support. I assembled a board of directors consisting primarily of friends in the industry: Ahmet Ertegun, John Hammond, Elliot Hoffman, Stanley Dance, Dick Hyman, Jimmy Owens, Bob Wilber, and Charles McWhorter. Mr. Bloom was also on the board, as were former mayor Robert F. Wagner and Mary Burke Nicholas from the Department of Housing and Urban Development.

Because I wanted the company to reflect a wide-ranging vision, I enlisted four musical directors during the first year. Sy Oliver, Billy Taylor, Gil Evans, and Stanley Cowell each had his respective realm of expertise. Together, they represented an understanding of jazz from its early years to the present age and beyond. Our "company" during the first season was not a defined group so much as a diverse pool of talent; over a hundred New York–based musicians agreed to affiliate themselves with the project. It was like a phone book listing of jazz musicians; every style and era was represented.

For example, I put twelve different drummers on call. First there was Tommy Benford, who had played with Jelly Roll Morton, Fats Waller, Django Reinhardt, Coleman Hawkins, Benny Carter, and Eubie Blake; his photograph in the program book appeared next to Ed Blackwell, whose résumé included work with Ornette Coleman, Eric Dolphy, Booker Little, and Randy Weston. The rest of the roster was no less prestigious—it included Jo Jones, Art Blakey, Roy Haynes, Billy Higgins, and Elvin Jones. This obviously wide range of talent gave the NYJRC a broader historical scope than any previous organization in the history of jazz. In addition to our cadre of performers, we made plans to feature prominent guest artists.

Still, jazz repertory was bound to be a prickly affair. We had to resist the temptation to play generic old arrangements. I didn't want it to feel as if we were dusting off an old, ill-fitting coat and trying it on. We needed new arrangements of older material; an approach that would sustain the character of the original pieces, but with a contemporary perspective. Copying a great painting requires discipline, skill, and attention to detail. But absorbing that painting's style and producing your own distinct canvas requires artistry.

Another important question arose: How does a repertory company address a music so rooted in improvisation? I didn't want to hear our soloists playing transcriptions of old improvisations—that would suck out the spontaneity. But it would be even more disastrous to have someone play a bebop solo over a Benny Goodman arrangement. I believed in the premise that a musician's playing could be creative and still relevant to a historical context. I felt, then as now, that improvisers have a responsibility to reflect the arranger's method and approach to music. These were issues I discussed at length with our musical directors and players.

The inaugural performance of the NYJRC on January 26, 1974, was a mélange of styles. We featured the music of Jimmy Lunceford, with original charts arranged by Lunceford alumnus Sy Oliver; a fusion segment called "Jazz in the Rock Age," with Gil Evans; and a performance by Charles Tolliver, a young trumpeter brought in by Stanley Cowell.

In our second concert, Dizzy Gillespie conducted the NYJRC in a program of his classic big band arrangements. Then Billy Taylor led the band in a program of the music of Oliver Nelson. Our third concert featured a performance by Sam Rivers; Sy Oliver's reinterpretation of the Tommy Dorsey Orchestra; and a modern quintet performance led by Billy Taylor.

We wanted our tributes to be as innovative as they were stirring. Our John Coltrane concert featured as guest artists former Coltrane sidemen Elvin Jones and Jimmy Garrison; it also showcased a highly creative use of solo transcriptions by saxophonist-composer Andrew White. Another concert was in part a salute to Fletcher Henderson, with rearrangements of his classic compositions; the second half was devoted to tenor saxophonist Bud Freeman, and featured cohort Bobby Hackett. Our Charlie Parker concert took the form of a sweeping retrospective, featuring not only erstwhile partner Dizzy Gillespie, but also former employers Jay McShann, Earl Hines, and Billy Eckstine—and prominent disciples Sonny Stitt, Phil Woods, Charles McPherson, and Jackie McLean. We explored Jimi Hendrix through the lens of Gil Evans, including arrangements that Evans had written for a collaboration (foiled by Hendrix's death). Our Thelonious Monk evening went immediately into the annals of jazz history, due to Thelonious's unscheduled personal appearance. Our Duke Ellington salute, which featured historical treatments of seldom-heard early Ellington as well as newly minted arrangements by our musical directors, preceded the Maestro's death by less than a month.

In addition to the impressive number of tribute events, the NYJRC attempted to produce creative programmatic performances. One show revisited Harlem's Savoy Ballroom, through the music of the Chick Webb, Don Redman, and Erskine Hawkins Orchestras, with Mr. Hawkins, the only surviving leader of that era, on hand. Another concert, "Jazz with a Spanish Tinge," explored the influence of Flamenco and Moorish folk music on jazz; on the same program, Tito Puente demonstrated the influence of jazz on Latin music. "52nd Street Revisited" revived the sounds of the John Kirby Sextet, the Count Basie Band, and the Art Tatum Trio, with Hank Jones tackling Tatum and guitarist Tiny Grimes reprising his old supporting role.

The NYJRC also presented its share of new and original work. On one occasion, Cecil Taylor performed with a thirty-piece orchestra. George Russell guest-conducted the company for a performance of his composition "Living Time," with soloist Bill Evans. Lennie Tristano made a rare and long-awaited public appearance with the company. Billy Taylor performed a third-stream composition by Howard Rovics.

Occasional miscommunications happened. When I asked Gil Evans to produce a concert that would spotlight his own illustrious career, I expected him to perform a retrospective, starting with the Claude Thornhill arrangements that were his earliest triumph. I also specifically requested material from *The Birth of the Cool* and *Sketches of Spain*. But what Gil finally provided was a montage, a sprawling composition that reflected his new direction and referred only fleetingly to those previous accomplishments. He didn't want to do the things exactly as he had done them before. Although I was initially disappointed, I eventually realized that Gil Evans was right. His concern for a contemporaneous spirit underscored our effort to keep jazz repertory a movement in the present tense.

We concluded our first season, at the end of 1974, with a deficit of over $40,000. Our audience attendance had been uneven; it was downright shameful during the more obscure productions. An evening honoring George Russell—the brilliant composer who had sparked the first interest in jazz modality—was especially embarrassing. The company played two of Russell's long pieces: "Living Time" and "Electronic Sonata for Souls Loved by Nature." The composer made a rare appearance as guest conductor, leading an ensemble consisting of three percussionists, three keyboard instruments, two bassists, and a dozen wind instruments. Bill Evans, one of the most lauded and influential pianists of his time, participated as guest soloist. Vibraphone virtuoso Gary Burton provided a complementary performance, interpreting a Mike Gibbs composition. It was a bold and terrific concert. But we sold only 200 tickets—less than *one-thirteenth* the capacity of Carnegie Hall.

We couldn't afford to endure similar woes again, and our second season took on a sense of urgency; the *New York Times* called it a "do-or-die stand." Everyone recognized the fact that we were establishing a standard; the fate of jazz repertory hung in the balance. "The funding agencies have not been programmed to deal with this type of music," Jimmy Owens told a reporter from the *New York Post*. He added: "If this company fails, no one will be able to start anything like it again for years."

After weighing the strengths and weaknesses of our first season, the NYJRC announced several key changes. We lowered top-line ticket price from $7.50 to

$5.50, to encourage better box office returns. We shifted the responsibility of producing each show to a planning committee (consisting of myself, Billy Taylor, Stanley Dance, Joe Newman, and Dick Hyman) that could work out the details of each program before distributing assignments to the musical directors. As for the musical directors themselves, there was a changing of the guard; for our second season, we bestowed the positions on Dick Hyman, Jimmy Owens, and Bob Wilber. Billy Taylor returned to his post for a second year.

We made a conscious decision to put more thought into the continuity and overall effect of each concert, eliminating what the *Village Voice* had branded "the schizoid programs" of the previous year. We had found that a lot of our audience members were walking out of concerts when there was an abrupt change in style emanating from the stage. Lovers of the old styles of music found it harder to accept newer music on the same program. We attempted to address this problem by planning uni-directional thematic concepts during the second season. Then we streamlined the company from a hundred members to roughly forty, having concluded that size and variety were no substitute for consistency.

With renewed grants from the State Council and National Endowment, the NYJRC also received financial support from record companies (with Atlantic and RCA each contributing $10,000) and private sources (including a sizeable portion of my company's funds). We announced a membership incentive; $30 made any patron a "Friend of the NYJRC," and included attendance to selected open rehearsals and post-show jam sessions, as well as a ticket to a retrospective show, "75 Years of Jazz in Concert." But halfway through the season, we had raised only $5,000 in memberships.

The NYJRC's "Tribute to Louis Armstrong," our second season premiere, was an auspicious event. We divided the tribute between two evenings; the first concert saluted Louis's work with the Hot Fives and Sevens in the 1920s, and the second dwelled on his later work with big bands and the Armstrong All-Stars. We put a great deal of thought into the production of the concert, which would ultimately include rearrangements of Armstrong tunes as well as archival recordings, informative narration, and rare film footage from the 1970 FestiFilms documentary. Stanley Dance wrote the script, which traced Armstrong's history and illuminated the background behind the performances. The overall effect was masterful. It was one of the first multimedia jazz concert events of its kind.

Dick Hyman created a book of arrangements for the evening that not only carried the concert, but also underscored the possibilities of jazz repertory. He took a number of early Armstrong solos—arguably the most consistently impressive body of improvisation ever executed—and arranged them in three-part harmony. The concept wasn't entirely new; an ensemble called Supersax had built a reputation through similar feats with Charlie Parker. (Dick half-jokingly referred to our concept as "Super Satch.") What made the arrangements so compelling was the fact that they acknowledged the trumpet solos as timeless, which they are. Magnificent improvisation holds up to the scrutiny of the ages; a musical solo is a composition unto itself. So a three-part trumpet arrangement of classic Armstrong makes for a far more fitting tribute than any number of Satchmo imitations by well-meaning soloists. Gary Giddins wrote in the *Village Voice*:

> For Armstrong's first recorded solo, on King Oliver's "Chimes Blues," Super Satch was used ingeniously. The house lights faded as the 1923 recording was played; when the Armstrong solo neared, trumpeters Mel Davis, Joe Newman, and Pee Wee Erwin jumped up and presto! there was the solo without surface noise or static.

For me, and for many others, that was the moment at which jazz repertory reached an aesthetic pinnacle.

Although Hyman's arrangements were the showpiece, there was much more to the concert. Bernie Privin and Doc Cheatham each revisited songs associated with Armstrong, and Ruby Braff played a duet rendition of "Rosetta" with Hyman (recalling Louis's classic recordings with Earl "Fatha" Hines). Ray Nance lent both his trumpet-playing and singing skills to the proceedings, including some lovely obbligato behind singer Carrie Smith on "You've Been a Good Old Wagon" and "St. Louis Blues." The night ended with footage of Mahalia Jackson dedicating "Just a Closer Walk with Thee" to Louis at the 1970 Newport Jazz Festival. The *New Yorker* called this "the most exhilarating number at the first concert"; the *Daily News* called it "a once in a lifetime stunner."

The second evening, which chronicled Armstrong's later work, was a good concert—but not as powerful as the first. Hyman's big band arrangements lacked the intense focus of his small-group charts.

John Wilson of the *New York Times* said that the programs "could serve as a model of imaginative, entertaining, informative and rewarding jazz programming." Jerry Wexler of Atlantic Records (who had become a member of our board of directors) was so moved that he decided to make an album of Hyman's arrangements. In the *New Yorker*, Whitney Balliett opined that the two concerts:

were the most successful the New York Jazz Repertory has given. They brought to the fore attractive and even brilliant copies of superb Armstrong recordings that had long ago sunk out of sight and that were completely unknown to a good many in the audience. And the musicians did their archeological work with an enthusiasm and intelligence that should send us all, neophytes or not, back to the originals. Which is what a jazz repertory company should be all about.

I was so elated that I decided to use the Armstrong tribute as the kickoff event in that summer's Newport Jazz Festival–New York—as I had done in 1974, with our Charlie Parker concert. My plans were changed, however, when officials in Moscow and Washington agreed that the NYJRC would be appropriate for a State Department–sponsored tour of the Soviet Union. A delegation of sixteen musicians from the company would head for the USSR on June 13, carrying the spirit of Armstrong (who we all thought would have been seventy-five that July) to Alma-Ata, Novosbirk, Yaroslavl, Kirv, and Moscow. They were scheduled to play twenty-three concerts.

Our second season continued with much more success than the first. We presented contemporary concerts like "The Music of Quincy Jones" and "We Love Miles . . ." alongside tributes to Jelly Roll Morton and Count Basie.

Our Bix Beiderbecke concert featured musicians who had played with the famed cornetist: Bill Challis (arranger of the original Jean Goldkette Orchestra in 1927), trombonists Bill Rank and Spiegle Wilcox, pianist Paul Mertz, drummer Chauncey Morehouse, and violinist Joe Venuti (the only musician of this lot still actively performing at that time). They played transcriptions of the original Goldkette recordings. In another part of the concert, Bob Wilber led a facsimile of Bix's Wolverines, with Pee Wee Erwin, Bob Rosengarden, Bucky Pizzarelli, and Kenny Davern. Dick Sudhalter, who had recently published a Beiderbecke biography, played some of the trumpet solos. It was rightfully hailed as a triumphant event; Beiderbecke's music was heard so rarely in concert that the strength and authenticity of our tribute was impressive.

Our "75 Years of Jazz" concert traced the history and evolution of jazz in one sweeping gesture. The company started with Scott Joplin's "The Entertainer" and an example of African-American spirituals, and blazed forward to Jelly Roll Morton and Louis Armstrong, through Dizzy Gillespie and Charlie Parker, and on to John Coltrane and Oliver Nelson. The crowning achievement of the program was a mélange of Ornette Coleman compositions, ingeniously arranged by Garnett Brown. Overall, the concert was an artistic success. The show illustrated, as the *Times* reported, "how much essential jazz territory the company's programs have covered in less than two seasons."

In that brief amount of time, the New York Jazz Repertory Company had become a sort of institution. Nowhere was this fact more aptly illustrated than in the formation of another jazz repertory group across town: the National Jazz Ensemble, led by bassist Chuck Israels. It was déjà vu; I still had crystalline memories of the rebel festival at Newport (which had also been led by a bassist). Whitney Balliett offered an analogy in the *New Yorker*: the NYJRC employed "a graduate-seminar approach," while the NJE more closely resembled "an undergraduate survey." There should have been room in New York, and in jazz, for both organizations.

Despite its growing success and its better financial straits, the NYJRC didn't last the duration of its second season. The New York State Council on the Arts had voiced some concern over my involvement with the company, and whether it reflected a conflict of interest. Even the hint of such an allegation rankled me; why should I be prevented from participating in this cause simply because I was a jazz promoter? To me, the NYJRC was not a business, but an ideal. The State Council never took their concern further than conversation, but I believe that they were very carefully monitoring our funding. Unfortunately, I didn't come to this conclusion until too late.

Sometime in the fall, Gil Evans came into my office and asked for a favor. He had applied for a grant from the State Council, in order to compose an original piece in honor of Wilhelm Reich. But Gil had no nonprofit organization; without one, the council wouldn't allocate the funding. So he asked if he could funnel the money through the NYJRC.

"Is there anything illegal about that?" I asked. Well, we checked, and there was nothing at all illegal about it. His commission was entirely separate from our foundational grant. So the NYJRC received the grant—some seven or eight thousand dollars—and awarded it to Gil. We scheduled a world premiere of the new composition as a New York Jazz Repertory concert.

But Gil never wrote the piece. We never did the concert. And before long, I received a call from the State Council's office. "We have you on record as receiving these funds. You're in default." Wait a minute. We're in *default*? This grant has nothing to do with the New York Jazz Repertory Company; we were just doing somebody a favor! But the officials were implacable. "Sorry," they said, "the records show that you're in default."

I got on the phone. "Gil, we've got to do a concert! Give me a piece of music—anything—and we'll call it 'The Wilhelm Reich Suite!'"

"No, I can't do that."

"Gil! You're going to kill us!"

But he wouldn't do it; Gil Evans was too much of an artist. As a result, the company went into default, and the council revoked our third-year application for funding. There was no power structure to save the NYJRC, no experienced fundraisers or financiers to keep us afloat. We had no choice but to call it quits. But not without a few parting salvoes.

In May 1975, the NYJRC traveled to the Kennedy Center in Washington, D.C., for a bicentennial salute to W. C. Handy. The show, a recreation of Handy's noted Carnegie Hall concert of 1928, was sponsored by Exxon and conducted by Dick Hyman. It featured not only classic Handy compositions like "St. Louis Blues," but also spirituals, work songs, and a performance of "Yamekraw," James P. Johnson's orchestral rhapsody. We had a full university choir on hand from Morgan State, and the additional vocal prowess of Bobby Short, Carrie Smith, McHenry Boatwright, and Geanie Faulkner. Katharine Handy Lewis, who had appeared in the original concert, was also on hand. On piano, "Juba Dance" by Dent was deftly handled by an old acquaintance of mine from Newton, Massachusetts, one Allen Booth, the same Allen Booth who had acted as my protector at Weeks Junior High School in 1939.

For all intents and purposes, with the exception of my using some of the programs on future festivals and tours, the New York Jazz Repertory Company experiment was finished. I have always felt that there were political reasons why the New York State Council of the Arts used the Gil Evans incident as an excuse to withdraw the little funding we had from them. There were many neighborhood cultural organizations looking for money and filing complaints asking why the council was giving money to Carnegie Hall and George Wein. The council was obviously happy to get the pressure off of its back.

*　　*　　*

Our 1973 festival was overly ambitious. My main challenge in 1974, then, was to produce a festival that was much smaller in scale, but no less in scope. The key word was consolidation. As festival season approached, I repeated this word to myself, to my staff, and to countless reporters.

On Friday, June 28, I kicked off the festival with a showcase for the New York Jazz Repertory Company, which had presented the Charlie Parker tribute earlier at Carnegie Hall. Once again the concert would consist of five parts, each devoted to a different band in Bird's career. The first of these was Jay McShann's Kansas City Orchestra. The other four were: the 1942–43 Earl Hines Orchestra, the 1943 Billy Eckstine Orchestra, a bebop combo led by Dizzy Gillespie, and a string ensemble reminiscent of Verve's popular "Bird with Strings" series. Though we couldn't reunite each of these bands, we did have their respective leaders. Jay McShann played the same arrangements that he had played in 1942. In each context, Parker's contribution was lovingly tended to by one of his stylistic inheritors: Sonny Stitt, Phil Woods, or Charles McPherson. The entire evening was unified by a script written by Dan Morgenstern and read by Willis Conover. It was a near-seamless performance; even better this time than it had been in the spring. John Wilson praised the concert for being "historic in its overview and contemporary in its performance." This was what jazz repertory, produced thoughtfully and presented in a proper context, could accomplish.

Another tribute concert at Carnegie Hall was a "Salute to Café Society." Barney Josephson, the original founder of the legendary Greenwich Village nightspot, was then 72 years old. He was still in business; he ran a restaurant on University Place called the Cookery. My Boston Storyville's entertainment policy—a staple of jazz artists alongside occasional folksingers and comedians—had been patterned after that of Café Society in the '30s and '40s. Frankie Newton, my mentor, had been among the first musicians to play there. Over the next few years, the club helped launch the careers of Hazel Scott, Lena Horne, and the comedians Zero Mostel and Jack Gilford. It also figured prominently in the early careers of Josh White, Harry Belafonte, and Sarah Vaughan.

The magnitude of this star power led me to believe that I could stage a spectacular program. I soon made a surprising discovery: none of the artists I approached were interested in participating. They didn't care about saluting Barney Josephson, despite the role he had played in their careers.

Desperate for a name attraction, I considered featuring Josephine Baker on the concert. Although Miss Baker had never actually performed at Café Society, she personified the spirit of the place. I don't know how or why, but she was in New York City at that time. Ruth Bowen, president of Queens Booking Agency, took me to see her perform at the Sherry Netherland Hotel. That evening, we arranged for her appearance on the festival. We soon busied ourselves trying to locate two Russian wolfhounds—one of the stranger stipulations in Miss Baker's contract. Our search was futile; as far as we could tell, there were no rentable Russian wolfhounds in New York City. But it ultimately didn't matter; Miss Baker canceled her appearance at the last minute, for health reasons. She died within a year.

The following night on July 1, Carnegie Hall hosted two separate concerts devoted to solo jazz piano. The first concert, at 7:30, featured more traditional players (I referred to them in the program as "melodists"): Teddy Wilson, Eubie Blake, Jess Stacy, Marian McPartland, Dick Wellstood, Eddie Heywood, Johnny Guarnieri, and Bill Evans. The highlight of the show was Eubie Blake—who, at ninety-one years of age, proclaimed that he was "glad to be here. Glad to be anywhere." Eubie's set, which closed the concert, was pure ragtime. He received a rousing standing ovation. Then we cleared the hall and readied ourselves for "Solo Piano II," which featured three leading young impressionists (at the time, I called them "meanderers"): Herbie Hancock, Keith Jarrett, and McCoy Tyner. Jarrett played one continuous forty-minute rumination, while McCoy transformed standards. Herbie took the stage with some electric keyboards; he called them his "toys." In terms of imagination, this concert traveled far afield. But it didn't match the joy or wonder of the earlier show.

On July 2, Harry James played at Carnegie Hall, where he had last played in 1938 with Benny Goodman. They were followed by Lionel Hampton, who took the stage with an all-star combo consisting of former cohorts Teddy Wilson, Milt Hinton, and Buddy Rich.

While Goodman alumni James and Lionel Hampton were packing them in at Carnegie, Avery Fisher featured a "Schlitz Salute to the Divine Sarah." I had presented Sarah Vaughan in Europe on many occasions, but this was the first solo concert she would perform for a New York audience. Like our Ella Fitzgerald tribute of the previous year, it was a highlight of the festival.

A "Schlitz Salute to Jazz and the American Song" was a continuation of the program we had presented with Alec Wilder in 1973. This year, the program made news primarily because it featured the pop singer Johnny Mathis.

Some critics had complained about the participation of Mathis on a jazz festival. He was a pop singer, to be sure; he had just made the *Guinness Book of World Records* for an album of greatest hits that had spent some 500 weeks on the *Billboard* charts.

But early in his career, Johnny Mathis had maintained a connection to the jazz world. He had played Storyville at Copley Square as early as 1952; I had paid him five hundred dollars for the week. Two months after that gig, he had the number one record in the country. I tried to get him back into the club, but he went instead to Blinstrub's Village, a big pop venue in South Boston. More than a decade later, sometime in the mid-1960s, I ran into him again. I was in London, on a tour I had arranged for Dave Brubeck. After our concert, we had headed over to Ronnie Scott's. Mathis showed up there; he had also played a concert in London that evening. He staggered over to our table; he was drunk.

"George Wein," he slurred, "someday you'll think I'm good enough to sing at the Newport Jazz Festival. When I played for you in Boston, you gave me the best rhythm section I ever had: Joey Masters, Champ Jones, and Marquis Foster." He not only remembered the gig; he recalled the Boston musicians I had hired for him.

The fact that Johnny Mathis, a major star, was so eager to work with me again in 1974 shows what the Newport Jazz Festival meant at that time. Pop artists sought the accreditation of the jazz world; Newport was like a cultural imprimatur. This ceased to be the case once rock and roll achieved its own cultural status.

The "Schlitz Salute to Jazz and the American Song" gave me an opportunity to finally present Johnny Mathis on the festival. And he wasn't doing a Johnny Mathis show; he was performing the songs of Richard Rodgers. He sang "Hello, Young Lovers," "Have You Met Miss Jones?" and "Falling in Love with Love." He also asked Mabel Mercer, a surprise guest, to sing a few songs. He had rehearsed with Mabel earlier in the week, and he treated her like the queen that she was.

Press and publicity, which had been impressive ever since I moved the festival to New York, were positively astounding this year. The *New York Times* not only printed a number of feature articles leading up to the festival, but also assigned a writer to cover each event. A review would hit the stands the day after a concert; critics were seeing concerts and then going over to the *Times* to churn out articles for the early-morning edition.

The final event of the 1974 Newport Jazz Festival–New York was another midnight jam session at Radio City Music Hall. It began with a drum battle. Buddy Rich, Max Roach, Art Blakey, and Elvin Jones went after each other gleefully, playing for an exhilarating hour. Then came the artist that everyone was waiting for: Diana Ross.

Just as Frank Sinatra had transfixed Festival Field in 1965, Diana Ross galvanized the crowd at Radio City Music Hall. The concert had sold out as soon as tickets were available; she was a major star. Presenting Miss Ross was consistent with my philosophy of working with popular artists who wanted credibility in a jazz context. What made it such a natural step this year was Diana Ross's recent portrayal of Billie Holiday on film.

The real diehards were complaining that the Hollywood film *Lady Sings the Blues* was a misrepresentation of the Billie Holiday story. Anyone who knew Billie (or even knew anything *about* her) recognized this fact. But I liked the movie. It did a lot to revitalize jazz, and it probably did more for Billie Holiday's reputation and legacy than anything that had ever happened before. For this, the City of New York gave Ross a Certificate of Appreciation. I presented her with something I called the "Golden Gardenia Award," from the Newport

Jazz Festival. Her portrayal of Lady Day had been fictionalized and glamorized, but it had also prompted thousands of people to reexamine Billie's life.

The show ended with a host of all-stars for the final session, including Milt Hinton, Eddie "Lockjaw" Davis, and Clark Terry. At one point, I sat at the piano in a spontaneous ensemble that included Charles Mingus on bass. Without counting off a tempo or calling a tune, I began to play the standard "On the Sunny Side of the Street." I took it at a relaxed tempo: nice and easy. I never explicitly stated the melody. Mingus joined in, and played it beautifully. Every one of his notes was perfectly chosen. Together, we played the song through. And after we finished, Charlie leaned over to ask me a question.

"Hey man. What tune was that?" He had no idea what we had been playing.

I replied: "We just played something I'm very happy about, Charlie. It was 'Sunny Side of the Street'—because I think the festival is on the sunny side of the street now."

After struggling to stay afloat in the Big Apple, we had finally come out on top. The festival was coming to a close after ten straight days. I was exhausted. But I knew that we had finally made it. Our compromises had been moderate. All told, it was a triumph, and playing that song was a very touching moment for me. I don't know whether it meant anything to Mingus. Whatever the case, at that instant I was on top of the world.

\*     \*     \*

Greenwich Village had enjoyed a heyday in the early sixties, when its bohemian atmosphere sparked activity in all forms of the arts. But the onslaught of rock culture had killed the jazz spirit, along with the small venues that sustained it. The Five Spot—a launching pad for Ornette Coleman and Cecil Taylor, and a proving ground for those who came afterward—had closed in 1968. The Village Gate, another prominent jazz room, had moved uptown in 1972 and died a slow death there, finally closing in 1974. Several lesser clubs had experienced the same ill fate. Only Max Gordon's Village Vanguard had been hardy enough to survive the lean times, never closing its doors and never forsaking jazz.

But there had been an awakening in Greenwich Village. By 1975, the Vanguard had been rejoined by both the Five Spot and the Village Gate. And there were a handful of new clubs—like Sweet Basil and Bradley's—that also featured jazz on a regular basis. Musicians who had struggled to find work a few years prior were now back in business. If clubs were the pulse and lifeblood of the city's jazz scene, then it seemed that an ailing patient had been jolted back to life.

The Newport Jazz Festival was not solely responsible for this resuscitation, but it was part of what made it happen.

Some artists naturally didn't see it that way. They were more concerned with how they had been "excluded" from the festival. So they complained to the press, and busied themselves with presenting a series of small-scale counter-festivals (a reaction to which I had grown accustomed). Sam Rivers kicked off a month-long Summer Music Festival at Studio Rivbea. A block west on Bond Street, vocalist Joe Lee Wilson ran a Summer Loft Jazz Festival at his place. In SoHo, Juma Sultan's Studio We presented concerts almost around the clock, while Rashied Ali played nightly at his Studio 77.

All of this activity had repercussions for Newport–New York. Ironically, the successful revitalization of jazz in the city—itself a by-product of the festival—now presented us with formidable challenges. Audiences were less hungry for the music than they had been just a year or two ago. I doubt whether we could have wrapped a line around the corner of Radio City for a jam session in 1975, the way we had in previous years.

A second result of the New York club boom was the end of our honeymoon with the critics. The festival was no longer an underdog in the jungle of New York City. We had become a fixture, an institution. Artists from the avant-garde were complaining about being ignored. Articles commented on the Newport Jazz Festival's "predictable," "conservative" programming. While I was looking to put on a festival that was a success, they were looking for me to provide a forum for cutting-edge art. I may love jazz, but I don't immediately accept everything that comes up the road. Newness doesn't make something significant; it has to prove itself one way or another.

Our situation was worsened by a fiscal crisis in New York City. With an old city budget expiring at the end of June, more than 37,000 city employees—sanitation workers, police officers, firefighters, parks workers, and corrections officers among them—were expected to lose their jobs. In response, there was a citywide sanitation strike. Garbage festered in the streets for weeks.

The most interesting concert in 1975 featured both the Thelonious Monk Quartet and the Keith Jarrett Quartet. It was Monk's first concert performance, besides his unscheduled appearance at a 1974 NYJRC tribute, in two years, and despite his age and his flagging health, Thelonious played beautifully. His quartet included Paul Jeffrey on tenor, Larry Ridley on bass, and son Tootie on drums. Keith Jarrett performed a set with his group that reflected Monk's music. Keith was respectful of Thelonious, and his band with Dewey

Redman on tenor, Charlie Haden on bass, and Paul Motian on drums was in good form. John Wilson noted that "the combination of the groups, with Mr. Monk, once considered a radical innovator, as the traditionalist centerpiece, was indicative of the broad musical range into which jazz has moved in the last 20 years."

John Hammond was directly involved with the "Schlitz Salute to the Jazz Hall of Fame," a concert organized by Dan Morgenstern. The evening honored a parade of older musicians with film clips, live performances, and plaques that were presented by Hammond serving as emcee. Film footage of Red Norvo playing with Benny Goodman led into Red Norvo's performance onstage; footage of Barney Bigard playing "C Jam Blues" with the 1942 Ellington Orchestra segued into Bigard onstage playing the same piece. The other musicians—Bobby Hackett, Vic Dickenson, Joe Venuti, Earl Hines, Teddy Wilson, Milt Hinton, and Jo Jones—were fêted in the same manner. Everyone shone brightly, although there was some embarrassment when Jabbo Smith, the long-lost trumpeter who had famously locked horns with Louis Armstrong in the 1920s, stepped forward for his solo. Jabbo could still play, but he got so nervous onstage at Avery Fisher Hall that he couldn't bring out any notes. We had to get Bobby Hackett to stand right behind him, ghosting a solo. Few people noticed the subterfuge.

\*     \*     \*

*Over the years, Newport has been justly accused of bloat, compromise, and conservatism, and though the last charge would seem to apply this year, I can't recall a more inventive and varied series of concerts.*

**—Gary Giddins**

There was a serious stand against the festival at this time by most jazz critics—too much crossover, not enough "new" music, the "same old thing"—were constant refrains.

A final complaint, and a newer one, was best articulated by John S. Wilson. Wrapping up the 1975 festival for the *Times*, he had expressed concern that Newport–New York had "boiled down to a series of concerts at Carnegie and Avery Fisher Halls. And one wonders if that, for a jazz festival, is sufficiently festive." This point was well taken; I was beginning to feel the same way myself. The original Newport Jazz Festival had derived much of its splendor from its surroundings; it gave city dwellers the opportunity to escape for a few days and enjoy the breezes on Narragansett Bay. Such a feeling was hard to come by in the New York area, but we had to try. So for the 1976 festival, our outdoor activities included not only the ever-popular Staten Island Ferry cruise, but also two new events.

The first of these took place in a pastoral environment—Waterloo Village, located on the Musconetcong River in northern New Jersey's Sussex County. Waterloo Village, adjacent to the town of Stanhope, had originally been settled in 1740 as a farming community. Its most lasting legacy had been the Andover Forge, an ironworks that had supplied raw materials for the armament of George Washington's troops during the Revolutionary War. Two businessmen had revived Waterloo Village, restoring a mill area near a stream. The town had become an historic site. Antebellum houses, tiny shops, and cozy taverns gave the town a quaint atmosphere.

Waterloo Village seemed an ideal spot for traditional jazz. It was a lovely, sprawling area, and there was a built-in audience—the New Jersey Jazz Society, an association of businessmen and assorted enthusiasts with a passion for early Ellington and Armstrong. I made plans to present three events at Waterloo: a gospel picnic hosted by Harlem's prominent Reverend Wyatt T. Walker, a traditional jazz picnic, and a concert featuring both Eubie Blake and the "Kid from Red Bank," Count Basie.

Our other outdoor innovation had much more urban surroundings. Nineteen seventy-six was the nation's bicentennial year, and the City of New York was promoting a number of special events. A significant moment in New York's cultural history was the heyday of 52nd Street. I proposed a 52nd Street Fair featuring several stages, food booths, and a strong lineup of jazz artists. The event would be free and would take place during the morning and afternoon of Monday, July 5. The city liked the idea, and agreed to block traffic on 52nd between Fifth and Sixth Avenues.

The fair served a double purpose for the festival. Not only did it contribute atmosphere, but it also provided an opportunity to present worthy artists. I always wanted the platform of artists to be wider; not necessarily bigger, but wider. The musicians I hired for the fair included: Sonny Stitt, Barry Harris, Gary Bartz, Roy Haynes, Zoot Sims, Joe Newman, Sam Rivers, Charlie Rouse, Clark Terry, Beaver Harris, Machito, Hannibal Marvin Peterson, the New Orleans Preservation Hall Jazz Band, the Original Traditional Jazz Band, and, from South Africa, the Jazz Ministers. I was able to pay for these bands because I had cut out our costly stadium concerts and other money-losers.

A midnight jam session planned for Radio City Music Hall became a benefit. It was a good idea; it enabled us to revive the midnight jam sessions while raising money for a good cause. In fact, there were two good causes. The concert was a tribute to the Reverend John Garcia Gensel, pastor of St. Peter's Lutheran Church. Through his work both within and without the church, Reverend Gensel served the whole jazz community. Everyone—from Bobby Rosengarden to Anthony Braxton, from Milt Hinton to George Benson—came out to salute him. Sarah Vaughan did several numbers with her trio and then was joined by Dizzy Gillespie. Count Basie led a combo peopled with all-star alumni like Clark Terry, Joe Williams, and Harry "Sweets" Edison. Bill Evans, Eddie Gomez, and Elvin Jones played behind a reunited Lee Konitz and Warne Marsh.

Half of the proceeds from the evening went to St. Peter's Lutheran Church; the other half went to pay the medical bills of Rahsaan Roland Kirk, who had suffered a debilitating stroke several months before, which immobilized the right side of his body. Kirk played at the benefit concert, and although he was still half-paralyzed, he was astounding. Hobbling onto a stage crammed with stars like Dizzy, Mingus, and Blakey, Rahsaan held aloft a custom-altered tenor and nearly blew everyone away. His tone was alarmingly full-bodied, given his fragile condition, and his ideas flowed as freely as ever. It was the peak of a magnificent evening.

The festival platform also briefly revived the New York Jazz Repertory Company. Although the NYJRC had not conducted a regular season, all of the charts (and musicians) were still around. It was time to use our resources in a final, monumental gesture: a salute to the musical career of the late Duke Ellington. Rather than condensing the tribute to a single program, I had decided to spread it out over four separate evenings—a night apiece for the 1920s, '30s, and '40s, and one night dedicated to an extended composition. So little of the Ellington music had been transcribed that we had to enlist the services of several additional arrangers. It was a formidable task; they were forced to score much of Duke's music from old, scratchy 78s. We used ten different arrangers over the course of the four programs.

The first installment of our "Ellington Saga" took place on the evening of June 27, with Dick Hyman leading a charge into the territory of the 1920s. The second installment, on June 29, featured Bob Wilber's musical direction, and material from the '30s. On both concerts, the band was impressively precise, tackling Duke's trademark sonorities with deceptive grace and ease. Critics noted, with mixed feelings, that an audience member could close his or her eyes and imagine a time warp; it was as if the old records had come to life. What troubled them most was the improvisation, which hewed close to the original solos. Musicians were hard-pressed to play a solo that captured the spirit of the original. The antidote to this problem was Cootie Williams, whom we brought out of retirement for these concerts. Cootie had been a part of Ellington's Orchestra since 1928, and he played this concert with a strength that scared the whole trumpet section. When Cootie blew, his section-mates—trumpeters like Joe Newman, Jon Faddis, and Doc Cheatham—just looked around at each other in not-so-mock disbelief.

Part III of our Ellington Saga featured a performance of "Black, Brown and Beige," the Maestro's "tone parallel to the history of the American Negro." There was a resonance to our event, not only because it was happening once again in Carnegie Hall, but also because we had one of the vocalists from the original performance: Joya Sherrill, who sang "The Blues."

The second portion of the evening, after this exhilarating, exhausting performance, showcased the Duke Ellington Orchestra under the direction of Mercer Ellington.

Part IV of our Ellington Saga, "the '40s," took place on the Fourth of July. The band, under the leadership of Joe Newman, included several prominent second-generation Ellington alumni: Quentin Jackson, Norris Turney, and Al Hibbler. This was arguably Ellington at his creative peak, with songs like "Chelsea Bridge," "Jack the Bear," and "Harlem Air Shaft." Approaching this repertoire was a daunting task, and the NYJRC struggled valiantly to keep the program afloat.

The only persistent criticism of the Ellington Saga was an obvious statement: No matter how impeccable the performances, it just wasn't the same without the Duke. Still, no one had ever mounted so ambitious a repertory project in the history of jazz.

This sort of repertory programming would thankfully resume in the '80s, when Gary Giddins and John Lewis worked together on the American Jazz Orchestra, and the 1990s, when Wynton Marsalis led the Lincoln Center Jazz Orchestra. It took nearly two decades for the cultural establishment to catch up with our thinking, and Jazz at Lincoln Center was the primary result. Our efforts provided a foundation and a precedent for what was to come.

If Duke Ellington hovered over the 1976 Newport Jazz Festival, as John Wilson noted, "like a ghostly presence," Count Basie received equal due as a living, breathing legend. The New York Repertory Company participated in a Saturday night program at Carnegie Hall, a "Schlitz Salute to Basie: Today

& Yesterday." I had organized a reunion band consisting of Basie veterans: players like Benny Powell, Al Grey, Frank Foster, Sonny Payne, and Frank Wess. This band held forth during the concert's first half. With Basie himself at the piano, they revisited "April in Paris," "Corner Pocket," and other classics, swinging on every note. It was as good as any of us remembered, and it posed a serious challenge to the working Count Basie band, which followed with a driving set of new arrangements. The evening was a true study in Basie; each band had its respective strong points, and both represented the spirit and feeling of their leader.

I had plans to put together a European tour for the Basie reunion band. After their smashing success at Carnegie Hall, promoters were anxious to get them. I called the group The Count Basie Alumni Band; as I recall, we had Nat Pierce on piano. But when Basie found out about this, he got quite angry. "Look, George," he said, "I'm not dead yet. You've got me competing against myself, and I don't think that's very nice." Embarrassed, I apologized, realizing that I had made a mistake. It was inappropriate for me to use the Basie name in conjunction with that group. Basie probably could have sued me for this infringement. He didn't force me to cancel that tour (he didn't want to knock his former guys out of work), but his admonishment ensured that I would never do this again.

\*     \*     \*

A pioneering concert in 1977 was entitled "Solo Flights," featuring solo performances by various jazz artists. I dedicated this evening to the memory of Erroll Garner, who had passed away early in the year. It featured such artists as Art Blakey, Gary Burton, John Lewis, Joe Pass, Charlie Mingus, Steve Swallow, and Joe Venuti.

Violinist Joe Venuti's career pinnacle was well in the past, but his virtuosity was still undiminished. In recent years, he had taken to playing with an amplifier. During the sound check, I heard him testing this amp, and it sounded terrible. It was just too loud. So when Joe came off the stage, I spoke to him.

"Joe, you sound wonderful. But you really don't need the amp. You're playing Carnegie Hall all by yourself."

Joe protested, but I persisted. His violin had such a singing, resonant tone—it made no sense to ruin that with bad amplification. I made such a point of arguing against the amp that Joe finally relented. He went out onto the stage that night and played acoustically, and it was lovely. But I don't think Joe Venuti ever forgave me for insisting that he lose the amp. He took issue with my interference. At Nice that summer, he was not overly friendly with me. He passed away a year later.

For some people, the centerpiece of the entire festival was the Ornette Coleman retrospective at Avery Fisher Hall. I had long been trying to figure out a way to present Ornette properly. The solution: We'd put on a concert representing the three major segments of his musical career. First we would feature the original quartet with Don Cherry, Charlie Haden, and Billy Higgins. The second segment would spotlight his sextet, which included Dewey Redman, Ed Blackwell, David Izenzon, and electric guitarist James "Blood" Ulmer. And finally, there was Prime Time, a new group. Ornette was happy to go along with my concept. To my knowledge, it was the first time he did a concert in this tripartite manner.

I felt at the time that this concert, with its historical scope, could be an important event. We were giving Ornette the freedom and incentive to paint a portrait of his own career. If it worked, the concert would go far to depict the roots of most of the directions jazz had taken in the previous seventeen years. The jazz public recognized this fact, and our advance ticket sales were fair. The concert would not be a washout; we anticipated that the hall would maybe be two-thirds full.

Then an unexpected thing happened. A few days before the concert, the *New York Times* published a full-page article outlining and applauding Ornette Coleman's career. Almost immediately, the remainder of the tickets were sold. Some 700 or 800 tickets flew out the door in those last two days. I was elated as I went back to Ornette's dressing room on the night of the concert. "Ornette," I beamed, "we sold out, and I mean we sold *every ticket*." It made me happy. Although he could be terribly inflexible in his business dealings, I was always fond of Ornette as a person. He was never confrontational with me. He has always been a kind man, with a gentle disposition.

Some years earlier, during the mid-sixties, Ornette had come over to my office on West Seventy-fourth Street. He was quite frustrated. He told me that he had a scrapbook of more than 750 articles discussing his importance to the continuing evolution of jazz. "But even with all this publicity," he said, "I can't get a decent paying gig." He thought that he had every right to earn the same amount as artists like Dave Brubeck, Miles Davis, and the Modern Jazz Quartet. Perhaps he did deserve more. But promoters around the world refused to meet his price. I booked him on several European tours during the 1960s, and presented him at Newport a few times. Otherwise, there was little I could do to help him; I couldn't meet his terms. The price of an artist at that time was determined by the public; nonprofit organizations had not become such an integral part of jazz funding.

The Ornette Coleman retrospective was a major coup. It was the triumph of the fifty-pound scrapbook; Ornette's adulatory reviews were finally putting people in the seats. Maybe this was a turning point, I thought. Perhaps I could now create a niche for adventurous music in the festival setting, in a manner that would also be financially feasible. These hopes would later be dashed, repeatedly.

All things considered, the 1977 Newport Jazz Festival–New York was a moderate but less-than-triumphant success. There were many highlights, to be sure. But the festival itself was not the attraction that it had once been. I was beginning to feel that the New York festival had run its course.

I missed Newport. Like a retired baseball star, not hearing the crack of the bat against the ball in spring training, I missed the big stage, the crowds, the sound of jazz under a wide-open sky. No matter what we did, the annual gauntlet of concerts in Manhattan would never approximate this feeling. So I looked into alternative sites outside the city for the festival. The most promising discovery was the Saratoga Performing Arts Center, in the upstate–New York resort town of Saratoga Springs. This facility was ideal for a festival presentation, and the people there were prepared to welcome us with open arms. I made my decision: the festival was going to move.

I called a press conference to announce this news in late summer: The Newport Jazz Festival was leaving New York for Saratoga Springs. I was prepared to hear criticism and complaints from jazz fans in the city.

Instead, my announcement met with a bewildering silence. Nobody cared. A few newspapers printed an item on the topic; there were no letters to the editor. And I got this uneasy feeling in the pit of my stomach. Had I done the right thing? What if the whole idea had been a mistake? Instead of becoming a larger-scale Waterloo Village, would Saratoga be my Waterloo?

Joyce rescued me. She ventured a wise and practical solution: "Why don't you do both?"

How simple! I still had a hold on the New York concert halls, although I had notified them of my cancellation. I could conceivably present festivals in both Manhattan and Saratoga Springs. So I called another press conference, about three weeks after my original announcement.

"You know," I remarked to a roomful of reporters, "as I drove over the George Washington Bridge, I noticed that they don't charge you to leave the city. But coming back costs $2.50. I think they're trying to tell me something. If I take the festival out of New York City, it will be hard to bring it back. So we're not leaving. I'm going to do Newport Jazz Festivals in both Saratoga and New York."

It was one of the smartest moves I ever made. I have Joyce to thank for it.

The deal I made with the Saratoga Performing Arts Center as partnership was the best kind of arrangement a promoter can make with a facility. As my partner, they waived the rent and the usual miscellaneous fees. So the expenses were the musicians, the advertising, and the staff working on the event that day. We split all expenses and profits equally. To this day, we still have the same arrangement.

That fall, Joyce and I retreated again to the home we had acquired in France. After the manic energy of another New York festival, this was just what we needed. Yet a producer's mind is rarely respectful of vacations. One afternoon in Vence, I hit the tennis courts with a man named Les Lieber, who rented a house in the next valley. Les was a public relations man by trade, and a saxophonist by hobby; he ran a weekly jam session called "Jazz at Noon," for other musically inclined businessmen and professionals. I didn't know him well, but we were friendly. That day, we got to talking about the festival. I mentioned that it would soon be twenty-five years since the First American Jazz Festival in Newport. "That's a big anniversary," Les pointed out. "You should be honored in some way. Why not an event at the White House?"

That, I thought, was not a bad idea.

I had been to the White House once before in 1969, during the first year of the Nixon administration. The occasion was a celebration of Duke Ellington's seventieth birthday. Richard Nixon presided over the event, and awarded Ellington with the Presidential Medal of Freedom. *Down Beat* would later attest that this was "the most popular thing he ever did in a public career spanning 30 years."

That may not have been an exaggeration; the Ellington party was a classic night. Despite my lifelong liberalism, I found myself standing in line to shake President Nixon's outstretched hand. Say what you will about his politics; Richard Nixon knew how to throw a party. The wine, whiskey, and food were plentiful. The musicians in attendance took part in a joyously informal jam session. Televised footage of the event includes a shot of me playing the piano next to Willie the Lion. And although Nixon excused himself from the celebration shortly after dinner, he left the rest of us there to enjoy ourselves. We stayed until the early-morning hours.

Nine years after that evening, much had changed. Nixon had resigned, Ford had taken his place, and Jimmy Carter had been elected by a narrow margin. In all that time, there had been no other presidential jazz galas.

During the first year of his term, President Carter had devoted evenings at the White House to rock and country music. Coming from Georgia, he had direct contact with the promoters in these fields of music. I felt that if he was going to pay tribute to the Allman Brothers and various Nashville country artists, he should do something comparable for jazz. The twenty-fifth summer anniversary of the Newport Jazz Festival, I realized, just might be the right hook.

But I didn't have the slightest idea how to set the necessary wheels in motion. Instinctively, I felt that it would be inappropriate to arrange the affair through a PR office.

Although my company no longer ran a festival in Newport we still called our main event the Newport Jazz Festival. The Rhode Island politicos who had been in office in the 1960s were still in place, and they had all been my guests, at one time or another during earlier festivals. I drafted a letter outlining my idea, and asking for help. I sent out three copies of this letter—to U.S. Senators Claiborne Pell and John Chafee, and to U.S. Representative Fernand St. Germain. I received responses from each of them.

Senator Pell sent a letter that basically read: "Dear George, this is a wonderful idea. There is not much I can do to initiate it, but if it comes up I will certainly endorse it."

Senator Chafee wrote a note saying: "Dear George, I think this is a wonderful idea. What artists would you bring to the White House? Send me a list and I will present it to the White House."

Rhode Island congressman Freddy St. Germain sent a letter that read: "You have an appointment with the social secretary of the White House." This story illustrates the various ways of dealing with a request. While each letter was encouraging, you can guess which was the most helpful.

In spring 1978, Joyce and I traveled to Washington, D.C., to meet with Gretchen Poston. We had our arguments ready; we were determined to convince Ms. Poston of this White House Jazz Festival idea. We discovered that our preparations had been unnecessary; Ms. Poston had already approved the festival, and was ready to begin making plans. "We'll set up a stage on the lawn," she said, "and do it during the first week of June."

Emboldened, I raised a point: "Wait a minute, Ms. Poston. Could we move the date to mid-June, shortly before our festival in New York? Many more artists will be available at that time." She checked her calendar and told us that would be fine. Then the three of us began discussing the festival together, like old friends. We talked about the program. We sketched out basic specs for the stage. Joyce came up with the idea of bringing people from New Orleans to prepare the food. The conversation continued in this fashion, and in one day, the concept for a White House Jazz Festival had progressed from pipe dream to scheduled event. As Joyce and I left the grounds and walked together down Pennsylvania Avenue, we marveled at the thought of it. The president of the United States was going to honor the Newport Jazz Festival's twenty-fifth year with a jazz festival on the White House lawn.

Within a week, we had sent Ms. Poston a letter outlining a hypothetical plan for the concert. This included what I called "a continually revolving program with musicians gradually changing from number to number in a very subtle manner." This would be a carefully coordinated afternoon.

In my letter to Ms. Poston, I included a list of 224 people—musicians, critics, industry people, and FPI staff—to be considered as potential invitees. We later narrowed this list quite a bit; the White House wanted an attendance of no more than 400 people, and they gave me one-third of this number for my guest list. The final list encompassed some forty musicians, as well as a number of family members, critics, and industry friends. I made sure to include the leadership of the Jos. Schlitz Brewing Company and Brown & Williamson, my two corporate sponsors. I also extended an invitation to Elaine Lorillard, without whom the Newport Jazz Festival would not have happened in the first place. We sent our invitations in early May. Despite this short notice (the event was scheduled for June 18), almost all of our invitees accepted. Most of the musicians on my list paid their own way to Washington, D.C. I helped only a few of them from New York with transportation and hotel expenses.

We kept in close touch with Ms. Poston, taking several more trips to Washington to map out every aspect of the afternoon. This was not going to be an indoor party, like the Ellington birthday tribute of 1969. It was to be a full-fledged outdoor concert, with almost all of the technical demands of a festival performance. There would be no tent; Ms. Poston was firm on this point. In case of rain, there was a backup plan which involved moving the function indoors and trimming the guest list.

During the course of our communications, I had many requests of Gretchen Poston. She answered every request with efficiency but no excess of sweetness. I later realized that this was merely the technique of a fantastic organizer who didn't want to commit herself and her office to something she couldn't honor. One example of this caution: I asked if it would be possible for the president to take an individual photograph with each of the participating musicians. Her answer: "I don't know whether that's possible. President Carter will be in Panama the night before; I hope he even gets back in time for the festival." The thought of presenting a White House event without the president was a distressing prospect. In any case, I understood that Ms. Poston was playing it on the safe side; she didn't want to make any promises. It was, after all, a rather important weekend for the president. That Saturday, June 17, he signed a treaty promising the return of the Panama Canal to Panama in the year 2000. He returned to Washington early Sunday morning, and immediately went to sleep.

That afternoon, I gathered the musicians on the South Lawn to run down the program. It was a remarkable assembly. Benny Carter next to Ron Carter. Clark Terry alongside Chick Corea. Sonny Rollins, Stan Getz, Zoot Sims, Illinois Jacquet—all in one place. Some of the artists were going to play together in groups; others would play solo. My biggest concern was time. I had been instructed to restrict the affair to two hours. In order to meet this demand, I had to impose time limits. After some quick calculations, I had it figured out. Solo artists would get five minutes apiece. Ensembles would get eight minutes.

Asking Cecil Taylor to play for only five minutes was not easy. But he, and everyone else, cooperated without complaint, although Eubie Blake, who would have been happy to play all night, did grumble good-naturedly.

At three o'clock, to our surprise, we were joined by a shirt-sleeved Jimmy Carter, with a White House photographer in tow. Not only did he stop to pose with every musician, he had words for each of them. Jimmy Carter had listened to New Orleans jazz radio broadcasts during his childhood, and had visited Greenwich Village as a young naval officer in the 1940s. "I saw you in a club in New York more than twenty years ago," he said to one musician. "You came to Atlanta once, and I saw you there," he said to another. To players he had never seen before, he said, "I haven't heard you yet, but I'm really looking forward to hearing you today." He didn't jive anybody. Within ten days of the event, every musician had received his or her autographed photo with the president.

A buffet—including jambalaya and pecan pie—was served outdoors, with rousing accompanying music by New Orleans's Young Tuxedo Brass Band. It was a bright, muggy, sunny day, with temperatures hovering around 90 degrees. But the 400 guests in attendance remained in high spirits.

President Carter ushered in the musical portion of the day with a heartfelt speech about the role of jazz in his own life and in America's cultural history.

He characterized jazz itself as "vivid, alive, aggressive, innovative on the one hand; and the severest form of self-discipline on the other. Never compromising quality as the human spirit bursts forward in an expression of song."

After President Carter's speech, I took the stage for a brief introduction, thanking the president for making the event possible. "I thank you," I said, "the musicians thank you, and to get personal for just one second . . . of all the people who thanks you the most, it's my father Dr. Wein—who has the best Father's Day present he ever had, in his eighty-fifth year." By coincidence, June 18 was Father's Day. As I made this pronouncement, I looked over at Doc sitting next to my mother on a folding chair. Yes, he *kvelled*.

Doc's age was nothing compared to the giant who opened the program. Eubie Blake was ninety-five years old, and still a commanding presence on-stage. He obediently (if grudgingly) played only two songs. They were "Boogie Woogie Beguine" and the more familiar "Memories of You."

The first of our ensembles—a septet featuring Teddy Wilson, Jo Jones, Milt Hinton, Roy Eldridge, Clark Terry, Illinois Jacquet, and Benny Carter—played "In a Mellotone" and "Lady Be Good."

Our second assembled group took a more modern approach. Sonny Rollins, Max Roach, McCoy Tyner, and Ron Carter did a modal blues—Rollins's "Sonnymoon for Two."

After this group, I stepped on stage to make a short announcement. Thanks to taped broadcast recordings of the event, my spontaneous address has been preserved.

> There's one more thing I want to do here. Ladies and Gentlemen, I want to ask you to acknowledge a man in the audience. He's one of the greatest musicians of our generation. He's a man whose courage and strength is only exceeded by his talent and creativity. He's sitting over here—Ladies and Gentlemen, I want you to stand up for this one. Because I want you to give as great a round of applause as he's ever had in his life . . . for Charlie Mingus, Ladies and Gentlemen!

President Carter walked over to the front row, where Mingus was sitting in a wheelchair, and embraced him. Charles Mingus had recently had a stroke. He also had advanced amyotrophic lateral sclerosis—Lou Gehrig's disease—and his condition had been getting progressively worse. At this point, he was almost totally paralyzed. I had taken special care to see that he had everything he needed. Still, it was wholly incongruous to see Mingus—a man who seemed to have been in perpetual, furious motion all his life—so immobilized. As President Carter leaned over and spoke to him, Mingus broke down and started to cry. Tears streamed down his face. The audience, on their feet, applauded him: his courage, his brilliance. For me, it was a spiritual moment. My voice quavering, I spoke.

"C'mon Mingus, stand up, will you? God bless you, Charlie Mingus." It was as if I was praying aloud. At that moment, perhaps, I believed that these people who stood and cheered, might have the power to restore a man's strength; to bring him out of that chair.

For many of us it was the last time we would see him.

I never considered this moment controversial until many years later, when I listened to a National Public Radio "Jazz Profiles" tape. The broadcast was an anniversary celebration of Charles Mingus's music, and an examination of his life. Near the end of the program, announcer Nancy Wilson mentions the White House Jazz Festival of 1978, and the fact that Mingus was a guest. "Ironically," she adds, "the man who emceed, Mingus despised. Jazz producer George Wein."

I couldn't believe my ears. A man Mingus *despised*? And as I kept listening, the NPR broadcast played part of my speech. "C'mon Mingus," I heard myself saying, "stand up, will you?" Then Nancy Wilson's voice again: "But standing wasn't possible. By then wheelchair-bound, Mingus—*Charles* Mingus, as he insisted on being called—could not."

I was shocked. Obviously, whoever prepared the script had looked no further than 1960, the year of Mingus's infamous rebel yell. But in the years since, we had worked together many times. We had a good relationship.

It doesn't do much good to protest this matter here, but the incident does illustrate a certain point. Despite the years of work devoted to jazz and the jazz musician, I remain a target. The Man. The Producer. The "Enemy." So it's tantalizingly easy to take shots at me. It must also be somewhat gratifying. I'm defenseless against such attacks, so I take them as they come. They don't destroy me. They used to leave a bitter taste in my mouth—but no longer.

Cecil Taylor's five-minute solo was a measured dose of creative mayhem; a fleeting glimpse of some kind of genius. After the last note faded, Jimmy Carter sprang up from the grass and rushed over to Cecil; Secret Service men scrambled to keep pace. The president took the pianist's two hands in his own, looking at them with wonderment and awe. "I've never seen *anyone* play the piano that way," he marveled.

The final scheduled set of the White House Festival—featuring Lionel Hampton, Chick Corea, Stan Getz, Zoot Sims, Ray Brown, George Benson, and Louis Bellson—was energetic and swinging. They did "How High the Moon," "Georgia on My Mind," and Hamp's theme song, "Flying Home," which he rechristened the "Jimmy Carter Jam." Illinois Jacquet came on to reprise his famous tenor solo.

In the midst of this gaiety, President Carter approached me. "When is this concert scheduled to end?"

Mindful of Gretchen Poston's time limit, I explained that we were prepared to cut it off at precisely 8 P.M. That time was almost nigh. "Sir, I was told to end the concert in exactly two hours. Unless those orders are countermanded, that's precisely when the show will end."

"Consider the orders countermanded," the president said, smiling. Soon afterward, he took the stage to signal the end of the official program. "I don't believe the White House has ever seen anything like this," he enthused. "This music is as much a part of the greatness of this nation as the White House or the Capitol down the way. Stan Getz and Lionel Hampton have been heroes of mine for a long time. Anybody who wants to is free to go, but I'm going to stay and listen to some more music."

The show kept going, on its own momentum. Pearl Bailey, who was in attendance not as a performer but as Louis Bellson's wife, jumped onstage to join Hamp. The vibraharpist, mildly threatened, tried to shoo her off. (He later claimed that without his glasses, he didn't recognize Pearl. He thought she was white.) Miss Bailey stayed on to sing a few tunes. Later Gerry Mulligan, another invitee not scheduled to perform, seized one of the Young Tuxedo Band's clarinets and got in some licks of his own. Dizzy and Max played a duet, and later Dizzy—in a magisterial air—summoned the president onstage. It was then that Jimmy Carter became the first president to take part in a bebop tune—singing "Salt peanuts, salt peanuts!"

\*     \*     \*

Five days later, we kicked off the festival in New York City. With events running back-to-back in Washington, D.C., New York, Stanhope, N.J., and Saratoga Springs, it's a wonder, and a testament to the commitment of FPI staff, that I managed to remain standing. Not to mention the just-finished New Orleans Jazz and Heritage Festival, and the still-to-come Grande Parade and KOOL festivals. It was a busy time.

The year 1978 found Latin jazz making a definite impact on the festival in "A Schlitz Salute to Jazz Latino"—featuring the Tito Puente Orchestra, Machito's Afro-Cuban Jazz Orchestra, Mongo Santamaria, and host Felipe Luciano.

Schlitz not only sponsored the evening concert; it also underwrote a Latin Roots Musical Exhibit at the Lincoln Center Performing Arts Library. This exhibit, curated by Mr. Luciano along with musicologist Joe Conzo and bandleader Charlie Palmieri, featured artifacts from the annals of Latin music history. The items on display ranged from the ancient, *claves* made from human bones, to the recent, a stage gown donated by Celia Cruz. And Latin Roots was not merely a smart festival tie-in; it was the first time any major New York museum had mounted an exhibit on Latin musical culture.

Irakere was an eleven-piece band from Havana, Cuba. Columbia Records had brought them to America to play at the festival. Because we feared political demonstrations by anti-Castro Cuban émigrés, we had decided not to publicize their appearance, but rather to add them onto an existing concert. And it worked. Their long set surprised everybody; the band danced, sang, and even paraded through the aisles of the audience like a New Orleans street band. And their musicianship was at a high level. The group's leaders were pianist Chucho Valdes and alto saxophonist Paquito D'Rivera. The band was tight, powerful, and flexible. Their lead trumpeter, a stocky young man named Arturo Sandoval, seemed to be setting a new standard for unbelievable high-note acrobatics. During Irakere's encore, the band welcomed American jazz heroes Stan Getz and Maynard Ferguson to the stand. Ferguson, who had always reigned unchallenged as king of the stratosphere, went head-to-head with Sandoval in a blowout duel. When it was all over, Maynard looked over at the Cuban virtuoso with an expression of total respect.

Music of the Americas resurfaced several more times during the festival. The Brazilian husband-and-wife team of Flora Purim and Airto Moreira played Avery Fisher Hall. And at Carnegie, we presented a program called "Brazilian Nights." This latter concert was a memorable affair commemorating the *samba* and *bossa nova*, and their relationships to jazz. Guitarist Charlie Byrd led a trio in playing the music of Heitor Villa-Lobos, both with and without the help of Stan Getz. Afterward, Getz brought on his own group, and played some of the material from his successful *bossa nova* albums. Then out walked João Gilberto. The unassuming singer and guitarist took a seat on a folding chair at center stage. Next to him, a single percussionist provided the only accompaniment. The music was magic; its lilting pulse cast a spell over the hall. João had not performed in the United States in roughly fifteen years, a statistic that rendered this moment all the more precious. The evening ended with Gilberto, Getz, and Byrd playing an impromptu "One Note Samba"—a fitting end to a perfect night.

Mindful of Ornette Coleman's sellout the previous year, I presented him again—this time, on a double-bill with Cecil Taylor. It was the first time that these two giants of the avant-garde were being presented together by me on a major concert. I was quite excited about this, and harbored hopes that it would go over with the public. After working successfully with Ornette in New York, and presenting both Ornette and Cecil at the White House, I felt some affinity with these artists. I recognized their significance in the world of jazz.

Unfortunately, my optimism was ill-founded. We sold less than half the house. A week earlier, Cecil had played a five-minute solo on the White House lawn that was breathtaking in its aggressive energy. I thought that Cecil might have learned something there about pacing his performances. I was wrong. At Carnegie Hall, he and his group played nonstop for an hour. After a while, their intensity had a deadening effect; it was exhausting.

A musician with an entire concert to himself was the keyboardist Chick Corea. In fact, he had two. "Chick Corea and Friends" sold out so quickly that we added a second show. Chick was one of those superior talents who had come up with a formula, call it "crossover" or what you will, for commercial success. Yet he hadn't forgotten the joy of being a musician. This concert featured not only Chick's thirteen-piece orchestra but also the Woody Herman Orchestra, frequent collaborator Gary Burton, vocalist Gayle Moran, and fellow keyboardist Herbie Hancock. The concert closed with Corea-Hancock duets, on both pianos and synthesizers. This musical saga, which somehow unfolded twice in one evening, hinted not only at the versatility of Chick Corea's artistry, but also the respect and rapport that he shared with some of his musical peers.

The following night, we staged a tribute to Lionel Hampton at Carnegie Hall. The irrepressible bandleader-vibraphonist was celebrating fifty years in music. The Borough of Manhattan had officially declared it "Lionel Hampton Day," and this concert was no disappointment. The seventeen-piece band we assembled for the occasion included Hampton alumni Cat Anderson, Joe Newman, Doc Cheatham, and Arnett Cobb.

We still continued our Schlitz Salute to the American Song. This turned out to be one of the festival's best concerts. It began with the eighty-three-year-old Alberta Hunter, singing her own compositions. The former blues singer and Broadway star, who had at one time played nightclubs with both King Oliver and Louis Armstrong, was back in business after nearly twenty years' absence. Her comeback had been a matter of chance; Charlie Bourgeois heard her at a party at Bobby Short's house, and recommended her for a long engagement at the Cookery. Her wildly successful performance there prompted Barney Josephson to manage her. He quickly became obsessed with her career (neglecting his own nightclub in the process). Josephson's devotion paid off; Hunter was once again a star.

And she had adopted a star's attitude. I was standing backstage as Ms. Hunter mounted the stairs to the stage. I heard her mutter under her breath: "It's payback time." That was sad to me. She regarded her festival appearance as a reciprocal favor, misjudging Charlie, whose motives in bringing her back were selfless, and me, who wanted to honor her artistry. She was showbiz till the end.

And that concluded the 1978 Newport Jazz Festival–New York. That same weekend, we had also invaded Saratoga Springs.

It was perfect summer weather on Saturday afternoon, when fans began streaming into the Saratoga Performing Arts Center. Our program bore the unwieldy title "Jazz Today and Tomorrow—A 12-Hour Salute to the 25th Anniversary of the Newport Jazz Festival." The list of artists participating in this concert was formidable; in the *New York Times*, John Wilson alluded to "a quantity of performers that was profligate even by Newport Jazz Festival standards." The musical marathon kicked off at noon, with a premiere performance of "Hannibal" Marvin Peterson's symphony "The Flames of South Africa," which had been commissioned by the Hanover Symphony Orchestra of West Germany. It continued with the Dave Chesky big band, with guest soloist John Lewis; Flora Purim with Airto; George Russell's Living Time Orchestra; and a salute to Charles Mingus, with a twenty-four-piece band directed by Paul Jeffrey.

The Mingus tribute was an instant highlight—with four trumpets, two trombones, eight reed instruments, a piano, four guitars, three basses, and two drummers, this was an ensemble befitting the bigness of Mingus's orchestral vision. The most striking solo of the set was an extended tenor essay by youngblood Michael Brecker; other high points were the contributions of guitarist John Scofield and baritone saxophonist Cecil Payne.

Chick Corea followed, reprising his now-familiar concert performance. Then came a monumental jam session: Dizzy Gillespie, Sonny Rollins, Dexter Gordon, Michael and Randy Brecker, Roy Haynes, Herbie Hancock, George Benson, Larry Coryell, Jean-Luc Ponty, Roy Haynes, and Tony Williams. At one point, their noble ranks were augmented by singers Dee Dee Bridgewater, Al Jarreau, and Andy Bey.

It was obvious that Saratoga had not been a mistake. Our Saturday box office was somewhere in the vicinity of 25,000. The crowd was happy, low-key, and peaceable. Concessions did well. The music was fine. And, most important, it captured the festive spirit of the old Newport.

For Sunday I had programmed an entire day of big-band jazz, a total of nine bands in all. It began at noon with the Woody Herman Orchestra, which covered familiar territory ("Early Autumn," "Four Brothers") as well as more recent arrangements (like a fiery "Giant Steps," with tenor solos by Joe Lovano and Bill Ross). The NYJRC went next. The band had originally planned to play charts from its formidable repertory library; instead it was forced to resort to Plan B, since someone had mistakenly left those charts in New York. Plan B involved some hastily scribbled twelve-bar blues arrangements by musical director Dick Hyman. Due to the high caliber of the musicians, and Hyman's quick and resourceful pen, this desperate measure produced some terrific music.

The Mercer Ellington Orchestra followed. Then Stan Kenton, still a bit shaky from a bad head injury the previous summer, emerged and led his orchestra. Then Harry James and his orchestra, the Buddy Rich Orchestra, the Count Basie Band, Maynard Ferguson's Jazz Rock Group, and the Thad Jones–Mel Lewis Orchestra followed in relatively quick succession. It was more big band music in one dose than anyone could remember. And with that behind us, we closed the chapter on Newport '78.

After counting the receipts, we realized that Saratoga had attracted over 35,000 fans. Even without a sponsor, we were successful. Obviously, the Newport Jazz Festival had a future in Saratoga; over twenty-five years later, the event still prospers. During that time, I have maintained a trusted relationship with Herb Chesbrough, the executive director of SPAC; we have never had a contract. Saratoga is one of the few places where ticket sales alone can pay the bills. In the past few years, we have had Freihofer Baking Company as a sponsor.

The 1978 Newport–New York festival was also somewhat of a triumph. With the help of a Silver Anniversary celebration, the prestige of the White House, and a well-organized schedule, we had put together the most impressive Newport festival to date. Public response was tidal; there was a feeling for the festival all through the city.

It was at around this time that I received a phone call from Dick Rosenzweig, an associate of Hugh Hefner at Playboy Enterprises. In past years, Dick and I had discussed the possibility of a Playboy Jazz Festival, but it had only been conversation. Now, early in 1979, he asked me to come to California for a meeting; it was *Playboy* magazine's twenty-fifth anniversary that year, and they were once again kicking around the idea of a jazz festival at the Hollywood Bowl. Beleaguered by my far-flung activities—in New York, in Nice, in New Orleans, and all over the country for KOOL—I bluntly told Dick that I was not interested in being part of a fishing expedition. I didn't want to fly to California unless he was serious about working with us, and not talking to other promoters. He took my gruffness in stride and assured me that he and Hefner wanted to work with Festival Productions, Inc.

Hugh Hefner had never forgotten the jazz festival he had promoted twenty years prior in Chicago, to celebrate his magazine's five-year anniversary. Although it had drawn over 60,000 people, that festival had not become an annual event. I gather that the Playboy management had realized that putting on a jazz festival was best left to professionals.

Which led them to us. FPI already had some experience in California, having done several KOOL festivals in San Diego. Darlene Chan, one of my most experienced producers, was already based in Los Angeles, so it was no problem to set up an office there. We scheduled the first annual Playboy Jazz Festival for June 15 and 16, 1979. In the program book, I noted that both *Playboy* magazine and the Newport Jazz Festival had started in 1954. "In their separate ways," I wrote, "[they] have become very much a part of the American scene."

Although it lasted only two days, that first festival was packed with stars. Bill Cosby was the emcee, and as always he brought his impeccable timing and humor along with his deep understanding and love of jazz musicians.

On Friday, the Playboy Jazz Festival presented not only Benny Goodman, Count Basie, Sarah Vaughan, Joe Williams, and Harold Land, but also Joni Mitchell, who had just collaborated with jazz musicians on an album dedicated to Charles Mingus. Joni's ensemble featured Herbie Hancock and Michael Brecker. In keeping with the Mingus tribute, we also presented a group consisting of his alumni; it included Ted Curson, Roland Hanna, Jimmy Knepper, and Danny Richmond.

Saturday was no less exciting, with Lionel Hampton, Willie Bobo, Weather Report, Flora Purim, and Chick Corea in duet with Herbie Hancock. The concert also included a jam session featuring the likes of Dizzy Gillespie, Stan Getz, Dexter Gordon, Freddie Hubbard, Stephane Grappelli, Gerry Mulligan, Art Blakey, and Ray Brown—artists with whom I had worked many times over the years.

Since we were running on a tight schedule, I had to figure out a way to feature all of these giants in one sixty-minute jam session. I gathered everyone together and suggested that they play a head arrangement to open the program, then each play a five-minute solo feature; the ensemble would close with another standard. No problem. That night, Dizzy broke up the crowd with his solo, and Mulligan scored with a lovely ballad. Then Dexter Gordon took center stage; I believe he had chosen "There Will Never Be Another You." He went into it, playing the melody and then two or three solo choruses, easily filling five minutes. Then he went into an off-tempo tag cadenza.

Five minutes later, he was still playing tags. It was as if he was stuck on a groove in a record; the feeling was that he might never stop. So I crept onto the stage and whispered to Dizzy: "Take him out." Dizzy got the guys together behind Dexter and played a chord, signifying the end of the tune. But Dex kept playing. Finally he did stop, a few minutes later; I think his segment took nearly fifteen minutes, which seemed like an hour, since the program was so strictly scheduled.

As the musicians came off stage at the end of the set, Dexter shuffled over to me, with a quizzical expression on his face. "George," he said, "when you ask a musician to play just five minutes . . . "—here he paused, furrowing his brow—". . . do you really mean it?"

The Playboy Jazz Festival was an instantaneous success in 1979, and has continued to improve with age. In 1980, the festival sold out well in advance, breaking the attendance record for a jazz festival in Southern California. A few years later, it broke the record for overall attendance at the Hollywood Bowl. In the years since, the festival has become established as one of the most important annual musical happenings in Los Angeles; for two consecutive evenings each June, 17,000 people fill the Hollywood Bowl. Box seats sell out months in advance, with Hollywood celebrities making a point to drink at the fountain of jazz.

I've always enjoyed the Playboy Jazz Festival, for a number of reasons. Darlene Chan does all the work and I get the credit. I have lunch with Hugh Hefner and Dick Rosenzweig every year, and make an annual pilgrimage to the Playboy Mansion for our press conference—at which I specialize in humorous, off-the-cuff jazz anecdotes. And because Bill Cosby has been our emcee for as long as we've produced the festival, Playboy essentially cemented our friendship. Cos is fond of Joyce and me, but he really works for Darlene. His cooperation has done much to ensure the festival's continued success.

\*      \*      \*

It was during the Christmas of 1978 that Joyce and I, vacationing at our house in Vence, saw a television show featuring the baritone Jean Sablon, whom we thought had long since retired. I faintly remembered that he had been a regular in the heyday of radio thirty years earlier, and that he had sung at the Versailles nightclub in New York in the 1950s. Hearing him on this TV special, I could hardly believe how beautifully he sang; he conveyed the masculine ease of Bing Crosby, yet also personified the boulevardier of classic French romance.

I knew the producer of the show, Jean Christophe Averti. I called him in Paris to ask whether Sablon was still singing. He answered in the affirmative, and gave me the singer's phone number and address. Wasting no time, I called Monsieur Sablon, who lived on the Mediterranean coast in Theoule, not far away on the west side of Cannes. I introduced myself and invited him to our house for dinner.

No longer young, Jean Sablon was still a handsome man. A thin Gallic moustache accentuated his charming smile. He carried himself with all the elegance befitting his occupation. Yet when I mentioned that I was interested in possibly bringing him to America for a concert, he was hesitant. While he had appeared on the television show (recorded the previous year), he had not performed in public for quite some time. But I was in love with this gentleman's singing, and over the course of months, I persisted until his interest was piqued. At that point, I called Bobby Short and told him that I was planning on bringing Jean Sablon to the States; would he want to be my partner in this venture? Bobby, a fan of Sablon's, agreed. Then, when I told Monsieur Sablon that Bobby Short would co-produce, he gave his final consent.

We brought Jean Sablon to New York with his companion, Karl Gamm, put them up at the Hotel Carlyle, and contracted a forty-piece orchestra led by Frank Sinatra's musical director of the time. The resulting concert was beautiful, but I was ashamed at how much money we lost. As my partner, Bobby Short shared this loss without hesitation. We agreed that the privilege of bringing someone like Jean Sablon to Lincoln Center was worth every cent. The bonus was the friendship Joyce and I and Bobby developed with Jean and Karl; we spent many days and nights together on the Riviera. Whenever Jean came to our house for dinner, listening to his theme, "Vous Qui Passez Sans Me Voir," he would always sing the final lines: "Au revoir—bon soir!—au revoir." Thinking of those moments never fails to make me smile.

\*     \*     \*

It's a testament to the friendship and trust of Bobby Short that, despite our failure with Jean Sablon, he didn't shy away from future partnerships. Just a year later, in 1980, we collaborated on a program with much potential.

An innovation of the 1979 KOOL Jazz Festival was a revue celebrating the African-American figures of Broadway theater from the first half of the twentieth century. Among the stars we enlisted for this tribute were Adelaide Hall, who had recorded "Creole Love Call" with Duke Ellington in 1927, and whom we brought to New York City from London for her first appearance in many years; Edith Wilson, who had appeared in the 1929 musical *Hot Chocolates* with Louis Armstrong and Fats Waller; and Diahann Carroll, sang Irving Berlin's "Supper Time," the story of a black woman waiting for her husband, who has been lynched, to come home for supper. Putting on this show was fun. But it also planted the germ of an idea: Why not produce a Broadway show reminiscent of this golden era? Along with Bobby Short, dancer Honi Coles, and writer-historian Robert Kimball, I began to explore this concept in earnest. After much discussion, we started rehearsal with no working title. I dubbed it "Black Broadway," declaring my title a temporary measure. As it turned out, Honi, Bobby and Robert liked it, and so *Black Broadway* was born.

I was not in a position to raise the many hundreds of thousands of dollars, now millions, necessary to produce a show on Broadway. Besides, many of our stars had contractual agreements that made them available for only a few weeks. So I booked Town Hall for three weeks in May 1980. Honi Coles of the most sophisticated tap-dance duo in history—Coles and Atkins—asked two of his buddies, Charles "Cookie" Cook and Lester "Bubba" Gaines, to join him. Mercedes Ellington organized a line of four beautiful girls, including herself. Veteran artists who would perhaps be making their last appearance in New York were Adelaide Hall—whom we brought once again from London, and who sang "I Must Have That Man" and "Creole Love Call"—and Elizabeth Welch, who had introduced Cole Porter's "Love for Sale" in a 1930 production of *The New Yorkers*. Miss Welch sang the beautiful, "Silver Rose" that Florence Mills made famous. The gracious Edith Wilson came from Chicago and sang her version of "He May Be Your Man But He Comes to See Me Sometimes." The climax of the first half of the program was John W. Bubbles's "Sportin' Life" from Gershwin's *Porgy and Bess*, singing, "It Ain't Necessarily So." Nell Carter, who had just won a Tony for her Broadway show *Ain't Misbehavin'*, was happy to perform with our legendary artists. She sang some of her Fats Waller material. The camaraderie that developed among this cast of legends was unique. Gregory Hines, who was not originally scheduled to be in the show, called me to say that he was free for a few weeks and wanted to be in *Black Broadway*. I told him that we didn't have much of a budget; he didn't care. He wanted to share the stage with the great pioneers of his field. Eubie Blake, who was not in the show, came in every other night to play a few of his songs. All of the 1920s artists had worked for Noble Sissle and Blake at one time.

*Black Broadway* received positive reviews from Doug Watt in the the *New York Daily News*, John Wilson in the *New York Times*, and in *Newsweek*, which acknowledged that it was the finest show of its kind. But because Town Hall was not a Broadway theater, theater critics would not deign to review the show. I believe we were also limited by our title. I always thought that "Silver Rose" would have been a better title. The theater-going public never picked up on *Black Broadway*. We did have a prestigious audience—Jackie Kennedy and Jack Lemmon were among those in attendance. Because I had kept the budget down, our losses were meager.

*Black Broadway* was, needless to say, my only attempt at being a Broadway producer. Many people imagine the producing of a Broadway show to be a glamorous act. But three weeks at Town Hall, despite all the joy and pride I gleaned from the experience, was enough to cure me of any desire to join the ranks of David Merrick and Alexander Cohen. Jazz festivals were difficult enough.

# 13

# *"Come Up to KOOL"*

THE STORY OF THE OHIO VALLEY JAZZ FESTIVAL begins in the bitter-cold winter of 1961, more than six months before the Newport Jazz Festival's first resurrection. Times were hard—I had no club or festival—and I found myself falling back on the piano as a means of income. With Ruby Braff, Pee Wee Russell, Marshall Brown, and Jack Six on bass, I managed to book a series of gigs for the Newport All-Stars in the Corn Belt. There wasn't much money in touring, but it kept us alive. One of our extended engagements had been in a Xenia, Ohio, club called Kenkels. As leader the gig paid me about $400 a week—just enough money for the rent of my office-apartment at Fifty Central Park West.

One night during our run, I spotted a familiar face in the crowd—the beaming, oval-shaped visage of Dino Santangelo, a former associate from my French Lick, Indiana, promotions. Dino had handled publicity and public relations for the Sheraton Hotel Corporation during those years, and we had struck up a friendship. Dino looked like a kindly padrone from an Italian hillside town, or a gregarious boniface in a fine restaurant who couldn't wait to recommend the best in the house.

I knew Dino also to be an incurable optimist. After nervous Sheraton officials had pulled the plug on our French Lick festival in 1960, he was determined to revive the fête under a different banner. He had scouted out possible locations. More important, he'd spent months drumming up local interest, and speaking with potential financial backers. By the time Dino heard about my plan to return to Newport, Rhode Island, in 1962, he had assembled a loose network of curious investors and jazz fans.

Dino delivered his idea to me in person, over cocktails at Kenkels. With fervor, he informed me that he wanted to make a Cincinnati jazz festival a reality. Everyone he knew remembered the Sheraton Festival at French Lick. A similar event in the Cincinnati region, he argued, would be a sure success.

Dino's buoyant enthusiasm was highly contagious, but I still managed to maintain my balance. I told him that I was interested in the idea, but couldn't make a definite commitment until after Newport. I had no idea whether Newport would sink or swim. Dino and I scheduled our hypothetical festival for late August, which would give us about six weeks after Newport to pull it all together.

The day after the Newport festival was over, I flew to Cincinnati to meet with Dino. I was accompanied on my trip by John Sdoucos, an associate from my club, Storyville. After the ordeal of Newport, we both were exhausted—and now we faced a new frontier. Upon arrival, John and I stepped onto the tarmac from the plane, and were immediately bombarded with a wall of blistering, 105-degree heat. The July humidity made it even more unbearable.

Despite the climate, we set to work immediately; we had just six weeks to piece together a festival. Promotional work was to be done in and around Cincinnati. It was to be a genuine grassroots campaign. We visited nightclubs every night; I'd sit in on the piano and be introduced as both the producer of the Newport Jazz Festival and the man behind a rapidly approaching festival in Cincinnati. John, Dino, and I took many excursions to Louisville, Dayton, and even as far as Detroit to plug the festival on whatever radio or talk shows would have us and to whichever newspapermen would talk with us. We hit local promoters and disc jockeys within a 150-mile radius of Cincinnati, and handed out press releases at every stop along the way. We even put up posters on telephone poles.

Nothing can beat that kind of grassroots promoting—where you make your personality known on a daily basis within the community. The locals had begun to feel an affinity for the event; we weren't just promoters buying space in a paper to advertise a product. Newspapers and radio shows adopted the Ohio Valley Jazz Festival as a calendar event that belonged in their hometown.

We also had to choose a venue for the Ohio festival. After negotiating unsuccessfully with officials from the Cincinnati Zoo, who had been frightened by the apocalyptic image of rioting jazz fans commingling with hippopotami and orangutans, Dino had decided that our best bet was the Carthage Fairgrounds. The fairgrounds was located about twenty minutes from downtown Cincinnati; the historic site had hosted an annual county fair more or less continually since 1884. More important for our purposes, it had a wooden grandstand that could seat up to 8,200 people—an ideal size for a festival crowd.

The Carthage Fairgrounds management was receptive to our proposal. But "jazz" was still a dirty word due to the 1960 Newport incident, and we soon encountered opposition from the Cincinnati City Council. Faced with the prospect of a jazz festival in the hallowed nineteenth-century Carthage Fairgrounds, City Building Commissioner Donald Hunter raised questions of safety. The seventy-five-year-old wooden grandstand, he reported, was strong enough for "normal sedate patronage," but "would not stand up under stomping and stamping about."

This objection was preposterous, and the local press rallied in our favor. A public rejoinder also came from Jim Devine, caretaker of the fairgrounds. "There's nothing wrong with our grandstand," he declared in one newspaper interview. "Those timbers will hold up anything." He later reiterated his point more colorfully: "You could run a herd of elephants through this grandstand!"

Finally, we settled the matter with some degree of mutual compromise. I agreed to stop the music if at any point there was an outbreak of either "stamping" or "stomping" in the grandstand.

Jazz was still battling for respect. Conscious of this continuing struggle, I asked Father Norman O'Connor to serve as the festival's master of ceremonies. Once again, Father O'Connor happily lent us the legitimacy of his collar. It didn't hurt, given the predominately Catholic population of Cincinnati.

Although the event's working title had been "The Cincinnati Jazz Festival," I decided that we should broaden the appeal. Our promotional efforts had carried us far beyond the Cincinnati city limits. Owing to the fact that Cincinnati is situated on the Ohio River, I felt the title "The Ohio Valley Jazz Festival" gave it a regional identity. The audience did in fact come from miles around.

A few glitches did occur on the festival's inaugural night. Dave Brubeck, who had been scheduled to open the festival, missed his plane. He arrived two hours late, forcing us to start the show with Duke Ellington and follow up with Louis Armstrong. This change in programming prevented a promised alto saxophone summit with Paul Desmond and Johnny Hodges. It also kept us from presenting an Armstrong-Ellington pairing as planned. Nevertheless, the 6,000 people who turned out saw some terrific music. I don't believe anyone requested their $3.50 admission back.

A young fighter from Louisville, Kentucky, named Cassius Marcellus Clay was a guest at the festival; this was just a few weeks before his scheduled match against veteran fighter Archie Moore. During the final night's concert, several people came up to me and told me that Cassius wanted to read some poetry to the crowd. It didn't matter to me whether he went onstage or not. But during a spare moment, I spotted him backstage. So I went up and introduced myself, and said, "I understand that you want to go onstage to read some poetry."

He eyed me blithely. "How much do you want to pay me?"

"Pay you? Cassius, we don't have any money to pay you. But you're welcome to go up during intermission to plug the fight."

He gave no intelligible response to this suggestion, merely mumbling a few more words about getting paid. I didn't give the matter any more thought until, during the intermission, I heard the sound of the young fighter's voice over the PA. Looking toward the stage, I saw that he was reading lines that had been scrawled on a roll of toilet paper. "When you come to the fight, don't block the aisle, and don't block the door. You will all go home after round four."

After a few minutes of this pointed verse, someone relayed a message from the food vendors: "Get him off the stage—nobody is buying any beer!" We managed to curtail Clay's monologue and hustle him off the microphone. None of us had any inkling that we had brushed against one of the great figures of the twentieth century. Incidentally, Archie Moore did go in four. It was one of many triumphs of Muhammad Ali's career.

All told, the first Ohio Valley Jazz Festival was a success. It wasn't that we made a lot of money—on the contrary, we just about broke even. That was no small accomplishment for an inaugural year. But we had poured the concrete for a foundation on which great things could now be built. Dino and I knew that the Ohio Valley Festival would have the benefit of a sequel—even though our investors, disappointed by our modest profits, pulled out after the first year. They had no faith.

Just how successful the future would be was a mystery that only time and fate could reveal.

\*     \*     \*

For the second Ohio Valley Jazz Festival, 1963, our artist roster included Dizzy Gillespie, Cannonball Adderley, Thelonious Monk, Rahsaan Roland Kirk, Oscar Peterson, and Gerry Mulligan. The potential for growth was now evident.

And with two Ohio Valley Jazz Festivals under our belts, 1964 marked Festival Productions's first year of accord with the ruling class of Cincinnati. We had become a part of the city's economic life; the hotels had discovered what a windfall a festival could be. People were flocking to Cincinnati from all over the Midwest for the jazz festival. This had only happened during baseball and football weekends. As for the Cincinnati Reds, they saw an opportunity to make some extra income by renting out the ballpark. So the Ohio Valley Jazz Festival now moved across town from the Carthage Fair Grounds to Crosley Field at the invitation of the Reds. Dino and I were entering the big time.

The 1964 Ohio Valley Jazz Festival at Crosley Field was nearly a disaster. The weekend began well, with an evening featuring the Woody Herman Orchestra, Thelonious Monk, Sarah Vaughan, Jimmy Smith, Stan Getz with Astrud Gilberto, and the Newport All-Stars. It was on closing night, August 15, that we ran into some problems. That program featured the Duke Ellington Orchestra, the Dizzy Gillespie Quintet, the Dave Brubeck Quartet, the John Coltrane Quartet, and an up-and-coming vocalist named Gloria Lynne. These last two artists were big attractions; Gloria Lynne had a hit record with the song "I Wish You Love," and Coltrane's rendition of "My Favorite Things" seemed to be on constant jazz radio rotation. So it caused some alarm when eight o'clock rolled around and neither artist had arrived.

In those days my office would sign a contract with an artist's agency and send in an advance payment, and hold it in good faith that the artist would show up. Here we were, putting on a major outdoor festival that drew crowds upward of ten to fifteen thousand—with only vague information about artists' arrival times or points of departure. The festival didn't have a weekend phone number where we could be reached in case of emergency. We would know where artists were when we were informed that they had checked into their hotels, after which we made arrangements to get them to the field. This haphazard system usually worked fine (Duke, Dizzy, and Brubeck had checked in and were ready to go), but what were we to do about Gloria Lynne and John Coltrane? We had received no word from either of them. I began to think, seriously, that something terrible might have happened.

Meanwhile, I had to make some decisions about the festival program. Normally I paced a show quite closely, with five artists performing just under an hour apiece; the last performer usually went on at midnight. But I knew that if Coltrane and Lynne failed to show, we would have a problem. We had one of the largest audiences of our three-year experience in Cincinnati, and I knew it was because of the popularity of Lynne's hit record. The crowd would not be happy if the concert ended at 11 P.M. and 40 percent of the talent advertised had not appeared.

I delayed the concert's opening by fifteen or twenty minutes, and asked Brubeck to play a seventy-five-minute set instead of the usual fifty minutes. Brubeck finished at 9:30 to a warm reception, and we then spent roughly a half-hour setting up and sound-checking the Ellington band. Duke went on at slightly past 10 o'clock, and took full advantage of my request to "play a good long set." He came off at 11:35 P.M.; Dizzy Gillespie went on at midnight.

I asked Dizzy to keep playing until I told him to stop. There had not been the slightest word from either Coltrane or Lynne; no telephone calls to Crosley

Field, no telegrams, no word whatsoever. I didn't know whether to be upset or have serious anxieties for the lives of these artists.

While Dizzy was playing, I called a meeting of festival security—which included members of the Cincinnati Police force—and apprised them of the situation. I told them that I would keep Dizzy going until around 1:30 in the morning. By then, more than half of the audience would have dispersed, as postfestival parties were always scheduled.

Sure enough, when Dizzy finished the crowd had thinned out. I got on-stage and made an announcement that we had no clue as to the whereabouts of Lynne or Coltrane, and we were deeply concerned. I told them that we had signed contracts and paid deposits. And I asked the people in the stands to pray for the safety of these two artists.

There were no howls of protest or cries of rip-off. The audience had heard more than five hours of excellent music, and the sincerity of our announcement reached them. The local all-night jazz stations repeated the story and begged people not to blame the festival promoters. No requests for refunds were asked for, as far as I can recall.

On Monday morning we discovered that Gloria Lynne had called her agent, Joe Glaser, at six P.M. Saturday night, telling him to get her out of the Cincinnati commitment. A disgusted Glaser had done nothing. Jack Whittemore, Coltrane's agent, told us that the saxophonist had never left his house that weekend. The artist hadn't even told his men about the engagement.

The whole experience was a valuable lesson. During future concert events, we would make it our business to know every artist's itinerary and schedule, including estimated time of arrival. Today the amount of preproduction detail in this area is extensive; each festival has its own transportation staff, coordinating artists' movement from airport to hotel, from hotel to festival site, and around the festival grounds.

*     *     *

As we prepared in 1965 to mount the fourth annual Ohio Valley Jazz Festival in Cincinnati, representatives of the Ohio State Fair called Dino and offered what seemed like a sweetheart deal: we could bring the festival to Columbus and play in the fair's grandstand, where overhead expenses would be far less than those at Crosley Field. But since we didn't want to seem as if we were deserting Cincinnati, Dino and I scheduled one night at Crosley and two at the Ohio State Fairgrounds. This way, we could give some of the artists two nights' work, which was always appreciated. Some of the featured musicians that year were Art Blakey, Woody Herman and his orchestra, with Milt Jackson as guest artist, Joe Williams, Dave Brubeck, and John Coltrane, in spite of his missing the previous year.

But our deal turned out to have an underside. The State Fair management wanted jazz fans to pay an entry fee to the fairgrounds and then pay an additional fee to enter the festival grandstand. I was furious when I heard about this manipulative condition. None of the administrators at the Ohio State Fair had mentioned it to us, and it wasn't until right before the festival that we made this discovery. It was an intolerable arrangement that would destroy the festival.

On the day before the festival, I contested this arrangement with the manager of the fairgrounds. A serious argument ensued; it was one of the few times in my life in which I nearly engaged in a fistfight. Finally, he told me that the only thing I could do would be to take my appeal to the governor of Ohio.

I managed to get an immediate audience with Governor James Rhodes, whose political longevity and success in the state of Ohio were already legendary. Governor Rhodes was quite amiable; but at first, he made no effort in solving the problem.

The audience for the Ohio Valley Jazz Festival consisted primarily of members of Ohio's African-American population. After discussing my problem in vain with Governor Rhodes for a few minutes, I remarked: "It would be sad if the jazz fans of Ohio felt that their governor was prejudiced against them." The message rang loud and clear.

Five minutes and one phone call later, the conflict was resolved. The Fairgrounds agreed to charge only one admission, for both the fair and the festival. It was our only experience with the State Fair; the Ohio Valley Festival would return to Crosley Field in 1966, and remain there for another five years.

\*   \*   \*

My company was producing a number of other festivals around the country. There was the Boston Globe Festival, a two-day event at the brand-new Prudential Center. In partnership with the management of the Atlanta Braves, we had created the Atlanta Jazz Festival. Along with my friend Rod Kennedy, we produced the Longhorn Jazz Festival in Austin, Texas. I had presented a two-day festival in Pittsburgh for the Catholic Youth Organization, and we had become involved with the Metropolitan Opera in a series of concerts in Lewisohn Stadium in New York. FPI's foreign activities—including tours of Japan with the Glenn Miller Orchestra and the Stan Getz Quartet—had generated some income.

With all this activity—and the Newport Jazz and Folk Festivals, in their new Connell Highway setting—it seemed that we might have a future in this business. There were no doubts in my mind that what we were doing was unique and contributed to the cultural life of both America and the world. FPI might not have been flying high yet, but it was clearly taxiing for takeoff.

*     *     *

What was interesting about the Ohio Valley Jazz Festival, aside from its success, was the evolution of its programming. Dino and I had gradually discovered that the funkier jazz groups—like Les McCann and Eddie Harris—were popular with our predominately African-American audiences. Herbie Mann with his hit record "Comin' Home, Baby" was for several years the hit of the festival. By this time we had started presenting the occasional soul or blues artist as well, like Roberta Flack, Chuck Berry, or B. B. King. Programming of this sort was what brought many thousands of fans to the stadium.

By the early seventies, the Ohio Valley Jazz Festival had achieved status as *the* musical event of the region. Audiences came from all directions, within a sprawling 150-mile radius of Cincinnati. This increase in attendance necessitated a move from Crosley Field (which seated just over 29,000 people) to Riverfront Stadium (which could accommodate nearly 53,000). Dino and I were finally beginning to make some money.

In 1971, we entertained a new thought: why not take the concept of the Ohio Valley Festival to other cities? We had established relationships in a number of cities during the Schlitz Salute to Jazz in 1968. In addition, we had created a festival in Hampton, Virginia, very similar in tone to the Ohio Valley Festival. With this experience under our belts, we felt that we could introduce stadium concerts in several other large cities. We chose Atlanta, Houston, and Oakland as our target markets.

Our first expansion attempt, in 1972, was an immediate success. The next year we fared just as well. By 1974 we were so encouraged that FPI added another festival—in Kansas City, Missouri. That summer our six stadium events drew more than 400,000 paying customers. Our patrons heard such jazz legends as Ella Fitzgerald, Sarah Vaughan, Herbie Hancock, and Chick Corea. But the real meat of our production was supplied by soul and blues artists: the likes of Al Green and B. B. King. Our 1974 Houston festival was staged at the brand-new Astrodome; one night, over 50,000 people gathered there for a concert featuring the O'Jays and Gladys Knight and the Pips.

In Atlanta that year, Aretha Franklin was the headliner on a show that included four other acts. We had sold some 40,000 tickets to the concert; that night the Atlanta Stadium would be nearly filled to capacity. Everybody was coming to "the festival"; when you start drawing 30,000 or 40,000 people, you're *the* event in town.

However, the day before the festival, Aretha sent word that she wasn't coming. Her father, the Reverend C. I. Franklin of Detroit's New Bethel Baptist Church, was apparently ill, and Aretha said that she wanted to be with him in Detroit. This was not unprecedented; Aretha had been known to skip a date on occasion. The timing couldn't possibly have been worse. My office went into damage-control mode; we needed another attraction, and fast. Somehow Marie St. Louis, who hired the talent from our office in New York City, managed to find a replacement for Aretha overnight: a band called Harold Melvin and the Blue Notes.

Harold Melvin and the Blue Notes was not a new attraction; the group had formed as a Philadelphia doo-wop group in 1954. But despite a few modest hits, the group had never been big, and was not generally considered a concert attraction. In the past couple of years, though, the Blue Notes's sound had changed; drummer Teddy Pendergrass was now singing lead. Buoyed by a new contract with the Philadelphia International label, the group was on a fast upward track.

I told our staff in Atlanta to put up a sign at all gates announcing that Aretha Franklin would not appear, but "Harold Melvin and the Blue Notes—featuring Teddy Pendergrass" would perform in her place. (This was in addition to four other groups on a star-studded concert.) I instructed our people to grant refunds to anyone who asked *before* entering the stadium.

It soon became clear that the festival itself meant more than any one star attraction. There were barely more than thirty refund requests. And at the beginning of the concert, the recently elected mayor of Atlanta, Maynard Jackson, took the stage.

"Aretha Franklin is in Detroit with her father," Mayor Jackson announced. "I want everybody to pray for Aretha and the Reverend." And Maynard Jackson, Atlanta's first black mayor (and one of the first African-American politicians in any such office in the South), got the fans—99 percent African-American—to hold up cigarette lighters and matches in a makeshift candlelight vigil. That was quite a sight, thousands of tiny flames flickering in the stands—all for Aretha and her father, who may or may not have been sick. The situation ended well for everyone involved; Aretha got to skip the date, Harold Melvin's Blue Notes played to perhaps their largest crowd yet, and the audience saw a marvelous concert. We made out, too—since the fee allocated for Aretha was much larger than what we paid Melvin's band.

We were swinging. We didn't know how long these festivals would last, but each one seemed to have a relatively secure future. There was no competition to speak of, and we realized there was room for even more growth. As the 1975 summer season approached, Dino and I made plans to present stadium festivals not only in Cincinnati, Houston, Atlanta, Oakland, Kansas City, and Hampton, Virginia, but also in the new frontier of San Diego. This was in addition to the Newport Jazz Festival in New York, which I produced on my own. Dino and I estimated that these eight Festival Productions, Inc., events would draw more than 650,000 patrons altogether.

Although FPI continued to present jazz, especially jazz of a funkier nature, the Ohio Valley Festivals were driving deeper into soul territory. For 1975, we made plans to feature artists like the Ohio Players, the O'Jays, the Spinners, Bill Withers, Aretha Franklin, and Bobby "Blue" Bland.

Producing and promoting these concerts was a momentous enterprise. In each of our cities, our office had to establish relationships with mayors' offices, chambers of commerce, convention bureaus, stadium administrations, and a host of local promotional and nonprofit organizations. We advertised each festival relentlessly: in daily newspapers, on radio and television shows, over print and wire services, in national magazines (primarily *Ebony* and *Jet*), and through grassroots efforts in retail stores and local clubs. Each festival drew from as large as a 300-mile radius, with roughly half of any stadium audience consisting of fans from out of town.

Dino bore the brunt of these responsibilities, since I often had my hands full with other affairs. I was in charge of not only the Newport Jazz Festival in New York, but also the New Orleans Jazz and Heritage Festival, the New York Jazz Repertory Company, and the Grande Parade du Jazz. Yet I was far from a passive participant in our nationwide soul concerts. Marie St. Louis in our New York office bought all the talent. Dino kept me apprised of every detail, no matter how trivial. And he always showed me a personal loyalty, although he was doing the lion's share of the work. We had both been dead broke when we started together in 1962. At that time, Dino had been working in Cincinnati for the Sheraton Hotel, out of an office the size of a closet. Partly due to this history together, and partly due to our friendship and mutual respect, we never had any arguments. We were in this business together for better or worse and never had a signed contract with each other.

Little did we know that things were about to get better. In mid-November 1974 Dino received a phone call from Leo Bell, an African-American employee (and there were precious few) of Brown & Williamson, the cigarette company based in Louisville, Kentucky. Mr. Bell had been coming to the Ohio Valley Jazz Festival for several years, and he thought it might be a good sponsorship opportunity for his company, which manufactured KOOL, a menthol cigarette. Dino and I had spoken with a number of potential sponsors over the years, and nothing had ever materialized. But the day after his conversation with Mr. Bell, Dino wrote and sent a letter outlining the breadth and scope of FPI's activities across the country. He was careful to point out that in 1974, our seven festivals had attracted just under 550,000 paying customers. He also noted such audience demographics as the average age of our attendees (approximately thirty years old) and their ethnic composition (ranging from 50 percent African-American in Oakland to 80 percent in Hampton). One month later, Dino and I were meeting with Brown & Williamson officials in Louisville.

After a few more meetings, the tobacco corporation agreed to sponsor the Ohio Valley Jazz Festival and its many satellite events. In May 1975 we made the big announcement: Dino and I, as FPI, were launching a nationwide series of "KOOL Jazz Festivals"—in Atlanta, Oakland, Hampton, Cincinnati, Houston, San Diego, and Kansas City.

Promotion for these festivals was overwhelming. Dino held press conferences in which Brown & Williamson distributed free menthol cigarettes to grateful reporters. Harold Melvin and the Blue Notes recorded a musical rendition of the brand slogan, "Come Up to KOOL"; this ditty, with Teddy Pendergrass on vocals, became a popular radio spot. Our toll-free telephone information line received over 100,000 inquiries; almost every caller requested information on more than one festival.

The artists we presented reflected a broad spectrum of African-American culture. Harold Melvin and the Blue Notes, which had done so well in Atlanta the year before, appeared on all but one of our 1975 festivals. We also presented the Ohio Players, B. B. King, Archie Bell and the Drells, the Stylistics, the Isley Brothers, the O'Jays, and Quincy Jones. At the same time, our roster was still roughly half-composed of jazz artists. Freddie Hubbard played in most of our cities; so did McCoy Tyner. The KOOL roster also featured Bobby Hutcherson, Ramsey Lewis, Stanley Turrentine, Donald Byrd, Stan Getz, Toshiko Akiyoshi, Gato Barbieri, Herbie Mann, Cannonball Adderley, Count Basie, Bobbi Humphrey, and "Brother" Jack McDuff.

In each city, the KOOL Jazz Festival was an event. Not only was it an opportunity to hear the music one loved; it was also the place to see and be seen. All the "folks" turned out for a festival. Local retail and department stores had their best week of the year right before a festival, because our audience (especially women) invariably dressed to the nines. Every night a fashion show literally took place in the grandstand.

Taking into account the increase in business for area hotels, restaurants, and retail merchants, each festival provided a major financial boost to its host city. We took this contribution a step further by donating portions of our profits to local charitable organizations. In 1975 KOOL and Festival Productions, Inc. presented grants to community groups like the United Negro College Fund, Houston's Eliza Johnson Home for Aged Negroes, and Oakland's Dimensions Dance Theater. Dino and I were especially aware of our relations with each city's African-American community, as we were two white promoters presenting black music to black audiences. Our relationships with local organizations and community leaders kept us from being hassled as "carpetbaggers" or opportunists. We did our homework.

Occasionally there were hassles with local music promoters, who maintained a territorial attitude even when they worked with us as partners. In Oakland, for example, we teamed up with Bill Graham, the reigning concert impresario of the Bay Area. Although he was purportedly our partner in Oakland's KOOL Jazz Festival, Bill wouldn't let us use artists who were scheduled to play his own concerts. We had tapped one of these artists, Roy Buchanan, to play a KOOL concert in a hall in town. Roy Buchanan was scheduled to play a Bill Graham concert later in the month, and we wanted Graham to cancel this date. He came back with a suggestion: If he guaranteed the KOOL concert, could he play Roy Buchanan in a couple of weeks?

"If you guarantee our concert," I said, "you can play him tomorrow night!"

As it turned out, our Roy Buchanan concert did not sell out, and Bill Graham was quite dismayed to discover that he had to buy out $6,000 worth of tickets. The woman who was Graham's own ticket manager said she had never heard Bill scream so loudly. Graham was renowned for his screaming.

The only substantial criticism that we received at all was most succinctly printed in the *San Francisco Chronicle*. Reviewing a concert at the Oakland Stadium featuring Aretha Franklin, the Isley Brothers, McCoy Tyner, and Ramsey Lewis, the paper's reporter noted that the evening had basically consisted of two separate events—"a superb soul concert, and a dismal jazz presentation." He ended his review with a hypothetical question: "Why doesn't the Festival management drop its pretensions to be a jazz festival and confine itself to soul?"

I had anticipated this line of criticism. After all, the Ohio Valley Jazz Festival had begun as a midwestern reflection of Newport, with a program geared almost exclusively toward mainstream jazz. The gravitational pull of soul music had taken place over the course of a decade, as our audience's tastes had grown more clearly defined.

Soul was the music of black America, in a way that jazz had not been for many years. And the soul performers we presented were consummate artists; the talent that these people had was unique. Aretha Franklin and Ray Charles were two of the shining icons of the twentieth century. Gladys Knight and Patti Labelle were magnificent artists. A group like the O'Jays could not only sing convincingly, but also put on an incredible show. And the Staple Singers, whom we presented in five of our seven cities, fit right in on the Newport Folk Festival. This was a world of music that could not be dismissed. Our position as the number one promoters of black music was a point of pride.

The KOOL Jazz Festivals bore no trace of rock and roll. There was a fundamental difference between soul and rock performances, a distinction that went further than the issue of sound or style; it had to do with the communication between artist and audience. The African-American soul performer conveyed a certain earthiness that resonated with the lives of the fans. By contrast, the rock performer conveyed an otherworldliness far removed from those lives. So while the soul artist presented a reflection of his or her audience's familiar longings and hopes and frustrations, the rock artist mainly sold a means of escape.

As for our "pretensions," I had made a conscious decision to continue calling the KOOL events "jazz festivals," despite the fact that jazz was drifting further and further from the heart of our productions. There was also some incentive to keep the name from a marketing standpoint; during the course of just one year, "KOOL Jazz" had become a catchphrase among African Americans across the country. The KOOL Jazz Festivals were hot, and I wasn't about to change the title. Everybody in town was going to "KOOL Jazz."

No one was happier about this development than Brown & Williamson, and they expressed interest in broadening the scope of the festivals for the 1976 season. I convinced Dino that we were in a good position to ask for more money.

This came at a time when we were both finally making a good living. For several years I had been struggling to pay off debts incurred during the disastrous summers of 1969 and 1971. By 1975 I had paid off every cent. Yet neither Dino nor I was truly financially independent. If KOOL decided to drop the festivals, we would be no better off than when we started.

Our meeting with Brown & Williamson took place at Brown & Williamson corporate headquarters in Louisville. KOOL wanted to add more cities to the series; Milwaukee and Washington, D.C. were mentioned as two possible markets. So I proposed an FPI fee of $200,000 per festival—a substantial raise from the existing agreement. But the executives were uncomfortable with this proposal; this was a lot of money in 1975. So I inhaled and took the biggest gamble of my life.

"Look, you're getting a national program here. If you don't want to pay us, let us go."

There was a long silence. I was sitting with my hands under the table, fingers crossed. Dino was sitting across from me with a blank expression on his face. I could tell that his heart was pounding just as hard as mine.

I swallowed and went on. "We love what you did for us last year; it was just great. But these festivals are big. And if you can't pay us what we feel they're worth, please let us go. Other sponsors have been impressed by what we've done. We'll just go with someone else." Frank McKeown, a B & W executive in charge of KOOL is now retired and lives in the Tampa Bay area, where I met him again recently while producing the 2001 Verizon Music Festival–Tampa Bay. Recalling the "old days," I told him about the finger-crossing under the table incident and how we were pulling a dangerous bluff; he told me that he wanted the program so badly that we could have gotten more money from him. So much for my business acumen!

To our great relief, Brown & Williamson did eventually approve our new budget. We started in earnest on the program for 1976. And as KOOL had requested, we included Milwaukee and Washington, D.C. We were now dealing with nine stadium festivals. Obviously, our work was cut out for us.

In addition to the usual groundwork—negotiations with city governments, stadium crews, local unions, and the like—we discovered that it was getting harder and harder to secure the artists. In a sense, the KOOL festivals had spoiled its performers; no one had ever played to stadium crowds like this before. The agents began holding us up. Prices escalated, and nobody would give us a firm commitment. Marie St. Louis was going out of her mind trying to negotiate the talent; it was getting to be a real hassle. But we did score a coup that year by signing up Marvin Gaye.

Gaye had been one of many hit-makers on the Motown Records roster in the early sixties. His first major hit, "I Heard It Through the Grapevine," had charted in 1968. Two subsequent albums—*What's Going On* and *Let's Get It On*—had yielded even greater success. By 1975, his place in the pantheon was incontestable; he was soul music's biggest star, and we wanted him for KOOL.

Marvin's manager was a Jamaican citizen by the name of Steven Hill. He happened to be passing through New York City that fall, so Dino and I had dinner with him to discuss the possibility of taking Marvin on tour. Dinner went reasonably well, and afterward we went up to his suite in the Americana Hotel in midtown. By this time we had been negotiating for a few hours; it was eleven o'clock in the evening.

At three in the morning we were still there. Dino and I had attempted to go home five times, thinking that we had a deal. But every time we got up, Steven Hill stopped us. In his Jamaican accent, he'd say: "Oh listen mon. One more ting." And he would add another item to his list of conditions. By the time Dino and I left his room, it was nearly four A.M. We were wiped out; totally and utterly exhausted. But we had signed Marvin Gaye to play every one of the festivals. Ten cities. It was the first time anyone had scheduled him for such an extensive tour.

Gaye had a well-deserved reputation as a difficult man. He himself knew this, and took no pains to counteract the image. But Dino, who was at all of the festivals, told me that they never had a problem. Marvin went up to him several times to say: "Don't worry, Dino, I'm going to play the date." This was a major relief; hundreds of thousands of dollars were on the line. If Marvin Gaye finked out on us, which he had been known to do, we would lose a lot of money.

Stevie Wonder was already an established headliner, but the KOOL Festivals introduced him to a new concert format. Stevie, who loved to play for two hours without a break, was aghast to learn that he would only be granted an hour-long set. But he complied. Afterward he told me: "George, you know, playing for just an hour wasn't so bad. After a couple of nights I got to know how to handle it, and it worked."

Our FPI team was obsessed with the details of production and community relations. This professionalism paid off. Nineteen seventy-six was our biggest year yet. The 1977 KOOL Jazz Festival empire encompassed not only the usual festivals in Cincinnati, Atlanta, San Diego, Hampton, Houston, Oakland, Milwaukee, Kansas City, and Washington, D.C., but also several one-nighters in the Louisiana Superdome in New Orleans, Texas Stadium in Dallas, and the Pontiac Silverdome in Michigan and a week-long venture called the First Annual Pacific KOOL Jazz Fair in Honolulu, Hawaii.

I had passed through Honolulu a number of times *en route* to and from the Far East, but I had never worked there. During the past year, some local promoters had convinced me that Hawaii was ripe for a major festival. One of them, a gentleman by the name of John Leonard, became FPI's island liaison. Brown & Williamson agreed to add Honolulu to the KOOL Jazz Festival roster, and we scheduled a jazz fair for the first week of May.

Instead of casting this event in the soul vein, we modeled the Pacific KOOL Jazz Fair after the Grande Parade du Jazz, which by this time was a succes in Nice, France: two stages running simultaneously, with food and crafts booths and an emphasis on traditional jazz. Our site for this fête was the Waikiki Shell, a large bandstand located in the heart of Kapiolani Park, just a stone's throw from Waikiki Beach. We hoped to tap into not only local music fans, but also the transient tourist population. The fair was slated to run for seven days, from early afternoons until well into the evening.

The musicians I gathered for this festival (mostly swing-era veterans like Benny Carter, Joe Venuti, Barney Bigard, and Clark Terry) were overjoyed to be spending a week in paradise; one could scarcely imagine a more enticing assignment. For my part, I was generally too wrapped up in promotions and production to take full advantage of the isle of Oahu. I never got to visit my little grass shack in Kealakekua which, I discovered, was located on another island. But we did get to experience some of the legendary local friendliness—the aloha spirit—as the festival got under way.

Unfortunately, it was soon apparent that that aloha spirit has no bearing on ticket sales. Despite a treasure chest of world-class traditional jazz artists, an evening concert with the full Woody Herman Orchestra, two great blues artists, Muddy Waters and Joe Williams, and a couple of popular names, trumpeter Chuck Mangione and singer Al Green, we couldn't get people out to the fair. Advance tickets had been priced at $5.00 per day; they were $6.50 at the gate. Children's tickets were $2.00. A seven-day pass cost a mere $25.00.

What we had failed to account for was the fundamental limitation of presenting concert events in Hawaii: geographic isolation. Unlike festivals in Newport or in New York City, which could draw people from surrounding cities and towns, the Pacific Jazz Fair was completely reliant on the local population. This population was small to begin with—fewer than a million people. We had no way of knowing how few of those were jazz fans. Counting our losses, I recalled the wise advice of my friend Ken Glancy. As the president of RCA Victor, Ken had seen sales figures for jazz records in the state of Hawaii. Hearing my plans to present a festival there, he had told me: "Why would you do that? There's nobody out there!"

# 14

# *KOOL to JVC*

Aᶠᵗᵉʳ ᵗʰᵉ ᵈᵉᵐⁱˢᵉ ᵒᶠ Nᵉᵂᵖᵒʳᵗ ⁱⁿ 1971, I had established the Newport
Jazz Festival–New York in July 1972. Joseph Schlitz Brewing Company
had long been a sponsor of Newport concerts, and its support subsidized part
of our efforts. But the president of Schlitz had just died, and in 1980 the company went into a tailspin. Ben Barkin reluctantly informed me that the company would not be able to contribute funds for the 1980 event.

I called upon my friends at KOOL. I had made a few misjudgments—
notably the Pacific Jazz Fair in Honolulu; an ill-fated attempt at presenting
country music ("KOOL Country on Tour," and the less said the better); and a
touring concert package that year featuring Mel Tormé, Gerry Mulligan, and
Sarah Vaughan. But our stadium soul concerts were always a hit. So I felt that
I could ask my colleagues at Brown & Williamson whether they would care to
step in as our sponsor of the Newport Jazz Festival–New York; they obliged
me.

Sponsors were becoming a necessity. When we first began the concerts in
New York, even though our ticket prices were low (tickets for our Carnegie
Hall concerts ranged from $4.50–$6.50), they were governed by the economics of the time; the festival was paid for from ticket sales. Now in the twenty-
first century, even with ticket prices as high as seventy-five or eighty-five
dollars and going higher, the need for commercial sponsorship increases every
year. This syndrome started back in 1980.

That spring I held a press conference in a hotel in New York City. Representatives from both Schlitz and the Brown & Williamson Tobacco Company
were there. It was then that Ben Barkin, my friend and Schlitz PR adviser,
symbolically handed the sponsorship of the Newport Jazz Festival to Brad

Broecker of KOOL special events. The torch had been passed. This little ceremony exemplified the relationships I had developed with my sponsors.

And the torch burned brightly. The 1980 KOOL Newport Jazz Festival–New
York was a smashing success. In order to counter suspicion among jazz enthusiasts that Brown & Williamson's sponsorship would engender a soul-music
takeover, I produced an event consisting almost entirely of jazz.

In effect, this festival was to be an extension of all that I had been doing in
the Big Apple for the past eight years. We continued to present concerts at
Carnegie, Avery Fisher, and Town Hall; in Waterloo Village, New Jersey;
at Manhattan's Roseland Ballroom; and on the Staten Island Ferry. We revived
the 52nd Street Fair, with free performances by the likes of John Abercrombie,
Don Pullen, Roy Haynes, Charlie Rouse, and Howard McGhee. We deepened
the focus of our concept programs—with a massive Charlie Parker tribute, a
salute to Fred Astaire, and a program called "The Blues Is a Woman," featuring vocalists Big Mama Thornton, Nell Carter, and Adelaide Hall. And as
usual, we staged a number of double-bills: Dave Brubeck and Carmen McRae,
Herbie Hancock and Arthur Blythe, Max Roach and McCoy Tyner, Gerry
Mulligan and Chick Corea, Dexter Gordon and Stan Getz.

But our sponsorship situation did have its detractors; a few in the press
complained about the carcinogenic legacy of the tobacco industry. More common was the sentiment that KOOL's conspicuous presence stretched the
boundaries of good taste. Whitney Balliett, writing in the *New Yorker*, sardon-
ically mused that other cultural institutions might follow suit (he mentioned
as examples "the Lark Metropolitan Opera" and the "Winston American Ballet
Theatre." I don't think even Whitney realized that he might have been pre-
dicting the future direction of corporate sponsorship of the arts).

Yet it was precisely the ubiquity of our sponsor's brand name that made the
KOOL Newport Jazz Festival such a win-win arrangement. In one season, we had
generated more positive publicity for the KOOL brand than any of their previous
promotions. Everywhere you turned, you saw or heard about "KOOL Jazz."

The Ketchum Public Relations firm in Pittsburgh had a system by which
brand-name recognition and public awareness could be rated on a numeric scale.
If your product achieved a rating of "1," you had a good public relations program.
That summer, they awarded the KOOL Newport Jazz Festival a "3," which was so
outstanding that it further cemented our relationship with Brown & Williamson.

At around the same time, *Fortune* magazine published a feature article on
our promotional campaign, lavishing the "KOOL Jazz" name with its highest
praise. But *Fortune* did have one point of criticism: How could KOOL be so
stupid as to endorse the "KOOL Newport Jazz Festival"—when Newport was
the name of another menthol cigarette?

When the Louisville executives of Brown & Williamson saw this item, I could hear the explosion all the way from New York. Within a week they were meeting with me in Manhattan. In no uncertain terms they told me that they wanted me to drop the Newport name.

This was troubling. Since 1962 I had owned the copyright for the "Newport Jazz Festival." It was my life. I had nurtured the festival in Newport from 1954 to 1971, missing only one year. I had even taken the Newport name to New York in 1972. It was my most valuable asset. But Brown & Williamson had a deal prepared. They were ready to offer me $1.3 million to surrender the Newport name.

One million three hundred thousand dollars. Cash, paid in annual installments over a period of five years. Three hundred thousand dollars a year.

This was 1980. I was making a good living, what with New York; New Orleans; Nice, France; and KOOL. My cumulative annual salary was somewhere in the vicinity of $100,000. But I had nothing put away; I still lived from year to year, hand to mouth. The festivals were barometers of my own stability, and FPI's overhead was steadily growing. In a sense I was indentured to my sponsor.

The money they were offering me now was in addition to my fees for the festivals. For the first time in my life, there was real money on the table, for the taking. This could grant the security that had eluded me all my life. I told them that I would seriously consider their offer.

During the next few days, I talked with many of my closest friends and advisers. Some of them echoed the sentiments of Elliot Hoffman, my attorney of many years. He didn't want me to take it. "George," he protested, "that's your legacy. You'll be giving that up."

"Elliot," I said, "what good is my legacy if I don't have any money? I could be starving in the streets! I have money now, I'm living well—but I don't have anything in the bank. If this sponsorship goes, I have nothing."

My history as the producer of the Newport Jazz Festival had always served me well. I had a good reputation, and it helped to form a lot of friendships. Most of these people were successful, and I had always felt a little insignificant. Friends in the record industry respected me for who and what I was, but I had the unshakable, nagging feeling that I wasn't in their league. There was no solidity behind me. All I had was my name.

I mulled over the decision. Dino, who was not a part of the deal because he had no stake in Newport, urged me to take the money. At one point I was discussing the matter with Joyce, and she fixed me with a direct but loving look. "George," she said, "take the money. You deserve it."

I signed a new five-year deal with Brown & Williamson to present KOOL Jazz Festivals in New York. We agreed to bill the event as the KOOL Jazz Festival–New York, with no mention of Newport. We negotiated in such a way that I was not actually giving up my license on the Newport name, but simply promising not to use it.

I knew that I had made the right decision. But the act of signing off on Newport left an uneasy feeling in the pit of my stomach. Now that the New York festival was purely a KOOL event, what could I do to preserve the memory of the old Newport Jazz Festival? The obvious answer: go back to Newport.

\*     \*     \*

In the ten years since I'd been away, some other promoters had tried to present jazz on Aquidneck Island. But you can't start a fire just by stirring cold ashes; despite some valiant efforts, every attempt had failed. No one but FPI had the instinct or experience to make a festival work there. So, now that I had achieved a degree of security in New York, it seemed appropriate to make my presence known in Newport once again. I asked my KOOL liaisons whether they would allow me to do this. I wasn't asking for sponsorship money, just their permission. They quickly granted it; they had no qualms about my producing a festival in Newport on my own. So I began to make plans. Festival Productions, Inc., was going to resurrect the Newport Jazz Festival, in its original home.

Most of the Newport city council was amenable to this idea. New Englanders seemed to appreciate the fact that I had preserved the Newport name, even after setting up shop in New York City.

But old habits are hard to break, and an otherwise painless reconciliation with the city of Newport was slightly soured by one demand. This concerned the permanent stage we had erected on Mariano Bucolo's field in 1966. After the festival's exodus in 1971, this 120-foot-long structure had remained standing—a hulking, skeletal reminder of things past—for several years. Finally Mr. Bucolo had requested that the city take the stage down. This was no small task, and it had been accomplished at considerable expense. Now, in 1981, the city of Newport wanted me to pick up the tab. Unless my company reimbursed the city $18,000 for the stage removal, they would not grant my festival license.

This was a rather bitter pill for me to swallow, as the festival's cancellation had occurred at the city's behest. The old Newport City Council had stabbed me in the back; now the new council was sending me the hospital bill. But I had no choice. I surrendered the $18,000 fee without a word of complaint. After this act of acquiescence, even our staunchest detractors could voice no logical opposition.

As for the press and people of New England, they welcomed back the Newport Jazz Festival without reservation. I was interviewed by countless newspaper reporters in the weeks preceding the event. The *Providence Journal* ran a front-page photograph depicting me with outstretched arms and a beatific smile. The headline read: "We're Back."

Fort Adams State Park is a large, abandoned, Civil War–era edifice on the northwest corner of Aquidneck Island. It's an ideal spot for a festival, with only one point of entry, which can easily be controlled. When the city council requested that we use this site, we happily consented.

The 1981 Newport Jazz Festival took place on the weekend of August 22 and 23, and featured a program nearly commensurate with the festivals of yore. On Saturday we presented the Buddy Rich Orchestra, the McCoy Tyner Quintet, the Dexter Gordon Quartet with Art Farmer, the Mel Lewis Jazz Orchestra with Zoot Sims, and the Classic Jazz Band (including Dick Hyman, Bob Wilber, Vic Dickenson, "Doc" Cheatham, and Ruby Braff). On Sunday the bill included Nancy Wilson, Dave Brubeck, Dizzy Gillespie with Milt Jackson, Art Blakey and the Jazz Messengers, and an all-star band led by Lionel Hampton.

The Newport City Council had issued a maximum capacity of 5,000 people—an excessively cautious but understandable condition, which we heeded scrupulously. With fewer than 5,000 people on the field, it was as if I knew almost everybody there. Most of our audience consisted of fans who had attended Newport festivals in the sixties, and they all came to me with their festival memories. Many of them I remembered personally; others knew me from seeing me on the festival stage. Everyone who approached me told me how good it was to have the festival in Newport again. It was like attending a class reunion. And it really did feel good to be back.

Meanwhile, New York beckoned. With a nine-year history behind us, FPI's biggest challenge was topping our own success. Despite the solid infrastructure of the festival in New York, it was difficult to conjure a suitably momentous schedule. Big concert series were not enough.

The 1981 KOOL Jazz Festival roared into action on Friday, June 26. There were a few innovations in the structure of the festival that year.

One of these was the utilization of the talents of guest producers, which I had done before. This year, I contracted nearly half of the big concerts to independent producers, many of whom were critics with little production experience. This was both a practical and a strategic move—practical because it alleviated my burden as a producer and diversified the tone of the festival, and strategic because it extended the hand of collaboration to some of our most outspoken detractors. ("I well realize," wrote Gary Giddins after this experience, "that not even the cruelest critical blows aimed from this page could restore my virginity, tattered thing that it was.")

These concerts, of course, varied in terms of production value, aesthetic worth, and financial success—but several of them were top-notch. Giddins's "The Art of Jazz Singing" concert (cohosted by Carmen McRae and Joe Williams and featuring the debut of Bobby McFerrin) fared well by all three measures. So did a "Portrait of Roy Eldridge" concert, coproduced by Giddins and Ira Gitler. Harriet Choice of the *Chicago Tribune* produced "Goin' to Chicago," an appropriately sprawling salute to Chicago jazz covering everyone from Jimmy McPartland to Roscoe Mitchell. Dan Morgenstern's evening of duets featured several inspired performances. And "A Portrait of Art Tatum," coproduced and cohosted by Dick Hyman and Billy Taylor, was superb.

The major event of the 1981 Kool Jazz Festival–New York, however, was the reappearance of Miles Davis after a five-year hiatus. This proved to be a public relations dream come true. Largely as a result, the press surrounding the festival was magnificent. Our corporate liaisons recognized that jazz had done more for KOOL's image in just two years than soul music had done. The strength of this sponsor relationship sowed the seeds for the corporate support that is now so crucial for jazz.

Brown & Williamson soon came to a bold decision.

"Let's cut out the soul festivals," they said. "Let's do jazz in every city." So just like that, our nationwide battery of stadium soul concerts (which had really peaked a few years earlier) was replaced by a program of week-long jazz events. And KOOL wanted to expand again; the roster for 1982 would include twenty American cities—with new outposts in Chicago, Dallas, Detroit, Los Angeles, Minneapolis, New Orleans, Orlando, Philadelphia, Pittsburgh, San Francisco, Seattle, and Washington, D.C.

Given this newfound focus on jazz, it made sense for KOOL to sponsor our festival in Newport. So, despite the conflict in nomenclature, the 1982 Newport Jazz Festival was a KOOL event. It took place once again in late August at Fort Adams State Park, and featured performances by Mel Tormé, George Shearing, Gerry Mulligan, the Modern Jazz Quartet, Oscar Peterson, Sarah Vaughan, Dorothy Donegan, Chick Corea with Gary Burton, guitarist Tal Farlow with Red Norvo on vibes, and the Great Quartet consisting of Freddie Hubbard, McCoy Tyner, Ron Carter, and Elvin Jones.

As FPI expanded the Kool Jazz program, we received some moral support from classical organizations. The Atlanta Symphony, for instance, agreed to endorse the KOOL Jazz Festival. Robert Shaw, the Atlanta symphony's brilliant conductor, was vacationing in France with his wife. They had been given our phone number at our house in Vence, where Joyce and I were also vacationing. We had a lovely time with Mr. Shaw and his wife, and shared some bottles of excellent Burgundy wine. When the Atlanta Symphony held its KOOL press conference a few months later, Robert Shaw introduced me in truly laudatory fashion. His oration was inspired; at one point he put me in the same company as Sol Hurok and Leonard Bernstein. I turned to a member of Mr. Shaw's staff just before my own ascent to the podium. I whispered, "See what a few bottles of Musigny '61 will do?"

In Minneapolis we were welcomed by Pinchas Zukerman, the renowned violist and head of the St. Paul Chamber Orchestra. Like Robert Shaw, Mr. Zukerman held a press conference in which he enthusiastically endorsed the establishment of a KOOL Jazz Festival in his city. Then I took the microphone to answer some questions. And the press were ecstatic; they were so jazz-deprived that the festival was like a cool rain after many years of drought. Reporters could barely conceal their glee. They were asking questions like: "Do you think you could get Dizzy Gillespie on the festival? How about Sarah Vaughan?" I felt like the Santa Claus of jazz.

Then a woman raised her hand, cleared her throat, and asked, "Mr. Wein, how do you justify the fact that you're proselytizing cancer by promoting cigarettes?"

At the time I wasn't prepared for that type of question. I followed my instincts, responding, "I don't smoke personally. I've never smoked in my life. But I *have* been involved with jazz all my life. And I'm very grateful to Brown & Williamson for making it possible to bring this important music, this American cultural phenomenon, to your city." I made no attempt to justify cigarettes. But in those few tense moments, I could almost see my sponsorship dispersing, like so much smoke, into thin air.

To be welcomed in city after city, just a few years after Newport's ignominious end, was gratifying. Jazz was no longer a dirty word. In fact, our only opposition came from those in existing jazz organizations who feared we would usurp their terrain. The producers of Chicago's free music festival in Grant Park were suspicious in this regard, until we persuaded them that KOOL merely wanted to give them a subsidy as well so they they could keep doing what they were doing. In San Francisco we encountered a similar problem with Ron Cowens, a successful businessman and a jazz fan who owned the local radio station KJAZ and ran a good but financially struggling festival. I convinced Ron that we had no intention of controlling or competing with his efforts. So we managed to work together—and in the process, forged not only an excellent festival but also a lasting friendship.

KOOL had decided to keep three stadium soul festivals—in Atlanta, Cincinnati, and San Diego. This didn't keep us from presenting some jazz in those cities. In San Diego, for instance, we produced not only a soul concert, but also a week's worth of jazz events around town.

Most of these San Diego jazz concerts took place at the Starlight Bowl, a beautiful outdoor amphitheater. I had scouted out the location earlier, and it seemed a nice little stage, ideal for jazz, with seating for approximately 5,000 people, and reasonable rent. We had been warned that the park was in the path of the San Diego airport. When we went to check it out, it was fine. I guess it was a slow moment in air traffic. We decided to use this venue for four separate concerts.

What a mistake. Each of our Starlight Bowl concerts was marred by the sight and sound of commercial airliners roaring overhead. You could almost count the ribs on the planes, they were so close. And they passed one after another, in a migraine-inducing succession. We had scheduled Ella Fitzgerald, Oscar Peterson, Benny Goodman, Sarah Vaughan, Weather Report, and the Modern Jazz Quartet at the Bowl, and every program was ruined. We should have known better.

In Los Angeles FPI teamed up with a New York–based new music organization called Outward Visions, Inc., in producing a five-day festival of the avant-garde. Lester Bowie shared a bill with the World Saxophone Quartet and the James "Blood" Ulmer Trio. Muhal Richard Abrams performed a duet concert with Anthony Braxton, opposite Air (Henry Threadgill's trio) and the John Carter Quintet. Braxton also gave a free afternoon lecture at the California Institute for the Arts. The Art Ensemble of Chicago played opposite the Nikolais Dance Theatre in Santa Monica's Civic Auditorium. And our final concert featured performance artist Laurie Anderson on a program with Leroy Jenkins's band called Sting, and Roscoe Mitchell and the Sound and Space Ensemble.

Though the Laurie Anderson concert sold out, the rest of our events did poorly in ticket sales, which was a distinct disappointment. I was never able to present the newer sounds with any measure of commercial success. So although press for this festival was good—some of the best advance publicity we ever received—the concert failed.

We incurred an even more spectacular failure in Orlando. KOOL had given us a $250,000 fee—significantly more than our fees for other cities—to produce a jazz and heritage fair there. I wanted to have the event in November. But Brad Krasner, our partner in Orlando, was positive that we would have a smashing success in early June. Kids would be out of school, and people would be there on summer vacation. Brad convinced us that summer was the right time.

Brad Krasner was a concessionaire who lived in Atlanta and later went on to make a lot of money. But in those years, he was struggling. The only reason he wanted to hold the festival in June was that he couldn't stand to wait—he needed the money—but the partners listened to him.

We had found a field with a lot of acreage and good possibilities for security. Multiple stages and an array of vendors were set up, in an intricate but sensible ground plan that mirrored the fairgrounds in New Orleans. We held press conferences touting the festival; Panama Francis, an Orlando native, became our honoree. Ray Charles was our major headliner. The price of admission was low, and we had promotional deals with retailers in the area; people could get festival tickets at 7-Eleven for only two dollars apiece.

The much-anticipated festival weekend came—and it was over a hundred degrees on the field, with nary a shady spot in sight. It was a total fiasco—nobody came. We lost the $250,000 KOOL had given us, and another $250,000 that the partners Dino, Quint Davis, Brad Krasner, and I had pooled. So the KOOL Jazz Festival–Orlando cost $500,000 altogether, with nothing to show for it.

A failure of a different sort occurred in Washington, D.C., where I had come up with an idea for a Kennedy Center jazz festival. We took over the entire Kennedy Center, with jazz running simultaneously in each of the building's performance halls. The idea had occurred to me after observing Paul Acket's success with the indoor multivenue format at the North Sea Jazz Festival, a concept that Acket, in turn, had borrowed after attending the multistage outdoor Grande Parade du Jazz in Nice. I knew Roger Stevens, the Kennedy Center's founder. During a dinner one night I had told him that I wanted to take over the whole center. He raised his eyebrows but said, "If you want it, you've got it." We rented the entire place and produced several major concerts. It was a unique event, and it should have succeeded.

What killed it was a lack of support from the local press. In the months leading up to the festival, I met with editors at the *Washington Post* several times. I told them that we wanted to make this into an annual event. But aside from a couple of meager articles, they dropped the ball, which was disappointing. If the *Post* had just backed us in Washington the way the *Times* backed us in New York City and the way the *Times-Picayune* had adopted the Jazz and Heritage Festival in New Orleans, we would probably still be producing a jazz festival there. Instead, it died. We sold fewer tickets for this festival than we would have for a single concert by any one of the featured artists. This was to be one of the greatest disappointments of my life.

KOOL's 1982 expansion may appear to have brought nothing but problems, but it was just a classic case of too much, too fast. If we had added just a few cities each year for several years, we would have been able to set in motion more grassroots promotion in each market. Instead we were struggling to catch up with ourselves.

Occasionally, these festivals approached moments that were sublime. In Philadelphia that summer, we produced a concert at the Academy of Music featuring the Great Quartet (Freddie Hubbard, McCoy Tyner, Ron Carter, and Elvin Jones) opposite the Wynton Marsalis Quintet.

Wynton Marsalis had made a big splash in just the past two years (1980–82), first as the new trumpet sensation in Art Blakey's Jazz Messengers and also as a classical artist playing Hayden trumpet concertos. In Philly that night, he locked horns with Freddie Hubbard during the finale.

Freddie threw in everything but the kitchen sink; he was in top form. But Wynton matched him, with unnerving poise. He was phenomenal. And Freddie left the stage drenched in sweat and out of breath, as if he had gone ten rounds in a heavyweight bout. He walked past me and, shaking his head, muttered: "That kid knows how to play the trumpet." It was as exciting a trumpet duel as any I had ever seen.

Just as KOOL had a serious impact on jazz at this time, jazz had an undeniable impact on KOOL. After adopting an all-jazz policy in 1982, Brown & Williamson changed the entire image of its major brand. The waterfall, that longstanding icon of KOOL cigarettes, disappeared. In its place, KOOL launched a massive advertising campaign featuring portraits of jazz musicians. They took dozens of color photographs, not necessarily featuring celebrities, but regular jazz players holding a trumpet or a trombone. Each image was emblazoned with a new slogan: "The only way to play it is KOOL."

As this campaign was launched, I was in nearly constant touch with several people at the company. To one of them I remarked, "It's really nice to be part of the mainstream of your promotion." He replied, "You're not part of the mainstream, you *are* the mainstream of our promotion." They were spending close to $150 million in advertising, and jazz was at the center of their image. In light of this development, I looked back upon my deal with KOOL; I should have received $10 million, not $1.3 for giving up the Newport name!

KOOL kept its line of jazz-related advertising for several years, with some success. But by 1984, the company felt they had exhausted the concept. Sales were as big as ever, but the brand's percentage of market had dropped—primarily because other cigarettes like Salem and Newport had started aggressively promoting their own menthol cigarettes. In an industry like this, percentage of market is the name of the game. So KOOL dropped the jazz-related ad campaign. This didn't bother me in the slightest. What did bother me was the fact that Brown and Williamson also wanted to annul the final year of our contract.

I said, "Gentlemen, what are you asking me?" They had already paid me the $1.3 million for the Newport name, but they were also obligated to sponsor festival activities for another year. Sponsorship for all the cities totaled a couple hundred thousand dollars. They wanted to back out of this fifth year, dropping the KOOL name in New York City and everywhere else.

"We have a contract," I told them. "If you don't want to continue beyond that point, fine. But this year, you're committed. Pay me the money, we'll do it, and then we'll quit." They were incensed. But I had to hold them to it; without their funds, there would be no festivals. Having them for that fifth year gave me time to look for another sponsor.

I was fortunate in this regard. In the summer of 1983, I was contacted by my friend and associate Nobunosuke Saito. He arranged a meeting with Miyoshi-san, who ran a Tokyo advertising agency, and his client from Japan Victor Company (JVC), Shibata-san. JVC, an electronics manufacturer headquartered in Yokohama, was making a push into the international market at that time and was particularly interested in sponsoring events in America. They had focused on Newport because of its prestige and the fact that Shibata-san was a jazz fan. JVC was serious, and shortly after we were working with Sugawa-san from the advertising agency Dentsu to help with the sponsorship.

Knowing that KOOL never regarded Rhode Island as a major market, I asked Brown & Williamson if they were willing to give up the Newport Jazz Festival. They were more than happy to oblige: they didn't want any further association with the name Newport. Thus the JVC Newport Jazz Festival came into being even though I was still under contract with KOOL in New York.

That initial meeting with Shibata-san has grown into JVC's relationship with FPI, which stands today at over 150 jazz festivals and audiences of more than 3.5 million people.

# *Interlude 3:*
# *Miles Davis*

EARLY IN 1952, STORYVILLE AT NEW HAVEN, a club I opened for a disastrous few weeks, welcomed a sextet that had been organized by Symphony Sid (Torin). Sid was the voice behind the live radio broadcasts from Birdland. He had worked with Shaw Artists to set up a tour for his bebop all-stars. The group consisted of Jimmy Heath on tenor saxophone, his brother Percy on bass, J. J. Johnson on trombone, Milt Jackson on vibraphone, Kenny Clarke on drums, and Miles Davis on trumpet.

At the beginning of the engagement, Symphony Sid told me not to give Miles any money. I was paying the group twelve hundred dollars for the week—from which all of their expenses, including Sid's managerial fee and the agent's percentage, were being extracted. I paid this amount directly to Sid, and he paid the musicians. Miles, who was deep into drugs at this time, probably owed Sid some money from their last gig.

Later that same night, Miles approached me.

"George," he said, "give me ten dollars."

"Sid told me not to give you any money, Miles. I can't do it."

"George," he said, as if he hadn't heard me, "give me five dollars."

"Come on, Miles, I can't do it. The man said not to give you any bread."

"George, give me a dollar."

"Miles—"

"Give me fifty cents, George. Give me a quarter. George, give me a *penny*."

That was my first conversation with Miles Davis.

\*    \*    \*

In 1955, during a trip to New York City that spring while I was planning the second Newport Jazz Festival, I stopped by the Basin Street East club. Miles Davis was sitting alone at a table in the corner. When Miles had played Storyville–New Haven, he'd been a pain in the ass. We didn't have much of a relationship. But when I walked into the club, he called me over and asked a question.

"Are you having a jazz festival up at Newport this year?"

"Yeah, Miles," I replied.

He looked me in the face and rasped: "You can't have a jazz festival without me."

"Miles," I said, "do you want to come to Newport?"

"You can't have a jazz festival without me," he repeated.

"If you want to be there, I'll call Jack," I said. Jack Whittemore was Miles's agent.

"You can't have a jazz festival without me," he said again. Miles had a way of getting his point across. Although I had already sketched out the program, I knew that I would somehow fit him onto the bill. Miles was in better physical shape in 1955 than he had been in recent years. But he didn't have a working group. The economics of jazz were such that it was difficult for *anyone* to keep a band. Players took whatever work they could get. So I added Miles onto a jam session that already featured Zoot Sims on tenor saxophone, Gerry Mulligan on baritone, and Thelonious Monk on piano. These musicians were all willing to work as individual artists, without their respective groups. Percy Heath and Connie Kay were already scheduled to play earlier in the same program with the Modern Jazz Quartet, so I asked them to serve as the rhythm section.

Because of his late addition to the festival, Davis's name wasn't even printed in our program book. But his presence was felt that night. He overcame the inadequacies of the sound system by putting the microphone right into the bell of his trumpet—and playing Monk's "'Round Midnight." The clarity of his sound pierced the air over Newport's Freebody Park like nothing else we heard onstage that year. It was electrifying for the audience out on the grass, the musicians backstage, and the critics—some of whom had opined that Miles's career was already over.

In his autobiography, Miles claims to have played "'Round Midnight" with a mute. This was the way he would record it a few years later on *'Round About Midnight* for Columbia Records. But he played the ballad with an open horn that night at Newport. My memory is as clear on that point as the sound that rang from the bell of the horn. Bootleg recordings of the jam session, taped from a Voice of America broadcast, confirm my recollection.

A point of interest in these tapes is that Miles does not appear to play well with Monk comping behind him (Hackensack). When Monk lays out, Miles swings easily—"Now's the Time."

Miles also writes about how he had struggled with "'Round Midnight" for a long time. Newport marked his victory over the tune. "When I got off the bandstand," he writes, "everybody was looking at me like I was a king or something—people were running up to me offering me record deals. All the musicians there were treating me like I was a god, and all for a solo that I had had trouble learning a long time ago. It was something else, man, looking out at all those people and then seeing them suddenly standing up and applauding for what I had done."

As Miles descended from the stage, he passed by me. His only words were in the form of a complaint: "Monk plays the wrong changes to "'Round Midnight."

I laughed. "Miles, what do you want? He wrote the song!"

Miles Davis had the jazz world in his pocket at that moment, and he knew it. He handled it with characteristic aplomb. But even Miles couldn't ignore the fact that this single performance had energized his entire career. His Newport appearance led to the beginning of what would be a longstanding relationship with Columbia Records. The fact that his comeback took place on the Newport stage helped to validate the festival among the jazz elite. In this way, July 17, 1955, was a good night for both of us.

*    *    *

One night at Birdland I was in the back of the room and listening to the sextet with John Coltrane and Cannonball Adderley. Miles finished a solo and walked off the stage—a habit for which he had become notorious. The band kept playing. Miles slinked around the perimeter of the club, finally stopping at the back where I was standing listening to the group. The trumpeter tilted his head slightly, and furrowed his brow in careful concentration. He was scrutinizing the sound of the band. I wondered if he heard the same things I did. I got my answer after a few wordless minutes, when he leaned over and rasped in my ear.

"Tell Philly Joe he plays too fucking loud."

I shot Miles an incredulous grin. "Miles, it's *your* band. Why don't you tell him?"

I don't know whether Miles ever got around to giving "Philly" Joe Jones this advice. It ultimately didn't matter; the drummer only remained with the group for another few months. That spring, a dispute over money led Philly Joe to quit; he was replaced by Jimmy Cobb. This substitution first took effect at Storyville in late May 1958; Cobb recalls getting Miles's call at six-thirty on the night of the gig. He rushed from New York to Boston with his drums, taking the stand in the middle of "'Round Midnight." From that point on, he was a member of the band.

Philly Joe wasn't the only band member who had recently been replaced. Just a month prior, Red Garland had stormed out of the studio during a take, leaving Miles to play piano. Soon afterward, Red left the band. He was replaced by Bill Evans. So it happened that Storyville was the first gig for this incarnation of the Miles Davis Sextet, with Evans and Cobb both on board. They would tour incessantly throughout the rest of the spring, and all summer, appearing at the 1958 Newport Jazz Festival. The following spring, they would record six sides, producing Miles's best-selling album, *Kind of Blue*.

This group has come to be seen as one of Miles Davis's two most important bands—and one of the most dynamic working groups in the history of jazz. But at the time, my enthusiasm for the sextet was tempered by a reservation; I thought that Miles let his guys play too long. In fact, I aired these views in one of my *Herald* columns that fall. Miles's sidemen, I noted, "just do not have the quality of general communication that is evident in the tender sensitive playing of Davis, the accredited jazz giant. Yet when one goes to hear the Miles Davis Sextet, for every trumpet chorus by the leader, the listener will hear four or five times as many choruses by his two featured saxophone players." I went on to examine the newly minted Columbia album *Milestones*, which contained two tracks on which Miles didn't even play. And, as I pointed out: "on the four other longer tracks his solo space is dwarfed by the time allotted to Adderley and Coltrane." It wasn't that I didn't appreciate these monumentally gifted saxophonists; I just wondered why Miles was acting like a sideman in his own band. I concluded the column by writing:

> The music on the album is good because it involves good musicians. Your avid modern jazz fans will enjoy it highly. I'm afraid however that the larger novice jazz public, which is so eager to learn about this music, will reject this album.
>
> The reader up to now might get the impression that I expect an artist like Miles Davis to make artistic concessions to the public. This is absolutely not true. I merely suggest to Miles that a better choice of material, some disciplining of his featured sidemen and a little more desire on his own part to feature himself, would result in an increasing acceptance of his very wonderful music.

This passage may illustrate why I never became a jazz critic.

\*  \*  \*

I knew Kenneth Tynan to be an iconoclastic, self-adulating, often brilliant critic who sought shock value in his work. It would be misleading to say we knew each other, but we were, for a time, involved in the same circles. An entry from his private journal, published posthumously, illustrates this point:

> Some time late in the 1950s I went to hear [Miles Davis]. Between sets he joined our table for a drink, and chatted in his rasping whisper quite amiably. Suddenly we were approached by a timid white teen-aged boy with an autograph album. Nervously he asked Miles for a signature and as Miles obliged he said: "I've always admired you, Mr. Davis. I play trumpet in my high school band and I think you have a wonderful embouchure. How do you get an embouchure like that?" Miles said casually: "I got it from sucking little white boys like you." The boy absolutely froze. We all did. The words were spoken without passion, but they taught me more about feeling towards whites than dozens of liberal fundraising sessions with Sidney Poitier and Harry Belafonte.

Tynan's anecdote, told in the first person, bears much resemblance to a story of mine from that era. Miles Davis had appeared at the first Sheraton Jazz Festival in French Lick, Indiana, in 1959, on the same night that the Newport All-Stars performed. Miles, who listened to the music that night, actually had something nice to say about my playing: "Man, you swing more than Marian McPartland." I was flattered by this apparent compliment, which I didn't believe because Marian plays more music in one chorus than I've played in a lifetime. Walking back to the hotel from the field, we were talking amiably when a young white boy with obvious stars in his eyes approached Miles. The rest of the story unfolds exactly the way Tynan describes it—right down to the wording of Miles's response. Only, unlike Tynan, I didn't freeze. After the astonished boy scurried off, I admonished Miles: "Man, why do you do things like that? What are you trying to prove?" Miles said nothing.

I'm sure that I told this story once or twice among friends, and it's highly possible that on one such occasion I even mentioned it to Peter Brook. Peter, a close friend of Tynan, would have passed it along. Until reading Tynan's account published in a recent *New Yorker*, I had planned to withhold the story from publication. It's much more likely to me that Tynan, whose appreciation for shock value was great, liked this anecdote so much that he claimed it as his own. Tynan's critics have noted this characteristic elsewhere in his journals. In any case, I never felt that Miles's behavior in this instance was racially motivated so much as purposefully provocative, and rude.

\*     \*     \*

While on tour with Miles in 1967, I had met him in Paris on a Thursday and paid him off with a check for the balance of dates, which ended in Spain on the following Saturday. Miles Davis arrived in Barcelona for his last European commitment, a double concert. I had negotiated all of the dates with Jack Whittemore, Miles's manager. When Miles got to Spain, he noted the double concert with surprise. Charlie Bourgeois called me from Barcelona the night before the concert.

"Miles isn't going to do the double concert here unless you give him more money."

I replied: "We don't have any more money. Put Miles on the phone."

When Miles picked up, I told him our situation. "Jack made up the contract," I said. "You signed that contract. It's two shows in Barcelona. I can't change that now."

"I'm going home," he said. "Tell Charlie to give me my plane tickets."

"Miles, I can't put a gun to your head. Go home if you really want to."

I told Charlie to give him his ticket.

That morning, Joyce and I flew home from Paris. As we landed in New York, I noticed there was also a flight arriving from Barcelona. In those days, there was a gallery in the airport where you could view arriving passengers going through customs. On a hunch, I told Joyce: "Let's wait here a minute."

Sure enough, who walks off the plane but Miles Davis. I turned to Joyce and uttered the incestuous obscenity that was so much a part of Miles's vocabulary. It wasn't until seeing him in New York that I knew he had really left Barcelona. The Spanish promoters had to cancel both Saturday concerts. It was a huge scandal.

I went to the bank at nine o'clock Monday morning and stopped payment on the check I had given Miles in Paris. On Wednesday, I received a call from Miles.

"George," he said, "why did you stop that check?"

"Why didn't you play that gig?"

"Fuck you," he snarled, and hung up on me.

Miles would cite the story in his own book as an example of the "bullshit" I've handed out over the years. But the conflict proved to be pivotal in our relationship. I believe it was at this moment that I began to win Miles's trust and respect. We never had any serious financial problems again.

Not that there weren't differences of opinion. I disagreed with many of Miles's decisions, and never hesitated to tell him so. One such instance occurred right after a tour, when Miles decided to fire his agent, Jack Whittemore, without cause or warning. He called to say that he didn't want Jack to be paid.

I protested: "Miles, that's not right. This man worked with me on this tour for months. He deserves the money you owe him. If you want to fire him, that's your call—but you've got to let him collect his commission for this tour."

"I don't want him paid," Miles said.

I called Jack, offering to deduct his commission and pay him anyway, even though this might cost me my association with Miles. Jack's response revealed a depth of feeling for his client: "Look, George—if Miles doesn't want to pay me, I don't want the money."

Jack had no contract with Miles, but they had worked together for years. He accepted his dismissal without complaint. This self-effacing behavior was atypical of agents, who are commonly portrayed as cold-blooded, but wholly typical of Miles's followers. Jack loved Miles Davis to the point of masochism, and Miles took full advantage of this fact.

At the "rock festival" I had created out of the 1969 Newport Jazz Festival, many musicians and critics felt betrayed. Not every jazz musician felt this way. During the festival concerts, I stood in the wings of the stage, as was my custom. Miles, who wanted to avoid the festival grounds and had arrived via sailboat the previous year for a truly perfunctory appearance, now stood at my shoulder all weekend. Every time I turned around, there was Miles Davis. Photographer David Redfern took a photo that captures the two of us in this position, peeking out attentively from stage right. While I was observing the concerts as a promoter and producer, Miles had different motives. He was intrigued by the rock phenomenon. He listened to every group. He watched the audience. He scrutinized every detail of each performance. He saw those thousands of young people and their enthusiasm—and decided that he wanted to be a part of it.

By chance, Miles and I happened to have the same flight from Providence back to New York City after the festival. Once we were airborne, he left his seat to talk to me. He was in a strangely introspective mood.

"George," he said, "what do you think I should do? I don't know what direction to go in."

"Miles," I answered, in a hoarse voice meant to mimic his, "play the melody." After the visceral assault of the rock groups at Newport, all I could think about was the sincerity of melodic jazz. Miles himself had achieved those heights before, with renditions of standards like "Bye, Bye Blackbird" and "It Never Entered My Mind."

"Play the melody"—it was my mantra. But Miles didn't say anything in response. His "Bye, Bye Blackbird" era had occurred ten years earlier; for him, it was ancient history. Melody was the furthest thing from his mind. What Miles wanted, more than anything at that point, was to reach young people. He had already been listening to some rock, at the urging of drummer Tony Williams. He had recorded an album earlier in the year with multiple keyboards and electric guitar. But Miles's concept was still rooted in jazz improvisation. This changed right around the time of the '69 Newport Festival. There's no telling how the experience of the festival—seeing the response of the crowds up close—influenced Miles. All we know is that one month later, he went into Columbia's studios in Manhattan with a dozen musicians and recorded the first three sessions of what would become *Bitches Brew*.

Putting a major tour of Europe together with a month-long itinerary for Miles was no small feat. In addition to the usual headaches of scheduling, making countless travel arrangements, filling out dozens of individual contracts, and tackling every little detail, there were also Miles's exasperating ways to contend with. I was familiar with such problems; the previous tour with Miles, in 1967, had ended with a no-show and a stop-payment on a check. This time around, trouble began brewing months ahead of time, as I was setting up concert dates. I received word from his agent that Miles was thinking of canceling the tour and going with another promoter. This news had come just a few weeks after the termination of the 1971 Newport Festival. At that time, I wrote Miles this letter:

July 20, 1971

Mr. Miles Davis
312 West 77th Street
New York, New York

Dear Miles:
I have always known you were evil but I never thought you were crazy. My firm offer is $130,000.00, twenty-six out of thirty-three days starting mid-October. If Arthur House and Larry Goldblatt can beat that offer, by all means go with them. If not, I will welcome you back with love.

Best regards,
George T. Wein

I thought the tone, although strong, was necessary; unless you were firm with Miles, you didn't stand a chance. In this case, it worked. Miles agreed to the tour package. But he also harbored some resentment. I wanted to smooth things over, and start the tour on a good note. So, just as I had taken a willful stand in July, I sent the following letter just a few days before Miles left for Frankfurt.

October 15, 1971

Mr. Miles Davis
312 West 77th Street
New York, New York

Dear Miles:
I'll see you in Paris. I think most of the problems of the tour have been solved and I hope you'll enjoy it.
My wife, Joyce, tells me she met you on the street a week or so ago. She says you feel I don't have any respect for you, and I should show you more respect.
Miles, I don't know what to say to this, except that you are wrong about this. I respect you both as a musician and as a man. You have as much talent and charisma as anyone I've ever met. You are not easy to work with and you know that only too well. But it is because of my respect for you that I want to continue to work with you.
You are a great artist and my life has been devoted to working with great artists. Miles, I could treat this entire thing lightly and make a few jokes. But I don't want to. Whatever the difficulties between us, and however straightforward I am with you when I feel I must tell you what is on my mind, lack of respect is never involved.
Have a great time on the tour and I'll see you soon.

Best regards,
George T. Wein

I met up with Miles in Paris on October 23, 1971. I had been in Europe for only a few days; I had just finished a Japanese tour with a Giants of Jazz unit. I was relieved to see that Miles's tour was going well. His band, consisting of saxophonist Gary Bartz, keyboardist Keith Jarrett, bassist Michael Henderson, drummer Leon Chancler, and percussionist James "Mtume" Foreman, had already played Frankfurt, Stuttgart, Munich, and Milan. They were scheduled to travel all over Europe for the next month, ending in Bordeaux on November 17. But in Paris Miles came up to me and said, "Do you want me to finish the tour?"

I shot him a look. "What do you mean, 'Do I want you to finish the tour?' I signed a contract that says you've got a tour. If you don't want to honor the contract, that's your business."

He was silent for a moment. Then he said, "Shit man, I don't know," and reached into his pocket, producing a watch. He handed it to me. It wasn't a particularly expensive watch, but it was a nice little present. I took it as a gesture of goodwill.

"Thanks Miles," I said. "Finish the tour."

This exchange was Miles Davis to a tee. He could come on very strong, but then at a certain point he'd say or do something that touched you, that made you think he cared a little bit. In this case, I think he was just generally in good spirits. While staying in Paris, he even phoned agent Jack Whittemore in New York, to talk about a Philharmonic Hall concert scheduled for late November. Miles wanted Jack to buy $2,000 worth of tickets for the concert, and then distribute them to young people who couldn't afford them.

*       *       *

It was the first year, 1972, of the Newport Jazz Festival–New York. Carnegie Hall's show for that evening was billed as "Miles, Sonny & McCoy." I had put together a show with the McCoy Tyner Quintet (which featured saxophonist Sonny Fortune), the Sonny Rollins Quartet, and the Miles Davis Sextet (with Keith Jarrett on piano and keyboards). This was a much-anticipated show, especially since Sonny Rollins had just emerged from a musical sabbatical.

Miles, who was shrewd about his publicity, had seen the press the festival had accrued. I don't know whether he felt overshadowed by the success of the festival itself, or perversely thought that he could get more attention for *not* playing than he would for playing. Whatever the reason, Miles took decisive action on the day of the Carnegie concert, issuing a public statement to the press claiming that he had never agreed to appear. If he was going to play two shows, he wanted double his fee. He referred to the festival as "George Wein's plantation," and insinuated that any participating musician was an Uncle Tom. And the festival, he opined, catered to older tastes by featuring musicians like Dizzy Gillespie and Sarah Vaughan.

The concert had already sold out in advance. So rather than begging and pleading with Miles, or canceling the show, I contacted Freddie Hubbard and asked him to get his group together. In the lobby of the hall, I posted a sign announcing that Miles Davis would not perform that evening. We didn't give any refunds; nobody asked. It was a great night. Freddie played well, and to an appreciative audience.

I think this perturbed Miles quite a bit. His pronouncement had had little effect on the concert. In fact, it backfired. There was some speculation in the press as to whether Miles's refusal to play signaled some insecurities. "The real reason may have been fear," Whitney Balliett noted in the *New Yorker*, "for he has played little in recent months, and a trumpeter's chops, if not used, can deteriorate in a week."

*　　*　　*

From 1976 into the early '80s, Miles Davis was a recluse. He had sickle-cell anemia and his joints were shot. In 1973, he had an operation on his left hip. I had arranged a number of summer concerts in Europe for Miles at around that time. But after the operation, it was clear to all parties that he would have to cancel the tour. In spite of my knowing this, I had given him several relatively large advances. Miles was touched by this gesture, which he mentions in his autobiography. We did the tour the following summer and I got back every cent I had advanced him.

Miles's second operation on his hip, late in 1975, was obviously more traumatic. I visited him in the hospital after surgery and the pain was obvious. He would later tell me that the nurses in the hospital, taking pity on his anguish, provided him with a steady supply of "painkillers," which might have been responsible for what happened following his hospital discharge. Miles resumed some old, self-destructive habits. He dropped out of sight, stopped playing, disappeared. He was a man in exile.

From time to time we still saw each other; Miles's house, a brownstone on West Seventy-seventh Street, was just a few blocks from the Festival Productions office, a brownstone on West Seventy-fourth. He would stop by every so often—usually when he needed some money. We never turned him away; whatever Miles wanted—within reason—he could have; he was very appreciative. Despite his defiant attitude, Miles remembered when you did nice things for him.

One afternoon, sometime in 1976, Marie St. Louis and I paid Miles a visit at home. His place was a total mess. There was rotting trash on the floor, clothes and papers strewn everywhere. All of the windows were shut tight; stepping inside was like entering a dungeon.

Miles was dressed only in a silk bathrobe. I could see that he had a pistol in his pocket. This made us a bit uncomfortable.

"Miles," I said cautiously, "what are you doing with that gun?"

"Man," he said, "they came here the other day, some of these guys, and they beat the shit out of me. I'll be ready for them next time."

I didn't know what this was all about. Suffice it to say that Miles's social set at the time was a less-than-charitable crowd. It was obvious that music had little bearing on his life anymore. Sex and cocaine were his two obsessions; he consumed both in unhealthy abundance. In just a matter of months, Miles Davis had undergone an alarming transformation. That afternoon we saw the quivering mess that he had become.

Eventually we left Miles's house and started back toward the office. I turned to Marie. "I guess that's the end," I said sadly. "We'll never hear him play again." We kept walking. I noticed a hum to the air that could have been either the traffic on the West Side Highway or the Hudson River beyond. "But you know," I added, "don't bet against him. He just might come back."

In the next couple of years, Miles took some steps toward recovery. By 1978 he was beginning to get back into music, although he was still ill. He would occasionally come into the office with tapes for me to hear. He had been working with George Butler and Teo Macero at Columbia Records.

After lending me a tape, Miles would call to ask: "What did you think of that?"

I thought it was terrible. He was using heavy electronics—synthesizers and programmed loops—that barely masked his poor playing. His chops were gone.

But he kept bringing me tapes, and they sounded a little better with every pass. He was working with younger musicians raised on rock and soul. Then one day, Miles had a tape that sounded nearly right. This was sometime in the fall of 1980. He had been off the scene for almost five years.

"You may be getting ready," I told him.

With a KOOL Jazz Festival on my hands, I decided to take the plunge. So in spring 1981, I invited Miles to the office to discuss a deal.

"Miles," I said, "we want to bring you back. And I'd like to show you just how much we want you. I'll pay you seventy thousand dollars to play a double concert in Avery Fisher Hall."

It was an astronomical offer. But with Miles coming out of such a long hiatus, I knew that both concerts were bound to sell out. I figured that we could scale the hall for roughly $120,000, and just about break even. The publicity these concerts would generate was worth more than money.

I wrote and signed a check for half of the sum—thirty-five thousand dollars—and handed it to him. He took it.

Shortly afterward, I received a call from Mark Rothbaum, Miles's manager. He was furious that I'd given Miles a check for so huge a sum. He was also amazed, because Miles had given him the check for safekeeping—

when Miles's inclination had always been to take the money and run. Miles had every opportunity to take that advance to the bank without performing.

I was unfazed. "Mark, look. Don't worry about it. If Miles cashes the check, I'll just have to figure out some other way to get the money back. That's my problem. I'm not worried because I know that he *won't* cash it. He wants to play that concert, and he knows I want him to play it. I think it's about time that he came back."

*    *    *

The 1981 KOOL Jazz Festival ended on Sunday, July 5, with Miles Davis's comeback performance. The attention this event received from the press was staggering; feature stories were in every music magazine and in newspapers across the country. It didn't hurt that Columbia Records had coordinated the release of Miles's new album, *The Man with the Horn*, to coincide with the concert. This of course was the most anticipated moment of the festival; the media speculated as to what sort of music (Electric fusion? Afro-funk? Standards?) Miles would now be playing. Both shows at Avery Fisher Hall sold out just two hours after the box office had opened.

Miles's group consisted of musicians who, for the most part, were young enough to be his offspring. He had Bill Evans on saxophone, Mike Stern on guitar, Marcus Miller on bass, and Mino Cinelu on percussion. Drummer Al Foster, at age thirty-seven, was the only holdover from Miles's pre-hiatus years. The KOOL concert was this group's official debut, but they had warmed up by playing four nights in Boston—at a club owned by Freddie Taylor, my old friend. Reports from this engagement were encouraging.

Miles was quite cooperative about the concert—although he did refuse to let James "Blood" Ulmer, a fellow Columbia artist, precede him as an opening act. He was a half-hour late for the first concert, but proceeded to play an hour-long set. The second concert lasted nearly an hour and a half. There were countless celebrities on hand—I recall Carlos Santana and Bill Cosby standing in the wings of the stage, riveted. It was an important moment for Miles, and as a comeback it was an unequivocal success.

Musically, for me, the concerts left much to be desired. I had never been interested in Miles's electronic vamp arrangements, and they were employed here to full, mind-numbing effect (even on a rendition of "My Man's Gone Now"—one of the few recognizable tunes).

Though jazz fans were reluctant to be too harsh on their hero, critics went to town on his group. Gary Giddins called it "the sorriest retinue assembled for a great jazz musician since Ellington sat in with the Boston Pops." But they spared the man with the horn. The *New York Times*'s Robert Palmer noted that

"Mr. Davis himself was in fine form. His solos were carefully sculpted, dramatically paced, and alive with fire and commitment. They consistently rose above their rather ordinary setting." Whatever criticism this music invited, the fact remained that Miles Davis was back.

\* \* \*

A few years after that concert, in 1986, Cicely Tyson threw Miles a star-studded sixtieth birthday party at a restaurant in New York City. Joyce and I attended with Charlie Bourgeois and Marie St. Louis from my office, both of whom Miles liked very much. We all sat at a table with David Franklin, Miles's lawyer and manager at the time.

Miles was sitting in the corner with a strange-looking guy, motioning for me to come over and sit down. I walked over and started a light conversation with Miles. We didn't have much to say to each other, so I didn't stay long.

"What did Prince have to say?" my table asked me when I returned.

"You mean that character is Prince?" I hadn't recognized him.

A few minutes later, Miles came over to our table.

"What did you think of Prince?" he asked me.

"To tell you the truth," I replied, "I didn't even know who he was."

"I bet you thought he was gay," Miles said.

"I wasn't worried about him, Miles, I was worried about you!"

Around this same time, during one of my trips to California in the mid-1980s, Miles invited me to his house in Malibu. It was a lovely day. Miles had a piano there, and he asked me to play. I sat down, and Miles took out his trumpet, and we played some blues, just the two of us. It lasted only a few minutes. For me, it was fun. As for my host: I'm sure it reaffirmed his conviction that I would never play in his band. But he said nothing disparaging. In fact, as we walked around the house, Miles—who had taken up painting—proudly showed me a number of his canvases. He told me to take my pick. I chose four of them, one of which he signed. I took these back with me to New York, and had them framed. I gave one of them to Marie St. Louis and another to Darlene Chan. I kept two for myself.

The next time I spoke to Miles on the phone, I said: "You should see these paintings you gave me." I had paid six or seven hundred dollars for each of the frames; they were expertly done.

"Well, I'll see them sometime," he said.

Two months later, I got a call from Miles. "I want my paintings back," he said.

"What do you mean, you want your paintings back? You gave them to me."

"I want my paintings back."

"Miles, I got them framed. They're my paintings now."

It was no use. When Miles wanted something, he persisted. So I relented, giving him back one of the paintings; I kept the one he had autographed "To George."

Some time later there was an exhibition of Miles's paintings in New York. I went there and, sure enough, there was my painting on the wall with a price tag of $15,000. I don't know whether that piece ever sold, but I often kidded Miles about it afterwards: "Fifteen thousand dollars! The least you could have done was pay me for the frame!"

In the summer of 1991, the French government nominated both Miles Davis and me for the *Légion d'Honneur*. I had long been fascinated by this heroic commendation; the artist Louis Kronberg was an *officier* in the *Légion d'Honneur*, and in my youth I had always been impressed by the little red button he wore in his lapel. As late as 1991, not a single jazz musician had ever received this noble distinction—they had been awarded *L'Ordre des Arts et Lettres*. In fact, I had been inducted into *L'Ordre* several years earlier. My induction into the Legion of Honor was realized thanks to a friend of Simone Ginibre, Alain Brunet, who was assistant to the minister of culture. He was an avid Miles Davis fan, and was highly appreciative of the contribution we had made to jazz in France in the proliferation of festivals that had grown because of our work at the Grande Parade in Nice.

At the ceremony, we were each kissed on the cheek by France's minister of culture, Jack Lang. Then the floor was opened to questions. At this point the power of celebrity became all too obvious, as the reporters in the room swarmed around Miles, obviously elated to be in his presence. It was like he exerted a gravitational pull. I was left talking to myself, "Hey, what about me? I got the award too!" My cry was to no avail.

After the ceremony, I invited Miles to a celebratory dinner in Paris, along with a few friends. Miles had played the previous evening in Montreux in Switzerland. He arrived at dinner bearing a beautiful canvas he had painted, which he gave to me. It was a lovely gesture—and a lovely painting—and it meant as much to me as the award we both had received that day.

\*     \*     \*

The last decade of Miles's career involved our office to a great extent; we arranged most of his tours of Japan and Europe and presented him on many U.S. festivals and concerts. The relationship was so strong that whenever he changed managers—and he had three or four different managers over the last five or six years of his life—he would tell each of them, "You can make decisions everywhere except where it's involved with George Wein or Simone Ginibre. Whatever they tell you to do is the right thing to do."

Miles had a warm feeling for Simone, whom he had known since earlier days in Paris, when she had had a short career as a jazz singer before she became Festival Productions, Inc., in Europe.

Miles Davis and Duke Ellington had one thing in common. They both paid attention and learned from the musicians that worked for them. This attitude manifested itself in different ways—Duke listened to riffs and melodies that his musicians might give him. He would arrange and harmonize them and create a song. It would become his—Duke's—music, part of the Ellington repertoire. Miles was the opposite. He was like a chameleon. He absorbed whatever music his sidemen were listening to or experimenting with. Bill Evans with his harmonies, Coltrane with his modal scales, and Tony Williams and Joe Zawinul's concern with fusion are examples. Miles wanted to be part of what was happening with youth. Williams and Zawinul knew, and influenced the directions taken by Miles in his latter years.

Miles came out of a generation—the first generation after the war—that marked the beginning of an era in which a black man had and practiced the right to voice displeasure about the problems of African Americans in the United States. Militancy was becoming common; during the era of Duke and Louis and Basie, musicians dared not speak out too freely. Ellington had spoken out through his music—"Black, Brown and Beige" and his *Liberian Suite* expressed his message. Louis did it in a way when he sang the 1934 song "Just a Gigolo." He put in the line: "When I die, I'll just be a jig, you know." The written law was against African Americans. They were viewed as second-class citizens and treated accordingly. But with the fight for civil rights in the fifties, which led to the passing of the Civil Rights Bill of 1964, there was a chance to voice one's feelings, particularly in the North.

People accused Miles of being antiwhite. He wasn't. Miles Davis was proud of being black—there's a difference. He resented the mistreatment of blacks by the society, and he spoke out against it. He appreciated his stature as the black Prince of Darkness. He liked that image. He liked the "black is beautiful" period that America went through. He wasn't anti-white, but anti-fool—white or black.

\*　　\*　　\*

I didn't love Miles Davis. I could never feel about him the way I felt about Duke Ellington or Dizzy Gillespie or Thelonious Monk. I loved those people. Miles was different. Perhaps I knew better than to love him. The people who loved Miles did so with a vulnerable blindness. Instead we operated on trust, which he held till the very end.

More than once, Miles asked me to become his manager. I told him that we had too good a working relationship. If I was his manager and got too close to him, it would only be a matter of months before the inevitable break. And in all likelihood, it would not be pretty.

During those last few years, Miles worked with us many times, on festivals at home and abroad. We received huge money for his international appearances. Interestingly, Miles usually did these concerts as a sole headliner, but never carried a New York festival concert alone. On the 1986 JVC Jazz Festival we packaged him with Spyro Gyra, a popular group of young musicians led by saxophonist Jay Beckenstein. The following year, we packaged him with Kenny G in a pairing that ultimately had a detrimental effect on Kenny Gorelick, who never considered himself a jazz performer—but whose name has consistently been invoked as a demonic representative of commercial "jazz." Miles was very happy to play with Kenny G, as well as Spyro Gyra; he didn't mind sharing a program with a group that had popular appeal. In 1988 we paired him with saxophonist Gerald Albright; in 1990, with the West Coast crossover group Hiroshima.

I arranged Miles's last two scheduled concerts. The first of these I organized with promoter Ron Delsener at Jones Beach on Long Island; Miles was part of a program that included four or five groups, including Wynton Marsalis's band. The second concert was in Los Angeles at the Hollywood Bowl, produced by my West Coast office in association with the Bowl.

By this time, Miles was ill and his health was deteriorating. But he was Miles until the very end. He called me and said: "I didn't realize these places were so big. I want more money."

"They can't give you more money, Miles," I said, "the budgets are already enormous." But Miles kept at it, until I finally said, "I'll talk to Ron Delsener, and to the Hollywood Bowl, and we'll see what can be done."

When I spoke with Delsener, he told me that he couldn't justify paying Miles any more than the original fee. "Well," I replied, "then don't. Just tell him to stay home. Put up a sign that says 'Miles Davis will not appear tonight, due to circumstances beyond our control.' Don't blame anyone, and don't tell any stories. You already have four major artists on the bill, so anyone who comes in will still get their money's worth. Give refunds to whoever asks." Ron took my advice, and to his credit, he did give refunds to people who came in the amphitheater after having seen the sign.

The Hollywood Bowl was another story. Miles was the only attraction on the bill, so the producers were more inclined to negotiate. They agreed to give Miles an extra ten thousand dollars, and he played the date. Shortly afterward, Miles checked into a hospital in California. He never checked out.

I spoke at his funeral, along with Bill Cosby, Mayor David Dinkins, the Reverend Jesse Jackson, Max Roach, Herbie Hancock, and some others. The core of my speech was an exchange Miles and I had had a few years earlier, when I was in bed with a serious back injury. Miles, who had recently played some dates for my office, phoned me. His first words were to the point.

"Where's my money?"

"Miles, for crying out loud! Here I am bedridden. People are calling to wish me well. All you can say is 'Where's my money?'"

"George, how are you feeling?"

"I'm doing a little better."

"You alright? You're going to be alright?"

"Yeah, I think so."

"Good." Then: "Where's my money?"

I also related the story of Miles's comeback—how I offered him a $35,000 advance, how he took it, and how his manager thought I was crazy. I described how I considered it a privilege to do that, since the world had not heard Miles Davis play in nearly five years. And I asked: "How many of you here who could, would be willing to give any amount of money to be able to hear Miles play again?"

At Miles's funeral, I saw at least four of the different women in Miles's life. Even though the respective relationships were over, they were still drawn to him. It was more than just his celebrity, or fame, or talent. There was a mystique about the man. George Frazier used to write that he had *duende*—a Spanish term often used to describe the bullfighter whose very presence sets him apart from the competitors, loosely translated as "a dazzling flash of charisma."

My long association with Miles meant a great deal to me. It was inevitable that we would figure largely in each other's lives. I've written before that jazz is like a deck of cards—there are only fifty-two cards in the deck. In producing jazz festivals, no matter how you shuffle the pack, you're still dealing the same cards. Miles was one of those cards. In fact, he was an ace. I was going to have to deal that hand if I was to work in jazz. And, despite our arguments and disagreements over the years, we worked out a good relationship. I had earned Miles's trust, and he had earned my respect.

I doubt Miles knew it at the time, but he once spoke the essence of our relationship. It defined his feelings about me, and I suppose it's also how I felt about him. "George," he had said, in that raspy whisper, "You're a motherfucker. But you're the best."

# 15

# *Grande Parade du Jazz*

SOMETIME IN 1973, I'D COME to the conclusion that I should start a festival in Nice, on the Côte d'Azur. This most populous of cities on the French Riviera was less than twenty miles from Vence, our home away from home. Nice was perpetually left out of international cultural events, while other coastal towns like Cannes, Cap d'Antibes, Cap Ferrat, and Monaco epitomized Mediterranean glamor. Intuitively, I recognized that a music festival in Nice would fill a void.

The absence of traditional jazz on European concert programs bothered me. By this time, "new thing" improvisers had established a firm foothold throughout Europe; a number of festivals there were devoted to this cause. In the 1960s I'd toured with such avant-garde icons as Archie Shepp, Albert Ayler, Ornette Coleman, and Cecil Taylor. The music of these and other experimentalists had been accepted on the Continent. This in itself did not bother me—it was a source of work for musicians, and I always appreciated that—but I was concerned with the prevailing critical indifference toward the music I loved. The swing era was long gone in 1974, but many of its giants were alive and well. Basie was still roaring. Ella Fitzgerald reigned as the First Lady of Song. Other influential artists—like Teddy Wilson, Fatha Hines, and Illinois Jacquet—were still active and playing.

Throughout Western Europe—and France in particular—there was a wealth of jazz fans who worshiped the music that Armstrong, Ellington, Basie, and Goodman had made in the thirties. The Hot Club de France, which founder Hughes Panassie still led, had chapters in dozens of cities in France.

Several summer jazz festivals had already been established in Europe. Antibes, on the Riviera, had hosted an eclectic jazz festival since 1960. The Pori

476 / MYSELF AMONG OTHERS

Jazz Festival in Finland had been up and running since 1966. And the Montreux Jazz Festival, in Switzerland, had been founded in 1967. Each of these festivals was an island unto itself; they would ask American musicians to come to Europe just for a festival appearance. None placed an emphasis on traditional jazz.

So a plan had begun to take shape in my mind. The multistage concept that we had established in New Orleans had never been utilized exclusively for jazz. Through my friend Guy Weiner, Pan Am Airlines's Nice bureau chief, I had found a site that could accommodate this concept: the Jardins de Cimiez, a space of several acres in Nice Nord. Cimiez, with its olive grove, 1,500-seat Roman amphitheater, and open spaces, seemed ideally suited to a New Orleans–style festival.

The next step, naturally, was to see if Cimiez Gardens was available for our use. My Parisian liaison, Simone Ginibre, arranged a meeting with the late Jacques Médecin, the city's mayor. Médecin was a brilliant man; he spoke fluent English and fully understood everything that I wanted to do at Cimiez. I had been hoping that perhaps the city of Nice would waive the rental charge for the gardens. I wasn't yet aware of the subsidies available to promoters who had ideas to promote tourism in French cities. I was pleasantly surprised when Jacques Médecin offered me a grant of 100,000 francs—approximately $20,000 at that time. He noted that the proposal would have to be approved by the City Council of Nice, then quickly assured me that it would not be a problem. I had just learned that the mayor of a French city held a degree of power nearly commensurate with the lord of a domain. Médecin was, in fact, a member of a ruling dynasty; his father, Jean Médecin, had been mayor of Nice before him, and their family had in effect presided over City Hall since 1934.

The chief of the Nice Opera, Ferdinand Ayme, was a man in his eighties who had served under Jean Médecin. His office organized all of the entertainment events and fairs that were a part of recreational life in the city. He was more than helpful; his office provided a box office, security, cleanup, stage construction, and just about every other logistical aspect of the production, at minimal cost. It was a pleasure to work with M. Ayme; he was a gentleman and he was honest.

But he was also skeptical. While he loved the idea and supported it wholeheartedly, he doubted the estimate of 1,500 people on the first night. I made a bet with him that we would exceed that figure; the wager was a lobster dinner, then, as now, an expensive indulgence in France.

Programming the seven-day festival was a full-time job in and of itself, because there had never been such an undertaking before. We were dealing mostly with over one hundred individual musicians, so the scheduling and transportation was a huge task. Arrangements were made to house the artists in a hotel in Nice—another tricky affair, because of the continual checking in and checking out taking place because the groups were appearing at so many other summer festivals in Europe.

The festival took place from July 15–21. We erected four stages in the Jardins du Cimiez. Each was booked with seven hours of continuous music, every day, lasting from five P.M. to midnight. All instruments were to be acoustic, so we were able to program fifty-minute sets with ten-minute set changes. More than any other festival in my career, this one reflected my influences and the reasons I became so deeply involved with jazz in the first place. Barney Bigard, Benny Waters, Joe Venuti, Eubie Blake, Cozy Cole, Jo Jones, Bud Freeman, Tiny Grimes, Milt Buckner, Jimmy and Marian McPartland, Buddy Tate, Eddie "Lockjaw" Davis, Vic Dickenson, Bob Haggart, Budd Johnson—these, and many other legends, were featured. In addition there were younger musicians of this style, like Michael Moore and Kenny Davern. We imported some New Orleans heroes like Kid Thomas, Harold "Duke" DeJan, Wallace Davenport, Milton Batiste, and others. And from France, we invited veteran artists Michel Attenoux and Gerard Badini among others, who represented the story of traditional jazz in France as it evolved after the Second World War. These French musicians were thrilled to be able to play with their American idols in jam sessions, both on the festival and at the hotel after hours.

We had set ticket prices at the ridiculously low figure of fifteen francs, which was then equivalent to roughly three U.S. dollars; this fare let you into the Gardens, where you could enjoy four separate stages of jazz. With such undervalued ticket rates, there was no way we could make money. But I was insistent on the price; I wanted people to feel that it was affordable. This policy worked, in that we drew over 20,000 people in the course of seven days. Mayor Médecin was ecstatic—not only because of the popularity of the event, but also because I was the first promoter who had lost money in Nice without asking the city to bail him out. This despite the fact that we were in the hole over $100,000. But things looked better for 1975, as Monsieur Médecin proffered a subsidy of 500,000 Francs, or $110,000. As for our opening night receipts, we counted 1,560 paid admissions—just over the optimistic projection of 1,500. Monsieur Ayme had lost the bet. He willingly took us to one of the best restaurants in Nice for a lobster dinner.

Some people on my staff thought I was courting insanity by starting a festival of these proportions—when I was already so swamped in the States. But we somehow made it work. The Grande Parade du Jazz, like the New Orleans Jazz and Heritage Festival, would survive its first few rocky seasons to become a successful and well-loved event. So ended the summer of 1974: we had presented a solid New Orleans Jazz Fest, the first financially successful Newport Jazz Festival–New York, and even kicked off the first-ever Grande Parade du Jazz.

*　　*　　*

The atmosphere of the Grande Parade was unique. Most of the musicians spent at least three (and sometimes as many as six) days at the festival. They all agreed to play in jam sessions. Many musicians would jump onstage in mid-set, even when they weren't scheduled to perform that day. Others became part of the audience.

Another distinguishing characteristic of the Grande Parade was the food concession, which had been Joyce's provenance since 1978. During the festival's first few years, the French *traiteurs* in charge had not done an adequate job. So Joyce, taking matters into her own capable hands, created a soul-food restaurant that became as much of an attraction as the music. She built a local team, and brought in the fabled Buster Holmes from his red beans and rice restaurant in New Orleans. Buster was idolized by the French cooks; they treated him as a master chef. Another festival chef imported from New Orleans was Susan Spicer, who went on to become a nationally ranked restaurateur; her restaurant Bayona is one of the Crescent City's finest. In Nice, Susan joined Joyce's busy team in preparing fried chicken, red beans and rice, and other down-home fare. They served hundreds of free meals for the musicians—and thousands more for paying festival-goers. During the Grande Parade, restaurants in Nice actually suffered, because many people came to eat this authentic New Orleans cuisine.

Our home in Vence became a social outpost during the festival. Joyce and I often had informal parties there, for musicians and festival staff. One year, Joyce taught Art Blakey to swim in our pool; she still marvels at how he could enter the water and simply sink to the bottom. Blakey somehow defied the laws of floating—until finally, Joyce got him to relax enough to float one time across the pool. Another memorable occasion was when we invited Miles Davis and B. B. King to lunch together. B. B. was in awe of Miles, and Miles respected B. B. for the blues that flowed through them both. Joyce prepared a meal suitable for the hot July climate: a cold puréed vegetable soup. B. B. took a spoonful and politely asked Joyce to heat it up; soup, in his opinion, was meant to be served hot. Miles agreed with this assessment, and

Joyce met their request. Later on I picked up the gist of an exchange between our two guests. B. B., who had never been short of female companionship, was telling Miles he envied him for the young girls that always seemed to follow in his wake. Such was the conversation of musical masters.

Well into the 1980s, our festival was the most successful event in France. Some years we had as many as 80,000 people pass through the Cimiez gates in an eleven-day period. Many practicing and would-be jazz promoters came, fascinated by the multistage concept. Paul Acket, whom I had met during my Newport International Band audition tour in 1958, transplanted this concept indoors, creating the Hague's North Sea Jazz Festival, one of the largest jazz festivals in the world today. Other festivals sprang up in smaller French cities, employing the same musicians that we brought to Nice from New York. Vienne started its jazz festival in an ancient Roman amphitheater. Bayonne, Montauban, Arles, Salon, and Nîmes each followed suit as well. We serviced all of these jazz events with our artists. Perugia, in Italy, and St. Sebastien, in Spain, also utilized our talent. The promoters of these and other festivals salute me as their inspiration, and all have become friends: Fritz Thom in Vienna, Inaki Anua of Vitoria, Miguel Martin of San Sebastien, Carlo Pagnotta of Perugia, Jyrki Kangas of Pori, Claude Nobs of Montreux, Jacques Launay and Paul Boutelier of Vienne, Gorgun Taner in Instanbul, Thorstein Granley and Rolf Bugge in Norway, and Paul Acket's successor, Theo Van Den Hoak, in North Sea. Their respect means a great deal to me. Another promoter, Hans Zurbrugg, whose Bern (Switzerland) Jazz Festival is held each spring, has become a fan of the Newport All-Stars. I've played in Bern on three separate occasions.

There was a downside to our cooperation with Europe's many other festivals: our attendance slowly diminished as those festivals grew. However, we were selling most of our musicians to the other promoters, which helped pay the cost of our own festival in Nice. In addition, our subsidy from the city grew each year—and eventually JVC, after becoming our sponsor in New York, began sponsoring the Grande Parade as well. Business was good.

Every year some of our jazz legends passed away, as did the jazz fans from the 1930s, '40s, and '50s. Younger people wanted more contemporary music, and the festival progressively changed to suit their tastes. The first musical shift occurred in 1979, when blues giants B. B. King and Muddy Waters, and rhythm and blues man Fats Domino, joined our roster of artists. Two years later, Chuck Berry made his first appearance; we presented him on the same program as Muddy Waters, and drew more than 10,000 people to the Jardins de Cimiez. It was our biggest crowd yet, and it sent me a warning signal; from that point on I was careful about how we presented any artists that might be too big for our venue. Yet the demand from other towns for our artists was so great that our booking business was growing by leaps and bounds. We could sell artists like Lionel Hampton and B. B. King to as many as ten or twelve different festivals. We were financially secure enough, in fact, to spread our own wings; to produce entirely new events.

England had an old Victorian Hall called Alexandra Palace, affectionately known as "Ally Pally." With an associate and friend of mine, Andy Hudson, as a partner, we made arrangements to produce a festival there in 1980. Ally Pally was situated in the north of London at the top of Muswell Hill. A manicured grassy slope descended from the building to the end of the property. Again, I utilized the multiple-stage concept and set up three performance areas at the bottom of the hill, creating a natural amphitheatre. There'd be no chairs; people would just seat themselves on the ground. The space was wide enough so that if we alternated the music intelligently, sound interference was negligible. It was a successful festival; by the response we knew that we could establish a yearly summer jazz event in London. I fondly remember one set I played there with Ruby Braff and the magnificent Benny Carter; Slam Stewart was on bass and Duffy Jackson was on drums.

That same summer of 1980, Fritz Thom from Vienna and Alexander Zivkovic from Yugoslavia became my partners in producing a festival in the Austrian lakeside village of Velden Am See, not far from the Italian border. This festival was a three-day event preceding Nice on July 4, 5, and 6; the dates for Nice were July 12–22. In addition to some of the musicians we were bringing to the Grande Parade—like B. B. King, Muddy Waters, Gato Barbieri, and the Basie alumni band—we presented John McLaughlin, Stanley Clarke, and Pharaoh Sanders. This was a broad spectrum of music that shocked the conservative little Alpine village. It was an experience they had never before encountered, and we were not invited back. This was sad because the festival had no crowd problems whatsoever, and the public enjoyed it immensely.

But Ally Pally, Velden Am See, and the Grande Parade didn't fill our plate that summer, as my friend Karl-Heinz Hein from Munich had convinced us to bring a festival to that Bavarian city. The Olympiahalle, which had been constructed for the 1972 Summer Olympic Games, was available; the venue's management, headed by a gentleman named Jurgen Kolbe, was happy to make an equitable deal with us. On July 10, 11, and 12, coinciding with the beginning of the Grande Parade, we put on three nights of music. Most of the artists were scheduled for Nice, but we bought quite a few groups from other agents to fill out our program. Some forty different groups appeared over the course of three days; they represented the broadest spectrum of jazz styles.

Because the Olympiahalle was a government institution and also that we were partners in the event, we had made arrangements that certain dreaded taxes would not be deducted from ticket sales. But in spite of the fact that this clause was in our contract, government tax agents came to the box office on the night of the concert and took the equivalent of $30,000 in German marks right out of the cash register. Fortunately, Jurgen Kolbe got this money back the next day, which was a minor miracle. It's just one example of the exigencies that so often make foreign promotions a hopeless game. Lack of awareness of European and Australian tax laws has scuttled many seemingly profitable ventures, a fact that I had learned while promoting Newport Jazz Festival tours since the 1950s. These tax problems would eventually curtail my European activities.

Despite these travails, the first Munich festival was financially profitable in its inaugural year, an exceedingly rare circumstance, in my experience. We attracted close to 25,000 paid admissions over the course of three nights. I was certain that we had created an event that would become an indelible part of the Munich cultural scene, and one that could be added to our list of festival institutions. Most of our press was good, despite sound problems in the cavernous Olympiahalle. The exception was Munich's major newspaper, which printed one of the most poisonous reviews I have ever encountered. The reporter for this newspaper had been drunk during the concert; he had spent the entire night in the dressing rooms badgering the artists, and never hearing a note of music.

My optimism proved premature. The following summer, Germany's leading rock promoter of the time, Fritz Rau—a man I had known as an old friend and an avid jazz fan—scheduled a huge concert the same week as our Olympiahalle festival. This rock event drew all the young people in Munich, many of whom had attended our jazz festival the year before. In addition, the same drunken reporter again killed us in the paper. I had never experienced such animosity—from promoters or the press—and it was clear that we could not continue to work in Munich with such an atmosphere. I don't know whether it was anti-Americanism, anti-Semitism, or purely the impulse of local promoters protecting their terrain. Whatever the case, we counted our considerable losses and canceled future plans for Munich.

Our second Ally Pally Jazz Festival in London had been due to open on July 11—the second night of our ill-fated Munich run. We had scheduled one concert in the hall itself, featuring both B. B. King and Ray Charles, which had sold out in advance; tickets for the rest of the festival, to be presented again on three stages at the foot of the hill, were selling briskly. We had a financial success on our hands before the first note of music was sounded. But fate was not to be on our side. On July 10, 1981, as I was backstage at the opening of the Olympiahalle Festival, I received a telephone call from London. It was Joanne Schmidt, a member of our New Orleans staff, and one of many Festival Productions employees who helped in producing European events. Our conversation went something like this:

"George, you won't believe it."

"What won't I believe?"

"You won't believe it. Ally Pally is on fire. It's burning down."

"I don't believe it."

Unfortunately, it was true. The old Victorian auditorium was a firetrap; fire department inspectors had politely ignored its deteriorating condition for years. When a workman who had been using an acetylene torch carelessly ignited a curtain, the whole building went up in flames. It was a major London fire; all the fire engines in the city couldn't keep the building from burning to the ground.

The fire had spread so fast that, had it happened the following night, many of our audience of five thousand might have perished. We were lucky, but it was the end of the Ally Pally festival. For a few years we tried to keep it alive in a continuing association with Andy Hudson and, later on, Capital Radio and John Burrows. We achieved varying degrees of success, but never captured the spirit or momentum of what we had at Ally Pally.

With the destruction of our English venue, antipathy in Munich, and vehement conservatism in Velden, we lost three potentially lasting events at once. But the Grande Parade continued, as did our business of bringing artists to Nice and making them available to local festivals in various European cities.

Out of these many tours one story stands out in my mind. I had just produced a festival with Andy Hudson at a soccer stadium in Middlesboro, in northern England. The next day, we had a Lionel Hampton date scheduled, believe it or not, for Carthage, Tunisia. Transportation was arranged from Middlesboro to London, from London to Paris, and from Paris to Carthage. While the schedule was difficult, the band would have plenty of time to make the engagement, a city-run festival presented in a Roman amphitheater. Unfortunately, as often happens, there was an air-traffic-controller strike in France, and it was impossible to get to Paris from London. So we rerouted the group to Brussels; they missed the Carthage date. Hampton was due to play a concert in Germany the next day, but the Tunisian producer begged us to send him to Carthage a day late, which was quite a dilemma. We would not have had a problem going from Brussels to Germany, and it would have been easier on everyone involved. But Carthage was an adventure, and the promoter, one Lotfi Belhassine, had become a friend. I finally notified the people in Germany that we wouldn't make their date. We flew to Tunisia and played the concert in Carthage.

Due to the date change, attendance for this concert was poor, so the Tunisian promoters decided not to pay us. They said that since the band had come a day late, our contract was broken, and their obligation waived.

I couldn't believe it. While I wasn't in Tunisia with Hamp and the band, I sent word to them to get out of the country as fast as possible. Then I called my friend Lotfi. "How could you do this to us?" I exclaimed. He promised to get the money. I later heard—from a young man in Louisiana who had worked in Lotfi's Paris office—that he did in fact get the money, but kept it for himself. Needless to say, I was wary about ever promoting concerts in Tunisia again.

And then there was Chuck Berry. Chuck, a likeable guy, had been cheated during his early years—and had determined that at this stage in his life, anybody who dealt with him would "do it Chuck's way." This was fine, except for the fact that "doing it Chuck's way" could be a harrowing experience. He demanded all his money in advance of any schedule tour before leaving America. And he wanted payment directly, not in escrow. In later years, as Chuck's fee grew higher, this meant that we were putting up as much as $150,000 in advance—knowing all along that if one thing went wrong, Chuck would refuse to board his plane, leaving us hanging.

One tour was scheduled to begin in Oslo, Norway. We had made arrangements with Air France to fly him to Paris and to connect with an Oslo-bound plane. According to this schedule, Chuck would arrive in plenty of time for the concert. But when Chuck got to the airport, he discovered that his first-class seat was not in the smoking section. He declared that he wasn't flying unless he could sit in smoking, first-class. The airline did everything they could to accommodate him. They told him they would give him two rows in tourist class all to himself, with first-class treatment, and he could smoke three packs of cigarettes if he so desired. But Chuck was stubborn, and the plane took off without him. Quint Davis, his road manager, called me from the airport and all I could say was: "Fuck it. I don't give a damn what Chuck does." I kissed our money good-bye. But Quint, characteristically, refused to give up. By some miracle he found a Pakistani airline flight with a first-class smoking section that left New York at 11:30 P.M. and landed in Brussels, where a connection could be made to Oslo. Chuck got on this flight, and he and Quint arrived in Oslo about an hour before the concert. Somehow or other, Chuck's musicians—who had taken the original Air France flight to Paris without anyone to guide them to the next flight—had also arrived; they played the show.

The rest of the tour unfolded in similar fashion. Every day was a crisis, with Quint solving every problem with poise. But the next time we presented Chuck Berry, I insisted that the William Morris Agency be held responsible for the advance that Chuck demanded. I don't think Dick Allen, the William Morris agent, has ever forgiven me.

\*       \*       \*

The Grande Parade du Jazz was the most enjoyable festival I ever produced. The festival lasted twenty years, from 1974 to 1993, and made many significant contributions to the cultural history of Nice. For example, in 1974 I convinced Jacques Médecin that it would be a good idea if we commissioned a bust of Louis Armstrong to be placed in the Jardins du Cimiez. We invited Lucille Armstrong, along with her friend Phoebe Jacobs, for the ceremony. Mayor Médecin invited Princess Grace of Monaco, who had appeared in *High Society,* the film set in Newport, with Satchmo. The bust was unveiled, and remains in a prominent position in the gardens. Some years later, Lionel Hampton indicated that it would be nice if he, too, could have a bust in Cimiez. So Jacques Médecin commissioned another sculptor to do Lionel Hampton's head. I'll never forget the way Hamp blessed himself as the bust was unveiled at the ceremony. He had probably suddenly realized that statues are usually created to honor the dead.

After reaching its peak attendance of 80,000 in the early 1980s, the Grande Parade leveled off at an average of about 60,000 admissions a year. But from 1984 on, the festival was sponsored by JVC, so our financial position was relatively secure. The musical image changed along with the talent budgets. Crossover groups like Spyro Gyra and the Crusaders, reggae king Jimmy Cliff, and Latin artists like Celia Cruz and Tito Puente, all joined our parade. In 1985 Miles Davis made his first appearance, as did blues guitar wizard Stevie Ray Vaughan and nascent pop star Kenny G. We presented Astor Piazzola, master of the tango. In 1987 we added George Benson to the list; in 1988, Carlos Santana and James Brown came to Europe. So the festival was taking on more popular appeal. In the nineties Gilberto Gil, João Bosco, and Astrud Gilberto imparted a Brazilian flavor, which climaxed with a rare appearance, in 1993, by the legendary Chico Buarque. I only pick out a few of these names to show how we gradually mixed world music artists with jazz originals. Regulars from the jazz world included Herbie Hancock, Wynton Marsalis, Branford

Marsalis, Lionel Hampton, Miles Davis, Dave Brubeck, Gerry Mulligan, and Dizzy Gillespie. Our roster also encompassed more pop-oriented artists like Chaka Khan, Roberta Flack, Grover Washington, Jr., and the Blues Brothers.

Yet we never lost our concern for the individual, traditional jazz musician. Doc Cheatham's last appearance in 1992 was memorable. Doc, then 87, still had a few years to live. But when he closed his performance on the garden stage with a vocal rendition of "I Guess I'll Get the Papers and Go Home," the audience, consisting mostly of English jazz fans who regularly made the pilgrimage to Nice and understood Cheatham's legacy, applauded for five minutes straight. You could sense their feeling that it might be the last time they would see him. And while Doc was a special figure, he was not the exception in Nice; we made it a point to present older musicians like Joe Pass, Clark Terry, Milt Hinton, and Al Grey. These veterans were the festival's heart right to the end.

That end, unfortunately, involves a set of circumstances that I am sad to have encountered. It's almost a Dorian Gray narrative, with Mayor Jacques Médecin as the central figure. Following the death of M. Ayme, chief of the Nice Opera and all other cultural and entertainment events, it seemed that greed took over the life of this brilliant man. I'm sure that Médecin had always had a hand in the corruption so common in French cities. Construction, road building, and other city contracts had always yielded their payments to politicos. But M. Ayme's replacement opened some additional coffers that had been closed during the tenure of the honest M. Ayme. This, of course, affected us.

The atmosphere grew increasingly sordid. The counts for our ticket sales had taken serious drops, despite sizeable attendance. Joyce and I had developed a good eye for determining the size of a crowd, but some evenings our estimates were as much as two thousand less than we had thought. Many things were happening that we could not understand. We were invited to take part in certain activities that would have put cash in our pockets. Because Simone Ginibre was scrupulously honest, and I was always concerned with propriety, we declined.

We were, nevertheless, friendly with the people exercising this corruption, and I asked them one night how they could justify what they were doing. Their answer was simple: "C'est la vie, George." I could only reply: "It may be your life, but it isn't mine." There were intense police investigations, and we often talked with the authorities. But our operations were never investigated; they knew our attitude toward what was happening.

In spite of the scrutiny, pressure from city officials to graft more and more money never stopped. The last time I spoke with Mayor Médecin was the day he was supposedly embarking upon a vacation to South America. He called from his home, shortly before going to the airport. I told him that his people were pressuring us in a way that made us uncomfortable. He said: "George, I will be back in a few weeks, and I will take care of everything. Do not worry." I made a toast to him at that moment; I was drinking a 1970 Château Giscours, a fine Bordeaux. I said: "Have a lovely vacation. I look forward to your return." He left, and did not return for several years. To many people, this came as no surprise. When the mayor did return to France, he was sent to prison in Grenoble. He served a short sentence, then was exiled once again to Uruguay, where he died. The casket of this destroyed man was returned home, and his body lay in state for several days in City Hall—while thousands of Niçoise passed the bier to pay homage to a man whose family had ruled the city for over sixty years.

Although the Grande Parade's attendance had been on the decline for several years, Simone and I had hoped to continue working with the new city administration. But it was not to be. The new mayor, who may have perceived us as part of the Médecin team, opened the festival up for bids from other promoters—with conditions that Simone and I knew would completely inhibit potential success. We knew, for example, that the festival could not open before the 14th of July (Bastille Day), because that is when vacations begin in France. The new contract proposed an earlier date. So we did not even apply for the license in 1994. It was the end of the Grande Parade du Jazz. Simone had registered the name, so the city could not use it. Since that time, at least four different promoters have been involved in producing the jazz festival in Nice. Enormous sums of money have been lost. I often think about the wonderful years we had there; sometimes I wonder whether we could bring that spirit back. But every time I fall prey to these idle thoughts, Joyce reasonably quells them. So the Grande Parade du Jazz remains a fond memory—one of the most joyous chapters of my life.

# 16

# *JVC and Beyond*

WITH A NEW SPONSOR SAFELY UNDER CONTRACT, I was looking forward to the next few years. Harry Elias, vice president for JVC in America, once told us that his company's rise in business in the States has coincided with its sponsorship of our festivals in Newport and New York. We know, as does JVC, that such a trend can be attributed to many factors beyond that of the festival sponsorship. Japanese companies uphold a tradition of loyalty, and JVC has always respected the work we do on their behalf. Mark Adachi, Shibata-san, Karl Bearnarth, and Hattori-san have become friends; as far as business goes, they maintain a hands-off policy regarding festival production. We have never had a better sponsor; they have allowed us to operate at the highest possible level. In addition to Newport and New York City, we have produced JVC festivals in Paris, Amsterdam, Miami, Denver, Chicago, Concord (California), Los Angeles, and Toronto.

The years since 1985 have not been kind to jazz. Most of the stars of the fifties have passed away. They had been regulars on the JVC Jazz Festival. In fact, we were often accused of playing the "same old thing." Since the "same old thing" was Sarah Vaughan, Miles Davis, Dizzy Gillespie, and Ella Fitzgerald, I paid this criticism little heed. As an example of our "same old," consider the 1987 JVC Jazz Festival, which featured Sassy, Dizzy, Basie, Stan Getz, Mel Tormé, Grover Washington, Jr., and the Modern Jazz Quartet. All of these artists are now gone. On the other hand, 1987 also saw appearances by Chick Corea, McCoy Tyner, and Herbie Hancock—anchors of jazz then and now—and the debut performances of Wynton Marsalis, Branford Marsalis, and Ruben Blades.

An artist who made an auspicious debut in 1987 was the pianist Michel Petrucciani, whom we had presented earlier that year in Nice. Michel was literally half a man, afflicted with a bone disease that had severely stunted his growth. His little legs dangled from his torso; he could not walk. We carried him to the stage. He was a fine pianist. He recorded two albums on the George Wein Collection label, issued through Concord Records. In the years before his death, his popularity in France was staggering. I always felt this related to Toulouse-Lautrec, the artist whose dwarfism was legendary.

Nineteen eighty-seven saw some changes that have proved important for jazz. First was the formation of the Lincoln Center Classical Jazz series, a string of concerts produced in August 1987. This would eventually lead to Jazz at Lincoln Center, now the most influential jazz-affiliated organization in the world. At approximately the same time, another movement was taking shape, downtown, on Houston Street. A young fellow named Michael Dorf had opened the Knitting Factory, a club dedicated to "new" music. Both of these organizations received recognition in the press, and deservedly so. However, the former group came under fire for its "institutionalization" of jazz; the latter, adopted as a hub for the marginalized avant-garde, was touted as the path to the future.

In 1990 the JVC Festival presented Pearl Bailey. Her husband, drummer Louis Bellson, backed her with his band. Pearl, who was much underrated as a singer because of her appeal as a comedienne, performed a stimulating concert. She sang Eubie Blake's "Memories of You," one of the most difficult entries in the standard songbook, as beautifully as anyone I have ever heard. For her finale, she asked Wynton Marsalis, who had taken part in the first half of the program, to play "The Battle Hymn of the Republic." Wynton waited over an hour and half backstage to play this one song. When it was time, he played it straight, with no embellishment. It reflected the deep respect Wynton felt for the artists—like Pearl Bailey—who preceded him. I believe this might have been Pearl Bailey's last public performance; she died several months later.

By 1990 Wynton's own professional career—then little more than a decade old—had already inspired a new generation of musicians to sound the call of "traditional" jazz. Many of these players showed quite a bit of promise. I got in touch with Larry Clothier and said: "Let's get a bunch of these young musicians together." Larry was managing one of them, the trumpeter Roy Hargrove. The resulting group, the Jazz Futures, played on the 1991 JVC Jazz Festival opposite the Wynton Marsalis Quintet. This received a lot of attention—negative as well as positive—because of the "Jazz Futures" name. Whether the music these musicians created reflected the future of jazz remains to be seen. Whatever the case, there's no question that the musicians in our supergroup—Hargrove, Marlon Jordan, Antonio Hart, Tim Warfield, Mark Whitfield, Benny Green, Carl Allen, and Christian McBride—have become staples on today's jazz scene, and will remain so for many years.

At the other end of the age spectrum was the Modern Jazz Quartet, which performed a fortieth-anniversary concert on the JVC Jazz Festival in 1992. This was a special moment for me, as the collective career of the MJQ had mirrored my own. They had started in the early fifties, played Storyville, and appeared at the first Newport Jazz Festival in 1954. John Lewis, Milt Jackson, Connie Kay, and Percy Heath projected a dignity and elegance in performance that had meaning then, as it does today. Lewis's song "Django" stands as one of the finest jazz compositions ever written.

I was somewhat apprehensive about presenting Nina Simone in concert in 1992, as our last Nina experience had been a no-show. But the concert sold out, and Nina gave a sparkling performance. She walked out onto the stage in a lovely white gown, stood at the microphone, and without saying a word, enjoyed a solid five minutes of tumultuous applause. At the end of the concert I exited the stage door to see Andrzej Gluchowski—who has worked with Joyce and me, as an all-around lifesaver, for quite a few years—running across the street. "He's got a gun," Andrzej was shouting, "he's got a gun! Call the police!" It took a moment to figure out what had happened. Andrzej had been sitting in our Mercedes waiting for me to come out. When he saw me exit, he had turned on the ignition—only to be accosted by a man with a gun, who jumped into the car and tossed Andrzej out. This guy backed the Mercedes from Fifty-sixth Street to Seventh Avenue and it was never seen again. Andrzej and I went to the police precinct to report the theft. I called Joyce and asked: "What do you want, the good news or the bad news?"

"What do you mean?"

"The good news," I said, "is that Nina sold out the hall and it was a wonderful concert."

"What's the bad news?"

"Andrew was carjacked at gunpoint. We don't have a car anymore."

Other festival mishaps were less dramatic, and of our own doing. The most painful of these mistakes involved Charlie Watts, drummer with the Rolling Stones. Charlie is a good drummer who loves jazz, and he had organized a good band of English jazz musicians. I said: "Wow, Charlie Watts is available?" I was under the impression that the entire world knew Charlie Watts; I thought that his fans would come to see him regardless of whether or not he was onstage with the Stones. We presented him in New York City, Saratoga, Newport, and several other places; I committed well over a hundred thousand dollars. And it was a fiasco. I learned, the hard way, that while the world knows the Rolling Stones, the guy sitting behind the drums is just that: a guy behind the drums. This was not the case with Phil Collins, whom we tried to get on the festival a few years later when he was touring with a Buddy Rich–inspired big band. Phil's agent asked us $75,000 for the band, which we thought was crazy. We countered with $40,000—still a lot of money. They were about to accept the date when we were outbid by rock promoter Ron Delsener—who offered $100,000 a night for ten dates. Every once in a while, we're reminded that the world of rock and roll occupies another plane.

Nineteen ninety-two also marked the year that I brought Michael Dorf's "What Is Jazz?" festival—which had been held at the Knitting Factory for the past several years—under the umbrella of JVC. Michael's festival spotlighted a portion of the music scene that performed a function that I wholeheartedly applauded. For the 1992 JVC Festival, I asked him to produce five concerts at Alice Tully Hall. He obliged with a series featuring Cassandra Wilson, Cecil Taylor, and John Zorn, among others. This venture lasted just one season. But it gave me an opportunity to know Michael. We became friends.

I've never felt a particular urge to defend my turf from encroaching rivals; if something is basically good for jazz, since that's my dedication in the first place, why should I object? This attitude prompted my welcoming response in 1960 (in the face of the Rebel Festival), in 1972 during the New York Musicians' Festival, and in the late-seventies to the early eighties when the Grande Parade triggered a wave of competing European festival events. Imitation, as the saying goes, should best be considered a form of flattery. Beyond that, you have to look upon it as if you've bought a house on a quiet street, and the next thing you know, it becomes a popular residential area—with a row of houses standing where there was once an open field. Whenever we started something, we had the field to ourselves, and in almost every case this was a luxury that didn't last. Such is life—so we were never resentful of competition.

The jazz press, however, has often seized upon emergent activity as an excuse to cast our festival in an adversarial role: as an institution to be opposed, even dismantled. This epidemic started as far back as the late fifties, the dawning of Newport's prominence. In summer 1959, my friend Nat Hentoff had gone so far as to publish an article for *Rogue* magazine comparing the festival to a "sideshow"—and presented as reasonable alternatives a few smaller events, including the festival at Monterey. Hentoff, a former member of our board of advisers, wrote:

> The Newport Jazz Festival has nothing to do with the future of jazz. It is a last if large gasp of the more expendable show-biz, con-

man, fast-talking-agent, tent shows, musicians-come-in-the-back-door past of jazz.

Such a statement crosses the line, in my opinion, from thoughtful criticism to spiteful slander. It was as if Hentoff—and the many writers who followed in his footsteps—wanted nothing less than the destruction of the Newport Jazz Festival. I often thought of answering these innumerable salvos, but always stopped myself—recognizing such an act as the ultimate losing battle. So I simply stayed in the kitchen, trying not to succumb to the heat.

I was ultimately rewarded for this patience, to a degree. Twenty years after the publication of "Sideshow or Culture?" Hentoff accepted an assignment to write an essay for the KOOL Jazz Festival program book. In it he marveled at the legacy and durability of the event whose demise he had once foreseen. "The Festival," he wrote, "is a continuing history of glory, as well as of occasional irrelevancy." These words went some distance in smoothing things over, even if they were set in motion by a festival commission. More recently, Hentoff has extended a hand of reconciliation on his own accord. In a May 2001 column penned for *JazzTimes* magazine, he described the long history of our personal friendship first forged at the Savoy Club, and apologetically dismissed his *Rogue* remarks as "more than a little hyperbolic." And he softened the memory of those harsh attacks with new praise: "Since Newport, [George] has expanded the audience for jazz more than any other promoter in the music's history."

Though there's some satisfaction in rapprochement, the larger issue remains: for many critics I'm an irresistible target, a fact that was even more clearly illustrated in the mid-1990s, as the jazz press rallied around the Knitting Factory and attempted to skewer JVC. Adopting the uncomplicated rhetoric of athletic combat, these writers tried to create a schism between Michael Dorf and myself—despite the fact that I had encouraged Michael at every stage of his emergence.

In the summer of 1996, *New York Times* critic Peter Watrous penned a venomous two-column article titled "A New Champion in Town." It described an epic struggle between "the ambitious young owner of the Knitting Factory" and "the wizened head of JVC." The Knitting Factory Festival, he argued, had gained the upper hand in this conflict—through more extensive, more eclectic programming that appealed not only to the downtown crowd but also to the core of a mainstream jazz audience. He wrote: "Mr. Dorf has been helped by Mr. Wein's own haplessness. Every year the 'What Is Jazz?' festival has taken on weight, while the JVC Jazz Festival has become increasingly irrelevant." With his use of the word "irrelevant" Watrous paid unintentional homage to Hentoff. But his words proved far more insidious, as the article surpassed mere distortion to engage in full-blown character assassination. The most offensive device in Watrous's arsenal was an obvious metaphor linking the "august but doddering JVC Jazz Festival" with the tired old man in charge; it was too easy to see the similarity between "the wizened head of JVC" and a festival that had allegedly become "a shrunken version of its former self." And as if this weren't enough, Watrous ended his attack with a gesture of disdainful dismissal: "With the demise of the JVC Jazz Festival as a central power, the king may be dying. But his death won't particularly matter."

The article was so vicious that two people I hardly knew—Randall Klein, producer of the San Francisco Jazz Festival, and Tim Jackson, producer of the Monterey Jazz Festival—felt compelled to act on my behalf. They were both friendly with Darlene Chan in my California office, and together they organized a roast in my honor. It was held in New York City at the Supper Club. Tickets were sold for $350, and all proceeds were donated to charity. I had nothing to do with the planning; I just sat there while Bill Cosby, Wynton Marsalis, and other friends got up and roasted me. It was a glorious night. Yet even this event was not without controversy, as it had unwittingly been scheduled for the same evening as a jazz awards ceremony presented by the Knitting Factory. This was cited, again in the *Times*, as further proof of my cantankerousness.

The schism between Michael Dorf and myself was greatly exaggerated. The truth is that when Michael was looking for several sponsors for his "What Is Jazz?" festival a year later, I advised him to reduce his search and give to one corporation the title sponsorship. He took my advice and soon had the Texaco Jazz Festival, which after the first year became the Bell Atlantic Jazz Festival.

The fact remained that Michael had not yet proven himself except in the press. I had been in the festival business, at that point, for just over forty years. I was seventy-one years old, and not yet ready to call it quits. It was important— and is still important—for me not to go out in such a way, with my tail between my legs. When I do decide to give up my title as "champion" (the *Times*'s word, not mine), it will be on my own terms, and at a time of my choosing.

In this situation time rewarded my conviction and restraint. FPI was invigorated by the challenge of criticism, and we worked hard over the next few years to stay on top. The JVC Jazz Festivals of 1998–2001 were aesthetically well balanced, commercially successful, and, for the most part, critically praised. We were proud to present Cassandra Wilson at Carnegie Hall, with Shirley Horn one year, and with Cape Verdean folksinger Cesaria Evora the next, and to participate in the meteoric rise of Diana Krall. It was gratifying, as well, to showcase Wayne Shorter and Herbie Hancock in duo; to witness the communicative power of Caetano Veloso; to see the astounding success of John McLaughlin's "Remember Shakti" tour and album; to hear the wonders Maria Schneider did with Gil Evans's charts for *Sketches of Spain* and *Porgy and Bess.*

\*　　\*　　\*

In 2001, Verizon Communications—which, as Bell Atlantic, had devoted major resources to two Knitting Factory jazz festivals in New York City—decided to change the direction of its programming. The company sent out a request for a proposal for its festival contract and, after a selective process, engaged FPI as its new partner in the Verizon Music Festivals. We produced three Verizon Music Festivals in 2001—in New York, Los Angeles, and Tampa.

In 2002 and 2003, we added a fourth festival in Washington, D.C. Working with Bruce Gordon and his team of Pat Hennebry and Dana Moscato is an enjoyable challenge.

\*　　\*　　\*

Technically speaking, 1993 marked the thirty-ninth Newport Jazz Festival. So it was not exactly a fortieth anniversary. But, it was close enough for jazz. I noticed during the campaign that Thelonious Monk's son, T. S. Monk, Jr., was President Bill Clinton's man for jazz. I knew that I could go directly to the social secretary of the White House, as I had before, but I felt it was best to call T. S. Monk first. The wife of Tom Carter, who was chairman of the Monk Foundation, worked for Vice President Al Gore. After speaking with T. S. Monk, I called Tom Carter and he set up a meeting with the social secretary Ann Stock.

Ann Stock was agreeable to the idea of a jazz evening. Plans were made to set up a tent on the White House lawn that could host 400 people to a sit-down dinner and concert. Because this was one of the first important social events of the Clinton administration, the president's staff had little experience in organizing such an evening. What started out to be a repeat of the glorious afternoon at the White House in 1978 ended up being a near nightmare that came close to destroying my relationship with T. S. Monk, Jr., whom I love dearly, and Tom Carter.

Where problems emerged, was when the first directive came down in reference to the invitation list. Where Gretchen Poston had given me one-third of the 400 invitees to invite as my guests, Ann Stock gave me none. As this was the first large reception at the White House, they wanted total control of the invitation list. For reasons I'll never understand, Clinton's staff made the pronouncement that they wanted no foreigners. This edict came down after I had invited the president of JVC Japan, who was coming to America to be my guest at the White House. I knew that this would not be a problem because Ann Stock would of course let me invite the president of JVC, who sponsored the Newport Jazz Festival. As it turned out I knew nothing. JVC's president was not allowed to come to the White House. He did come to New York for the JVC Gracie Mansion party, and I will be forever grateful to Mayor David Dinkins, who gave him the key to the city of New York and a plaque that commemorated JVC Jazz Festival week in New York City. I apologized with tears in my eyes, to this man who was president of the company that kept me in business. He understood the problem even though neither of us spoke a word in each other's language.

The irony of all of this is that on the same afternoon of the evening of jazz at the White House, President Clinton held a press conference and announced that Walter Mondale was to be the ambassador to Japan because it is so important to establish necessary favorable relationships with Japanese industry and business; and meanwhile the White House staff was insulting an important Japanese businessman who had come to America for the singular purpose of attending the fortieth anniversary of an event his company now sponsored. I can't recall ever being so embarrassed. In the Japanese tradition "of losing face," this could have been a disaster.

This was to be only the tip of the iceberg of the problems. Most of the few guests and family that I was finally allowed to invite were notified as late as the evening before the event that they could come to the White House the next day.

T. S. Monk and I chose the musicians for the concert. It was a reasonable representation of the world of jazz in 1993. Charlie Haden, Clark Terry, Illinois Jacquet, Al Grey, Dorothy Donegan, Bobby McFerrin, Herbie Hancock, John Lewis, Christian McBride, Elvin Jones, Red Rodney, Jon Faddis, Jimmy Heath, Joe Henderson, Joe Williams, Grover Washington, Jr., Michel Camilo, Dick Hyman, T. S. Monk, Jr., himself, the Wynton Marsalis Septet and, at the request of the White House, Rosemary Clooney.

This entire group arrived at the White House for an afternoon rehearsal. The program was being televised and I had to present all these artists in one hour. The professionalism of the artists came through. With cooperation, I organized a program that could be edited into a one-hour television program. Ann Stock wished T. S. Monk to be the master of ceremonies, which was fine with me. T. S. has a nice stage manner and was quite eloquent, if we didn't let him talk too much. I planned a program where I would make a thirty-second announcement, welcoming everyone to the White House and introducing Monk as the emcee. I was then told that I was not to go on the stage at all. I was furious. It wasn't Tom Carter or Jr.'s fault, but I was so angry that I had words with them that could have destroyed our relationship. I'm very grateful that they did understand my pique. Here was a party honoring my festival, where my guest list was not honored and I was "told" not to go on stage during a program that I had produced in its entirety. I was so distraught that I almost made the decision not to go to my evening at the White House. Then I realized that nobody except my personal friends would really care if I stayed home.

President Clinton came to the rehearsal to be photographed with the musicians as a group. I chose not to be in the group picture and sat and watched the photo being taken. If I was not wanted on the stage, I didn't need to be in the photo. John Schreiber and John Phillips from my company were quite upset about this. As President Clinton was walking on the lawn back to the White House, they grabbed hold of me. We approached the president. Surprisingly, we had no problem doing this because it was in the confines of the White House. They introduced me as the producer of the program and the founder of the Newport Jazz Festival. As I stood next to the president, John Phillips and the White House photographer took pictures of me with President Clinton. And, perhaps as a gesture of reconciliation, Joyce and I were invited to a small private reception in the White House just before the program was to begin. President Clinton told me he had always wanted to go to the Newport Jazz Festival but never had the opportunity because he was too busy either studying or working.

I never blamed Clinton himself for that day's problems. Politically, I have always supported him. But I have always held it against his staff. When the president delivered his remarks later that night, he introduced me from my table. I had been advised that I should stand up and take a bow. This was a very incidental part of the program and had little meaning to me. But Jack Namath, editor of the television show, saw to it that my introduction with the nice words said by President Clinton and my polite bow were included as a permanent acknowledgment of my being at the White House that stressful evening.

\*     \*     \*

Since 1984, FPI has produced festivals for Mellon Bank of Pittsburgh and Philadelphia. This was a direct result of KOOL's desertion as a sponsor. Festivals discontinued in places like Atlanta, San Diego, and Detroit, much to the disappointment of local jazz fans. In Pittsburgh there was such an outcry that a trio of regional businesses—Mellon Bank, Citiparks, and KDKA TV—asked us to continue producing a jazz festival there under their combined sponsorship. I gave the task to John Schreiber, then president of FPI. Schreiber produced the first Pittsburgh Jazz Festival in 1984. The Mellon Corporation was so impressed by this effort that they assumed sole sponsorship in 1985. Moreover, they asked me to produce a second festival in Philadelphia, where they had just taken over the Main Line's venerable Gerard Bank. This was the start of the Mellon PSFS Jazz Festival.

John Schreiber and I had worked closely in producing each of the Mellon festivals, but he had been FPI's primary point man with the sponsor. As a result, when John left FPI to form his own company, Mellon expressed concern over who would take his place. The answer was simple: me. I'd been getting lazy, and it was time to get back on the road. I took over producing the Mellon Jazz Festivals myself, working with my FPI assistant Deborah Ross and our associates in both cities. I enjoyed doing the press conferences, and the people that John had cultivated as friends were reassured. The healthy business relationship continued, and, in a sense, John's leaving got me back to the grassroots level that had worked so well in years past. In the years since, I delegated the festivals' production to others in my company; Dan Melnick produced both events with heart and vision. Mellon, as a bank, no longer exists.

*   *   *

Meanwhile, in light of successful JVC Jazz Festivals in Newport and New York City, I began to think about reviving another institution: the Newport Folk Festival. By 1985 this dream seemed economically feasible. Joyce and I began to discuss the possibility of re-creating the folk foundation and working in the same manner as we had during the unforgettable sixties. We called some of our old board members: Pete and Toshi Seeger, Peter Yarrow, and a few others. For a few minutes it was just like old times, as we picnicked in the basement of the Festival Productions office on West Seventy-fourth Street. But, you can't go home again. The world had changed in the two decades since the Newport Folk Foundation's peak. The musical atmosphere was different, rock and roll had taken over, and costs had multiplied. There was no basic incentive for a folk revival. We all decided it was best to preserve the folk world of the sixties as a beautiful memory. Yet this didn't exclude the possibility of a reimaged Folk Festival.

Together with Bob Jones, our erstwhile folksinger, and his teenage daughters, Nalini and Radhika, who were well versed in an emergent modern folk scene, we decided to give it a try. In 1985, after a fifteen-year hiatus, the Newport Folk Festival was revived—no longer under the aegis of a nonprofit foundation, but as a Festival Productions event.

Interest in folk music—with its reverence for artists like Pete Seeger, Joan Baez, Judy Collins, and Arlo Guthrie—was now being fueled by stirrings from a younger generation of singer-songwriters whose audience haunted clubs, bars and concert halls. Bob Jones conceived and produced the 1985 festival at Fort Adams State Park as a sister event to the JVC Jazz Festival–Newport. Intrigued by the prospect of a new generation of young audiences, I fully endorsed Bob's dream.

The 1985 Newport Folk Festival was a moving reunion of artists who had performed in the festival's earlier years: Doc and Merle Watson, Mimi Fariña, Taj Mahal, Dave Van Ronk, Ramblin' Jack Elliott, Joan Baez, Judy Collins, and Arlo Guthrie, to name a few. Crowds were small but enthusiastic. It was evident that the Folk Festival, in its third incarnation, would continue for some time.

By 1986, the Folk Festival began to include up-and-coming artists, some of whom have since achieved international prominence. Alison Krauss made her first festival appearance at age fourteen. Nanci Griffith and Patty Larkin were among the new faces. Bob and Nalini Jones developed a winning policy, striking a balance between contemporary performers and the extraordinary musicians who had carried folk music from one generation to the next. In the years since its rebirth, the Newport Folk Festival has presented veterans like Odetta, John Lee Hooker, Willie Nelson, and Sweet Honey in the Rock—as well as younger artists like Shawn Colvin, Billy Bragg, Michelle Shocked, Dar Williams, Lyle Lovett, Ani DiFranco, Natalie Merchant, and Suzanne Vega. The Indigo Girls made the first of several wildly successful Newport appearances in 1990; Sarah MacLachlan made her festival debut in 1993. James Taylor returned to Newport in 1998, twenty-nine years after his "New Faces" debut; his performance, which drew a capacity crowd of 10,000, was important to the stability of the festival.

The two artists most connected in legend to the early folk festivals are Joan Baez and Bob Dylan. Though Joan has made several appearances over the years, we had never been able to convince Bob Dylan to come back until 2002. Dylan, who happened to be on the road at the right time, agreed to play at the folk festival. His management asked us to treat it like any other date on a tour, but they must have known that this was an impossible request. We made no effort to capitalize on its significance, but the long-awaited return of Bob Dylan to the Newport Folk Festival was an international event.

He arrived quickly and without fanfare and headed straight for his trailer. When Dylan finally emerged nearly a half-hour past schedule, he was dressed like a cowboy—complete with white hat, false beard, and a wig of long straight hair. He played for nearly two hours backed by a good band. They revisited many of the old songs, "The Times They Are A-Changin'," "Tambourine Man," "Blowin' in the Wind." But they all sounded new to me as Dylan gave each song a different melodic interpretation. Many of us didn't even know the songs he was singing until we heard the title in the chorus. He never said a word to the audience. His fans felt secure in knowing that they were witnessing musical history in the making. The media went crazy: the *New York Times* devoted the equivalent of four full pages to the story. I think it has given a new life to the folk festival. We had made news again, and not merely for nostalgic reasons.

*        *        *

The festival's shift from nonprofit to profit prompted virtually no objections from the folk world. But it was clear that our sponsor's identity and image were crucial. In 1987, Bob Jones arranged partial sponsorship through a friend at Nestlé, the Swiss chocolate company. A chocolate sponsorship seemed ideal, since most of FPI's other sponsorships over the years had involved cigarettes or beer. We had no idea that Nestlé had incurred deep animosity from environmentalists around the world by distributing instant baby formula in third-world countries. Some of our folk performers refused to perform on a festival sponsored by Nestlé. We did our best to work with the company on this public relations problem, and some artists—Arlo Guthrie in particular—commended Nestlé for "turning around" its policies. Ultimately, however, the company wasn't fully dedicated to sponsoring musical events.

We formed a more lasting and less controversial union in 1988, with a unique ice cream company based in the New England town of Waterbury, Vermont. Ben Cohen and Jerry Greenfield were idealistic flower children, products of the sixties, who had brought their independent business to international prominence. They loved the idea of sponsoring the folk festival, with its traditions hewing so close to the social and political feelings they shared. For just over a decade, Ben and Jerry's and the Newport Folk Festival maintained an ideal association. The sponsorship fee they paid us, while not large, was a necessary underwrite for the continuation of our business. Ben and Jerry would come to the festival each year with their families, and everybody backstage would have free ice cream. They would take the stage and preach to the choir, airing their latest liberal thoughts in an entertaining way.

The dream ended in 1999, when capitalism reared its ugly head and our sponsors were forced to sell the company to a larger ice cream manufacturer with little interest in their mission. We were sad to learn that the idealism of Ben Cohen and Jerry Greenfield did not extend to their business association with Festival Productions. They left us high and dry in 2000 with little notice and with no sponsorship—a precarious position that endangered the very existence of the Folk Festival. We were fortunate to find help from a new sponsor, Apple & Eve, a producer of fruit drinks. But with or without sponsorship, it's probable that the astonishing legacy of the Newport Folk Festival will carry on.

*     *     *

My life has been a succession of dreams, both realized and unrealized. One such dream was to create a celebration of African-American contributions to world culture and the American way of life. This celebration could include visual arts, dance, classical music, and sports in addition to popular music.

I made no secret of my idea, and in 1993 I found myself discussing it with Harry Belafonte. Along with Lena Horne, he had been one of the first African-American performers to be accepted by white America in cinematic roles that were more than "Aunt Jemima" or "Uncle Tom." Harry Belafonte had not only endangered his professional career, but also put his life on the line during the civil rights movement of the fifties and sixties. He was receptive to the concept of a cultural celebration, and we began to talk in earnest. Over a period of months, and many meetings and dinners, we outlined a huge concept for a week-long festival. We met with several potential investors and sponsors. Unfortunately, the venture's budget was enormous, and it was impossible to find adequate funding at that time. When this fact became clear, my relationship with Harry dissolved.

But dreams don't die easily with me. A year earlier, at the 1992 Playboy Jazz Festival, Bill Cosby had introduced me to his friend Ed Lewis, the CEO and co-founder of *Essence* magazine, a successful publication directed toward the African-American woman. Ed and I had mutual friends besides Cosby; his goddaughter Heather Fierce was at that time working in public relations for FPI. So we continued our acquaintance. One afternoon late in 1993 we were having lunch and I mentioned the fact that my plans with Harry Belafonte had fallen through.

Ed Lewis is a laid-back guy whose enthusiasm for any project is usually concealed by the shyness of his demeanor. He already knew the general premise of my idea; I had told him about it during our first meeting. He now said he would like to pursue the idea. Quint Davis, Heather Fierce, and I arranged a meeting with Mr. Lewis, his then-partner, Clarence Smith, and Susan Taylor, whose vibrant personality and philosophy of feminism are the soul of the *Essence* message. Having realized that the notion of a massive week-long celebration was impractical, I scaled back my expectations and modeled my proposal after our many years of Ohio Valley and KOOL stadium festivals.

*Essence* magazine has a profound influence on the lives of its many readers. I knew the power that a national publication could have in terms of ticket sales, having witnessed the continuing success of the Playboy Jazz Festival. So Quint Davis and I sold Ed Lewis on the idea of an Essence Music Festival in New Orleans. We agreed that it would be held at the Louisiana Superdome on the weekend of the Fourth of July.

The Fourth of July? In New Orleans? Many of my New Orleans friends thought I was crazy. The heat and humidity of that city is almost unbearable at that time of year. But the Superdome is air-conditioned, and can hold up to forty or fifty thousand people. I knew that New Orleans was the ideal city because our Jazz Fest staff was intact. To create this sort of production organization in another city would not be impossible, but it would be more than difficult and prohibitively expensive. I also understood that African Americans from all over the region were eager to attend and had the means to travel. Heat would not bother them because the entire East Coast and southern region are humid for most of the summer. It's not so cool in Mississippi in July. The Fourth of July is a holiday, but New Orleans hotels were empty because the city had never been able to develop a thriving summer tourism industry.

After outlining the concept of the festival, Ed made the decision to move forward with the idea. I agreed to be 50/50 partner with them in both profits and losses. People in business are more willing to take a chance with you if you will take part of the financial risk.

The next step, as in any urban production effort, involved our relationship with the city. I had had contact with the city of New Orleans since the first Jazz and Heritage Festival. Administrations had come and gone. We had seen Ernest "Dutch" Morial elected in 1978 as the first African-American mayor of New Orleans. A powerful political figure, Dutch had held the office for two four-year terms and could have been elected for a third, had the city constitution allowed it. He was succeeded by Sidney Barthelemy, who served from 1986 to 1993. In 1994, the political dynasty that Dutch Morial had established took over city hall once again, as his son Marc Morial took office. The younger Mayor Morial had the strength and charisma of his father.

Marc Morial wanted the Essence Music Festival in New Orleans. He saw the potential for major economic impact and promised the city's full cooperation in this high-risk venture. But he asked one question: Why was *Essence* not working with an African-American promoter? This was a matter of some concern to both Clarence and Ed. Naturally, it bothered me. I was a partner in the Essence Festival. I told my partners at *Essence* that I would handle the situation directly. I wrote a letter to Mayor Marc Morial that read, in part:

> Dear Mayor Morial:
> My associate Clarence Smith of Essence Communications, Inc., with whom I have formed a joint venture to produce "Essence '95," a celebration of the African American contributions to America's musical heritage on July 4th weekend in New Orleans, has advised me that in a meeting with you on Wednesday, October 5, you expressed some concern that if this event happens that the African-American community should benefit and that African-American businesses be included for meaningful participation. It seems that you may have some reservations about possible negative reactions to the fact that Essence's partner in this venture is a primarily white company like Festival Productions, Inc.
> This is ironic to me. In 1962 I was invited to New Orleans to a meeting of the power structure (Mayor Schiro, Seymour Weiss, etc.) to discuss producing a possible Newport-type jazz festival. I explained to the gentlemen that it was impossible to produce such an event because the Jim Crow local laws prohibited Blacks and whites from working together. Now, in 1994, in New Orleans, could it be possible that I cannot do business with an African-American firm because I am white?

I went on to touch upon my lifelong embrace of African-American culture, and the work I had done on its behalf. I advised him of Quint Davis and how we had produced and created the New Orleans Jazz and Heritage Festival, and the contributions we had made to New Orleans's cultural and economic life. And in reference to the proposed plans for the Essence Music Festival, I wrote:

> The state, the hotel association, and the various tourist agencies have all given their blessing, but we cannot proceed without your help and cooperation. I have advised *Essence* that if you do not approve of our team that we should cancel the event. Mayor Morial, we want you with us. I request of you, please sit down with Quint

Davis and his associates and discuss your concerns. We believe what you believe. With *Essence*'s approval, anything we can do to work with you that will not damage the delicate structure of such a difficult festival, we will do.

On Columbus Day in October of 1994, at approximately 11 o'clock in the morning, the unlisted telephone in my New York apartment rang. A voice with that beautiful New Orleans accent said, "Jarge, this is Marc Morial. Welcome to New Orleans."

I thanked the mayor and breathed a sigh of relief. Since that time, New Orleans has supported the Essence Festival without reservation. The event has become a destination for hundreds of thousands of African-American men and women. More than that, it has given a huge boost to the summer economy of New Orleans.

In the festival's first year, 1995, tens of thousands of African Americans reveled in the music of artists such as Patti LaBelle, Aretha Franklin, Frankie Beverly, and a host of others. The Essence Music Festival in the Superdome was unique in that besides the artists on the main stage, who could perform for an audience of 40,000, there were four quadrants, each with a capacity of approximately 2,000, that presented different African-American-related music. Jazz, funk, gospel, and blues were all part of the festival—and in the afternoons, festival attendees could enjoy the Essence Empowerment Seminars created by Susan Taylor. FPI is no longer a partner in the Essence Music Festival, but we are still the producers. I dissolved our partnership when I realized that *Essence* as a magazine had a different agenda than FPI. I had no control over our own destiny. Quint Davis and his staff have nursed the festival's growth to the extent that in July 2002, the opening-night crowd of 50,000 broke all records and total attendance to the paid and free events exceeded 200,000.

\*     \*     \*

The Essence Festival was only one of many ancillary projects we undertook during this time.

I still augmented my KOOL activity with other endeavors. In 1982, my longtime translator and representative in Japan, Saito-san, had suggested that I follow up on a lead in the ski resort town of Madarao, in the Nagano Prefecture. My involvement with promotion in Japan had cooled considerably since the sixties and seventies; looser regulations and monetary exchange restrictions now allowed Japanese promoters of jazz to work directly with American booking agents, diminishing the need for our services. I listened to Saito-san's recommendation and flew to Madarao, a quaint little village high in the mountains.

The owner and founder of the Madarao ski resort, a gentleman by the name of Kunio Ogawa, expressed his desire to boost business in the dead summer months. I explained that we might make Madarao a jazz village, with daylong activities. He and his investors, small hotel and pension owners, agreed to the idea, and we scheduled a press conference in Tokyo to announce the first-ever Newport Jazz Festival at Madarao. Shortly after setting the press date, however, a business obligation arose for Ogawa-san, and he asked us to reschedule. Having met his wife, Hiroko, a charming woman who spoke English remarkably well, I made an unusual suggestion: Why not have Hiroko conduct the press conference? This was quite unconventional in Japan, but both Kunio and Hiroko accepted. This cemented a bond of friendship with the Ogawas.

The first Newport Festival in Madarao featured the Gerry Mulligan Big Band, the Great Quartet (Freddie Hubbard, McCoy Tyner, Ron Carter, and Tony Williams), Dizzy Gillespie, Carmen McRae, and Spyro Gyra. A format was established by which musicians held clinics in the morning before playing afternoon and evening concerts on a stage erected at the base of the mountain. Jam sessions would run into the early hours. It was a total jazz experience.

The simple country folk whose pensions funded the resort became my friends, making the Madarao experience different from any of the tours I had arranged in previous years. These people had invested their lives in developing this resort. They loved the festival, despite the fact that it became something of a financial burden. Nakajo-san and his family adopted me as an American cousin.

The Madarao Festival has continued, with just one interruption, since its inception in 1982. We have brought many fine artists to the Nagano Prefecture: among them, B. B. King, Dave Brubeck, Wayne Shorter, and Michael Brecker. Jon Faddis was a favorite at Madarao; his buoyant personality endeared him to the Japanese, and he became an annual attraction.

Their cooperation was due, to some extent, to the nature of the festival itself. Spending a week at Madarao was like going on vacation, since the musicians had time to swim, play golf or tennis, and generally enjoy the amenities of the resort. For a time, I endeavored to play a little tennis myself. I wasn't good, but I loved the game. One year—it was 1986—Branford Marsalis challenged me to a game of tennis. I was sixty-one years old at the time, and Branford boasted that he was going to run the old man into bad health. There was only one problem: Branford did not know how to play tennis at all. I had him running all over the court. After a half-hour of this, his knee—which had caused him some trouble a few years earlier—began to act up. He had to go to the hospital. We still sometimes joke about the day he was trounced by the overweight "old man."

At the 1987 Madarao festival, Lionel Hampton led a jam session packed with stars. He asked me to play piano with him. I replied: "Hamp, I'll gladly play with you—but only if we play songs, instead of 'Hamp's Boogie Woogie' all night." Lionel agreed. We started off the set at a nice, relaxed pace; we selected a few seldom-heard standards. I thought the music was wonderful. But after two or three tunes, he felt nothing was happening with the crowd. He turned around before the fourth tune, called "'Hamp's Boogie' in C," and we were off. At the jam session's end, the applause was thunderous. I tried to get Hampton off the stage—no easy task, when the crowd is roaring—and ended up leaving him onstage alone.

A jam session at another Madarao festival involved three tenors: Lew Tabackin, Scott Hamilton, and Wayne Shorter. This was a rare act for Wayne, who doesn't usually take part in impromptu jams. Before they went on, I heard the tenor men talk over their game plan. Wayne Shorter, turning to Scott Hamilton, asked: "Do we have to play changes?" His question was met with a blank stare. It was a strange performance. The same could be said for the following evening's finale, featuring all of the musicians—including B. B. King and his band. We played "When the Saints Go Marching In." Wayne Shorter joined us, and to this day I haven't the slightest idea as to what he played.

Tragedy struck Madarao in 1994. Kunio Ogawa's beloved wife Hiroko took a walk one evening and was found dead on the side of the mountain the next morning. Her death remains a mystery. Kunio never recovered from this loss (he died in 2003), and his son took over the operations of the resort. One result of this shake-up was that no festival was held from 1995–97. When we were asked to return in 1998, I passed the reigns to John Phillips, then and now president of FPI. Under his direction, the Madarao Jazz Festival is more successful than ever.

\*     \*     \*

Nineteen ninety-one was the 100th anniversary of the opening of Carnegie Hall. The late Judith Aaron, then executive director, and Catherine Gevers, the artistic director, asked me to produce two concerts to commemorate the hall's association with both jazz and folk music.

On April 30, I asked Pete Seeger to produce "A Celebration of Folk," a tribute to the folk music of New York City and featuring music from the

Puerto Rican, Jewish, Irish, African-American, and Greenwich Village cultures that contribute to the colorful kaleidoscope that is New York City.

A "Celebration of Jazz," which I produced myself, was a smash success and featured, in the first half of the program, Wynton Marsalis, Mel Tormé, George Shearing, and Gerry Mulligan. It was a reflection of the historic first union of Torme, Shearing, and Mulligan that had occurred some years earlier at Carnegie Hall. The second half of the program featured Dizzy Gillespie with an all-star orchestra with Jon Faddis as musical director. This band was called the "Centennial Jazz Orchestra."

The program met with such a favorable response that I was asked to institute an annual jazz program for Carnegie Hall subscribers. I had always known Jon Faddis was one of the world's finest trumpet players, but seeing him rehearse and direct this group of all stars of the stature of Tommy Flanagan, Ron Carter, Slide Hampton, Al Grey, Terence Blanchard, Freddy Hubbard, and Lew Soloff left an indelible impression upon me. How about having a "Carnegie Hall Jazz Band" with Jon as musical director? Judith Aaron and Catherine Gevers agreed and gave us a schedule of presenting four concerts a year. Our problem was to determine a theme and concept for the work that this band would do that would appeal to the demographics of the Carnegie Hall loyalists; and at the same time, not compete with what Lincoln Center Jazz was doing and avoid the pitfall of recreating the New York Jazz Repertory Company.

We realized the programming must allow Jon Faddis, the musicians in the band, and the arrangers to have a certain freedom of expression. The concerts would also have to have a familiar ring to the average jazz fan and to the Carnegie Hall subscribers.

We produced a total of some forty concerts over a period of ten years, with Faddis and I working as a team. I'd come up with ideas and titles, and Jon would either agree or not. Once we had determined the image for the concert, the music itself was directly in the hands of Faddis. We'd then speak to our arrangers, who would each write original charts for the proposed concert. For example, we'd do an evening of the music of Benny Goodman. We commissioned Jim Mc Neely to write an arrangement of "Sing, Sing, Sing." Mc Neely did not ask a clarinet player to play Benny Goodman's choruses; instead, he utilized the soprano saxophone, which could feature band member Dick Oates or a guest artist, such as Dave Liebman, who each played in his own individualistic style. While the listener knew he was hearing echoes of the Goodman smash hit of the 1930s, he was being swept up in a new experience. The *New York Times* referred to the CHJB version of "Sing, Sing, Sing" as a standard of what jazz repertory should be.

For the millennium the CHJB created a suite in four parts entitled, "Jazz: The Twentieth-Century Musical Miracle." The first segment was composed and arranged by the late Manny Albam, to reflect jazz of the 1920s, '30s, and early '40s. Slide Hampton took over the second segment with a salute to bebop. Jim McNeely prepared a unique twenty-minute segment that related to the Coltrane era of jazz. We asked the legendary avante-gardist Muhal Richard Abrams to dedicate the fourth and last segment to the emergence of free jazz.

Watching Jon Faddis direct the band during eighteen rehearsal hours, observing the respect for Jon and the excellence of the musicians who performed some of the most intricate big band arrangements I have ever heard, was a lesson in how to achieve greatness with a big band.

In 2002, Carnegie Hall engaged as executive director Robert Harth, with whom I had worked many years earlier when he was with the Los Angeles Philharmonic and Darlene Chan and I were producing a series of concerts for the LA Philharmonic at the Hollywood Bowl. Harth is a good friend. Unfortunately, one of the first moves Harth made was to tell me that he wished to discontinue the Carnegie Hall Jazz Band. I must admit I will never fully understand his reasoning. Regardless of what was said, the small deficit incurred by the CHJB concerts was not the reason for the demise of the band. My respect for Robert Harth has never ceased. I still serve on the board of trustees at Carnegie Hall. I decided not to fight a decision with which I was in total disagreement. Experience taught me that you should only get in a fight if you have a chance of winning. If I had challenged him, I would have lost him and my fellow board members as friends and still could not have saved the CHJB. It was a lose-lose situation. The press tried its best to make Carnegie Hall realize that it was a mistake to abandon the CHJB, but the decision was final.

The last performance of the Carnegie Hall Jazz Band was the first night of the JVC Jazz Festival–NY in 2002. Young pianist Brad Mehldau opened the concert. After intermission I personally wanted to introduce each member of the band and then see that Jon Faddis got the welcome he deserved. But as the band walked onto the stage, the entire audience rose up and started to cheer. I saw what was happening and told Jon, "No introduction is necessary for you. Get out on the stage!" As he walked to the microphone, the sound of the faithful, screaming appreciation for the ten years of dedication, reached its peak. Jon Faddis and I and the members of the orchestra will never forget that moment. It was a fitting finish to an adventure that never should have ended.

\*     \*     \*

The enjoyment of life makes living worthwhile. In addition to music, art and wine have for many years served this purpose for me. These interests have expanded my social and professional world. One story perfectly illustrates this idea.

In 1983 my friend Robert Pirie and I each purchased over thirty cases of 1982 Premier Grand Cru Bordeaux. I invested roughly $13,000 in the total purchase; today that investment would be worth over $100,000. At a recent auction, the Petrus '82 sold for $18,000 a case.

As the prices of '82s and other wines in my collection rose astronomically, I felt guilty about opening and drinking them. With the needs of so many people in our society, to casually open a thousand-dollar bottle of wine was an extravagance and even a waste.

I came up with a way to assuage my guilt. I called Ken Chenault, now CEO of American Express, with whom my company had been doing business, and suggested we cohost a dinner for charity. I would contribute the wine and he could contribute the dinner. Ken agreed and suggested the Rheedlen Foundation, a community-building organization devoted to improving conditions for Harlem children and their families, be our recipient.

For our first dinner, there were twenty invited friends who paid $1,000 apiece. That dinner was noted for the opening of a magnum of Mouton-Rothschild '45 and some Petrus '55. Since then, our guest list has expanded to more than forty friends who each pay $1,200, and in eight years, we've raised over $250,000 for the Rheedlen Foundation, now known as the Harlem Children's Zone.

Checks from our invitees are made out directly to the foundation, without any deductions for expenses. A good example of the wine tasting was in 1999, when we did a vertical drinking of Château Latour—from 1967, '55, '75, '78, and '86. Another year it was a horizontal drinking of '82s: Château Mouton-Rothschild, Château Margaux, Château Latour, Château Trotonoy, and Château Cos d'Estournel. Not only do Joyce and I get a good feeling about these wine dinners, but Ken and Kathy Chenault have become close friends. The joy of these evenings brought me into contact with Dick Parsons, CEO of AOL Time Warner, who has asked me to be on the board of the Apollo Theatre Foundation, and Bruce Gordon, president of Verizon Retail, who with his wife, Tawana, share Joyce's and my love for jazz and art and wine.

Joyce and I have become involved in the cultural life of New York City. She serves on the board of the Studio Museum in Harlem. I am a one-man committee for jazz on the board at Carnegie Hall, and a member of the board of directors of Jazz at Lincoln Center. At the Museum of Modern Art I am on a committee called Friends of Education, which raises money for the purchase of works by African-American artists; at my request, both Wynton Marsalis and

Cassandra Wilson have performed at benefits for this important cause. Joyce and I continue to tend to our own African-American visual art—one of the better private collections in the city, with works by acknowledged masters (Romare Bearden, Jacob Lawrence, Norman Lewis, Eldzier Cortor), older heroes (Robert Duncanson, Henry Ossawa Tanner), and contemporary greats (Elizabeth Catlett, Faith Ringgold).

So wine and art have each played an inadvertent but integral role in both my personal and professional life, increasing the scope of my acquaintances and forging bonds with interesting people. The same could be said for opera, cuisine, world travel, and sports. Joyce's culinary expertise, our combined passion for Pavarotti, my hatred of the Yankees—all have served as grist for the social mill.

Whatever fluctuations occurred with the festivals, my primary motivation continued to be my concern for the musicians themselves. I still considered myself one of them, despite the fact that I had made my living, and built my reputation, on the other side of the stage. The relationships I had developed over the years were precious to me. It was one thing to work with artists; quite another to know and love them as human beings.

Joyce and I knew many jazz musicians as close friends; John Lewis and his wife, Mirjana, were two of our closest. And as the years went on, we met many new friends whose lives intertwined with ours. Among them were Howard Alden, Scott Hamilton, Warren Vaché, Clark Terry, Al Grey, and Lew Tabackin—all of whom joined me on Newport All-Star tours of the 1980s and '90s.

Other musicians, whom I knew less intimately, could surprise me with their gestures of kindness. Once in the late seventies I was bedridden with a horrific case of gout, the result, no doubt, of an excess of food and wine. During my convalescence on the Upper West Side, I received a number of concerned phone calls and visits. One of these was unexpected; at around eight o'clock one night, there was a knock at the front door. I opened it and was surprised to see Gil Evans.

"Gil," I exclaimed, "what are you doing here?"

Gil said, "I heard you had the gout." Then, proffering a large glass jar, he added, "Cherries are supposed to be good for the gout. So I brought you some." Surprised and touched, I thanked him warmly and invited him in. But Gil politely declined my invitation, said good night, and departed. I never forgot his thoughtfulness. The cherries were delicious—although the allopurinol prescribed by my doctor was, I suspect, more directly responsible for my recovery.

For every Gil Evans, there was someone else who took years to regard me as a friend. Benny Goodman, one of my earliest heroes, fell into this category. Having been a student of Teddy Wilson, I had always wanted to at least sit in and play even one or two numbers with Benny. But despite my many years' acquaintance with the clarinetist, I was never asked. One day I told him how, as a high-school kid practicing the piano in Newton, it had been my dream that Benny Goodman would drive by, hear me play, and ask me to join him. Benny was less than amused by this anecdote. Making a face, he said: "I don't want to hear about that." I never mentioned it again.

One summer, sometime in the late seventies or early eighties, Benny was scheduled to play at *Jazz d'Antibes à Juan-les-Pins*, the jazz festival on the French Riviera. Norbert Gamson was the producer of *Jazz à Juan*, and although we were competitors (Antibes is not far from Nice, where I produced the *Grande Parade du Jazz*), we were also friends. Norbert called me to say that he had a serious problem: Benny had sent word from London that he was not feeling well, and was canceling his engagement. This was Norbert's most important concert; he had sold every ticket. He asked me to call Benny and convince him to play. I didn't know whether this would work, but I called Benny's number in London to try.

"Benny," I said when he answered, "it's George Wein. I've just heard terrible news. I heard that you're ill and can't play at Antibes. Is this true?"

"It's just that I'm not feeling well," Benny replied. "Is it an important festival?"

"Sure, it's important," I said, "but nothing is more important than your health. If you're not feeling well, you should go home."

"Do you really believe that?"

"Of course I do. Benny, you are an important person. It will make international news if you're ill. The world cares about you."

Benny thought for a while and finally said: "Well, maybe I can spend another day in Europe before I go home." He flew down to Nice, spending a pleasant day at a hotel on Cap d'Antibes. We had lunch, and were joined at one point by a topless beauty who came over for Benny's autograph. He had a good time. He played the concert without negative incident, and then returned to the States. If I had begged him to play the concert and said that the Antibes festival would be ruined without him, he wouldn't have cared at all. It was when I told him that his "illness" would make headlines that the problem was solved.

I was never personally that close with Benny, even though we had spent a number of hours talking backstage at concerts or in his Manhattan apartment. This changed after Joyce and I bought a home in Easton, Connecticut—a half-hour drive from Benny's clapboard house in Stamford. We had never been invited to Benny's home. The extent of his hospitality had been a lunch or two in New York where, to my surprise, he'd picked up the check. But when Benny heard that I had purchased a house in Connecticut, he called to ask where it was. I told him Joyce and I would love to have him over; I would drive to his place and pick him up. He said it wasn't necessary, he'd drive himself. Forty-five minutes later, Benny Goodman, driving alone, appeared at our home in Easton. We welcomed him into the house, and he evinced interest in seeing it. He proceeded to examine every room of the house: our bedrooms, kitchen, and bathrooms. And after having tea he departed. He must have approved of the way we lived, because shortly afterward we received an invitation to lunch at his home in Stamford. We had passed the test, and were close to being accepted as possible equals. The whole episode confirmed my suspicion—that Benny Goodman was perhaps the biggest snob I had ever known.

For the 1985 JVC Jazz Festival–NY, I had organized a tribute to the ailing John Hammond. George Benson and Stevie Ray Vaughan were part of the program along with a salute to the Benny Goodman sextet with Buck Clayton, Dick Hyman, Benson, a rhythm section, and Phil Bodner playing the clarinet role of Benny. On a hunch, I telephoned Benny and told him about the program. Would he like to play? To my surprise and delight, he agreed. The evening did not pass without some scary moments, but it was more than a success. It brought Benny back to the music scene. He reorganized his big band and enjoyed working for most of the following year. He passed away on May 6, 1986. Carole Phillips wrote me the most touching letter after the funeral. She said the last year of Benny's life was a happy one because he was playing again. She said it was my getting him to appear at the John Hammond Tribute that gave him the confidence and courage to come out of retirement. I have to add that it could not have happened without the help of Carole Phillips herself, who was Benny's companion in the years following the death of his wife, Alice.

\*       \*       \*

Another artist synonymous with difficulty was the legendary Buddy Rich. But we had developed a good relationship over the years, even playing together in Newport. The last summer Buddy played for me in Europe, his band had an engagement at a jazz festival in Lugano, Switzerland. The next day, they were to drive to Milan and then fly to Palermo, Sicily, for a concert. Buddy decided that he was too tired to go. I was informed of this decision via a long-distance phone call from the road manager; I was in Nice, working on the Grande Parade. I said, "Tell Buddy I want to talk to him." After holding the telephone for a few minutes, my roadie returned and said: "Buddy won't talk to you. He doesn't want to go to Sicily. And he says that if he talks to you, you'll convince him to go." That was the end of that. The date in Sicily had been sponsored by the power structure of that island, most likely a branch of Cosa Nostra. My associate in Italy, Alberto Alberti, who had booked the date, was afraid to show his face on that island for several years.

Of all artists with whom I worked closely, Sarah Vaughan was the toughest. I never fully gained her trust. But in this regard, I'm in good company; I don't think Sassy ever trusted anyone completely.

She was like the little girl with the curl: When she was good she was very good, and when she was bad, it was miserable. I don't know exactly how many concerts and festivals she worked on with me, or how many tours we did together around the world, but it was a lot. Probably I was the single most significant source of income for Sarah Vaughan during her entire career. She was a superior vocalist, and made a lot of money. But she never cracked the upper echelon of the entertainment field, as did Ella Fitzgerald and Nat King Cole. She could have done this. But throughout her life, she never allowed anyone capable to manage her career.

The last concert Sarah performed for me was in June 1989 at the JVC Jazz Festival–New York. I went back to see her in the dressing room before the concert. I went to give her a hug and wish her luck. All she could say to me was: "Why do you pay Ella more than you pay me?"

Sarah's bitchiness in the dressing room got me down, and I wasn't going to stay to hear the concert. As I was leaving the hall, I stopped at the sound booth just to see that everything was correct. Her first two songs confirmed the fact, to me, that it was going to be a terrible evening. But with the third tune, something happened on stage. It was miraculous; the magic took over. It's the way I like to remember her. But I'm afraid that even with my respect for Sassy as an artist, our many conflicts overshadow my memories of her, and even cloud my enjoyment of her recordings.

I was far from alone in being professionally burned by Sarah. A day or two after her JVC concert, she was supposed to leave from New York for a fifteen-performance tour of Europe. This tour was going to net Sassy a considerable income. Her musicians had their equipment packed and they all had their tickets. But at the last minute, Sarah canceled. No one knew how ill she was at this time, not even Sassy herself. She just decided that she didn't care what happened. It was a disaster; her fans in Europe were looking forward to her appearance. I had a lot of problems with various festivals in Europe who blamed me for her cancellation. In her usual stubborn way, she had refused to get a note from a doctor saying how ill she was. It took about two weeks to get a doctor's certificate, and even after I received it many of the promoters were unsympathetic. Only when Sassy died eight months later did they understand how sick she had been.

Today Benny Goodman is gone, along with Buddy Rich and Sarah Vaughan, and most of the figures from jazz's golden era. I have attended more jazz funerals than I can recall; I have spoken at dozens of them. It would make little sense to enumerate the names of the deceased here—the list grows mercilessly longer month-by-month. I do remember each of these good-byes vividly, and can usually recall what I've said. Some in particular have stayed with me.

One such example: the funeral of Roy Eldridge early in 1989. I kept my comments short; as is often the case, there was little to say that hadn't already been said. The thrust of my eulogy was the fact that Eldridge was known, for years, as "Little Jazz"—an epithet that acknowledged both his small physical stature and his enormous musical presence. Eventually musicians dropped the diminutive adjective. They would say: "Hey man, Jazz is in town." No one ever had to ask who "Jazz" was; Roy Eldridge was in town, and a greater compliment could not have been paid him by any musician.

Roy's funeral, held at St. Peter's Lutheran Church on Lexington Avenue, was paid for by Norman Granz. Norman had been Roy's man since the late 1940s; he had presented the trumpeter on countless Jazz at the Philharmonic tours, had paid him well, had essentially become his sponsor. In return, Roy gave Norman everything he had. He played his high notes—unmatchable in their fire and swinging freedom—night after night, for years. By the late 1950s, this grind took its toll, as Roy lost the clarity and spirit—and chops—of his heyday. Though I can't blame Norman Granz for this deterioration, JATP was what wore down Roy.

My thoughts on this subject may have been tainted by the fact that, due to Norman's surveillance, I could never get as close to Roy Eldridge as I wished. Whenever Marie St. Louis called Roy to play one of our festivals, he would turn to Granz for advice. More often than not Norman would tell Roy to ask for much more money, which we could not and would not pay.

It was a bitter irony, then, to learn Norman's feelings after Roy's funeral. He had arrived late, and, not thinking to reserve a seat for himself, was forced to stand in the rear of the church. He happened to be standing next to Marie, and she asked him what he thought of my speech. "It was alright," Norman replied, "but he should have given him more gigs when he was alive."

I can't help but remember an early New Orleans Jazz and Heritage Festival, in which I presented Roy at an all-star concert in the Municipal Auditorium. Before bringing him on, I delivered a glowing introduction describing his place in the history of the music—outlining how he was the link between Armstrong and Gillespie, and how his playing so clearly illustrated a unique and compelling style. As Roy walked out, he said to me: "Thanks for the introduction, George. Man, I hope I don't fall flat on my face."

A more positive image from Roy's later years, and one that I remember more fondly, dates from a Mellon Jazz Festival in Pittsburgh. Eldridge—who was being honored as one of Pittsburgh's gifts to the world of jazz—had stopped playing the trumpet by this time, for physical reasons. But one night at the festival, as he listened to a set by the Newport All-Stars, he asked if he could come up and scat a few choruses. Our band at that time included Warren Vaché, Jr., Scott Hamilton, Harold Ashby, and Norris Turney. Of course we invited him on—and Jazz nearly swung us off the bandstand.

Roy belonged to a generation of musicians who shared a common experience working during the thirties and forties. They had developed personalities and characteristics toward people that were, in a sense, a form of survival. You had to have friends, man, in order to survive. Living on the road, whether it was North or South, you couldn't afford to be arrogant. Your life and livelihood depended on your ability to allow people to be comfortable with you. I was always touched to encounter the gentleness of Buddy Tate; the sensitivity of Buck Clayton; Clark Terry's sincere concern for others. And I still marvel at the love Benny Carter gave to all who knew him; at Doc Cheatham's warmth; at the ability of Harry "Sweets" Edison to lighten up any occasion. And at the leadership and counsel "The Judge" Milt Hinton gave to his fellow musicians both young and old. This list could go on and on.

Most of these people were sidemen during the prime of their careers, but due to their reputations ended up as sometime-leaders and important all-stars. What set them apart was their humanity—which went even beyond that of an artist playing from his heart. In some musicians the feeling for communication transcends the music itself and becomes a part of their personal life. Buck and Buddy and Sweets and Clark and a number of others like Willie "The Lion" Smith—all had something very, very special as human beings. It's not that they weren't independent; they were strong people, and had tremendous pride in what they could do. But if you showed them respect, their egos would not come into play. And if you met them more than halfway, they would meet you—and with a sense of trust. Whatever was needed to make a show work, they would do. This was a rare and special characteristic among musicians, almost as special as the music that flowed through their bodies. Mainly for this reason, these musicians will always represent jazz for me—despite their relatively marginal position in the history of the music. They might not have been the geniuses, but they were the troops. They made jazz happen, and we owe them an unfathomable debt.

# Coda

IN MY CAREER OF OVER FIFTY YEARS, the question I've most often been pressed to answer is: "What do you think is the future of jazz?" My stock answer was that only the musicians could determine where jazz was going, and as long as there were young artists taking up the art, it would stay alive and well. The statement, while true, is somewhat evasive—an attempt to forestall any further inquiries along those lines. I believe the issue is far more complicated than it may initially seem.

Looking at the broader picture of jazz in the past seventy-five years, it's clear that the art was fed by two primary sources. First and foremost, it was informed by a black experience, a culture steeped in the blues and in church music. Second, it was related to American popular music. Listening to jazz in that era was enjoyable, an enhancement of life. It was not that different from the lifestyle of a previous generation, my parents' generation. While the true aficionado had strong likes and dislikes—swing fans dismissed Dixieland and rejected bebop, while bebop fanatics ridiculed swing—it was clear that the many styles of jazz were still part of a larger genus.

The culture experienced a transformation in the rock-and-roll era. With the Beatles and the Rolling Stones, a new standard of listening took over. Music was no longer an enhancement, but an escape from life. The volume of the music rose to such levels that social conversation was impossible. Concerts, as they grew stranger and more surreal, shut out the everyday experience. Widespread audience drug use created an ambience that was otherworldly. Rock concerts could last three or four hours, with a single group playing without cease. The audience never wanted to leave. Bands wanted their performances to completely envelop the listener. There was no precedent for this phenomenon in any previous generation—except perhaps in the realm of mysticism and religion.

While this was happening in the rock world, jazz saw its own transitions. Improvisation, the heartbeat of jazz music, had been given an expanded role. This was to some degree a matter of technology; in the days of seventy-eight-RPM recordings, musicians rarely played more than two choruses of a song. LPs changed that—but the change was hardly seismic. Well into the 1950s, musicians edited their solos, realizing that unfettered improvisation was best kept to the jam sessions and the shed. In the early '50s, I went with Stan Getz to an after-hours jam session. Without getting up from his chair, Getz played chorus after chorus on one song; I sat in awe as I heard him go on for fifteen, twenty minutes without stopping. He had an unceasing flow of ideas; it was breathtaking. Yet Stan would never have played for such extensive length at Storyville. Restraint was still the commanding precept in jazz presentation.

If I had to pinpoint the moment at which this changed, I would look to 1956. This was the year in which Paul Gonsalves played an unprecedented twenty-seven choruses, in a performance that immortalized that summer's Newport Jazz Festival and accounted for the best-selling album of Duke Ellington's career. A paradox was emerging in the jazz world. It was becoming apparent that the musical personality of one individual utilizing lengthy improvisations could reach out to the jazz audience. Sonny Rollins exiled himself from the music business, practicing alone on the Williamsburg Bridge. John Coltrane, playing in Miles Davis's band, began taking marathon solos. Both Rollins and Coltrane would become the standard-bearers for the next age in jazz, each musician approaching improvisation with a long-distance runner's stride.

Groups given an hour's stage time on a festival were now playing three or four songs at most, lasting fifteen or twenty minutes apiece. If the audience demanded an encore, I had to exercise good judgment; a twenty-minute encore could throw a wrench in my schedule. Beyond the matter of timing, young saxophonists were beginning to form trios and quartets with just a rhythm accompaniment; they were attempting to carry an entire night's worth of music with just one horn. This was no small feat for Rollins and Coltrane; for their followers, it proved difficult, if not impossible. Jazz records stopped selling, and as of this writing, command the lowest market share in history.

Yet jazz will survive, because it has to. At its most fundamental level, the recognizable element of swing is the thread that weaves every facet of jazz in the twentieth century—from New Orleans second-line music to the modal explorations of Coltrane—into a single dimension. While many contemporary jazz artists have played down the element of swing, we can't ignore them; they must be fostered. Swing may not be a matter of concern to these younger players; it makes no difference. Youth is still the spirit of what happens as far as the growth and future of this music. As a producer, I have to recognize this fact. I attempt to do so.

But what is jazz? If the critics don't agree what jazz is—as is often the case—then the public will never know. The disagreement stems, simply, from fierce allegiances in taste. Critics need to have a broader sense of what jazz is: both the champions of the avant-garde who refuse to listen to traditional jazz, and the traditional-jazz fans who ignore new things. And it's much more important for the avant-garde critics to pay attention to traditional jazz than for the traditional jazz critics to pay attention to the new—because the traditionalists will soon be gone. Musicians are going to play what they want to play in any case. Regardless of their own guidelines, they should respect all the music. There was a time when bebop musicians were putting down everything that came before; later on they started to hang out and play with those older guys. That was a natural coming-together, because they were all musicians. There was a real jazz community then, not just a series of isolated mini-communities. What needs to happen now is a movement back toward that; jazz must become a family again.

Defining jazz involves defining who is a jazz musician, and this is a practice best left to the musician himself. In part, it's a way of life. It's an attitude of how you get up in the morning with your horn and figure out where you're going to play your gig, and whom you're going to play with. It involves what your purpose is, musically, in life. These things have nothing to do with age or era or style. And this is, ultimately, the only plausible way in which to assess the definition of jazz. Does a player consider himself to be a jazz musician? Or does he see himself as somebody who's trying to make a hit record or play any type of music to make a living? That's the only definition I can find that has any meaning. George Benson, for instance, does not consider himself a jazz musician when he's playing "On Broadway." But when he says "Man, let me get my guitar, I want to play with McCoy Tyner," then he is.

Since 1950, I have worked with and gained the trust of many artists who have been the source of jazz in the twentieth century. Trust was initially established because I always paid what the contract called for and musicians knew that their money was secure. But there is much more to it than that.

Many of these artists were ravaged by drugs, which often was responsible for mental and physical illnesses. But the expression "sick genius" was never part of my lexicon in dealing with them. Most jazz musicians have a touch of genius, but I treated them as professionals. They had a job to do, and I had responsibilities. My job was to see that they got paid, were presented properly, and got cared for.

I can only think of a few minor occasions when any of the so-called unreliable artists ever let me down in a professional sense. Stories about Billie Holiday, Charlie Parker, and others are legendary; but they don't come from me and my association with them. They knew what I expected from them and vice versa.

This relationship that I had with so many jazz artists was never brought home to me more vividly than when I was in bed for four weeks with a bad back in 1990. I received a telephone call from hall of fame trombonist, J. J. Johnson. J. J.'s words were moving; he said, "George, you can't be down. You are the rock on which we all lean." I have never forgotten these words. There were innumerable times when musicians made commitments to me and they had to go back on their word for one reason or another. But regardless of the circumstances, the expression, "You will never work for me again" was never used by me. I have never thought I was the panacea to the ills of jazz musicians, and I can't always do what is asked of me. But every day is a new day, and in any negotiation I treat the musician as an equal.

My love and respect for the jazz musician has deepened. Perhaps more than any other human being blessed with a God-given talent, he or she gives up the most to develop and practice his or her art. Except for the few who have achieved fame and financial reward, the insecurity and work conditions of his or her life is difficult to imagine unless you have lived or been part of it.

\*     \*     \*

Jazz festivals have become as diverse (some would say "diluted") as jazz itself. There is a reason for this development. The declining sales of jazz records are reflected in diminishing ticket sales, and you can't have a festival without people. Success for my work lies in compromise between commercial and artistic pursuits. I keep sponsors not only because my shows draw people, but also because I do so while maintaining a certain artistic credibility. In this way, I'm no different now than I was in Newport in 1954.

At the beginning, I had jazz stars with broad appeal to lean upon while I also presented Cecil Taylor or Ornette Coleman. I've always done those things. But now, I have a problem of reaching different segments of the jazz community. They won't come to me. I have to go to them.

For this reason, among others, cultural institutions are crucial to the welfare of jazz. Lincoln Center, being the leader in this field, has suffered a maelstrom of criticism. In attacking the Lincoln Center Jazz program, critics in a sense may be attacking jazz itself. They are looking for something that Lincoln Center is not doing at this time. Granting exposure to emerging artists is only part of LCJ's mission. Their lack of involvement in new music has little effect on those creative impulses. You can't stop new things from happening, because the energy of newness is always there. It'll always find a cellar or a joint or a school or somewhere to be played. But cultural institutions like Lincoln Center have chosen to utilize and maintain the traditions of the artists who shaped the course of jazz. The continual challenge is to play this music with an individuality and creativity that doesn't put it in the pigeonhole of mere reproduction.

At present, Lincoln Center Jazz faces an imperative that grows in significance with each passing year. It must begin to court the milieu of young people, listeners who would never consider seeing a sixty-dollar concert at Avery Fisher Hall. I have thought of suggesting that Lincoln Center and Carnegie Hall establish outposts (Lincoln Center Downtown and Carnegie Hall Downtown), which could present music every night: progressive jazz groups, rehearsing dance groups, way-out classical music, musique concrete, or whatever—and charge ten or fiteen dollars. The musicians' fees could be covered by a subsidy, which is already standard practice for the cultural establishment. This sort of institutional support could make a huge difference. Musicians who play clubs exclusively often end up not getting paid, or working for the door. It's a system that should not be romanticized. I'm glad we have that to a degree, but that's not the only way it should be.

Jazz musicians don't have the option available to classical musicians, thousands of whom earn salaries from symphony orchestras and as teachers. Jazz artists have finally reached the point where many of them are employed by schools, but what is needed more is a cultural base where they can perform under the best possible circumstances.

I like to think that our festivals still bear a standard of dedication to jazz. In this age of nonprofit cultural institutions, I may be the last of the independent promoters. But I'm still cognizant of presenting jazz in its widest definition. This is as true as it was in 1954—although fulfilling this agenda is much more difficult now than it was then.

The accomplishments of those few years come as no small point of pride. In light of what I knew to be pervasive cynicism, I was compelled to prove something, as much to myself as anyone else. I wanted to know that, in spite of whatever challenges arose, I was still capable of success. In fact, as I get older, I'm more motivated by success—by a sense of achievement—than by any other aspect of the business. Money is merely incidental to this feeling. The success of a venture is what thrills me.

I don't equate success with profit—yet without profit there is no success. That profit may come from a subsidy, or a sponsor, it may come entirely from ticket sales. Whatever the case, a venture has to be paid for in one way or another. Artistry alone cannot create a success—although it is the critical ingredient. I've had a plethora of losing artistic successes, and they leave a bitter taste in your mouth. In a way, this represents a complete change of perspective since the days of Storyville, when I was happy to be able to present Duke Ellington even to a half-empty house.

Once in a while, there's a moment that represents both material success and the elusive thrill of those early days. One example would be a 1998 JVC Jazz Festival appearance by João Gilberto, who had not performed in the States for some time. The concert was a sellout. The bossa nova legend walked onto the Carnegie Hall stage with just an acoustic guitar, and played a spellbinding concert. The hall felt like a cathedral; the awe and reverence were palpable. I sat through every moment of that performance, as transfixed as anyone else. That night I was proud to be a producer.

Two years later we presented João Gilberto again in Carnegie Hall, and again the house was full. We were hoping to recapture some of that magic. But curtain call came and went, with no João. We knew that he was staying at the Parker Meridien Hotel down the block, and a phone call confirmed that he was still in his room. Eight o'clock, eight-fifteen, eight-thirty, eight-forty-five. There was no telling when he would emerge. The crowd grew increasingly restless. I went onstage for a brief announcement: "Ladies and Gentlemen, thank you for your patience. I just want you to know that João Gilberto is here; he's in his room at the hotel next door. He will be here soon, and he'll play a wonderful concert. What can I say, except that João is João." A ripple of laughter, then applause, signaled to me that the audience understood.

Then I left the hall and walked down the block to the Meridien lobby. "João," I cried when he answered the phone. "You're destroying my reputation in New York?" I could almost hear him snap to attention. A moment later the elevator doors opened and João Gilberto emerged, guitar tucked under his arm. He glided past me, saying a quick hello, and ran in the direction of the hall. He took the stage, over an hour late, to tumultuous applause. Whatever grudge the crowd had felt about the delay was assuaged by his presence. The only noteworthy complaint we received that night was from the theatrical producer Hal Prince, who was outraged by what he saw as an utter lack of professionalism. I don't know whether it ever occurred to Mr. Prince that the concert, unlike a Broadway play, cannot go on without its principal star. We had no understudy for João.

João played an extra-long concert that night—close to two hours—without a break. In fact, I had to go onstage once again to bring him off, as I had no intention of letting the concert go past Carnegie Hall's curfew. When I announced the end of the concert ("Ladies and Gentlemen, João Gilberto!"), he immediately started to leave the stage. As he passed by me, he put an arm around my shoulders and said: "I love you, George."

The music had been beautiful as always. But I wasn't moved, as I had been at his previous Carnegie concert. The evening, a success by the standards of both the music and the revenue, was tainted by the stress of the situation.

Sometimes I am still thrilled by musical content alone. This happened when we presented Michael Brecker on a John Coltrane tribute concert in the mid-nineties with the Carnegie Hall Jazz Band. Brecker had informed us that he would be playing a long series of extended improvisations on Coltrane's modal themes; I could hardly imagine a duller concept. But the tenor saxophonist played that night with astonishing passion and control. I wrote him a letter of appreciation after the concert.

Another example would be the Newport Millennium Band, a touring ensemble we assembled in 2000 for performances overseas. I heard them play one night at the Blue Note club in New York. Lew Tabackin, Cedar Walton, and Nicholas Payton were in the band, on tenor saxophone, piano, and trumpet, respectively. The music they played that night—full of life and conviction—was jazz, and I was moved. I seek out those moments, and I always hope that my festivals will bring them to being.

My own tastes grow to accommodate new things, but remain fundamentally intact. The things that I loved I still love, whether it's Pee Wee playing the blues or Bud Freeman playing "Have You Met Miss Jones?" or Frankie Newton playing "Blues my Baby Gives to Me." Music still has the ability to reach me. I'm moved when I hear Bobby Hackett, or when I listen to Roy Eldridge in his prime. Then there's Duke and Louis, Basie, Pres, and Buddy Tate. And the early Billie recordings of course (or anything Billie sang, even on her worst days). While good music regardless of style or era can thrill me, the music of the masters or the source that I had the joy of being so close to for so many years remains in my musical psyche.

I have no intention to retire because I'm having too much fun. The festivals —JVC, Verizon, and New Orleans, among others—still present a formidable challenge, and I remain involved in each event.

I would like to see my legacy continue. With any luck, this book will shed some light upon the importance of those of us who have dedicated our lives to the presentation, rather than the performance, of the music. Whether it's one of the many festival producers throughout the world, or the concert promoters, or the individual nightclub owners struggling night to night—their contributions are essential to the history and future of this music. I'm glad to have been part of this process: in the development of the jazz festival; the acceptance of this music as art; the efforts to bring jazz to a larger audience worldwide. Here I have illuminated some of that process, along with my motivations and ambitions. Hopefully it has also reflected the joy with which I approach my career. Believe me, if I'm the greatest festival producer in the world, it's alright with me. Jazz is a dirty word no longer.

I am immeasurably proud of, and grateful for, my affiliation with so many unique artists in the past half-century. The years spent in the trenches with them are priceless, and brought joy along with the pain. But, as I look back, the thing that brings me the greatest happiness was the playing. When Lester Young said to me that night in Storyville: "You and me are going to be alright, Pres." That was as good as it can get.

I know my weaknesses, what I can't play. But I know what I can play, and I'm happy when other people recognize it on a professional level. Because playing with Lester Young and Sidney Bechet—that's a professional level. It's not that I can play with them. They know I'm not in their league. It has nothing to do with that. They're saying: "I can play with you, man." That's the thing that has given me the most gratification in my life.

I wrote a letter once to Warren Vaché, Scott Hamilton, and Howard Alden and the guys about the enjoyment I had touring and playing with them. Because you really get to know what jazz is, what the life of a jazz musician is. You're not apart from the scene; you *are* the scene. Yet, I would have only been a musician full-time if I felt I was good enough. I settled for not being that good, but good enough to enjoy it. It's just by accident that I became a jazz producer. In the long run, it's the music. I call that the raison d'être. That's why I'm here.

# George Wein Discography

**George Wein's Storyville Band**
*Jazz at Storyville*
1951 Storyville Records, Inc. LP 303, LP
Edmond Hall, Vic Dickenson, Johnny Windhurst, Jo Jones, Ruby Braff, John Field, George Wein

**Lee Wiley**
*Live: Look At Me Now!*
1951 Sitono Yado Live at Storyville, CD

**Sidney Bechet**
*At Storyville*
1953 IWS License Corp. 9014–2, CD
Sidney Bechet, Vic Dickenson, George Wein, Jimmy Woode, Buzzy Drootin

**Pee Wee Russell**
*By Arrangement Only*
1954 Storyville Records, Inc. LP 308, LP
Pee Wee Russell, Vic Dickenson, Doc Cheatham, Buzzy Drootin, John Field, Al Drootin, George Wein

**Wild Bill Davison, Pee Wee Russell & Vic Dickenson**
1954 Storyville Records, Inc. LP 319, LP
Wild Bill Davison, Vic Dickenson, Pee Wee Russell, Buzzy Drootin, Stan Wheeler, George Wein

**Jazz at the Boston Arts Festival**
1954 Storyville Records, Inc. LP 311, LP

Vic Dickenson, Samuel Margolis, Ruby Braff, Dick Lefave, Buzzy Drootin, John Field, Al Drootin, George Wein

**George Wein**
*Wein, Women and Song and more*
1955, LP
Ruby Braff, Sam Margolis, Stan Wheeler, Marquis Foster, Bobby Hackett, Jo Jones, Bill Pemberton

**Dixie-Victors**
*Magic Horn*
1956 RCA Victor LPM 1332, LP
Ruby Braff, Jimmy McPartland, Vic Dickenson, Peanuts Hucko, Buzzy Drootin, George Wein, Milt Hinton, Bill Stegmeyer, Ernie Caceres

**Vic Dickenson**
*Vic's Boston Story*
1956 PA 6010, LP
Vic Dickenson, Buzzy Drootin, George Wein, Arvell Shaw, Jimmy Woode

**Sidney Bechet**
*Recorded in Concert at the Brussells Fair*
1958 Columbia CL 1410, LP
Sidney Bechet, Buck Clayton, Vic Dickenson, Arvell Shaw, Kansas Fields, George Wein

**Newport All-Stars**
1959 Atlantic LP 1331, LP

Buck Clayton, Vic Dickenson, Pee Wee Russell, Bud Freeman, George Wein, Champ Jones, Jake Hanna

**George Wein and the Storyville Sextet**
*Metronome Presents Jazz at the Modern*
1960 Bethlehem Records BCP 6050, LP
George Wein, Harold "Shorty" Baker, Tyree Glenn, Pee Wee Russell, Mickey Sheen, Bill Crow

**Newport All-Stars**
*Midnight Concert in Paris*
1961 Smash Records MGS 27023, LP
George Wein, Pee Wee Russell, Ruby Braff, Vic Dickenson, Buzzy Drootin, Jimmy Woode

**Newport All-Stars**
1962 Paramount Records, Inc. Impulse Mono A–31, LP
George Wein, Ruby Braff, Marshall Brown, Pee Wee Russell, Bud Freeman, Bill Takas, Marquis Foster

**Various**
*Great Moments in Jazz Re-Created at the Newport Jazz Festival*
1965 RCA Victor RCA Victor LP 3369, LP
Muggsy Spanier, Joe Sullivan, George Brunis, Wingy Manone, Edmond Hall, Joe Thomas, JC Higginbotham, Bobby Haggart, Bud Freeman, Max Kaminsky, Lou McGarity, Peanuts Hucko, Slam Stewart, George Wettling, Buzzy Drootin, Jo Jones, George Wein

**Newport All-Stars**
*Newport Jazz Festival '66*
1966, CD
Buddy Rich, Jerry Mulligan, Ruby Braff, Bud Freeman, Jack Lesberg, George Wein

**Newport All-Stars**
*George Wein is Alive and Well in Mexico*
1967 Columbia CS 9631, LP
Pee Wee Russell, Ruby Braff, Jack Lesberg, Don Lamond, George Wein

**Newport All-Stars**
1967 Black Lion BLP 30115, LP
Ruby Braff, Buddy Tate, George Wein, Jack Lesberg, Don Lamond

**Newport All-Stars**
*In Japan*

1969 Union Records UPS 49, LP
Berney Kessel, Ruby Braff, Red Norvo, Cliff Leeman, George Wein, Larry Ridley, Joe Venuti

**Newport All-Stars**
*Tribute to Duke*
1969 MPSD MPS 15255, LP
Joe Venuti, Ruby Braff, Red Norvo, Barney Kessel, Kenny Burrell, George Wein, Larry Ridley, Don Lamond

**Newport All-Stars**
1969 Atlantic Records SD 1533, LP
Red Norvo, Tal Farlow, Barney Kessel, Ruby Braff, George Wein, Larry Ridley, Don Lamond

**Red Norvo**
*Rose Room*
1969 BYG 529–123, LP
Red Norvo, Larry Ridley, Barney Kessel, George Wein

**Ruby Braff**
*Plays Louis Armstrong*
1969 BYG Records BYG 529 123, LP
Ruby Braff, George Wein, Barney Kessel, Larry Ridley, Don Lamond

**Ruby Braff and Red Norvo**
*Swing That Music*
1969 Affinity AFF 45, LP
Ruby Braff, Red Norvo, George Wein, Barney Kessel, Larry Ridley, Don Lamond

**Stephanie Grappelli and Joe Venuti**
*Venupelli Blues*
1969 Affinity AFF 29, LP
Stephane Grappelli, Joe Venuti, George Wein, Barney Kessel, Larry Ridley, Don Lamond

**Newport All-Stars**
*That Newport Jazz*
1973 Columbia JCS 8979, LP
Al Grey, Bud Freeman, Ruby Braff, George Wein, Wendell Marshall, Roy Haynes

**Tribute to Count Basie**
1974 RCA Victor RCA FXL1 7158, LP
Wallace Davenport, Ruby Braff, Bill Coleman, Vic Dickenson, Buddy Tate, Eddie Lockjaw Davis, Gerard Badini, George Wein, Jimmy Leary, Panama Francis, Willie Mabon

**Sidney Bechet Jazz Allstars**
*Tribute to Sidney Bechet*
1979 William P. Gottlieb, CD
Bob Wilber, George Wein, Wycliffe Gordon, Ed Polcer, Vince Giordano, Mark Shane

**Newport All-Stars**
*Live-Mitschnitt Villengen*
1985 Stern Edition Stern Edition, LP
George Wein, Slam Stewart, Norris Turney, Harold Ashby, Scott Hamilton, Warren Vaché, Jr., Oliver Jackson, Carrie Smith

**Newport All-Stars**
1985 Concord Jazz, Inc., CD
George Wein, Scott Hamilton, Oliver Jackson, Slam Stewart, Norris Turney, Warren Vaché, Jr., Al Cohn

**Chicago Jazz Summit**
1986 Atlantic Records 818844–1, LP
Wild Bill Davison, Yank Lawson, Max Kaminsky, Jimmy McPartland, Eddie Miller, Art Hodes, Clarence Hutchenrider, George Wein, Milt Hinton, Key Robinson, Barrett Deems, Truck Parham, Kenny Davern, Frank Chase, Vince Giordano and the Nighthawks, Franz Jackson, George Masso, Marian McPartland

**Newport All-Stars**
*European Tour*
1988 Concord Jazz, Inc. Bern 1987, CD
George Wein, Harold Ashby, Scott Hamilton, Oliver Jackson, Slam Stewart, Norris Turney, Warren Vaché, Jr.

**Harumi Kaneko and the Newport Jazz Festival All-Stars**
*My Romance*
1990 Nippon Phonogam Co., Ltd. Clinton Recording Studio, CD
Harumi Kaneko, George Wein, Norris Turney, Lew Tabackin, Randy Sandke, Warren Vaché, Jr., Eddie Jones, Howard Alden, Oliver Jackson

**Newport All-Stars**
*Bern Concert '89*
1990 Concord Jazz, Inc., CD
George Wein, Ricky Ford, Scott Hamilton, Oliver Jackson, Eddie Jones, Gray Sargent, Norris Turney, Warren Vaché, Jr.

**Legendary Pioneers of Jazz: George Wein & the Newport All-Stars**

*Swing That Music*
1993 Sony Music Entertainment / Columbia Records, CD
George Wein, Howard Alden, Al Grey, Illinois Jacquet, Eddie Jones, Flip Phillips, Clark Terry, Warren Vaché, Jr., Kenny Washington

**Sidney Bechet**
*En Concert*
1993 Europe 1, CD
Sidney Bechet, Andre Reweliotty, Guy Longnon, Roland Hug, Buck Clayton, Jean-Louis Durand, Vic Dickenson, Yannick Singery, George Wein, Georges "Zozo" d 'Halluin, Arvell Shaw, Marcel Blanche

**Duke Ellington**
in Sweden 1973, Highlights from the Swedish Radio Jazz Archives
1999 Caprice Records/Sveriges Radio 2
George Wein appears with Band on "A Train", CD
Harold Money Johnson, Johnny Coles, Barry Lee Hall, Mercer Ellington, Rolf Ericson, Vince Prudente, Art Baron, Chuck Connors, Ake Persson, Russell Procope, Harold Geezil Menierve, Harold Ashby, Percy Marion, Harry Carney, Duke Ellington, Joe Benjamin, Quentin Rocky White, Alice Babs, Anita Moore, Tony Watkins, and guests: Nils Lindberg and George Wein

**George Wein**
*Wein, Women and Song and more*
2002 Arbors Records, Inc., CD
George Wein, Ruby Braff, Sammy Margolis, Bobby Hackett, Warren Vaché, Jr., Howard Alden

**Ruby Braff**
*Hear Me Talkin*
Polydor 2460, 127 Select, LP
Vic Dickenson, Buzzy Drootin, George Wein, Don Lamond, Ruby Braff, Jack Lesberg

**Ruby Braff**
*Hustlin' and Bustlin'*
World Records LAE 12051, LP
Ruby Braff, Vic Dickenson, Edmond Hall, George Wein, John Field, Jo Jones, Sam Margolis, Kenneth Kersey, Milton Hinton, Bobby Donaldson, Dick LeFave, Al Drootin, Buzzy Drootin

# *Notes*

## 1: NEWTON BOY

12   "I'll never do nothin' for nobody, no time"; Ann Charters, *Nobody: The Story of Bert Williams* (London: Collier-MacMillan Limited, 1970), p. 9.

## 2: THAT'S A-PLENTY

46   "catalytic for Communism"; Undated FBI Report, "Communists and Pro-Communists for Wallace," Truman Presidential Library, p. 1.

52   "the talk of the town for several days"; Manfred Selchow, *Profoundly Blue: A Bio-Discographical Scrapbook on Edmond Hall* (D-Westoverledingen: Uhle & Kleimann, 1988), p. 241.

53   "it was a great disappointment and shock to me"; Ibid., p. 245.

## 4: STORYVILLE

75   "where jazz was born . . . "; Nat Hentoff, liner notes, *Jazz at Storyville* (Storyville Records STLP 303), 1954.

88   *Stan Getz at Storyville—Vols. 1 & 2;* Originally on Roost Records, but has since been reissued on CD as Roulette CDP 7945072.

88   has circulated as a bootleg recording for years; These items, and other Storyville performances by Holiday, can be found on the import CD *Lady Day—The Storyville Concerts*, Jazz Door 1991.

100   was made by a friend, Mel Levine; I have learned that this recording can be found in the Library of Congress archives.

103   he had returned to the stage, finishing the show; Stanley Eames, "Busy George Wein's Nightspots Modeled For Youth and Parents," *Boston Herald*, 23 February 1953.

106   John McLellan's WHDH broadcast dated September 22, 1953; Ibid.

107   WHDH broadcast the Tuesday night set, as usual; *Lady Day—The Storyville Concerts*, Jazz Door 1991.

108   very good Bechet, and some excellent Dickenson; Originally released as *Jazz at Storyville* on Storyville Records (STLP 301), this recording session was later issued on CD in 1988 (as Black Lion BLCD–760902) and in 2000 (as 1201 Music 9014–2).

109   which was released in early April of the following year; *'Round Midnight,* with Teddi King accompanied by Beryl Booker. Storyville STLP 302

112 *Storyville Presents Bob Brookmeyer, featuring Al Cohn*; Storyville STLP 305, Rec. 1/7/54.

115 released the second volume of Sidney Bechet's performance; Originally released as *Jazz at Storyville Vol. II* on Storyville Records (STLP 306), this recording session was later included on CD reissues in 1988 (as Black Lion BLCD–760902) and in 2000 (as 1201 Music 9014–2).

115 Mahogany Hall All Stars and the Jo Jones Quartet; Jo Jones Quartet featuring Ruby Braff. *Jazz at Storyville, featuring Mahogany Hall All-Stars*; Originally released as Storyville STLP 307.

115 Pee Wee Russell in the ranks of the Mahogany Hall band; Originally released as Pee Wee Russell's *By Arrangement Only* (Storyville STLP 308).

115 *Serge Chaloff and Boots Mussulli, featuring Russ Freeman*; Storyville STLP 310, reissued in 1990 as part of a CD called Serge Chaloff, *The Fable of Mabel* (Black Lion BLCD760923).

117 Storyville released *Joe Newman and the Boys in the Band*; *Joe Newman and the Boys in the Band*, Storyville STLP 318.

121 cited it as the best record he ever made; Manfred Selchow, *Ding! Ding! A Bio-Discrographical Scrapbook on Vic Dickenson* (Eekeweg: Westoverledingen Germany, Uhle & Kleimann).

121 Boston Arts Festival featuring Vic with Ruby Braff; *Jazz at the Boston Arts Festival*, Storyville STLP 311.

121 another Lee Konitz record; *Konitz*. Storyville, STLP 313.

121 the vocal duo Jackie Cain and Roy Kral; *Spring Can Really Hang You Up the Most*, Storyville.

121 another Joe Newman small-group session; *I Feel Like a Newman*. Storyville STLP.

121 and a second album featuring Teddi King; *Storyville Presents Miss Teddi King*, Storyville STLP 314.

121 solo piano effort by Ellis Larkins; Larkins, Ellis. *Perfume and Rain*. Storyville STLP 316.

121 The result was *Rudy Vallee's Drinking Songs*; *Rudy Vallee's Drinking Songs*, Storyville STLP 315.

126 and recorded a live album for Pacific Jazz; Gerry Mulligan Quartet. *Recorded in Boston at Storyville*. Pacific Jazz 1228.

## 5: NEW THING AT NEWPORT

133 "could ever be a torrent of jazz"; George Frazier, *Boston Herald*, 1 July 1962.

134 "millionaire" had first appeared in print; Cleveland Amory, "High Society Blues," *Holiday*, July 1956.

143 the morning after the festival's close; Howard Taubman, "Newport Rocked by Jazz Festival," *New York Times*, 19 July 1954, front page.

143 "The first Newport Jazz Festival was a sensation"; William Keogh, "Jazz Fans Fill Newport Casino as Festival Ends," *Providence Journal*, 19 July 1954.

144 "opened a new era in jazz presentation"; Jack Tracy, "13,000 at Newport Show Jazz Concerts Have Come of Age," *Down Beat* 21, no. 17 (August 25, 1954).

146 distant parts of the arena; "10,000 Jazz Fans Expected at Festival Opening Tonight," *Newport Daily News*, Vol. 111—No. 236, Friday, July 15, 1955. p. 6.

146 "one impresario could handle"; Hammond.

147 "It may take twenty years to run this festival smoothly"; Louis Lorillard, speech delivered at a meeting of the board of directors, 12/9/55, p. 3.

147 "America's jazz aficionados have a new mecca"; "Newport Jazz Festival," *Ebony*, October 1955.

148 "Bach's 'Art of Fugue'"; Harold C. Schonberg, "Music: Jazz Comes of Age in Newport," *New York Times*, 18 July 1955.

148 the atmosphere of Newport to that of Tanglewood and Salzburg; Roger Maren, "A Few False Notes at Newport," The *Reporter*, 8 September 1955.

148 "and it certainly isn't jazz"; Schonberg.

148 "in which to move and operate"; Alan Morrison, speech delivered at a Meeting of the Board of Directors, 12/9/55, p. 19.

149 "What is the difference?"; Partial transcription, meeting of board of directors at Marshall Stearns's apartment, 12/9/55, pp. 18–19.

150 been expected to be found in America; John Hammond, speech delivered at a meeting of the board of directors, 12/9/55, pp. 10–11.

150 "the first jazz concert ever done under water"; Eddie Condon, quoted in James T. Kaull Jr., "3,500 Jazz Fans Brave Rain to Launch Festival Program," *Newport Daily News*, 6 July 1956.

150 "the show goes on!"; "Jazz Festival Starts Tonight 'Rain, Shine or Hurricane,'" *Newport Daily News*, 5 July 1956.

151 the terms of a contract in a tent backstage; Derek Jewell, *Duke: A Portrait of Duke Ellington* (New York: W.W. Norton & Company, 1977), p. 113.

153 "don't stop until I tell you"; Burt Goldblatt, *Newport Jazz Festival* (New York: The Dial Press, 1977), p. 28.

153 in front of a much larger crowd; Schaap, p. 30.

154 Paul was in fact a devotee of Webster; Jewell, *Duke*, p. 113.

**INTERLUDE 1: DUKE**

157 "I was born at the Newport Jazz Festival"; This was a frequent remark; it has been documented in Derek Jewell's *Duke: A Portrait of Duke Ellington* (New York: W. W. Norton, 1977), p. 110.

175 London bobbies watching the great and famous arrive; Don George, *Sweet Man: The Real Duke Ellington* (New York: G. P. Putnam's Sons, 1981), p. 248.

**6: A LONG STEP FORWARD**

179 "Dear Gentle Folk of Newport"; Bing Crosby (as Dexter Haven), *High Society*, Metro-Goldwyn-Mayer, A Sol Siegel Production, 1956.

179 "all over the uncivilized world"; Cleveland Amory, "High Society Blues," *Holiday*, July 1956.

179 "to break down class and racial barriers"; Elaine Lorillard, "Hot Time in Old Newport," *Collier's*, 20 July 1956.

180 comparing it to a vaudeville show; Jack Tracy, "Newport!" *Down Beat*, 24 August 24, 1955.

180 "a caricature of himself"; Whitney Balliett, "Jazz at Newport: 1955," *Saturday Review*, 30 July 1955.

184 "it came through the Spanish Civil War"; George Wein, "Lisbon Exciting First Stop on European Talent Tour," *Boston Herald*, 21 March 1958.

185 "an organization such as the Newport Festival"; John S. Wilson, "A Jazz Festival That Was Not a Grab Bag," *New York Times*, 1958.

186 "'people to people'"; Richard Nixon letter cited by Bert Goldblatt, *Newport Jazz Festival* (New York: The Dial Press, 1977), p. 45.

187 "mincemeat of Benny Goodman night"; Cerulli, p. 18.

189 (100,000 feet of exposed negative color stock); Goldblatt, p. 47.

192 "the June German in the North Carolina"; John McLellan, "Monk, Basie, Ballet, Ellington Standouts at Newport Festival," *Boston Traveler*, 6 July 1959.

192 "the annual affair is getting more sedate every year"; "Jazz: Has Less Display; Is More Sedate," *Evening Journal-Bulletin*, 3 July 1959.

194 in the *Village Voice* the previous year; Nat Hentoff, "Whose Festival?" *Village Voice*, 24 June 1959.

194 "to combat from the beginnings of jazz"; Nat Hentoff, "Sideshow or Culture?" *Rogue*, May 1959.

195 ordered the deployment of state troopers; Ted White, "Riot at Newport," *Rogue*, p. 32.

197 "exposed the blues to the whole world"; Francis Clay, interview with Sandra B. Tooze, in *Muddy Waters: The Mojo Man* (Toronto: ECW Press, 1997), pp. 171–72.

197 the now legendary album *Muddy Waters at Newport, 1960*; Ibid., pp. 172–73.

## 7: BROTHER, CAN YOU SPARE A DIME?

201 "Thereafter will be only noise and silence"; Hayden Carruth, "What a Wonder Among the Instruments Is the Walloping Trombone!" *Brilliant Corners* 3, no. 2 (1999).

211 "a program of music for the many"; Ibid.

215 a loss of $60,000; Editorial, "Wein Updates Jazz Festival Format," *Boston Traveler*, 5 June 1962.

## INTERLUDE 2: MONK

222 "that note that is right yet different"; George Wein, quoted by Sinclair Traill in *Jazz Magazine*, September 1961.

222 "literally a reed in the wind"; John Ephland, liner notes, *Miles Davis & Thelonious Monk Live at Newport 1958 & 1963* (Columbia/Legacy C2K 53585).

223 praised Pee Wee's "personal poetry"; Ira Gitler, *Down Beat*, 1963.

223 "on the same platform at the same time"; John S. Wilson, *New York Times*, 1963.

## 8: THE FESTIVAL IS ME

231 "The festival is me"; Cited in George Forsythe, "Newport Festival Now His," *Boston Traveler*, 26 April 1962; and "Glad to Be Back," *Billboard Music Week*, 12 May 1962.

232 "than anything else in the world"; "Jazz Festival Has New Note," *Boston Sunday Advertiser*, 22 April 1962.

232 "with the new festival promoter"; "'Meaning of Jazz' Is Theme of This Summer's Festival," *Newport Daily News*, 19 April 1962.

233 500 senatorial staff members; "Senate Samples Newport Jazz," *Pawtucket Times*, 19 June 1962.

233 appeared the following morning on NBC's *Today Show*; "Wein's Jazz Group on 'Today' Tuesday," *Boston Sunday Globe*, 17 June 1962.

233 Boston Arts Festival on July 2; "Boston Arts Festival Open June 20 to July 8," *Hartford Times*, 16 June 1962.

236 "A triumvirate, not a trio"; Duke Ellington/Charles Mingus/Max Roach, *Money Jungle*, United Artists UAS 15017, available on CD as Blue Note CDP 7 46398 2.

237 refunds to anyone who didn't like the show; Gene Santoro, *Myself When I Am Real: The Life and Music of Charles Mingus* (New York: Oxford University Press, 2000), p. 203.

238 edited product as *Town Hall Concert*; Charles Mingus, *Town Hall Concert*, United Artists UAJ14024/UAJS15.

238 reassembled and remastered; Charles Mingus, *The Complete Town Hall Concert*, Blue Note CDP 7243 8 28353 2 5.

238 Rollins and Hawkins to record together; *Sonny Meets Hawk!*, RCA Victor LSP–2712; reissue 09026 63479–2.

245 "festival fans are not wanted"; "A Cold Shoulder for the Newport Festival Fans," *Providence Journal*, 4 January 1965.

246 "in search of seats to a Beatle bash"; Jack Tubert, "Sinatra Overshadows Newport Jazz Festival," *Worcester Telegram*, 27 June 1965.

247 "kills you when the wind isn't blowing"; Robert F. Flynn, "Newport Jazz Fete's Sweet Sounds May Be Wafted On Smelly Breezes," *Portland Press-Herald*, 21 June 1965.

247 Cassius Clay–Sonny Liston prize fight; "Jazz Festival Coming Up," *Boston Globe*, 25 June 1965.

247 larger than previous festival stages; James A. Gourgouras, "Newport Stage Is Portable," *Worcester Gazette*, 3 July 1965.

248 an "exercise in cacophony"; Arnie Reisman, "Newport Avant Garde," *Quincy Patriot-Ledger*, 3 July 1965.

248 "hugging Rich and lifting him off the ground"; Dan Morgenstern, "Newport Report," *Down Beat*, 12 August 1965.

249 dispersed by an attentive police force; James T. Kaull, "Festival's Finale Attracts 15,000; All Arrive Early," *Providence Journal*, 5 July 1965.

## 9: CONFLICTS AND CONCERTS

253 "handling the festivals is sheer demagoguery"; "A Shameful Bid to Arouse Fear of the Festivals," *Providence Journal*, 17 January 1966.

253 "published it for town-wide distribution"; "Middletown and Festival" (editorial), *Newport Daily News*, 18 January 1966.

254 "distribution of the Middletown Voice at any time"; "Opposition's Tactics 'Irresponsible' –Wein," *Newport Daily News*, 13 January 1966.

254 "registered to the Diocese of Providence"; "Bishop an Author of Letter Objecting to Festival Area," *Newport Daily News*, 14 January 1966.

254 "the friends of the Jazz Festival"; "Two Statements," *Providence Visitor*, 14 January 1966.

254 "developed a more sophisticated set of values"; Ibid.

255 "the entire purpose of our Novitiate"; Bishop McVinney, quoted in "Festival Story Background," *Providence Visitor*, 14 January 1966.

255 "a decline in moral and spiritual values" to Aquidneck Island; "Where We Stand on the Festivals," editorial, *Providence Visitor*, 14 January 1966.

255 "with the proposed upgrading of the quality of the programming"; Frederick L. Yarger, secretary, Newport County Clergy Association, personal letter, December 14, 1965.

255 Dozens of other residents complained of similar encounters; "Council Samples Festival Feuding," *Newport Daily News*, 18 January 1966.

259 "I wasn't born yesterday, and my answer is 'no'"; Bishop Bernard M. Kelly, quoted in "2,127 Oppose Festival Site," *Westerly Sun*, 20 January 1966.

259 "liquidate the spiritual benefits of the novitiate"; Bishop Bernard M. Kelly, quoted by Andrew F. Blake, "The Show Went On and On and," *Providence Bulletin*, 20 January 1966.

259 "he has done—God bless him"; Ibid.

259 "Win, lose, or draw, I have won"; Andrew F. Blake, Ibid.

259 we consider a move to that city; "For Festivals in Providence," *Providence Journal*, 5 February 1966.

259 University of Rhode Island campus; "URI Offer 'Excellent Choice,'" *Providence Bulletin*, 8 February 1966.

260 find alternate festival sites on Aquidneck Island; "Group Seeks to Keep Festivals in Newport," *Providence Journal*, 23 January 1966.

260 "one of the cultural centers of the world"; "Fact-Finding Group in Favor of Festivals," *Providence Journal*, 2 February 1966.

260 "the decision of the Middletown Council Monday night"; "Wein Abandons Middletown; Newport Will Keep Festivals," *Newport Daily News*, 4 February 1966.

261 "what a lovely place it would be to have a Festival"; Ibid.

261 "They recognized then that times do change"; Leonard Panaggio, "Musically yours, Newport," program of the 1966 Newport Jazz Festival, p. 44.

262 before the onset of the Jazz Festival; "Festival Field Christened; 'History Made,' Wein Claims," *Newport News*, 29 June 1966.

263 Jimmy Garrison on bass; Lewis Porter, *John Coltrane: His Life and Music* (Ann Arbor: University of Michigan Press, 1998), p. 266.

264 "Permanence has arrived at last"; Whitney Balliett, "Newport Notes," *New Yorker*, July 1966.

264 grateful that our performance was recorded and later released in Britain; *Newport Jazz All-Stars: July 1966*. Flyright Records, Bexill-on-Sea, East Sussex, UK, 1995. EBCD 2120–2.

267 on par with Cornelius Vanderbilt's best efforts; Marjorie Sherman, "Gilded Picnic Launches Newport Opera Fete," *Boston Globe*, 13 July 1966.

267 he admitted to "thoroughly enjoying" them; James T. Kaull, "Met Would Like Two Weeks at Newport in '67," *Providence Journal*, 15 July 1966.

268 (about half that of the 1966 Newport Jazz Festival); "Newport Hoping for More Opera," *New York Times*, 18 July 1966.

268 "in an acoustically disagreeable one"; Michael Steinberg, "The Met Opera at Newport—A Troubled Marriage," *Boston Globe*, 14 July 1966.

268 "having a marvelous time"; Barbara Marsh, "Newport Delights 'The Met,'" *Newport Daily News*, 15 July 1966.

269 "prominent and permanent place among international musical events"; Rudolph Bing, "A Foreword by the General Manager," Metropolitan Opera at Newport program, 1967, p. 4.

271 voted unanimously to make me an honorary citizen; "George Wein, Honorary Citizen," *Newport Daily News*, July 26, 1966, p. 8.

275 *George Wein Is Alive and Well in Mexico; George Wein Is Alive and Well in Mexico,* Columbia CS 9631.

276 $25,000 sponsor subsidy; Burt Goldblatt, *Newport Jazz Festival* (New York: The Dial Press, 1977), p. 141.

283 "But is it JAZZ?"; George Wein, "Foreword from the Producer—Newport," program for the 1969 Newport Jazz Festival.

283 10,000 on the adjacent hillside; Dan Morgenstern, "Newport '69: Bad Trip," *Down Beat*, 21 August 1969.

286 "the rock experiment was a resounding failure"; Morgenstern, p. 45.

294 "and see what they were doing"; Louis Armstrong, interviewed by George Wein in Festi-Films tape #3 ("New Orleans"), 1970.

295 "late 19th century charm and grace"; Morgenstern, *Down Beat*.

296 Mahalia had suffered some poor health in recent months; Laurraine Goreau, *Just Mahalia, Baby* (Waco: Word Books, 1975), p. 534.

296 "I don't think you really know how to love"; Mahalia Jackson, FestiFilms tape #4 ("Finale"), 1970.

298 "he knows who to get, and where to place 'em"; Armstrong, Festi Films tape #1, 1970.

298 "the kind of night festivals seem to be made for"; Morgenstern, p. 12.

299 "from the first day I started working for him"; Louis Armstrong, quoted in Bergreen, p. 278.

299 "He was the greatest for me and all the spades that he handled"; Bergreen, 490.

302 "we were going to get the hell out of there"; Count Basie and Albert Murray, *Good Morning Blues: The Autobiography of Count Basie* (New York: Da Capo, 1995), p. 360.

303 "George had his father along with him on the trip"; Basie and Murray, p. 360.

304 "There will always be a Newport, somewhere, somehow"; Dan Morgenstern, "Newport: All Is Not Lost," *Down Beat*, 16 September 1972.

311 "was out of his head and high on something"; George Wein, quoted by James T. Kaull, "A Tearful Wein—'Don't Blame All'" *Providence Journal*, 5 July 1971.

311 "They are America's disgrace"; George Wein, quoted by Dee Allen, "Silenced by the Madding Crowd," *Groton News*, 9 July 1971.


10: THE NEWPORT FOLK FESTIVAL

313 "the most influential festival of the urban folk revival"; Robert Cantwell, *When We Were Good: The Folk Revival* (Cambridge, MA: Harvard University Press, 1996), p. 294.

314 "a catalogue of current trends and styles in American folk music"; Robert Shelton, "Folk Music Festival," *The Nation*, 1 August 1959.

315 "thongs that laced up to just below the knee"; Baez, p. 60.

316 "an unquenchable burst of protest"; Herbert P. Zarnow, "Kingston Trio Hit of Festival—Huge Crowd Demands 'More,'" *Newport Daily News*, 13 July 1959.

316 "fiddle playing, and songs in many different languages"; Pete Seeger, "The American Folk Song Revival," program for the Second Newport Folk Festival (1960).

317 "a likely successor to Leadbelly"; Harry Oster, "Angola, 1959," in Ibid.

317 "what he feels is most meaningful and honest"; Seeger, Ibid.

317 "they moved quickly from song to song without talking very much"; Susan Montgomery, "The Folk Furor," *Mademoiselle,* December 1960.

317 "in short, the best of everything"; Jean Ritchie, ed., *The Newport Folk Festival Songbook* (New York: Alfred Music, 1965), p. 6.

319 "a mixture of old blood and new"; "Proposal for the Newport Folk Festival to be held in Newport July 1963 on the 26th, 27th and 28th," cited in Appendix B of Cheryl Anne Brauner's *Study of the Newport Folk Festival and the Newport Folk Foundation*, p. 254.

321 Freedom Singers organize a cross-country collegiate tour; Cantwell, *When We Were Good*, p. 301.

321 March on Washington scheduled for the following month; Ted Holmberg, "Newport Rights Rally Features Festival Star," *Providence Journal*, 28 July 1963.

322 fewer than a hundred people were in attendance; Brauner, p. 106.

323 "Blues dwell in everyone. It's all in the soul"; Lightnin' Hopkins, "Whose Blues?" program for 1963 Newport Folk Festival.

324 evoked the afternoon's only standing ovation; Brauner, p. 96.

326 were instrumental in reviving a languishing Cajun culture; Brauner, p. 192.

329 COMPLICATED CIRCLE; Bob Dylan, "—for Dave Glover," program for 1963 Newport Folk Festival.

329 The new song was an "electric epic"; Goodman, p. 90.

330 "Let's find out if these guys can play it at all"; Paul Rothchild, quoted in Eric von Schmidt and Jim Rooney, *Baby, Let Me Follow You Down: The Illustrated Story of the Cambridge Folk Years* (Garden City, NY: Anchor, 1979), p. 253.

332 in secret in a Bellevue Avenue mansion; Shelton, *No Direction Home*, p. 302.

334 "people were on their way home"; Robert J. Lurtsema, "On the Scene," *Broadside of Boston*, 18 August 1965.

335 "represent a new trend"; "Concert Program," program for 1966 Newport Folk Festival.

335 surplus of approximately $80,000; Newport Folk Foundation secretary's report, prepared by Elliott Hoffman and printed in program for 1967 Newport Folk Festival, p. 41.

335 resulted in a deficit $15,661.49; Newport Folk Foundation treasurer's report, prepared by Arnold London and printed in program for the 1957 Newport Folk Festival, p. 45.

339 to prove we could in agony contain yet more; program for 1968 Newport Folk Festival, p. 4.

340 "to be like this I'd of stayed in Kentucky"; Brauner, p. 93.

342  Jean-Bosco Mwenda to Newport from Africa cost us $2,000; Brauner, p. 156.

342  cost the Folk Foundation another $14,000; Brauner, p. 157.

## 12: NEWPORT JAZZ FESTIVAL—NEW YORK AND THE NYJRC

377  "clearly the top American music story of 1972"; Albert Goldman, "Jazz—Out in Front Again with All the Old Sidemen," *Life* 1972.

383  "a few yards from where he had started"; McCandlish Phillips, "Jazz: Kaleidoscopic Sounds, Syncopated Visions," *New York Times*, 8 July 1972.

391  "on the old 78 r.p.m.s becomes brand-new again"; Whitney Balliett, *New Yorker*, 7 April 1975.

392  "exclusion of already established contemporary and traditional jazz"; George Wein, program for the 1974 Newport Jazz Festival–New York.

395  and a dozen wind instruments; John S. Wilson, "Russell Presents His Episodic Jazz," *New York Times*, Monday, 10 March 1975.

395  called it a "do-or-die stand"; John S. Wilson, "Jazz Company's 2d Season to Be Test," *New York Times*, Tuesday, 5 November 1974.

395  "no one will be able to start anything like it again for years"; Jimmy Owens quoted in "A Jazz Group Has the $ Blues" by Peter Keepnews, *New York Post*, 16 December 1974.

396  had branded "the schizoid programs" of the previous year; Gary Giddins, "Jazz Repertory and the Jazz Moment," *Village Voice*, 21 November 1974.

396  we had raised only $5,000 in memberships; John S. Wilson, "Repertory Jazz," *New York Times*, 30 March 1975.

397  "there was the solo without surface noise or static"; Giddins, 21 November 1974.

397  "exhilarating number at the first concert"; Whitney Balliett, *New Yorker*, 23 December 1974.

397  called it "a once in a lifetime stunner"; A. H. Tannenbaum, "The Era of Satchmo," *Daily News*, 13 November 1974.

397  "imaginative, entertaining, informative and rewarding jazz programming"; John S. Wilson, "Jazz: A Lively Mixture of Armstrong," *New York Times*, 10 November 1974.

398  "Which is what a jazz repertory company should be all about"; Whitney Balliett, *New Yorker*, 23 December 1974.

398  They were scheduled to play twenty-three concerts; Harriet Choice, "Newport Preempted: Ambassador Satchmo Is Russia's Choice," *Chicago Tribune*, 8 June 1975.

398  "have covered in less than two seasons"; John S. Wilson, "N.Y. Jazz Repertory Company Surveys 75 Years of Changes," *New York Times*, 20 April 1975.

399  while the NJE more closely resembled "an undergraduate survey"; Whitney Balliett, *New Yorker*, 7 April 1975.

400  to my staff, and to countless reporters; "Wein Announces Smaller Newport Festival," *Down Beat*, 23 May 1974.

401  "in its overview and contemporary in its performance"; John S. Wilson, "Be-bop Pioneers Mark Parker Era," *New York Times*, 30 June 1974.

402  "glad to be here. Glad to be anywhere"; Ernie Santosuosso, "Newport Hails Jazz Pianists," *Boston Globe*, Tuesday, 2 July 1974.

402  he called them his "toys"; John S. Wilson, "Return of Unaccompanied Pianists," *New York Times,* 2 July 1974.

402  some 500 weeks on the *Billboard* charts; Ernie Santosuosso, "Songwriters have their night at Jazz Festival," *Boston Globe*, 5 July 1974.

404  that also featured jazz on a regular basis; John S. Wilson, "It's Not the Same Old Jazz as Newport Festival Opens," *New York Times*, 27 June 1975.

405 Rashied Ali played nightly at his Studio 77; Les Ledbetter, "Festival Fans Stream to Lofts and Studios," *New York Times*, Tuesday, 1 July 1975.

405 "predictable"; Peter Keepnews, "There Were Few Surprises at the 22d Jazz Fete," *New York Post*, 2 July 1975.

405 "conservative"; Gary Giddins, "Festival Notes, Highs and Lows," *New York*, 30 June 1975.

406 "into which jazz has moved in the last 20 years"; John S. Wilson, "Full House for Thelonious Monk," *New York Times*, 5 July 1975.

406 "varied series of concerts"; Gary Giddins, "Newport and Elsewhere: Where to Hear It," *Village Voice*, 28 June 1976.

406 "is sufficiently festive"; John S. Wilson, "Festival Crowds Found Disappointing," *New York Times*, 8 July 1975.

409 "like a ghostly presence"; John S. Wilson, "Ellington Concert Lacks Duke's Touch," *New York Times*, 6 July 1976.

413 "in a public career spanning 30 years"; *Down Beat*, "Live—From the White House," 1978.

415 "from number to number in a very subtle manner"; George Wein, letter to Gretchen Poston, 1978.

417 "spirit bursts forward in an expression of song"; Jimmy Carter, speech delivered June 18, 1978. Cited from a transcription in *Down Beat*, "Statement from the White House," 1978.

417 "best Father's Day present he ever had, in his eighty-fifth year"; George Wein, speech delivered June 18, 1978. Cited from a transcription of NPR "Jazz Alive" Broadcast.

418 *"Charles* Mingus, as he insisted on being called—could not"; "Jazz Profiles," National Public Radio.

419 "I'm going to stay and listen to some more music"; Jimmy Carter, quoted in Ira Gitler's "White House Whirligig," *Radio Free Jazz*, July 1978.

420 had mounted an exhibit on Latin musical culture; Robert Palmer, "Manhattan Will Bounce with the Latin Beat," *New York Times*, 23 June 1978.

422 "even by Newport Jazz Festival standards"; John S. Wilson, "It's Like Newport of Old at Saratoga Springs Fete," *New York Times*, 3 July 1978.

## 13: "COME UP TO KOOL"

430 (. . . commingling with hippopotami and orangutans); Dale Stevens, "Jazz Producer Seeks to Have Festival Here," *Cincinnati Post & Times-Star*, 16 March 1962.

430 hosted an annual county fair more or less continually since 1884; "Jazz Mixes with History at Carthage," *Cincinnati Post & Times-Star*.

431 "would not stand up under stomping and stamping about"; Report by City Building Commissioner Don Hunter, quoted in "Fair Grandstand Sturdy Enough for Fete, Is View," *Cincinnati Enquirer*, 26 July 1962.

431 "Those timbers will hold up anything"; "Fair Grandstand Sturdy Enough for Fete, Is View," *Cincinnati Enquirer*, 26 July 1962.

431 The audience did in fact come from miles around; "Jazz Festival Advance Sale Assures Success," *Cincinnati Post & Times-Star*, 24 August 1962.

432 "You will all go home after round four"; Quoted in David Remnick, *King of the World* (New York: Random House, 1998), p. 122.

436 our six stadium events drew more than 400,000 paying customers; Dino Santangelo, letter to Leo Bell, Brown & Williamson Tobacco Company, November 19, 1974.

438 events would draw more than 650,000 patrons altogether; Festival Productions, Inc. "Total Identification with the Jazz Festivals" proposal submitted to Brown & Williamson Tobacco Company, p. 6.

439 ranging from 50 percent African-American in Oakland to 80 percent in Hampton; Santangelo letter.

440 "confine itself to soul?"; Thomas Albright, "Jazz Festival—A Great Night for Soul, Rock," *San Francisco Chronicle*, 16 June 1975.

## 14: KOOL TO JVC

446 and the "Winston American Ballet Theatre"; Whitney Balliett, "Jazz: Number Twenty-six," *New Yorker*, 21 July 1980.

450 "could restore my virginity, tattered thing that it was"; Gary Giddins, "Medium Kool: A Nonvirgin's Report," *Village Voice,* 8 July 1981

## INTERLUDE 3: MILES DAVIS

459 "and applauding for what I had done"; Miles Davis and Quincy Troupe, *Miles: The Autobiography* (New York: Simon & Schuster, 1989), p. 191.

459 From that point on, he was a member of the band; Jimmy Cobb, May 1999 interview with Ashley Kahn. Quoted in Kahn, *Kind of Blue: the Making of the Miles Davis Masterpiece* (New York: Da Capo Press, 2000), p. 79.

460 leaving Miles to play piano; "Sid's Ahead," on *Milestones,* Columbia CL 1193 / Sony 65340.

460 (appearing at the 1958 Newport Jazz Festival); Their Newport set can be heard on *Miles Davis & Thelonious Monk: Live at Newport 1958 & 1963.* C2K 53585.

460 "by his two featured saxophone players"; George Wein, "Miles Davis Won't Accept Challenge to Win Wide Public," *Boston Herald*, 28 September 1958.

460 "time allotted to Adderley and Coltrane"; Ibid.

460 "an increasing acceptance of his very wonderful music"; Ibid.

461 "with Sidney Poitier and Harry Belafonte"; Kenneth Tynan journal, entry dated January 11, 1974. Reprinted in *New Yorker,* 7 August 2000.

462 the "bullshit" I've handed out over the years; Davis & Troupe, p. 288.

466 featuring musicians like Dizzy Gillespie and Sarah Vaughan; Jack Chambers, *Milestones: The Music and Times of Miles Davis* (New York: Da Capo, 1998), p. 231.

467 "and a trumpeter's chops, if not used, can deteriorate in a week"; Whitney Balliett, *New Yorker.*

469 "since Ellington sat in with the Boston Pops"; Giddins, p. 47.

469 "They consistently rose above their rather ordinary setting"; Robert Palmer, "Jazz: The Comeback of Miles Davis," *New York Times,* 6 July 1981.

## 16: JVC AND BEYOND

491 "come-in-the-back-door past of jazz"; Nat Hentoff, "Sideshow or Culture?" *Rogue,* May 1959.

491 "as well as of occasional irrelevancy"; Nat Hentoff, program for the 1978 Newport Jazz Festival.

491 "more than any other promoter in the music's history"; Nat Hentoff, "George Wein: A Life in, and for, Jazz," *JazzTimes,* May 2001.

492 "the JVC Jazz Festival has become increasingly irrelevant"; Peter Watrous, "A New Champion in Town," *New York Times,* 16 June 1996.

# Index